MARYHELEN VANNIER
Professor and Director, Professional Preparation
Department of Health and Physical Education
Southern Methodist University

DAVID L. GALLAHUE
Associate Professor and Assistant Dean
School of Health, Physical Education, and Recreation
Indiana University

sixth edition

teaching PHYSICAL education in elementary schools

Illustrated

W. B. SAUNDERS COMPANY
Philadelphia   London   Toronto

W. B. Saunders Company: West Washington Square
Philadelphia, PA 19105

1 St. Anne's Road
Eastbourne, East Sussex BN21 3UN, England

1 Goldthorne Avenue
Toronto, Ontario M8Z 5T9, Canada

Library of Congress Cataloging in Publication Data

Vannier, Maryhelen, 1915–

Teaching physical education in elementary schools.

Includes bibliographies.

1. Physical education for children.   I. Gallahue, David L.,
   joint author.   II. Title.

GV443.V35 1978   372.8'6   77–80752

ISBN 0–7216–8979–5

Teaching Physical Education in Elementary Schools   ISBN   0-7216-8979-5

Last digit is the print number: 9   8   7   6   5   4   3

This book is dedicated to our Mothers

MRS. MAUDE VANNIER

MRS. LORETTA GALLAHUE

who taught us to love children and instilled in us the desire to help each child discover the joy, wonder, and miracle of our own childhoods and lives.

I keep six honest serving men;
(They taught me all I knew)
Their names are *What* and *Where* and *When*
And *How* and *Why* and *Who*.

RUDYARD KIPLING

PREFACE

This book is first a presentation of physical education—what it is and what its place should be in our rapidly changing world and educational system. Second, it is a source book of physical education activities for children in nursery school, kindergarten, and grades 1 through 6. Third, it contains methods for teaching children through these activities, as well as for directing the numerous sports, rhythms, dances, games, and movement exploratory activities that have been included.

It has been written for five groups: (1) the specialized physical educator, (2) the classroom teacher, (3) the college student who is professionally preparing to become an elementary-school teacher, (4) those primarily interested in school curriculum improvement, and (5) elementary school physical supervisors and principals.

This sixth edition is a major revision. Most of the text has been either rewritten, reorganized, or greatly expanded. Briefly stated, these major changes include

1. The addition of two new chapters: Developing Neuromuscular Abilities in Children and Movement and Self-Concept Development.
2. The addition of around 150 new activities in such areas as movement exploration, basic skills for individual and team sports, games, rhythms and dance, and self-testing activities.
3. The chapters on The Exceptional Child, Physical Fitness and Youth Development, The Elementary-Grade Child, and Stunts and Tumbling have all been extensively revised and enlarged.
4. All reference materials, suggested teaching aids, record sources, and suggested reading lists have been revised to include the latest and best materials available.
5. Over 50 new photographs and drawings have been added.
6. The chapter on Movement Exploration now includes a wider variety of movement exploration activities.
7. The chapter on The Teacher includes new materials on teacher aids, the use of squad leaders, older students, and para-professionals with suggested techniques for training these last to become better helpers to the teacher, especially those with large classes.
8. The chapter on The Exceptional Child now contains over 25 suggested activities to teach each type of handicapped child, including the obese and clumsy child, as well as the mentally retarded, emotionally disturbed, blind, deaf, cerebrally palsied, epileptic, orthopedically handicapped, and other kinds of exceptional children.

9. The latest, best suggested techniques for understanding and working successfully with children in our fast-changing society have been added, which should enable the teacher to become a more effective and positive influence upon the lives of children.
10. The activity section of the text has been considerably rewritten and revised.
11. Each chapter now contains an opening quotation or poem that either stimulates thought or summarizes in a few words what the chapter's basic concepts are.
12. The Appendices now contain recommended films and filmstrips, film sources, sources for equipment and supplies, playground and gymnasium floor markings, suggested placement of outdoor apparatus, and a self-evaluation score card for the physical education program.
13. The latest and best suggested records, special equipment, and other teaching aids have been added.

It is imperative that every teacher make each and all physical education class periods more meaningful and purposeful, linking more securely what is learned today with what has been mastered yesterday. Likewise, the elementary-school physical education program must become more skillfully and better planned to contain a wider variety of progressively more difficult and challenging educational experiences. The aim of education, through its curriculum, should be to develop all youths physically, socially, mentally, and morally to their highest potential so that they *do* become well-rounded, happy, intelligent, socially sensitive, and productive, democratic citizens, as youngsters as well as adults. To this great endeavor, each teacher on every educational level, regardless of his or her area of specialization, has much to contribute. May this book help each one to discover significant ways for doing so through the successful teaching of physical education activities in the elementary school.

MARYHELEN VANNIER

Dallas, Texas

DAVID L. GALLAHUE

Bloomington, Indiana

ACKNOWLEDGMENTS

The authors are indebted to many persons who have made this book possible. Special gratitude and appreciation are due our families and professional colleagues for submitting photographs for illustrations and helpful suggestions for improving the contents of this sixth edition.

We are thankful to numerous students in our classes, both on the elementary and college level, who have helped us to learn and play the games and other activities presented in this book, as well as to collect new materials.

We are especially grateful to Mildred Franz of Louisville, Kentucky, Douglas Gallahue, Clarence Biedenweg, Rudy Heis, and Fred and Ervina Deinhart. We are also grateful to Ellie, David Lee, and Jennifer Gallahue for their support and encouragement and also to John Snyder of the W. B. Saunders Company.

Acknowledgments for Photographs Used in this Book

The authors wish to thank the following companies for the use of their splendid photographs to illustrate this book:

School-Tech, Inc.
745 State Circle
Ann Arbor, Michigan 48104

The Delmer F. Harris Company
P.O. Box 288
Concordia, Kansas

The Instructor
Instructor Park
Dansville, New York 14437

Montessori Academy
14545 Noel Road
Dallas, Texas 75240

Kanakuk-Kanakomo-Kamps
702 Thomas
College Station, Texas 77840

Northlake Elementary School
10059 Ravensway Street
Dallas, Texas

Lind Climber Company
807 Reba Place
Evanston, Illinois 60202

Board of Education
348 West First Street
Dayton, Ohio 45402

Smiley's Photo Marketing Systems
3480 W. Vickery
Fort Worth, Texas 76107

Jayfro Corporation
P.O. Box 50
Montville, Connecticut 06353

Refugio Public Schools
Refugio, Texas

Things From Bell, Inc.
P.O. Box 26
90 Clinton Street
Homer, New York 13077

Snitz Manufacturing Company
104 South Church Street
East Troy, Wisconsin 53120

Documentary Films
3217 Trout Gulch Road
Aptos, California 95003

Tucson Creative Dance Center
3131 North Cherry Avenue
Tucson, Arizona 85719

Ed-Nu, Inc.
5115 State Highway No. 38
Pennsauken, New Jersey 08109

J. A. Preston Corporation
71 Fifth Avenue
New York, New York 10003

Things From Bell
30 North Main Street
Homer, New York 13077

Nissen Corporation
930 27th Avenue S.W.
Cedar Rapids, Iowa 52406

Flag-A-Tag Company
P.O. Box 11010
Tucson, Arizona 85706

Game Time, Inc.
900 Anderson Road
Litchfield, Michigan 49252

Raven Industries, Inc.
P.O. Box 1007
Sioux Falls, South Dakota 57101

Hazelton Area School District
Peace and 20th Streets
Hazelton, Pennsylvania 18201

Gym Scooter Company
Winfield, Kansas

Shield Manufacturing Co.
9 Saint Paul Street
Buffalo, New York 14209

Creative Playground Corporation
RR23 1234 East 99 Drive
Terre Haute, Indiana 47802

CONTENTS

PART ONE

Your children are not your children.
They are the sons and daughters of Life's longing for itself.
They come through you but not from you,
And though they are with you they belong not to you.
Yet you may give them your love but not your thoughts,
For they have their own thoughts.
You may house their bodies but not their souls,
For their souls dwell in the house of tomorrow, which you cannot
      visit, not even in your dreams.
You may strive to be like them, but seek not to make them like you.
For life goes not backward nor tarries with yesterday.
You are the bows from which your children as living arrows are sent
      forth.
The archer sees the mark upon the path of the infinite, and He
      bends you with His might that His arrows may go swift and far.
Let your bending in the archer's hand be for gladness;
For even as He loves the arrow that flies, so He loves also the bow
      that is stable.

                                                    Kahlil Gibran

THE WHY

CHAPTER ONE

THE PLACE OF TODAY'S PHYSICAL EDUCATION IN CHILD DEVELOPMENT

A child is God's opinion that the world should go on.
Carl Sandburg

Movement is at the very center of the lives of children. It is a central focus of their development and has vast implications for their cognitive and affective development as well as for their motor development. A well-planned, well-taught physical education program geared to the needs, interests, and developmental level of the children it is intended to serve will make important contributions to their total development. The use of a term such as "total development" may sound grandiose or trite to the casual reader, but the astute student of child development will recognize the truth of these words when they concern children in a *quality* physical education program.

Movement provides children with a concrete means with which to act in, interact with, and react to the world around them. It is their way of exploring, experimenting, and discovering the countless wonders of life. Movement is a primary information-gathering device for children, one which helps them acquire increasingly complex knowledge. Movement serves as the primary vehicle by which they expand their conceptions of themselves and their world. It is their primary mode of expression, for unlike adults, children are in the process of "becoming" rather than in the process of "being." Adults express themselves best through words, but children express themselves best through movement; we must provide them with ample opportunities for expression. As educators, we must realize that children are not miniature adults ready to be programmed to perform as such. Yet throughout our nation the period of time generally referred to as "childhood" is constantly shrinking as a direct result of the ever-increasing demands that we place on our children to enter the adult world of behavior, logic, and concepts before they are developmentally ready. We must cease to "adultize" our nation's youth and allow our children to be children.

Movement is the essence of all life. To move is to be alive. All of our covert as well as our overt behaviors are reflected in some form of movement, no matter how subtle. If our heart does not beat or if our lungs cease to exchange old air for new air, we soon die. Even the supposedly motionless state of cortical thought involves minute forms of movement in the brain, which can be detected and recorded by special devices.

Our primitive ancestors depended upon their skill to move in order to stay alive. Their very existence in a hostile environment depended upon their ability to secure food, erect crude shelters, and do battle with their enemies.

Just as primitive people had to learn to use their bodies wisely or else perish, so must modern society, for biologically both are almost identical. Our ancestors needed vigorous activity to keep themselves fully functioning, and so do we today. We depend on movement for survival in perhaps a less obvious and direct way, but the difference lies only in degree. Human beings, primitive and modern, have the same basic physical, emotional, social, and mental needs. By necessity, primitive people placed primary emphasis on the satisfaction of physical needs. Satisfaction of other needs was secondary because of the constant struggle for survival. Today we are faced with an increased intensity of emotional, social, and mental needs without a corresponding decrease in physical needs. We are *total* beings, and as such we must develop in all areas if we are to function to our fullest potential.

Movement is central to our complete development as fully functioning, contributing members of society. The body and mind exist in an inseparable unit. The notion that one functions independently of the other is absurd and without scientific basis or support. The movement experiences of a quality elementary school program have a profound effect on all aspects of children's development.

THE AIMS OF PHYSICAL EDUCATION

The aims of physical education have been variously stated by a variety of authors and leaders in the profession. Lofty ideas and flowery platitudes have often clouded the fact that the aims of physical education may be simply and succinctly stated as *learning to move* and *learning through movement*.

The learning-to-move aim of physical education is based upon the recognition that the central focus of any quality physical education program is on helping each individual learn how to use his or her body more efficiently and effectively in a wide variety of fundamental movements, sports, dances, and aquatic skills. Elementary-school children need to learn how to use their bodies better. Their motor development is not a process of maturation alone but relies heavily on quality and quantity experience. The sedentary lives led by a great many school-age children have been brought about by busing, television, and parental apathy. Lack of gross motor play, vigorous activity, and an opportunity for systematic physical education instruction prevents many children from satisfying the learning-to-move aim of physical education. The mere process of getting older will *not* result in the development of mature patterns of movement and improved performance levels. Children must have encouragement, opportunities, developmentally appropriate experiences, and quality instruction if they are truly going to learn to move with joy and efficiency.

The learning-*through*-movement aim is based on the realization that physical education can make positive contributions to the many cognitive and affective facets of children. While children are learning to move, the understanding teacher is also taking advantage of numerous opportunities to help them learn through movement. The cognitive and affective domains of human behavior are not separate and distinct, as is often implied. They are closely related and complexly intertwined with the child's motor development and movement behavior.

The two aims of physical education are focused on the development of the total individual. The growth and development of children through directed physical activities should affect the complete child. Physical, social, mental, and emotional growth are closely related. The teacher of physical education must understand these interrelationships and conduct a well-planned and progressive physical education

FIGURE 1–1. If it is true that each child is an individual, then we must teach him individually and know his own unique growth pattern. (Courtesy of Lind Climber Company, Evanston, Illinois.)

program. This program should serve as an integral part of the total school curriculum and make positive contributions to each individual child.

WHAT IS ELEMENTARY SCHOOL PHYSICAL EDUCATION?

The realization that movement is an important contributor to our total development as fully functioning individuals enables us to view *quality* physical education as a useful educational tool. This tool makes major contributions to the broad aims of education (1) by helping children learn how to use their bodies more effectively and efficiently and (2) by helping them learn about their world and those in it through movement.

The elementary physical education program should be looked upon as a vital contributing portion of the total school curriculum. It should never be viewed as a frill or appendage that can easily be left out of the school program. The values of sound physical education programs that are well taught by dedicated teachers are seldom questioned by parents, colleagues, school boards, or taxpayers, for the benefits of such programs to the child's total education are readily seen. What people *do* object to is a poor physical education program that is poorly taught. Unfortunately, many programs that are lacking in clearly stated objectives and that are poorly taught and developmentally unsound for children still exist throughout the world. The elementary school program is sometimes looked upon as a "watered down" high school program, and too often it is just that.

Elementary school children are not miniature adults. Their needs, interests, and capabilities are considerably different from those of adolescents. Nor is the elementary

FIGURE 1–2.   Hand-eye coordination should be learned early in life. (Courtesy of Ed-Nu, Inc., Pennsauken, New Jersey.)

school physical education program a recess or free-play period. It is a learning laboratory in which children are involved in the important task of learning to move and learning through movement.

The primary objective of the physical education program is not fun. Fun may be the child's primary objective, but it should not be the teacher's. Fun is a worthy by-product of good physical education, just as it is a desired by-product of all good education. The term "education" means to lead forth. Physical education is that aspect of the educational process in which there is both education *of* the physical and education *through* the physical.

THE GENERAL OBJECTIVES OF PHYSICAL EDUCATION

The unique contribution of physical education is in the realm of physical development. Physical education makes contributions in this area that no other type of education does, by enhancing the child's movement abilities and increasing his level of fitness. This does not mean, however, that physical education is limited to the physical aspect of development only. On the contrary, well-organized, well-taught, and developmentally appropriate movement experiences make a very real and highly positive contribution to the child in all phases of development. Quality elementary physical education is that aspect of the total school curriculum that enhances the child's movement abilities in a wide variety of locomotor, manipulative, and stability activities. The general objectives of elementary physical education are in the areas of (1) neuromuscular skill development, (2) physical and motor fitness development, (3) perceptual-motor development, (4) self-concept development, (5) development of academic understanding, and (6) development of wise use of leisure time.

Neuromuscular Skill Development

Neuromuscular skill development is the unique contribution of physical education to the well-being of the child. As such, it can be looked upon as the primary objective of the elementary program and the vehicle by which the other objectives are achieved. Through the interaction of both maturation (aging) and experience (learning), the child develops and refines a wide variety of locomotor, manipulative, and stability skills. The reciprocal interaction between maturation and experience plays a major role in determining the onset and extent of development of the movement repertoire of the child.

For example, teachers of preschool and primary grade children are *not* overly concerned that their pupils develop *high* degrees of skill in specific games, sports, or rhythmic activities. They realize that children must proceed from simple to complex skills in the acquisition of movement abilities and that they must be developmentally ready to learn before they will benefit to a measurable degree from specific forms of instruction. As a result, the teacher of young children is concerned with enhancing their fundamental abilities to move in an *acceptable* manner in a wide variety of ways. The teacher of intermediate and upper elementary grade children is more concerned that his students develop form, skill, and accuracy in the performance of selected games, sports, and dances. At this grade level, children are developmentally ready to be involved in a program of movement experiences that require more complex combinations of movements and the selection of the "best" ways of performing in a wide variety of activities.

The role of the teacher in neuromuscular skill development is to (1) recognize learning readiness, (2) motivate the learner, (3) provide an atmosphere conducive to learning, and (4) use teaching approaches suitable to the individual child. Improved performance in fundamental movement patterns and general movement skills can be developed through practice under the direction of a teacher skilled in implementing each of the above criteria.

Fitness Development

Because it is impossible to separate the mind and body, there is no such isolated thing as "physical" fitness in the literal sense of the word. Actually, the mutually dependent and inseparable components of total fitness are mental, emotional, social, and spiritual, as well as physical and motor. Thus, fitness is a total phenomenon. Taking part in vigorous activities contributes to organic development and a sense of general well-being. To build intelligent and socially sensitive youth we must work toward that goal. The muscles of their bodies will grow in strength, size, and tonus through exercise and vigorous physical activity, which growth will in turn enhance their total development.

The vital organs of the body are likewise favorably affected by exercise. Through activity, the rate and force of heartbeats are increased, breathing becomes deeper and more rapid, production of body heat and waste is stepped up, appetite and sleep improve, and accelerated energy build-up and breakdown result. In children, physical activity serves as a stimulus to growth.

Fitness development is the result of planned activity; regular exercise, sleep and rest, eating, and play or recreation; and the maintenance of emotional well-being.

FIGURE 1–3. All children crave adventurous activity. (Courtesy of Game Time, Inc., Litchfield, Michigan.)

Abundant, buoyant health gives one the drive to work, to play, and to live with a zest for life.

Children need about four hours of vigorous big-muscle activity a day in order to be in good health. Obviously, the school's physical education program alone cannot provide the time for all the activity a child needs. School children are seldom involved in more than one and one half hours of organized physical education per week. The contributions that physical education can make toward the fitness development of the child are through (1) fostering positive attitudes in the child toward the importance of physical fitness, (2) motivating the child to have a desire to increase his level of fitness, (3) increasing his knowledge of how to gain or maintain an optimal level of fitness, and (4) actually *helping* him develop increased levels of fitness.

Perceptual-Motor Development

From the moment of birth, children begin to interact with their environment. This interaction is a perceptual process as well as a motor process. Because these two processes are not independent of each other, the term "perceptual-motor" has come into vogue in recent years. It means (1) that effective and efficient movement is dependent upon accurate perceptions of the environment and (2) that the development of one's perceptual abilities is dependent, in part, on movement.

The terms "eye-hand coordination" and "eye-foot coordination" have been used for many years by physical educators to indicate the dependency of efficient movement on accurate perceptual information. What has not been recognized or generally accepted until recently is that the movement experiences of preschool and primary grade children play an important role in the development of their perceptual abilities. The development of perceptual abilities is a process controlled by both maturation and experience; thus, each child develops these abilities at his or her own individual rate. Not all children are at the same perceptual ability level upon entering the first grade. Children must be perceptually ready for reading and other forms of schoolwork before they can benefit to any great extent from school. Perceptual readiness is an important aspect of total readiness for learning. A well-planned physical education program that incorporates appropriate movement experiences that contribute to the development of the young child's perceptual abilities.

Self-Concept Development

One's sense of personal worth or worthlessness is generally referred to as "self-concept." The concept one has of oneself, particularly at the elementary school level, is influenced greatly by movement. Through movement, children learn about themselves and develop their *body images* (knowledge of the movement potential of one's body). They learn whether their classmates consider them to be "swell hitters" or "easy outs." The body images that children develop influence their self-concept development. Most children place high positive value on moving well. Those who run the fastest, throw the hardest, and perform well in games and sports are generally the best-liked, most sought-after playmates on the schoolyard. On the other hand, children who are "only" average or below average in their movement abilities are generally less popular and less sought after by their peers.

An atmosphere of acceptance, challenge, and success in the gymnasium can do much to foster the development of a positive, stable self-concept in children. The very fact that they place such value on moving well makes it crucial for physical education teachers to carefully structure their programs in such a manner that all children are given plenty of opportunity and encouragement to achieve to their unique levels of ability. The quality physical education program is one in which children are recognized as being individuals and, as such, not all at the same ability level. In the quality physical education program it is also recognized that success and challenge are important to children and adults alike and that the program can and must be structured in such a way as to include these two important attributes.

Self-concept development is too important to be left to chance. We must do all that we can to foster the development of stable, positive self-concepts in our children. We can do this, in part, through a quality physical education program.

The acceptance of oneself is prerequisite to the wholesome acceptance of and the successful interaction with others. Children learn much through the use of their bodies. It is the role of the teacher not only to provide meaningful and progressive learning experiences but also to help each pupil shape constructive attitudes toward himself, life, the rights of others, his parents and family, and adults in general, as well as to help him gain respect for the value of learning and education. A positive self-concept makes it easier to accept others. Because people are dissimilar in many ways as well as similar in many, the skilled teacher is constantly aware of "teachable moments" that will help each child develop his or her unique self.

Academic Concept Development

Elementary physical education can contribute to the development of the child's academic understanding by integrating movement experiences with science, social studies, mathematics, and language arts. This is not meant to imply that the physical education program can or should replace classroom instruction in the teaching of these areas. It does mean, however, that the physical education program can often be

FIGURE 1–4. This boy is physically experimenting with abstract ideas. (Courtesy of John Bennett, Hanover Public Schools, Ashland, Virginia.)

effectively used in conjunction with the academic program as a tool to aid learning. All people learn best through active participation because there is more relevancy and a greater sense of immediacy in active participation. They generally regard movement as "fun" and do not equate it with the routine "work" of the classroom, owing to its recreational nature and the sheer joy found in moving well. As such, physical education can serve as an effective motivator and stimulus to learning. Active participation in the learning of academic concepts also permits the child to use a greater number of sensory modalities, a factor that aids learning and promotes retention.

Many children, particularly those from culturally deprived environments, are not "turned on" to the needs, values, and joys of gaining an education, which takes work and effort. They consider school to be unstimulating drudgery, and the teacher often finds them difficult to reach. The physical education program offers an excellent medium for integrating material generally reserved for the classroom by allowing it to "come alive" through the use of movement activities. For example, the child's understanding of social studies concepts can be enhanced by integrating games and dances of different nations with various units of study or by having pupils participate in modified activities such as jousting, which was a recreational activity of previous civilizations. Understanding of many science concepts can be enhanced in the gymnasium by integrating classroom instruction with movement activities involving experiments with the mechanical principles of balances and levers and with Newton's Laws of Motion. The child has an increased need to learn how to use numbers when involved in movement activities that include counting, addition, subtraction, multiplication, and division. Keeping score, computing batting averages, and determining the number of couples in a square dance set are examples of how children can learn mathematic concepts through movement.

Careful planning and cooperation between the elementary physical education teacher and the classroom teacher are necessary for effective integration of movement experiences with academic concept development. The potential for achievement of this worthy objective is so great that it must not be overlooked. Educators are constantly looking for new and better ways of teaching children. Not all children learn best from the same method of instruction. The master teacher finds unique ways to motivate each individual child to *want* to learn. For the majority of them, this desire is often sparked by the fun approach to learning. Physical education, however, must be regarded as far more than just "fun" for children by their parents and other teachers in the school system. Active participation has been found to be an excellent facilitator of learning, particularly in young children. Thus, the contribution that physical education can make to academic concept development is of utmost importance and needs to be greatly stressed by physical educators and more widely recognized by all teachers and parents.

Development of Constructive Leisure Time Use

Play is one of the great physical needs of people, along with food, rest, elimination, and sex. It is leisure-time activity voluntarily selected and done that brings satisfaction and recreation to the individual. Life abounds with the rhythms of work and play, energy breakdown and energy build-up, sorrow and joy, and health and sickness. "All work and no play makes Jack a dull boy," but it can also make Jack a sick boy. People need to get away from the drabness, dullness, and monotony of their lives whether they are 6, 16, or 60. They need a change to do activities that are challenging, adventurous, and fun!

What is work for one person may be play for another. The manual laborer who lays brick upon brick eight hours a day for five days is working. Winston Churchill, on the other hand, when prime minister of England, was known to lay bricks for fun; it was one of his many hobbies. It has been said that the main difference between work and play is the degree of pleasure that comes from them. What is hard work for one brings much joy to another. What one does during the hours of free time is recreational if it brings deep satisfaction and release from tension, is done voluntarily without pay, and

FIGURE 1–5. As many classes as possible should be coeducational. (Courtesy of Thelma Goodwin, Central College, Pella, Iowa.)

gives one a change from the usual routine. Children need to be taught to play as much as they need to be taught to work, for play and work are inseparable. We work so that we can play, but we play so that we can work more productively, whether we are young or old.

DESIRED OUTCOMES OF THE PROGRAM

The outcomes of the quality elementary physical education program should be directly related to the six general objectives of physical education briefly reviewed above. Outcomes are generally considered to be more specific in nature than general objectives. They are usually observable and measurable in some form, and they usually contribute to the general objectives of the program. Table 1–1 presents a list of the outcomes of a good elementary program. Each of these categories is classified under one of the six general objectives of elementary school physical education.

TABLE 1–1.   OUTCOMES OF A QUALITY ELEMENTARY-SCHOOL PHYSICAL EDUCATION PROGRAM

Neuromuscular Skill Outcomes

Enhanced fundamental movement abilities
Increased general sport skill abilities
Improved specific sport skill abilities

Fitness Outcomes

Enhanced level of muscular strength
Enhanced level of muscular endurance
Enhanced level of circulatory-respiratory endurance
Increased flexibility
Increased motor fitness (speed, agility, coordination, balance, power)

Perceptual-Motor Outcomes

Greater body awareness
Greater spatial awareness
Greater directional awareness
Greater temporal awareness

Self-Concept Outcomes

Increased harmony with self
Increased ability to get along with others
Increased ability for self-expression and creativity

Academic Understanding Outcomes

Enhanced understanding, interest, and/or performance in
Science
Mathematics
Social Studies
Language Arts

Leisure-Time Outcomes

Increased ability to play well
Beginning skills gained in lifetime sports
Ability to find joy in moving well
Ability to entertain oneself constructively

FIGURE 1–6. Movement accuracy should precede the development of agility, speed, body flexibility, and the use of body explosive power through correct timing. (Courtesy of Thelma Goodwin, Central College, Pella, Iowa.)

SPECIFIC OBJECTIVES OF THE PROGRAM

Statement and achievement of the aims, general objectives, and desired outcomes of the elementary school physical education program are necessary and important. They are worthy goals for which to strive. The reality of these goals, however, is not measured in terms of what should be but rather in terms of what can be and what is. In other words, given the aims, general objectives, and desired outcomes of the elementary program, each individual teacher of physical education must determine for herself or himself the specific objectives of her or his particular program. The specific objectives of one's program are a function of (1) the needs, interests, and developmental level of the children being taught, and (2) the environmental circumstances under which the program is being implemented.

The teacher must carefully ascertain where children are in the development of their movement abilities. This may be done through formal sport-skill testing or through observation of the general quality of the children's movement behavior. Their interests also need to be taken into account. The teacher must carefully observe factors within the school and community that point out general types of interests typical for the various age levels. The teacher must carefully note children's maturity levels at each grade level. With this information (needs, interests, and development level) the teacher can begin to formulate specific objectives for his or her program that will be meaningful and worthwhile to the majority of his or her students.

The environmental circumstances in which the physical education program is to be taught will also significantly affect the specific objectives established for the program. Factors such as facilities, equipment, time, weather, and climatic conditions are important determiners of specific objectives.

The aims, objectives (general and specific), and outcomes of a good physical education program are all related to one another. The four might be likened to a freight train. *Aims* represent the locomotive that is pulling the remainder of the train to its destination. *General objectives* represent the various types of freight cars that are being pulled by the locomotive. *Desired outcomes* may be characterized as the payload that is being carried in each of the freight cars. *Specific objectives* represent the actual contents within each of the payloads in each freight car. The end result of this process is represented by the train reaching its destination.

IMPLEMENTING THE PROGRAM

Achievement of the aims, general objectives, outcomes, and specific objectives of elementary school physical education is brought about by involving children in a series of developmentally appropriate movement experiences. These experiences consist of participation in a variety of movement activities, which are the tools of the modern physical education program. Games and sports, rhythms, self-testing, aquatic activities, and outdoor education activities should be used as means to an end rather than as ends in themselves. That is, instead of utilizing an activity for activity's sake, each and every movement experience engaged in by children in the quality physical education program should contribute to clearly stated objectives. These specific objectives should and must be directly related to the desired outcomes, general objectives, and aims of the physical education program.

A variety of teaching approaches should be used to aid children in learning to move and learning through movement. The time-honored teacher-centered and direct-teaching approaches utilize a sequence of presentation that involves (1) explanation, (2) demonstration, (3) practice, (4) error correction, and then (5) performance of the skill in an appropriate activity. This traditional approach to teaching physical education is primarily concerned with the *product* of the learning experience and less

FIGURE 1–7. Children learn as much from one another as they do from their teachers—and often much more. (Courtesy of Thelma Goodwin, Central College, Pella, Iowa.)

concerned with the *process* in which the child is involved on the way to achieving the goal. As a result, it sometimes neglects individual differences among children.

In recent years, indirect teaching approaches have come into vogue. These approaches are child-centered and involve each child in problem-solving experiences. This movement-education approach pays greater attention to the *process* of learning that the child is involved in and is less concerned with the *product* of the activity. Greater attention is paid to individual differences by allowing more freedom and self-direction in solving movement problems.

Considerable controversy has arisen in recent years concerning whether the teacher-centered (direct) command and task approach of traditional physical education is as good as or better than the child-centered (indirect) exploratory and problem-solving approaches to movement education. The authors believe that the separatist views expounded by many "traditional physical educators" and "movement educators," which advocate blind adherence to one approach or the other, are not realistic. A great deal of good has come out of the direct-teaching approaches of the past 100 years, but the "newer" indirect approaches also offer a great deal to the development of children. The skilled teacher makes use of a variety of teaching approaches and does not adhere solely to one approach. *A variety of teaching approaches should be used in an effort to make the greatest contribution possible to the total development of the child.*

WHEN IS ONE EDUCATED?

One is never completely educated, for opportunities for more learning are everywhere at all times. When the desire for learning is gone, one is in a rut. The only difference between a rut and a grave is depth. Education involves learning, which in its last analysis means changed behavior. If a person's behavior does not change through education, there has been no learning. Time and energy have been wasted. Increasingly one is considered educated because of what one *does* rather than what one knows. Education should and must make a difference in behavior.

One is educated when one:

1. Has command of fundamental communicative arts and has something of real value to communicate.
2. Can face, adjust to, and solve personal problems and is working toward a solution for them. Is actively engaged in helping to solve the bigger problems of society.
3. Knows how to live abundantly and knows the things to do in order to use the total body best as a child, youth, adult, and aged citizen.
4. Can make a living doing the things that bring personal satisfaction, that are personally creative.
5. Can accept sorrow, find happiness, and live a balanced life.
6. Can live and act rationally by using education in daily life experiences.
7. Can face courageously the many ever-changing complexities of life by utilizing what one knows and believes in as a human being.

WHEN IS ONE PHYSICALLY EDUCATED?

One is never completely physically educated, for each year of life brings new adjustments that must be made and new techniques that must be mastered. Physical education, like education in general, is continuous. It can be measured or evaluated by what one does, how one lives, and how one utilizes oneself.

The kind of education children receive affects the kind of adults they will be. What type of product do we want to turn out from our schools and colleges? What kind of boys and girls do we want to put our stamp of approval on or pass in our classes as physical education teachers and professional educators?

An individual in our culture is physically educated when he or she

1. Knows about the body and how to use it wisely whether he or she is 6, 16, or 60, and possesses organic health and vigor.
2. Knows how to play several individual sports and gains satisfaction from having participated.
3. Knows how to play several team sports and gains satisfaction from participating.
4. Knows how to move gracefully in rhythm and knows how to perform many social, folk, and square dances.
5. Knows how to save him- or herself from drowning and has adequate skill in first aid, in safety and survival techniques, and in the avoidance of injury related to activity.
6. Knows how to use the body without undue fatigue.
7. Can move at different speeds with ease, can change directions, and can judge distances.
8. Can throw balls of various sizes with accuracy and skill.
9. Can hit, strike, kick, and catch moving objects with accuracy and skill.
10. Can hit stationary and moving targets with accuracy and skill.
11. Takes part in a wide variety of activities during leisure time regardless of age.
12. Has positive, beneficial, and regulated daily health habits.
13. Knows the role physical activity plays in relationship to weight control, prevention of fatigue, stress, aging, degenerative diseases, poor mental health, and psychosomatic disorders.

This list is incomplete but should serve as a guide for youths and adults, pupils and educators. Teachers of physical education, like all other educators, need to determine for themselves *what* they are trying to do through their teaching and *how* they are going to bring about learning, or changed behavior, in their students. Each pupil must understand *what* physical education is, *why* it is important, *how* to have and maintain total fitness, and how to be and keep in good condition.

Teaching may be compared to taking a trip. First you must choose the place you want to go to; next you must discover how you are to get there in the most economical way with regard to time, money, and energy; and then, to gain the real satisfaction from your planning and your dreams, you must go. The skilled physical educator helps students *go* forward to better things in life.

Whether civilization will endure depends on the greatest race in the world—the race between education and world destruction. Education of the present type will neither cure nor save the world. If education is to win the race, it must find new and better methods of changing selfish "I" drives to "we" drives in people and nations. It must devise new ways to change immaturity into maturity. It must help sick societies full of feelings of fear, frustration, and futility become healthy ones full of courage and strong moral convictions. It must help each person find and live an abundant life. This is a goal that every teacher, regardless of his or her field of specialization, must accept, believe in, and work for with united and dedicated effort.

SUGGESTED READINGS

American Alliance for Health, Physical Education, and Recreation (AAHPER): *Essentials of a Quality Elementary School Physical Education Program: A Position Paper*. Washington, D.C., 1970.
AAHPER: *Promising Practices in Elementary School Physical Education*. Washington, D.C., 1969.
AAHPER: *This is Elementary Physical Education*. Washington, D.C., 1965.
AAHPER: *Tones of Theory*. Washington, D.C., 1973.

Caplan, F., and Caplan, T.: *The Power of Play*. Garden City, New York, Anchor Press/Doubleday and Company, Inc., 1973.

Cratty, B. J.: *Intelligence in Action*. Englewood Cliffs, New Jersey, Prentice-Hall, Inc., 1973.

Ellis, M.: *Why People Play*. Englewood Cliffs, New Jersey, Prentice-Hall, Inc., 1973.

Gallahue, D., Werner, P., and Leudke, G.: *A Conceptual Approach to Moving and Learning*. New York, John Wiley & Sons, Inc., 1975.

Gilbert, A. G.: *Teaching the Three R's Through Movement Experiences*. Minneapolis, Burgess Publishing Company, 1977.

Helms, D., and Turner, J.: *Exploring Child Behavior*. Philadelphia, W. B. Saunders Company, 1976.

Humphrey, J. H.: *Child Learning; Through Elementary School Physical Education*. Dubuque, Iowa, William C. Brown Company, Publishers, 1974.

Kalakian, L., and Goldman, M.: *Introduction to Physical Education: A Humanistic Perspective*. Boston, Allyn & Bacon, Inc., 1976.

Logsdon, B. J.: *Physical Education for Children: A Focus on the Teaching Process*. Philadelphia, Lea & Febiger, 1977.

Miller, A. G., Cheffers, J. T. F., Whitcomb, V.: *Physical Education: Teaching Human Movement in the Elementary Schools*. Englewood Cliffs, New Jersey, Prentice-Hall, Inc., 1974.

Sweeney, R. T. (ed.): *Selected Readings in Movement Education*. Reading, Massachusetts, Addison-Wesley Publishing Company, Inc., 1970.

CHAPTER TWO

DEVELOPING NEUROMUSCULAR ABILITIES IN CHILDREN

Movement is the source of all learning.
The Authors

The unique and primary contribution of the physical education program to the growth and development of children is in the area of neuromuscular skill development. In recent years a great deal has been written and said concerning the potential contributions of physical education to the perceptual, academic, social, and emotional development of children. Chapters 4 and 5 deal with perceptual-motor and self-concept development, respectively, as important potential outcomes of the well-planned and well-taught physical education program. The fact is, however, that the development and refinement of a wide variety of movement patterns, movement skills, and specific sport skills is the unique contribution of physical education to the education of children and, through this, the development of physical fitness and worthy use of leisure time.

Physical educators can contribute to many other areas of child development, but they are not alone in this. The classroom teacher makes important contributions to the perceptual, social, emotional, and academic concept development of children. Physical education programs centering on the development and refinement of a variety of neuromuscular skills can, in fact, make many important contributions to other areas of development through sensitive teaching and the use of "teachable moments."

EXPERIENCE AS A VARIABLE IN MOTOR DEVELOPMENT

Until recently, the assumption had been made by many that children somehow automatically develop neuromuscular skills and that instruction, practice, and experience are of little or no real importance. It was thought that maturation alone accounts for the development of mature patterns of movement. As a result, the elementary physical education period, particularly at the preschool and primary grade levels, was looked upon as little more than a glorified recess period in which an endless variety of games ranging from Duck-Duck-Goose to Brownies and Fairies were played. Little thought was given to using the physical education period as a time for helping children learn how to use their bodies with greater efficiency and control. It was instead viewed as a time to get away from the pressures of the classroom, have fun, and "blow off steam."

It is now recognized that experience is an important aspect of neuromuscular skill development and that children do, in fact, need opportunities, encouragement, and time to develop their neuromuscular skills. The preschool and early elementary years are the critical years for developing fundamental movement abilities, and maturation alone will not account for the mature development of these basic abilities. Although it is now clearly recognized that (1) opportunity, (2) encouragement, and (3) time are crucial for the development and refinement of children's movement abilities, these are often difficult commodities to come by. They are discussed in the following paragraphs.

THE MOTOR DEVELOPMENT DILEMMA

Many of today's children are born and raised in the congested atmosphere of the city; they live in high-rise apartment buildings, cramped housing complexes, and sprawling suburbs, all of which are too often poorly equipped to meet their physical and recreational needs. There is often little space to play ball, fly a kite, or play a game of tennis. The facilities that do exist and have been set aside for public use are hotly contested for by children and adults alike. All too often the needs and interests of the children are preempted by those of the adolescent and adult, and young boys and girls are left to fend for themselves in the pursuit of vigorous movement experiences. Opportunity for practice in neuromuscular skill development is also often limited by lack of proper equipment. The cost of basketballs, baseball gloves, and hockey sticks, for example, is high. In most schools and community centers it is prohibitively expensive for each child to have his own pieces of equipment for practice and use. Homemade equipment can help to fill this gap but not completely. Also, many parents cannot afford the cost of sports equipment for their children, making it impossible for them to practice at home.

Many of today's children do not receive sufficient encouragement to develop their movement abilities. The fast-paced society of today is one in which both father and mother are often employed. As a result neither has the time nor the energy for active physical involvement with his or her children. Children learn by example and are quick to notice and imitate Mom and Dad in their pursuit of the "good life." They are often witnesses to a "workaholic" work ethic, which leaves little time for family activities, leisure, and purposeful recreational pursuits. Or they may be part of a family in which the cares of the workday are left behind to be replaced by the mind-dulling escape of the television set. This failure to stimulate, encourage, and motivate children to active involvement in physical activity because the parents lack time, energy, or interest or because they set a poor personal example for children to follow results in the failure of many children to develop mature patterns of movement.

A third factor affecting the development of neuromuscular skills in children is time. A cursory look at the daily schedule of most school-age children readily reveals little free, unstructured time during the day for the pursuit of movement activities. A great many of today's children are bused to and from school. The bus ride to school followed by five or six hours of schooling and the bus ride home leaves only the after-school hours for vigorous activity. All too often these hours are spent staring at the television set. By the time the television set is turned off, dinner eaten, homework completed, and another hour or two of television watched, it is time for bed. Where are the three to four hours of daily vigorous physical activity that educators and physicians agree are necessary for the normal, healthy development of children? The sad fact for a very large number of today's children is that the time does not exist because of a lack of sufficient opportunities during the school day and a lack of adult encouragement.

A SOLUTION?

Some may counter the argument that children do not have sufficient opportunity, encouragement, or time set aside in their daily routine for vigorous activity. They may claim that interscholastic sports and community athletic programs, intramurals, and free time on weekends provide plenty of opportunity for developing and refining movement skills. This may be true—*for some*. All too often, however, the interscholastic community athletic programs cater to the physically gifted children who make up no more than 20 per cent of the total population. Is it really fair to say that these programs offer opportunities for "all?"

Intramural programs at the elementary school level offer great potential for active involvement in physical activity. Intramurals go beyond the interscholastic and community athletic program concept by being geared to the interest and ability level of most children, or the 80 per cent of the population who are not classified as the physically gifted. Unfortunately, however, intramurals in a great many of our nation's elementary schools are more of a myth than a reality. The potential is great, but the opportunity is often limited. Schools with extensive busing programs find it difficult to permit children to stay after school for intramural activities, and a noon-hour program is often limited because of dual use of the gymnasium as a lunchroom.

What about using free time on weekends to engage children in purposeful physical activity? Again, the potential is great, but a look at many American homes is sure to reveal millions of children watching hour after hour of television on Saturday morning, followed by a host of afternoon movies or televised sporting events.[1] It is not enough to participate in sports through watching television and being a sports fan. Active involvement is crucial. You can't sit and be physically fit! Nor can you learn skills by watching someone do them. *You* have to do them.

The fact is that unless we are willing to use a portion of the school day for instruction and practice in a variety of movement patterns and skills, a large segment of today's children will not develop these abilities on their own. The elementary school physical education program that is developmentally sound, well planned, properly conducted, and of sufficient duration is the best possible solution for assuring the neuromuscular development of the greatest number of children. A commitment is required on the parts of parents and educators alike to see that children receive the best possible education both academically *and* physically.

CRITICAL PERIODS

Failure to develop and refine fundamental movement patterns and sport skills during the elementary years often leads to frustration and failure during adolescence and adulthood. Failure to attain these basic abilities makes it extremely difficult to find

---

[1]Research shows that children three to five years old average 54 hours of TV viewing time each week. The prekindergartener spends more than 64 per cent of his time watching TV. By the time he graduates from high school, he will have spent roughly 22,000 hours watching television, compared with 11,000 hours in school.

success, satisfaction, and enjoyment in leisure-time activities involving vigorous physical activity and in lifetime sport participation. Failure to develop the mature patterns
of throwing, catching, and striking, for example, makes it quite difficult to experience
success and enjoyment in a recreational game of baseball or softball. The inability to
swim makes it impossible to enjoy swimming as a leisure-time activity. In other words,
one cannot take part with success in a specific sport as an adult if one did not develop
the essential movement abilities contained within that activity as a child. This does not
mean that the adolescent or adult cannot develop and refine basic movement skills
with practice, but the fact is that he or she is beyond the critical period of childhood in
which it is easiest to develop these abilities. Several factors contribute to this situation.
One important cause is an accumulation of bad habits from improper learning.
Learned behaviors, whether they take the form of correct or incorrect performance, are
very difficult to erase, for it is much harder to "unlearn" faulty movement patterns than
to learn to do them correctly in the first place. Self-consciousness and embarrassment
are other factors. "He has two left feet," "I'm all thumbs," or "what a klutz" are all
derogatory phrases we use to describe our poor performance or that of others. A third
factor is fear. Fear of being hit in the face by an approaching ball and fear of drowning
are very real anxieties that contribute to the difficulty in developing mature patterns of
movement later in life. It is crucial that children develop *fundamental movement
abilities* and *efficient sport skills* during the elementary school years in order to help
avoid frustration, failure, and rejection of physical activity later in life.

FUNDAMENTAL MOVEMENT ABILITIES

The period ranging from about two to seven years of age is most critical for the
development of fundamental movement abilities. It is during this time that boys and

FIGURE 2–1.   Mastery of hand-eye coordination is basic to learning all major
movement skills. (Courtesy of Thelma Goodwin, Central College, Pella, Iowa.)

FIGURE 2–2. I like pushing and pulling activities! (Courtesy of *The Instructor*. Photograph by Edith Brockway.)

girls develop and refine basic patterns of movement in three areas: locomotion, manipulation, and nonlocomotion.

Locomotor movement abilities are generally considered to be those by which the body is transported in a horizontal or vertical direction from one point in space to another. Such activities as running, jumping, hopping, leaping, galloping, and skipping are considered to be fundamental locomotor abilities.

Manipulative movement abilities are considered to be those that involve giving force to objects or receiving force from objects. Throwing, catching, kicking, trapping, and striking are among those considered to be fundamental manipulative abilities.

Nonlocomotor movement abilities are ones by which the body remains in place but moves around its horizontal or vertical axis. Nonlocomotor movements place a premium on gaining and maintaining equilibrium in relation to the force of gravity. Axial movements such as reaching, twisting, turning, bending, and stretching are fundamental nonlocomotor abilities, along with lifting and carrying, and pushing and pulling.

As pointed out earlier, the development of fundamental movement abilities to their mature state is not an automatic process. Experience is vital. Recent research reveals that the development of efficient patterns of movement generally occurs in three stages: initial, elementary, and mature.[2]

Initial Stage

During the period of infancy (birth to two years of age) children are involved in a process of acquiring rudimentary movement abilities. These early forms of movement serve the infant's basic survival needs. The infant develops a variety of crude locomo-

---

[2]McClenaghan, B., and Gallahue, D. L.: *Fundamental Movement: a Developmental and Remedial Approach.* Philadelphia, W. B. Saunders Company, 1978.

SELECTED RUDIMENTARY MOVEMENT ABILITIES (up to two years of age)

Locomotion	Manipulation	Stability
1. Forward Thrusting	1. Reaching	1. Control of Head
2. Crawling	2. Corralling	2. Control of Neck
3. Backward Creeping	3. Palmar Grasp	3. Control of Upper Trunk
4. Forward Creeping	4. Pincer Grasp	4. Sits with Support
5. Walking with Support	5. Uncontrolled Release	5. Sits Alone
6. Cruising	6. Controlled Release	6. Pull to Stand
7. Walking Unaided		7. Stands with Support
		8. Stands Unaided

FIGURE 2–3. The sequence of emergence of selected rudimentary movement abilities.

tion, manipulation, and stability abilities in a sequential manner. Figure 2–3 presents a list of some of the major rudimentary movement abilities acquired during infancy in the order in which they appear. The rate of appearance may vary from child to child depending upon environmental circumstances, but the *sequence* of their emergence is fairly rigid. Only extreme conditions within the environment will have any measurable effect on the sequence.

As the infant emerges from the rudimentary movement ability phase of motor development as a toddler, he or she enters the initial stage of the development of fundamental movement abilities. The distinction between the two phases is not clear-cut or easily discernible, but the second phase is generally considered to begin around the second birthday.

In the initial stage the child makes the first observable purposeful attempts at performing fundamental movement patterns. This phase is characterized by crude, uncoordinated movement. The child makes valid attempts at throwing, catching, kicking, jumping, and the like, but major components of the mature patterns are missing. Rhythmical, coordinated execution of movement patterns at the initial stage is absent.

Elementary Stage

The elementary stage of fundamental movement pattern development follows the initial stage and is characteristic of the typical movement performance of four and five year olds. The elementary stage of development appears to be primarily dependent upon maturation. It is relatively easy to predict the manner in which a nursery school child will throw, catch, kick, and perform numerous other fundamental movements. The elementary stage is a transitional period between the initial and the mature stages. Coordination and rhythmical performance of movements improve and the child gains greater control over his movements. Movements at this stage may still appear awkward and lack fluidity of motion because some aspects of the pattern are still missing or performed incorrectly.

Many adults are only at the elementary stage in such basic activities as throwing, striking, and catching. Such comments as "He throws like a girl," "You swing like a rusty gate," and "She looks like she's catching eggs" are unfortunate but all too often true of many adolescents and adults. They have progressed to the elementary stage in

FIGURE 2–4. You shift your weight forward as you throw. (Courtesy of Documentary Films, Aptos, California.)

their fundamental movement abilities by virtue of maturation, but because of lack of experience they have failed to progress to the mature stage of performance.

Mature Stage

The mature stage of fundamental movement pattern development can be seen in six and seven year olds, provided there are abundant opportunities for practice and experience. Children pass through these developmental stages at varying rates. Some may be delayed in their motor development and pass through them more slowly than may be expected, whereas others may be advanced and pass through them more rapidly. It is important to keep in mind, however, that if development is delayed over a period of years, the child may never achieve mature patterns of movement without considerable effort and outside influence.

The mature stage of fundamental movement is characterized by integration of all the component parts of a particular pattern into a well-coordinated, efficient act. Performance improves rapidly from this point. The child, with increases in physical fitness, motor fitness, and practice, is able to throw farther, run faster, and jump higher as he gets older. A mature pattern may be continually refined, combined with other mature patterns, and finally utilized in sport-related activities.

SPORT-SKILL ABILITIES

Around the eighth year, children begin to develop a keen interest in sport-related activities. Boys and girls alike select their favorite sports heroes, don football jerseys and baseball caps, select their favorite running shoes, and carry a basketball or a baseball glove to school.

They begin to develop basic skills in a wide variety of sports and are eager to learn them all. Efficient sport-skill development is based on the proper development of fundamental movement abilities and continues into adulthood. There are three stages of sport-skill development, ranging from the general through the specific to the specialized stages of development.[3]

General Sport-Skill Stage

The general sport-skill stage begins around eight years of age and extends to about ten years. Boys and girls at this stage generally have a high degree of expressed interest in all sports but little ability in any. They are eager to learn many sports, and the physical education program should be one in which the sport skills and basic rules for a wide variety of sport and dance activities are introduced. The student should be given opportunities to further refine specific fundamental movements and to use them as sport skills in lead-up activities. For example, the fundamental movement pattern of kicking may now be applied to the sport skill of using the instep kick in soccer. This skill is practiced and may be applied in a lead-up game such as line soccer or circle soccer. At the general sport-skill stage boys and girls do not play the official sport; rather, they are exposed to the basic skill aspects of several sports through skill drills and lead-up game activities.

Specific Sport-Skill Stage

The specific sport-skill stage is typified by the middle school or junior high school student, who is about eleven to thirteen years of age. Boys and girls at this stage have begun to select the *types* of sports they prefer. Their preferences are generally based on previous successful experiences, body build, geographical location, and emotional and social factors. Some may prefer dual sport activities, whereas others may prefer team sports. Some may enjoy contact sports, whereas others may prefer noncontact sports. Some may particularly enjoy water sports, others court sports, and still others dance activities. The narrowing of interest at this stage brings with it an increased desire for competence. Form, skill, accuracy, and standards of good performance are all stressed at the specific sport-skill stage. Individuals begin pursuing their favorite activities through intramurals or interscholastic competition or on a recreational basis. More complex rules, strategies, and skills are developed during this time, and the first real exposure to the official sport should occur during this period.

Specialized Sport-Skill Stage

The specialized sport-skill stage is the third and final stage of sport-skill development. It generally begins around the fourteenth year and continues throughout adulthood. It is at this time that individuals select two or three sport activities that they particularly enjoy and want to participate in as lifetime pursuits. Generally at this stage high interest in an activity is evidenced by active participation in it on a regular

---

[3]Gallahue, D. L., Werner, P. H., and Luedke, G. C.: *A Conceptual Approach to Moving and Learning.* New York, John Wiley & Sons, Inc., 1975.

out-of-school basis at either a competitive or recreational level. The development and refinement of a variety of fundamental movement abilities and sport skill abilities to a level at which one may take part in several sport-related activities on a regular, enjoyable, purposeful basis for life is the ultimate objective of the physical education program throughout the elementary and secondary school years.

Figure 2–5 is a visual representation of the two phases of motor development discussed in the above paragraphs and their corresponding stages.

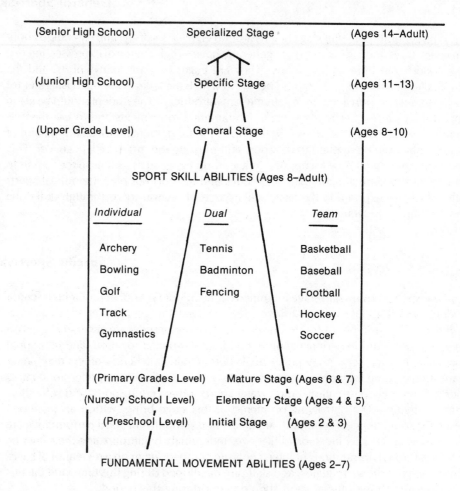

(Senior High School)	Specialized Stage	(Ages 14–Adult)
(Junior High School)	Specific Stage	(Ages 11–13)
(Upper Grade Level)	General Stage	(Ages 8–10)

SPORT SKILL ABILITIES (Ages 8–Adult)

Individual	*Dual*	*Team*
Archery	Tennis	Basketball
Bowling	Badminton	Baseball
Golf	Fencing	Football
Track		Hockey
Gymnastics		Soccer

(Primary Grades Level)   Mature Stage (Ages 6 & 7)
(Nursery School Level)   Elementary Stage (Ages 4 & 5)
(Preschool Level)   Initial Stage   (Ages 2 & 3)

FUNDAMENTAL MOVEMENT ABILITIES (Ages 2–7)

Locomotor	*Manipulative*	*Non-Locomotor*
Walking	Throwing	Stretching and Bending
Running	Catching	Swinging and Swaying
Hopping	Kicking	Turning and Twisting
Jumping	Trapping	Pushing and Pulling
Skipping	Stripping	Lifting and Carrying
Galloping	Bouncing	Falling
Leaping	Rolling	

FIGURE 2–5

DEVELOPING FUNDAMENTAL MOVEMENT ABILITIES

As discussed earlier in the section on acquiring fundamental movement abilities, children pass through various stages in the acquisition of mature patterns of movement. The following is a compilation of several fundamental locomotor, non-locomotor, and manipulative movement abilities. A brief description of the mature performance of each pattern is given, followed by lists of common faults observed in children, teaching tips, and appropriate learning experiences.

LOCOMOTOR MOVEMENTS

Walking

This movement carries the body through space forward, backward, in a circle or square, or on a diagonal. It is the act of transferring body weight that occurs as one foot and the opposite arm move forward while the other foot and arm move backward, with one foot always remaining in contact with the floor. The movement should be rhythmical and relaxed, the head and back erect, and the eyes ahead rather than looking down at the feet.

COMMON FAULTS

Walking with feet turned out, or waddling; walking with the feet pigeon-toed, or on the toes or heels too much.
Dragging heels rather than lifting them.
Walking on the outer borders of the foot (ankle supination) or on the inner borders of the feet (ankle pronation).
Drooping and shuffling along instead of moving erectly with vigor.
Incorrect arm and foot action. As one moves forward, the other should move backward in rhythm.
Being too stiff or too collapsed.
Thrashing the arms too much to pump the body forward.

TEACHING TIPS

Stand tall. Keep all three parts (head, trunk, buttocks) of your body balanced like stacked boxes.
Relax, and move like royalty. Hold head up and chest out, suck stomach in, and tighten hips.

LEARNING EXPERIENCES

Walk around the room, pushing your head toward the ceiling.
Walk and change directions on a signal.
Walk fast, slow, hard like a giant, soft like a midget. Step high, then low.
Walk like an elephant, bird, and other animals.
Walk in tempo to music; walk in double time.
Walk crossing one foot over the other in a zigzag step.
Walk carrying a heavy suitcase, a balloon.
Walk in 2s, 4s. Walk in a straight line of ten, keeping in step.
Walk as fast or as slowly as you can.

Running

A run is a speeded-up walk except that there is a momentary loss of contact with the floor by both feet as the body moves forward. The knees are bent more and the legs are lifted higher and put down more forcibly as the body leans slightly forward. Again, as one foot moves backward the opposite arm moves forward. The continuing interchange of arm and foot positions should be rhythmical.

COMMON FAULTS

Running too erectly, stiffly, and awkwardly.
Arms remaining down at the sides instead of being bent and moving forward or slightly across the body.
Not lifting knees high enough.
Running with heels instead of toes touching the floor first.
Running pigeon-toed or spraddle-legged.
Throwing the legs and feet out to the sides too much.
Running with knees too stiff and leaning the body forward too much.

TEACHING TIPS

Run on the balls of your feet.
Swing arms and hands forward.
Keep your head up and back straight.
Look ahead, not down.
Run lightly, quickly, and as though you are happy.
Run rhythmically.

LEARNING EXPERIENCES

Play simple games involving running found elsewhere in this book.
Run in place; run in circles, in squares, on a diagonal.
Run in rhythm with a partner; run in rhythm in 3s, 5s, 7s, 10s.
Run fast and stop suddenly on a signal; run forward, backward, and to the side, and stop.
Run, combining this movement with a hop, gallop, skip, wide jump, high jump, and low jump.
Run through a turning rope; run in and jump between two ropes turning "Double Dutch," then run out. Run in, jump ten or more times, run out.
Run zigzag, with a partner; run zigzag in 3s, 5s, 7s, 10s, with all keeping in rhythm.
Run lightly to a drumbeat or to music and listen to the rhythm of your movements.
Run like a deer fleeing a hunter; run and creep through the bushes like an Indian stalking an animal.
Run as fast and as slowly as you can.
Run as lightly and as hard as you can.
Run in relay races.
Run and jog for one half, then one or more miles.

Leaping

A leap is like a run except that it involves increased ankle and knee height. In the leap, body weight is transferred from one foot to the other while the body is in the air. The push-off should be from the supporting foot to propel the body high and far into the air. The take-off is on one foot, with the opposite arm back, and landing is on the other, with a bent knee. When the body is in the air, the arms move upward. Although a leap can be done from a standing position, it is best for children to run-run-leap or to take several running steps before leaping.

COMMON FAULTS

Landing flatfooted, on one foot, or on the heels.
Landing with knees stiff.
Failing to swing the arms forward and to stretch and reach with the legs.
Not pushing off with enough spring.

TEACHING TIPS

Push U-P, S-T-R-E-T-C-H, and R-E-A-C-H with your forward foot as you leap.
Swing your arms up and out.
Leap O-U-T.
Run, run, *leap!*

LEARNING EXPERIENCES

Run and jump over a folded mat, over one rope raised higher on each successful try, between two ropes moved wider apart each time.
Run and leap over a small hurdle, then over several hurdles spaced apart that are placed increasingly higher.
Leap as far as you can, as high as you can.

Hopping

In this movement weight is transferred from one foot back to that same foot. On the upward body thrust, the toes of that foot are last to leave the floor, and the arms move sharply upward to lift the body up into space above the head. Landing is done on the same hopping foot, and weight is transferred quickly from the ball of the foot to the heel. It can be done on either foot.

COMMON FAULTS

Landing with a thud; landing flatfooted instead of on the ball of the foot.
Inability to hop very far up into space as a result of being too earthbound.
Taking off on one foot and landing on the other one.
Falling because of balance loss.

TEACHING TIPS

Hop high! Hop high!
Swing your arms forward to help you jump higher.
Keep your body erect and head up to make a straight vertical line with your body.

LEARNING EXPERIENCES

Hop in place ten times on your right foot, ten on your left foot.
Hop in a circle, around a square, on a diagonal.
Hop as low to the floor as you can, then up higher from this position on each hop.
Hop forward, back, to the side as fast as you can, as slowly.
Hop in rhythm with a partner, in 3s, in 5s, in 10s.
Hop to a 4/4, 3/4, and 2/4 rhythm. Change your arm and body positions on each hop.

Galloping

This is a forward movement done in a side stride position with one foot always leading. Weight is transferred from that foot to the rear one, then quickly back to the front causing a rocking motion. The toes of the rear foot should come close to the heel of the lead foot to propel the body forward. A gallop is an uneven leap-and-walk step that moves the body forward.

COMMON FAULTS

Moving the body too far forward; the body should be erect.
Keeping the knees and body too stiff; the movement should be a rhythmical one.
Bobbing instead of moving gracefully. Moving on the heels instead of on the balls of the feet.

TEACHING TIPS

Relax, and glide forward.
Clap out a three-beat uneven rhythm, emphasizing the first beat.
Swing your arms freely forward and backward.

LEARNING EXPERIENCES

Gallop like a pony around the room.
Gallop in rhythm with a partner and in 4s, 6s.
Gallop as fast as you can, as lightly, as slowly, as hard.
Reverse the lead foot on the count of 5, 10, 15.
Gallop in a circle, in a triangle, a square, on diagonal lines, in a rectangle.
Gallop moving your body as close to the floor as you can, as erectly as you can.

Skipping

A skip is a combination of an uneven, short hop and a long walk step done on one foot and then on the other to an uneven rhythmic beat. Spring from the ball of one foot, and land back on it as you step with the other foot and transfer your weight to it. Alternate swinging your arms forward and backward.

COMMON FAULTS

Inability to hop from one foot to the other. This is basic in learning to skip. When the child can hop on his right foot on the count of 1 and then on his left foot on the count of 2, he can more quickly learn to skip.
Landing flatfooted instead of on the ball of the foot.
Being stiff instead of moving the arms and body rhythmically.

TEACHING TIPS

Lift up your knees.
Step forward and hop up on the same foot.
Swing your arms in time with your legs.

LEARNING EXPERIENCES

Skip to music in as many different directions as you can.

Skip with a partner, in 4s, in a straight line of ten with all keeping together.
Can you skip backward?
Alternate the lead foot every ten skips.
Skip high, low, fast, slowly.
Hold skipping relays.

Sliding

A slide is a combination of a step and hop that is usually done sideways with the same foot always leading. Land to the side from a slight spring, transferring weight to the ball of one foot. Step to bring the feet together as you move to an uneven rhythm.

COMMON FAULTS

Not gaining distance by moving body too high in the air.
Not shifting body weight from the lead to the following foot and vice versa.
Landing on the heels instead of the balls of the feet. (Children should learn to gallop and skip before learning to slide in order to learn how to land properly).
Turning the body too much to the right or left rather than sliding with the body turned to the side and moving in a straight line.

TEACHING TIPS

Move in rhythm on to "slide, slide, slide" and a drumbeat first, then do so to music. Keep your body up and slide lightly and rhythmically.
Always lead with the same foot.

LEARNING EXPERIENCES

Slide with all facing in a circle, then with all facing out.
Slide around the room.
Slide facing a partner, both moving in rhythm.
With four, eight, then ten in a line all face right and slide in rhythm together to the end of the room; all turn and slide back.
Slide as fast as you can, as slowly.
Face a partner, slide four counts, turn back to back, slide four counts; keep on reversing positions on five, seven, nine counts.
Combine a slide with a skip, run, or walk, with partners making up their own pattern.

Landing and Stopping

Jump off an object and land on both feet. Bend the knees, take the weight on the balls of the feet, and keep the body erect. To stop when running or skipping, bend the knees somewhat, lean back slightly, take a quick catch step, and hop to stop the body's forward momentum.

COMMON FAULTS

Landing

Keeping knees locked, without enough "give" to absorb the jolt of the floor contact.
Not keeping the body erect or not coming back to an erect position quickly enough after landing.
Landing on the whole foot instead of on the balls of the feet.

Stopping

Not absorbing the movement by bending the knees slightly.
Losing balance after stopping.
Jumping forward instead of hopping slightly upward to regain body balance more quickly when stopping after a skip.

TEACHING TIPS

Landing

Extend your arms out to your sides to add style.
"Give" with your body as you land.
Keep your chest out, head up, and body in a straight line.

Stopping

Give and lean backward slightly, then come quickly to an erect position.
Land with your feet inside the shoulder girdle line, not far apart.

LEARNING EXPERIENCES

Landing

Jump from various heights on a mat from a standing position.
Run, jump, and land facing forward, sideways, and backward.
Jump over a folded mat and land, over a crouched partner as in leap frog, over two persons.
Jump, land, and then run, skip, slide, gallop, and so forth.
Jump and turn one, two, three times in the air.
Jump and touch your toes as in a jackknife dive, your toes with your legs out to the sides, your heels behind your body.
Jump, click your heels together twice, and land with feet apart.
Jump on the trampoline or minitramp or from a springboard to perfect skills in jumping and take-off positions after landing.

Stopping

Run forward fast and stop as quickly as you can. Do the same moving sideways, backward.
Skip, and stop when the whistle blows; turn and run and stop; combine other locomotor movements with stopping suddenly on signal.
Run 10, 20, 30, 40 steps, stop, turn, and run in a different direction.

Dodging

Dodging is a quick sharp movement that directs the body away from a moving person or stationary object by changing the motion of the body to avoid or lean away from an oncoming obstacle and by moving quickly in another direction to escape contact. It is done by bending the knees while moving forward to lower the center of gravity and then twisting the body away from its original direction.

COMMON FAULTS

Not bending the knees.
Holding the body in any one position too long.
Being too stiff and inflexible.

TEACHING TIPS

Stop and twist away quickly.
Bend your knees and snap away or you will be hit or hurt. Move quickly in the opposite direction.

LEARNING EXPERIENCES

Play tag games with a partner.
Shadow box with a partner.
Run to an obstacle, avoid it, and keep moving forward.
Play line or circle dodgeball.
Try to avoid body contact as a partner tries to kick you any place between the knees and stomach. (Boys only, using a mild type of karate-style kick.)

NONLOCOMOTOR MOVEMENTS

Stretching and Bending

Bending is contracting or flexing the body; streching is extending it. These two movements go together, as in opening and closing the fingers.

COMMON FAULTS

Being able to do one movement well and the other poorly or too slowly.
Losing balance when flexing and extending the body or while standing on one leg and bending and stretching the other.
Being too fat or lacking physical strength to be able to bend and extend fully the trunk, arms, or legs.

FIGURE 2–6.   Exploration of stretching and bending movements. (Courtesy of the Detroit Public Schools, Detroit, Michigan.)

FIGURE 2–7. Hanging activities develop upper arm and shoulder girdle strength. (Courtesy of Creative Playgrounds Corporation, Terre Haute, Indiana.)

TEACHING TIPS

Curl up into a ball, then stretch out and reach for the sky.
Bend way down, come up, and S-T-R-E-T-C-H.
Make yourself as little as you can and then as tall as you can.

LEARNING EXPERIENCES

Bend, then straighten your whole body while standing, lying down on your back.
Bend and straighten your legs while lying on your back, use a bicycle-pedaling motion, making circles as big as you can.
Bend and straighten your arms, your fingers, each finger, your whole hand, your neck.
Bounce like a ball up and down; bounce close to the floor, then as low and as high as you can, alternately, for ten counts.
Hang from a chinning bar in full extension; bring your legs up to "sit" on the air while hanging.
Bend one arm and extend the other 20 times. Do the same in turn with the fingers on one hand and your hands at the wrist joint. Sit and swing your legs in opposite directions.
Discover how many ways you can bend and stretch your body.

Swinging and Swaying

Swinging is done mostly with the arms and legs and the upper part of the body, in a circular or pendular motion. Force and speed can be applied to the swing by adding a more vigorous drop. To stop, discontinue the force of the downward recovery swing. To sway, move rhythmically and shift weight easily.

COMMON FAULTS

Being rigid instead of limber.
Swinging and swaying too hard, causing loss of body control.
Fear (which retards learning speed) of swinging from high objects such as bars and rings (show how to land should one fall).

TEACHING TIPS

Relax and swing and sway!
Swing and sway rhythmically and lightly.

LEARNING EXPERIENCES

Swing your legs, arms, trunk, and head to music.
Swing and sway from the waist with your arms overhead; move your arms in as many ways as you can as you bend.
Sway like a tree in the wind, like a clock pendulum.
Swing one arm backward and forward and the opposite leg forward and backward; next use the other arm and leg.
Jump onto and swing on a hanging climbing rope.
Swing and sway your whole body like a rag doll.
Swing your hips while standing in place; swing as many other parts of your body as you can as you do so. Then sway, using your whole body in a complete body swing up and down, from side to side, around in a circle.
Find out how many body parts you can swing at one time; swing them in opposite directions, swing as slow as you can, then as fast as you can. Using a hula hoop, see how many times you can make it go around your body without missing.

Turning and Twisting

A turn is a circular movement through space in which the whole body completely revolves. Twisting is the rotation of the entire body or any of its parts from a stationary base. On the turn, a slight initial twist in the opposite direction will add momentum.

COMMON FAULTS

Having the skill to turn one way (usually right) but not the opposite.
Fearing loss of balance, which can result in an actual fall.
Moving too fast and losing body control.

TEACHING TIPS

Turn and twist and have fun!
Relax and let yourself go but control your movements.

LEARNING EXPERIENCES

Turn as many parts of your body as you can; do this as you twist your body in all kinds of ways you discover.
Turn and twist as fast as you can, as slowly.
Find out how many parts of your body you can twist, how many you can turn.
Turn and twist standing on one leg, standing on your head, lying on your back, lying on your stomach.
Turn after skipping ten times forward and go the other way; stop and twist after 5, 10, 15 hops.

Turn with a partner in as many different ways as you can.
Ring the Dishrag. Face a partner. Hold hands and by raising one arm together turn so you are back-to-back with one turning clockwise and the other counterclockwise and return facing each other.

Falling

Relax, tuck your head in, land on padded areas of the body, give with the knees, and go into a roll.

COMMON FAULTS

Landing with a thud, instead of melting or collapsing.
Getting up too quickly.
Trying to break the fall with the hands and arms rather than absorbing the fall with the whole body.
Not tucking head in.

TEACHING TIPS

Relax and fall easily
Bend your knees.
Roll before you land.
Take the fall on your shoulders and tuck your head and tail in.
Make yourself into a soft, round ball.

LEARNING EXPERIENCES

Fall gradually from a standing position forward, backward, to one side.
Rise slowly and erectly from a crouched position on the mat; squat slowly down and move back to get the feel of the fall recovery.
Roll forward, backward, and to each side in a tucked position.
Jump from a low object and roll forward on a mat.
Roll around in a circle, making yourself into a tiny ball. Then jump from a low object and roll forward twice before coming into an erect position.

MANIPULATIVE MOVEMENTS

Throwing Overhand

For the right-handed player, the ball is held in the right hand with the first two fingers on top of the ball, the third and fourth fingers spread comfortably to the side, and the thumb supporting the ball from underneath. Do not allow any part of the palm to touch the ball.

With the feet in stride position, the weight equally distributed, and the left foot forward, the left shoulder turns toward the target, moving the body at right angles away from the target. As the right arm moves back to a position behind the head at about ear level, the weight shifts to the rear leg. The elbow points away from the body with the upper arm parallel to the ground. The wrist is cocked backward. On the release, the forward leg extends in the direction of the target, the shoulders turn parallel to the target as the body rotates, the hips move forward, and the arm is brought forward in a semicircular motion. The hand passes forward past the ear, the elbow straightens, the wrist uncocks, and the ball rolls off the first two fingers. The power of the swing carries the arm down and across the body, rotating the body so that the shoulder of the throwing arm points toward the target.

COMMON FAULTS

Not facing the target sideways.
Holding the ball in the whole hand instead of in three fingers.
Having the wrong leg forward, leaving the body unbalanced instead of having one arm forward on one side of the body and one leg back on the opposite side.
Not shifting weight from front to back to front again.
Releasing the ball above or below shoulder height.
Not leading the throwing motion from the elbow.
Failure to follow through in a rhythmical motion.

TEACHING TIPS

Move the arm forward and backward, bring it around in a circle, and T-H-R-O-W, pointing to the target at shoulder level. Your elbow leads.
Throw the ball with three fingers, not your whole hand. A-I-M, and throw.
Make a big circle with your arm and release the ball with your arm at shoulder level.

LEARNING EXPERIENCES

Use bean bags and soft playground balls instead of regulation softballs for the youngest children first.
Throw at clown targets or areas drawn on the wall.
Play lead-up games to softball, involving throwing and catching skills.
Play pitch-and-catch with a partner.
Throw a softball, handball, and football for accuracy.

Throwing Underhand

The underhand throw is used for a quick throw when there is little time to stand or to take a full backswing after fielding a grounder. The ball is held with the thumb on top. The first and second fingers are under the ball, and the third and fourth fingers are on the side of the ball. The body is crouching more than for the overhand throw, and the ball is held below shoulder level. The arm swings back, bent elbow restricting backswing, parallel to the ground, and wrist cocked. The forward foot extends, and the arm swings across the body at waist level as the body follows.

COMMON FAULTS

Not shifting weight properly from the front foot to the opposite back leg and then back to the front.
Failure to bring the arm back far enough on the backswing.
Stepping forward on the wrong foot.
Releasing the ball at the wrong time and place instead of when the arm is at a right angle to the target.
Body imbalance caused by not moving the opposite arm back when the ball is released.

TEACHING TIPS

Throw at the center of the target. The pitching arm moves straight down from in front of the body, then back, and then forward to T-H-R-O-W.
Twist your body on your arm swing down to give you power.

LEARNING EXPERIENCES

Play lead-up games to softball.
Practice throwing at a target on a wall.
Play catch with a partner.
In 2s, see which couple can throw back and forth to each other without missing the ball using good form.

Catching

If the ball is above the waist, the hands and thumbs are held together upward; if it is below the waist, the little fingers are together and the hands held down. The feet should be in line with the ball in a forward stride position. The player should move forward to meet the ball as it approaches if on the ground. When the ball is caught, it should be pulled toward the body.

COMMON FAULTS

Being afraid of the ball.
Not being in line with the oncoming ball.
Not "giving" with the ball when it is caught.
Not curving the fingers around the ball enough so that it gets away.
Failure to widen the stance for an oncoming fast ball.
Remaining too long in a crouched position after catching the ball instead of changing to an erect position, and stepping forward quickly on one foot to throw the ball.

TEACHING TIPS

"Give" with the ball.
Stay in line with the ball.
Go out to meet the ball if it is on the ground.
Keep hands up and together for a high ball; keep hands down and together for a low one.

LEARNING EXPERIENCES

Play pitch-and-catch with a partner.
Throw and catch by yourself, working on getting the ball at different levels.
Practice catching balls thrown from different distances and different speeds.
Catch for someone hitting the ball to you (fungo batting).
Throw the ball as high as you can and catch it. See how far away you can be to catch successfully.
Use bean bags and throw to a partner 3, then 5, then 10 feet away.
Throw a ball into the air, clap your hands one, two, three, five times before catching it.
Throw a ball into the air and see how many times you can turn around before you catch it.

Batting

A right-handed player places her left hand around the bat several inches above the end. The right hand is placed above the left and touches it. The natural grip is firm but not tense. The second joints of the fingers of the top hand are aligned with the knuckles of the lower hand. Batters attempting a power hit often use the end grip, bringing the hands as far down on the bat as possible. For more accurate and less powerful hits, a player may move her hands up the handle of the bat. This "choke" grip is particularly useful to a player who swings late because of weak arm and shoulder strength.

STANCE.   A comfortable, natural stance is taken in the batter's box. The distance from the plate is gauged by the individual's reach and swing. Feet are comfortably spread and knees are relaxed to support the upright trunk facing the plate. The bat is held up and back by an almost straight left arm and a bent right arm. The elbow of the right arm is pointing toward the ground and away from the batter. The batter looks over her left shoulder toward the pitcher.

STRIDE.   Just before the ball reaches the strike zone the batter slides her left leg several inches toward the pitcher. The body moves forward as the swing begins.

The bat moves forward in a level plane as the hitter watches the ball moving toward the plate. The hips pivot forward, and the body turns toward the pitcher with the bat moving rapidly forward. As the bat meets the ball, the arms extend, and the wrists snap and roll into the follow-through. As the hands and wrists roll, the body weight shifts to the forward foot. Near the completion of the follow-through the hands are completely over, with the back of the right hand uppermost, and the right foot, free of body weight, strides toward first base.

COMMON FAULTS

Missing the ball by not keeping your eye on it, or swinging too fast, slow, high, or low.
Feet too far apart.
Not facing sideways.
Punching and chopping at the ball instead of swinging to hit it.
Inability to judge correctly the speed of the ball.
Tensing up and trying too hard.
Not swinging rhythmically.

TEACHING TIPS

Relax, swing, and hit the ball.
Take an easy stance; relax your knees.
Keep your eye on the ball.
Swing in a straight line.
Keep your hands together.
Bring your bat back far and swing rhythmically.

LEARNING EXPERIENCES

Hit balls thrown to you by the teacher or partner.
Practice hitting balls thrown at various levels and speed.
Throw the ball up and hit it to a partner (fungo batting).
Play lead-up games to softball.
Play regular games of softball and baseball.

PLAY AND SPORT-SKILL DEVELOPMENT

Play means being absorbed in an activity for the sheer joy of it and not just to satisfy or accomplish a particular end or purpose. It is the enjoyment of an activity, any

FIGURE 2–8.   Children need plenty of opportunity to explore their environment. (Courtesy of Jayfro Corporation, Montville, Connecticut.)

activity, for its own value or merit, without external motives. Play is *fun*. It is the fun of playing that keeps people involved in play. Play takes many forms. First, there is gross motor play, which may range from climbing a tree or hiking to swimming or water skiing. Second, there is sensory play, which includes watching a sunset, listening to a symphony or a rock band, or tasting a cake one has just made. A third type of play is intellectual in nature. It involves such things as attending a lecture, seeing a movie, or reading a book. Through recreational play activities both the child and the adult become refreshed and revitalized. The value of play to children and adults is immense. It is an important means of escape from the cares, tensions, and worries of everyday life. Play is therapeutic in that it permits the individual to engage in it for the sheer sense of enjoyment and pleasure that it brings him.

One very important type of play, and the primary concern of this chapter, is gross motor play. Since many children sit during most of their time in school and are directed in their many activities by an adult, they must become more active and self-directed in their play during their free time. Our children are watching television and sitting at home too much. According to a recent study conducted by the American Academy of Pediatrics, a child spends more hours watching television before he goes to kindergarten than a college student spends in the classroom in his four years of college. This same child spends about 64 per cent of his waking hours in front of the television, a fact that clearly indicates that many parents have abdicated their daily responsibilities of involving their child in worthwhile pursuits that will contribute to his growth and development.

One of the important contributions a good elementary physical education program makes is to enable children to make better use of their leisure time. It helps to provide them with the "tools" they need to play more effectively and efficiently as children and, later, as adults.

FIGURE 2–9. Using the latest kinds of equipment will add zest to your program. (Courtesy of Creative Playgrounds Corporation, Terre Haute, Indiana.)

The Value of Play to Children

Children are dynamic, exploratory creatures. The vast portion of their early learning comes from and through movement. One is amazed at the number of things a one year old child can do. The greatest learning period of a person's life is between one and six years of age, and the more children see, hear, and do, the more they want to see, hear, and do. By the age of three, children have learned to a large extent how they *should* and *will* deal with their worlds. If they are normal, throughout life they will continue to add skill upon skill until a peak is reached. Children find deep satisfaction in the big-muscle movements of running, skipping, hopping, and jumping. Joy comes in pretending, in moving to sounds, in playing tag, and in chasing and being chased. Some adults have erroneously believed that children, because they naturally seem to enjoy movement, pretense, and rhythm, do not need to learn how to play. Although play is universal, each child in each culture (whether he or she is an Eskimo, Pygmy, or a freckle-faced American boy or girl) must be and is taught by adults the games of the clan, tribe, or city block, plus those most favored ones of his own sex, race, and religion. Both tradition and education influence the child through the adult. Games such as Run, Sheepie, Run, Fox and Geese, and Red Rover are passed down to children. They are eager to learn them, for children crave to be like grownups, to do the things adults would like them to do, to play games favored by adults. Often the cry is, "Teach us a game you played when you were little."

The play of children up until the age of three is largely narcissistic play, or playing alone. This isolated period of play is followed by parallel play, in which they can play for a short time with one or two other children. They refuse to share their playthings and will scream in anger when the child next door grabs their toys and runs away. As they grow older they become more social in their play interest and will voluntarily play with two, three, or four others. They also become more socially conscious, more willing to share. Just how many games they will play and how many other children they want to and can play with successfully depends upon their age, how well they were taught to play, when they were taught, and by whom. The first grader who has learned to play well with others in a small group and can follow simple directions has learned much indeed.

Children from rural areas need directed play just as much as city children, in spite of the fact that they have wide fields in which to roam and trees to climb. In fact, among rural children this need to learn how to play with others is often intensified.

Through play, the child learns about himself and the world around him, as well as to accept or work around his own limitations and those set for him by adults. Perhaps most important of all, however, is the fact that play reduces a child's world to manageable proportions. It is through play that the child first discovers how to use his own body and its many intricate interdependent parts. He soon learns, too, that through play he can gain power over his own peers as well as over adults who will continue to pick up the toys that he continues to throw out of his playpen. Among very young children, play is marked by the conflicting desire to become independent from and yet to remain close to his mother. Play also provides children with outlets for feelings and strong emotions that cannot be expressed through words and helps them to rid themselves of forbidden desires and "dirty thoughts" without feeling guilty or actually carrying them out in actions. As children learn to play with others they also quickly come to see that they can include or exclude others if they wish, and gradually they begin to form a protective group out of which one will emerge as the leader.

Speech develops rapidly through play, and the more the child learns to use words to substitute actions (for example, saying "I will hit you!" rather than actually hitting), the more he can organize his thoughts and verbalize them to others, which will enable him to fit into and contribute to groups. It is through exploratory play that movement skills are learned and refined.

Perhaps the greatest value of play to a child is as the greatest builder of self-concept. A child can play without fear of failure. Play also gives him a chance to be a "holy terror" without being punished; thus, it is a great safety valve, keeping the child emotionally balanced. Through play a child learns how to gain control of his own body, how to get his arms and legs to move rhythmically together. For a change, it gives him a chance to do what *he* (not an adult) wants to do. Play is the most significant thing a child does. It is a mirror that reflects him as he really is. *If you want to know what a child is like, watch him play. If you are concerned about what he will become, guide his play.*

The Value of Play to Older Youth

Because of differences in strength, play interests, and physical capacity, boys and girls are usually separated at the fourth grade for instruction in physical education. Boys tend to like rugged games in which they can show their strength, while girls tend to favor rhythmical activities and team games. As each sex grows older, activities are favored in which they can meet members of the opposite sex. During the adolescent period, which has been called often the time of temporary disorganization, the youth is awkward, ill-at-ease, moody, and rebellious. He is more apt to bridge the gap successfully between childhood and adulthood if he can play several sports with more than average skill, and if he has mastered some social graces fairly well or at least well enough not to be completely miserable at a social gathering. Above all, it is vastly important that somewhere between the ages of 10 and 15, skill patterns laid down in previous years be refined, reinforced, and relearned. Unless youth can dance, play tennis, swim, ride horseback, or do other sport skills well, their chances for learning to do so at the age of 20, 30, 40 or later are very small. As one grows older he is more fearful of losing face among his peers. It is only the unusual adult who learns how to swim or play golf or other sports unless basic movement patterns similar to those found in these activities were learned during early life.

The Value of Play to the Adult

As a person grows older he tends to become physically, emotionally, and mentally sluggish. Too often he is a victim of heartburn, headaches, or ulcers. One reason why heart disease is the chief cause of death among American people is that people burn themselves out too early; they become frustrated and unhappy, not from physical fatigue, but from overworking their emotions and their minds. Some medical authorities claim that modern man works all day and worries all night. Many American adults tend to be pleasure-mad without finding real or abiding enjoyment in many of the things they do or seek. They rarely spend their leisure time leisurely or recreatively. Recreation alone will not cure our contemporary national problems or the personal problems of each citizen. It can help, however, especially if one knows how to choose the physical and recreational activities best suited for his age and finds meaning, joy, release from tension, and renewed purpose from doing them.

Whether or not one develops a state of physical, emotional, and mental fitness depends, among other things, upon practicing good health habits regularly. Routinized daily health habits of early childhood become habitual and tend to carry over to later life. A healthy, happy childhood is the foundation upon which a healthy, happy adulthood rests.

SUGGESTED READINGS

Corbin, C. (ed.): *A Textbook of Motor Development*. Dubuque, Iowa, William C. Brown Company, Publishers, 1973.

Cratty, B. J.: *Perceptual and Motor Development of Infants and Children*. New York, Macmillan, Inc., 1970.

Espenschade, A., and Eckert, H. M.: *Motor Development*. Columbus, Ohio, Charles E. Merrill Publishing Company, 1967.

Gallahue, D. L., Werner, P. H., and Luedke, G. C.: *A Conceptual Approach to Moving and Learning*. New York, John Wiley & Sons, Inc., 1975.

Gallahue, D. L.: *Motor Development and Movement Experiences for Young Children*. New York, John Wiley & Sons, Inc., 1976.

Gerhardt, L.: *Moving and Knowing: The Young Child Orients Himself in Space*. Englewood Cliffs, New Jersey, Prentice-Hall, Inc., 1973.

Gilliom, B.: *Basic Movement Education For Children*. Reading, Massachusetts, Addison-Wesley Publishing Company, Inc., 1970.

Godfrey, B., and Kephart, N.: *Movement Patterns and Motor Education*. Appleton-Century-Crofts, 1969.

Herron, R. E., and Sutton-Smith, B.: *Child's Play*. New York, John Wiley & Sons, Inc., 1971.

Larrick, N.: *Children of television*. Teacher Magazine, September 1975.

McClenaghan, B., and Gallahue, D. L.: *Fundamental Movement: A Developmental and Remedial Approach*. Philadelphia, W. B. Saunders Company, 1978.

Piaget, J.: *Play, Dreams and Imitation in Childhood*. New York, W. W. Norton and Company, Inc., 1962.

Rarick, L.: *Physical Activity: Human Growth and Development.* New York, Academic Press, Inc., 1973.
Singer, N. C.: *The Psychomotor Domain: Movement Behavior.* Philadelphia, Lea & Febiger, 1972.
Walters, H.: *What TV does to kids.* Newsweek, February 21, 1977.
Wickstrom, R. L.: *Fundamental Motor Patterns.* Philadelphia, Lea & Febiger, 1977.

SUGGESTED RECORDS FOR USE WHEN TEACHING BASIC MOVEMENT SKILLS

Creative Rhythm Album. Bowmar Records, 622 Rodier Drive, Glendale, California.
Get Fit While You Sit; And The Beat Goes On; Creative Movement and Rhythmic Exploration; Simplified Folk Songs For K–3; Mod Marchers; Roomnastics I and II; To Move Is To Be; Keep on Steppin'; Clap, Snap and Tap. Educational Activities, P.O. Box 392, Freeport, New York.
Popular and Folk Tunes For Dancing and Rhythmic Movements. Hoctor Records, Waldwick, New Jersey.
Coordination Skills; Modern Dance; Jumpnastics; Movement Exploration; Music For Creative Movement, Series 1 and 2; Movement Fun; We Move to Poetry; Animal Rhythmics. Kimbo Education Records, Box 55, Deal, New Jersey.
Fundamental Steps and Rhythms, Album 20. Folkraft, 1159 Board Street, Newark, New Jersey.
Elementary Rhythms. Phoebe James Productions, Box 134, Pacific Palisades, California.
Freda Miller Records For Dance. Albums 1 through 5. Freda Miller Records, Box 55, Deal, New Jersey.

CHAPTER THREE

PHYSICAL FITNESS AND YOUTH DEVELOPMENT

The physical vigor of our citizens is one of America's most precious resources.

John F. Kennedy

Physical fitness is a topic of great interest throughout America. In recent years professional as well as lay literature has devoted considerable coverage to the fitness status of our nation's youth. This was brought about largely by the results of tests comparing the physical fitness of American children with that of European and Asian youth. The tests revealed that American boys and girls were in poorer physical condition than their Italian, German, English, Japanese, and Chinese counterparts. Although some physical educators and physicians challenged the reliability of these tests and questioned the sweeping generalizations made from them, much has since been achieved in developing public awareness of the importance of developing and maintaining acceptable standards of physical condition. Further refinement of fitness-testing devices, accumulation of more evidence, reduction of parental apathy, and improved physical education programs for many children have been important by-products of the heightened interest in our youth's physical fitness.

Since the administration of Dwight D. Eisenhower each president of the United States has been actively involved in improving and promoting the fitness of our children. A committee on youth fitness was established by President Eisenhower in 1956 as a result of the distressing comparison of our youth's fitness with that of youth from other nations. President Kennedy further supported this effort by establishing the President's Council on Youth Fitness. The council has continued to be a viable organization disseminating information and promoting fitness programs, testing, and public interest throughout the administrations of each succeeding president. The efforts of the Youth Fitness Council as well as those of concerned parents and teachers must continue if we are to adapt to an ever-changing world and increasingly complex society.

There is no doubt that in our present period of drastic change, which has no historical precedent, American parents tend to be overly indulgent and our children sit too much watching mediocre spectator activities. The increased mechanization of our farms, the automation in our factories, and the population explosion will in the future bring us more leisure, more wealth, more self-indulgence, and a whole set of new and challenging problems of great magnitude. Certainly there is an abundance of evidence that in this time of shifting values, our present problem of the "soft" American who already has leisure and is throwing it away is minute in comparison with what the problem will be in the future. Likewise, we know that although our "creature comforts" are increasing rapidly, man has not changed biologically. Children have a compulsive drive for movement; their need for it is as basic as that for sleep or food. The curtailing of vigorous activity for children of all ages can lead to faulty structural development and alarming results. There is an abundance of scientific evidence that (1) there is a strong correlation between vigorous health and educational progress and success, (2) play activities are directly related to good mental and emotional health, (3) the status of a child in school in relation to his peers is dependent to a great extent upon his motor skills and sportsmanship, (4) the problem of obesity begins early in life and is due as much to underactivity as to overeating, (5) regular activity increases the density of bones of the body and produces organic changes that increase resistance to stress and strain and greatly improve the function of the organs and systems of the body, and (6) children who are strong and energetic have fewer absences from school. Physical activity *is* essential to human growth and development.

Collectively, the fitness of all people is one of our greatest assets, for as President John F. Kennedy said, "The physical vigor of our citizens is one of America's most precious resources. If we waste or neglect this resource, if we allow it to dwindle or grow soft, then we will destroy much of our ability to meet the great and vital challenges which confront our people."[1]

WHAT IS FITNESS?

The word fitness is difficult to define objectively, for it means many things to many people. In 1956, 100 delegates to the AAHPER Fitness Conference proposed the following components that must be achieved in order for one to function efficiently and to do his part in contributing to the welfare of society:

One is physically fit when he has

1. Optimum organic health consistent with heredity and the application of present health knowledge.
2. Sufficient coordination, strength, and vitality to meet emergencies as well as the requirements of daily living.
3. Emotional stability to meet the stresses and strains of modern life.
4. Social consciousness and adaptability with respect to the requirements of group living.
5. Sufficient knowledge and insight to make suitable decisions and arrive at feasible solutions to problems.
6. Attitudes, values, and skills that stimulate satisfactory participation in a full range of daily activities.
7. Spiritual and moral qualities that contribute the fullest measure of living in a democratic society.

Fitness is the ability to live a life that is balanced and complete. It is a state of physical, mental, emotional, social, and spiritual well-being. The concept of fitness is a totality of all the functions of man operating in harmony interdependent upon one another (see Fig. 3–1).

---

[1]Kennedy, J. F.: *The soft American*. Sports Illustrated, December 26, 1960.

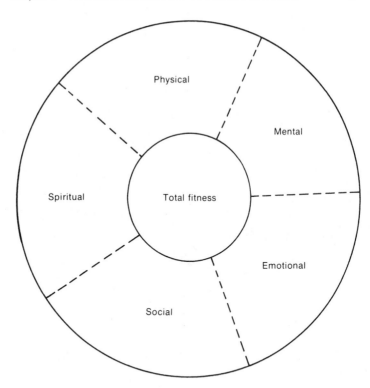

FIGURE 3–1. The aspects of total fitness.

WHAT IS PHYSICAL FITNESS?

Physical fitness is one aspect of total fitness. It is interrelated with the other aspects of fitness and may be defined as the ability to perform life's daily tasks without undue fatigue and still have ample reserves of energy left to meet emergencies and enjoy recreational pursuits. Being physically fit is relative to the tasks in which the individual must engage. The degree of fitness required of one individual to meet the daily requirements of living may be quite different from another. For example, a bricklayer or postman will require a different type of fitness from an accountant or a bank teller to adequately perform his job. The student who plays on an athletic team requires a type and degree of fitness different from what is required by the student who is on the debating team.

There are three factors that play an important role in the development and maintenance of physical fitness. First, the health status of the individual establishes the upper and the lower limits of fitness that can reasonably be expected. Second, the nutritional status of the individual can greatly inhibit or enhance the level of physical and mental functioning. Third, the genetic structure of the individual sets the upper limits of fitness that can be attained. Parents, teachers, and leaders of youth must understand the influence of these factors on fitness and also possess knowledge of the components and the principles of developing physical fitness.

COMPONENTS OF PHYSICAL FITNESS

There are generally considered to be four health-related components of physical fitness: muscular strength, muscular endurance, circulatory-respiratory endurance,

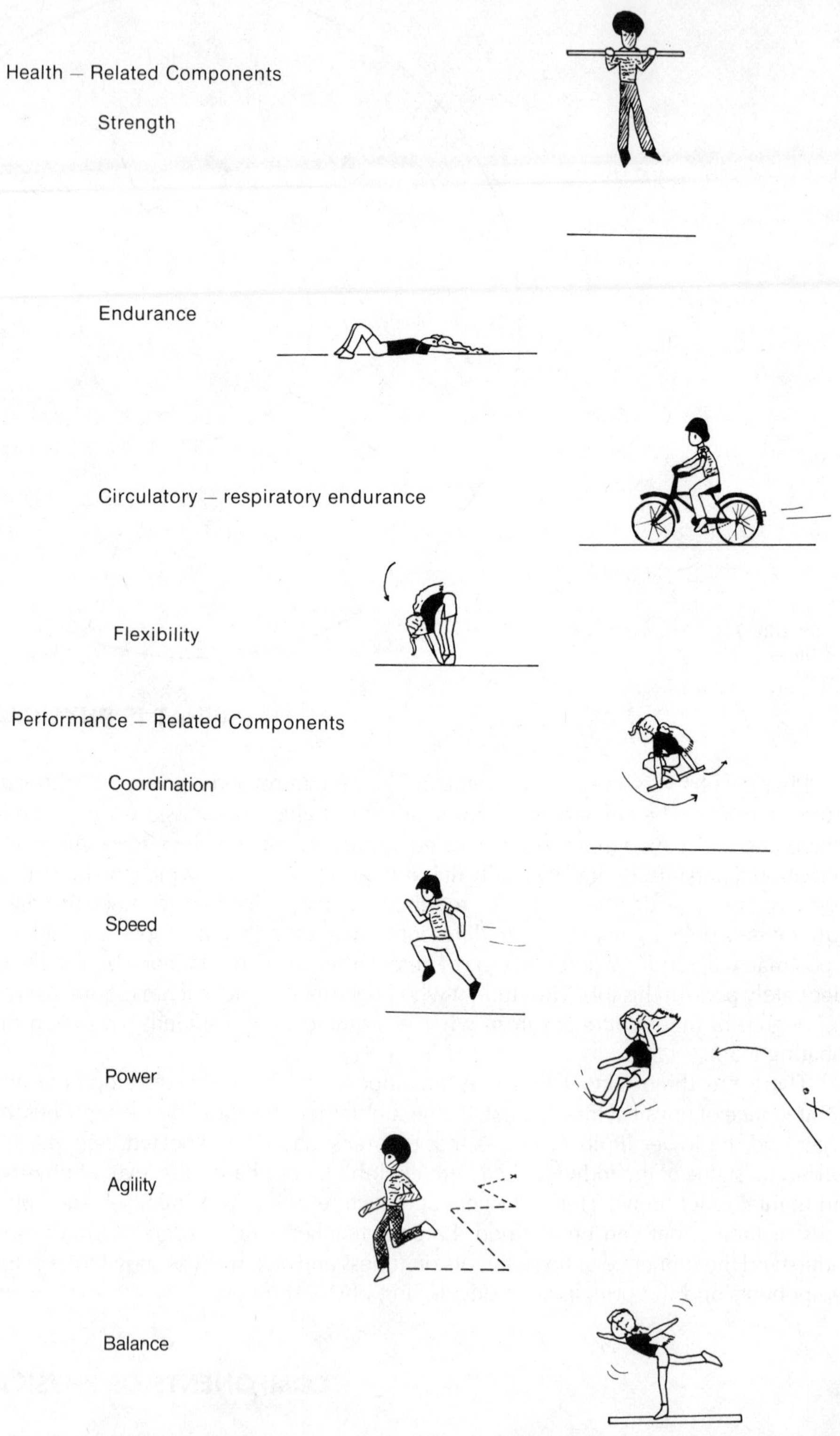

Health — Related Components

Strength

Endurance

Circulatory — respiratory endurance

Flexibility

Performance — Related Components

Coordination

Speed

Power

Agility

Balance

FIGURE 3–2.   The components of physical fitness.

and flexibility. There are also five performance-related components of physical fitness: coordination, speed, power, agility, and balance.

Muscular Strength

Muscular strength is the amount of force that can be exerted by a single muscle or a group of muscles in one single maximal effort. Strength is influenced by the size of the muscle and its quality. The normal process of maturation, exercise, heredity, and good nutritional habits affect the size of the muscle. Strength is specific to the muscles exercised and can only be increased if the muscles are required to perform a greater amount of work than they are accustomed to do. There must be an ever increasing amount of resistance against which the muscles work before they grow stronger and produce increased body strength.

Muscular Endurance

Muscular endurance is the ability of a muscle or group of muscles to continue contracting over an extended period of time against a moderate resistance. It is closely related to strength but differs primarily in that it involves a greater number of contractions with moderate resistance; strength development involves fewer contractions but greater resistance. In order to improve muscular endurance, one must increase the number of repetitions of a movement. If he wishes to increase strength, he does not increase the repetition but does increase the resistance.

Circulatory-Respiratory Endurance

Circulatory-respiratory endurance is a highly specific form of muscular endurance that is concerned primarily with the heart, blood vessels, and lungs. Circulatory-respiratory endurance is enhanced by placing continual stress on large-muscle groups for a long period of time through such activities as running, swimming, and cycling. The circulatory and respiratory systems are taxed to a point at which they are required to supply greater quantities of oxygen to the muscles so that they may continue to work. The increased work loads required of the two systems result in increased circulatory-respiratory endurance.

Flexibility

Flexibility is the range of motion present at a given joint. It is increased through moderate progressive stretching and is specific to each joint in the body. Flexible joints are an important factor in efficient movement and the safety with which one may engage in sports activities.

There are several performance components of physical fitness. These components are more directly related to one's ability to perform skills well and to be able to enjoy participation in leisure-time activities than the health-related components of physical fitness discussed previously. They are, however, intricately related to strength, endurance, and flexibility. The following is a brief description of the motor fitness aspects of physical fitness.

Coordination

Coordination is the effectiveness and rhythmical efficiency with which one moves one's body. It involves the harmonious working together of all the many body parts. The various sensory modalities, i.e., vision, touch, and kinesthesis (feel), play an important part in coordinated movement. The terms "eye-hand coordination" and "eye-foot coordination," along with the familiar statements "She is getting the feel of it" and "He is developing his touch," are all indications of the perceptual and motor systems of the body working smoothly together.

FIGURE 3–3. Rope jumping is a vigorous aerobic activity requiring considerable coordination. (Courtesy of Things from Bell, Homer, New York.)

FIGURE 3–4. The cargo net develops strength, agility, and coordination. (Courtesy of Things from Bell, Homer, New York.)

Speed

Speed is the ability to perform rapidly successive movements over a short period of time in a single direction. The speed of an individual is related to both his reaction time and his movement time. Reaction is the length of time it takes to move after being stimulated to do so. For example, the length of time between the sound of the starter's pistol in the 100 yard dash to the time it takes the individual to make his initial movement out of the starting blocks is a measure of his reaction time. Research indicates that reaction time is innate and is not affected greatly through practice. Movement time (the time it takes from your first movement to the completion of that movement) learning can be improved through practice and concentration upon improved techniques of efficient movement shortcuts.

Power

Power is a combination of both speed and strength. It is the ability to perform one maximum *explosive* effort in the shortest time with the greatest efficiency. Power is involved in jumping, throwing, and kicking objects for distance and can be improved through practice on the specific item of interest and by increasing the strength in the muscles involved in the act.

Agility

Agility is the ability to make successive movements in different directions as efficiently and as rapidly as possible. It is important in activities involving dodging, quick starts, stops, and changes in direction. Agility is closely related to speed, strength, and coordination and can be improved through participation in activities that involve these factors.

Balance

Balance is the ability to maintain equilibrium when one's center of gravity and base of support are altered. Balance is controlled by the semicircular canals located in the inner ear, the proprioceptor nerve endings located in the muscles and joints, and the focus of the eyes during movement. There are two types of balance—static and dynamic. Static balance is the individual's ability to maintain equilibrium while his center of gravity remains stationary, as in the act of standing on one foot. Dynamic balance is the ability to maintain balance while the individual's center of gravity is shifting, as in the act of walking on a balance beam or jumping rope on one foot. Good balance is important because it is involved in one form or another in virtually all game, sport, and dance activities. Children can improve their balance through practice in activities that place a premium on gaining and maintaining balance, such as walking on a balance beam.

PRINCIPLES OF FITNESS DEVELOPMENT

There are certain principles that must be recognized by parents, teachers, and children in the improvement and maintenance of a person's level of physical fitness. Each of the following factors should be taken into consideration when determining the type of fitness program to establish and the amount of activity the children are to do!

Overload Principle

In order to increase fitness, a person must perform more work than he is generally accustomed to doing. This may be accomplished by either increasing the amount of work done (such as by doing 20 push-ups rather than 10) or by reducing the time period in which the same amount of work is accomplished. An overload of the specific systems will enhance one's level of fitness. The amount of overload must be progressively increased in order to promote continual fitness improvement and to gain increased strength.

Principle of Specificity

Improvement in the various components of fitness is specific to the type of training engaged in and to the muscles being exercised. Even though the components of fitness and the various systems of the body are related, specific types of training result in developing specific qualities of fitness and produce greater amounts of change in the parts exercised. Strength activities, for example, will not have much influence on improving muscular and circulatory-respiratory endurance. Coordination is not generally improved through the performance of push-ups, and the shoulder-girdle muscles are not strengthened by running or playing a game of Alley Soccer.

Principle of Use and Disuse

Utilizing a part of the body in various activities will either improve its efficiency or help it remain at about the same state. Failure to use the body part will cause it to diminish in its efficiency. Muscles that are used regularly will grow or increase in size, whereas muscles that are not used regularly will atrophy or decrease

FIGURE 3–5. Climbing and chinning activities help children gain needed shoulder-girdle and arm strength. (Courtesy of Jayfro Corporation, Montville, Connecticut.)

in size. This can be aptly demonstrated by observing an arm or leg that has just been removed from a plaster cast. The limb is loose, flaccid, and smaller in size than its counterpart. Use promotes improvement, while disuse leads to regression. That which is used will live and grow; that which is neglected will die and slowly fade away. This applies to all living things, including plants, animals, and people.

Principle of Individual Differences

Each person improves his level of fitness at his own rate. This is due to several factors, i.e., age, body type, nutritional status, body weight, health status, and motivation. There are no criteria for individual rates of improvement, and each child will respond in a manner peculiar to his own particular environmental and hereditary characteristics.

WHY SHOULD WE BE CONCERNED ABOUT PHYSICAL FITNESS?

In recent years professionals and experts in early childhood education and elementary education have stressed the importance of the early years in learning and in establishment of lifetime patterns in many areas. The lifetime pattern for physical development, just like that for cognitive development, is often cast during these early years, so teachers and parents must do all they can to enhance the child's development during this critical time. However, the need for carefully planned activities to enhance physical fitness throughout the child's education is also obvious.

Recent studies have shown that vigorous physical activity is necessary in the early years because exercise in the form of play stimulates bone growth, develops lung capacity, and aids in blood circulation.[2] It has also been shown that good motor development and physical fitness contribute to academic achievement. Children are more alert and pay more attention to their classwork when they are physically fit.

Another very important reason why we should be concerned about physical fitness of children is its implications and effect upon the general health of the child. The relationship between a lack of physical exercise and numerous health disorders has been emphasized by competent authorities. For example, in recent studies conducted by medical experts a strong parallel existed between muscle status and pain disability. It is believed that exercise throughout life does much to prevent pain caused by muscular deterioration.[3] Authorities also have evidence that supports the belief that physical exercise helps prevent degenerative diseases by preserving the heart and blood vessels.[3] It is also believed that physical fitness will help protect the body against stress by toughening the nervous system.[4] From this, one can conclude that physical fitness should be developed because it (1) stimulates physical growth, (2) is essential to the well-being and safety of the child, and (3) helps to prepare for physical and emotional emergencies.

---

[2]Moffett, M.: *Physical play—it's vital.* The Instructor Magazine *82*:48, January 1973.
[3]Hunsicker, P.: *Physical fitness:what research says to the teacher.* Washington, D.C., National Education Association (NEA), 1963, p. 11.
[4]Cureton, T. K.: *Health and fitness in the modern world and what research reveals.* Journal of Physical Education *70*:238, September 1972.

FIGURE 3–6. The achievement of optimal fitness during the formative years is basic to the education for the building and maintenance of fitness in adulthood. (Courtesy of AAHPER, Washington, D.C.)

Obesity and weight problems are found in children as well as in adults and should be of concern to parents and teachers. As reported by Corbin, studies have shown that inactivity is a more relevant factor than overeating in childhood and adolescent obesity.[5] Physical exercise and physical fitness are important in controlling one's weight. The obese person has less energy for activities and often a shorter life expectancy owing to a greater incidence of various diseases in the overweight person. In addition to these problems related to obesity, the person who is overweight may also develop a negative self-image as a result of his or her appearance and inability to function well in physical activities both as a child and as an adult.

PHYSICAL FITNESS TESTING

Physical fitness testing has become quite common in our nation's schools. The results of these tests are used for (1) determining the physical status of each student, (2) identifying those who are deficient in certain areas and need special help, (3) classifying students, (4) measuring progress, and (5) aiding in activity selection and program

---

[5]Corbin, C. B.: *A Texbook of Motor Development.* Dubuque, Iowa, William C. Brown Company, Publishers, 1973, p. 100.

FIGURE 3–7. Children respond well to exercises, for many are motivated by a desire to play on an athletic team. (Courtesy of *The Instructor*. Photograph by Edith Brockway.)

planning. The results of each child's performance on tests of fitness should be placed in the cumulative record and made available to parents in order that they may be apprised of particular strengths and weaknesses. Parents should be encouraged to promote activities for their children that will help them overcome their deficiencies in physical fitness. It has been found that the majority of adults are eager to do whatever they can to help their child's physical functioning, and it is strongly urged that fitness test results and recommendations regarding each child be sent home with the child.

It is not recommended that fitness testing be begun before the third or fourth grade. Children below this grade level generally are not very interested in putting forth maximal effort when taking the tests. As a result, the information that is obtained is often inaccurate, misleading, and of very little concern to the child in the primary and lower intermediate grades. Children in the fourth grade and beyond, however, are developing a keen spirit of competition and are interested in knowing their performance abilities. They can be easily motivated to do their best and generally exhibit a great deal of enthusiasm in taking fitness tests.

When selecting a test for inclusion in the program, the teacher should be sure that it suits her purposes and meets certain criteria. She should have information concerning its reliability, objectivity, validity, norms, and ease of administration. A test that has *reliability* is one that measures whatever it is measuring consistently. A test with *objectivity* yields the same results even though it may be administered by different teachers. A test with *validity* is one that measures what it is supposed to measure and not something else. *Norms* are standards of performance that have been established in order that comparisons may be made within groups of children and between groups of children. Norms may be established on a school, city, state, or national basis, and they permit the teacher to judge pupils' performances in relation to other students' performances. A test that has *ease of administration* is one that can be given in a reasonable amount of time with a minimal amount of equipment. Physical fitness tests can play an important role in the total program *if* the results of these tests are used to aid the teacher, pupils, and parents in improving our nation's (1) level of fitness, (2) attitude toward the importance of physical fitness, and (3) knowledge of how to achieve higher levels of fitness.

Many tests have been developed that measure some of the components of physical fitness. These tests can be divided into two types: those taken when the child is resting or in a quiet state and those taken when he is going through physical performances. Each of these has value in assessing the child's level of physical fitness.

Those tests taken in a quiet state are usually in the form of medical examinations given by physicians to determine the child's physical condition. Since fitness programs involve physiological stress, it is important that the child receive an examination before beginning strenuous physical activity. Although the classroom teacher is not responsible for diagnosis, the teacher should be informed of the child's condition, so that she can relate it to the physical fitness program.

The tests that indicate how well a child can function in physical activities are of great value. Since a number of agencies and individual researchers have developed tests on the measurement of physical fitness, the teacher should not have any difficulty in obtaining suitable physical fitness tests. A list of standardized fitness tests and where they may be obtained may be found at the end of the chapter.

The American Alliance of Health, Physical Education, and Recreation (AAHPER) Youth Fitness Test (revised edition, 1976) is by far the most popular test of fitness used in our schools today. The Kraus-Weber Test of Minimum Muscular Efficiency is also used extensively, particularly with young children. In addition to these widely used tests there are other tests that have been developed by various school systems for their own use. These tests can be just as valid and useful as standardized tests and provide motivation for practice. You can make up your own physical fitness test by combining elements of various standardized tests. The following is a list of some things you may wish to measure under each component of physical fitness:

1. Muscular endurance. Muscular endurance of the abdominal muscles may be measured by such test items as trunk curls, leg lifts, bent-knee sit-ups, and the V-sit.
2. Muscular strength. This may be measured by use of the dynamometer and tensiometer. The use of hand grips, as well as isometric and isokinetic activities, will improve strength.
3. Circulatory-respiratory endurance. Test items may include cycling, hiking, rope jumping, 600-yard run, 6, 9, and 12 minute runs, and distance swimming.
4. Flexibility. This may be measured by performing lateral bends, trunk flexion activities, back lifts, floor touching, and other activities.
5. Agility. Leg thrusts, the shuttle run, side-step squat thrusts, and the zigzag run are all good measures of agility.
6. Balance. Static and dynamic balance may be measured on the balance beam and balance board.
7. Power. Explosive arm and shoulder power can be measured by testing the ability to throw a medicine ball, softball, or basketball for distance. Leg power may be measured by such activities as the mountain climber, vertical jump, standing long jump and standing high jump.
8. Speed. Timing children in the dashes ranging from 30 to 100 yards is a good measure of speed. Having them run for a stipulated number of seconds to see how much distance they can cover in 5 or 10 seconds is a good measure also.

There are basically three factors that are prerequisites to physical fitness. These are (1) plenty of rest, (2) good nutrition, and (3) regular exercise. The teacher must help provide these three conditions. For example, if young children require additional rest periods during the school day these should be provided. The teacher can also help the child to know what is good nutrition and how to make wise food choices. Moreover, the teacher can provide physical activity regularly and help the child to develop physical skills. Most importantly, the teacher can help the child to develop good attitudes regarding these three areas of rest, nutrition, and exercise.

Another important concept is that physical fitness is individual and that it exists in various degrees. When motivation and opportunities are provided, practically all students can improve their physical fitness status.

One must keep in mind that achieving and maintaining physical fitness is a lifetime job. Good physical condition is not a permanent condition. With this fact in mind, the teacher should strive to help children realize that they need physical activity throughout life.

SCREENING TESTS FOR FITNESS

Although it is not recommended that all children below the fourth grade be involved in formal fitness testing, it is recommended that the teacher establish a battery of informal tests that can be administered periodically as a screening device for children with suspected physical deficiencies. It is not necessary or recommended that the entire class be involved in this testing procedure in the lower grades. The teacher will get a better measure of the child's true capabilities if the tests administered are given on an individual or small group basis. Appropriate items from several other formal tests may be selected and utilized and minimum levels of achievement established. Children in the lower grades, for example, can be tested for joint flexibility along with back and abdominal strength (which are only two of the several components of physical fitness) by means of the Kraus-Weber test.[6] This is the test in which 57.9 per cent of the American children failed one or more of the items shown below, in contrast to 8.7 per cent of European youngsters in the same category. Although some children may pass this test with ease, many will be unable to pass all six items. Again, it should be pointed out that this test measures only the minimum strength of the trunk muscles of the body and thus is concerned with only one aspect of fitness.

Although many schools increased physical fitness activities after the results of the Kraus-Weber test were made public, recent studies show that the resulting actual fitness gains have been minor and that once again our children are not as fit as they should be.[7]

THE KRAUS-WEBER TEST

Test I.   Clasp the hands behind the neck, and roll up to a sitting position as someone holds both feet on the floor.

Test II. Bend the knees, clasp the hands behind the neck, and roll up into a sitting position as someone holds both feet on the floor.

Test III. With hands clasped behind the neck and legs extended straight, raise the heels 10 inches from the floor. Hold this for 10 seconds or as someone counts, "One thousand and one, one thousand and two, one thousand and three," and so forth.

---

[6]A modification of the Junior Physical Fitness and Proficiency Test of the Amateur Athletic Union of the United States is also recommended. Copies can be obtained from this organization, 233 Broadway, New York, New York.

[7]Hunsicker, P., and Reiff, G.: *Youth fitness report.* Journal of Health, Physical Education, and Recreation, January 1977.

  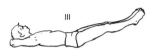

Test IV. Lie face down with a pillow under the abdomen. Clasp hands behind the neck; then raise head, chest, and shoulders off the floor. Hold this for 10 seconds or ten counts as in Test III.

Test V. Place the hands under the head and a pillow under the abdomen. Raise both legs off the floor, and keep knees straight. Hold this for 10 seconds or ten counts as in Test IV.

Test VI. Keep feet together and slowly bend forward, keeping knees straight; see how nearly you come to touching the floor with your finger tips. Do not bend the knees or bounce down. If you can touch the floor with the finger tips for three seconds or counts of "One thousand and one," and so forth, you pass the test; if not, it is a failure. (This is the one item most of the American children failed.)

The Revised AAHPER Youth Fitness Test

The revised AAHPER Youth Fitness Test (1976) is the most widely used physical fitness testing battery in the United States today. It is a direct outgrowth of the President's Youth Fitness Council. It is a six-item test that can be easily administered with a minimum of equipment and has established national norms for boys and girls in grades 5 to 12. Norms have also been established for mentally retarded youngsters between the ages of 8 and 18. The tests can be given outdoors or in the gymnasium. The test battery includes (1) *pull-ups (flexed-arm hang for girls),* for determining arm and shoulder girdle strength; (2) *bent-knee sit-ups,* for judging the efficiency of the abdominal and hip flexor muscles; (3) *shuttle run,* for judging speed and agility; (4) *standing long jump,* for determining power of the leg extensors; (5) *50-yard dash,* for measuring speed; and (6) the *600-yard run* (with optional runs of 1 mile or 9 minutes for children aged 10 to 12, and 1½ miles or 12 minutes for children aged 13 and older), for determining circulatory-respiratory endurance.

Test I. Pull-Ups (Boys)

Action: Grasp the chinning bar with the palms facing forward and the legs dangling free of the floor. Pull the body up until the chin is placed over the bar. Lower the body until the arms are fully extended. Repeat as often as possible.

Rules: The pull must not be a snap. The knees cannot be raised. No swinging is permitted. Kicking the legs is not allowed. One trial is permitted.

Equipment: Horizontal bar or wooden ladder with rungs about 1½ inches in diameter.

Scoring: Number of completed pull-ups is recorded.

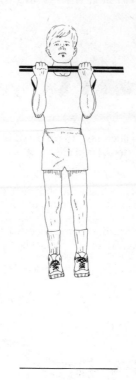

Test I. Flexed-Arm Hang (Girls)

Action: Grasp the chinning bar with the bar at standing height and the palms facing forward. Raise the body with assistance so that the chin is above the bar, the elbows are flexed, and the chest is close to the bar. Hold this position as long as possible.

Rules: The watch is started as soon as the flexed hanging position is assumed, and stopped when the chin touches the bar, the head tilts back in order to remain above the bar, or the chin drops below the bar.

Equipment: Horizontal bar or doorway gym bar about 1½ inches in diameter set at pupil's approximate standing height.

Scoring: Number of seconds to the nearest tenth is recorded.

Test II. Sit-Ups

Action: Lie on the back with the legs bent, feet on the floor, heels not more than 12 inches from the buttocks, and hands clasped on the back of the neck with the fingers interlaced and elbows on the floor. The feet are held by a partner. Curl up, and touch the elbows to the knees. Return to the starting position with the elbows on the floor before beginning another sit-up.

Rules: One trial per pupil is permitted. There shall be no resting between sit-ups. Only those sit-ups are counted in which the fingers remain clasped behind the neck, both elbows are brought forward in starting the sit-up, and the body is returned with the elbows flat on the floor before sitting up again.

Equipment: Mat on floor, or turf, and stopwatch.

Scoring: The number of correctly executed sit-ups performed in 60 seconds is recorded.

Test III. Shuttle Run

Action: Two parallel lines are marked 30 feet apart on the floor. Two blocks of wood are placed behind one of the lines and the pupil behind the

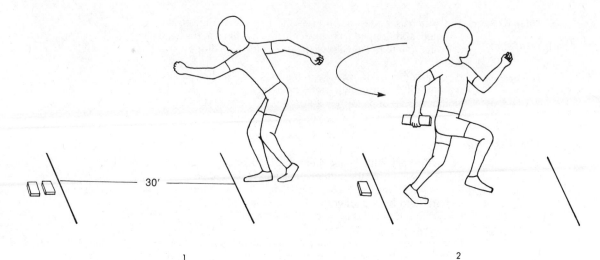

30'

1

2

other. On the signal "Ready? Go!" run to the blocks, pick one up, and run back to the starting line. *Place* the block behind the line. Run back for the second block, and carry it across the starting line.

Rules: First block must be placed down behind the starting line. Two trials with some rest between are given.

Equipment: Two wooden blocks, each measuring $2 \times 2 \times 4$ inches, and a stopwatch.

Scoring: Better of two trials to the nearest tenth of a second.

Test IV. Standing Broad Jump

Action: Stand behind the restraining line with the feet a comfortable distance apart. Perform a broad jump the greatest distance possible.

Rules: A 2-foot take-off and landing are required. Three trials are given, and the distance is measured from the front edge of the restraining line to the heels (or the closest part of the body to the restraining line that touches the floor).

Equipment: Tape measure or yard stick, and floor mat or jumping pit.

Scoring: Best of three trials in feet and inches to the nearest inch.

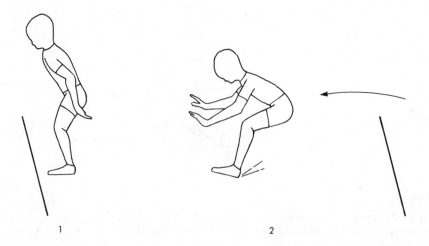

1

2

Test V. 50-Yard Dash

Action: On the verbal signal "Ready? Go!" two pupils will run as fast as possible over a level course marked off by two restraining lines 50 yards apart.

Rules: Children must run in a straight line, and record the length of time between the signal "Go!" and the time the pupils cross the finish line.

Equipment: Two stopwatches.

Scoring: Seconds to the nearest tenth are recorded.

Test VI. 600-Yard Run

Action: From a standing start at the signal "Ready? Go!" run a 600-yard course in the shortest time possible. The running may be interspersed with walking if necessary. Pupils pair off, and one runs while the other listens for and remembers his partner's time as the instructor calls it out when he crosses the finish line.

Rules: When walking, move to the outside of the course.

Equipment: A level, marked off area and a stopwatch.

Scoring: Record in minutes and seconds.

Two to five class periods are needed to administer the entire test. The tests should be given the first and last months of the school year. All pupils should go through a conditioning program before any part of the test is taken. The test scores should become part of each pupil's cumulative record and be used as a guide for program planning based on the needs of the pupil.

Teachers must be ever cognizant that there is far more to fitness than having the ability to chin oneself or being able to run a certain distance in the national average time. The value of fitness testing lies in the fact that the results can be used

1. To determine the extent to which a child gains and retains a standard of physical fitness.
2. As one way of determining the strengths and weaknesses of the physical education program in terms of achieving the physical fitness objective.
3. To place students in a physical education program based on their physical needs.
4. As a means of motivating children to achieve and maintain physical fitness.
5. To interpret to administrative personnel the purpose and value of physical education programs.
6. To convey to lay groups the meaning and value of physical education in our schools.[8]

MOTIVATING CHILDREN TO BE CONCERNED ABOUT FITNESS

During their early years, children are usually eager to participate in play activities. Too often it is assumed that since young children do participate in play activities during much of the time, they do not need a special fitness program. When this attitude is taken, the teacher often neglects to teach motor skills that are necessary for participation in many physical activities. These skills should be taught to young children especially, because in many cases the rate of learning will be much faster at the younger ages. By building these skills at an early age, children can maintain a high level of fitness and enjoy participating in activities when they are older. Children will participate in those activities that have been taught in the schools and those in which they have developed sufficient skills to enjoy their participation. Since it is during the early years that desirable attitudes and abilities for physical activity begin to be established, it is important that our schools have this as one of their goals.

In addition to providing challenging experiences, the teacher can also provide a great range of activities. By getting to know the individual student and assessing his interests and abilities, the teacher can plan activities that are appealing and that are appropriate to the child's age and developmental level. This is extremely important because it can help prevent experiences that are unsuccessful and frustrating to the child. It is essential that the student have a positive self-image and a good attitude toward participation in physical activities.

It is also important to note that girls in our society are less likely to achieve their full potential of physical fitness than boys. Motivational factors created in our society seem to be one reason for this difference between boys and girls. Therefore, educators should be particularly concerned about motivating girls and creating attitudes of acceptance of girls in vigorous physical activities.

WHAT CAN WE DO TO PROMOTE PHYSICAL FITNESS IN CHILDREN?

Because many believe that lifelong habits of activity are being established in young children, it is important that a good physical education program be established in our schools to develop positive physical activity patterns. It is necessary that we begin with a program in the nursery schools and continue with programs through high school, since a major portion of the child's formative years are spent in school. Positive attitudes toward physical fitness and an opportunity to develop the components of

---

[8]American Alliance of Health, Physical Education, and Recreation (AAHPER): *Youth Fitness Test Manual*. Revised ed. Washington, D.C., 1976, pp. 59–60.

FIGURE 3–8.   The stress challenge course is a real fitness builder. (Courtesy of Creative Playgrounds Corporation, Terre Haute, Indiana.)

physical fitness are important goals that all teachers should aim for in their school programs.

In any type of program, the teacher's attitude can have a great effect upon the students. The example set by the teacher is critical because a child will often imitate what he sees. If the teacher sees physical education as being unimportant, or if she simply ignores it or even dislikes it, then the child will frequently develop a similar attitude. So teachers, as well as parents, must keep in mind that they are models for young children.

Schools have often put children into environments that demand rigid conformity to inactivity. In these programs the scheduled physical education classes and the recess periods are the only times children can be physical during the school day. This situation is changing in today's schools and especially in the primary grades, where physical activity is most important. Today many teachers realize children need to be active and to move about the classroom and explore their environment. Because of the nature of the child, classrooms are often set up so that children have more freedom to move. In the next few years, one can expect to see even more provisions made for physical activity in the classroom.

A new, workable concept in the classroom is that of a fitness center. We have had math, science, language arts, and many other interest centers in the past. Why not a physical fitness center? This is a place in the classroom where one or several children can go during the day to use exercise and fitness equipment. There are a great variety of materials that can be used in making a fitness center. With some imagination and initiative, there can be valuable, healthful physical activity right in the classroom.

It is important that the teacher have a planned program and not leave physical activity to chance. Physical fitness is accomplished mainly through participation in vigorous exercise or activities that increase endurance, strength, circulation, respiration, and heart power. Some activities contribute more in one way than in another, so a

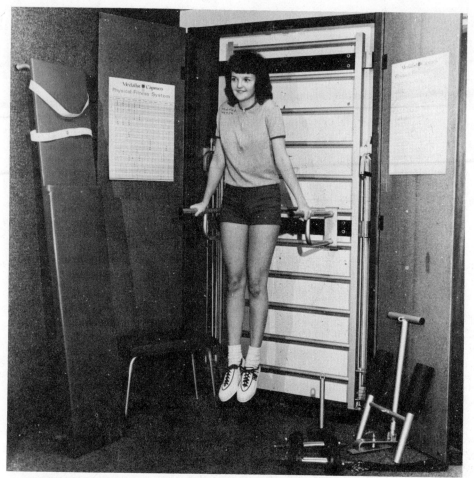

FIGURE 3–9.   A physical fitness area may be set up in a small corner of the gym. (Courtesy of Things from Bell, Homer, New York.)

variety of activities are needed. It is possible to provide many types of physical activities that will also interest children and motivate them to exercise on a regular basis. Activities that can be performed for a few minutes, for a long period of time, with others, or alone are important in the planning of physical fitness activities that children can do at home. It is good to give the children challenges that they can practice or perform after school hours.

Because of its implications for physical fitness, the teaching of skills must also be emphasized in the program. Physical fitness will result from participation in activities that require skill and interest on the part of the participant. Seeing that skills are developed so that avenues are opened for recreational pursuits is an important responsibility of the teacher, as well as parents. The school must offer the opportunity for children to develop the basic movement skills and then those skills that are essential for self-direction in recreational activities. The program should provide instruction in a variety of activities, with the goal that participation will result in enjoyment and satisfaction for the child.

The last area in which teachers can have an influence is that of parent education. Many parents are concerned when their child is not physically active, but they do not always know what to do to help the child. Also, many parents have lost or never developed the habits of physical exercise on a regular basis. Programs to help parents gain a better understanding of physical fitness and its importance to children should be conducted by the physical educator. Parent education programs should be established in which interested parents attend meetings to learn about various topics such as the child's physical development, family fitness programs, and physical fitness activities for children at home. The teacher could establish a committee of parents to help plan the topics and the type of meetings. For example, these meetings could be lectures, group discussions, films, or activity workshops, depending upon the topic, needs, and interests of the parents involved. These meetings would provide an excellent opportunity to involve professionals and experts of the community in the school programs. Operating alone, the school can have only limited success. Physical fitness is a year-round objective, so there must be a cooperative effort on the part of both the home and the school to develop and maintain the physical fitness of the young child.

To establish a program that accomplishes all of the above objectives is a great challenge to the teacher. It also takes considerable time and effort to provide an environment that will motivate children and parents to become and to stay physically fit. Because of the physical educator's impact on children and their physical development, however, it can be very rewarding and satisfying to know that you have made the effort.

SUGGESTED READINGS

Alexander, J. F. (ed.): *Physiology of Fitness and Exercise*. Chicago, The Athletic Institute, 1972.
Allison, P. T., and Harrison, J. M.: *Fitness for Life: An Individualized Approach*. Dubuque, Iowa, William C. Brown Company, Publishers, 1976.
AAHPER: *Youth Fitness Test Manual*. Revised ed. Washington, D.C., 1976.
AAHPER: *Special Fitness Testing Manual*. Washington, D.C., 1976.
American College of Sports Medicine: *Guidelines for Graded Exercise Testing and Exercise Prescription*. Philadelphia, Lea and Febiger, 1975.
American Heart Association: *Beyond Diet: Exercise Your Way to Fitness and Heart Health*. Washington, D.C., 1974.
Annarino, A. A.: *Developmental Conditioning for Women and Men*. St. Louis, The C. V. Mosby Company, 1976.
Cooper, K.: *Aerobics*. New York, Bantam Books, Inc., 1968.
Cooper, K.: *The New Aerobics*. New York, Bantam Books, Inc., 1970.
Cundiff, E.: *Fundamentals of Functional Fitness*. Dubuque, Iowa, Kendall/Hunt Publishing Company, 1974.
Fox, E. L., and Matthews, D. K.: *Internal Training: Conditioning for Sports and General Fitness*. Philadelphia, W. B. Saunders Company, 1974.
Kuntzleman, C. T.: *Activetics*. New York, Peter H. Wyden/Publisher, 1975.
Wallis, E., and Logan, G.: *Exercise for Children*. Englewood Cliffs, New Jersey, Prentice-Hall, Inc., 1966.

STANDARDIZED FITNESS TESTS

Amateur Athletic Association (AAU) Physical Fitness and Proficiency Test. National AAU Office, Attention: Physical Fitness Program, 3400 West 86th Street, Indianapolis, Indiana 46268.
Centennial Athletic Programme Testing Program. Canadian Association for Retarded Children, 4700 Keele Street, Downsview, Toronto, Canada.
Elementary School Physical Fitness Test for Boys and Girls Ages Six to Twelve. State Department of Public Instruction, Olympia, Washington 98501.
Kraus-Weber Test of Minimum Muscular Fitness. In Kraus, H., and Hirschland, R.: *Minimum muscular fitness test in school children*. Research Quarterly 25:178–188: May 1955. AAHPER, 1201 16th Street, N.W., Washington, D.C. 20036.
Mr. Peanut's Guide to Physical Fitness. Standard Brands Educational Service, P.O. Box 2695, Grand Central Station, New York, New York 10017.
Physical Fitness Test Battery for Mentally Retarded Children. Hollis Fait, School of Physical Education, University of Connecticut, Storrs, Connecticut 06268.

Physical Fitness Test for the Mentally Retarded. Metropolitan Toronto Association for Retarded Children, 186 Beverly Street, Toronto 2B, Ontario, Canada.

Physical Fitness Motor Ability Test. The Governor's Commission on Physical Fitness, 4200 North Lamar, Suite 101, Austin, Texas 78756.

Special Fitness Test Manual for the Mentally Retarded. AAHPER, 1201 16th Street, N.W., Washington, D.C. 20036.

Youth Fitness Test. AAHPER, 1201 16th Street, N.W., Washington, D.C. 20036.

To add variety to your testing program, you should write for information about all of the tests listed. You'll find all of them useful in devising your own physical fitness tests.

SUGGESTED FILMS

Evaluating Physical Fitness. Athletic Institute, Room 805, Merchandise Mart, Chicago, Illinois.

I Am Joe's Heart (16 mm., color, sound, 25 min.). Audio-Visual Center, Indiana University, Bloomington, Indiana.

The Heart: Counterattack (16 mm., color, sound, 30 min.). Audio-Visual Center, Indiana University, Bloomington, Indiana.

The Time of Our Lives (16 mm., color, sound, 28 min.). Association Films. Free rental.

Vigorous Physical Fitness Activities (16 mm., sound, color and black and white, 13 min.). President's Council on Physical Fitness, Washington, D.C.

Your Child's Health and Fitness (16 mm., color, filmstrip, 33⅓ r.p.m. record). American Association for Health, Physical Education, and Recreation, Washington, D.C.

Youth Physical Fitness—A Basic School Program (16 mm., color and black and white, sound, 13 min.). President's Council on Physical Fitness, Washington, D.C.

Youth Physical Fitness, A Report to the Nation (16 mm., color, sound, 28 min.). Equitable Life Insurance Company, 1285 Avenue of the Americas, New York, New York. Free loan.

PHYSICAL FITNESS ACTIVITIES TO MUSIC

And the Beat Goes On For Physical Education: Album KEA5010. Two records, manual, $12.00. Educational Activities, Freeport, Long Island, New York 11520.

Chicken Fat: Capital CF-1000. Instructions available from U.S. Junior Chamber of Commerce, Box 7, Tulsa, Oklahoma 74101, $.35 per copy.

Elementary School Exercises to Music: Record No. 4008. Vocal instructions for exercises, and music. Hoctor Dance Records, Inc., Waldwick, New Jersey 07463.

Exercise is Kid Stuff (Grades K to 2): Album K2070, $7.95, Educational Activities, Freeport, Long Island, New York 11520.

Fitness Fun for Everyone (Grades K to 3): Album HYD 24. $12.95. Educational Activities, Freeport, Long Island, New York 11520.

Get Fit While You Sit (Grades 3 to 8): Album AR516, Manual included, $7.95. Educational Activities, Freeport, Long Island, New York 11520.

Jumpnastics: Album KEA6000. Two records, manual, $12.00. Educational Activities, Freeport, Long Island, New York 11520.

Kimbo Kids (Grades 2 to 3): Album K1066, Album, manual, and wall charts, $7.95. Educational Activities, Freeport, Long Island, New York 11520.

Kimbo Kids—Rhythmics: LP1066. Album, manual, and wall charts available, $7.95. Record #209. Vocal commands, Side A; Instrumental version, Side B. Illustrated teacher's instructions included. Kimbo Records, Box 55, Deal, New Jersey 07723.

Modern Dynamic Physical Fitness Activities (Primary grades): Album HYP14. Album and manual, $12.00. Educational Activities, Freeport, Long Island, New York 11520.

Music for Physical Fitness No.1: Bowman Records 2851. Arm, shoulder, leg, and trunk development as well as flexibility and coordination, $5.95. Record Center, 2581 Piedmont Rd. N.E., Atlanta, Georgia 30324.

Physical Fitness For the Younger Set (Grades 1 to 3): Album K1055. Album, manual, and wall charts, $7.95. Educational Activities, Freeport, Long Island, New York 11520.

Primary Grades 1 to 3: Album 14, *Upper Elementary Grades 4 to 7:* Album 15. Each album contains four 78 r.p.m. records. Illustrated manual free with each album, $12.00 per album. Educational Activities, Inc., P.O. Box 392, Freeport, Long Island, New York 11520.

Primary Physical Fitness: Record RRC-803. *Intermediate Physical Fitness:* Record RRC-903. Rhythm Record Company, 9203 Nichols Road, Oklahoma City, Oklahoma 73102.

Rhythmic Activities and Physical Fitness (Grades K through 2): LP1055. Album, manual, and wall charts available, $7.95. Kimbo Records, Box 55, Deal, New Jersey 07723.

Rhythms for Group Activities: Record No. 22. Hoctor Dance Records, Inc., Waldwick, New Jersey 07463.

Rhythms for Physical Fitness: R.R.2. David McKay Company, Inc., 119 W. 40th St., New York, New York.

CHAPTER FOUR

PERCEPTUAL-MOTOR DEVELOPMENT AND ITS MEANING IN MOVEMENT

If a child develops a good image of his body, he will have a sound base upon which to build the perceptual skills which will be needed in future classroom activities.

William Braley

WHAT IS PERCEPTUAL-MOTOR DEVELOPMENT?

The study of perceptual-motor development attempts to answer the age-old question of how man comes to know his world. The nature of the perceptual process and the meaning of the term perceptual-motor development have been of considerable interest to pediatricians, physical educators, psychologists, physiologists, and educational specialists in recent years.

From the moment of birth, the child begins to learn how to interact effectively and efficiently with the environment. This interaction is a perceptual as well as a motor process, aspects that should not be considered separately. Historically, textbooks have devoted individual chapters to the motor and perceptual aspects of the developing human organism. They have created an artificial division between these two domains of performance that has perpetuated itself in our thinking for hundreds of years.

The hyphen in the term "perceptual-motor" is there for two specific reasons. First, it signifies the dependency of voluntary motor activity upon perceptual information. All voluntary movements involve an element of perceptual awareness of some sort of sensory stimulation. Second, it indicates that the development of one's perceptual abilities is dependent to a large degree on motor activity. Perceptual abilities are learned abilities and as such depend on movement as a medium for this learning to take place. There must be a reciprocal interaction of motor data with perceptual data in order that both abilities may develop adequately in the child.

It has long been recognized that the quality of one's movement performance depends on (1) the accuracy of perception and (2) the ability to interpret these perceptions into a series of coordinated motor acts. The terms "eye-hand coordination" and "eye-foot coordination" have been used for many years by physical educators as means of expressing the dependency of efficient movement on the accuracy of one's perceptual information. The youngster in the process of shooting a basketball free throw has numerous sensory inputs that must be sorted out and expressed in the final perceptual-motor act of shooting the ball. If the perceptions are accurate and they are put together into a coordinated sequence, the basket is made. If not, his shot misses. All voluntary movement involves the use of one or more perceptual modalities to a greater or lesser degree, depending on the motor act to be performed. What has not been recognized until recently is the important contribution that movement experiences have on the development of the young child's perceptual abilities.

Clifton[1] has aptly defined perception as "the process of organizing incoming data with stored data which leads to the overt act or motor performance." Based on this definition of perception, perceptual-motor development may be described as a process of attaining increased skill and ability to function involving the following elements:

1. *Input*—receiving various forms of sensory stimulation by way of specialized internal and external sensory receptors and transmitting them in the form of a pattern of neural energy to the brain.
2. *Organization*—collecting and indexing all sensory stimulation at any given point in the time from the input portion of the cycle and making it available for future use.
3. *Integration*—matching new information with information that has previously gone through the process of organization and has been stored.
4. *Output*—translating integrated information into a new pattern of neural energy that leads to the response.
5. *Response*—the actual overt act of perceiving or moving.
6. *Feedback*—the overt response being fed back to the stimulus portion of the cycle, causing the generation of modified stimuli and inputs (see Fig. 4–1).

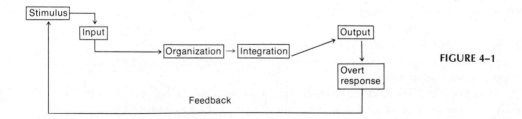

FIGURE 4–1

The feedback mechanism is the key to the concept of perceptual-motor development, for it ensures that perceptual and motor learning proceed together. The motor response feeds back information to correct the perception, and this altered perception leads to an altered response. This process continues until the motor data and the perceptual data are congruent. For example, when you throw a ball, feedback is utilized. If you miss the target on the first try, you make adjustments in the force applied to the ball and its angle of release on the second try. You continue to make these adjustments based on your perceptions of your previous response as you continue throwing. Thus, we see that in reality all voluntary motor acts are perceptual-motor acts.

---

[1]Clifton, M.: *The role of perception in movement.* In *The Academy Papers No. 1,* American Academy of Physical Education, Department of Physical Education for Women, University of Arizona, Tucson, Arizona, March 1968, p. 22.

THE SENSORY MODALITIES

The bodily equipment by which we transmit sensory stimulation to the brain and interpret this stimulation into a perception may be classified as follows:

1. Visual perception (seeing).
2. Auditory perception (hearing).
3. Tactile perception (touching).
4. Kinesthesis (feeling).
5. Olfactory perception (smelling).
6. Gustatory perception (tasting).

The transmission of messages from the various sensory end organs is made possible by special receptors in each perceptual modality. A vast network of afferent neurons forms a direct path from these sensors to the brain. The sensory impressions that are formed in the cortex are organized, categorized, and combined with other sensory impressions and stored information. At this point, an interpretation of the sensory impressions is formed. As a result, the child seees, hears, touches, feels, smells, or tastes. These initial organizations and interpretations change and become more sophisticated as the child grows older. He gradually places more meaning on what his perceptual modalities tell him and begins to rely on one or two particular modes for most of the information received about the environment.

Vision is basic for gaining accurate knowledge of the world around us. The other senses are organized around vision and are generally not as highly developed unless specifically trained and are often taken for granted. If deprived of all of your senses except vision, your tactile receptors would no longer give you information concerning heat and cold or painful and pleasurable sensations. Your kinesthetic receptors would not be functioning, and, as a result, you would not have any knowledge of where your body was in space unless you could actually see it. You would even have to look at your feet as you walked in order to guide them in the right direction. If your auditory receptors were not functioning, you would no longer be aware of the numerous auditory cues that influence your movement. You would be unable to localize sounds and determine their origin. As a result, your performance in numerous sports (basketball, track, football, and so forth) would be hindered and your world would consist of only what you could see. Your peripheral vision probably would not be as well developed. You would also be unable to distinguish the composition, size, or texture of objects by the sound that they made. Failure of your olfactory and gustatory receptors to function would prevent you from enjoying the many varied smells and tastes of the food you eat. In short, failure of your sensory modalities to function would deprive you of a great deal of information necessary for effective interaction with your environment. Evidence exists that indicates that if our brain is deprived as nearly as possible of all outside stimulation, we will begin to manufacture our own stimuli in the form of hallucinations and other personality aberrations.

VISUAL PERCEPTUAL DEVELOPMENT

Vision is the core of our perceptual world. As the child passes through the normal stages of development, his visual perceptual abilities become more acute and refined. This is due to the increasing complexity of the neuromuscular apparatus and sensory

FIGURE 4–2.   Developing perceptual motor abilities using a ladder. (Courtesy of Elsie Burton.)

receptors and partly to the increasing ability of the organism to explore and act. Piaget[2] reported that there is little differentiation in the infant between sensory experiences and little or no perception of objects as objects. He has traced the gradual development of perception from crude meaningless sensations to the perception of a stable spatial world.

The newborn child receives all sorts of sensory stimulation through various sensory receptors. Responses are made to these stimuli, but they are limited in their utility and are more or less automatic. The infant is unable to combine these sensory impressions or attach precise meaning to them, for the process of organizing incoming information and integrating it with stored information is a monumental task. Only when sensory stimuli can be combined with past experience do these sensations take on meaning and express themselves in a form of altered behavior that warrants being called perception. For example, light rays impinge on the eyes, register on the retinas, and are transmitted to the appropriate nerve centers in the sensory area of the cortex (input). The newborn's reaction is simple (sensation): if the light is dim, the pupils dilate; if the light is bright, the pupils constrict and some of the stimulation is shut out. Soon the infant blinks at the stimulus. These simple reflex actions persist throughout life, but after a while, the infant begins to attach meaning to the visual stimulation he receives (organization and integration). Soon a certain face becomes "mother"; a blob is identified as having three or four sides (perception). As the child grows older, he begins to identify the three- or four-sided figure as a triangle or a square (concept). He becomes increasingly able to attend to certain stimuli, organize them, and apply increasingly complex meaning to them. The child is now developing and refining the powers of visual perception to a degree necessary to enable him to function effectively in society. (This example applies to all the other sensory modalities as well.)

---

[2]Piaget, J.: *The Construction of Reality in the Child,* New York, Basic Books, Inc., Publishers, 1964.

Visual-motor experiences are of tremendous importance to the developing child. He relies heavily on motor information as a primary source of gaining information about the world in which he lives. As he grows older, he relies increasingly on the role of vision as an information-gathering process. As the child's perceptual world develops, he tries to construct it with as much stability as he can in order to reduce variability as far as possible. As a result, he learns to differentiate between those things that can be ignored, are easily predictable, or are wholly unforeseen and must be observed and examined in order to be understood.

The majority of our perceptions, and visual perceptions in particular, result from the elaboration and modification of certain basic reactions that occur spontaneously in the developing child. However, they are a minor part of the total perceptual process, which depends most heavily on experience as the major contributor to the development of the child's perceptual abilities. When we speak of a child's being "perceptually ready to learn," we are referring to when he has sufficiently developed his perceptual abilities to benefit from going to school. Movement experiences serve as a vehicle by which these capabilities are developed and refined. The physical education teacher plays an important role in the development of the young child's perceptual abilities through the varied movement experiences that are incorporated into a graded and developmentally sound physical education program.

AREAS OF STUDY IN PERCEPTUAL-MOTOR DEVELOPMENT

The study of the influence of movement on perceptual-motor development falls into two broad categories: (1) the perceptual process and outcomes in nonimpaired adults and children, and (2) the deviational aspects of perceptual-motor development among groups containing some form of sensory, intellectual, physical, neurological, or emotional deficit.

The young child's perceptions are not a carbon copy of the adult's. Until relatively recently, the majority of research in perception had been done using adults, with only occasional reference made to children. All too often these studies looked upon the child's perceptions as mere modifications of the adult's. Visual perceptual ability is a developmental quality that is linked to the young child's motor development. The concept of readiness training takes this fact into account and utilizes movement experiences as a phase of the total readiness program.

The study of deviational aspects of perception deals with specific limitations and their influence on perceptual development. Children with specific sensory defects, such as those who are totally or partially blind or deaf, are affected at the input level of the perceptual process. Their sensory receptors are unable to receive and transmit sensory stimulation to the brain. Mentally retarded persons are affected primarily at the organization and integration stages of the process. They are unable to use accurately adequate amounts of stored information. Individuals with physical disabilities are affected primarily at the output portion of the process. They are unable to translate accurately perceptual data into appropriate motor responses. Neurologically impaired children have some form of brain damage or cerebral dysfunction, which may be located at various sites in the brain. These children, as well as emotionally disturbed children, may experience breakdowns anywhere in the perceptual process, a fact that makes it difficult to pinpoint their problem.

The primary concern of the physical educator interested in the study of perceptual-motor development is in the influence of planned programs of specific

FIGURE 4–3.   Some children have perceptual-motor problems and need special help.
(Courtesy of James Wheeler of the Dayton Public Schools, Dayton, Ohio.)

movement experiences on the preventive (readiness) and remedial (learning disability) aspects of perceptual-motor development. Readiness programs are preventive and geared toward the preschool and primary grade child in an attempt to get him "ready" for school. Remedial programs are directed at those children in the normal classroom who for unexplained reasons are failing to keep pace with their classmates. They do not have any apparent physical, neurological, or intellectual disabilities, but they do not succeed and they fail to react to their potential. As a result, they are referred to as being dumb or retarded, but they may have a learning disability and must receive remedial help if they are ever to succeed in school.

There is now ample evidence to suggest that perceptual-motor training programs are making a positive contribution to the perceptual-motor development of the child.

PERCEPTUALLY BASED LEARNING DISABILITIES

The quality and quantity of movement experiences engaged in by children have an effect on the development of their perceptual abilities. The matching of perceptual data with motor data is necessary in order to develop a stable spatial world. If such a match is not made, the child comes to live in two worlds: one in which he sees, hears, and feels, and another in which he responds to overt movement.[3] Consider the case of Billie who is eight years old and in the third grade. His schoolwork is below average, and he is failing in nearly every subject. Billie reads at less than a normal first grade level, he can hardly write his name, arithmetic is completely beyond him, he does not pay attention to directions, and he is easily distracted. He also is clumsy and has

---

[3]Kephart, N.: *Perceptual-motor aspects of learning disabilities.* Exceptional Children, December 1965, pp. 4, 31, 201–206.

FIGURE 4–4.   There are many ways of detecting the child with a perceptual-motor learning disability. (Courtesy of James Wheeler of the Dayton Public Schools, Dayton, Ohio.)

considerable difficulty in controlling his body in locomotive, manipulative, and balance activities. Billie has caused deep concern in his parents and teachers and has been labeled a slow learner and mentally retarded. However, a series of intelligence tests indicates that Billie has the potential brain power for success in school but is lacking in some particular quality necessary for that success.

Billie has a perceptually based learning disability. Many children with problems similar to his are found in *every* school in the United States, for it has been estimated that from 10 to 20 per cent of all school-age children have a perceptually based learning problem of varying degrees. These children may be below average, average, or above average in their intelligence but are unable to fully develop perceptual abilities. This lag may result in problems of direction in which the child sees a word such as TAR and reads it backward as RAT or reads the number 63 as 36. A perceptual readiness lag may cause him to see and write words upside down or prevent him from grouping letters and numbers into meaningful units. It may cause him to constantly lose his place on a printed page, skip lines, or leave out entire sentences when reading. The young child must be proficient in these and numerous other perceptual skills *before* he can be successful in school. He often shows little improvement in his school work but is passed on, as in Billie's case, to the next grade in the hope that somehow he will catch up. This is probably the greatest injustice that can be done to this type of child. The stress of new, more difficult lessons piled on top of previously unlearned material is likely to cause great emotional stress and increased difficulty in learning. Eventually, the child rebels as Billie has done. He becomes disobedient, doesn't pay attention, is moody, and is disgusted with himself.

READING READINESS AND MOTOR ACTIVITY

Although perceptual-motor training programs have gained prominence primarily in the area of remediation of learning disabilities, there are implications for their inclusion in the readiness training of the young child for reading. Visual perceptual readiness for learning is a developmental process, and perceptual-motor activities play an important part in helping the young child achieve this general stage of visual readiness. Specific perceptual readiness skills, such as visual perceptual readiness for reading, are affected by the quality and quantity of perceptual-motor experiences engaged in by the child. Oxendine has stated

A second group of motor skills is those which are essential for the further development of educational objectives. This group includes communicative skills such as handwriting, which are used as tools for more advanced learning. The primary grade teacher is concerned with this type of motor learning, and teachers throughout the elementary schools are interested in the development of the perceptual-motor skills necessary for effective reading.[4]

Being able to read involves a number of abilities of which visual perceptual ability is an important one. Reading is a process dependent upon the use and understanding of language and perception. Considerable research has been conducted in the first two areas, but the third has only begun to be explored. The perceptual phase of reading involves the identification and recognition of words on a printed page. Visual perception has its greatest amount of development between the ages of three and seven years. These are the crucial years preceding and during the time that the child begins to learn to read. He is perceptually ready to read when he has developed a sufficient backlog of information that enables him to encode and decode sensory impressions at a given point in time with previous learning experiences. A sufficient number of children enter the first grade without the necessary perceptual abilities for learning how to read. As a result, these children frequently become the lowest in academic achievement and the most poorly adjusted children in the classroom.

Reading is one of the highest levels of neuromuscular behavior of which man is capable, for many highly refined *learned* activities are involved in the reading process. The eyes must be able to move smoothly from left to right, stop at the end of the line, and then sweep back to the next line and continue this process hundreds of times. They must be able to see letters and group them into words, and also pick out relevant details in distinguishing between letters. Failure to do these activities with precision and accuracy results in reading problems. In part, these perceptual problems may be *due to the improper or incomplete motor development of the child.*

If there is indeed a relationship between the motor and the perceptual aspects of behavior, a program of directed movement experiences (a perceptual-motor training program) may play a part in the prevention and remediation of perceptually based disabilities. However, it would be erroneous to conclude that a perceptual-motor training program alone will overcome all the perceptual problems of the under-achiever, or that participation in such a program will necessarily enhance the academic achievement of all children. There are no panaceas in remedial or readiness training, and a perceptual-motor program must be reviewed as only *one* avenue by which the perceptual abilities of the young child may be enhanced. We do know from the research conducted to date, however, that practice in perceptual-motor activities will enhance perceptual-motor abilities. What we do not know is whether improved perceptual-motor abilities have a direct effect on improved performance in the

[4]Oxendine, J.: *Psychology of Motor Learning.* New York, Appleton-Century-Crofts, 1968, p. 13.

academic classroom. A possible result of the many quality perceptual-motor programs throughout North America is a positive effect on children's self-concepts, or their "I can" attitudes. It just may be that this improved perception of themselves as being successful and worthwhile has spilled over into the classroom work of many children. Thus, their improved performance in the academic classroom becomes a factor based on improved self-esteem, with perceptual-motor experiences serving as the *vehicle* for this improvement rather than as the direct cause.

REMEDIAL AND READINESS TRAINING PROGRAMS

The study of the development of visual perception and its relationship to motor activity can best be made at and have implications for the preschool and elementary school child. The theoretical positions of Strauss and Lehtinen[5] and Piaget[6] underguard most prominent readiness and remedial training programs that utilize movement activities as a portion of their program. Both of these theories point out that a broad base of gross motor-learning experiences in the early years is a prerequisite to proper perceptual and conceptual development. On the basis of these two theoretical positions, one might view motor or perceptual-motor experiences as a foundation for future perceptually and conceptually based learnings. If this base is weakened, late in developing, or incompletely developed, it may contribute to the child's encountering problems in achieving a state of perceptual readiness for his schoolwork. A planned program of sequential movement experiences incorporated into the total school program will play a vital part in the prevention and the remediation of perceptually based learning disabilities.

Three programs that have been designed as both remedial and readiness programs for schoolwork will be discussed shortly. Each program utilizes perceptual-motor activities as an integral part of their evaluative and training programs. Each views movement experiences as an important contributor to a child's perceptual development.

Kephart

Newell Kephart's program for the development of perceptual skills is directed at readiness training and the remediation of omissions in the perceptual development of

FIGURE 4–5

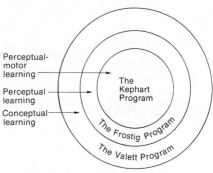

[5]Strauss, A., and Lehtinen, L.: *Psychopathology and Education of the Brain-Injured Child.* New York, Grune & Stratton, Inc., 1947.

[6]Piaget, J.: *The Origins of Intelligence in Children.* New York, International Universities Press, 1952.

the child. He felt that special training is necessary because of factors in our environment that make it difficult for many children to obtain the necessary background of movement experiences that are a prerequisite to performing tasks normally expected of their age group. The complexity of our modern society often deters the child from experiencing a sufficient variety of movement experiences. Many children never have the opportunity, encouragement, or motivation to climb a tree, walk a rail, jump a stream, swing from a rope, throw a ball, or perform many of the physical activities considered to be a natural part of childhood. Well-meaning but overprotective parents are constantly warning their children not to touch or to stay away from situations that offer a wealth of motor and perceptual information. They become slaves to the television set and miss out on many of the movement experiences that contribute to their development. Kephart feels that, as a result, perceptual information, which is based on motor information and must be integrated with it, becomes confused and distorted. The portion of Kephart's training program that utilizes motor activities is designed to enhance each of the following perceptual abilities:

1. *Laterality.*   An *internal* awareness of the two sides of the body and the ability to use each side independently of the other or in conjunction with it.
2. *Directionality.*   An external projection of laterality into external space. It involves the ability to relate the position of objects to the observer (egocentric localization) and the ability to relate them to one another independently of the observer (objective localization).
3. *Body image.*   The impression the child has of the nature of his body and its potentialities for movement. Development of an adequate body image involves knowledge of the body parts, what they are capable of doing, how to make them do it, and how much space they occupy.
4. *Temporal projection.*   The development of a time structure within the child (the preceding perceptual abilities referred to the development of a space structure). There are three aspects of temporal projection that must be coordinated together for effective perception of time in movement:
   a. Synchrony.   The harmonious working together of all body parts. It requires balance, changing of direction, or speed of a movement.

FIGURE 4–6.   A child who learns to crawl learns early in life how to use both sides of his body. (Courtesy of Barbara Mettler, Tucson Creative Dance Center, Tucson, Arizona.)

FIGURE 4–7. Spatial and body awareness can be developed through the inclusion of this type of activity. (Courtesy of Refugio Public Schools, Refugio, Texas.)

   b. Rhythm.   The purposeful performance of repeated synchronous acts in a regular succession as is seen in marching.

   c. Sequence.   Sequence refers to the proper step-by-step progression in performing a task. Proper sequencing requires the ability to arrange dissimilar events into a logical order as is seen in the proper sequencing of a golf swing or a baseball hit.

   In order to develop these perceptual abilities, Kephart and his associates have developed a series of movement experiences that rely heavily on perceptual information, stressing variety, adaptability, and ability to move in a variety of ways to a given stimulus. Generality of movement is stressed rather than specificity. Allowing the child to be adaptable in his movements gives him numerous opportunities to explore his environment and match perceptual and motor information. Kephart classifies these generalized movement abilities into four broad categories:

1. *Balance and posture.*   This category is basic to all others, for it involves maintaining a constant relationship to the force of gravity and the ability to make fluid adjustment to changes in their force.
2. *Contact.*   This involves those activities that incorporate the handling of objects. With these activities, the child has an opportunity to investigate relationships within objects such as reaching, grasping, or releasing.
3. *Receipt and propulsion.*   These involve giving force to objects and receiving force from objects, such as throwing, catching, kicking, and trapping.
4. *Locomotion.*   This involves activities in which the body moves through space in a variety of ways, such as running, walking, hopping, or galloping.

   Kephart's belief that physical education plays an important role in the prevention and remediation of perceptually based learning disabilities constantly appears in his writings. His feelings can probably be summed up best in the following statement:

   There may, however, be an additional goal for physical education—to contribute to the overall learning ability of the child. Perhaps we should stop thinking of "physical" education as different from "academic" education and recognize the mutual contribution of both. Then physical education can become a basic part of a total educational program for the whole child.[7]

Frostig

Marianne Frostig's training programs are organized sequential readiness and remedial perceptual training programs that utilize perceptual-motor activities as a portion of the entire training program. Both programs are designed to be used with all children in order to help prepare them for success in their schoolwork. Frostig's programs emphasize the development of visual perception and utilize motor activities as an integral part of the training sessions. It is her contention that children need to be proficient in five basic visual perceptual skills before they can be successful in school:

1. *Visual-motor coordination*.   The ability to combine movement of the body with vision in a coordinated manner.
2. *Figure-ground perception*.   The ability to distinguish an object as distinct from its background. The "figure" is the center of one's attention, while the "ground" is only dimly perceived.
3. *Perceptual constancy*.   The ability to perceive objects in the environment as constants despite inconsistencies in shape, color, size, or dimension.
4. *Perception of position in space*.   The ability to perceive objects in relationship to one's own body. Accurate perception of your position in space enables you to identify objects as being to the left or right of you, above or below you, or in front of or behind you.
5. *Perception of spatial relationships*.   The ability to perceive the position of objects in relationship to each other without regard to self.

The Pictures and Patterns Program[8] by Frostig is designed for use with preschool and primary grade children as a perceptual readiness program. It aims at developing perceptual abilities through a coordinated program of progressive activities that include perceptual-motor experiences, three-dimensional activities, and paper and crayon activities.

The Frostig Program for the Development of Visual Perception[9] is a remedial program for use by children with known or suspected perceptual problems. It also makes use of perceptual-motor, three-dimensional, and paper and crayon activities, but unlike the readiness program it divides these exercises into the five perceptual skills measured by the Frostig test. This is done so that specific perceptual problems may be remedied through specific remedial activities.

Valett

Robert Valett[10] has developed a training program to help the child with a learning disability. The program also has direct application to the readiness training of normal children. Valett's ideas are an outgrowth of the work of Frostig, Kephart, and Getman. The program is similar to numerous other independent remedial and readiness training programs that are currently in use or are being developed in that it does not adhere to any one theory or training technique but is eclectic in nature.

---

[7]Kephart, N.: Foreword. In Ismail, A. H., and Gruber, J. J.: *Motor Aptitude and Intellectual Performance.* Columbus, Ohio, Charles E. Merrill Publishing Company, 1967, p. VIII.

[8]Frostig, M.: *Pictures and Patterns.* Chicago, Follett Publishing Company, 1966.

[9]Frostig, M., and Horne, D.: *The Frostig Program for the Development of Visual Perception.* Chicago, Follett Publishing Company, 1964.

[10]Valett, R.: *The Remediation of Learning Disabilities: A Handbook of Psychoeducational Resource Programs.* Palo Alto, California, Fearon Publishers, 1968.

The training uses movement experiences as a means of enhancing the abilities of the child in the first three of the six major areas of learning: (1) gross motor development, (2) sensory-motor integration, and (3) perceptual-motor skills. It goes beyond the majority of perceptual-motor and perceptual training programs because it places considerable emphasis on the development of language, conceptual, and social skills:

1. *Gross motor development.* The development of the child's large muscle abilities in a variety of locomotor activities and the development of an awareness of the body and its parts.
2. *Sensory-motor integration.* The integration of gross motor activities with fine motor activities through the manipulation of objects.
3. *Perceptual-motor skills.* The ability to utilize basic visual-motor, visual, and auditory skills in a functional manner.
4. *Language development.* The functional use of speaking, reading, writing, and spelling.
5. *Conceptual skills.* The developing of the child's general reasoning abilities.
6. *Social skills.* The development of accepted social behavior.

Each of these six major areas is divided into a total of 53 subcategories of learning. The first three areas and subcategories of the program are of particular concern to the physical educator. These three areas include subcategories that are designed to enhance

1. Locomotor abilities.
2. Body image.
3. Physical fitness.
4. Balance abilities.
5. Laterality and directionality.
6. Temporal projection.
7. Manipulative abilities.

The Valett program is a comprehensive program for the remediation of learning disabilities. It does not rely on any one technique for remediation or regard perceptual-motor training as a panacea for all learning disabilities. The importance of this point cannot be overemphasized. All training programs for the child with learning disabilities should make use of a variety of approaches rather than restricting themselves to the views of one or two individuals. Adequate detection of the perceptually handicapped child will aid in the selection of appropriate training techniques.

Table 4-1 is a summary chart of the areas of interest of the Kephart, Frostig, and Valett programs. Although the terminology is different for each, and each program places major emphasis on different levels of development, there is considerable overlap in the perceptual-motor aspects of the three programs.

The observant teacher is able to detect many problems through informal observation of his students in the classroom, in the gymnasium, or on the playground. Any one of the following physical, academic, emotional, or social characteristics or a combination of them may indicate that a child has a perceptually based learning disability:

1. Inability to perform movements normally expected of children his age.
2. Poor eye-hand and eye-foot coordination resulting in the inability to play games and sports well.
3. General clumsiness and hesitancies when performing simple locomotor movements. Slowness in learning new movement skills.
4. Difficulty in tying shoes, buttoning buttons, or performing similar tasks requiring fine motor coordination.
5. Difficulty in understanding directional words, such as left, right, up, down, in, and out.
6. Easy distraction by minor intrusions into his focus of attention.
7. General carelessness, disorganization, and inability to locate objects clearly within his view.

TABLE 4–1. SUMMARY CHART OF THREE REMEDIAL AND READINESS
TRAINING PROGRAMS

Program→	Kephart	Frostig	Valett
Areas of concern →	Laterality Directionality Body image Temporal projection	Visual motor coordination Figure ground perception Position in space Spatial relations	Gross motor development Sensory motor integration Perceptual- motor skills
Developed through →	Body-awareness activities Spatial-awareness activities Directional-awareness activities Temporal-awareness activities		

8. Excitability or hyperactivity caused by the unreliable appearance of his visual world.
9. Seeing and reproducing letters or words backward or upside down.
10. Poor self-concept and peer relations.

While the teacher may believe that a child has a learning disability based on these informal observations, it is wise to utilize formal tests that have been developed for this purpose in order to help substantiate this belief. A variety of performance and paper-pencil-type tests can be given, but no one test should be considered as an absolute predictor. Rather, several should be utilized and considered in conjunction with the teacher's observations before a plan of remediation is attempted. In this way there is a greater likelihood of locating specific aspects of the child's perceptual disability and of employing appropriate remedial techniques. The following test battery is often administered:

1. The Purdue Perceptual-Motor Survey (PPMS).[11]

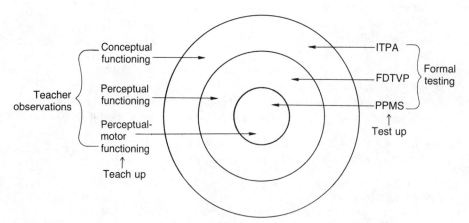

FIGURE 4–8. Ways of detecting learning disabilities at various levels of cognitive functioning.

[11] Roach, E., and Kephart, N.: *The Purdue Perceptual-Motor Survey.* Columbus, Ohio, Charles E. Merrill Publishing Company, 1966.

2. The Frostig Developmental Test of Visual Perception (FDTVP).[12]
3. The Illinois Test of Psycholinguistic Abilities (ITPA).[13]

The PPMS, the first of the three tests to be administered, is a performance-type test and can easily be used by the physical education teacher with a minimum of special training. The PPMS is given first because it is concerned primarily with the child's perceptual-motor functioning. If the child has problems on this test, a perceptual-motor training program similar to Kephart's or Getman's and Kane's will serve as an effective starting point for the remediation of these perceptual-motor disabilities. If the child does not encounter any difficulty on the PPMS, then the FDTVP is administered. This is a paper-pencil test that can be effectively given by the physical education teacher or the classroom teacher who has received a limited amount of training and practice in the administration and scoring procedures of the test. The FDTVP primarily measures the child's visual perceptual functioning rather than his perceptual-motor functioning, and tests an aspect of perceptual ability that is not as dependent upon motor information. If the child has difficulties with this test, a training program similar to Frostig's may be used. This type of program strives to remedy problems in visual perception through the use of three-dimensional, paper-and-crayon activities and to remedy problems in perceptual-motor functioning through movement experiences. If the child does not have difficulty performing either the PPMS or the FDTVP but a learning disability is still suspected, then the ITPA should be used. This test is a combination paper-pencil and performance test, and requires special training for its administration and effective interpretation of the results. It should be given only by a trained school psychologist or psychomotorist. The ITPA measures aspects of the child's conceptual functioning, as well as his perceptual functioning. The child who has problems with this test may be given remedial training, utilizing a program similar to Valett's, in which perceptual-motor, perceptual, and conceptual abilities are developed through a series of training activities.

In detecting children with a perceptually based learning disability one must make use of both informal and formal means of evaluation. Care should be taken to administer formal tests that attempt to get at the heart of the child's learning disability. Not all disabilities are perceptual-motor in nature; some may be due to problems in perceptual functioning, and others may be due to problems in conceptual functioning.

IMPLICATIONS FOR ELEMENTARY PHYSICAL EDUCATION

The elementary classroom teacher and physical education specialist concerned with the prevention and remediableness of perceptual-motor learning disabilities should know that

1. Not all children are at the same perceptual ability level upon entering the first grade. Perceptual development is a process of both maturation and experience and as such proceeds at the child's own individual rate.
2. Adequate visual perception is a prerequisite to success in school. Inaccurate perceptions lead to difficulties in academic concept formation. Perceptual readiness is an important aspect to total readiness for learning.

---

[12]Frostig, M.: *Developmental Test of Visual Perception.* Palo Alto, California, Consulting Psychologists Press, 1963.

[13]Kirk, S., et al.: *The Illinois Test of Psycholinguistic Abilities.* Urbana, Illinois, University of Illinois Press, 1970.

3. Perceptual abilities can be improved through specialized training programs.
4. The percentage of perceptually based learning disabilities is great enough to initiate readiness programs for preschool and elementary-school children even though the evidence is not conclusive that readiness training has a prolonged effect on later learning.
5. Deprivation of perceptual-motor experiences at an early age may hinder the development of the child's perceptual abilities.
6. Perceptual-motor training programs enhance the visual perceptual abilities of the young child and should be included as a vital part of readiness training programs.
7. There is a relationship between certain perceptual-motor abilities and reading achievement among certain groups of low-, normal-, and above-average-intelligence children.
8. A well-planned physical education program that incorporates a variety of movement activities provides many of the perceptual-motor experiences that contribute to the development of the young child's perceptual abilities.

Artificial means must be devised to provide additional opportunities in a variety of movement experiences that are often absent in the life of present-day children. Providing the child with substitute experiences that he is unable to receive or fully explore on his own will have a positive effect on the development of his perceptual abilities. The elementary physical education teacher plays a *vital role* in the child's educational curriculum. Any physical education program that is primarily oriented toward the movement education concept provides many of the movement experiences that contribute to the development of the child's perceptual-motor abilities. *This fact alone means that elementary physical education must advance in both quantity and quality far beyond what is offered in the majority of schools at the present time.*

THE MOTOR THERAPIST

The elementary physical education specialist can play an important role as a member of the total therapy team by working with the child with learning disabilities. The child with a perceptual-motor learning disability generally possesses other disabilities that interfere with his functioning. He may have academic, emotional, social, or physical disabilities and require the aid of trained professionals in one or more of these areas. The remedial reading teacher, the speech therapist, the school psychologist, the physician, and the motor therapist are all members of the total therapy team. The motor therapy portion of the program should be conducted by a professionally prepared physical educator rather than by someone without background knowledge of the structure and function of the human body and experience in directing a progressive program of movement activities.

SPECIALIZED ACTIVITIES FOR THE CHILD WITH A
PERCEPTUAL-MOTOR LEARNING DISABILITY

Although the movement experiences found in the regular physical education program are by nature perceptual-motor activities, there is a difference in emphasis in the motor therapy program of the child with learning disabilities. Emphasis is placed on perceptual development through the medium of movement rather than on gross motor development as in the regular physical education program. The following locomotor, manipulative, and stability activities are classified according to the perceptual-motor qualities they enhance: (1) body awareness, (2) spatial awareness, (3) directional awareness, and (4) temporal awareness. These activities should be incorporated into the specialized training program and used in conjunction with the activities found in the regular program. Several balance-type activities have also been included. These activities have been found to be helpful in developing and refining a variety of perceptual-motor abilities.

ACTIVITIES TO DEVELOP BODY AWARENESS

These activities are designed to help the child gain a better understanding of the nature of his body and the functions of its parts.

1. Name the body parts by pointing to them and identifying them by name:
   a. *Head:* hair, eyes, ears, nose, mouth, lips, teeth, tongue, chin, cheeks, forehead, eyebrows, eyelashes, neck.
   b. *Trunk:* shoulders, chest, stomach, side, back, hips, waist.
   c. *Limbs:* arms, elbows, wrists, hands, palms, fingers, thumbs, knuckles, legs, thighs, knees, ankles, toes, heels.
2. Move specific body parts on command:
   a. *Head:* Nod your head; wrinkle your forehead; wiggle your nose; close your eyes; flutter your eyebrows; chatter your teeth; open your mouth; pop your lips; jut your chin; blow up your cheeks; turn your head.
   b. *Trunk:* Stick out your chest; stick out your stomach; shrug your shoulders; bend at the waist; arch your back; tuck your trunk; pike at the hips (L position).
   c. *Limbs:* Bend your elbows; clap your hands; wiggle your fingers (toes); snap your fingers; bend your knees; stamp your feet; click your heels.
3. Name a specific task and have the child indicate the body part that is used to perform it:
   a. *Head:* I comb my_____.
   I brush my_____.
   I see with my _____.
   I hear with my _____.
   I smell with my_____.
   I taste with my _____.
   I wink (blink) with my_____.
   I chew with my_____.
   I talk with my _____.
   I lick with my_____.
   b. *Trunk:* I shrug with my_____.
   I bend at the _____.
   Food goes to my_____.
   I sleep on my _____.
   c. *Limbs:* I write with my_____.
   I wave with my_____.
   I clap with my_____.
   I throw with my _____.
   I catch with my_____.
   I kick with my_____.
   I walk with my _____.
   I squat with my_____.
   I jump with my_____.
4. **Angels In the Snow.** The child lies on his back in an "attention" position. The teacher points to or names a limb and the child responds by moving it through its full range of motion, keeping it in contact with the floor:
   unilateral movements (moving one limb at a time),
   bilateral movements (moving both arms *or* both legs at the same time),
   cross-lateral movements (moving one arm and the opposite leg at the same time).
5. Identify body parts and their function on another person or a doll.
6. Fill in the missing parts of a man drawn on the blackboard or flannel board.

7. Construct a picture of a man on a flannel board when supplied with all the parts.
8. Draw a man on a piece of paper or blackboard.

ACTIVITIES TO DEVELOP SPATIAL AWARENESS

These activities are designed to enhance the child's awareness of the movement potentials of his body and the amount of space that it occupies as it moves about.

1. Instruct the child in the performance of various fundamental locomotor movements:
   a. walking.
   b. running
   c. hopping.
   d. jumping.
   e. galloping.
   f. sliding.
   g. skipping.
2. Instruct the child in the performance of various fundamental manipulative movements:
   a. throwing.
   b. catching.
   c. kicking.
   d. trapping.
   e. dribbling.
   f. rolling
3. Instruct the child to explore the movement potentials of each body part in isolation from others.
4. Instruct the child in exploring the movement potentials of each body part in conjunction with others.
5. Perform each of the above movements at various levels and in various floor patterns:
   a. tall.
   b. short.
   c. medium.
   d. straight lines.
   e. zigzag lines.
   f. curved lines
6. Provide opportunities for each child to experience activities that help him become aware of how much space his body occupies:
   a. Tunnel crawling (use tumbling mats or automobile tires).
   b. Cube maze (see appendix).
7. Have each child lie on his back on a large sheet of paper. Instruct another child to draw around him and cut out the outline of his body. The tracings should be hung up and identified by the child's name. (Color-code various parts to enhance body awareness.)

ACTIVITIES TO DEVELOP DIRECTIONAL AWARENESS

These activities will enhance the child's awareness of his body as he projects it into external space. Directionality gives dimension to objects in space. The concepts of left, right, up, and down take on meaning when the child has established directional awareness.

1. Move the body in different directions:
   a. forward.
   b. sideward.
   c. backward.
   d. diagonally.
   e. left.
   f. right.
   g. up.
   h. down.
2. Station oneself in relationship to another person or object:
   a. in front.
   b. behind.
   c. under.
   d. between.
   e. to the side.
   f. left.
   g. right.
   h. near.
   i. far away.
3. Move *on* various pieces of apparatus:
   a. over.
   b. under.
   c. through.
   d. on top.
   e. around.

4. Have the children close their eyes and point to or face familiar objects that are located in the gymnasium or classroom:
   a. door.
   b. clock.
   c. flag.
   d. windows.
   e. bulletin board.
   f. drinking fountain.
   g. apparatus.
   h. chalkboard.
5. Be sure to identify direction when issuing commands or giving instructions:
   a. "Stand to the right of David."
   b. "Turn to your left."
   c. "Move clockwise." (or counterclockwise)
   d. "Pivot on your right foot."
   e. "Pass to the left forward."
6. Instruct the child to imitate specific arm and leg movements that you make from an eminent, erect "attention" position.
   a. Unilateral movements (movements involving the use of one limb at a time).
   b. Bilateral movements (movements involving the use of both arms or both legs at the same time).
   c. Crosslateral movements (movements involving one arm and the opposite leg at the same time).
7. **Mat maze.**   Place the folding-type gymnasium mats in various configurations to form a maze through which the child can find his way.

ACTIVITIES TO DEVELOP TEMPORAL AWARENESS

Temporal awareness refers to the development of a time structure within the child, enabling him to coordinate the movements of his eyes and limbs together in an efficient manner. The terms "eye-hand coordination" and "eye-foot coordination" are an end-result of fully developed temporal awareness. The child who is developing temporal awareness is in the process of learning how to synchronize his movements in a rhythmical manner and to put them into the proper sequence or order. Striking a stationary object with the hand or an implement or kicking an object requires the development of temporal awareness.

The specialized training program uses the same activities found in the regular program but modified to the child's ability level. A suspended ball hung in a stationary position or allowed to swing in an arc is often used in the specialized program. The following ball activities are used to help develop temporal awareness:

1. Stationary ball:
   a. Contact it with an open hand and a fist.
   b. Alternate left and right hands.
   c. Contact it with various body parts.
   d. Contact it with various implements moving from shorter to longer levers.
   e. Adjust the height of the ball and repeat all the above activities.
2. Swinging ball:
   a. Repeat the above activities while the ball is swinging.
   b. Catch the ball with both hands.
   c. Catch the ball using one hand.
   d. Catch the ball with both eyes closed (use a yarn ball).
   e. Visually track the ball as it swings without moving the head.
   f. Visually track the ball and point at it as it swings.
3. *Target throwing.*   Use targets of varying sizes and have children throw beanbags or balls at them:
   a. Hoops.
   b. Auto tires.
   c. Wastepaper baskets.
   d. Wall-mounted targets (see appendix).

4. *Hit the Clown.*   Paint a picture of a clown on a window shade (or use a decal). Attach the window shade to a firm support. Instruct the children to throw beanbags at the clown. When hit properly, the shade will roll up and the clown will disappear (see appendix).

BALANCE ACTIVITIES TO ENHANCE PERCEPTUAL-MOTOR ABILITIES

These activities are used to enhance the development of the child's stability abilities. These activities will contribute to the development of the child's body image (body image is used here to represent a combination of body, spatial, and directional awareness, and the development of a stable time structure in which events must be sequenced properly for correct performance). The balance beam, balance board, bounding board, and trampoline are four pieces of inexpensive equipment that are used in the specialized program.

1. Balance beam:
    a. Walk forward, backward, sideward.
    b. Walk with one foot always leading.
    c. Walk alternating lead foot.
    d. Walk with arms in various positions.
    e. Walk with arms on various body parts.
    f. Walk while balancing beanbag on head.
    g. Walk while balancing eraser on head.
    h. Walk and step over wand or ruler.
    i. Walk and step under wand.
    j. Walk and crawl through hoop.
    k. Walk and carry objects in hands.
    l. Stand with eyes closed.
    m. Walk with eyes closed.
    n. Pick up an object on the beam.
    o. "Cat walk" on beam (both hands and both feet in contact with beam).
    p. Crawl on "all fours" on beam.
2. Balance board:
    a. Balance with feet apart.
    b. Balance with feet together.
    c. Balance with legs straight.
    d. Balance with legs together.
    e. Balance with arms in various positions.
    f. Balance with arms touching various body parts.
    g. Balance with beanbag or eraser on head.
    h. Balance with eyes closed.
    i. Balance with eyes fixed on various targets.
3. Bounding board.
    a. Bounce with feet apart.
    b. Bounce with feet together.
    c. Bounce on right foot.
    d. Bounce on left foot.
    e. Bounce using a combination of left and right feet.
    f. Bounce and make quarter turn.
    g. Bounce and make half turn.
    h. Bounce forward, backward, and sideward.
    i. Bounce with eyes fixed on various targets.
4. Trampoline:
    a. Balance on hands and knees in the center of the canvas.
    b. Stand erect.
    c. Balance on one foot, then the other.

d. Walk around on the canvas.
e. Balance on the canvas while another person is on the trampoline.
f. Repeat the bounding activities from above, stressing symmetrical use of the arms and legs.
g. Toss and catch a soft ball while bouncing.
h. Clap hands in various ways while bouncing.
i. Clap to the rhythm of the bouncing.
j. Bounce while moving the arms in various positions.

SUGGESTED READINGS

AAHPER: *Foundations and Practices in Perceptual-Motor Learning–A Quest for Understanding.* Washington, D.C., 1971.
AAHPER: *Approaches to Perceptual-Motor Experiences.* Washington, D.C., 1970.
AAHPER: *Perceptual-Motor Foundation: A Multidisciplinary Concern.* Washington, D.C., 1969.
AAHPER: *Motor Activity and Perceptual Development–Some Implications for Physical Education.* Washington, D.C., 1968.
Braley, W., et al.: *Daily Sensorimotor Training Activities.* Freeport, Long Island, New York, Educational Activities, Inc., 1968.
Chaney, C., and Kephart, N.: *Motoric Aids to Perceptual Training.* Columbus, Ohio, Charles E. Merrill Publishing Company, 1968.
Clifton, M.: *The role of perception in movement.* In *The Academy Papers No. 1.* American Academy of Physical Education, Department of Physical Education for Women, University of Arizona, Tucson, Arizona, 1967.
Cochran, E. V.: *Teach and Reach That Child.* Palo Alto, California, Peek Publications, 1973.
Cratty, B. J.: *Developmental Sequence of Perceptual-Motor Tasks.* Freeport, Long Island, New York, Education Activities, Inc., 1967.
Cratty, B. J.: *Trampoline Activities for Atypical Children.* Palo Alto, Caifornia, Peek Publications, 1972.
Ebersole, M., et al.: *Steps to Achievement for the Slow Learner.* Columbus, Ohio, Charles E. Merrill Publishing Company, 1968.
Espenschade, A.: *Perceptual-motor development in children.* In *The Academy Papers No. 1.* American Academy of Physical Education, Department of Physical Education for Women, University of Arizona, Tucson, Arizona, 1967.
Frostig, M.: *Pictures and Patterns.* Chicago, Follett Publishing Company, 1966.
Frostig, M., and Horne, D.: *The Frostig Program for the Development of Visual Perception.* Chicago, Follett Publishing Company, 1964.
Frostig, M., and Maslow, P.: *Move: Grow: Learn.* Chicago, Follett Publishing Company, 1969.
Getman, G. W., and Kane, E.: *The Physiology of Readiness.* Minneapolis, Programs to Accelerate School Success, Inc., 1966.
Godfrey, B., and Kephart, N.: *Movement Patterns and Motor Education.* New York, Appleton-Century-Crofts, 1969.
Harvat, R.: *Physical Education for Children with Perceptual-Motor Learning Disabilities.* Columbus, Ohio, Charles E. Merrill Publishing Company, 1971.
Kephart, N.: *The Slow Learner in the Classroom.* Columbus, Ohio, Charles E. Merrill Publishing Company, 1971.
Lerch, H. A., et al.: *Perceptual-Motor Learning: Theory and Practice.* Palo Alto, California, Peek Publications, 1974.
McCarthy, J., and McCarthy, J.: *Learning Disabilities.* Boston, Allyn & Bacon, Inc., 1969.
Piaget, J.: *The Origins of Intelligence in Children.* New York, International Universities Press, 1966, pp. 21–341.
Pulaski, M. A.: *Understanding Piaget.* New York, Harper & Row, Publishers, 1972.
Valett, R.: *The Remediation of Learning Disabilities.* Palo Alto, California, Fearon Publishers, 1968.

SELECTED TESTS OF PERCEPTUAL-MOTOR FUNCTIONING

Ayres, J.: *Southern California Perceptual-Motor Tests.* Los Angeles, Western Psychological Services, 1970.
Bender, L.: *Bender Visual Motor Gestalt Test.* New York, The Psychological Corporation.
Berry, K. E.: *Developmental Test of Visual-Motor Integration.* Chicago, Follett Corporation.
Doll, E. (ed.): *Oseretsky Motor-Proficiency Tests.* Circle Pines, Minnesota, American Guidance Service, Inc., 1955.
Frostig, M., et al.: *The Marianne Frostig Developmental Test of Visual Perception.* Palo Alto, California. Consulting Psychologists Press, 1963.

Kirk, S., et al.: *The Illinois Test of Psycholinguistic Abilities.* Urbana, Illinois, University of Illinois Press, 1971.

Perceptual Testing-Training Kit for Kindergarten Teachers. Winter Haven, Florida, Winter Haven Lions Research Foundation, Inc.

Perceptual Testing-Training Kit for First Grade Teachers. Winter Haven, Florida, Winter Haven Lions Research Foundation, Inc.

Roach, E., and Kephart, N.: *The Purdue Perceptual-Motor Survey.* Columbus, Ohio, Charles E. Merrill Publishing Company, 1966.

Valett, R.: *Valett Developmental Survey of Basic Learning Abilities, With Student Workbook.* Palo Alto, California, Fearon Publishers, 1968.

SUGGESTED FILMS

Bridges to Learning (16 mm, sound, color, 30 min.), 1970. Palmer Films Inc., 611 Howard Street, San Francisco, California.

Perceptual-motor activities are incorporated into kindergarten to sixth grade physical education programs.

Bright Boy Bad Scholar (16 mm, sound, black and white, 27 min.). Indiana University Film Library, Bloomington, Indiana (rental).

Care studies of bright children with high IQ's who are unable to learn. Shows examples of perceptual-motor problems and points out that 15 per cent of those in school have a learning disability.

Developmental Physical Education (16 mm, sound, color, 28 min.). Simensen and Johnson Educational Consultants, P.O. Box 34, College Park, Maryland.

A developmental approach to teaching physical education for learning-disabled children. Perceptual-motor activities, creativity, and physical fitness activities are stressed.

Moving Is Learning (16 mm, sound, color, 18 min.). Canadian Association for Children With Learning Disabilities, 88 Eglinton Ave. E., Toronto 315, Ontario, Canada.

Perceptual-motor training activities for the learning-disabled child are demonstrated.

Physical Education—Lever to Learning (16 mm, sound, color, 20 min.), 1969. Stuart Finley Inc., 3428 Mansfield Road, Falls Church, Virginia.

A physical education program for educable mentally retarded children is shown with emphasis on fitness and perceptual-motor development through the use of inexpensive equipment.

Sensori-Motor Training (16 mm, sound, color, 24 min.). Dayton Public Schools, Division of Federal Assistance, 3201 Alberta Street, Columbus, Ohio.

Presents a training program for developing preschool readiness in three and four year old children.

Thinking, Moving, Learning (16 mm, sound, color, 20 min.), 1970. Bradley Wright Films, 309 North Dunn Ave., San Gabriel, California.

Twenty-six perceptual-motor activities for preschool and primary grade children are demonstrated in this film.

Visual Perception and the Failure to Learn (16 mm, sound, color, 20 min.). Churchill Films, 622 N. Robertson Blvd., Los Angeles, California.

Visual perceptual disabilities are related to learning disabilities. Frostig visual perception tests are used to identify disabilities.

Why Billie Couldn't Learn (16 mm, sound, color, 40 min.), 1967. California Association for Neurologically Handicapped children, P.O. Box 604, Los Angeles, California.

Diagnostic procedures and teaching approaches utilized in a classroom for learning-disabled children.

CHAPTER FIVE

MOVEMENT AND SELF-CONCEPT DEVELOPMENT

The basic purpose of all human activity is the protection, the maintenance and the enhancement, not of the self, but of the self-concept.

Yamamoto

The term "self-concept" refers to how we feel about ourselves and how we think others feel about us. It includes one's awareness of one's personal characteristics, abilities, limitations, and worthiness. The view that one has of oneself is unique. A person absorbs constantly the sights, smells, sounds, tastes, and tactual feelings from the surroundings. The perceptions received from this sensory information provide the data for one's self-concept. Meaning is attached to the sensory data, and the individual comes to conclusions about his worth or worthlessness. The ideas and thoughts that one has about oneself develop into attitudes that have an emotional quality. Because self-attitudes are directed inward the emotions aroused are particularly powerful. If a person has negative self-attitudes, it is very difficult for him to escape from them without considerable individual and group effort.

The experiences an individual has in everyday life indicate whether he is competent or incompetent, worthy or unworthy. These experiences help to form the self-concept, but the self-concept is also an active ingredient in shaping the person's experiences. An individual's actions in various situations are determined, in part, by his self-concept. It determines how he will behave in a wide range of situations. Usually one will not act in a way inconsistent with one's self-concept. If a person feels he cannot do a task, then he is likely to act that way and quite literally be unable to perform. One's self-concept is also a determinant because it shapes the way in which individual experiences are interpreted to the inner self. A third part of the self-concept's power and influence is that it determines what one expects to happen.

William James, one of the early students of self-concept, considered the perceptions that an individual has of himself to be an important variable in understanding human behavior. He once remarked that when two people meet, there are really six persons present. There is each person as he is, each as the other sees him, and each as he sees himself. The view that each has includes feelings and perceptions about self that are distinct from or different from reality, but each feeling is important.

People who are plagued by doubt of their worthiness have great difficulty receiving and giving love. They fear that the exposure that comes with such intimacy will reveal their inadequacies and cause them to be rejected. People whose performance does not match their personal aspirations evaluate themselves as inferior no matter how high their attainments may be. They also are likely to have feelings of guilt, shame, and depression. Probably the major cause of anxiety is conditions that threaten to expose personal inadequacies. Belief in oneself and the conviction that one can force or impose order upon a segment of the universe are basic prerequisites for creativity. People with low self-esteem tend to be more conforming than those who have high esteem. In children, dominance, rejection, and severe punishment have a great negative impact on self-esteem. Self-esteem is a *personal* judgment of worthiness that is expressed in the attitudes the individual holds toward himself.

THE CHILD AND THE DEVELOPING SELF

One aspect of self-concept that is agreed upon almost universally is that the self-concept is learned. In the early years of life, parents serve as the primary models for the developing behavior of the child. They are the child's primary feedback agents; through them the child can know how his behavior is influencing others. Parents also serve as the primary evaluators of behavior. They give "moral" or "worth" meanings to the activities of their children.

Children face two problems, one of *security* and the other of *status*. Children's security comes from identification with their parents and teachers. This fact has several

FIGURE 5–1.   The cargo net is an excellent builder of confidence as well as strength and coordination. (Courtesy of AAHPER Update, Washington, D.C.)

important implications for self-concept. One is that identification provides a sense of belonging. Children begin to make the self become more like the revered adult. Another implication is that the sense of belonging provides a secure place so that children know they are safe and can operate from this safe base without fear. This place of security also gives children a measure of what they perceive to be power, since the wishes of parents and teachers now become the wishes they adopt.

In the matter of status, children are incompetent in most tasks in the early years of life, but considerable learning is going on during early and middle childhood. The struggle throughout life is not so much between being competent and incompetent but in perceiving oneself in a positive way in spite of the incompetencies that may be present. Children seek status and must look at incompetencies as learning tasks rather than as personal defects. The response of adults needs to be "You can't do it now, but you will be able to do it!" Just as children receive much feedback of incompetence, they also receive continual feedback of newly developing competencies. As they progress through childhood, they increase their number of competencies and decrease the amount of new learning that takes place.

The toddler begins to learn that there is more to the world than his family. His sense of belonging is enlarged to include the fact that people "out there" like him or dislike him. Another primary task that becomes important in this period is that of sexual identity. The process of sex typing, or of learning the differences between male and female behaviors, begins early. By age 2, children can identify traditionally male activities with a high degree of accuracy. At two and a half years of age, children can identify items by appearance and task according to sex linkage with 75 per cent accuracy, and by three years, they can judge a wide range of activities according to

FIGURE 5–2. The Activity Tower provides plenty of opportunity for fun and adventure. (Courtesy of Creative Playgrounds Corporation, Terre Haute, Indiana.)

traditional sex appropriateness. Sex differences in preferred play activities and in actual play are noted by age 3.[1] Sex-typing behavior may become somewhat blurred with the continued efforts of the feminist movement, but it is probably safe to assume that it will continue to exist in varying degrees for years to come.

As the school-age child spends more time with peers, competencies are evaluated by age mates. His sense of competence or incompetence is likely to be enlarged or diminished. This is a time when children must face harsh criticism from age mates because their peers have not reached the level of maturity required to temper criticism on the basis of other people's needs. Competence begins to become enmeshed with competition during the elementary school period, and judgment begins to be made on the basis of how well a child does in comparison with others rather than in comparison with his past performances.

As children venture more into the world it is possible for their sense of competence to grow. They now have a larger set of evaluators and feedback agents. They receive information from more people so that there is the possibility of more positive evaluation. In cases in which parents have unrealistic expectations for their child, this feedback can be very important to the child's self-concept. Playmates and increasing facility in language usage and comprehension are two other factors that play a role in developing the sense of competence in elementary school children.

With competition comes also the increased possibility of failure. Yamamoto states that "the sense of failure is aggravated by three possibilities. The first is objective losses and damages; for example, no supper or dessert, exclusion from play activities,

---

[1]Margolin, E.: *Young Children, Their Curriculum and Learning.* New York, Macmillan, Inc., 1976, p. 282.

FIGURE 5–3.   The Cable Race is a thrilling adventure. (Courtesy of Creative Playgrounds Corporation, Terre Haute, Indiana.)

or physiological injuries. The second is social devaluation, namely, a lowering of one's stature in the perception of others; and the third is self-devaluation. Both the second and third types of experience can directly contradict one's self-concept."[2]

Children become increasingly aware of themselves as members of a group. They enjoy their growing independence as they try to take care of their own needs in routine activities and in play. Their developing skill in gross motor activities helps them play on equal terms with peers.

As the self-concept develops more completely, children act in ways consistent with that concept. *Significant others* in children's lives, such as parents and teachers who serve as models and mediators, play a crucial role in determining the results of learning. The self-concept grows only in the presence of other people. One of our tasks as adults is to see to it that a profound sense of respect for the self is nurtured in our children and that the willingness to accept the self be continually fostered.

REQUIREMENTS FOR A POSITIVE SELF-CONCEPT

There are three basic prerequisites for a positive self-concept: *belonging, competence,* and *worthwhileness.* Each plays an important role in the child's feelings of self-esteem. *Belonging* means that an individual is a part of the group and is accepted and valued by the other members of that group. Not only is it necessary for the group to regard the individual as belonging, but also it is essential that the individual regard himself as belonging. He must see himself as an accepted and valued member of the group. *Competence* refers to self-evaluation on the basis of how efficiently one accomplishes what one sets out to do. Competence is often an inner feeling and is not always observable. If the feeling about the past is negative, it is possible that this can be changed. This potential for change is important for self-concept development. One of the steps individuals need to take in the process of improving the self-concept is to reinterpret the past so that the meaning of past experiences is changed, especially if the experiences were negative. It should be kept in mind that it is the individual's perceptions of his competence that influence self-esteem. *Worthwhileness* develops out of an individual's seeing himself as being worthy because of the kind of person he is and because he sees himself as being worthwhile in the estimation of others. An action that is meant to express love and concern is not always pleasant (as in the case of a parent spanking a child), but it is crucial for the person's sense of worth that he perceive actions that express the concern of other persons important to him as being so.

Three other important conditions for high self-esteem in children are *total or near total acceptance by parents, clearly defined and enforced limits,* and *respect for individual actions* within these limits. *Accepting* parents are concerned about their children and willing to exert themselves on their behalf. They are also loyal sources of affection and support. They express their acceptance in a variety of ways, with expressions of interest and concern being perhaps the major underlying feature of their attitudes and behaviors.

Clearly defined and enforced limits are associated with high self-esteem. Concerned parents and teachers permit greater rather than less deviation from conventional behavior, and there is freer individual expression. Families with clear limits generally use less drastic punishment. Coopersmith stated that "parents who have

---

[2]Yamamoto, K. (ed.): *The Child and His Image.* Boston, Houghton Mifflin Company, 1972, p. 9.

definite values, who have a clear idea of what they regard as appropriate behavior, and who are willing and able to present and enforce their beliefs are more likely to rear children who value themselves highly."[3]

Respect and latitude for individual action within the defined limits is a final condition for high self-esteem. Parents and teachers who are attentive to their children structure their worlds along lines they believe to be proper and appropriate and are then able to permit relatively great freedom within the structure they have established. It should be noted that the limits need to be reasonable and appropriate for the age of the child. They are not inflexible and arbitrary limits.

At first it may seem surprising that well-defined limits are associated with high self-esteem, but limits provide children with a basis for evaluating their performance, and they define the social geography (for example, safety and hazards, means of attaining goals, how others judge success or failure). When the "map" drawn by parents or teachers is a realistic and accurate depiction of the goals of the larger social community, it serves as a guide to the expectations, demands, and taboos of that community. It clarifies ambiguities and inconsistencies of social behavior. It also gives such behavior meaning and purpose. If this map is provided early and accurately enough, and if it is upheld by behavioral and verbal reinforcement, limit definition gives the child a conviction that there is indeed a social reality that makes demands, provides rewards, and punishes violations. Limits thus help in self-definition. Children from homes where there are definite limits tend to be more creative, less dependent, and more capable of expressing opinions and accepting criticism. In such a home a child can judge for himself whether he has attained the goal, made progress, or deviated. He can rely on his own judgment. This focus is internal and personal.

There is no definite pattern of conditions necessary to produce high self-esteem. *Not all* of the six ingredients discussed above have to be present, but probably at least three of the six conditions must be there in order to provide a wholesome atmosphere for positive self-concept development.

ENHANCING POSITIVE SELF-CONCEPT DEVELOPMENT

Donald Felker, author of the excellent book *Building Positive Self-Concepts,* proposed an interesting plan by which teachers can help children develop better self-concepts. Each of these "Five Keys to a Better Self-Concept" is outlined in the following paragraphs.[4]

ADULTS PRAISE YOURSELVES. This is very difficult for adults to do, but if a teacher is to help children feel good about themselves, the children must know that it is all right to feel good about oneself. Children learn from models and from imitation. If the teacher feels good about herself but never says anything in words, the children have no way of knowing how she feels. Such feelings must be verbalized. In order to teach self-referent praise and reinforcement, the teacher should reinforce and praise herself vocally in front of the pupil. This is a very difficult thing to do. You can begin praising yourself by expressing praise and satisfaction in areas where objective criteria are absent. You might say how you feel about something you have done or made. "I really felt good when I looked at the bulletin board I put up." If someone in the class responds with "I don't think it is so great," it is appropriate to say "I didn't

---

[3]Coopersmith, S.: *The Antecedents of Self Esteem.* San Francisco, W. H. Freeman and Company Publishers, 1967; p. 236.
[4]Felker, D.: *Building Positive Self-Concepts.* Minneapolis, Burgess Publishing Company, 1974, pp. 65–90.

FIGURE 5–4. Teachers who give children a helping hand when needed become a significant influence upon the development of their self-concept. (Courtesy of Northlake Elementary School, Dallas, Texas.)

say it was great, but things don't have to be perfect for us to feel good about them.'' Teachers should regard this self-reinforcement and positive self-referent language as a teaching activity. The purpose is *not* to enhance the teacher's self-image but to teach children how to feel good about themselves. One can begin by praising one's own work and then move to praising personal qualities. One can begin with things that are not highly personal, so that the possible attacks on one's self-concept will be minimized. But it is important at some point to move into the more personal qualities so that the children begin to see that the model in the situation is allowed to say nice things about herself and not only about what she makes or does. It is helpful to tell the class what you are doing. This helps them to know it is all right to say nice things when they feel good about what they have done and that one of the joys of life is to share our good feelings with one another and to tell ourselves about it. For most adults, praising themselves is a new activity and something that does not come easily. You should force yourself to say positive things out loud until you get accustomed to hearing yourself say such things.

TEACH CHILDREN TO EVALUATE REALISTICALLY. This is an important factor that is often ignored in many achievement situations. Children do not naturally develop a basis for realistic evaluation and self-reward. They tend to be overly harsh with themselves and give themselves fewer rewards than adults would deem appropriate. To maintain a positive self-concept the evaluation of self must be accurate and realistic. If you are dealing with true failure, look at it from the standpoint of learning. Improvement and learning extend the possibility of turning the experience of failure into one that can build up the individual's self-concept. If there is inaccurate assessment and unrealistic evaluation, however, it is not a problem of learning and gaining skills; it is a problem of false interpretation of what has been done. Failure must be faced by children, but the unrealistic evaluations that many children are taught only compound the problems of real failure. The purpose of realistic evaluation is not to have children completely avoid negative evaluations. Some realistic evaluations may be negative. But a negative evaluation that is realistic provides a basis for change that will allow positive performance and, therefore, positive evaluation.

Teachers should learn to give reinforcements in specific small areas of good and poor performance. The child needs to be given statements that cushion failure with success: "You will do better next time"; "You only got two right, but how unlike you"; "You were wrong this time, but you will probably be right the next time." This helps to connect the failure with hope and the present with reinforcing past performances. One way of handling evaluation is to have children keep track of their performances. This can be done by simple cards or charts on which the child marks his own performance.

TEACH CHILDREN TO SET REALISTIC GOALS.   Such goals must be individual, must be made in relation to past performance, and must have both a goal and an end in view. If a student is to have a commitment to reach a goal, it is very important that he have some part in setting the goal. The goal should be *slightly* higher than that reached by previous performance. This may be far below the eventual performance toward which a child is striving or toward which the teacher is aiming. But the lower level is reasonable, in the sense that it is attainable. This gives the child some reinforcement from the achievement of a near goal on the way to achieving a larger goal.

TEACH CHILDREN TO PRAISE THEMSELVES.   If children are to develop and maintain positive self-concepts, they need to become their own evaluators and reinforcers. Their behavior should be largely self-controlled, and the teacher or parent should no longer be their total reinforcer. It may be easier for a teacher to think of this as self-encouraging, rather than self-praising. Also, it might be easier to use group praise first, such as "The group did a tremendous job" or "Our class can do it," before using individual self-praise. Question asking is one of the tools that teachers should use to get children to praise themselves. A question such as "Don't you think you did well on that?" can give children a chance to praise themselves.

TEACH CHILDREN TO PRAISE OTHERS.   Self-praise and praise of others are positively related. It appears that learning to praise is a general skill that is applied to similar situations and is increasingly applied to self and others. When children learn the skill of praise giving, each individual becomes the reinforcer for the other individual. As a result, they are more likely to meet with positive responses, which will increase their praising behavior. Children need to be taught how to give praise to others and also how to receive praise from others.

We have been taught early in life to be critical and point out mistakes and incorrect behavior but to ignore good behavior. If children are playing happily, parents tend to leave them alone, but if they start walking on the sofa, one of the parents soon pays attention to them.

MOVEMENT AND THE DEVELOPING SELF

Very little research has been done to date that clearly reveals the unique contribution of human movement to the development of a positive self-concept in children. The number of variables influencing such research is formidable. This does not mean, however, that quality physical education programs cannot or do not have an impact on self-concept development. It simply means that at this time, we are unable to precisely measure the extent of the influence. Child development specialists, psychologists, and educators are quick to recognize that although it is difficult to measure self-concept

FIGURE 5-5. Great fun!
(Courtesy of Creative Playgrounds
Corporation, Terre Haute, Indiana.)

development, it is relatively easy to observe positive changes in children who have been involved in a quality physical education program that (1) *is success oriented,* (2) *is developmentally appropriate,* (3) *has reasonable goals,* (4) *is challenging,* (5) *individualizes instruction,* and (6) *provides plenty of positive reinforcement.*

A child's movement skill level is often controlled by factors that are outside of his influence. Such things as physical stature, health-related conditions, lack of experience, and lack of quality instruction make it impossible for many children to meet the standards of their peer group. Movement is not the only influence on a child's self-concept, but it is an important one. If movement skills are poorly developed, chances are that this fact will have a negative effect on self-concept development. If one begins to feel one is not able to do things, one becomes less willing to participate and to try to develop these skills. Also, if other children show that they do not hold a child in high regard because of his or her lack of ability, the child is more apt to feel negatively about his abilities, for the self-concept is to a large degree dependent on what we think *others* think of us.

It is important that children develop a proper perspective on success and failure. Children must be somewhat more exposed to success so that they can develop positive self-concepts. The use of a problem-solving approach in the teaching of movement skills is an excellent way in which to ensure a degree of success on the part of all children. The use of a problem-solving approach permits a variety of "correct" solutions by the child.

The ratio of success and failure that children experience should emphasize success to the point that they are conditioned to expect further and greater success. Persons of low self-esteem wish just as much as others for success, but they do not believe they have the necessary qualities to achieve success. Children will gain little by repeating a task for which their responses are inappropriate, their ability inadequate, or their information insufficient. Children need to have some sense that eventually they will be able to master the condition, or they will not be willing to continue trying. This suggests the importance of analyzing the movement situations children are engaged in and the resources at their disposal for accomplishing movement tasks successfully.

Individualizing instruction is another way of programming for success. The activities are designed in accordance with the skill levels at which the child is operating, so that there is some stretching and growing, but the step forward is small enough that the child can be assured of successful performance. Developmentally appropriate activities are necessary for the balanced and wholesome development of children.

Children respond often to scary or daring challenges, and so adventure activities will lure children to perform new and more challenging feats. There is a need to consider what is developmentally appropriate in the challenge. The task must be sequenced according to difficulty. This is of crucial importance in determining a child's sense of success or failure. Competition should be reserved for the time when children have learned the fundamental movement patterns and developed some degree of skill in them. There is plenty of time after that to introduce competitive team sports.

Another area in which movement can be an influence on children's developing self is in helping them establish reasonable expectations for themselves. Reaching the goal is an important boost to the self-concept. However, once a goal has been reached, a new one that is challenging needs to be set. Since self-concept is based in large part on what we think others think of us, it is important that adults working with a child make known their expectations to the child.

When praise and verbal and nonverbal encouragement are used they must be sincere, for the child can soon detect if they are false. Nonverbal communication is just as important as the verbal. The way a child is treated also tells him whether he is valued and whether he is living up to expectations. Adults working with children need to be accepting and nurturing. There is no place for sarcasm, devastating criticism, or shame. Each of these can affect the self-concept drastically, and once the self-concept is firmly established, it is very difficult to change.

Childhood is a critical period in acquiring movement skills. Overprotection at this time is likely to hamper a child's motor development and instill fear and doubt, which will make it difficult for him to mature later on. Because of this retardation, he may be unable to participate with his peers satisfactorily. The effect of such a deficiency may snowball, so that the child will fall further and further behind his peers.

Motor development plays a significant role in social skills even at an early age. The first contact with other children is generally through parallel and manipulative play, in which toys circulate from one child to another. By age 4, children want to be with other children and to share in vigorous activities. Espenschade and Eckert state that "there would appear to be a reciprocal action between the motor behavior of a child and his emotional responses, in that activity promotes a child's well being and this, in turn, coupled with success in the performance of the activity, leads to expansive action on the part of the child."[5] This is illustrated in the fact that children tend to repeat motor skills recently acquired.

Evaluation of progress in the areas of motor development and self-concept is made primarily through observation. The progress is visible. It can be observed daily without any special efforts on the part of the teacher or parent. One simple method of evaluation is to take careful note of a child's performance periodically, date these observations, and indicate the levels of skills and abilities achieved to that date. A card file or folder can be used to retain anecdotal records of how the child is progressing.

---

[5]Espenschade, A. S., and Eckert, H. M., *Motor Development*. Columbus, Ohio: Charles E. Merrill Publishing Company, 1967, p. 107.

The person who works with children in developing motor skills needs to be a warm, caring adult, for children need more than anything else in their early years the trust and endorsement of such a person. Only a person who enjoys nurturing and helping others grow should be working with children.

Although there is as yet little scientific research to support it, there can be no doubt that development of skills in motor patterns enhances the self-concept of young children. Caring teachers who are interested in helping children develop to their fullest potential should look seriously at the level of motor skills a child has attained. Although a program of motor development is not a panacea for all educational problems, it is one area that needs to be explored and used more intensively than it has been in the past.

SUGGESTED READINGS

Block, S.: *Me and I'm Great:* Physical Education for Children Three Through Eight. Minneapolis, Burgess Publishing Company, 1977.

Coopersmith, S.: *The Antecedents of Self-Esteem.* San Francisco, W. H. Freeman and Company Publishers, 1967.

Cratty, B. J.: *Human Behavior: Explaining Educational Processes.* Wolfe City, Texas, University Press, 1971.

Espenschade, A. S. and Eckert, H. M.: *Motor Development.* Columbus, Ohio, Charles E. Merrill Publishing Company, 1967.

Felker, D. W.: *Building Positive Self-Concepts.* Minneapolis, Burgess Publishing Company, 1974.

Gallahue, D. L.: *Motor Development and Movement Experiences for Young Children (3–7).* New York, John Wiley & Sons, Inc., 1976.

Hendrick, J.: *The Whole Child.* St. Louis, The C.V. Mosby Company, 1975.

Margolin, C.: *Young Children, Their Curriculum and Learning Processes.* New York, Macmillan, Inc., 1976.

Yamamoto, K.: *The Child and His Self-Image.* Boston, Houghton Mifflin Company, 1972.

SUGGESTED FILMS

All the Self There Is. AAHPER, Washington, D.C., 1975.

Every Child A Winner. AAHPER, Washington, D.C., 1972.

Gallahue, D. L.: *Yes I Can! Movement and the Developing Self.* Bloomington, Indiana, Phi Delta Kappa, 1975 (filmstrip).

PART TWO

CHILDREN LEARN WHAT THEY LIVE

If a child lives with criticism,
  He learns to condemn.
If a child lives with hostility,
  He learns to fight.
If a child lives with ridicule,
  He learns to be shy.
If a child lives with shame,
  He learns to feel guilty.
If a child lives with tolerance,
  He learns to be patient.
If a child lives with encouragement,
  He learns confidence.
If a child lives with praise,
  He learns to appreciate.
If a child lives with fairness,
  He learns justice.
If a child lives with security,
  He learns to have faith.
If a child lives with approval,
  He learns to like himself.
If a child lives with acceptance and friendship,
  He learns to find love in the world.

Dorothy Law Nolte

CHAPTER SIX

THE PRESCHOOL CHILD

Movement is the essence of life: It is a primary vehicle through which young children learn.
The Authors

For preschool-age children (2 to 5 years old), movement is at the very center of life. The play experiences of young children serve as a primary vehicle by which they learn about themselves and their environment. Play and work are not opposites, as is often thought. For children, play is a way of exploring and experimenting while they gain information about themselves and their world. The child at play is learning how to come to grips with the world, cope with life's tasks, master fundamental movements, and gain confidence in himself as an individual.

LEARNING TO MOVE

Preschool children have passed through the period of infancy and are no longer immobilized by their basic inability to move about freely or by the confines of the crib or playpen. They are now able to explore the movement potentials of their bodies as they move through space (locomotion). They no longer have to maintain a relentless struggle against the force of gravity because they are gaining increased control over their musculature in opposition to this force (stability). They no longer have to be content with the crude and ineffective reaching, grasping, and releasing of objects characteristic of infancy because they are rapidly developing the ability to make controlled and precise contact with objects in their environment (manipulation). The development of effective patterns of movement permits children to move about freely in complete control of their bodies. Learning to move with control and efficiency during early childhood does not imply developing high degrees of skill in a limited number of isolated processes or forms of movement. During this period we are concerned with developing the child's ability to move in a variety of ways in response to a given stimulus. The ability to move in response to unexpected as well as expected situations is stressed along with the ability to combine fundamental movements into more complex forms of movement behavior. Children who are learning to move with greater efficiency are constantly exploring, experimenting, practicing, and making a variety of spontaneous decisions based on their perceptions of the moment and their past experience. They are involved in a continuous process of sorting out their many daily experiences in order to gain increased knowledge about their bodies and their potential for movement.

FIGURE 6–1. The turning bar provides both fun and learning experiences. (Courtesy of Creative Playgrounds Corporation, Terre Haute, Indiana.)

LEARNING THROUGH MOVEMENT

While involved in learning to move, young children are simultaneously involved in learning through movement, a process that involves utilizing movement as a means to an end rather than as an end in itself. The child that is involved in learning through movement uses his body to gain increased knowledge about himself and his world. He explores and experiments with all that is within his grasp. Children's primary means of exploration and experimentation is movement. Their basic inability to conceptualize at a sophisticated level makes it exceedingly difficult for them to learn without the use of some form of movement as the primary agent of their experimentations. A three year old, for example, may be learning to move by pouring water into different-sized containers. The coordinated act of pouring may be an end in itself if the child is learning how to pour. But as he is mastering the art of pouring he is also learning through his movements. He is gaining increased knowledge about the nature of water, its viscosity, and its texture. He is also expanding his knowledge about the water-holding capacity of various containers and learning the concept of volume. He is using movement as a means of increasing his fund of knowledge. Learning through movement is not limited to enhancing one's knowledge about one's physical self. For the young child, movement serves the vital role of enhancing his intellectual, emotional, and social capabilities as well as his physical ones.

THE VALIDITY OF PLAY

Parents, teachers, psychologists, and pediatricians are aware of the critical need for the young child to move about freely in order that he may grow and develop to his maximal potential. The literature on child growth and development is replete with information indicating that the child's *experiential* background in movement as well as

FIGURE 6–2.   Creative play is not new, but its possibilities are comparatively untouched. (Courtesy of Los Angeles City Schools, Los Angeles, California.)

his hereditary background plays an important role in his *total* growth and development. Movement is a biologic necessity through which growth takes place. Growth is a social, emotional, and mental process as well as a physical process, and movement is a prime contributor to each of these processes.

The so-called play experiences of young children are actually vital learning experiences. There is a growing acceptance by knowledgeable persons that the quality and quantity of experiences engaged in by the child affect the development of his intelligence.[1] Realization of this fact enables one to extend oneself beyond the notion

---

[1]Lavantelli, D. B.: *Piaget's Theory and Early Childhood Curriculum.* Boston, American Science and Engineering, 1970.

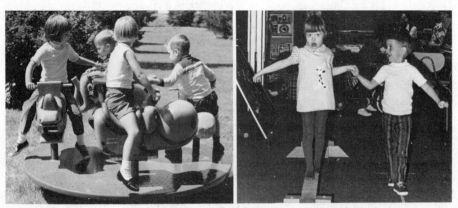

FIGURE 6–3.   Children learn as much from each other as they ever learn from their teacher. (*Left,* Courtesy of Game Time, Incorporated, Litchfield, Michigan. *Right,* Courtesy of Northlake Elementary School, Dallas, Texas.)

that the play of children, particularly young children, is of little or no educational value. On the contrary, play experiences serve as a vital learning medium that enables children to learn through movement while they are learning to move. With this important concept in mind it is possible to view the supposedly "silly" active games of Brownies and Fairies or Crossing the Brook or the singing games of Head and Shoulders or Inky Dinky Spider in a new light. Now we can look at them for their educational value as well as their free-play value. We can view the preschool years as important years that ready the child for all that lies ahead of him in the world of cognition, concepts, and abstract thinking.

CHARACTERISTICS OF NURSERY SCHOOL–AGE CHILDREN
(Ages 2 to 4)[2]

The preschool-age child is beyond the infancy and "toddler" periods, which range from birth to three years of age. The preschool-age child of today may be found at home with his mother or involved in a nursery school program of which there are an ever-increasing number and variety (see pages 111–127 for a description of various types of preschool programs). The following is a compilation of a variety of significant physical, social-emotional, and mental characteristics of the preschool-age child that have implications for physical education.

Physical Characteristics

1. Perceptual-motor abilities are rapidly developing, but confusion often exists in body awareness, directional awareness, temporal awareness, and spatial awareness.
2. Good bladder and bowel control is generally established by the end of this period, but accidents sometimes still occur.
3. Children during this period are rapidly developing a variety of fundamental movement abilities. Bilateral movements such as skipping, however, often present more difficulty than unilateral movements.
4. Children are active and energetic and often prefer to run from place to place rather than walk, but they still need short, frequent rest periods.
5. Motor abilities are developed enough for children to begin to learn how to dress themselves, although they may need help straightening and fastening articles of clothing.
6. The body functions and processes become regulated. A state of physiological homeostasis (stability) becomes well established.
7. The body build of both boys and girls is remarkably similar. A back view of boys and girls reveals no readily observable structural differences.
8. Fine motor control is not established, but gross motor control is developing rapidly.
9. The eyes are not generally ready for extended periods of close work because of the farsightedness that is characteristic of preschool and primary grade children. Also, binocular vision is often not completely established.
10. Little difference exists between boys and girls in their performance level of fundamental movement skills, although boys do perform slightly better.

---

[2]Adapted with permission from Gallahue, D. L.: *Motor Development and Movement Experiences for Young Children (3–7).* New York, John Wiley & Sons, Inc., 1976, pp. 37–48.

Social-Emotional Characteristics

1. They are egocentric in nature. They assume that everyone thinks the way they do. As a result they often seem to be quarrelsome, and they exhibit difficulty in sharing and in getting along with others.
2. They are often fearful of new situations, shy, self-conscious, and unwilling to leave the security of that which is familiar.
3. They are learning to distinguish right from wrong and beginning to develop a conscience.
4. Two and four year olds are often "out-of-bounds" in their behavior, whereas three and five year olds are often viewed as being stable and conforming in their behavior.
5. Their self-concept is rapidly developing. Wise guidance, success-oriented experiences, and positive reinforcement are especially important during these years.

Mental Characteristics

1. Their ability to express thoughts and ideas verbally is constantly increasing.
2. They have fantastic imaginations that enable imitation of both actions and symbols with little concern for accuracy or proper sequencing of events.
3. They are continuously investigating and discovering new symbols that have a primarily personal reference.
4. The "how" and "why" of their actions are learned through almost constant play.
5. They experience a preoperational thought phase of development that results in a period of transition from self-satisfying behavior to fundamental socialized behavior.

Implications for Physical Education

1. Plenty of opportunity for gross motor play must be offered in both undirected and directed settings.
2. The movement experiences of the preschooler should primarily involve movement explo-

FIGURE 6–4.   Children can be totally absorbed in learning what *they want* to learn. (Courtesy of The Montessori Academy of Dallas and Ann Melvin.)

ration and problem-solving activities in order to maximize the child's creativity and desire to explore.

3. The movement education program should include plenty of positive reinforcement in order to encourage the establishment of a positive self-concept and reduce the fear of failure.

4. Stress should be placed on developing a variety of fundamental locomotor, manipulative, and stability abilities that progress from the simple to the complex as the children become "ready" for them.

5. The interests and abilities of boys and girls are similar, so that there is no need for separate programs at this stage.

6. Plenty of activities designed to enhance perceptual-motor functioning are necessary.

7. Care should be taken to provide ample opportunities for short rest periods during vigorous performances.

8. Advantage should be taken of the child's great imagination through the use of a variety of dramatic and mimetic activities.

9. In view of their often awkward and inefficient movements, be sure to gear movement experiences to maturity level.

10. A wide variety of activities that require object handling and eye-hand coordination should be provided in order to aid in the development of binocular vision.

11. The teacher should begin to incorporate bilateral activities such as skipping and alternate galloping and hopping after bilateral movements have been fairly well established.

12. The children should be encouraged to take an active part in the movement education program by "showing" and "telling" others what they can do in order to help overcome tendencies to be shy and self-conscious.

13. Convenient access to toilet facilities should be provided and the children encouraged to accept their responsibility on their own.

14. Individual differences should be provided for, and each child should be allowed to progress at his own individual rate.

15. Plenty of climbing activities and activities in which the upper trunk muscles are utilized as well as those of the legs and lower trunk should be encouraged.

16. Standards for acceptable behavior should be established and abided by. Wise guidance should be given children so that they establish a sense of what is right and proper and what is wrong and unacceptable.

17. The motor development program should be prescriptive and based on *each* individual's maturational and readiness level.

18. A multisensory approach should be utilized by the instructor, that is, one in which a wide variety of experiences are incorporated using several sensory modalities.

CHARACTERISTICS OF KINDERGARTEN-AGE CHILDREN
(Ages 5 and 6)[3]

The kindergarten-age child is five or six years of age. Most children in this age bracket are involved in some form of formal schooling in either public or privately sponsored kindergartens. This is an important time of readiness development for the stresses of the academic world of the elementary school. The following is a compilation of significant physical, social-emotional, and cognitive characteristics of the kindergarten-age child and their implications for physical education.

Physical Characteristics

1. Growth is beginning to slow down, especially toward the end of this period. There is, however, a slower but steady gain in height and weight.

[3]Adapted with permission from Gallahue, D. L.: *Motor Development and Movement Experiences for Young Children (3–7).* New York, John Wiley & Sons, Inc., 1976, pp. 37–48.

2. The body begins to lengthen but with only a two- to three-inch annual gain in height and a three- to six-pound yearly gain in weight.
3. The cephalocaudal (head to toe) and proximodistal (center to periphery) principles of development are now quite evident, for the large muscles of the body are considerably better developed than the small muscles.
4. Girls are generally about a year advanced beyond boys in physiological development.
5. Hand preference is firmly established, with about 90 per cent preferring the right hand and only about 10 per cent preferring the left.
6. Reaction time is still quite slow, causing difficulty with eye-hand and eye-foot coordination.
7. Both boys and girls are full of energy, but they often possess a low endurance level and tire easily.
8. The visual perceptual mechanisms are not yet fully established. Such perceptual qualities as figure-ground perception, speed of vision, perceptual constancy, and spatial relationships are generally established by the end of this period.
9. Children are often farsighted during this period and are not ready for extended periods of close work.
10. Loss of several baby teeth occurs during this time and is emphasized by the loss of the two front teeth.
11. Stability abilities are defined. Both static and dynamic balancing abilities are improved.
12. Basic skills necessary for successful play are fairly well developed.
13. Activities involving the eyes and limbs mature slowly. Such things as catching, kicking, striking, and throwing need practice.

Social-Emotional Characteristics

1. The interests of boys and girls are quite similar.
2. These children are generally self-centered, and they play poorly in large groups during extended periods of time, although small group situations are handled well.
3. They are often aggressive, boastful, self-critical, and over-reactive. They accept defeat and winning poorly.
4. They manifest an inconsistent level of maturity. Owing to parental influence they are often less mature at home than at school.
5. They are responsive to authority, "fair" punishment, and discipline.

Mental Characteristics

1. Their attention spans are generally short. Nevertheless, boys and girls of this age will often spend hours on activities that are of great interest to them.
2. They are eager to learn and to please adults, but they need assistance and guidance in decision making.
3. They have good imaginations and extremely creative minds.
4. They are interested in songs, fairy tales, television, movies, rhythmic games, and gymnastic-type activities.
5. They are not capable of abstract thinking. They deal best with concrete examples and situations.

Implications for Physical Education

1. Opportunities to refine fundamental movement abilities in the areas of locomotion, manipulation, and stability to a point where they are fluid and efficient should be provided.
2. It is important to assure these children that they are accepted and valued as human beings,

so that they know they have a stable and secure place in both their school environment and their home environment.
3. Abundant encouragement and positive reinforcement from adults are necessary in order to promote continued development of a positive self-concept.
4. Opportunities and encouragement to explore and experiment with their bodies and objects in their environment through movement enhance perceptual-motor efficiency.
5. Exposure to experiences in which progressively greater amounts of responsibility are introduced helps promote self reliance.
6. Adjustment to the rougher ways of the school playground and neighborhood without becoming rough or crude is an important social skill to be learned by children this age.
7. Opportunities for gradual introduction to group and team activities should be provided at the proper time.
8. Story plays and other imaginary and mimetic activities may be effectively incorporated into the program because of these children's vivid imaginations.
9. Activities that incorporate music and creative rhythmics are especially enjoyable at this level and are valuable in enhancing fundamental movement abilities, creativity, and basic understanding of the components of music and rhythm.
10. Children at this level learn best through active participation. Integration of academic concepts with movement activities provides an effective avenue for reinforcing academic concepts in science, mathematics, social studies, and language arts.
11. Activities that involve climbing and hanging are beneficial to the development of the upper torso and should be included in the program.
12. Play situations involving such topics as taking turns, fair play, cheating, and sportsmanship should be discussed so that a more complete sense of right or wrong can be established.
13. These children should be encouraged to "think" before engaging in an activity. Help them recognize potential hazards in order to reduce their often reckless behavior.

PRESCHOOL EDUCATION

The education of young children has traditionally been left in the hands of the family. The types of learning experiences or play situations that the child is involved in are left to the discretion of the parents. Until recently little consideration was given to any form of preschool education outside the home other than the custodial services provided by local day-care centers. Americans scoffed at the Soviets' practice of involving their young in a coordinated series of learning experiences outside of the home. We looked at the education of young children as being the sole responsibility of the home. In recent years, however, there have been two important developments that have caused a reassessment of this position. They have led to a reevaluation of the role of nursery schools and their function as a valid form of enrichment or instruction for the young child. First, our society is undergoing a marked change in its social and economic structures, causing a tremendous increase in the number of mothers seeking employment. As a result, there has been a marked increase in the number of children enrolled in some form of preschool program. Second, there has been a dramatic growth of professional interest in young children and the contribution of their early experiences to later development. The eminent Swiss psychologist Jean Piaget[4] was the first to emphasize the importance of the child's early learnings on future development. His stress on the importance of perceptual-motor experiences as a facilitator of cognitive development, as well as physical development, has been a prime factor in stimulating this interest. As a result of these two factors, there has been a tremendous increase in the number and variety of preschool programs throughout America.

[4]Piaget, J.: *The Origins of Intelligence in Children.* New York, International Universities Press, 1952.

CHARACTERISTICS OF A GOOD PRESCHOOL PROGRAM

The preschool programs of today are no longer looked upon as a "parking place" for children by most parents. The selection of a program suitable to the child's needs is an important task that should not be taken lightly. For the child who is ready for a group experience, the nursery school helps many busy mothers enjoy their children more and to be enjoyed more by them when they are together. A reduction in the *quantity* of hours that the child is under the direct supervision of the parent often results in an increase in the quality of time spent together. The nursery school gives the child an opportunity to work with people his own age under the guidance of specially trained and skilled individuals. He is placed in a different environment that offers many new, exciting, and challenging experiences. There are a wide variety of preschool programs available. All programs should be based on the following criteria:

1. There should be an adequate amount of indoor (35 square feet) and outdoor (75 square feet) space for each child.[5] There should be ample space for both active and quiet play to go on undisturbed both indoors and out.
2. Safe, sanitary, and hygienic conditions must be maintained at all times.
3. A pediatrician should be on call, and a person trained in first aid should always be available. There should be adequate first-aid supplies stored out of the reach of children.
4. The child's health should be protected and promoted. A medical examination should be given by the family physician at least once a year and required before admitting any child into the program.
5. The program should provide daily opportunities for outdoor play and a balance between vigorous and quiet activity.
6. There should opportunities for a rest period and nutritious meals at appropriate intervals during the day.
7. An adequate amount of appropriate equipment and play materials should be made available for each child's enjoyment and growth.
8. There should be an adequate number of teachers and assistants for the group. Younger children require a smaller teacher-pupil ratio (one teacher to every four to six students) than older children (one teacher to every six to eight children).
9. There should be no more than 15 to 20 children in any one group.
10. The school should assist the child in concept development and in the use of language.
11. The child should be provided with experiences that provide him with direct first-hand contact with the environment within the school and in the neighborhood.
12. The teacher should encourage the creative use of materials and equipment rather than insisting on following stereotyped uses of them.
13. The teacher should have a clear understanding of the growth and development characteristics of young children, their needs, and their interests.
14. A conscious effort should be made to assist the child in adjusting to the social demands of society. Taking turns, sharing, and considering the rights of others should be stressed.
15. Adequate records should be kept of each child's progress and development as well as records of his physical examinations and any special problems or needs.
16. The school should recognize the importance of regularity in the life of young children without overstressing routines or rigid programming.

MATERIALS AND EQUIPMENT

Preschool children play with and learn through the different equipment and materials available to them during informal play periods. The amount, durability, and versatility of the equipment are very important. Too little equipment leads to quarreling, and too much equipment forces the child to make decisions that he is unable to make. They prevent him from being able to focus his attention on anything. The

[5]*Some Ways of Distinguishing a Good School or Center For Young Children.* Washington, D.C., National Association for the Education of Young Children.

FIGURE 6–5. The first time on the horizontal ladder can be scary, but what a challenge! (Courtesy of Creative Playgrounds Corporation, Terre Haute, Indiana.)

following is a list of some equipment and materials that should be included in the program. This list is not complete. The innovative teacher is constantly on the alert for new equipment that contributes to the child's development.

1. Small Equipment

   Blocks
   Paints
   Modeling clay
   Puzzles
   Beads
   Games
   Puppets
   "Dress-up" clothes
   Rhythm instruments
   Carpentry tools
   Gardening tools
   Soft balls
   Beach balls
   Playground balls
   Hoops
   Jump ropes

2. Large Equipment

   Climbing ropes
   Jungle gym
   Ladder
   Mats
   Balance board
   Balance beam
   Bouncing board
   Large crawling cubes
   Wading pool
   Sand box
   Tricycles
   Bicycle
   Wheelbarrows
   Wagons

FIGURE 6–6. It takes coordinated movements and determination to climb on top of a walk-through block. It can be used to help children develop courage as well as to teach them how to climb. (Courtesy of Northlake Elementary School, Dallas, Texas.)

CHALLENGE ACTIVITIES

The young child is constantly exploring and experimenting with the many movement potentials of his body. The teacher may aid him in this process by motivating him with a variety of movement challenges. A challenge is an open-ended statement phrased in the form of a question or problem. It is not a command. The child is given the freedom to solve the problem as he sees fit within the limits of his abilities. There is no one "correct" way of performing. A variety of interpretations of the questions may be possible if exploration is the primary goal of the lesson and the questions are loosely structured: "How can you roll the ball?" or "Can you run in a different direction?" If skill development is the goal, the challenges are more narrowly stated: "Can you roll the ball and knock down all the pins?" or "Can you run backward while still facing me?" The following challenges are stated under the three broad headings of locomotion, manipulation, and stability. A variety of examples are given in the locomotor section using only one form of movement (running). By inserting a different locomotor movement, such as jumping, skipping, or galloping, or combining it with manipulative or stability activities, an infinite variety of responses are possible:

1. *Locomotion* (walking, running, hopping, jumping, skipping, galloping, leaping)

>   Can you run in different ways?
>   Can you run in different directions? (forward, backward, sideward, diagonally?)
>   Can you run at different levels? (high, medium, low?)
>   Can you run at different speeds? (fast, medium, slow?)
>   Can you start running fast and finish slow?
>   Can you start running slow and finish fast?
>   Can you run to the beat of a drum?
>   Can you take long (short) steps while running?

Can you run happy? (sad, angry, tired?)
Can you run in a big circle? (square, triangle?)
Can you run in a small circle?
Can you run following this design? (Draw shapes on chalkboard.)
Can you run toward me?
Can you run away from me?
Can you run away from me while still facing me?
Can you change directions while running?
Can you change directions in response to my hand signals?
Can you do something with your arms while running?
Can you do something with your head while running?
Can you run with a partner?
Can you run on the foot opposite the one your partner is running on?

2. *Manipulation* (throwing, catching, rolling, bouncing, kicking)

   a. Balls
   Can you throw the ball up and catch it with both hands? (one hand?)
   Can you bounce the ball and catch it?
   Can you throw the ball up, clap your hands, and catch it?
   Can you bounce the ball, clap your hands, and catch it?
   Can you bounce the ball to a partner?
   Can you roll the ball?
   Can you roll the ball and knock the pins down?
   Can you roll the ball to a partner?
   Can you throw the ball hard? (easy?)
   Can you throw the ball to a partner?
   Can you throw the ball with both hands?
   Can you throw the ball with one hand?
   Can you throw the ball underhand?
   Can you throw the ball overhand?
   Can you throw at a target?
   Can you close your eyes and throw at a target?
   Can you catch a ball thrown by a partner?
   Can you kick the ball?
   Can you kick the ball to a partner?
   Can you kick the ball at a target?
   Can you kick the ball into the air?
   Can you kick the ball so that it stays on the ground?

   b. Beanbags
   Can you toss the beanbag up and catch it?
   Can you toss it higher?
   Can you toss, clap, and catch the beanbag?
   Can you toss, turn, and catch the beanbag?
   Can you toss the beanbag up with one hand and catch it with the other?
   Can you toss the beanbag up and catch it with your eyes closed?
   Can you throw the beanbag as far as you can?
   Can you throw the beanbag overhand?
   Can you throw the beanbag underhand?
   Can you throw the beanbag sidearm?
   Can you throw the beanbag to a partner?
   Can you catch the beanbag?
   Can you hold the beanbag between your knees and jump forward?
   Can you balance the beanbag on different body parts? (head, foot, shoulder)

3. *Stability* (static balance, dynamic balance)

   a. Balance Beam
   Can you balance on the beam with both feet?

Can you balance on one foot?
Can you balance on one foot with your hands at your side?
Can you balance on one foot with your arms out like an airplane?
Can you balance on one foot with your eyes closed?
Can you walk the length of the beam?
Can you walk the beam heel-to-toe?
Can you walk the beam without looking at your feet?
Can you walk the beam with your arms at your side?
Can you walk sideways on the beam?
Can you walk to the middle of the beam, turn, and walk back?
Can you step over a stick while walking the beam?
Can you crawl under a stick while walking on the beam?
Can you stoop down and pick something up off the beam?

b. Ropes
Can you balance on the rope with two feet?
Can you balance on one foot?
Can you balance on one foot with your hands at your side?
Can you balance on one foot with your hands out like an airplane?
Can you balance on one foot with your eyes closed?
Can you walk sideways on the rope?
Can you walk backward on the rope?
Can you walk to the middle, turn around, and walk back?
Can you hop on one foot the length of the rope?
Can you leap from one end of the rope to the other end?
Can you walk low?
Can you walk on your toes?
Can you walk with a partner on the rope?
Can you pass your partner on the rope?
Can you jump from one rope to another?

c. Balance Board
Can you balance on the balance board?
Can you balance and look at your feet on the board?
Can you balance and look at someone else?
Can you touch your head? (shoulders, knees?)
Can you balance and hold an object?
Can you balance on one foot? (the other)
Can you pick up an object while balancing?
Can you balance and turn around on the board?
Can you balance with your knees bent? (straight?)
Can you balance on your toes?

ANIMAL WALKS

Animal walks are a form of mimetics in which the child is given an opportunity to imitate the movements of various animals. Preschool children have vivid imaginations and are very interested in animals. The principal characters in the majority of the television cartoons that they watch and the storybooks that they "read" are animals. As a result, young children find it very easy to identify with animals such as lions, bears, dogs, or elephants. Imitation of animals stimulates the child's creativity while providing him with an opportunity to explore the movement potential of his body. There is no single "best" way to imitate the following movements. The situation should be left open-ended, allowing the child to explore and experiment with many possibilities.

However, suggestions for performance are provided as an aid to the teacher who may find it difficult to "let herself go" and explore on her own:

1. *Bear Walk*. Bend over at the waist and the touch the floor with the hands. Keeping the legs and arms stiff and the head up, walk forward in a crosslateral fashion (left leg, right arm, and so forth).
2. *Elephant Walk*. Bend at the waist, drop the hands and let them hang limp. Take large lumbering steps with the legs and sway the arms from side to side.
3. *Puppy Run*. Run forward with both hands and both feet on the floor.
4. *Lame Puppy Run*. From a position with the knees bent, with both hands and both feet on the floor as above, raise one foot off the ground and proceed forward.
5. *Bunny Hop*. From a squat position with the hands on the floor, place the weight on the hands and hop forward with the legs; move the hands forward and repeat.
6. *Rooster Walk*. Strut forward with the knees stiff and the hands at the side of the chest. Wiggle the elbows like flapping wings.
7. *Galloping Horses*. Gallop forward placing both hands in front as if holding the horse's reins.
8. *Kangaroo Jump*. Stand erect with the feet together, and bend the elbows out from the body letting the hands dangle limply. Do a deep knee-bend, jump forward, and come to a semisquat position.
9. *Frog Jump*. Come to a full squat position with the hands on the floor outside of the knees. Jump forward, landing in the same position.
10. *Prancing Horses*. Fold the arms across the chest while standing. Prance around lifting the feet high and pointing the toes. Throw the head up and back while prancing.
11. *Birds*. Stand on the toes and wave outstretched arms slowly up and down. As the "wings" flap faster run faster.
12. *Stork*. Stand on one foot and grasp the opposite foot in back. Hop forward and backward a few steps at a time.
13. *Crab Walk*. From a squatting position, reach backward and place both hands flat on the floor. Raise the hips and proceed forward or backward.
14. *Seal Walk*. From a position flat on the floor, push the upper body off the floor with the arms. Proceed forward dragging the legs behind.
15. *Ostrich Walk*. Bend forward at the waist and grab the ankles. Keep the knees stiff and walk forward moving the head in and out.
16. *Mule Kick*. From a squatting position with the hands on the floor outside the knees, shift the body weight forward to the hands and kick both legs backward.
17. *Monkey Jump*. From a squatting position with the back straight, spread the knees and let the arms dangle between them. Push off with the hands and legs and jump forward.

RHYMES AND FINGER PLAYS

Rhymes and finger plays are favorite activities of young children. They provide a great deal of enjoyment for the child and serve to enhance his sense of rhythm, knowledge of his body parts, and fine motor coordination. The following activities have been found to be very popular with young children:

Here Is The Church

Here is the church (fingers interlaced,
    knuckles up),
Here is the steeple (index fingers point
    up and touch),
Open the doors (move thumbs to the side),
And look at all the people (turn hands
    over and wriggle fingers).

Ten Little Indians

Ten little Indians standing in a row
  (hold fingers straight up),
They bow to the Chief, very very low
  (bend fingers),
They march to the left, then they march to
  the right (wiggle fingers to the left,
  then right),
They all stand up straight, ready to fight
  (straighten fingers again).

Inky Dinky Spider

An inky dinky spider climbed up the water
  spout (use fingers to represent climbing
  up),
Down came the rain (fingers wiggle downward like raindrops),
And washed the spider out (make sweeping
  motion with hands),
Out came the sun (make large circle with
  arms),
And dried up all the rain (make sweeping
  motion with both hands in opposite
  directions),
So the inky dinky spider climbed right back
  up again (repeat climbing motion with
  fingers).

Heads and Shoulders

Touch head and shoulders, knees and toes,
  knees and toes,
Touch head and shoulders, knees and toes,
  knees and toes,
Touch head and shoulders, knees and toes,
Eyes, ears, mouth, and nose, mouth and nose
  (touch the body parts indicated as the
  melody is sung, repeat verses faster, or
  leave words out).

Where Is Thumbkin?

Where is Thumbkin? Where is Thumbkin?
  (make a fist and hide thumb inside),
Here I am. Here I am (thumb pops up).
How are you today, sir? How are you
  today, sir? (thumb of one hand wiggles
  as if talking to the other thumb).
Very well, I thank you. Very well, I thank
  you (opposite thumb repeats action).
Now run away, run away (both thumbs run
  off together).
        (Repeat, using
            Pointer—index finger,
            Biggie—middle finger,
            Ringer—ring finger,
            Pinky—little finger.)

Hands

I can knock with my two hands;
Knock, knock, knock.
I can rock with my two hands;
Rock, rock, rock.
I can tap with my two hands;
Tap, tap, tap.
I can clap with my two hands;
Clap, clap, clap.
    (Do actions suggested by the words.)

Ten Little Gentlemen

Ten little gentlemen standing in a row.
Bow, little gentlemen, bow down low;
Walk, little gentlemen, right across the
    floor,
And don't forget, gentlemen, to please
    close the door.
    (Use fingers to simulate the action
    suggested by the words.)

Five Little Mice

Five little mice went out to play.
Gathering up crumbs along the way;
Out came a pussy-cat
Sleek and black,
Four little mice went scampering back—
Four little mice went out to play (and so on).
    (Use fingers of one hand for the mice
    and the other hand as the cat.)

Ten Galloping Horses

Ten galloping horses galloping through town.
Five were white and five were brown
Five galloped up and five galloped down;
Ten galloping horses galloping all around.
    (Use fingers as horses.)

The Duke of York

The grand old Duke of York,
He had ten thousand men.
He marched them up a hill
And marched them back again.
So when you're up, you're up (stand tall),
And when you're down, you're down (sit down);
And when you're only half-way up (crouch position)
You're neither up nor down (stand up, sit down).
    (March across the room making appropriate
    actions.)

Looby Loo

Chorus
Here we go Looby Loo,
Here we go Looby Light,
Here we go Looby Loo,
All on a Saturday night.
Verse
You put your right foot in,
You put your right foot out,
You shake, shake, shake,
And turn yourself about.
(Repeat chorus, then the verse, using
Left foot,
Right hand,
Left hand,
Whole self.)

Two Little Blackbirds

Two little blackbirds sitting on a hill
(children crouch down low),
One named Jack and the other named Jill
(boys jump up to a stand on the word
"Jack," girls on "Jill"),
Fly away Jack, and fly away Jill (make
flying motions with the arms and legs
all around the room),
Come back, Jack, come back, Jill
(fly back to original position).

Old McDonald

Old McDonald had a farm
E—I—E—I—O.
And on his farm he had some cows,
E—I—E—I—O.
With a moo-moo here,
And a moo-moo there,
Here a moo,
There a moo,
Everywhere a moo-moo,
Old McDonald had a farm
E—I—E—I—O.
(Repeat, using
Duck,
Pig,
Horse,
Sheep.)
(Use only single chorus with young children.)

Gay Musician

I am a Gay Musician
And I'm from _____.
I can play sweet music,
On my little drum.
Ratta—tat—tat—tat,
Ratta—tat—tat—tat.

And I can play sweet music,
On my little drum.
    (Repeat, using
        Trumpet,
        Clarinet,
        Violin,
        Accordion.)
(Children walk in a circle during verse and
stop to mimic instruments during chorus.)

STORY PLAYS

Story plays are simple dramatic interpretations of a story told by the teacher. Preschool children are quite uninhibited and enjoy acting out stories. Their vivid imaginations permit them to "lose themselves" in the story and perform the various actions of the story as if they were actually experiencing it. A good story play is one that provides a variety of creative opportunities and plenty of vigorous activity. It should also give the child freedom of response within the bounds of the story and allow him to participate at his own level of ability. A successful story play is one that

1. Has a clear story basis.
2. Is well planned and thought out.
3. Is enthusiastically presented.
4. Offers key words for possible actions.
5. Provides a variety of movement responses.
6. Is informally organized so that all can see the teacher.

There are numerous traditional stories familiar to most children that they thoroughly enjoy acting out. A partial list of favorite stories follows. They can be rewritten and adapted, using only the main points of the stories to direct the children's movements:

Lady and the Tramp	The Pied Piper
Winnie the Pooh (several stories)	Henny Penny
Jack the Giant Killer	Mother Goose Rhymes
The Three Little Pigs	Peter and the Wolf
Little Hiawatha	The Gingerbread Man
Dumbo	The Ugly Duckling
Little Red Riding Hood	Frosty the Snowman
Goldilocks and the Three Bears	

There are numerous experiences of both children and adults that can also serve as the basis for a story play. The following suggestions can be elaborated upon and developed into dramatic stories, as illustrated in the next few pages:

1. Special Occasions	2. Special Places
Christmas Day	A Trip to the Zoo
Thanksgiving at Grandmother's	A Day at the Park
Halloween Night	A Day on the Farm
The Easter Parade	Let's Go to the Circus
The Fourth of July	A Day at the Ocean

3. People's Jobs

    Fireman
    Astronaut
    Deep-Sea Diver
    Jet Pilot
    Road Builder
    Construction Worker
    Housewife

4. Playing

    Winter Sports
    Summer Sports
    Playing in the Leaves
    Going on a Bear Hunt
    Going Trout Fishing
    Going Moutain Climbing

Playing in the Leaves

"It is autumn and the leaves from the trees are all falling to the ground. Soon winter will be here. Let's go outside and play in the leaves."

MOTIVATING IDEAS

1. "Put your sweat shirt on; it's chilly."
2. "Run up the big hill, and back down."
3. "Walk through the leaves, and kick them with your feet."
4. "Stoop down and fill your arms with leaves, and take them over to the big pile."
5. "Rake leaves into the pile."
6. "Run and jump into the pile of leaves."
7. "Lie down in the pile, and cover yourself up with leaves, starting at your feet."
8. "Imitate the movements of a leaf as it falls to the ground."
9. "Walk across a little stream, balancing carefully on the stepping stones."
10. "Jump back across to the other side."
11. "Run up and back down the big hill again, and run back to the house."

Let's Go Trout Fishing

MOTIVATING IDEAS

1. "Put on your hip boots, and lace them up all the way."
2. "Put on your rubber coat."
3. "Reach up over the fireplace to get your fishing pole and net."
4. "Open the door and go outside."
5. "Let's run down to the stream (skip, gallop). Be sure to pick those heavy boots up high."
6. "We are here; let's wade into the stream. Be very quiet so we don't scare the fish."
7. "Spread out so we don't get hooked together."
8. "Put your bait on the hook very carefully."
9. "Put your rod over your shoulder and then cast out your line."
10. "Do you feel a fish biting? Reel him in."
11. "Now get your net out and catch him as you pull him in."
12. "How big is he?"
13. "Put him in your container, and let's try to catch some more."
14. "It's time to get these fish home so we can have dinner. Let's run back home."
15. "Take your boots and jacket off, and place your fishing pole back up over the fireplace."

Firemen

"The firemen are our friends. They put out fires and help us when we need them. Let us pretend we are firemen today."

MOTIVATING IDEAS

1. "The firemen are sleeping in their beds."
2. "The alarm rings. We must get dressed very quickly."
3. "Slide down the pole."
4. "Jump up onto the fire truck."
5. "Help steer the big fire engine to the fire."
6. "Unwind the hose, and hook it up to the fire hydrant."
7. "Hold the hose, and squirt the fire."
8. "Climb up the ladder to the roof of the burning building."
9. "Chop a hole in the roof."
10. "Squirt water through the hole."
11. "Climb back down, roll up the hose, and ride the fire engine back to the fire station."

GROUP GAMES

The following games are examples of simple group games that have been found to be successful with young children. Numerous games that are played in the primary grades can be adapted to the developmental level of preschool children. In selecting games for young children, the teacher should

1. Be aware of the developmental level of the students.
2. Provide for modification appropriate to the children's level of development.
3. Select activities that require a minimum of team effort.
4. Select games with simple rules to follow.
5. Select games that allow for maximum participation by everyone.
6. Recognize that young children want to move now and not wait their turn.
7. Select games that will hold the children's interest.
8. Be prepared to make on-the-spot modifications and revisions in the game.
9. Be prepared to present more than one or two games in a lesson; the attention span of young children is very short.

Animal Chase

Skills:	Ball handling
Equipment:	Two large balls
Players:	10 to 12 per group
Formation:	Circle
Directions:	The teacher starts one ball (rabbit) around the circle. After the "rabbit" has a fair start, she starts another ball (dog) after the "rabbit." As children improve in ability to handle the ball, start a "wolf" after the dog and then a "hunter" after the wolf. Any child who has two animals at once drops out of the game, but *only* until another is caught in the same predicament.

Animals and Wind

Skills:	Running, chasing, fleeing, tagging
Equipment:	None
Players:	Entire class
Formation:	Two parallel lines facing each other
Directions:	The players are divided into two equal groups—the animals and the wind. At opposite ends of a playing court and 50 to 75 feet apart, lines are drawn parallel to each other. The "animal group" go to their end of the playing court, and choose the name of an animal, which they keep secret from the wind. Then this group comes to within 4 feet of the base of the "wind group." A spokes-

man for the animal group may tell the wind group the color of the animal, its size, and the beginning initial. As soon as the wind group guesses the name of the animal correctly, they chase the animal group back to their base. All players caught must join the wind group. The game is repeated with the groups reversing. (The "wind group" now becomes the animal group and vice versa.) The game may be varied by using various locomotor movements of animals.

Brownies and Fairies

Skills:	Running, pivoting, starting, stopping, tagging
Equipment:	None
Players:	Entire class
Formation:	Two parallel lines facing each other
Directions:	Goals are set up about 40 feet apart. The players are divided into two equal groups; half are known as brownies and the other half as fairies. Each group is lined up on their goal line. The brownies turn their backs to the fairies who try to steal up to the brownies very quietly while the teacher says, "The fairies are coming." When the fairies come close, she says, "The fairies are here!" At that signal, the brownies turn and chase the fairies back home. Those that they tag become brownies. The game continues with the fairies turning around and the brownies approaching them silently. At the end of the game, the team having the most on their side wins.

Cat and Mouse

Skills:	Agility, running, dodging
Equipment:	None
Players:	10 to 12 per group
Formation:	Circle
Directions:	The children form a circle with their hands joined. One child is chosen to be the mouse and stands inside the circle. Another is chosen to be the cat and is on the outside of the circle. The cat says, "I am the cat." The mouse says, "I am the mouse." "I will catch you," says the cat. "No, you won't," says the mouse. Then the chase begins. The players in the circle help the mouse by raising and lowering their arms to let the mouse in and out as he wishes, but they try to prevent the cat from getting through the circle. When the mouse is caught, both players join in the circle after each has chosen a player to take his place in continuing the game. It is wise to replace the cat and the mouse within two or three minutes if the cat cannot catch the mouse.

Center Base

Skills:	Tossing, catching, running, tagging
Equipment:	Beanbag
Players:	Eight to ten per group
Formation:	Circle
Directions:	Children form a circle with "It" in the center. He throws a beanbag to someone in the circle. As soon as he throws it he runs away. The person thrown to catches the beanbag, places it in the center of the circle, and then chases "It." "It" tries to get back and pick up the beanbag before he is tagged. If he does, he may choose the next "It," but if he is tagged, that one becomes "It."

Crossing the Brook

Skills: Jumping
Equipment: None
Players: Entire class
Formation: File
Directions: Two diverging lines are marked on the ground or floor to represent a brook. The children start at the narrowest part of the two lines and jump over them. As the game progresses the children move farther down the line and continue to do so until they "fall into the brook." If a child fails to jump across the brook, he must stay at that point and "practice" until he can cross at that point. The game continues until one child is left at the widest part of the brook.

Hot Potato

Skills: Ball handling, tossing, catching
Equipment: Ball
Players: 10 to 12 per group
Formation: Circle
Directions: Have children form a single circle and face the center. A ball is passed quickly around the circle from one player to the next. The one who has possession of the ball when the signal is given to stop is out of the game (for one turn only). Also, if the child throws the ball or deliberately drops it, he must step out of the circle for one turn. Sometimes two balls are used to add more fun to the game.

Magic Carpet

Skills: Listening, starting, stopping
Equipment: Record, record-player
Players: Entire class
Formation: Large circle
Directions: Large spaces are marked on the floor in a circular formation. Players form a single circle over these "carpets." At a given signal or when the music begins, they march over each of the carpets. The object is to be on one of the carpets when the music stops or a signal is given. Anyone caught outside these spaces is eliminated from the game for one turn. Continue until all have failed to be on a carpet at least once. For variation, use running, jumping, hopping, or galloping.

Mouse Trap

Skills: Dodging, agility
Equipment: None
Players: 20 per group
Formation: Circle
Directions: The class forms a single circle holding hands. Choose six or seven players to be the mice who will go in and out of the circle under the children's raised arms. When the signal (the teacher may say, "Snap") is given to close the trap, the children in the circle drop their arms immediately. All mice caught in the trap will return to the circle and aid in catching the others. Continue until all are caught. Choose the same number again, and start over. Be sure each child gets a chance to be a mouse.

Poison Ball

Skills:	Rolling, ball contact
Equipment:	Ball
Players:	10 to 12 per group
Formation:	Circle
Directions:	Have children form a single circle sitting on the floor close together, and have them face the center. All players must have their legs crossed in Indian fashion. The ball is poison and is put in play by the teacher. As soon as the ball is in the circle, the players use their hands to pass or push it as quickly as possible to someone else in the circle. Should the ball stop in front of a player or hit any part of his body except his hands, the player will be poisoned. The poisoned players must drop out of the game for *one* turn.

Roll Dodge Ball

Skills:	Rolling
Equipment:	Ball
Players:	10 to 12 per group
Formation:	Circle
Directions:	The children form a small circle. Put two children in the center (after the game is learned, the number may be increased to three or four). The children roll the volleyball and try to hit either of the two in the center. If someone in the outside circle does succeed in hitting someone in the center with a rolled ball they exchange places. The children who are in the center may jump, dodge, or run inside the circle to keep from being hit. If one child is successful in hitting someone more than twice, he may choose someone to take his place.

Run for Your Supper

Skills:	Running, following directions
Equipment:	None
Players:	10 to 12 per group
Formation:	Circle
Directions:	The children form a circle with their hands at their sides. One of the children is chosen to be "It" and goes inside the circle. He walks around the inside of the circle, and stops between two players, places his hands on their shoulders, and with a slight tap, says, "Run for your supper." Both players run in opposite directions around the circle. The one who returns to touch the outstretched hands of the starter first becomes "It," and he may start the next two. The one who loses sits on the floor, as does the one who has just finished being "It." In this way all children will have the opportunity to run. (Be sure to teach the children to pass one another on the right side in order to avoid collisions.)

Duck-Duck-Goose

Skills:	Running, chasing, fleeing
Equipment:	None
Players:	10 to 12 per group
Formation:	Circle
Directions:	The children sit on the floor in a circle with their legs crossed. One player is chosen to be "It" and starts the game by running

around the outside of the circle and tapping a person on the head and saying, "Duck." He goes on, taps another, and says, "Duck." When he taps a third player he says, "Goose." This third child immediately jumps up and chases "It" around the circle, trying to tag him before he can get back to the place that was vacated. If "It" is caught, he must go to the center of the circle until another is caught; if not, he remains standing in the circle. The game continues with the chaser becoming "It," and tapping three players, and being chased by the Goose. (After having a turn, the child sits down so others may be chosen.)

Teacher Ball

Skills:	Tossing, catching
Equipment:	Ball
Players:	10 to 12 per group
Formation:	Circle
Directions:	A circle is formed with one child in the center (the "teacher"). He tosses the ball to any child in the circle, who in return tosses the ball back to him. He continues around the circle until all have had a turn. Quick, accurate throwing and catching should be stressed. Variation: Toss the ball to anyone in the circle. In this way all must be alert, not knowing when their turn might come. Variation: The ball may be bounced instead of tossed. If the class is large, more circles and more "teachers" may be used.

Superman

Skills:	Running, dodging, chasing, fleeing, tagging
Equipment:	None
Players:	Entire class
Formation:	Single line
Directions:	Two parallel goal lines are drawn 50 to 75 feet apart. All players but one stand on one of these goals. The odd player, or "It," is Superman. He stands midway between the two lines. He calls, "Who is afraid of Superman?" Players answer, "Not I" and run across from one goal to the other. All children who are tagged by Superman become his helpers. The last child to be caught is the new Superman for a repetition of the game.

There are many more games and variations of games that can be played by young children. The above are only suggestions for games to be played. They should be used in conjunction with the learning of specific fundamental movement skills.

SUGGESTED READINGS

Baker, K. R.: *Let's Play Outdoors.* Washington, D.C., National Association for the Education of Young Children, 1970.

Block, S.: *Diamond Me and I'm Great: Physical Education Three through Eight.* Minneapolis, Burgess Publishing Company, 1977.

Caplan, F., et al.: *The Power of Play.* Garden City, New York, Anchor Press/Doubleday, 1974.

Frostig, M., and Marlow, P.: *Move, Grow, Learn.* Chicago, Follett Corporation, 1969.

Gallahue, D. L.: *Motor Development and Movement Experiences for Young Children 3–7.* New York, John Wiley & Sons, Inc., 1976.

Gallahue, D. L., Werner, P. H., and Luedke, G. C.: *A Conceptual Approach to Moving and Learning.* New York, John Wiley & Sons, Inc., 1975.

McClenaghan, B., and Gallahue, D. L.: *Fundamental Movement: A Developmental and Remedial Approach.* Philadelphia, W. B. Saunders Company, 1978.

Mondale, W. F.: *Day care: education or custody?* National Elementary Principal *51*:79–83, 1971.

Mosston, M.: *Developmental Movement.* Columbus, Ohio, Charles E. Merrill Publishing Company, 1965.

Smart, M. S., and Smart, R. C.: *Preschool Children: Development and Relationships.* New York, Macmillan, Inc., 1972.

The Significance of the Young Child's Motor Development. Washington, D.C., National Association for the Education of Young Children, 1971.

CHAPTER SEVEN

THE ELEMENTARY SCHOOL CHILD

*I love these little people; and it is not a slight thing, when
they, who are so fresh from God, love us.*

Charles Dickens

All children react to others according to their own particular growth patterns. Although parents and teachers have long claimed allegiance to this belief, too many of them compare Johnny, age 10, with Jackie, age 10, or Mary, age 6, with Alice, age 5, or lump all children in one grade together as a group, comparing this year's group with last year's.[1]

If it is true that all children are individuals, then we must teach them individually and know the unique growth pattern of each. Johnny, age 5, may be an uncooperative bully, but his social growth by his tenth year, when compared with the behavior patterns of his first five years, may show remarkable progress.

Growth is influenced by many environmental and physical factors. Proper development can be retarded by sibling rivalry, constant criticisms, and rebuffs; it can be unbalanced by lack of praise for things done well or even tried, or by feelings of guilt welling up within from being called "bad" or "naughty." Lack of love and security, the right amount of proper foods, and sunshine and rugged outdoor play can hold a child back from developing along lines in his own unique growth channels. Increasingly, parents are wearing their children out by pushing them into many activities. Boys and girls who are going to school have room in their already full lives of work and play for one or, at the very most, two additional activities a week. Foolish are the parents who have their child taking dancing, music, and figure-skating lessons or other outside activities during the busy school year, for childhood should be the time for few responsibilities and the high adventure of discovery.

Growth might be compared to a ladder, each rung representing a developmental stage. Each child must progress up three such ladders, one marked "physical growth," the second "social growth," and the third "mental growth." Every boy and girl must climb up to, and pass, each developmental rung. The best adjusted youngsters are those whose progress up all three growth ladders is relatively even. Thus, adults will claim that a child reacts like most other ten year old children if that child is ten years in physical growth, socially advanced to levels of behavior characteristic of the average

---

[1]The authors recommend that any person teaching children should read the book THE WORLD OF CHILDREN by Paul Hamlyn. This beautiful book contains approximately 400 photographs of children and includes a supplementary text written by some of the leading authorities in childhood education. It is available at the Paul Hamlyn Publishing Company, Drury House, Russell Street, London.

ten year old child, and capable of learning materials suitable for his mental age. Other youngsters may be five in chronological age and physical development, eight from the standpoint of mental age, but comparable with only the average three year old child in social development. It is imperative that all teachers study the special needs and growth patterns of each individual child. Although growth cannot be forced, it can be encouraged, for children, like plants, grow best in a warm, favorable environment. Both plants and children suffer from neglect and overnourishment. Skillful, wise handling can aid all growing things to find the best that life contains.

Teachers need to learn more about each pupil, his family and environmental background, rate of development, and present developmental stage. Chronological age of a single year's space is of little help. Age groupings that include a two- or three-year span may be more accurate and meaningful. Although it is relatively easy for the teacher to distinguish between boys and girls, and between black and white children, it is more difficult to see maturation levels. Thus, not all children in the first grade can and will learn to skip correctly even though a majority may do so. The child who has difficulty may not learn to skip until he reaches the third grade, but meanwhile he may learn to perform other skills better than anyone else in the class. It is imperative that the teacher discover with each child activities in which he can succeed and gain positive peer recognition. This will yield more fruitful results than concentrating on trying to bring all pupils up to an unobtainable average in a chosen activity. Each child needs to be helped to accomplish the best he or she can do according to his or her own ability. Teachers should study each child carefully to discover what his maturation levels are as well as his differences, for these provide the basis upon which a developmentally sound physical education program may be built.

The age span during which most children attend the elementary school is a difficult one to study. In seeking greater independence children often become hostile toward adults or listen more to their peers than to their parents. Motives for actions are often concealed. From their point of view, children are removed from any age groups other than their own. Mere babies are children a year younger; adults are but one or two years beyond. Faced with the dichotomy of "acting like a man" and being treated as a baby, of being "too big to cry" and not being trusted out of sight, children are more confused than we adults realize we have made them. Although grownups, including the teacher, often count for little in the eyes and world of children, adults must provide much more guidance and help them grow in their own sight and their own world. Greater knowledge is needed about *when* to help children in their stages of confusion and *when* to keep hands off. Teachers, if they are worthy of the name, push children gently away from them and gradually lead them to greater independence.

It has often been said that the difference between an adult and a child is the difference between *being* and *becoming*. This implies that one must grow into adulthood, and that children change into adults slowly and often painfully. Above all, the teacher should help all children develop their own strengths and uniqueness. Studies show that children placed in an environment wherein they are *expected* to learn will learn the most. Consequently, every teacher must have a high degree of expectancy for each pupil. How the teacher regards each learner and the teacher's own temperament are as important as, perhaps more than, skill to teach children in the many areas of the school curriculum, for in the final analysis what any good teacher really teaches is a reflection of himself and his love for life, learning, and other human beings.

Research discloses that *inconsistent* teachers are more damaging to children than strict or lenient ones. Today we desperately need in our schools teachers who are eager to learn and who love to learn about many things in our exciting, ever-changing world. Such teachers will bring joy and individual challenge back into the school curriculum.

SIGNIFICANT FACTS ABOUT TODAY'S ELEMENTARY SCHOOL CHILDREN

Although all children are basically alike, each is as unique and different as each grain of sand or each snowflake. In order to be a successful teacher of youth, the teacher must know as much as possible about each pupil, his rate of development, his current developmental stage, and his family background and living conditions, as well as about his special needs, interests, desires, and problems. Likewise, the teacher must know (1) the characteristics of all children according to their class in school and what to expect of them as a group, (2) what materials to teach each grade, and (3) what methods are best to use to educate each pupil and the entire class most effectively.

We are living in a time of drastic changes, violence, and uncertainty—all of which are having a tremendous impact upon our children. America is rapidly changing geographically, socially, economically, and morally. The smothering of the individual is but one of the many prices (along with the breakdown of the family and of our moral structure and shifting values resulting from a more open and daringly erotic lifestyle) we pay for being basically a nation of bigness and affluence, as well as of great diversity of population.

Geographical Change

It is estimated that by 1980 almost 90 per cent of our population will be living in a big city or a nearby suburb. Not only will we be faced with increased crime and violence owing to the intensity of the population, but family mobility will be even greater than it is at the present time, in which the average family moves at least five times between the birth of its first child and the time that child reaches adulthood. We will become, even more than we are now, a "nation of strangers." Thus, it will be harder for children and adults to feel love, security, and belonging and to be recognized as unique persons.

RISING DELINQUENCY. Our 20 million teenagers have created a subculture of their own, which has set up a chain reaction often resulting in tyranny against the values of the mature world. Preteens are now joining them in rapidly increasing numbers. Although juvenile delinquents actually make up only 3 per cent of the total number of teenagers, this is a startling number of people, for many crimes are committed by youths who elude the police. Today one of every ten youths becomes an arrested delinquent. Legally, a delinquent is any youth caught and taken into custody for breaking a law. Arrests of juveniles in America have increased more than three times faster than the juvenile population. Delinquency is a social cancer that is spreading at an alarming rate. It results from several factors, including lack of parental acceptance, love, and discipline, as well as maladjusted personality, improper use of free time, and even prosperity. Reformatories and prisons are not the preventive answer to this social malady, for it costs the public around three thousand dollars a year to keep a child in a reformatory, far more than it costs to keep him in a public school. Approximately 80 per cent of all youths sent to such correctional institutions return as repeaters and later enter the adult criminal world. Studies show that crime, including murder, is being committed increasingly by children who are in the 8 to 14 year old age bracket.

Newspapers, movies, paperback books, television, and other media of communication have made us a crime-centered nation. Emotionally unstable youth and adults are greatly affected by what they see and hear. Such individuals are ripe for learning more about how to revolt against law and order. Inconsistent value and behavior patterns of adults, who can gain status quickly through materialism, do much to confuse youth further concerning what is right or wrong.

At the present time there are thousands of jobless youths, as well as older people, who are no longer looking for work. These are the drifters seen in the streets, parks, and bars of every city. These are our uneducated, unskilled, and most vulnerable youths, and their numbers are increasing. Many of these children are involved in the violent murder of their peers, their parents, and in some cases, people they have never even seen before. Thus, every effort must be made to keep youths in school and to teach them saleable skills.

Social and Economic Change

In our credit card society those seeking status are often on a merry-go-round ride that has trapped them deeply in debt. Things (the backyard swimming pool, the large house with two cars parked in front, and so forth) have become more important than people. Great social mobility is being experienced by those in the middle class. The poor remain trapped at the bottom of the social totem pole largely because of lack of education and vocational skills and because they come from minority groups; those already highest on the pole continue to remain aloof.

In America, in spite of the availability of the Pill, illegitimate births among teen-agers are increasing at an alarming rate. Statistically, the average American family is composed of 3.48 persons.

Currently 51 per cent of all mothers are working, and two thirds of these have full-time jobs.[2] One of every three working mothers in the latter group has children at home or in day-care centers who are below school age. At the present time many working parents are too busy or tired to spend time with their children. It is estimated that many fathers are now spending only 15 to 20 minutes a day with their children on a one-to-one basis.

DRUG USE AMONG YOUTH.   A recent statewide survey in Massachusetts showed a 92.7 per cent increase in the use of alcohol by teenagers, and 59.4 per cent of the students questioned said they had been drinking within the past year. Other recent surveys of students from all over the nation have shown that alcohol is increasingly becoming the favorite drug of teenagers. Many parents are so relieved that their children are not on "hard drugs" that they tend to look the other way in the case of alcohol indulgence. The sales to teenagers of "pop" wines have also increased rapidly, rising from three million gallons in 1968 to 33 million gallons in 1973. In some areas of the country even junior high and elementary school youngsters are often getting drunk. In America car accidents involving drunken teenagers in the 13 to 17 year old age group are also increasing. Alcoholics Anonymous has reported a sharp rise in teenage membership as well as the fact that some of its youngest members are ten year olds who are trying to remain sober.

It is well known fact that many children are hooked on drugs other than cheap

---

[2]Who's raising the kids? Newsweek, September 22, 1975.

wine, cigarettes, and alcohol. Even five year old children have already learned much about the drinking and smoking habits of their parents, others in their family, or other adults seen on TV.[3]

Studies show that youths begin using drugs because they are (1) curious, (2) under peer pressure, or (3) trying to escape an unpleasant situation. Those who do become involved seem to have a poor self-concept, lack respect for authority, have an unstable home situation, and be incapable of making responsible decisions on their own.

CHANGING STANDARDS OF VALUES AND CHOICE.   Ours is rapidly becoming a thrill-seeking, hedonistic culture in which anything goes and the more shocking behavior is, the better. Our movies and television programs largely revolve around crime or those who commit it and, like our cheap, brightly packaged magazines prominently displayed in newsstands and elsewhere, are full of shock and sex. Each citizen is urged to do "his own thing," and the race is on to become the most perverse and most revolting in actions, as well as in looks. The cheap and the tawdry are destructive elements found in the blowing winds of change, which are threatening to distort the vision of us all.

THE BREAKDOWN OF FAMILY LIFE.   The change that most deeply affects our children is the breakdown of family life. Recent statistics indicate that for every two marriages made in any one of the past few years, one divorce has been granted. Even in many families in which children have both parents, home is merely a rest stop and filling station, a place in which there is little communication, real love, or security. Because of family separation, children today rarely have aunts, uncles, and grandparents around to help teach them values and socially accepted behavior patterns. Television has become the babysitter, teacher, hawker, and parent substitute in the majority of American homes.

Today over one million youths below the age of 16 run away from home, becoming drifters, drug addicts, and young prostitutes. Many of these lose their lives through violent sexual abuse.

Child beating, or the battered child syndrome as it is known technically, which is found largely among those of low income or who are unemployed, is a national disgrace. It is also increasing, and an alarming number of children are being murdered in the cruelest and most inhumane ways by their rage-filled parents.

By the age of 18, one of every ten young women is a mother. Venereal disease among both sexes of teenagers is now at an epidemic level.

As already insecure children move from the spontaneous, pressureless environment of the home to the harder structured and directed learning environment of the school, far too many of them become early victims of frustration and failure. Although busing of school children has many advantages, it also has many disadvantages. Chief among these is the fact that children are cooped-up and inactive far too long while riding in the bus. Many face hostility and rejection at the school they are forced to attend when finally they do arrive there. The experience of an unhappy home life coupled with an unhappy school life is playing havoc with far too many American children.

Every child needs freedom to wander and wonder, to move and to explore in a world in which he is accepted *as a child*. The longer and happier their precious period of childhood is, the more likely the children who truly experience this magical exploratory time are to become mature, well-adjusted, productive, and happy adults in our society.

---

[3]Vannier, M.: *Teaching Health in Elementary Schools.* Philadelphia, Lea & Febiger, 1976, p. 302.

FIGURE 7–1. Excellent apparatus for developing the upper torso. (Courtesy of The Delmer F. Harris Company.)

BASIC NEEDS OF ALL CHILDREN

Needs basic to all children may be categorized as (1) physiological, (2) social, and (3) ego or self needs. If children are to grow in the friendly, warm, healthy environment of school, gymnasium, and playground, needs must be met. If and when they are ignored, submerged, or thwarted, the child becomes disturbed, rebellious, and delinquent. Although ideally the home, community, and school should work together as a team to provide for these inward urges, there are some cases of alarming neglect of any or all of the three in many of our public schools. When home or community factors exert negative influence the school must assume greater responsibility. Teachers need to be much more informed of the background of each pupil than they are; only then can behavior otherwise unexplainable become understandable.

Physiological Needs

Food, elimination, rest, exercise, and fresh air are the center of all human needs. Proper balance between rest and activity is of great importance to the health of the elementary school youngster. Children must have from four to six hours daily of big-muscle activity that involves running, jumping, and hopping. They need eight to ten hours of sleep nightly, plus one hour daily of quiet, restful activity. Many elementary schools provide cots or pallets for mid-morning and mid-afternoon naps. Little, if any, homework should be assigned so that the children are free to choose what they want to do in their leisure time after school. It is important that children use this time to explore, roam, wander, and play games with their peers in which there are no set rules and no one giving them directions. Children who play well together away from watchful adults grow as individuals and as group members. It is the lonely, isolated child suffering from deep fears of insecurity who often is frail and sickly. Such "loners" are often a great cost to society, for many end up in prisons or mental institutions, as did the Boston Strangler and the "Son of Sam."

Social Needs

These needs are especially strong among people of all ages. We all need to (1) belong, (2) feel secure, (3) gain recognition, (4) be loved, and (5) feel successful in learning attempts. These inner pressures are often intensified among children.

Behavior patterns are laid down early in life. Personality problems among adults usually are traced back to early home or school conditions or incidents. Children,

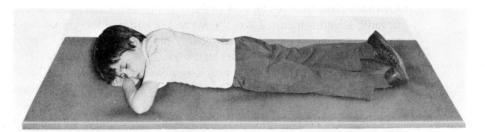

FIGURE 7-2.   Children need lots of exercise, rest, and good food in order to grow. (Courtesy of Jayfro Corporation, Montville, Connecticut.)

regardless of age, need to belong, to be a part of a group. Those who have few, if any, friends, who are always alone or the last ones chosen, who are crowd-fringers rather than joiners, are greatly in need of a friend. The teacher can best help such a child belong by aiding him to develop extra skills and abilities. She can push the youngster gently forward in the eyes of the other children. Care must be taken that the child does not cling to the teacher-friend but is gradually weaned away.

Children must feel secure in what they are doing if they are to do their best. Two circumstances contribute greatly to insecurity: (1) feelings of not being wanted and (2) a disturbed home life. Instability resulting from either or both can literally wreck a boy or girl, or an adult.

Day-by-day relationships with adults can build feelings of security. Teachers must, like parents, be consistent in methods of dealing with youth. One can not laugh on one occasion at conduct that may bring punishment or disapproval two days later. Insecure adult teachers who vacillate between being a friendly advisor and a hostile enemy confuse children. They cause those who are already insecure to be more so. Nonverbal communication through voice tone and facial expressions and in other ways can do much to help children feel more secure both at school and in their homes.

Studies show that children favor teachers who are firm and strict but fair, who do not show favoritism, and who are friendly and really like them. They dislike most teachers who are bossy, who do not know what to do in a situation but try to bluff their way out of it, and who are careless in their own appearance.

Children crave to be noticed, to be "first," and to be singled out. When this need is thwarted and they fail to gain such recognition legitimately, they will get it by negative methods. Deceitfulness, tattling, bragging, stealing, or other such measures may be resorted to in extreme cases. "I can run further than *you*" and "My Dad can lick *your* Dad" are expressions of this normal need. Recognition should be given to all not only by the adult but by the other children as well. This can be made in the form of simple phrases such as "Johnny, you are really getting that step now" or "Mary did the best in this group today" or "Alice learned how to do this faster than anyone yesterday." It can also be given by posting on bulletin boards the names of those who won class honors and class events, or of squad members who played most cooperatively for a two-week period. Children are not as interested in elaborate awards, such as cups or pins, as they are in receiving earned praise from adults and their peers. Although older youth crave the approval of adults, still more they crave recognition from their friends.

Children also need love—the kind that says, "I trust you," "I know you can do it," and "Let's figure out how we can do that better," the kind that is consistent. Boys and girls need the security of knowing that adults will be available for help if they need it. They need to feel that the adult cares about their welfare and their pressing problems. Adults need to remember that love or friendship is not a weapon, a big stick, or a favor to be used, denied, or removed when "Johnny is bad." In our society today we need to love each other truly, using love in the religious sense and not as in the popular songs or radio advertisements. Love, the highest emotion of the human being, is too often expressed by our cheapest phrases. Thus, foreigners find it difficult to understand how we can *love* that flavor or *adore* that book.

American schools all too often have neglected to answer the basic needs of children. Too frequently, little balance between activity and rest has been maintained; often only superior children or the poorly coordinated are singled out for praise or ridicule; all too often the extreme, pressing need of the pupil for the approval of his classmates is overlooked; all too readily we like children only when they do what *we* want them to do or perform according to our adult standards.

Children are *not* miniature adults. They are developing persons, who can and will grow into adults. As teachers we can help them or we can be their stumbling block. We can aid them by providing for their basic needs. We can retard them or even be their albatross when we teach games, sports, or facts, instead of primarily teaching children *through* these activities. Educators must realize the great importance of helping all children have as many kinds of successful learning experiences as possible.

Ego or Self Needs

The need to be loved, to feel wanted, to achieve, and to be secure, which is pressing among all children, should be met in the school as well as in the home. Children must also develop a sense of pride in themselves, a type of self-respect without egotism. They will acquire this self-respect from others according to their achievements. Teachers are morally responsible to see that each pupil receives praise for what he has accomplished each class period.

Youth must be aided to accept and make necessary compromises with life. They must know how to accept limitations and how to work, play, and live effectively within these boundaries. Those who are physically handicapped need to learn early in life how to compensate for their handicap and how to work around it.

In order to have good mental and emotional health every child needs to feel and know that:

1. He is loved and matters very much to someone
2. His parents and other adults will always accept him, even though often they may not approve of the things he does
3. He belongs to a group or a family and that there is a place where he truly belongs
4. Adults are there to help him when he faces strange, unknown, and frightening situations
5. He has a set of socially approved moral standards to live by
6. He has grownups around him who show him by example how to behave and get along with others at school and elsewhere
7. He must learn self-control, and although it is all right to feel jealous or angry, he cannot be allowed to hurt himself or others when he has these feelings

The desire for recognition is apparent in all age groups. Some gain it in socially approved ways; others find it through exceptional or antisocial behavior. In class some children will gain peer recognition early by being fair players or cheaters, by being physically adept or poorly coordinated, by being willing followers or rebellious leaders. The drive to display or improve skill mastery is intensified in some children. Pupils must receive recognition and praise legitimately from adults and their classmates. Every child can do some things better than anyone else and should receive recognition for that ability, provided it is socially approved.

CONFLICTS THAT ARISE FROM UNFILLED NEEDS

Physical, egotistic or self, and social needs fuse together and become closely interwoven to cause behavior. If a child's needs are gratified, he is a happy, well-balanced individual; when they clash or become thwarted or submerged, atypical behavior often results unless the child can be taught to sublimate or rechannel these drives into socially approved patterns. Regression, introversion, segregation, rationalization, dissociation, and projection are escape mechanisms through which the child may avoid self-realization or insight.

FIGURE 7–3.   Some children mature more quickly than others. (Courtesy of Kanakuk-Kanakomo-Kamps.)

Regression means returning or going back to childish behavior. First-graders who do not get their way with their playmates often resort to foot-stamping, temper tantrums, or other antics characteristic of three year olds.

Introversion frequently results from deep fears of inadequacy from which the child may escape through excessive daydreams. Children unskilled in play techniques often wander off from the group and sit watching others have fun. Basically such children often want to join their peer group but are held back by the fear of failure.

In all children there is the ever-present possibility for the flood waters of pent-up feelings to gush out when ideas and emotions clash. Unless they have mastered the fine art of self-control, mere trifles that exert pressure upon an emotional sore spot can send them flying off into a rage. They become upset, broken up, or dissociated at tiny incidents that previously left them untouched. They may not only "fly off the handle" but strike back at classmates verbally and otherwise as well. A pupil who is teased by his peers because he is afraid to be at bat in a baseball game may suddenly turn on them and lash out at these tormentors. The child may or may not be aware not only of his fear of batting but of many other fears as well. Because he wishes to hide his "horrible secret" from others he may suddenly charge at them like a wild animal. This action expresses a form of dissociation common among children.

At school the child who deeply distrusts or resents the adult teacher may be afraid to show these feelings. He feels safe, on the other hand, in releasing his pent-up frustrations upon his classmates. They, not the teacher, become the butt of his pugnaciousness. Prejudice, intolerance, excessive criticism, and cynicism are closely related to projection. One becomes adept in discovering those discrepancies others display that one knows are also one's own, regardless of age.

Wise is the teacher who recognizes that sudden antisocial behavior in pupils often expresses a need for adventure. Allowing the child to behave in this way is not the answer if the actions are repeated. However, the child has had the thrill of trying and usually passes on into his next growth pattern stage. Here again the teacher's attitude toward the child is the most important. It is suggested that the other children find how they can help the offender solve the problem.

CHARACTERISTICS OF PRIMARY-GRADE CHILDREN
(Ages 6 to 8)

Boys and girls in the primary grades range from about six years of age to eight years old. The primary grades are generally considered to be grades 1, 2, and in some cases, 3. Boys and girls in these grades are experiencing many new and exciting changes in their lives. The world of reading, cognitive thought, active games, and play is taking on greater importance. The following is a compilation of significant physical, social-emotional, and mental characteristics of typical primary-grade children:

Physical Characteristics

1. They still use the big muscles of the body best.
2. Their hand-eye and foot-eye coordination is still poor, but it is improving rapidly.
3. This is a period of rapid growth.
4. Imitative play patterns still predominate until the end of this period.
5. They lose baby fat if they are heavy and gain weight if they are thin.
6. They enjoy rugged big-muscle activities.
7. Motor skills are becoming important for acceptance and leadership.
8. Respiratory diseases are easily acquired.
9. They show more daring exploratory behavior.
10. They are less attentive to cleanliness.
11. Postural difficulties become more noticeable by the age of 8.
12. The lungs are relatively small, the heart is rapidly increasing in size, and pulse and respiration rates are increasing.
13. They show a gradual increase in speed and accuracy, and they have better hand-eye coordination by the age of 8.
14. They average weight gain during this period is 5½ pounds; the average gain in height is 2 inches.
15. Reaction time is still slow, but it is improving.
16. They are ready to learn to swim during this period or before.
17. Girls are better at stunts and tumbling than boys.
18. Boys show superiority over girls in throwing and batting because of cultural circumstances.

Social-Emotional Characteristics

1. They still tend to be self-centered until the end of this period.
2. They are sensitive to criticism.
3. They are fearful of being left alone, of failure, of loss of adult approval.
4. They seek and give affection readily.
5. They cry easily; those most insecure bite their nails or develop other nervous habits.
6. They have emotional outbursts because of their inability to control their environment.
7. They seek approval for more aggressive behavior.
8. They have poor group spirit and team loyalty, but this improves by the age of 8.
9. "Acting out" by the saying of cruel, taunting things takes the place of physical aggressiveness.
10. They "play" the roles of rough characters (e.g., the Bionic Man, Wonder Woman) in their games in order to gain confidence and power.

11. Sex roles are more easily identified by eight years of age.
12. Sex stereotyping has a great effect at this age.

Mental Characteristics

1. These children tend to be curious, full of questions, and very eager to learn.
2. Their creative abilities are developing and often outstanding. Creativity tends to be stifled unless encouraged.
3. They like definite, clear, concise directions.
4. They are often inattentive and talkative.
5. They take school seriously and are eager to learn.
6. Their interest and attention spans are both longer.
7. Girls tend to develop reading and writing skill more easily than boys.
8. Boys tend to grasp number concepts more easily than girls.
9. They have short-range mental goals.
10. They tend to have good memories.

Implications for Physical Education

1. Stress rhythmic activities and combinations of locomotor movements, such as hops with runs.
2. Arrange many large-group games, and provide a happy, secure, noncompetitive social climate in grades 1 and 2.
3. Use a wide variety of exploratory movement skills with many kinds of equipment, such as climbing equipment, jumping ropes, equipment of various heights for jumping, balance beam, stilts, and so forth.
4. Use graduated-sized balls for throwing- and catching-skill development.
5. Stress big-muscle activities such as running, jumping, hopping, and skipping in grades 1 and 2; begin skill refinement in grade 3.
6. Introduce a variety of games for small groups (six to eight pupils), such as Crows and Cranes or Frog in the Sea.
7. Stress climbing, hanging, and balancing activities.
8. Develop arm strength in stunts and tumbling activities such as wheelbarrow races, kneeling-position half push-ups, and inchworm relays.
9. Use dual and combative stunts to develop strength, such as pull-across-the-line, Indian leg and arm wrestle, and so forth.
10. Avoid highly competitive activities for children during these formative years. They will often push themselves too far.
11. In the second and third grade stress chasing and fleeing games that require agility, change of direction, and speed.
12. Help each child "feel" through rhythmic movement the differences between up and down, quick and slow, soft and hard, and heavy and light.
13. Provide opportunities for each child to experiment with ball skills in games such as O'Leary; start modified basketball shooting in the third grade using a volleyball and lowered basket.
14. Discuss play situations, "cheating," taking turns, and behavior problems with the class; let each express what he feels, sees, or thinks.
15. Provide opportunities to keep hands and bodies busy in grades 1 and 2; change activities often.
16. Have children help to make rules regarding safety and the use of equipment, and other rules they are expected to understand and obey.
17. Begin swimming instruction. Provide shorter periods for those not physically able to keep up with the group or those who chill easily.
18. Stress good posture, health habits, desirable social behavior, and developmental activities.
19. Provide many opportunities for each child to make suggestions by providing free-play choices and small-squad activities.
20. Stress joyful activities.

21. Proceed slowly with sport-skill development.
22. Emphasize safety while at play, work, and home, and coming to and from school.

CHARACTERISTICS OF INTERMEDIATE-GRADE CHILDREN
(Ages 8 to 10)

Boys and girls in the intermediate grades range in age from about eight years six months to 10 years old. Children in this age period are generally in the third, fourth, and fifth grades. At this level there are rapid learning, increased physical development, and increased influence of the peer group; sports receive more emphasis than previously. The following is a list of significant physical, social-emotional, and cognitive characteristics typical of the intermediate-grade child:

Physical Characteristics

1. There is a rapid increase in strength, especially in boys.
2. They tend to be robust, active, and noisy.
3. By age 10 they have better coordination, and skills are becoming "automatic."
4. They have growth spurts, with early physical development for some.
5. Some girls begin menstruating and develop pubic hair and breasts.
6. These children may have imaginary and far-removed romantic attachments.
7. Girls show increasing concern for their complexion, appearance, and figure.
8. Boys have abundant energy and huge appetites.
9. They begin developing skills in sports.
10. Boys often lag behind girls in developing skill in use of the small muscles of the body.
11. There is a steady increase in size; arms and hands grow longer and bigger.
12. Girls are taller and heavier than boys.
13. The small muscles become more developed; the large muscles are growing.
14. Most are in good physical condition; a few fatigue easily and should be watched for over-activity.
15. Poor posture becomes more apparent and should be corrected.

FIGURE 7–4. Girls grow and mature faster than boys. (Courtesy of Jayfro Corporation, Montville, Connecticut.)

16. Their eyes focus well near and far; nearsightedness develops in some.
17. Their locomotion is steadier, and they move with more grace and skill.
18. Sex differences become more pronounced.
19. These children recover quickly from illness and display increasing resistance to disease.
20. The average gain in weight is 7 pounds; the average gain in height is 2 inches.
21. This is often considered to be the golden age of skill development.
22. Boys and girls perform equally well in many activities.

Social-Emotional Characteristics

1. Intermediate-grade children are emotionally unstable in stress situations.
2. They tend to show less attachment to adults and rely less on their approval.
3. They have strong peer ties; groups and clubs develop.
4. They seek independence from adults but recognize their limitations.
5. Their enthusiasm often exceeds wisdom.
6. They become increasingly conscious of others and their feelings.
7. They chose heroes and heroines and emulate them; sports heroes are particularly common.
8. They still look to their families for security when in a difficult situation.
9. They are sensitive to criticism, especially from adults.
10. They are inquisitive about human relationships.
11. They are slowly developing an interest in the opposite sex and in sexuality.
12. They have conflicting needs for independence and security.
13. Peer acceptance is paramount in their thinking.
14. They experience increased anxiety over school work and over their status in their peer group.
15. They like challenges and adventure.
16. They have an increased need for independence and recognition.
17. They are easily discouraged and excited.
18. They are more sulking and resentful at home; they become quickly angry at their parents.
19. Loyalty to the peer group is strong; a feeling of belonging is a vital need.
20. They have short-lived and widely varied interests.
21. They value good sportsmanship, loyalty, and moral conduct and strive to do the right thing.

Mental Characteristics

1. They are interested in the world and the community and they want to improve both.
2. Children are often restless, and they are easily discouraged at learning attempts.
3. They show initiative and are creative and curious if encouraged in a positive, helpful manner.
4. They are idealistic and like to read about great people.
5. They enjoy learning new things but often have short interest spans.
6. They desire adult approval of their school work.
7. They are concerned with justice and with what is right. They have a clear-cut understanding of right and wrong.
8. They are often preoccupied with thoughts of sex.
9. By 11 years of age, most outgrow the tendency to laugh at others; intellectual growth parallels a developing sense of values and humor.
10. Boys like to fight, yell, and tease; girls tend to be more sedate and mature.

Implications for Physical Education

1. Provide longer activity periods in which skill instruction gradually receives more stress.
2. Provide opportunities for groups and individuals to release emotions and tensions through more rugged physical activities and through cheering for a team.
3. Stress vigorous exercise; help pupils know how exercise aids growth; alternate strenuous activities with less active ones.

4. Stress good body mechanics, posture, and movement in daily life as well as in sports.
5. Gradually emphasize movement accuracy and good form.
6. Avoid highly competitive activities; stress good sportsmanship, player consideration, and team loyalty.
7. Provide many activities that involve rhythm and balance, and teach social, folk, and square dances to coed classes.
8. Give as much individual attention and help to each pupil as possible in skill development tasks; develop good rapport with each child and with the group as a whole.
9. Provide a variety of activities using apparatus for chinning, vaulting, balancing, and hand traveling.
10. Develop a longer, more active class program for every pupil.
11. Provide for the need for belonging through team and squad games and relays.

THOUGHTS ON ELEMENTARY-SCHOOL CHILDREN

Not all children will fit into the growth characteristics listed above, but the majority of them will. The teacher should realize that a child of five to seven is undergoing a most important transition. Because of his boundless energy and never-ending curiosity as a "doing" creature, adults must see that he maintains a careful balance between active and passive play.

As children grow in age, skill, and ability to play with others, they should not engage in competition with children less advanced. The transition from early childhood to adolescence is one of remarkable progress. In schools, children should have increased opportunities for real responsibilities, as well as increased freedom to select, do for themselves, and evaluate their own program. Growth, like education, is a long and sometimes tedious process.

The characteristics of a healthy child are an abundance of vitality; bright, clear eyes; lustrous hair; good muscle tone; clear skin; good teeth; a hearty appetite; and freedom from remedial defects. Such a child gains progressively in weight and height. A healthy child is happy: he radiates and sparkles. An unhealthy child tires rapidly, is irritable, seems listless, and is dull.

Although today's children are one or two years more advanced than those of a generation ago, their interests are still wide-ranging and their need for instructional help in learning how to use their total capabilities well in work and play is perhaps even more intense.

The Six Year Old

Six year olds are eager to learn! They are often overactive and tire easily. Although they are less cooperative than they were at five, they are beginning to learn how to use their whole bodies. Often they are boastful and eager to show others how well they can fight. Interest periods are relatively short but are gradually increasing in length. Acting things out, as well as all other forms of spontaneous dramatization, is a favored pastime.

Children of this age need increased opportunities to take part in big-muscle activities of many kinds. Teachers can best work with them by giving them indirect supervision with minimum interference. Increased opportunities for making decisions may be provided.

All need encouragement, ample praise, warmth, and much patience from adults. The importance of the kindergarten and first grade teachers in the life of a child is vast. Some psychiatrists believe that if a child does not like his first grade teacher or sense

FIGURE 7–5. It's my ball and I love it! (Courtesy of the Montessori Academy of Dallas and Ann Melvin.)

love, acceptance, and security in her presence, he is a potential school dropout. Since all children of this age need a wide variety of activities involving the use of the large muscles of the body, as well as much freedom to explore, adult supervision with a minimum of interference is best.

The Seven Year Old

The seven year old suddenly seems to become sensitive to the feelings and attitudes of adults. Fear of their disapproval causes him to be less anxious to try many things than to do a few well. Fairy stories, rhymes, myths, nature stories, and comic characters bring delight to him. Although he is becoming more capable of some abstract thinking, he learns best in concrete terms and through activity. Boastfulness and exaggerated cocksureness show that he often prefers the word "fight" to the act of fighting.

Both teachers and parents should help the seven year old find the right combination of independence and dependence. Warm, encouraging, friendly relations between the child and the adult are imperative.

The Eight Year Old

Although the eight year old regresses, becoming dependent upon mother or teacher again, he also is gradually becoming more interested in others. Group life becomes a part of his play pattern. Although he may appear to adults to be noisy, aggressive, and argumentative, he tends to favor adult-supervised activities. Collections of all kinds fill his pockets, his bedroom, or the family den. He may have more accidents than the seven year old because of his increased daring.

Special needs of the eight year old include receiving much praise and encouragement from adults. Wise supervision from friendly grownups can help him belong to groups. Opportunities to develop control over small intricate muscles should be provided. Wood carving, model-airplane making, sewing, sketching, and other forms of arts and crafts can furnish needed channels for creative urges.

Nine and Ten Year Olds

By the age of nine most children have formed a reasonably strong sense of right and wrong, although they may argue long and loud over fairness in games or the decisions of referees. Their interest spans are becoming longer, and they have a greater tendency to make careful plans. Stories of other lands and people and love for their country cause them to desire to become good citizens and good people. They spend much time with members of their groups discussing people and events in their own environments. Active rough and tumble play keeps nine and ten year olds on the go.

Children of this age need to be given frank answers to their questions about sex. They need to belong to a group they can be loyal to, and they should have increased responsibilities in the home, school, and community. Training in advanced movement skills, such as learning to kick a ball or hit a target in the correct way, should gradually be added to the physical education program for both sexes.

The Preadolescent

Although there is a wide range of individual differences in maturity levels in this age group, certain generalizations can be made. The preadolescent prefers his group of male friends to his girlfriend and will be often more loyal to them than to his own parents. Although there is a marked interest difference between the sexes, both tend to like team games, pets, television shows, radio programs, and comic books. Teasing and other forms of antagonism between boy and girl groups is a favorite pastime. Although the majority of preadolescents tend to be overcritical and rebellious and have an "I know it all" attitude, some do not display these characteristics. Nailbiting, daydreaming, and often impudence show a regression to habits characteristic of younger children. Fear of ridicule, of being different, becomes a nightmare.

The preadolescent needs to know about and understand the emotional and physical changes happening within him. A sense of belonging to a peer group and increased opportunities for independence are paramount. Adult guidance that is friendly and unobtrusive enough not to threaten his need for freedom is necessary. Increased opportunities for the preadolescent to earn and spend his own money, pick out his own clothes, and set his own daily routine should be provided. Membership in clubs that work toward a "worthy cause" should be encouraged.

Skill mastery is one of the great desires of youth. They long to surpass others in strength, speed, and accuracy. Strict physical training to gain team membership is willingly accepted and should be encouraged.

ENLISTING THE COOPERATION OF OTHERS

Teachers sometimes need help in understanding each child more fully. Cooperation with the parents and other teachers and pupils can often prove fruitful. Frank discussions should be held with parents, but these should be carefully planned by the teacher. Suggested techniques for successful parent-teacher conferences are

1. quickly establishing the feeling that, like the parent, you want to help the child, that you are working together;
2. finding out as much about the child as you can without probing or prying; and
3. visiting the parents in their home, if possible.

THE USE OF BEHAVIOR RECORDS

Children express their inner strengths and weaknesses through their behavior. The more the adult can hear and see a child in action, the more he can learn about each one. Likewise, the more *he* talks, the less he will learn about a child, for the more freely a youngster can communicate and identify with him, the greater the learning and character-shaping result will be. Suggested questions to ask yourself when observing children at work and play include the following:

1. Are there children who maintain leadership after the activity or game has been continuing for 5 or 10 minutes?
2. Are there children who are noisy, but who are on the side lines rather than in the center of activity?
3. Are there children in your class who are remaining in group activity only as long as they can have their own way?
4. Which children are always on the fringe of activity?
5. Are there some children who are using teasing as a source of power?
6. Are some children so considerate of others that they have little time to attend to their own work?

All children performing the types of behavior described are problem ridden; many of them are preneurotic. If growth is a slow process, the teacher must know more about ways in which the child needs to develop and must aid him to help himself. If the teacher would teach the child, she first must know the child's developmental level in as many areas as possible.

In appraising the developmental rate of each child, the teacher should make, keep, and carefully study cumulative behavior records of each pupil. Although this is time consuming, it leads to better pupil understanding and teaching.

SUGGESTED READINGS

Cratty, B.: *Learning About Child Behavior Through Active Games.* Englewood Cliffs, New Jersey, Prentice-Hall, Inc., 1975.

Gordan, I. J.: *Human Development: A Transactional Perspective.* New York, Harper & Row, Publishers, 1975.

Helms, D., and Turner, J.: *Exploring Child Behavior.* Philadelphia, W. B. Saunders Company, 1976.

Herndon, J.: *The Way It Spozed To Be.* New York, Bantam Books, Inc., 1966.

Humphrey, A.: *Heaven in My Hand.* Stanton, Virginia, Knox Press, 1955.

Kagan, J.: *Understanding Children: Behavior, Motives and Thought.* New York, Harcourt Brace Jovanovich, Inc., 1971.

Lugo, J. O., and Hershey, G. L.: *Human Development: A Multidisciplinary Approach to the Psychology of Individual Growth.* New York, Macmillan, Inc., 1974.

McCandless, B. R.: *Children: Behavior and Development.* New York, Holt, Rinehart and Winston, Inc., 1976.

Morris, D.: *How to Change the Games Children Play.* Minneapolis, Burgess Publishing Company, 1976.

Pringle, M.: *The Needs of Children.* New York, Schocken Books Inc., 1975.

Smart, M. S., and Smart, R. C.: *School-Age Children: Development and Relationships.* New York, Macmillan, Inc., 1973.

Smart, M. S., and Smart, R. C.: *Children: Development and Relationships.* 2nd ed. New York, Macmillan, Inc., 1972.

Weiner, I. B., and Elkind, D.: *Children Development: A Core Approach.* New York, John Wiley & Sons, Inc., 1972.

CHAPTER EIGHT

THE EXCEPTIONAL CHILD

Who will help these children if you do not?
Robert Kennedy

Every community and school system contains some children who are physically, mentally, or emotionally handicapped. Their handicaps may be mild or severe, single or multiple, temporary or permanent, but all of these children possess one common characteristic—a limitation in some measurable way in their ability to participate in physical activities that are characteristic of normal children their own age. The philosophy of education in the United States includes the doctrine that every child is entitled to an education to the limit of his ability. Physical education as a part of the total education spectrum is also committed to this doctrine. The physical educator contributes to the atypical child's development by meeting many of his needs through the medium of movement.

Children should not be excused from the physical education class because of a disability. They need to learn how to live successfully with others and with themselves in our highly competitive society. They must learn how to interact effectively with their environment and how to use their leisure time wisely. The handicapped child should be a part of a class and be with normal children, but *only* if he is assigned learning tasks within the range of his capabilities and through these activities can gain a greater degree of total fitness. If the child needs to be in a special class, he should be placed with a group in an adapted physical education class taught by a trained specialist, and he should receive much individual attention.

SPECIALIZED PHYSICAL EDUCATION FOR THE HANDICAPPED

The exceptional individual is first of all a human being, and second, a person with some unique kind of handicap. Although most exceptional people are acutely and painfully aware of their physical limitations, almost all of them are totally ignorant of their physical development potentialities.

Until recently, many schools excused atypical students from physical education classes. Those with only slight handicaps were often allowed to do such things as keeping score during activities. Such practices are apt to do more harm than good. *All* children need to learn how to play and to be taught basic body control and movement skills. The unskilled child, if he is further handicapped by being physically disabled, is in for a lonely, isolated, unhappy future. It is through specially devised physical education programs that thousands of handicapped individuals are being educated to face and realize their limitations and to learn how to work around them.

Today there are three basic kinds of specialized physical education programs: adapted, corrective, and developmental. Adapted physical education is a modification of physical activities according to the physical limitations of an atypical individual or group. Corrective physical education is a program of specific exercises and activities designed to improve body mechanics in standing, sitting, or moving through space. Developmental physical education is concerned with the improvement of the physical fitness and motor coordination of those who are below established standards as measured by various diagnostic tests.

In addition to a knowledge of and skill in the type of teaching needed to successfully conduct a wide variety of physical activities, a teacher working with exceptional students should have a vast understanding of the human body, first aid, and the causes, nature, and effects of handicapping disabilities. This person must have a basic understanding of human behavior as well as a "feel" for teaching and people. Most crucial is (1) the patience to work with exceptional individuals (because their progress in learning skills is often painfully slow) and (2) total acceptance of such pupils (because many of them may be repulsive looking and even grotesque). The more one knows about individual pupils and their particular handicaps, the more successfully one can reach and teach them. Parent conferences will prove helpful; if they are well planned there will be a feeling of rapport, support, and willingness to work together. Such conferences can help the teacher establish controls necessary for protecting students from physical or emotional injury.

Horace Mann, the famous American educator, once declared that "the teacher who is attempting to teach without inspiring the pupil with a desire to learn and improve himself is hammering in vain upon cold iron." John Ruskin believed that "education does not mean teaching people what they do not know. It means teaching them to *behave* as they do not behave."

SOCIAL ADJUSTMENT AND THE EXCEPTIONAL CHILD

Extreme care must be taken to make school experiences positive ones for the handicapped child. The teacher must not only accept the child and his limitations, but must help other students to gain respect for this person too.

A major problem of the exceptional child is social adjustment. This problem appears to be the result of two separate influences. The first of these influences is external. It is brought about by the society and the environment in which the child lives. Internal influences are the second and most important cause of problems of social adjustment. They are related to an incomplete or distorted concept that the handicapped individual often has of his body and its potentialities for movement in space.

External Influences

The historical attitudes toward the treatment of the handicapped have had a great effect on modern man's attitude toward them. In the past they were treated as freaks, feared as beings sent by Satan, cursed, given improper medical care and treatment, beaten, and killed. Only recently has the emphasis begun to shift from the individual's disabilities to his abilities. This new way of seeing the disabled has had a great effect on their education, but unfortunately many of the old fears and much of the social stigma of the past still exist today.

The modern adapted physical education program is based on the premise that handicapped individuals want to be accepted in the community as well-adjusted, contributing members of society. Despite the great progress in treatment and social services for the disabled, social prejudice still exists against them, and they carry an inferior social status. The greatest obstacle to more rapid strides in rehabilitation is public prejudice.

The past has greatly influenced our present concept of handicapped persons and hence has affected the handicapped individual's concept of himself. Our feelings about ourselves are greatly influenced by the views and reactions of others toward us. Acceptance by others would go a long way toward promoting self-acceptance in the handicapped individual and would eliminate many of the social and psychological problems that he faces. Physical, mental, and emotional disabilities are phenomena on which high negative value is placed by society and the individual himself. The problem of adjustment to these limitations is a problem of creating favorable situations for the individual and social acceptance by a majority of the nonhandicapped population.

Although the mistakes and the negative attitudes of the past cannot be altered, physical education may have a profound positive influence on the adjustment of the disabled individual and his functioning in society. A good adapted program will influence his future acceptance by society and hence the individual's acceptance of himself. The nonhandicapped population must be made to realize that the handicapped person is not looking for concessions or sympathy but wants to be like others within the limits of his disability. Integration of the handicapped person with nonhandicapped persons as a functioning part of the normal physical education class whenever possible will lead to future acceptance. Integration will promote understanding (not pity), encourage favorable attitudes toward the disabled, and lead to their public and self-acceptance. If the negative attitudes toward the handicapped are eliminated future history will undoubtedly record a brighter picture of their self-acceptance, which is a key factor in social adjustment.

Internal Influences

We all possess some sort of awareness of our own body and its possibilities for movement and performance. This quality, or body image as it is commonly called, is a learned concept that results from observation of the movements of parts of the body and the relationship of these different parts to each other and external objects in space.

A well-developed body image is important because we do not deal in absolutes in our perceptions of ourselves or the world about us. If the child does not form a reasonably satisfactory body image as a result of appropriate movement activity, his self-concept is likely to be distorted and he will be retarded in his emotional and social development. The extent to which the child's body image is developed depends largely on his movement performance. Both the quality and the quantity of the movement activities are important. These various experiences lead to a better orientation and give him information about his body that he would be unable to obtain otherwise. Movement performance enables him to gain sensory information concerning changes in tonus. The more information that he receives, the better the quality of the information and the more the body image is developed. The movement experiences and diverse gross motor activities inherent in a well-planned physical education program contribute a great deal to the development of a stable body image, which in turn enhances one's self-concept.

If a child is restricted from vigorous physical activities over a long period of time his body image will not develop to its maximal potential. If his body image is retarded or distorted, it follows that his perceptions of himself and the world about him will be distorted. This is the plight of the handicapped child. He is either restricted from vigorous activities or is handicapped in such a way that his performance is atypical. As a result, he fails to form a complete body image or develops one that is distorted. This imperfect image further affects his perceptions of himself and his external world. These distorted perceptions contribute a great deal to undermining the child's self-assurance and confidence in himself. They often lead to social and psychological problems, which are indicative of problems of social adjustment.

Being able to perform a movement task in an acceptable manner contributes to the child's confidence and self-assurance. These two intrinsic by-products of an adequate body image are important elements in the development of a personality that negates the possibility of problems of social adjustment. If the disabled child is given an opportunity to develop his performance abilities to their maximal potential and to improve his body image, his confidence and self-assurance will increase. If his confidence and self-assurance are increased, his personality will be reinforced and the likelihood of problems of social adjustment will diminish.

Every child, including those who are physically, mentally, or emotionally handicapped, should be given the opportunity to engage in physical activities that will develop him totally to the limits of his abilities.

It is through the performance of large-muscle activities that a child experiences his first feelings of self-confidence or the lack of it, feelings of self-worth or worthlessness. If the handicapped individual is given the chance to participate in these activities, he will develop a more stable self-concept, which will lead to proper social adjustment by meeting many of his physical and psychological needs.

The adjustments that must be made by the atypical child may be modified by the environment in which he lives. The physical educator is a part of this environment. Working as a team, parents, teachers, and rehabilitation workers can contribute to the child's physical and psychological development.

NEEDS OF EXCEPTIONAL CHILDREN

The needs of exceptional children can be met if the following facts are recognized:

1. Their needs and interests are practically the same as those of normal children.
2. They usually profit more from being with normal groups than from being segregated; they need to be encouraged to mix with those who are normal.
3. In more ways than not they are like normal children.
4. Normal children can often help them to recognize their abilities as well as their limitations. Children are often cruel; however, when approached properly by an understanding adult they can be a tremendous asset to the atypical child's acceptance of himself and others.
5. Few children can be helped to any great extent who have been too sheltered by parents who have allowed them to remain helpless over a long period of time.
6. They need challenging movement experiences that are within the limits of their abilities.
7. They need to have ample opportunities to solve problems for themselves and to develop a sense of independence rather than dependence.
8. They need a variety of movement experiences that are designed to break down the artificial limitations that are often built up around their original defect.
9. They do not need pity or to be constantly reminded that they are "different."
10. They need to be accepted and treated as potential contributors to society.

FIGURE 8–1. Lennie is learning to walk using his crutches. (Courtesy of Northlake Elementary School, Dallas, Texas.)

11. Work and play programs must be geared to their limitations, environment, and ability, yet be challenging enough so that the children can and will progress.

THE ADAPTED PROGRAM

All exceptional children should be encouraged and required to take part in the physical education program just as are all normal children. Points to be remembered by the teacher with an adapted program are the following:

1. The program must be built on the individual needs and capabilities of each child.
2. The program should be for all students who cannot fully participate in the regular program.
3. The program must be conducted under the supervision and direction of a recognized medical authority.
4. The teacher should have specialized professional preparation to enable him to do this work successfully.
5. The program should not be limited to children with physical defects, but should include those with mental and emotional disabilities as well.
6. Recommendations for the extent of participation in the program must be made by the physician and not by the parent. Parents have a tendency to be overprotective and set needless restrictions on their child.
7. The parents' cooperation must be sought and secured.
8. The program should provide for children with temporary limitations, such as one recuperating from an illness or injury, as well as those with permanent limitations.
9. The children should participate in the regular program whenever possible but must not exceed the limits of their restrictions.

10. The children should follow the same procedures and rules in as many things as possible in the normal class, including class participation, costumes, and grading. In this way the concept that they are "different" is kept to a minimum.
11. The goals for atypical children participating in the regular program are not the same as for the others. Goals need to be adjusted for them.
12. A conscious attempt must be made by the teacher to assist the atypical child in gaining status with his peers. Giving him an opportunity to demonstrate some accomplishment or knowledge can be an important factor in enhancing his self-concept.
13. Classes for children that cannot be integrated into the regular program should be kept small. The type of limitation will determine grouping possibilities. Malnourished children, for example, may have classes with those suffering from cardiac and respiratory defects.
14. Complete records should be kept for each child, including results of the physician's physical examination, a health history, observations and data from his family, reports sent to other staff members, a record of his behavior, and his personality rating.
15. Most elementary schools do not have the facilities and equipment recommended for carrying out a good adapted program, particularly when it comes to the special equipment recommended for children with physical limitations. Consequently, the teacher must improvise and make the best use of what is available at school and in the community.
16. The teacher will need to develop modified activities that can be successfully participated in by the exceptional child. As such he should have specialized professional preparation to enable him to do this successfully.

PROGRAM OBJECTIVES

The aim of the adapted program should be to enable each pupil to obtain his optimal physical, social, and emotional level of functioning in a well-planned, progressive program built around his special needs, interests, and limitations. The teacher of atypical children must realize that the objectives he sets and the outcomes that he desires are often quite different from those sought by the child. It is difficult for us to put ourselves into the "shoes" of the exceptional child. Understanding his abilities, interests, and feelings is difficult, but we must avoid the pitfall of selecting activities to satisfy the program objectives based on *our* own abilities, interests, and feelings. We must remember that we are teaching not just activities but *people* as well. The objectives of the adapted program are classified into three categories:

1. *Physical objectives:*
   a. Development of total fitness.
   b. Development and improvement of physical skills and movement efficiency.
   c. Improvement of general physical health and appearance.
   d. Improvement of posture and body mechanics.
   e. Development and improvement of coordinated controlled movements of the body.
   f. Enhancement of more balanced growth.
   g. Development of physical strength, flexibility, power, balance, and movement efficiency.
2. *Social objectives:*
   a. Development of a wide variety of leisure-time recreational skills appropriate for the individual's abilities.
   b. Provision of socialization experiences that aid in the pursuit of increased independence.
   c. Becoming a tax-paying contributing member of the community.
   d. Ability to adjust to the demands of the social setting and become a part of it.
   e. Recognition from his peers for his abilities rather than his disabilities.
   f. Becoming more outgoing, and widening his circle of friends.
3. *Emotional objectives:*
   a. Development of an enhanced self-concept.
   b. Improvement of personal pride and self-respect.
   c. Development of a happy attitude and a wholesome philosophy of life.
   d. Feeling of security in a great number of circumstances.
   e. Use of activity as a socially acceptable way of releasing inner tensions.

Each child should also be asked to list what *he* wants to learn through his physical education experiences. Thus, the program should be built on the desires of the student *and* those objectives, goals, and expected outcomes the teacher sets for each class *and* each child in it.

TEACHING APPROACHES

Success in teaching atypical children lies in the teacher's ability to individualize his teaching in order to meet the unique needs and interests of each child. It is the teacher's responsibility to establish a climate that is conducive to learning. This climate must be one in which the child feels free to learn, to probe, and to explore. It should be one that establishes freedom within limits. These limits should act as guidelines rather than restraints, and produce a nonthreatening environment that enables the teacher to start with the child at whatever level he is on, and take him forward as far as he can go. Implementing the following suggestions for activity selection will enable the physical education teacher to develop workable approaches to teaching the atypical child:

1. Select activities that help the child overcome his lack of confidence and sense of failure.
2. Interrelate movement activities with the child's total educational program whenever possible.
3. Activities should be selected to satisfy the program objectives.
4. Select activities that contribute to the needs and interests of the child.
5. Select activities that are at an appropriate functional level for each child.
6. Activities should be designed so that the child is competing with himself and his previous performances rather than against others.
7. Select some activities that each child can do easily in order to assure at least a minimum of achievement.

The leader's role is a multiple one—part servant, friend, policeman, teacher, counselor, learner, and specialized experimental expert. He must constantly explore, improvise, and search for new and better ways to help each child. The teacher's tasks center on helping each child learn to help himself, to learn many new skills for personal development. He must be able to make what is being learned interesting, challenging, and fun.

CLASSIFICATIONS OF EXCEPTIONAL CHILDREN

Exceptional children fall into four broad and often overlapping categories:

1. *Physically disabled.* These children are characterized by the faulty functioning of their sensory receptors or their musculature to a point at which their ability to function normally in society is limited.
2. *Mentally disabled.* These children represent a condition characterized by the faulty development of intelligence to a point at which their ability to learn and to adapt to the demands of society is impaired.
3. *Emotionally disabled.* These children exhibit behavior that has a detrimental effect on their development and adjustment and interferes with the lives of others.
4. *Learning disabled.* These children fail to achieve satisfactorily in their schoolwork but do not fit into any of the above categories. See Chapter 4, pages 74 to 77, for a discussion of the child with a learning disability.

Within each of these groups each child differs greatly from the others. No two are alike any more than are any two normal children. There is often considerable overlapping of disabilities. For example, a single child might be mentally retarded and also have a physical disability. He may exhibit signs of emotional disturbance and fail to achieve his potential in the classroom. Both of these factors may or may not be brought about as a direct result of his mental or physical disability. The atypical child often exhibits perceptually based learning disabilities that influence academic performance.[1] We should keep in mind, however, that many physically, mentally, and emotionally disabled children experience some form of learning disability that prevents them from realizing their intellectual potential.

THE PHYSICALLY DISABLED CHILD

The child with a physical disability may suffer from one or more of numerous possible handicapping conditions. These handicaps may be mild or severe, single or multiple, temporary or permanent, but they all have one common characteristic: they limit the child's ability to function effectively in society. Examples of physical disabilities found among children in the school classroom are:

1. Crippling
2. Visual
3. Auditory
4. Respiratory
5. Cardiac
6. Nutritional
7. Diabetes
8. Congenital deformities
9. Lowered vitality
10. Cerebral palsy
11. Epilepsy

---

[1] These learning disabilities were discussed in detail in Chapter 4.

FIGURE 8–2.   Hockey is fun for everyone! (Courtesy of Shield Inc., Buffalo, New York.)

Heart Disease

Over half of all deaths in our country are due to heart disease. Those having heart disorders of a serious nature below the age of 25 are the victims of congenital heart abnormalities or rheumatic fever, which now affect more than 500,000 children. Although some of these children can attend school only part of the time, many must be taught at home by a visiting teacher.

Cardiovascular disorders include rheumatic fever, congenital heart involvement, hypertensive heart disease, coronary heart disease, and cerebrovascular disease. It is imperative that the physical educator especially, as well as other teachers, know which students have heart trouble and the seriousness of each condition. Rheumatic fever and congenital heart disease affect more children than adults, although many of the latter have heart damage of which they may or may not be aware as a result of rheumatic fever, which has symptoms similar to those of the common cold. Teachers and parents need to be on the lookout for children who seem listless, fail to gain weight, have frequent colds and sore throats, and complain that their legs and joints ache (too often erroneously thought to be "growing pains"). Often the disease recurs (in 50 to 70 per cent of cases), and almost always its victims break out in a rash and have high fever and pain. The brain can become affected as a result, by what is called St. Vitus dance, and the heart valves can be damaged.

Adjustment Problems

Often those with a diagnosed heart malfunction become extremely anxious and shun physical exercise. Those born with a congenital heart defect tend to be better adjusted and less cautious than those who develop it later in life. An alarming number of adults who suddenly have heart attacks panic and become almost complete invalids. Others, thinking their life is almost over, start burning the candle at both ends, thus shortening their lives even further.

All persons of school age having heart involvements should have a periodic physical examination, receive guidance and counseling, be provided with transportation if necessary, receive vocational guidance, be placed properly in classes from which they will receive the greatest benefit, and have frequent rest periods throughout the school day.

The Physical Education Program

Cardiac students should be placed in the physical education class best suited to their needs as determined by a physician, for the program must be composed of activities within the physical capacity level of each student. The daily instructional period should include short activities followed by longer periods of rest. Elementary children should be more closely supervised than those on the secondary level. For them, suggested activities are

1. Movement exploration
2. Rhythms and dance
3. Croquet
4. Table games
5. Tag and "it" games
6. Leadup games to sports such as Newcomb for volleyball
7. Jacks
8. Small table billiards
9. Archery
10. Circle games
11. Bag punching
12. Camping and campcraft activities
13. Fishing, hiking
14. Juggling

15. Horseshoes
16. Badminton and tennis doubles
17. Bowling with rubber balls
18. Table tennis
19. Bicycling
20. Relays
21. Simple games
22. Darts and quoits
23. Story plays
24. Miniature golf
25. Roller and ice skating
26. Rope spinning
27. Swimming and water games
28. Shuffleboard
29. Paddle tennis
30. Ring toss
31. Volleyball
32. Pitch and putt golf
33. Social and folk dancing

Auditory Impairments

Hearing difficulty is one of the most common defects found in children and adults, and hearing loss ranges from partial to complete. Many children are mistakenly labeled as retarded or slow learners when their learning problem is actually caused by deafness.

The *hard of hearing* can hear enough to learn how to speak and may or may not wear a hearing aid. Those classified as *deaf* (from birth) cannot hear or speak unless taught to do so by a speech specialist. *Hearing acuity* is measured in tone or pitch and *intensity* by decibels. All school children should be given a screen hearing test annually, and the tester should be a trained audiometry technician.

Types of screen tests include the sweep check audiometer test and the Massachusetts pure-tone test. Those with hearing loss should be given a more complete examination by an otologist, who can trace the source of hearing loss in order to determine if the defect is caused by excessive ear wax, involvement of the inner ear, or improper sensorineural development. Because speech and language are vital in our society, every effort should be made to correct defects as early as possible. It has been estimated that at least 5 per cent of all school-age children have serious hearing problems, that there are approximately 760,000 youths and adults who are totally deaf, and that hearing loss is on a rapid increase throughout the nation, especially in metropolitan areas.

Characteristics

Various types of hearing impairments include

1. *Psychogenic deafness*—associated with mental illness and emotional disturbance and not physiologically caused.
2. *Central deafness*—caused by diseases of the brain such as tumor, arteriosclerosis, cerebral hemorrhage, or multiple sclerosis.
3. *Sensorineural impairment*—due to prenatal factors (the Rh factor and infections such as measles and flu in the first three months of pregnancy), natal causes (meningitis, measles, mumps, head injuries, acoustic trauma), and postnatal causes (tumor, degenerative diseases, accidents).
4. *Conductive loss*—caused by impairments in the outer or middle ear or the eustachian tubes.
5. *Congenital deafness*—caused by nerve injury during birth or an inherited defect.

It is important that all persons having hearing defects receive help. Children should have assistance as early as possible and be well placed in either a special school for the deaf or in a regular school where speech or reading specialists teach deaf students how to communicate with others.

The following may be signs of hearing impairment:

1. Faulty speech patterns; faulty pitch, tone, or volume.
2. Holding the head to one side, inattentiveness, excessive daydreaming, inability to follow directions.
3. Inability to detect who is speaking and what is being said.
4. Emotional instability; hostility or extreme withdrawal.
5. Failure in school.
6. Difficulty in maintaining balance.
7. Inability to join class discussions and group games.
8. Social inferiority.

Those who are diagnosed as having nerve deafness (markedly severe or complete deafness) should be placed in schools for the deaf, for this type of disability is incurable and prohibits the successful use of hearing aids. Deaf people and those who are hard of hearing respond better if they are separated in school for instructional purposes. In most cases the teacher will need medical assistance if a deaf child is to be placed in a class with normal children. Special teachers are needed to instruct the child in lip-reading and speaking.

Most deaf persons are behind their normal peers educationally, physically, and socially. Those with partial hearing tend to be more stable, more outgoing, and more socially sure than totally deaf people. They also tend to talk loudly and a lot as well as use many facial gestures and rapid hand movements. Many deaf people are shy, sedentary isolates. Often they are overweight and many lack good physical skills, balance, and coordination. There is a great variation among the deaf; some can lip-read and talk; others are totally mute and seemingly in a daze. All need assistance in developing communicative skills.

Teaching Suggestions

It is possible for a teacher who is skilled in teaching normal students to learn to become a master physical educator of the deaf, assuming he or she has (1) a willingness to experiment in order to develop the best methods of communicating and teaching and (2) the ability to profit from failures.

It is important for the teacher-leader to be visible to all members of the class. Colorful visual aids are relied on heavily in teaching the deaf. Above all, class groups should be kept small; rapport must be quickly established between the teacher and learner; and every student must be given an abundance of approval and affection and a sense of achievement. Mastery of these three A's is basic to success for any educator, but especially to those working with handicapped persons.

The Physical Education Program

Many deaf and partially hearing students can be successfully placed in a regular physical education class or a modified one in which there are students with other kinds of handicaps. However, this can only be successful if the teacher realizes the seriousness of problems of communication each person has; skill in teaching through clear demonstration as well as through verbal instruction is necessary. The key decision concerns which type of class would best meet the needs and interests of the student and the class as a whole. Those who have severe or recent hearing loss can profit most from an individualized program for a small homogeneous group of eight to ten.

Many of the hard of hearing wear hearing aids, and most of them are afraid to run, jump, skip, or hop for fear of damaging this device. Difficulty in hearing instructions may cause seemingly rude or disinterested behavior in the hard of hearing. To avoid this, all game and safety rules should be made clear before the instruction or free-play periods begin. Deaf students usually need more factual knowledge concerning sports and games than do normal students; these can often best be understood through a liberal use of visual aids such as movies, slides, posters, and charts.

Ideal class size for groups of the total deaf is ten. Clear-cut class beginning and ending cues are needed. All the students should be arranged in fan formation for instructional purposes rather than in a single formation, so that all can see the teacher.

A wide range of activities should be taught to young children. These include simple and creative games such as Red Rover and games the children make up, leadup games to sports such as Newcomb for volleyball (in this game, the ball is caught and then thrown back across the net instead of being hit over it), Kickball for softball, and Twenty-one for basketball. Because deaf children, like many other handicapped persons, tend to be overweight owing to a lack of physical activity they may lack body coordination and the ability to balance when moving through space. Thus, a physical activity program can be of great value to this group. The program should also include activities in movement exploration, in which the child may be led into activity by such questions as "Can you show how you would . . .?"

Visual Impairments

There are many kinds of vision problems as well as degrees of blindness. Uncorrected faulty vision can cause deep-seated learning, emotional and physical problems. Hyperopia (farsightedness), myopia (nearsightedness), color-blindness, and strabismus, or muscular imbalance (which results in a cross-eyed condition or marked facial squint), are all common problems among thousands of children and adults in our society.

Visual acuity is most often measured in schools by the Snellen Eye Chart Test, in which the letters on each line of the chart are smaller than those of the line above. Normal vision is 20/20, meaning that a person can read the letters of the line marked for 20 feet. The E test also is often used for preschoolers and others. In this test, the person being tested points his fingers or hand the way the legs of the letter E point. Because most of our learning comes through our eyes and ears, it is vitally important that all children have their vision and hearing checked and corrected by the age of four, and that those with problems have them treated before starting school. Today it has been estimated that there are over 18,000 children who must read Braille or large-type books to gain their education.[2]

Blindness at birth is far more handicapping than that occurring later in life, for it prevents the person from understanding visual symbols and such concepts as big-little, near-far, beautiful-ugly, clean-dirty, and so forth.

Characteristics

Blind people tend to be overweight owing to lack of large-muscle activities, such as running, jumping, and skipping. Many have poor posture and coordination. Pecul-

---

[2]Buell, C.: *Physical Education for Blind Children.* Springfield, Illinois, Charles C Thomas, Publisher, 1966, p. 3.

iar mannerisms known as *blindisms* are common, especially among children. Examples are rocking back and forth, frequent eye rubbing with the fists, turning around and around like a spinning top, hand waving in front of the face, and head nodding. Among both the blind and the partially sighted are often found individuals who tend to be

1. Educationally retarded in comparison with normal individuals.
2. Awkward when moving through space and poor at activities that call for coordinated movement of the small muscles of the body.
3. Socially immature and ill at ease, especially when meeting strangers or in new social situations.
4. More likely to have emotional and personality problems.
5. Afraid to try to master new things, especially new kinds of physical activities.
6. Sedentary, solitary, and engaged in fantasies and daydreams.
7. Often depressed; they often feel rejected by parents, family, and normal peers.
8. Keener of hearing, feeling, tasting, and smelling than the normal child, with a more marked kinesthetic sense, so that they avoid running into walls or stumbling over curbs (referred to as *obstacle perception*).
9. Reluctant to take part in activities that require speed, strength, skill, and physical endurance.
10. Fearful of the future, which they feel holds no opportunities for marriage and parenthood.
11. Overprotected by parents and smothered by too much attention and guilt-centered parental "love."

Causes

Blindness can be caused by accidents, diseases such as trachoma, ophthalmia, or gonorrhea (which leads to prenatal blindness), and heredity. Scarlet fever, typhoid fever, smallpox, and measles can also result in serious eye defects. Accidents, the chief cause of death among elementary school children, often cause total or partial blindness.

It has been estimated that there are over a quarter million blind people (including children) in the United States, and there are twice as many who are only partially sighted.[3] As Wheeler and Hooley point out, partially seeing and blind children share the following common characteristics:

1. They favor solitary pursuits that permit them to start and stop and move about in space as they will. The activities they choose protect them from injury and from the failure that might result from competition with others, yet provide them with the satisfaction of having moved. Often their choice is sedentary activities in contrast with the more active occupations chosen by the normal child. Seldom do they participate in activities that lead to strength, speed, and endurance.
2. They may display symptoms of fear, frustration, concern over the future, and worry about social maturity, especially with regard to the opposite sex.[4]

Definitions

The *blind* person has a vision acuity of 20/200 or less. Such an individual may be totally blind in both eyes or in one or barely able to distinguish motion or light. Blind children are usually enrolled in special schools for the blind.

---

[3]Daniels, A., and Davies, E.: *Adapted Physical Education*. 3rd ed. New York, Harper & Row, Publishers, 1976, p. 261.
[4]Wheeler, R., and Hooley, A.: *Physical Education for the Handicapped*. Lea & Febiger, 1969, pp. 251–252.

The *partially sighted* person has visual acuity ranging from 20/70 to 20/200 and can see some light, forms, and bright colors, as well as black and white, and can detect some movements. He may be enrolled in a special or regular school, depending upon the degree of his visual defect. Increasingly today, those who are partially sighted attend regular schools wherein they have specialized instruction in the communicative arts and attend certain other classes with normal children.

Internal strabismus is a type of muscular imbalance that causes the eyes to turn inward. *External strabismus* causes the eyes to turn outward. *Alternating strabismus* causes the eyes to turn inward and then outward. *Hyperphoria* causes the eyes to turn upward or downward. All these defects can usually be corrected by an *ophthalmologist,* who is a licensed physician. (An *optometrist* is a nonmedical practitioner certified to prescribe and fit glasses as well as treat eye defects without surgery or drugs; an *optician* is licensed to grind lenses and fit glasses.) Often an ophthalmologist is assisted by an *orthoptist,* who directs eye exercises as prescribed by a physician.

All children need vigorous physical activity in order to grow and maintain a healthy body. The handicapped, who have many additional kinds of problems, must learn to accept their limitations and find ways to work around them. At school the primary responsibility of the teacher is to establish and maintain the best kind of learning environment possible for *all* students so that each one can learn, grow, and develop according to his own unique pattern for self-improvement. Extreme care must be taken when working with blind and partially sighted children to assure that the tasks provided for them are conducted in the safest kind of an environment possible. The teacher-leader must not rob any child of learning experiences by doing things *for* him instead of *with* him or by letting his peers do so.

Vigorous physical activities should be a vital part of the educational program for both the normal and the handicapped student. Dr. Charles Buell, a nationally recognized authority on physical activities for the blind, has declared:

> Physical fitness is important for all of us, but particularly for blind individuals. A blind person must expend much more energy to reach the same rung of success as an individual who has normal vision. Regardless of limitations in budget, facilities or physical handicap, we must provide our children, including those who are blind, the daily minimum of vigorous exercise they need for physical development.[5]

Teaching Suggestions

Teaching the visually handicapped requires the possession of the finest kind of instructional skills. Above all, the teacher must have empathy for her students, coupled with much patience, and be keenly interested in helping each person learn desired physical skills. Often the feet and hands of the sightless should be guided by the teacher, so that they get the kinesthetic feel of the movement, whether they are learning to throw a softball or kick a soccer ball. This individualized attention, however, should be given in such a way that at the same time the rest of the class is busily engaged in other learning tasks. The teacher must also be skilled in giving brief and accurate verbal communication. Often by blindfolding her own eyes or closing

---

[5]Buell, *Physical Education for Blind Children,* p. 5.

them she can better grasp the complications involved in learning various movements. Some helpful teaching hints follow:

1. Use a whistle to signal the class to move or stop.
2. Use a turning point for outdoor races that will guide the feet of the runners. Mats should be used for this purpose for indoor races or relays.
3. Clearly mark field dimensions and safety hazards in bright colors.
4. Use a bell or whistle ahead of the ball in order to help the players know where it is on the field in team games.
5. Have the students read game rules and other information in Braille before actually playing a game.
6. Use many auditory cues to help the student gain a quicker understanding of space and distances.
7. Use sighted assistants. (Teenagers are especially fine helpers, for they often are strongly motivated to be of service and tend to be more objective about handicapped children than are adults.)
8. Set definite goals with and for the student, and objectives to be reached.
9. Use music often both for relaxation and for motivation.
10. Include as many strenuous big-muscle activities as possible.

Almost all the activities suitable for normal children can be modified for use with handicapped children. Free play times as well as individual instruction should be given to these children. Above all, the class should not number more than fifteen students—less if there are many who need special help. Generally speaking, homogeneous skill grouping is best rather than age or sex grouping. Because many of the students lag far behind normal children of the same chronological age, games and activities suited for much younger children can be used. The teacher must accept the child where he or she actually *is* in relation to skill mastery and then help that child advance to a higher level of achievement.

Special Equipment

Balls used by blind students should have bells or rattles inside them and be painted yellow or white; they should also be larger and softer than those used by normal children. The play area for children should contain jungle gyms, turning bars, monkey ladders, swings, teeter-totters, and sandboxes. The play area should be fence enclosed and relatively free of natural hazards. Guide wires that runners can grasp should be used for track events, for they will enable the students to run freely at top speed. These can easily be made by stretching wires above head level over the running area and attaching short ropes with metal rings on the other end. The runner holds a pair of rings to enable him to move quickly in safe lines as the ropes slide along the wires.[6]

Other suggested equipment aids to teaching blind students include

1. Swimming—inflated swim trainer belts, which leave the instructor's hands free to assist the student
2. Softball—base paths in dirt or of raised cement for contrast
3. Trampoline—a bell under the center for placement and some type of sounding device at the end of the trampoline for direction
4. Basketball—metronomes on the backboard for shooting direction; orange-colored circle in center for partially sighted

---

[6]See *Recreation for the Blind*, the excellent color film of the many kinds of physical activities and equipment for the blind available for rental from Dr. Charles Buell, California School for the Blind, 3001 Derby Street, Berkeley, California.

5. General exercises—activity records for smaller children to make activities more interesting

An audible goal locator is available from the American Printing House for the Blind in Louisville, Kentucky. Gym scooters can be made by putting four casters and wheels on boards. A portable aluminum bowling rail can be purchased from the American Foundation for the Blind in New York City. Many teachers use their ingenuity as well as their knowledge of the particular problems of blind persons to design equipment for students to use. Some of the best ideas for usable equipment can come from the students themselves and their parents.

The Physical Education Program

Activities that are best suited for instruction of the blind and the partially sighted student in physical education include

Dance

Folk	Social
Square	Tap
Modern	

Individual Activities

Bag punching	Physical fitness testing
Camping and hiking	Rope jumping
Fly and bait casting	Rowing
Baseball	Swimming and diving
Basketball	Shuffleboard
Billiards	Stunts and tumbling
Bowling	Trampolining
Gymnastics	Volleyball
Horseshoes	Weight lifting
Hiking	Wrestling
Ice and roller skating	Movement exploration

Rope jumping, ice and roller skating, bowling, trampolining, swimming, hiking, dancing, physical fitness testing, and wrestling are the most popular activities. In many of these activities a sighted person acts as a partner of the blind or partially sighted person. Many blind people can play golf exceedingly well.

Orthopedic Impairments

The child with an orthopedic impairment has a motor disability. This disability may have been caused by accident, injury, disease, osteochondrosis, or birth defects.

Some possible causes are:

Amputation	Arthritis
Spina bifida	Muscular dystrophy
Musculoskeletal difficulties	Posture deviations

Crippled children who are able to be in school should be assigned to classes in physical education. Those who have mild defects may have classes with normal children. Those wearing braces, using crutches, or in wheelchairs may be assigned to the special corrective class.

Although programs in muscle re-education for these children must be built almost entirely upon specific exercise prescribed by medical authorities, the child can often receive great benefits from functional activities found in sports and games. Recreational activities high in social and carry-over values need to be stressed.

The victims of orthopedic conditions above all need to learn to do things for themselves. They should never be waited upon or pampered. They should mingle with normal children as quickly and as much as possible.

Suggested activities for those in wheelchairs include

Table games	Card games
Darts	Archery
Bait and fly casting	Swimming

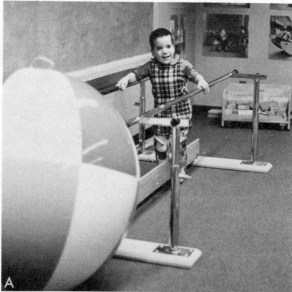

FIGURE 8–3. Some paraplegic children can learn to walk by using parallel bars. (Courtesy of Northlake Elementary School, Dallas, Texas.)

FIGURE 8–4. Children wearing braces should learn how to develop shoulder girdle strength. (*A*, Courtesy of Jayfro Corporation, Montville, Connecticut; *B*, Courtesy of Northlake Elementary School, Dallas, Texas.)

Activities suitable for those wearing leg braces, or using crutches, include

Archery	Individual stunts and self-
Shuffleboard	testing activities
Camping and outing	Tether ball
Swimming	Bait and fly casting
Horseshoes	

Activities suggested for those having paralysis of one arm are

Social dancing	Swimming
Runing and other relays	Individual stunts and self-
using the legs	testing activities
Camping	Roller skating
Rope jumping	Hiking

The physical education program for this group of handicapped children should be carefully planned around the specific movement, health, physical, and social needs of each child. It may be conducted on an individual or small-group basis; the class may be made up of all crippled children, or certain individuals may be put in a class made up of children with a wide variety of physical handicaps.

Cerebral Palsy

Brain-injured children who are the victims of cerebral palsy often have keen intelligence. Authorities claim that approximately 60,000 of the half million children affected are highly educable. Formerly, many persons believed that many of these children were feeble-minded because they looked that way. We now believe that if the child is mentally capable of learning, is emotionally stable, and can get around well enough without a special attendant, he will be better off in a public school than in a special one. Often when cerebral palsied and other exceptional children are too carefully shielded by their parents they become spoiled and maladjusted. For these children especially, the value of attending a public school is great.

Cerebral palsy victims have suffered damage to motor control centers of the brain as a result of a disease, anomaly, or accident before, during, or after birth. Cerebral palsy results in a motor disability that may affect many parts of the body or only a limited group of muscles anywhere in the body. It can cause weakness, lack of coordination, involuntary motions, paralysis, drooling, facial grimaces, and excessive rigidity or body stiffness, depending upon the severity and location of the brain damage.

Characteristics

In addition to their muscular handicaps, those with cerebral palsy usually have multiple handicaps. Many are also retarded, have hearing and vision loss, are emotionally disturbed, and are social outcasts because of their appearance and behavior. It is generally believed that most cerebral palsy victims are lower in intellectual ability than the "normal" population, although many have normal and superior intelligence.[7] It is not surprising that many have an excessive need for affection and independence. Although some victims appear docile and submissive, these feelings often hide underlying hostility and inward rebellion. Many have marked feelings of inferiority and escape reality through excessive daydreaming.

There is no cure for this disease, for the brain damage is permanent. Each person should be carefully evaluated by medical and special education experts. Remedial physical and school programs should be geared to build functional developmental patterns for the operative parts of the body that remain. Braces, drugs, surgery, and rehabilitation and physical therapy are used as treatment.

The cerebral palsied person, like all handicapped persons, must learn to live in a society that is mostly normal. Throughout the nation there are sheltered workshops in which those with vocational training can work for various manufacturing companies. The work often requires repetitive movements, and thus, it is well suited to many cerebral palsy victims (as well as other disabled people) and enables them to be financially self-supporting.

Causes

Approximately 30 per cent of the cases are a result of failure of the fetal brain to develop properly, infection of the mother during early pregnancy (usually German

---

[7]Kraus, R.: *Therapeutic Recreation.* Philadelphia, W. B. Saunders Company, 1973, p. 120.

measles during the first three months), maternal syphilis, fetal anoxia, cerebral hemorrhage during the fetal stage, the Rh blood factor, and other severe metabolic disturbances in the mother.

The majority of cases (60 per cent) occur *during* birth. If birth is too rapid, the tiny brain cells may explode, causing brain damage. If it is too slow, anoxia or lack of oxygen may also destroy the brain cells. Head injury resulting in cerebral hemorrhage is another cause. (Contrary to popular belief, only a small percentage of cases result from the faulty use of forceps.) Premature babies are often victims because the weakness of the tiny blood vessels in their brains results in hemorrhage. Vitamin K deficiency in the infant is thought to be another causative factor of this malady.

Only 10 per cent of cerebral palsy cases have been caused by head injuries following birth. These may involve accidents, combat in war, or infection in the central nervous system from such diseases as meningitis or from a brain abscess or tumor. A lack of oxygen to the brain as a result of, for example, gas poisoning or choking can also cause cerebral palsy.

Classifications of Cerebral Palsy

The five different types of this malady are the following:

THE SPASTIC GROUP. Stiffness and limited voluntary control of movement resulting from contracted hypertonic muscles are the chief characteristics of this type. The muscles of the arms and legs contract rapidly when passively stretched. Often the legs are rotated inward and flexed at the hip, with knees adducted. The arms are stiff and elbows flexed, and the lower arms and fingers are pronated. Body movements are jerky and uncertain.

The spastic person is usually introverted, extremely sensitive and fearful of new situations, tense, and awkward. This type of cerebral palsy is the most prevalent; its victims are often mentally retarded.

THE ATHETOID GROUP. This is the second most common type. Its victims have almost constant involuntary jerky, purposeless movements. When injury of the basal ganglia of the brain (which sort out and permit desired movements to occur) is great, control of speech as well as of the hands and swallowing is minimal. Often a movement starts where a person wants it to but ends up at a different place than intended. These movements vary from very fast to extremely slow responses. Frequently the toes turn back, feet rotate inwardly, and the head is thrown back with the mouth open and drooling. Facial grimaces are common.

THE ATAXIC GROUP. A disturbed sense of balance, direction, and coordination characterizes this group. Ataxics tend to walk in circles and are wobbly; standing upright or still is a real problem. They are also awkward and have many characteristics of the athetoid. Since kinesthetic awareness is lacking in this group, it is difficult for ataxics to see in three-dimensional space; frequently the eyeballs are involved in rapid, involuntary movements. Although the ataxia victim can understand the basic concepts of reach, grasp, and release, he cannot perform these movements accurately. When he throws a ball, it will go sideways instead of straight; he often spills his food and has much difficulty doing two-handed tasks such as lacing shoes or buttoning. He cannot do school work or other work in a poorly lighted place. Ataxics make up 5 to 10 per cent of all cerebral palsy cases.

THE RIGIDITY GROUP. Mental retardation is also often prevalent in this group, which is characterized by extreme body stiffness or rigidity and the lack of the stretch reflexes. This type is the result of a diffuse rather than a localized brain hemorrhage and

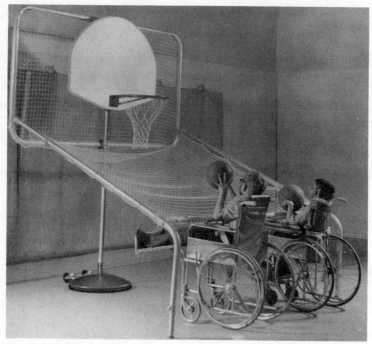

FIGURE 8–5. Even if you are in a wheelchair you can shoot baskets or throw to a target. (Courtesy of Jayfro Corporation, Montville, Connecticut.)

is often caused by encephalitis. Often normal movements suddenly are replaced by jerky ones (intermittent rigidity) and resistance to passive movements may often be continuous.

THE TREMOR GROUP.   In this type of cerebral palsy, tremors appear as uncontrollable movements, and their speed is constant. The tremors are often mixed with muscle rigidity. However, body movements are usually superior to those made by people in the other four palsied groups, and the learning of new movement skills is not such a gigantic struggle. As is true in all types of cerebral palsy cases, however, victims are often in both a social and emotional dilemma—too often they live in a world of social isolation. This group makes up about 5 per cent of the total of cerebral palsy cases.

The following terms are also used for classifying the cerebral palsied:

Degrees of Severity
1. *Mild*—ambulatory, understandable speech, and satisfactory use of arms and legs.
2. *Moderate*—partially disabled, with difficulty in moving, speaking, and performing tasks of daily living.
3. *Severe*—involvement complete, with confinement to bed or wheelchair.

Involvement Degree
1. *Monoplegic*—one limb involved.
2. *Paraplegic*—both legs only.
3. *Hemiplegic*—one leg and arm involved on same side of the body, with the arm often being more so than the leg.
4. *Triplegic*—involves both legs and one arm; generally spastic.
5. *Quadriplegic*—all four extremities involved; in spastics, the legs are the most affected; the arms are the most damaged among the tremor and athetoid groups.

The Physical Education Program

Many cerebral palsied persons need custodial care and are placed in special schools or hospitals where educational programs are provided for them. Some cannot go to school but are serviced by visiting teachers. Others attend special classes in public schools. Some few attend regular school with children of normal intelligence. Regardless of where the child does go to school, the educational program must be tailored to fit his very special needs. Extensive effort must be made by the teacher and an environment that is warm and friendly, yet challenging, must be provided in order to help the child want to learn.

The physical education program should be developmental and closely related to physical therapy. The teacher should be a part of the rehabilitation team, working closely with the parents, physician, classroom teacher, and physical therapist. Specific movement exercises—such as movement of the patient's various body parts by the teacher or therapist, followed by the patient making the same movements on his own —are often used. Learning to walk with crutches or alone through lowered parallel bars is often taught at special schools or treatment centers.

Those with only slight handicaps and movement problems can often be in a class with normal children, although activities should be adapted to their limitations. The fun and peer acceptance that develops through playing games should be stressed. Throwing larger balls, catching bouncing balls instead of thrown ones, kicking stationary rather than moving objects, and activities that require the large muscles rather than intricate movements are best. Square and social dancing for older children and rhythmical games for younger children are highly recommended. Skill perfection is not as important a requirement for this group as are the gaining of pleasure and the acceptance of others. Swimming is an ideal activity for most, for being in the water is relaxing and allows for greater movement possibilities. Doing exercises to music will prove beneficial, especially since many cerebral palsy victims are obese or cannot move their bodies rhythmically. However, because the needs of affected individuals are so different, the program must be uniquely designed for each one. Rest periods should be frequent, and students should be taught the various kinds of relaxing techniques.

If the class is composed entirely of cerebral palsied students, the teacher must realize that they, whether spastic, athetoid, or ataxic, differ greatly. The spastic child can be more successful in activities requiring constant, flowing movements. Among the athetoid students, relaxation should be stressed. Balance activities are not suitable for ataxic persons. All in the class, however, should be encouraged to develop smoother movement patterns and be taught activities with high carry-over value for later life and for present leisure-time activities.

Suggested activities include

Archery	Running games and relays
Billiards	Shuffleboard
Bowling	Simple folk and square dances
Camping and outing	Simple games
Croquet	Swimming
Horseshoes	

Epilepsy

A pupil suffering from epilepsy has the same desires, interests, and drives for play as any other child. But, unlike others, he is faced with the great problem of living in a society or group where his affliction is met with great prejudice, ignorance, superstition, and fear. Even the word "epilepsy" carries great stigma. Fear of rejection from peers and adult associates is constant and may be greatly magnified.

Epilepsy is caused by irritative injuries to the brain. The specific symptoms depend upon which part of the brain has been irritated. The symptoms vary from seizures lasting only a few seconds (petit mal or "little sickness") to twitching and convulsions in which the person becomes unconscious (grand mal or "big sickness").

Accurate statistics on the number of cases are not available, owing primarily to concealment and stigma. It is, however, a major health problem, and from the standpoint of numbers, it is far more prevalent than most people realize. Some medical authorities now state that one out of every 100 persons in the United States has some form of epilepsy.

Children whose seizures are mild may and do attend public schools. Those with more serious difficulties are in special classes in public schools, or in private schools. Afflicted persons are educable and many are extremely intelligent, but a few are feeble-minded and noneducable in the usual sense.

Increasingly, medical authorities are turning their attention to epilepsy. The new drugs diphenylhydantoin (Dilantin), trimethadione (Tridione), paramethadione (Paradione), methylphenylethyl hydantoin (Mesantoin), and phenacemide (Phenurone) have been found to be most effective; proper use of these medications has reduced the number of seizures in about one half of the cases. Diagnostic techniques are being improved constantly. The electroencephalograph, an instrument for measuring electrical impulses of the brain, has proved to be of great diagnostic value.

If the epileptic child is in school, he can be helped by understanding teachers who can help the other teachers and pupils to realize that, except for the fact that he may have a seizure, the child is normal in other ways. Should a seizure occur, the teacher can help the child by not showing fear, horror, or repulsion at the sight. By setting this pattern that the pupils will copy, the teacher can then explain to the others that Johnny is having an attack that does not hurt him, that he is temporarily asleep or unconscious, and that when he wakes up he will not even know what happened but will be very tired. The child, after the attack, should be taken to the first-aid room and be allowed to sleep or rest until he wants to get up. When he regains consciousness following a seizure, the first sight that he beholds should not be a circle of classmates and the teacher standing over him terror-stricken. During the seizure the teacher should place a tightly-rolled handkerchief between the child's back teeth and place him on the floor where he cannot injure himself from convulsive reactions.

Epileptic children placed in school with normal children must be under the care of a physician, who should work closely with the physical education instructor in selecting activities suitable for them. Because they rarely have seizures while engaging in play activities, group participation with the normal children should be encouraged. Activities that call for concentration might well be stressed. The controlled epileptic child may benefit greatly from competitive sports and team relays that require physical conditioning and much concentration.

Suggested activities include as many as possible that other children do, and increased rhythmic activities calling for concentration, such as learning intricate tap-, social- or folk-dance steps.

Lowered Vitality

Children who are underweight, overweight, or anemic, or who have had operations, rickets, tuberculosis or other chest ailments, fall into this group. All should be given a modified school program, little if any homework, and few responsibilities in both the home and school. Regular physical checkups, an appropriate, balanced diet, sleep and rest, and proper amounts as well as kinds of exercise should be recommended to the pupil and parents by the teacher and the physician. Allowing the pupil to rest or sleep during his physical education class may be for some of these children the type of physical education they most need. However, the child should also learn quiet games and take part in modified sports as a part of this program.

Suggested activities include

Archery	Jacks
Bait and fly casting	Table games, such as checkers,
Building games	pick-up sticks, and so forth
Hiking	Table card games
Camping and outing	Ping-pong
Games of low organization	Self-testing activities
Marbles	Social, folk, and square dancing
Singing games	Swimming

Physical education has much to contribute to the enrichment of the lives of all children. No child with defects need be restricted or denied the opportunity to learn how to play skillfully or the joy of playing with his classmates and friends. In as much as possible, afflicted children should play the same games as their peers, but the teacher should have the approval of a physician of the suggested individual program for each such child in her group.

THE MENTALLY DISABLED CHILD

Mental retardation is a national problem, and it is growing. In 1960 there were an estimated 5.5 million mentally retarded people; in 1970 the estimate rose to more than 6 million. This is a number equivalent to slightly over 3 per cent of our total national population. The physical education teacher can make a definite contribution to the total education of the mentally handicapped child. Until recently very little had been done to gain insight into the physical status of the intellectually subnormal child and to implement sound physical education programs designed to meet his needs. The reasons for this are varied, ranging from indifference to fear to lack of adequate facilities and financing. The potential for helping the mentally retarded child become a contributing member of society through physical activity rather than a constant drain on the tax rolls is great. Community, institutional, teacher-preparation, and research programs are now underway that are concerned with the education of the mentally deficient child.

1. COMMUNITY PROGRAMS.   There are few community recreation departments in the United States that have a comprehensive program for retarded people that approaches the quality of the programs offered to individuals with physical limitations. This is changing, however, thanks to help from the Joseph Kennedy Foundation, the AAHPER, and the federal government. The work has only begun, but there are encouraging signs that community recreation programs for the retardate are increasing in quality and quantity.

2. INSTITUTIONAL PROGRAMS.   Most public institutions for the mentally retarded claim to have a physical education or recreation program, but more often than not, these programs are staffed by poorly trained, underpaid, overworked full- or part-time employees who must substitute enthusiasm and dedication for professional knowl-

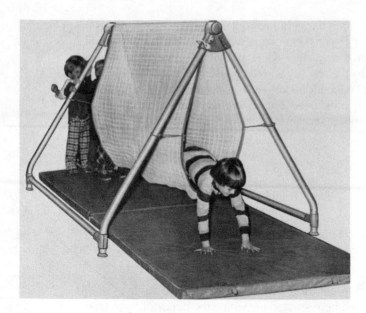

FIGURE 8–6. The child who learns to crawl and creep is least apt to have learning or posture problems. (Courtesy of Jayfro Corporation, Montville, Connecticut.)

edge of scientifically based physical activity programs. It is safe to say that not a single public institution in the United States has a well-organized physical education program that is integrated into the total school curriculum of the child and is designed to serve as an integral part of his education.

3. TEACHER PREPARATION.   Until recently teacher preparation programs in our colleges and universities have been negligent in the preparation of physical educators to work with the mentally retarded. As a result, there is often an undisguised fear of these children, considerable reluctance to involve them in the physical education curriculum, and a general lack of knowledge of appropriate movement experiences and teaching approaches.

4. RESEARCH.   There is a dearth of research available in the area of the physical abilities of the retarded child and the contribution of physical education to physical and cognitive functioning. There has been considerable conjecture regarding its benefits, but surprisingly little in the way of "hard data" is available to support the belief that physical education and recreation programs are important and can be of benefit to the total functioning of the retarded child. Sound research evidence is the key to more adequate institutional and teacher-preparation programs. Such research evidence will serve as a foundation for more comprehensive physical education and recreation programs for the retarded child.

Causes of Retardation

Mental retardation is a condition characterized by faulty development of intelligence, which impairs the individual's ability to learn and to adapt to the demands of society. The causes of mental retardation may be classified as

1. *Organic.* Organic mental retardation is characterized by damage to the central nervous system that is not hereditary in nature. Organic conditions may arise before birth (prenatal), during birth (perinatal), or after birth (postnatal) and can be brought about by injuries, diseases, or toxic conditions.
2. *Genetic.* Genetic mental retardation is inherited through deviations or incompatibilities in

the parents' genetic structure. Down's syndrome (mongolism), phenylketonuria (PKU), and familial mental deficiency are the most common forms of genetic retardation.

3. *Cultural.* Cultural retardation refers to environmental and socioeconomic factors as causes of mental retardation. The environment has a definite effect on suppressing or accelerating the child's intelligence within the range of his inherited capabilities. Inadequacies in maternal diet, as well as in the child's diet, and the deprivation of experiences have been shown to be contributing factors to retarded intellectual development.

Classification

Children with low intelligence have been classified in a variety of ways. Educators use the rate of learning that the child is capable of or the degree of the defect in terms of his IQ. The following categories are those used most frequently by educators:

1. *Slow Learner* (70 to 90 IQ). The slow learner is not actually mentally retarded. He is capable of achieving a reasonable degree of success in the regular classroom, but at a slower rate than the average child. A child may be classified as a slow learner because of a perceptual-motor learning disability, emotional disturbance, cultural deprivation, or motivational problems.
2. *Educable Mentally Retarded* (55 to 70 IQ). This child is characterized by his inability to benefit to any great degree from the curriculum offered by the regular school. He does, however, possess the potential for the development of minimum academic, social, and occupational skills to a degree that he can function independently in the community and assume partial or complete occupational support of himself at a marginal level.
3. *Trainable Mentally Retarded* (40 to 55 IQ). This child is characterized by his inability to profit from the program offered the educable mentally retarded child. He does, however, have the potential for learning self-care and personal hygiene, economic usefulness in the home or sheltered workshop, and getting along in the home or neighborhood but not the total community.
4. *Custodial Mentally Retarded* (0 to 40 IQ). This child is profoundly subnormal in intelligence. He is unable to perform the basic requirements of self-care, economic, and socialization skills that the trainable child is able to do. This type of child requires constant supervision throughout life. He is totally dependent upon the help of others for survival.

Physical Status of the Mentally Disabled Child

The mentally retarded child, in addition to being below normal in his intellectual functioning, is generally below the performance level of his normal counterparts on tests of motor ability, motor fitness, and physical fitness. This situation is due, in part, to the cognitive aspect that is part of all physical activity, as well as to a general lack of opportunity for activity on the part of the retarded child. This statement should not be viewed simply as another means of demonstrating the vast differences between the exceptional child and his chronological peers. It should, however, be recognized that to a large degree this state of affairs is due to the gross neglect that retarded people have suffered for years. What more can be expected if one's life is spent in endless hours of boredom brought about by constant inactivity? It would be a rare intellectually normal individual who would not degenerate into a physical wreck from year after year of inactivity. All we need to do is to look at the average white-collar worker who sits behind a desk day in and day out and gets no real large-muscle activity. His scores on tests of physical fitness and motor ability would most likely look like those of the retardate simply because of a gross lack of vigorous activity. The human machine needs physical activity in order to continue functioning at its optimum, no matter what its intellectual capabilities. We cannot expect the mentally retarded child to approach his normal counterparts in terms of his physical functioning if he does not have sufficient movement experiences and sound guidance in the development of his physical abilities. Although we must recognize that the ability of the retarded child's mind to function places the outer limits on the potential functioning of his body, we must not let this distract us from striving for maximal performance within the limits of his abilities.

Physical education and recreation programs can add to the reduction of the halo of physical inadequacies that contribute to the child's being labeled "retarded." The halo of disability that often surrounds the mentally retarded child is an ever-expanding circle of artificial disabilities that develop around the original and unalterable mental defect. Most mentally retarded children have developed a halo of disability, as is evidenced by their performance on numerous tests of physical status. A well-planned program of motor activities will contribute to its reduction. This is not to say that physical education is a panacea for *curing* mental retardation. Such a naive assumption is absurd. It is merely meant to say that the halo effect can be reduced through a good physical education program, and that the retarded child can be enabled to progress at a *rate* similar to that of the normal child even though he may still be unable to perform at the same *level*.

Those who are mentally retarded are often also physically retarded and score poorly on tests for physical fitness, motor ability, and physical coordination. Some do well, however, in some sports and physical activities including boxing, track and field events, football, tumbling, and simple games. Often those who are behind normal children in skill mastery have led sheltered lives and have not had an opportunity for activity. Many could learn to do and enjoy sports and games but greatly need to be patiently taught the basic movement skills needed for doing so.

Physical educators and recreation leaders can do much to help retarded children catch up with their normal peers in skill mastery by providing them with a well-planned graded program of activities that gradually increase in complexity and require greater coordinated movement accuracy. Thus, simple games and skills, when mastered, should be replaced by others that are more fun, challenging, and satisfying to do. Although the retarded child or adult will require much more help, praise, and other motivational encouragement than the normal person the leader will be rewarded, just as much as the learner, when the latter can say with glee "I did it! I did it!" when he does learn to hit or kick a ball after many failures to do so, or to jump the rope and so forth.

The Physical Education Program

Most retarded children have motor and perceptual difficulties and often have extremely poor motor coordination. They can learn an amazing number of physical activities from a teacher with great patience who shows them much loving care and understanding. In teaching the mentally retarded it is suggested that one

1. Stress big-muscle movement activities involving locomotion, manipulation, and stability movements.
2. Know each child's name and be sure that he knows yours.
3. "Show" more and explain less.
4. Be sure that instruction is slow, progressive, and brief.
5. Keep rules simple.

6. Provide for many kinds of rhythmical activities.
7. Stress the "fun" element in play.
8. Provide manual assistance in certain activities for the children who need it.
9. Include outdoor and camping activities in the program whenever possible.
10. Reduce each skill to its simplest component so that the child can cope with it.
11. Name the movement or skill being taught to help develop vocabulary.
12. Be sure that practice periods are short, with frequent changes in activities in order to reduce frustration.
13. Let a child repeat his successes several times and enjoy his feeling of accomplishment.
14. Reward all accomplishments, including the smallest, with praise.
15. Keep each child active.
16. Set standards of acceptable behavior by praising good performance.
17. Introduce new activities early in the lesson, because of the susceptibility to fatigue.
18. Stress the development of fundamental movement patterns and general movement skills.
19. Whenever possible include the retarded child in the normal class.

THE EMOTIONALLY DISABLED CHILD

The emotionally disturbed child is characterized by behavior patterns that have a detrimental effect on his adjustment and interfere with the lives of others. It is now estimated that between 10 to 14 per cent of all schoolchildren in America are emotionally disturbed. Until recently, the needs of the child with emotional problems had been almost completely ignored. Only the most severe cases were diagnosed and treated. They became the charge of the mental health profession. As psychiatric patients these children received psychotherapy and medication, but little was accomplished in providing them with sufficient resources to cope with society. Milder cases of emotional disturbance (those found in the regular school classroom) were ignored or dismissed as being "behavior problems," "bad boys," "incorrigibles," "introverts," or "wallflowers." However, it is now recognized that these children have definite problems that can be overcome with guidance and understanding. The prevalence of emotional disabilities in the regular school setting is considerably greater than previously thought.

Therapeutic education and the habilitative values of physical education are now recognized as major factors in the reduction and elimination of many cases of both severe and moderate emotional disabilities. This recognition is based on speculation and empirical observation. We should, however, consider the following factors as indicators of the contribution that physical education can make to the emotional habilitation of the disturbed child:

1. Tension reduction has been demonstrated to be one of the positive influences of activity on one's emotional status. Individuals often report that they *feel* better when they exercise, although no change in physical status may have been recorded.
2. The general psychological and social values of physical education have been demonstrated with normal children and should also prove to be beneficial to emotionally disturbed children.
3. Physical activity has been a common form of therapy with mentally ill adults for many years and has met with good results. The same values may be realized with disturbed children.
4. The positive value of well-planned and executed physical education programs on the social and emotional performance of normal and mentally retarded children has been demonstrated in a variety of investigations.
5. Severely disturbed children have been shown to exhibit severe deficiencies in perceptual-motor functioning. A good physical education program will enhance these skills. Improved perceptual-motor abilities may serve as an important means of reducing the child's disturbance.

Causes of Emotional Disturbance

The causes of emotional disturbance are not completely clear or understood. A variety of factors have been recognized as *potential* contributors to it, but it is not clear why some individuals react in a negative fashion while others do not exhibit any signs of emotional problems. An equal number of perfectly normal functioning children can be produced for every emotional handicap that can be directly related to one or more of the following factors:

1. *Psychological factors.* These factors are the outcome of constant frustration. They result from the child's inability to meet the requirements of his environment. Inability to cope with the real or imagined pressures placed on him by society results in feelings of anxiety, insecurity, fear, and hostility, which are manifested in inappropriate behavior patterns.
2. *Sociological factors.* The early home experiences of the child and the socioeconomic aspects of his environment contribute to his emotional stability or instability. Many of these children are victims of their parents' violence. The number of battered children in our nation is increasing.
3. *Physiological factors.* Brain damage, chemical imbalances in the brain, and a variety of glandular disturbances may produce emotional problems in the child. Overriding physical or mental disabilities may also be a contributing factor.

Signs of Emotional Disability

Children that are emotionally disturbed may exhibit anxiety reactions, frustration, fears, phobias, or impulsive behaviors. The following list of signs and symptoms may aid in the detection of these children:

1. A tendency to have accidents.
2. Hyperactivity.
3. Imaginary fears and phobias.
4. Regressive immature behavior.
5. Aggressive hostile behavior.
6. Withdrawal into fantasy (the daydreamer).
7. Abnormal fear of failure and criticism.
8. Unexplained poor school achievement.
9. Frequent disciplinary visits to the principal's office.
10. Inability to relate properly with the peer group.

Principles of Teaching the Emotionally Disabled Child

The following principles should be followed in teaching emotionally disturbed children:

1. The teacher will do much better if he understands that disturbed children need someone stable and orderly to serve as an example of steadiness.
2. The teacher will do better if he structures the learning environment in such a fashion that the child knows exactly what is expected of him. A teacher-centered teaching approach works best.
3. The teacher should expect the unexpected. You can always count on disturbed children to *over*react to any new or potentially threatening situation.
4. Limits should be set on what the child can and cannot do. The child needs a clear definition of what is acceptable and unacceptable behavior. The process of limit setting should be done in the spirit of helpful authority. Disturbed children feel safer when they know the boundaries in which they may operate.
5. Limits must be set in such a way that they arouse little resentment.
6. Limits should be phrased in language that does not challenge the child's self-respect (for

example, say "Time to put the balls away" instead of "Don't shoot another time, John. Put the ball away immediately!").

7. The teacher must learn to accept the fact that there may be little progress in the first month or two. This will depend on the severity of the disturbance. A sense of trust and rapport must develop between teacher and child.
8. Nonverbal reactions and facial expressions of the teacher often give away your thoughts. The disturbed child depends a great deal on nonverbal clues of acceptance, resignation, disappointment, pride, and so forth. Learn to attend to the signs that you communicate to the child as well as to the ones that he conveys to you.
9. The teacher should help the child express his feelings and vent his hostilities through socially acceptable channels.
10. The teacher should allow the child a safety valve for his behavior in order to prevent him from "blowing up."
11. It is important to help the children become contributing members of society.
12. The teacher should give opportunities for immediate satisfaction and feelings of progress by tailoring the activities to the specific achievement levels of each group member.
13. The activities should be made stimulant for further related activity.
14. The activities should be geared to the real interests of the group.

The specialist in this field must work closely with a psychiatrist, case worker, and other youth specialists. There must be full access to all records so that the specialist can learn as much as possible about each child. Then with great love and utmost patience, a recreation program can be provided that is planned and taught so that these unhappy youngsters may be helped in the best way possible.

The Physical Education Program

The following suggestions have proven to be beneficial in teaching the disturbed child:

1. Be firm and consistent in your discipline, but discipline in a manner that conveys an attitude of helpfulness, not authority.
2. Establish routines that the child can learn to expect and depend on.
3. Learn every child's name and let him know yours. Refer to him by name.
4. Structure activities for success. Every child should be able to achieve an element of success in order to help overcome his sense of failure and lack of confidence.
5. Utilize immediate positive reinforcement for desired behavior.
6. Avoid imposing standards or limits that are not within the child's capabilities.
7. Be cognizant of individual differences and modify activities to meet these needs.
8. Avoid elimination activities.
9. Activities should be within the individual's capabilities but must be challenging. If they are too easy he will not perform. If they are too hard he will not perform or will quit.
10. Do not let small incidents "snowball." The child must know who is the "boss" and respect that position. Nip violations in the bud.
11. Be thoroughly prepared, overplan, and try to anticipate problems before they occur.
12. *Be patient, understanding, and forgiving.*

OTHER CONDITIONS REQUIRING SPECIAL HELP

The Overweight and Underweight

Three of every ten American adults are 10 to 20 pounds overweight. Most of them are too fat because they are "mouth people"—they eat too much at meals and snack on the wrong kinds of foods throughout the day. Most often their overeating is caused by loneliness, boredom, and emotional problems. They are physically soft and under-exercised. Obesity among teenagers and children is increasing rapidly. According to medical findings, of every ten persons who are more than ten pounds overweight at 30, only six will live to age 60 and only three to 70. The average life span of the American woman is now around 74.6.[8]

Implications for Physical Education. If one's weight is just right for one's age and height, vigorous daily physical activity will help keep it that way. Remember, though, that the proper kind and amount of exercise (which affects shape) must be accompanied by a well-controlled diet (which affects weight). A total body workout for 20 minutes daily is a must. The fat child tends to be lazy. Every effort should be made to motivate him to take part in vigorous physical activities through which he can find success.

The Clumsy Child

Mental retardation, organic behavioral problems, epilepsy, cerebral palsy, and birth defects can all cause clumsiness. How a child thinks and feels about himself is reflected in how he moves and reacts to others. Numerous movement skill tests have been devised that assess the strengths and weaknesses of such children. These tests involve movement tasks such as target throwing, bead stringing, low balance-beam walking, shuttle runs, one-foot hopping, balancing backwards, bouncing, turning, swinging, and so forth.[9]

THE PHYSICAL EDUCATION PROGRAM

It is important that clumsy children be taught individually as well as in small groups. Muscle tension release through imagery activities such as "Imagine you are floating on a cloud" are an important part of the initial program. The program should be built around

1. *Many kinds of locomotor movements and a combination of several* (for example, hopping on your right foot, jumping off a box, and running to the end of the line).
2. *Balancing activities* (for example, catching balls while seated or walking sideways using the crossover step).
3. *Body and space perception activities* (for example, touching another child's knee, or playing Follow the Leader's movements in front of a mirror).
4. *Rhythms and temporal awareness activities* (for example, marching to cadence or skipping to the rhythm of a drumbeat).
5. *Rebound and airborne activities* (for example, jumping around a tractor tire or bouncing on a trampoline).
6. *Projectile activities* (for example, bouncing, catching, and then throwing a large ball to a partner or catching a hula hoop the teacher throws to the child).
7. *Management of daily movement tasks* (for example, pushing a box to the end of a line or pegboard activities).
8. *Selected play skills* (for example, long-rope jumping or hopscotch).
9. *Motor fitness* (for example, doing push-ups or wheelbarrow walking).

---

[8]Mayer, J.: *Overweight: Causes, Cost and Control.* Englewood Cliffs, New Jersey, Prentice-Hall, Inc., 1968, pp. 26–29.

[9]See Chapter 4, Assessing Factors in Clumsiness, in *The Clumsy Child* by Daniel Arnheim and William Sinclair (St. Louis, The C. V. Mosby Company, 1975) for suggested tests for diagnostic use.

10. *Aggressive activities* (for example, cockfighting or Indian leg wrestling).
11. *Aquatic activities* (for example, water games and basic swimming strokes).

SUGGESTED READINGS

AAHPER: *Physical Education and Recreation for Impaired, Disabled and Handicapped Individuals . . . Past, Present, and Future.*

Arnheim, D., et al.: *Principles and Methods of Adapted Physical Education and Recreation.* St. Louis, The C. V. Mosby Company, 1977.

Beter, T., and Wesley, C.: *The Mentally Retarded Child and His Motor Behavior.* Springfield, Illinois, Charles C Thomas, Publisher, 1972.

Cratty, B.: *Motor Activity and the Education of Retardates.* Philadelphia, Lea & Febiger, 1974.

Daniels, A., and Davies, E.: *Adapted Physical Education.* New York, Harper and Brothers, 1976.

Fait, H.: *Special Physical Education: Adapted, Corrective, Developmental.* Philadelphia, W. B. Saunders Company, 1972.

Gearheart, B.: *Learning Disabilities: Educational Strategies.* St. Louis, The C. V. Mosby Company, 1973.

Gearheart, B.: *Organization and Administration of Educational Programs for Exceptional Children.* Springfield, Illinois, Charles C Thomas, Publisher, 1974.

Kirk, S.: *Educating Exceptional Children.* Boston, Houghton Mifflin Company, 1972.

Kraus, R.: *Therapeutic Recreation Service: Principles and Practices.* Philadelphia, W. B. Saunders Company, 1973.

Long, N., et al.: *Conflict in the Classroom: The Education of Emotionally Disturbed Children.* Belmont, California, Wadsworth Publishing Company, Inc., 1969.

Lowry, T. (ed.): *Camping Therapy: Its Uses in Psychiatry and Rehabilitation.* Springfield, Illinois, Charles C Thomas, Publisher, 1974.

Moran, J., and Kalakian, L.: *Movement Experiences for the Mentally Retarded or Emotionally Disturbed Child.* Minneapolis, Burgess Publishing Company, 1977.

Sherrill, C.: *Adapted Physical Education and Recreation.* Dubuque, Iowa, William C. Brown Company, Publishers, 1976.

Stein, T., and Sessoms, H.: *Recreation and Special Populations.* Boston, Holbrook Press, Inc., 1977.

Vannier, M.: *Physical Activities for the Handicapped.* Englewood Cliffs, New Jersey, Prentice-Hall, Inc., 1977.

ORGANIZATIONS FROM WHICH HELPFUL INFORMATION CAN BE OBTAINED

American Federation of the Physically Handicapped, Inc. 1376 National Press Building, Washington, D.C. 20004

American Hearing Society 817 14th Street, N.W., Washington, D.C. 20005

American Heart Association, Inc. 1790 Broadway, New York, N.Y. 10019

American Legion National Rehabilitation Committee 1608 K Street, N.W., Washington, D.C. 20006

Association for the Aid of Crippled Children 345 East 46th Street, New York, N.Y. 10017

Children's Bureau, Department of Health, Education and Welfare, Washington, D.C. 20014

Comeback, Inc. 16 West 46th Street, New York, N.Y. 10036

Dallas Association for Retarded Children 3121 N. Harwood St., Dallas, Texas 75201

Dallas Services for Blind Children, Inc. 3802 Cole Ave., Dallas, Texas 75204

Goodwill Industries of America, Inc. 744 N. 4th Street, Milwaukee, Wisconsin 53201

Institute for the Crippled and Disabled 400 1st Avenue, New York, N.Y. 10010

Muscular Dystrophy Association of America, Inc. 1790 Broadway, New York, N.Y. 10019

National Association for Mental Health 10 Columbus Circle, New York, N.Y. 10019

National Council on Rehabilitation 1790 Broadway, New York, N.Y. 10019

National Epilepsy League 208 North Wells Street, Chicago, Illinois 60606

National Organization for Mentally Ill Children 171 Madison Avenue, New York, N.Y. 10010

National Society for Crippled Children and Adults, Inc. 11 South LaSalle Street, Chicago, Illinois 60603

National Society for the Prevention of Blindness, Inc. 1790 Broadway, New York, N.Y. 10019

National Tuberculosis Association 1790 Broadway, New York, N.Y. 10019

Scottish Rite Hospital for Crippled Children 2201 Welborn St., Dallas, Texas 75219

United Cerebral Palsy Association 50 West 57th Street, New York, N.Y. 10019

United States Office of Education, Department of Health, Education and Welfare, Washington, D.C. 20202

Vocational Rehabilitation Administration, Department of Health, Education and Welfare, Washington, D.C. 20202

Volta Bureau 1537 35th Street, N.W., Washington, D.C. 20007

REMEDIAL EXERCISE EQUIPMENT

Stationary Equipment

Single-section stall bars
Stall bar chinning bar
Triplex wall-pulley weights
Shoulder wheel
Pronator-supinator machine
Wall horizontal bar
Horizontal ladder
Shoulder ladder
Staircase, corner type

Stall bar bench
Floor and chest pulley weights
Latissimus dorsi exerciser
Wrist roll machine
Multi-chinning bar
Horizontal bar
Peg climb board
Adjustable height striking bag

Movable Equipment

Elgin exercise unit
Footstool
Heavy-duty N-K unit
Rowing machine
Densifoam mat with mat hooks

Exercise table
Abdominal incline boards
Treadmill with handrails
Bicycle exerciser
Ankle and leg exerciser

Posture Training Area

Posture training mirror, stationary
Foot inversion tread
Arthrodial protractor

Adjustable sitting posture training stool
Posture grid screen and evaluation kit

Resistance Training Equipment

Dumbbell set
Weight caddy with disc-type weights
Sandbag set
Press bench
Quadriceps boot with bar and collars
Wrist cuff
Ankle cuff
Shoulder strap
Tension hand grips

Dumbbell rack
Barbell set and weights
Medicine ball with ball rack
Foot stirrup
Thigh cuff
Head strap
Back weight pan
Grip exerciser

Group Exercise Equipment

Cage ball
Indian clubs
Exer-gym
Rubber exerciser
Balance board
Maxie club

Wands with wand rack
Indian club hangers
Spring pull exerciser
Jump rope
Scooter board

Testing, Measurement, and Anthropometric Devices

Body-weight scale
Lange skinfold caliper
Flexometer
Chest-depth caliper
Hand dynamometer
Back, leg, and chest dynamometer
Timer

Dry spirometer
Gulick anthropometric tape
Shoulder breadth caliper
Transparent goniometer
Push-pull attachment for dynamometer
Stopwatch
Electric rhythm metronome

Gymnastic Equipment

Low balance beam
Low parallel bar
Trampoline
Side horse
Still rings

Balance beam
Parallel bar
Mini-tramp
Climbing rope

Recreation Area Equipment

Gym scooter set
Table tennis table
Tetherball set
Shuffleboard set, indoor
Rubber quoit set
Beanbag game
Croquet set
Fun balls
Nok hockey set

Lightweight bowling set
Scoopball kit
Combination volleyball/badminton set
Rubber horseshoe set
Professional hockey set
Suction dart game
Paddle-racket set
Safe-T play bats
Cage balls

CHAPTER NINE

HOW CHILDREN LEARN

Man wonders over the restless sea, the flowing water, the sights of the sky, and forgets that of all wonders, Man himself is the most wonderful of all.

The Dallas Health and Science Museum

Children are in love with life! Watch any child having his very first "finding-out-about" experiences as he looks closely at a butterfly, holds a puppy ever so gently, tries to turn a somersault or roller skate. Such total absorption, delight, and sheer determination!

The desire to learn is a natural current in all human beings, but in youth it is a strong and forceful flood. To learn means to discover, to find ways to make a satisfactory adjustment to a new situation. It also means changed behavior in relation to achieving desirable educational goals. Children need not be driven to learn the things *they* want to learn, although they sometimes must be prevented from learning or experiencing some harmful things too early in life. Our old folk saying "You can drive a horse to water but you cannot make him drink" is truer than was once realized, for the learner, not the teacher, controls the learning situation. Pupils discover early in their school experiences how to tune the teacher out and still give a false impression of full attentiveness.

The desire to learn spurs the child on and often gets him into all kinds of trouble, for he usually acts first and thinks later in his trial-and-error attempts to find out. Any child who fails to learn may be stymied by physical or emotional stumbling blocks that must be removed before any real progress can be made. Sometimes these clogs are due to an inability to see or hear, to fear of failure, or to dread of loss of parental love. A six year old in a school in Dallas who refused to take part with his class in any type of supervised activities on the playground finally, after many tears, confessed to his teacher that he was afraid to play because he would get dirty, and consequently his "Mamma wouldn't love [him] anymore; she hates dirty boys." Regardless of what deterring factors are present, these must be discovered and dealt with before the child will give his whole self to his trial-and-error attempts to learn.

Learning involves the entire child, for there is no separation from one's physical, mental, or emotional self. One cannot draw a picture, catch a ball, read a book, or master any learning task by only "using one's head" or "learning it through one's muscles." The mind of man is a central clearing-house, a transfer station, a switchboard that can function only as messages come to it and are received, sorted, clarified or filed, and sent back out again. As William Kilpatrick has said, "What we live, we learn." Where we live, with whom we live, toward what ends we live—these things determine what we learn. The whole community educates, but the learner teaches himself. There is great truth in George Bernard Shaw's statement, "If you teach me, I

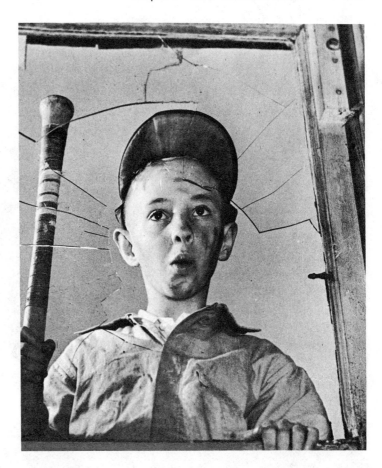

FIGURE 9–1. Learning takes place wherever there is life. (Courtesy of AAHPER, Washington, D.C.)

shall never learn,'' for *no one can really teach anyone else to do anything.* The best learning results will accrue when

1. The activities are child-centered.
2. The individual needs, interests, and capacities of each pupil are fully understood.
3. Teachers aid children to explore and discover things for themselves.
4. Pupils are free to create their own responses in a situation.
5. Pupils are taught and guided by teachers who are really interested in them.
6. Pupils believe in what they learn and believe it will be valuable to them.
7. That which is learned will increase the pupil's power to make intelligent decisions in life.
8. That which is learned will build a greater appreciation for life, our cultural heritage, other people, aesthetics, and health.

The person who is learning does so within himself by some magical process that includes his own fumbling trial-and-error attempts. Most of our learning comes from making mistakes and then catching on to how to avoid them. Without failure there can be no success. The role of the teacher is to guide the learner around pitfalls that are sure to stop him or end in failure, to encourage him to keep trying until he succeeds (until he can ride the bicycle after falling so many times, or turn a cartwheel and so forth), and to lead him to new learning thrills and adventures he never dreamed existed. All learning can be speeded up if the learner sees its relationship to himself and to his own goals. A child's past experiences, goals, and drives are the foundation upon which his present, and often more lasting, experiences are built.

FIGURE 9–2. The learner teaches himself. (Courtesy of Ed-Nu, Inc.)

LEARNING THEORIES

Most of what children learn comes through their senses of hearing, seeing, tasting, and touching; the more these can be stimulated, the richer the learning experiences will be. A child learns when he

1. Develops and uses new skills.
2. Forms new habits.
3. Develops new attitudes.
4. Builds new interests.
5. Gains new understanding.

FIGURE 9–3.   If I stretch more, I can balance this one on that one. (Courtesy of The Montessori Academy of Dallas and Ann Melvin.)

6. Makes generalizations and uses learned facts.
7. Develops social skills.
8. Becomes more concerned about his environment and other people around him.

The most commonly accepted learning theories are (1) conditioning, (2) connectionism, and (3) field theory. All of these theories stress that one learns from doing, or from experiences.

Conditioning

The simplest type of learning is conditioning, or setting a patterned reflex to the same repeated stimuli. Pavlov, in his famous dog experiments, proved that the animal could be conditioned to salivate when a bell was rung and food was expected. We all show that we have been conditioned when we automatically pick up the phone when it rings, stop at the red light, turn over and sleepily turn off the alarm on the clock at our bedside when it jars us awake, or do numerous other automatic acts in response to the same repeated stimuli because within us a behavior-patterned habit has been formed. The pupil who can give back the right response when asked to spell the word C-A-T or add 2 + 2 or name the capital of Texas has been trained to do so.

Conditioning has many uses and values for the teacher. It is both a great time saver and a great energy saver. However, in order to condition, the same stimuli must be given over and over again until the desired response is achieved each time. Approval, praise, or other rewards desired by the pupil who is being conditioned must also be given

FIGURE 9–4. Gaining a good self-concept is basic to learning. (Courtesy of Northlake Elementary School, Dallas, Texas.)

consistently in order for success to accrue. Students can be conditioned to automatically

1. Stop and listen when the teacher is talking.
2. Wash their hands every time after going to the toilet, and before eating.
3. Move safely inside the gymnasium or on the playground.
4. Keep themselves neat and clean.
5. Develop any other health habits.
6. Develop good work and play patterns.

Connectionism

This theory, which results largely from the work of Thorndike, stresses that humans voluntarily select activities that bring them the most pleasure and satisfaction, and that best fill their needs. Although similar to conditioning, this theory contends that learning must be on a higher plane, and that the purpose of education is *not* to create robots or human vending machines who will give back to the teacher the sought answer upon demand, but to develop educated citizens who can solve their own problems as well as help solve group problems intelligently in many ever-changing situations.

Simply, this concept, known also as the S-R-Bond theory of learning, means that when a stimulated (S) response (R) is made that is accompanied by satisfied feelings, the response tends to be repeated and long remembered (Bond). The intensity of these positive feelings can produce either an advancing positive response (choosing it again, joy, satisfaction), or a retreating negative one (avoidance of choosing it again, anger, disappointment, frustration). Pleasure and annoyance become selective factors, as is seen in the case of the teacher-frightened pupil who shows visible signs of annoyance or frustration when the instructor comes near. This same child, if given the opportunity to select his own teacher, would quickly reject the one who frightens and frustrates him, and would choose instead one who is more friendly and interested in him and makes him feel at ease.

The greater the desire the pupil has for learning, the more productive are his attempts to satisfy this need. All human beings, children and adults alike, have certain common needs. These drives make up the underlying causes of all human behavior:

1. Physiological needs (food, water, air, temperature regulation, rest, exercise).
2. Love needs (sex, mutuality, acceptance, affection).
3. Love for esteem (recognition, mastery, approval, status, adequacy, self-respect).
4. Self-actualization (desire to succeed at tasks for which one is best suited).
5. Need to know and understand.
6. Adventure (to seek ever-greener pastures, and discover what is behind the ranges).

Thorndike's three well-known laws of learning will, if adhered to, increase the effectiveness of all teaching and the depth and breadth of all learning. These are (1) the Law of Readiness, (2) the Law of Exercise, and (3) the Law of Effect.

THE LAW OF READINESS.   Educators have long been aware that pupils learn best and retain concepts longer when they are ready to learn. Teachers are cognizant that there is a "reading readiness," yet few realize that there is also the right time or state of readiness for learning each thing—whether it be riding a bicycle, throwing a ball, or memorizing the multiplication tables. Every learner is ready when he has reached just the right stage in his development (his maturation level)—when he not only has a keen desire to learn, but is ready physically, emotionally, and mentally. Then is he most likely to succeed. Although teachers often give lip service to this concept they are but vaguely aware of, until they understand the fullest significance and truth in it, they are only wheel-spinning when they could be making real progress. The pupil is "ripe" for any learning experience when he can learn with ease, succeeds, and is spurred on to continue his efforts until he masters his task. Readiness varies with each child, yet can be generalized upon too, for just as some pears ripen and fall to the ground long before others, they all will fall within a certain season of the year.

Childhood belongs to every child. Every youngster needs this time of life to be filled with joy, wonder, and freedom. Each must have many "first-finding-out-about" experiences that are rich enough to last a lifetime and strong enough to help him endure the sorrows and tragedies that come with adulthood. All must discover the joy of solitude and have gloriously rewarding free hours to roam and explore, and to *think, feel,* and *see.* They should be encouraged to go lazily along, stopping where they will—instead of being forced by eager and often status-seeking adults to scurry along and to take part in many outside-of-school activities. Patterns for adulthood and for happiness are established in childhood.

THE LAW OF EXERCISE.   Practice does not lead to perfection *unless* one practices correctly, for it is harder to unlearn something than to learn it. According to this law, the learner must know *what* and *how* he is doing, as well as *why* in relation to what he wants to learn. Likewise, he must have a clear understanding and picture of the correct way to do the thing he is learning.

All pupils should have a feeling of success as they are learning, for nothing is as spirit-quenching as failure. Success is a spur, failure is a check-rein. Repeated failure not only may damage the ego, but may also lead to feelings of inadequacy, inferiority, or worthlessness. This connotes that the teacher must help pupils set realistic heights on learning standards for themselves.

THE LAW OF EFFECT.   How the learner feels about what he is learning is of vast importance. Elementary school children especially are often much keener about learning many things *outside* of school rather than in school (especially after their initial taste of school). This is but one of many reasons for their eagerness to go to camp, ride in an airplane, or have such a wide variety of other "first-time" experiences. Teachers must be cognizant that there is learning wherever there is life, and that it by no means can be confined to a school or remain hidden in books. The child not only learns everywhere but is totally affected by what he learns. All learning is most fruitful and lasting when the child *has definite goals* in mind and *can be guided to select wisely* what he will learn, *to plan his method of attack* toward solving learning problems, and *to evaluate* his final results.

Motivation is the key to all learning. Just as adults are paid for their work, the child seeks his reward, too. For him, this is found in reaching desired goals and, in the elementary school, largely by pleasing adults, including his teacher. Those slower to learn must be guided to tasks in which they can find improvement (however slight it may be), security, and confidence in themselves. For the gifted and normal children, group status or self-improvement often serves as an effective motivator. An occasional pat on the back and words of encouragement are often enough to give the normal child an incentive to keep trying. Grades spur others on, but only if obtaining superior marks results from effort and brings status and recognition. Gaining even slight feelings of success often helps those having learning difficulties.

The teacher must know all students well and be able to determine what stimuli can best be used to fan each one's interest into a flame. For some this may be accomplished by praise, while for others it may require some widely different technique. The teacher must likewise keep in mind that when a pupil sees his own improvement, he will try even harder. Punishment in the form of ridicule, disapproval, or rejection should be avoided, for although the pupil may, finally, learn something under such treatment, he will not receive pleasure from any fleeting, unmeaningful, or dreaded task, which all too soon will be forgotten anyway.

Gestalt Field Theory

This theory, developed first by Koffka and Koehler, and later fostered by Hartmann and Wertheimer, stresses that one learns best by grasping whole concepts. It holds that one learns from one's trial-and-error attempts plus "insight"—or suddenly realizing how to do something. Anyone who has ever tried repeatedly to ride a bicycle usually was battered and bruised before he suddenly could do it! The beginner in crawl swimming has learned to do this stroke in that great moment of triumph when he *could* synchronize his arm and leg movements with his head-turning and breathing and move magically through the water using all these synchronized movements. Insight is "getting the hang" of anything we are learning, and can result only from previous trial-and-error attempts. The task of the teacher is to give the learner a pep talk so that he continues to muddle through his learning attempts until he achieves this thrill of accomplishment. Here again, the teacher must be fully aware that she must not nip learning struggles in the bud by being too much of a perfectionist or overly critical and impatient.

FIGURE 9–5.   We learn only by our own trial-and-error attempts; after repeated tries we suddenly learn just how to do it. (Courtesy of Jayfro Corporation, Montville, Connecticut.)

This concept of learning, which is also known as Gestalt (i.e., whole) psychology, places the major importance in any learning experience upon the learner and stresses that he knows more about his own values, desires, capacities, and preferences than the teacher. The instructor's main task is to help the learner to (1) set his own goals, (2) determine his action plans, and (3) judge the results. This does not imply that the teacher is unnecessary, but does imply that her main task is that of guiding and directing, and that more learning will consequently result from doing this than from telling students what to do, for there will be less friction and more rapport, fewer failures and more success.

If the main purpose of education is to help each person increase the number of socially approved things he can do well that will prove beneficial to him and society, teaching is more than either an art or a science, for it becomes a combination of them both, plus something else composed of a magical X quality called leadership ability by some, personality by others. The teacher must (1) provide the best kind of warm, friendly yet controlled learning environment possible; (2) motivate pupils' desire to seek worthy goals and make these goals as attractive as possible; (3) make even disagreeable tasks seem agreeable, or make them seem interesting to a bored, uninterested learner by changing negative attitudes to positive ones; and (4) help the learner develop finer and deeper appreciation of himself, others, and what he is doing.

Gestalt psychology also stresses that the best learning will accrue when the learning environment is used to its fullest extent. Furthermore, it emphasizes that the learner can and only will learn when *he* has a need to do so, and that he will learn best

FIGURE 9-6. Old tires can be used in a variety of exciting and challenging ways. (Courtesy of AAHPER, Washington, D.C.)

FIGURE 9–7. Discarded equipment can be recycled for fun and fitness. (Courtesy of AAHPER, Washington, D.C.)

when he can do so under the friendly, consistent guidance of a firm teacher who regards him as a unique human being. It also contends that learning through mastery of whole material will come faster and be more lasting. Educators call this the whole-part-whole method of teaching and learning and are in agreement that it is usually superior and usually brings desired results quickly. A teacher should teach each individual in each class as much as can be learned each class period.

KINDS OF LEARNING

The three kinds of learning are (1) primary, (2) associated, and (3) concomitant. They are intertwined, and all may occur almost at the same time. *Primary* learning means learning a specific skill, such as how to hit a baseball. *Associated* learning is marginal; it surrounds skill mastery and includes all kinds of fringe knowledge, such as the parts of a tennis racket. *Concomitant* learning is primarily concerned with attitude shaping and character development. Almost every learning situation abounds with character-shaping and value-developing opportunities. Because character can often best be *caught* rather than taught, the behavior and attitudes of the teacher in all situations are of paramount importance, for children are eager and skilled copycats of those they admire. Leadership through example is the best way to help children develop attitudes and to show them how to behave in socially accepted ways as developing youngsters.

BASIC PRINCIPLES COMPATIBLE TO ALL THEORIES OF LEARNING

Although there are a number of learning theories and ideas on how children develop motor abilities it is interesting to note that many principles are *compatible* to all theories of learning. Among them are the following:

1. Learning results in progressive changes in behavior.
2. Motivation is central to learning. Incentives, interests, tensions, urges, drives, and purposes are various aspects of motivation.
3. Concepts must develop, and there must be perception and understanding; the learner must know what he is about.
4. Learning depends on sensory preceptors: Sight, hearing, touch, taste, and smell represent the paths to learning. Kinesthetic perception is of primary importance in motor learning.
5. Trials or attempts must be made. Practice is essential to motor learning and seldom occurs solely through insight.
6. Learning is an active process. It may be mental or physical or both, but learning requires activity on the part of the learner.
7. Perfection of complicated motor skills requires practice of correct form.
8. Social development depends upon experiences with others in social situations.
9. Emotional development and adjustment depend on the complex interaction of the individual with his environment. Adequate adjustment to conflicting feelings is basic to desirable emotional development. Successful experiences are required for adequate development.
10. Learning is individualized. Ability to learn depends on innate capacity and previous experiences that make the child what he is. Wide variation in knowledge and skills, attitudes, and emotions make the effectiveness of learning experiences a variable for every individual.

GUIDELINES FOR MAKING LEARNING FASTER AND MORE EFFECTIVE

The following is a list of some guidelines for making the learning of motor skills faster and more effective.

1. Teach skills the right way. Trial-and-error learning is inefficient and results in incorrect patterns or defeat.
2. Correct a fault as soon as it appears. Repetition aids habit. Teach elementary skills early so the child has a foundation on which to build complex skills.
3. Teach one new skill at a time. Too many skills at once result in confusion and discouragement. Allow time for practice. Lack of practice results in loss of skill.
4. Concentrate on the skills for which the child has use at that time in his development. There is no incentive to learn something for which one has no use.
5. Make sure the child has incentive, or learning will be half-hearted. A boy will not want to dance before he is interested in girls.
6. The best teacher is one who teaches the learner how to teach himself. Fundamentally, all learning is the result of self-teaching; we cannot really "teach" anything; all we can do is make self-teaching easier.

MOTOR LEARNING PRINCIPLES

Basic beliefs and action guides are educational principles. They result from experience, research, and education. The best learning accrues if the following principles are used as action springboards:

1. *Children learn experimentally.* Trial-and-error plus insight produces changed behavior, or learning. In this process, mistakes are necessary, and success comes *from* failure.

FIGURE 9–8.   Children teach themselves body control. (Courtesy of Creative Playgrounds Corporation, Terre Haute, Indiana.)

2. *Learning is "doing" activity.* Discovery results from searching. We learn from doing, not from being told or watching others perform. In order to learn, one must try out things for oneself and through one's own experience gain skill, understanding, knowledge, and appreciation.

3. *The learner controls the learning situation.* If the learner is in situations in which he feels secure and confident, his rate of progress becomes greater. He will be handicapped when dominated or told by adults what, when, and how he is to learn. Knowledge of his progress in relationship to that of others can be an asset or a liability, depending upon the amount of self-confidence and emotional drive the learner has, and the degree of his desire to learn.

4. *Each pupil learns in his own unique way.* Every learner goes about learning tasks differently, and each develops his own progress curve that leads to victory or defeat. For the majority, this curve will rise sharply at first, taper off to a plateau, then rise again as the pupil becomes increasingly aware that he is reaching his desired goal. Learning is as personal as one's own toothbrush.

5. *Overlearning results in longer retention.* Practice of the correct pattern until what is to be learned is mastered or becomes automatic will keep it longer in the body's memory storehouse. The more a learned skill or concept is used and reviewed, the more valuable it will become. Just as unused silver tarnishes quickly, so do once-learned facts fade from memory.

6. *Emotions retard or accelerate learning.* Learning occurs more rapidly if both the pupil and the teacher are enthusiastic about and see purpose in what is to be learned. Fear and insecurity are clogs that dam up desire until it stagnates; confidence and encouragement plunge learning on.

7. *Brief practice periods are more productive than long, drawn-out ones.* The length of each practice period should be determined by the pupil's interest level and potency of desire to accomplish the learning task. Practice will be fruitful only if it brings satisfaction to the learner and is recognized as a basic task necessary for improvement. A "cooling off" period is needed before a renewed and recharged learning pursuit can become potent enough to lead to final victory, for a learning pause can bring real refreshment, as well as desired results more quickly.

8. *Transfer will occur when situations are recognized to be alike.* The transformation of anything learned in one situation to another will take place only when the learner sees similarities in the two situations and continues to do in the second one what he did in the first. The pupil who can see and feel the relationship of the baseball throw to the tennis serve will learn the latter more quickly if he can throw a baseball correctly.

9. *Learning is an exciting and challenging adventure.* To see the truthfulness of this principle one has only to watch the happy face of any youngster who first discovers that he can swim, recite the multiplication tables, or sing *all* the way through any song without a single mistake. The child who *wants* to learn what *he* has chosen to master can have a glorious time doing so. The real teacher is one who can inspire him to want to make many new and thrilling learning discoveries.

10. *Evaluation is an essential part of learning.* Improvement and evaluation are inseparable, for one can only improve when he sees his mistakes and cares enough about what he is attempting to avoid them. It is a difficult task for the teacher to know *when* to stop muddled learning attempts or *how* to go about it, for doing so at the wrong time and in the wrong way may destroy the pupil's zest and zeal to reach his desired learning goal to such an extent that he will give up trying. There is truth in Pope's wise statement that "only fools rush in where angels fear to tread."

SUGGESTED READINGS

Association for Supervision and Curriculum Development: *Learning More About Learning; Freeing Capacity To Learn; Theories of Instruction; The Elementary School We Need; New Curriculum Developments; Supervision in Action; Toward Better Teaching.* Washington, D.C., National Education Association.

Broer, M.: *Efficiency of Human Movement.* 3rd ed. Philadelphia, W. B. Saunders Company, 1973.

Cratty, B.: *Movement Behavior and Motor Learning.* 3rd ed. Philadelphia, Lea & Febiger, 1973.

Ginsburg, H., and Opper, S.: *Piaget's Theory of Intellectual Development.* Englewood Cliffs, New Jersey, Prentice-Hall, Inc., 1969.

Humphrey, J.: *Child Learning Through Elementary School Physical Education*. Dubuque, Iowa, William C Brown Company, Publishers, 1975.

Lawther, J. D.: *The Learning of Physical Skills*. Englewood Cliffs, New Jersey, Prentice-Hall, Inc., 1977.

National Association for Physical Education of College Women, National Association for Physical Education for College Men: *Quest* (A symposium on motor learning—entire issue). Monograph VI, May, 1966. New York, N.Y. Board of Education of the City of New York. *Education Through Recreation: Kindergarten Experimental Education,* 1965.

Robb, M.: *The Dynamics of Motor-Skill Acquisition*. Englewood Cliffs, New Jersey, Prentice-Hall, Inc., 1972.

Stallings, R.: *Motor Skills Development and Learning*. Dubuque, Iowa, William C. Brown Company, Publishers, 1973.

CHAPTER TEN

THE TEACHER

A child becomes what he experiences. While parents possess the original key to their offspring's experience, teachers have a spare key. They, too, can open or close the minds and hearts of children.

Dr. Haim Ginott

The teacher of physical education on the elementary level may be the regular classroom teacher or the specialized physical educator. Often in smaller schools it is the classroom teacher, who in a self-contained classroom assumes the responsibility of teaching all subjects offered in the curriculum. In the larger city system, however, it is generally the trained physical educator who is in charge of the program.

WHO SHOULD TEACH PHYSICAL EDUCATION IN THE ELEMENTARY SCHOOL?

There are arguments pro and con regarding this question. Some educators believe that it is better for the children in the primary grades to have their physical education classes and playground periods supervised by their own classroom teacher. Those who believe in this school of thought claim that since play is so significant it is important for this teacher, who will be with the children for the longest period of time, to see how they play so that she can best guide them into desirable physical and social growth patterns. Other educators hold that only those persons certified to teach physical education activities should do so. Those who cling to this line of thought believe that children learn faster when they are taught correctly from the beginning by a professionally prepared physical educator.

THE ROLE OF MEN IN ELEMENTARY SCHOOL PHYSICAL EDUCATION

The preschool and elementary physical education program has traditionally been the domain of women; however, the trend today is toward greater male influence in this area of education. There appear to be three primary reasons why more men are entering the area of teaching young children. First, the recent surge in interest by all members of the academic community in the influence of movement experiences on

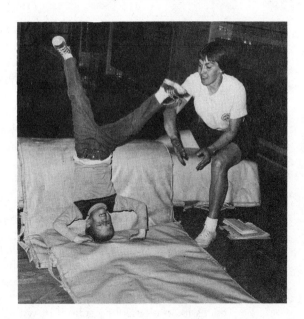

FIGURE 10–1. Just being close by if help is needed can aid some children in feeling more secure. (Courtesy of *The Instructor*.)

the *total* development of the child has caused many males to realize that good preschool and elementary school physical education programs are not babysitting services. They provide many of the vital learning experiences that are necessary for the optimal physical, mental, emotional, and social development of the child. Second, the male elementary teacher is often the only male teacher in the school, and it is now recognized that he provides a necessary masculine image with which youngsters can identify. Furthermore, he often serves as a father figure for many children without fathers. The third reason why more men are entering preschool and elementary school physical education is the ongoing cultural revolution in our nation that has broken down many of the traditional stereotypes of what is suitable work for men and for women. The future is bright for both men and women interested in the education of young children. A greater balance between the two in this area of education will help to ensure a more rounded education for the child.

In smaller schools the classroom teacher usually is the only one available to give instruction in all subjects offered in each grade. This includes basic instruction in the broad fields of language arts, physical education, art, and music. In schools organized under the self-contained classroom plan the teacher must be a jack-of-all-trades. Too often he is master of none, or of fewer than he might be had he fewer responsibilities.

It is imperative that the person selected to teach physical education be the best one available. Above all, the teacher should be the one most skilled in methods of teaching children through physical activities as well as the one who teaches them a wide variety of physical activities. Such a person may well be the classroom teacher, especially in the first three grades.

TEACHER PREPARATION

Physical educators must be certified to teach by the state in which their training was received. Although states vary considerably in specific requirements, the majority require over 20 hours of specialized professional preparation for a major in this field.

Broad educational areas center on theory and practical courses in activities, organization, administration, and principles and methods of teaching physical education. Ten to 12 hours in the biological sciences including anatomy, kinesiology, physiology, and hygiene are usually required. Supervised practice teaching is required in most states for certification. Gradually teacher certification standards are being raised throughout the country on both the elementary and secondary levels. This is a hopeful trend, for better-selected and prepared teachers should produce better educational results.

Trends

According to a recent national survey, physical education departments throughout the nation are increasingly offering a major in elementary physical education on both the graduate and undergraduate levels.[1] Some universities offer a choice for a major to become a K–12 or a K–6 physical education specialist. Others are now offering courses leading to specialization in preschool and primary grades or for the middle elementary grades. Most courses include actual teaching or field work experiences in an elementary school or with children at a recreational center.

Increasingly, colleges and universities are having their students in elementary physical education conduct physical education programs in a nearby public or parochial elementary school, a learning laboratory, or a demonstration center, so that their learning experiences are more practical. Some students are placed in complete charge of a group of children either in the gymnasium or on the playground. Still others conduct noon-hour or intramural programs.

Some teacher preparation institutions now offer new courses and combinations of them, including the following:[2]

1. A major in physical education with either a major or minor in elementary education. Programs with a dual major lead to certification in physical education and elementary education. Courses in the elementary school curriculum, child psychology, reading, and other elementary school content areas are usually included in the elementary education course requirements in this approach.
2. Programs leading to K–12 or K–14 certification, which follow two patterns. The first gives equal time to elementary and secondary school physical education, with most courses relating to the entire K–12 or K–14 spectrum and the student-teaching experience equally divided between the two levels. The second pattern also concerns the K–12 or K–14 range in most program experiences but provides additional opportunities for elementary specialization. Additional specific course work is required, and a greater amount of time is spent in the student-teaching experience at the elementary school level.
3. The elementary school physical education major program, which is one of the more dramatic departures from the traditional physical education professional preparation program. Course work and other experiences are all focused on the elementary child. Some programs with emphasis include a minor in elementary education.
4. A concentration in physical education for the elementary education major. In addition to the one or two courses usually required, the concentration includes course work in the scientific foundations of human movement, movement analysis, and various content or activity areas.
5. Graduate programs that have been structuring more work directly relating to elementary school physical education. Personnel at the master's and doctor's degree levels with elementary school classroom experience are doing graduate work in elementary school physical

[1]Hoffman, H.: National survey of preprofessional preparation for the elementary school specialist. *Journal of Health, Physical Education and Recreation.* February 1972, pp. 25–28.

[2]American Association for Health, Physical Education and Recreation: *Promising Practices in Elementary Physical Education.* Washington, D.C., 1969, pp. 20–21.

FIGURE 10–2. A good teacher can help you learn to do a lot of things well. (Courtesy of Documentary Films.)

education. They are generally required to do additional work to make up differences in their undergraduate preparation.

Program Emphasis

Since physical education is only a part of the total elementary school program, courses preparing teachers for this field should include many materials relating to the children's growth and motor developmental patterns, basic needs, and characteristics, as well as to the social and psychological factors that affect their developing self-image concepts and personalities. The program should also help students gain knowledge and understanding of the fundamentals of human movement.

Courses should include actual teaching experiences with children in the classroom as well as in the gymnasium or on the playground. At many colleges and universities students seeking certification in teaching physical education spend several semesters teaching on the elementary, junior, or senior high school level. Such programs help students gain a basic understanding of the need for a well-planned curriculum based upon a graded program. They also help students preparing to enter the teaching profession to find the age group to which they can make their greatest educational contribution as professional physical educators.

THE ROLE OF THE SUPERVISOR

It is increasingly becoming the practice in many American schools for the classroom teacher, who may be unprepared to teach physical education, to be under the supervision of an experienced physical education specialist. This form of guided in-service training can be of invaluable assistance. Together the expert and novice in this specialized field should plan, carry out, and evaluate a physical education program for which each particular grade teacher has responsibility. All such teachers in the entire elementary school should have regularly scheduled group conferences with the supervisor to establish goals to be accomplished, program content for each grade, and testing procedures to be used. In this way each grade teacher can see the way in which her program is related and contributes to those of all other teachers in the school.

The role of the supervisor should be that of guiding the teachers, and he or she will be most successful if democratic methods of leadership are used. Guidance in its broadest sense means helping others to help themselves. Democratic leadership rests upon the principle that a real leader makes more leaders. As the expert consultant, the supervisor should help all teachers grow in their understanding of the importance of skills for teaching children through physical activities. The supervisor should visit each classroom teacher periodically to observe the effectiveness of both her teaching and her program—their strengths and weaknesses—and, acting in the role of a co-worker, should aid the teacher to improve in those areas in which assistance is needed. The regular classroom teacher should be visited under her poorest and best teaching situations. Above all, no special program should be prepared to impress the supervisor. A friendly atmosphere should prevail throughout the supervisor's visit. In modern education "snoopervision"—as supervision was once called and practiced—is as outdated as teacher-dominated classes and dictatorial school administrators.

It is imperative that the supervisor have a broad understanding of the physical education curriculum, have successful teaching methods, know a great deal about the growth and development of children, and be able to evaluate objectively teaching results. She should also have had training in health and safety, be able to help those with whom she works to be conscious of safety hazards in physical education, and know how to help children protect themselves and others while playing in class, intramurals, or elsewhere. Also, she should aid teachers in capitalizing upon teachable moments in health education in their work with children.

The following list contains the duties usually performed by supervisors of physical education:[3]

1. They provide a plan for the development of a philosophy and objectives with teachers.
2. They interpret various phases of a program, such as curriculum guides and test data, to teachers.
3. They read and comment on teachers' lesson plans.
4. They prepare bulletins for teachers.
5. They develop standards for the use of others in the supervision of instruction.
6. They provide specialized resources upon which teachers may draw for meeting needs.
7. They rate teachers with a rating scale.
8. They assist teachers in the development of skills and the use of all types of instructional materials.
9. They develop a plan for the self-analysis of teachers, such as checklist for teacher self-evaluation.
10. They provide for intervisitation of teachers.
11. They do demonstration teaching.
12. They work with teachers to help them do demonstration teaching.
13. They hold conferences with teachers.
14. They visit teachers in their teaching situations.
15. They confer with teacher-education institutions regarding preservice education.
16. They participate in the planning of workshops and physical education clinics.

[3]Humphrey, J., Love, A., and Irwin, L.: *Principles and Techniques of Supervision.* Dubuque, Iowa, William C. Brown Company, Publishers, 1972, p. 47.

17. They participate in planning teachers' institutes.
18. They promote professional growth of teachers by encouraging them to participate in professional organizations, to attend graduate schools, and so forth.

QUALITIES NECESSARY FOR THE PHYSICAL EDUCATION TEACHER

The qualities most desired in a physical educator are the same as those desired in any other teacher. All good teachers in any field must have technical skills, personality, integrity, and good health. They must have a genuine and sincere feeling for people, in contrast to a feeling for things. They must know how to use desirable methods of democratic leadership, realizing that a good leader is also a follower at times and that a real leader aids others to develop good leadership traits. A teacher is like a good parent—both want to help children to help themselves to grow into strong, healthy, useful individuals and group members.

Teaching requires much stamina. One has to be physically fit to withstand the wear and tear of being with children over a long period of time. Too often weary teachers project their own feelings of fatigue, disappointment, anger, and pent-up emotions upon children. This is a fairly safe choice of victim, for children are less apt to fight back than adult colleagues. Teachers, like their youngsters, need to be able to get away from it all through recreative play. Increasingly, they must do themselves what they want others to do. Emerson's phrase, "What you *are* sounds so loudly in my ears that I cannot hear a word you are saying," is well worth remembering! If one wants to teach physical education, one must be well educated oneself, as well as have a deep desire to help others become educated in this field.

FIGURE 10–3. Even though you can't see too well, a good teacher can help you in many ways. (Courtesy of Northlake Elementary School, Dallas, Texas.)

EXCELLENCE IN TEACHING

The excellent teacher is one who through planned means of instruction is able to bring about positive change in the learner. Such change occurs in an environment that is meaningful and nonthreatening and that aids in developing a thinking and acting individual.

The following is a compilation of characteristics that contribute to excellence in teaching. They have been classified under three headings: Personal Qualities, Conducting the Class, and Evaluation. The possession of these characteristics is an *ideal* to be strived for and is often difficult to achieve fully in many of the teaching-learning situations that exist in our nation's schools.

Personal Qualities

Upon entering the classroom or gymnasium the student "sees" the teacher. A variety of personal characteristics display the teacher's attitude toward the subject matter, individual students, and class itself. The following is a list of personal traits that are characteristic of the excellent teacher:

The excellent teacher is one who

1. Displays personal interest in students as individuals but refrains from being "buddy-buddy." This indicates to students that the teacher really cares about them as persons as well as students.
2. Is honest with himself and his students. He is never condescending or afraid to admit to a mistake or lack of knowledge. This shows the student he can be trusted.
3. Is alive with enthusiasm about the subject matter and is eager to share his knowledge. This tends to help make the student want to learn rather than making him feel he has to learn.
4. Is human. He smiles, has an aura of warmth about him, and has a sense of humor. Students want to believe that teachers are human; only by acting human can the excellent teacher display his true concern for the class.
5. Is a good speaker with a clear voice and a vocabulary geared to the students' level. It is a pleasure to listen to a teacher who speaks well and is easily understood.
6. Is confident in his abilities and does not find it necessary to enhance his ego through his students. He is able to be a leader and be sensitive to the needs of the group. This enables the student to find comfort in the teacher's leadership without feeling threatened.
7. Recognizes that although it is superficial, personal appearance does have some effect on how students view him. He dresses neatly and appropriately for his age. This helps create a positive image of the teacher and enhances enjoyment of the class.
8. Possesses in-depth knowledge of his subject matter, is well read, and remains up-to-date in his knowledge. This helps ensure that the student will receive high quality, current, and correct information.

Conducting the Class

As the teacher enters the classroom or gymnasium, the process of rigid scrutiny by the student begins. There are a variety of factors involved in the teacher's actual conduct of the class period that play an important role in the quest for excellence. The teacher who makes maximal use of the time allotted and the resources and media available, and who applies a humanistic attitude toward education, is often viewed as excellent by students. The following is a list of items that form a solid base for the teacher striving to achieve excellence in conducting the class:

The excellent teacher

1. Arrives early for class. This illustrates enthusiasm and interest in the students. It also gives time for questions, comments, or conversation.

2. Provides a brief verbal or visual (blackboard) outline of the material to be covered during the class period. This enables the student to follow more closely the material being presented.
3. Always remains open to students' questions and comments and creates a forum for idea exchange. This encourages thinking and synthesizing of knowledge on the part of the student.
4. Carefully plans each class period so that all of the time allotted is used wisely. The excellent teacher never drags out a period simply to fill in time or cancels a class without prior notice. This makes the student feel that his time in class is well spent and worth the effort he makes to attend it.
5. Recognizes the necessity of practical application of ideas and concepts to the student's everyday life. He illustrates the relevancy of the material for the student and enables him to more accurately and personally apply the information.
6. Is objective, consistent, and constructive in the application of disciplinary measures and recognizes the individuality of each student. This assures the student that he will be fairly dealt with.
7. Uses a variety of outside resources, when applicable, to enhance learning and vary the normal class routines. This serves to broaden the students' scope of knowledge and enhance interest in class.

Evaluation

All teachers are faced with the responsibility of evaluating students, but it is the student who must cope with the variety of techniques employed. Every student is an individual and as such prefers certain types of evaluative methods to others. The following is a list of some basic feelings that most students have in common concerning the process of evaluation and how it directly affects them:

The excellent teacher is one who

1. Does not evaluate students by totally objective or subjective means. He combines objectivity and subjectivity in testing situations to help make the evaluative experience meaningful.
2. Takes the time to develop behavioral objectives for his students and for himself. The student needs to know what he is going to be tested and evaluated on and for. The teacher must know what goals he wants his students to reach and how he is going to go about helping them achieve those goals.
3. Employs valid instruments to measure students' mastery of the subject matter. Each evaluation should be based on a testing situation relevant to that particular subject matter.
4. Realizes and makes concessions in view of the fact that people perceive things differently. This indicates to the student that the teacher is interested enough in the student to listen to his interpretation of a question and the reasons for his answer.
5. Gives meaningful feedback to his students as quickly as possible. He corrects assignments and tests and returns these as soon as possible with meaningful comments on them to give the student an indication of his strong and weak points.
6. Recognizes that there are external factors that may affect a student's performance on a test. He takes the time to learn about his students and what they are involved in other than his own course.
7. Steadfastly refuses to let personal prejudices, biases, or preferences interfere with fair and honest grading. This assures the student that he will be evaluated on what he knows or can do, and not on artificial criteria such as hair length, style of dress, or likeability.

Excellence in teaching is a worthy goal for which to strive. Only experience and a great deal of personal effort will help in the quest for excellence. There are worlds of difference separating a poor teacher, a good one, and a master educator.

TEACHER AIDES AND OTHER PARAPROFESSIONALS

Some states have programs for teacher aides who work with the certified physical educator as an assistant and are paid by the state government. They are classified in two categories: (1) educational and clerical materials assistants, and (2) instructional assistants.

Aides, who work under the supervision of and in the presence of certified physical educators, may not assume the educational responsibilities of the teacher. Also, they may not be used by any school or district to replace teachers, to substitute for those certified as educators, or to change the pupil-teacher ratio.

Basic Qualifications[4]

1. High school diploma or the equivalent.
2. Minimum age of 21 years (unless enrolled in college).
3. Interest in physical education.
4. Emotional maturity, dependability, and sound character.
5. Completion of the standard first aid course or the equivalent.
6. Ability to do clerical work.
7. Ability to get along with people.
8. Good health.

Auxiliary personnel must comply with all general requirements applicable to other school employees, such as giving the school access to their health records.

Restrictions

Teacher aides should not be permitted to perform the following duties of a certified teacher:

1. Administering tests.
2. Organizing curriculum.
3. Evaluating students.
4. Interpreting results of tests.
5. Ordering equipment.
6. Taking charge of fire drills.
7. Instructing students unless directed to do so under the teacher's supervision.
8. Assuming teacher's responsibility.
9. Supervising intramural activities.
10. Assuming complete coaching responsibilities.
11. Administering corporal punishment.

Teacher aides should be required to participate in preschool institutes and in-service workshops. Conferences between aides, teachers, and supervisors are also necessary.

---

[4]These recommendations concerning teacher aides were made by a task force committee with representative numbers from the Society of State Directors of Health, Physical Education, and Recreation. They also incorporate suggestions from City Directors of HPER and members of the Texas Education Agency staff.

Duties

An *educational materials assistant* should prepare materials for instruction, maintain bulletin board displays, and operate audio-visual equipment. He should also

1. Keep the locker room orderly.
2. Launder and distribute uniforms and towels.
3. Operate the shower controls and oversee the shower room conduct.
4. Take care of the equipment room.
5. Make periodic safety checks, and maintain and repair equipment.
6. Clean the gymnasium and store equipment.
7. Set up the gymnasium for various activities.
8. Mark instructional areas.
9. Help maintain indoor and outdoor instructional areas.
10. Help construct instructional materials.
11. Maintain timely and neat bulletin boards.
12. Procure, set up, operate, and return audio-visual equipment.
13. Be responsible for valuables checked by students.
14. Check doors and windows at the beginning and end of the period.
15. Ensure proper lighting.
16. Mark uniforms and other supplies.

A *clerical assistant* should provide clerical assistance, duplicate materials, maintain student records, collect money, and perform some of the duties of an educational materials assistant. He should

1. Check attendance.
2. Check uniforms.
3. Check lockers and assign locks and lockers.
4. Unpack, count, and store new equipment.
5. Distribute and collect equipment.
6. Make a periodic inventory of equipment.
7. Assist in the initial health screening—check eyes, height, and weight and record health information.
8. Type and mimeograph stencils for tests.
9. File correspondence.
10. Transfer grades from the record book to marking forms.
11. Take care of records for classes made up.
12. Compile credits for extracurricular attendance and awards.
13. Mimeograph, correct, and change instructional material or curriculum outlines.
14. Record scores on physical fitness test forms.
15. Score objective test papers.
16. Type reports requested from the teacher by the administration.

The *instructional assistant* should demonstrate skills, assist individual students, and perform some of the assigned duties of a clerical worker or educational materials assistant. He should

1. Assist at fire drills.
2. Enforce safety rules.
3. Assist the chaperone or sponsors and other student groups.
4. Help with first aid but only when properly trained.
5. Assist at playdays, exhibitions, and sports days with publicity, tickets, and supervision of groups.
6. Supervise nonparticipating students.
7. Assist in the swimming program. (He should hold a Water Safety Instructor's Certificate or Red Cross lifesaving certificate.)
8. Assist with examinations.
9. Assist on field trips.

Professional Preparation of Teacher Aides

School districts that use teacher aides should develop guidelines for professional preparation, such as the following:

The teacher aide must

1. Enroll in a physical education program at a two year or four year institution.
2. Complete a two year curriculum at a two or four year institution that is aimed at preparing physical education aides.
3. Participate in staff development workshops held before, during, and at the end of the school year that are especially prepared for teacher aides in physical education. This in-service program would be geared to helping the aide achieve the maximum in assisting in the coordination and cooperation in the teacher-learning process.

DESIRABLE PRINCIPLES AND PHILOSOPHY

Principles, or basic beliefs regarding what is known in all fields of knowledge, should guide all teachers; these are the foundations upon which one's philosophy of teaching, of education, and of life are built.

Teachers continually search for short cuts in their work, practical ways in which to solve their problems. Such solutions come best out of each individual's experiences. They cannot be passed on very successfully from one person to another. Bernard Shaw believed that if you teach a man anything he will never learn. Materials in this book can be valuable to the readers only when tried and improved upon, modified, or reshaped to fit into their own unique situation, and added to things learned from their own experiences. Suggested teaching methods, materials, and books, however, will be most valuable to readers when they have been rooted in

FIGURE 10–4.   Demonstration is the first D of good teaching. (Courtesy of Ed-Nu, Inc.)

educationally sound principles. Both basic beliefs and objectives require continual modification as we push further to explore regions previously marked "unknown." One's philosophy must keep pace with the results of man's eternal quest to *know,* to find out *why,* and to *grow*.

PRINCIPLES OF TEACHING

Teaching is both an art and a science. To some it is a struggle, a bore, a job in which one does too much work for too little pay. To others teaching is a joy, an adventure, a challenge. To still others it is a leadership service to be rendered for the development of mankind.

Each teacher's philosophy—whatever it is—governs, colors, spurs on, or retards his or her results in working with others. The best and most fruitful results can come only from the skilled teachers who enjoy working with others. Such teachers improve constantly in their methods and continue to grow professionally.

Principles basic to education are the following:

1. People can be educated.
2. Every experience from which people learn involves their whole being.
3. Education goes on wherever there is life. It can be good or bad depending upon the teacher in the learning environment.

Principles basic to teaching are the following:

1. Everyone can learn something.
2. Learning means changed behavior.
3. The learner masters materials more readily if he shares in the planning, doing, and evaluation of what he is to learn.
4. Teaching is largely motivating people to *want* to do things.

FIGURE 10–5.   The teacher may occasionally enjoy participating in the lesson with her students. (Courtesy of Central College, Pella, Iowa.)

FIGURE 10–6. Come, let me help you. (Courtesy of Northlake Elementary School, Dallas, Texas.)

5. The learner, in reality, teaches himself. The role of the teacher is to help him find short cuts toward mastery and satisfaction in accomplishment.
6. Good teaching is guiding people to help themselves.
7. Teaching can be a conducted tour shared by the teacher and learner through a thrilling world of experience.
8. The most fruitful results accrue in a warm, kindly, friendly atmosphere, in which the learner feels secure.
9. Good teaching is progressive. Skills, knowledge, and appreciation are built upon one another and become increasingly more difficult.
10. Good teaching develops initiative, self-reliance, confidence, and independence in each child.

Each teacher should discover his or her own methods based upon these and other educational principles. It is this leader who is the key to successful accomplishments in physical education, more so than adequate or elaborate facilities and equipment, small classes, or sufficient time given to the program. Often the best instructors in the field have the poorest equipment with which to work and the most crowded room space. Creative master teachers are few. Resourcefulness, coupled with enthusiasm, can sometimes produce better results than superior technical knowledge and training.

FIGURE 10-7.   The teacher should set up a number of learning stations around which individual children or groups of children rotate. (Courtesy of Jayfro Corporation, Montville, Connecticut.)

Integration

Physical education offers many opportunities for integration with other subjects, such as:

1. Arithmetic—counting, scoring, and laying out courts.
2. Art—making costumes, posters, scenery, and charts and creating dances.
3. Language arts—speaking distinctly in games, dramatizing stories, choral speaking, reading and writing game rules, and keeping squad records.
4. Music—working with rhythms of all types; making and playing various kinds of instruments.
5. Social studies—folk dances, playing period games, developing understanding and appreciation of other persons and groups, developing group consciousness, leadership-"followership" activities.
6. Science and health—building desirable health habits and attitudes, developing physical fitness and good body mechanics, planning one's daily schedule for rest, work, and play.
7. Practical arts—making and repairing game equipment; laying out play areas.

PROFESSIONAL GROWTH

Preliminary professional education is but one aspect of effective teaching. Each professional leader is obligated to do her best and contribute to the growth and improvement of her own chosen specialized field. There are many challenges that a teacher faces, but perhaps none is more important than the ever-deepening desire every real educator has to improve herself and her teaching ability. There are two chief ways to grow professionally: through (1) in-service training programs and (2) engaging in further professional pursuits.

Continued Professional Enrichment Programs

In-service education is an on-the-job self-improvement program. Educators must learn how to teach; they can do so by capitalizing upon their own trial-and-error

FIGURE 10–8. One of the teacher's responsibilities is to make available the latest in equipment and teaching techniques.

attempts. The old folk sayings "Live and learn" and "Experience is the best teacher" are only true if one is wise enough to profit from experience. For some, the longer one stays in the profession, the greater the temptation becomes to teach in the same old way and stay in the same old well-worn groove. Fortunately, most teachers have high professional goals and are keenly interested in improving their effectiveness as educators.

The physical education supervisor working with classroom teachers can do much to improve elementary physical education programs through careful supervision and well-planned follow-up conferences, as well as by conducting teacher-education workshops. One of the finest means of in-service education can be found in the development of a graded course of study by a group of teachers aided by the physical education specialist for each school system or for each school in smaller towns.

Staff Meetings

Democratically led staff meetings with fellow teachers can be a splendid way to grow in understanding and appreciation of the unique and valuable contribution each makes to the school program. Such meetings should be well planned, and real problems that affect all who attend the school should be studied carefully. The old saying "Two heads are better than one" is not necessarily true, for this depends largely upon the kind of "heads" involved. Likewise, merely bringing a group of teachers together after a long school day to discuss cooked-up business is a waste of time and effort. In order that staff meetings be beneficial, each participant must feel that he has a real contribution to make for the benefit of the group as well as be aware that his time is being well spent in a pursuit that will help him become a better teacher and a member of an important educational team. Short, frequent staff meetings in which an agenda is followed are better than long ones. Everyone should contribute both to the making of the agenda and to the meeting itself.

Curriculum Study

Rather than compelling them to take part in curriculum improvement projects during after-school hours, schools are increasingly providing released time for teachers to work on curriculum improvement, and they regard such work as part of the teachers' job. All schools should periodically and continuously evaluate their objectives and programs and be assisted in this task by a small group of experts. The total school program should be revised at frequent and needed intervals, but no special area needing revision should be allowed to remain as it is until the time comes for a major "house cleaning" or curriculum change.

Surveys

Although community surveys will not provide teachers with the needed answers to educational problems, it is imperative that educators know much more than they do about the locality in which they work. Those who engage in community surveys or capitalize upon the information gained by local community social agencies or a community council *will* know more about the area in which they work and the kind of backgrounds and homes from which their pupils come. All teachers should conduct or take part in various surveys of their own school in order to gain valuable information that will enable them to become more productive and understanding youth leaders. The more any teacher knows about each student the better she can help each child develop to realize his potential as a human being capable of contributing to the society of which he is a vital part.

Research

Many teachers fail to realize that research and experimentation that they do on their own teaching situation, teaching effectiveness, and learning outcomes can be far more valuable and meaningful to them and lead to their own professional growth much more than reading about the research findings of others. All great teachers are those who have found their own unique teaching methods and have dared to be different and creative.

Workshops

Teacher workshops are rich sources for self-improvement. These often provide opportunities to obtain new teaching methods and materials, as well as help instructors gain a renewed interest and enthusiasm for their work. Such workshops should be carefully planned by a steering committee that should select, from returned questionnaires sent to teachers, problem areas they want to learn more about. The services of physical education specialists or supervisors or both as resource persons will add much to the value of such an experience.

FIGURE 10–9.   Good teaching develops initiative, self-reliance, self-confidence, and independence in each child. (Courtesy of Shield Manufacturing Company, Buffalo, New York.)

Home Study

Correspondence extension courses are now available in most communities. Although there may be merit in securing materials via the correspondence course method, most teachers will profit more from attending an extension course and gaining inspiration, along with other things, from working with a well-known educational authority and exchanging ideas with other teachers from other schools. Even if only one teacher from each building in the system attends such a course, her fellow instructors can profit from her experience by reading suggested new materials and by having her share with them the new ideas and concepts she has learned.

Professional Organizations

All teachers should be members of and contribute to professional organizations. Likewise, each should read the official publications of these groups, as well as contribute articles to them either individually or with others in a committee. All should attend as many local, state, regional, and national meetings of their professional organizations as possible.

Organizations that teachers of health and physical education can join with profit are The American Alliance for Health, Physical Education, and Recreation, the American School Health Association, and the National Education Association.

TRAVEL AND HOBBIES

Although aimless wandering is fun for a few days, travel for the purpose of gaining new or deeper understandings is far more rewarding. Increasingly, teachers are going abroad as exchange instructors, graduate students, or tourists. Those with keen interest in their work and specialized field will return home from any trip with newly gained enthusiasm and new materials for their work and will pass these on to pupils. Teaching is a de-energizing business, as anyone knows who has been in it long. Those who are the most successful educators are those who have learned not to take school home with them nor to identify too closely with their pupils, realizing that each child must learn to live his own life; such persons have leisure hours through which they gain recreation and refreshment. Only faulty planners have no leisure for themselves. Those who declare "I haven't time" need to be gently reminded that everyone has the same amount of time—24 hours, no more and no less—every single day. What one does with it is a matter of values, for first things do come first for those who make them so. Experts tell us that in order to be healthy, all people, regardless of age, need to spend some time every day doing things that bring pleasure and joy. Those who have recreative leisure usually become the most productive workers. Experienced teachers are those who have profited from their experiences and have learned many short cuts in their work, so that they do have free time in which to enjoy life. Hobbies can add much to one's joy in life, for they lead to an ever-widening new world of interests and friends.

Further Professional Education

Most large school systems require that teachers take a refresher course in their field every three years. Increasingly, those with a bachelor's degree are going on for advanced work or to receive their master's degree. This usually takes one year or about 35 hours of advanced work in summer school or night courses. Some institutions require a written thesis; others require the student to take additional hours and write one or more long research papers.

Those who wish to advance themselves professionally, teach on the college level, or become national leaders in their field usually study beyond the master's degree. Supervisory and administrative positions increasingly are requiring broad professional experience and the doctor's degree. If candidates qualify for admission and pass preliminary examinations, they then work toward the Doctor of Philosophy or Doctor of Education degree. Both degrees are similar in admission standards, matriculation procedures, residence, and other time requirements. The Ed.D. differs largely in that it tends to be more appropriate for those who wish to become education specialists. The Ph.D. is largely aimed at a more finely specialized subject area of knowledge. Graduate teaching fellowships, assistantships, scholarships, and loans are available for those qualified to receive them.

Every teacher, regardless of the educational level he or she works on, must be well selected, well prepared professionally, and a leader who continues to grow in productive skill as an educator. Through the united efforts of every such individual, a happier, healthier, safer, and better world can become a reality.

SUGGESTED READINGS

AAHPER: *Organization Patterns for Instruction in Physical Education,* Washington, D.C., 1971.

Bucher, C.: *Foundations of Physical Education.* 7th ed. St. Louis, The C. V. Mosby Company, 1975.

Cochran, E. V.: *Teach and Reach That Child.* Palo Alto, Peek Publications, 1971.

Dowell, L.: *Strategies For Teaching Physical Education.* Englewood Cliffs, New Jersey, Prentice-Hall, Inc., 1975.

Fabricius, H.: *Physical Education for the Classroom Teacher.* 2nd ed. Dubuque, Iowa, William C. Brown Company, Publishers, 1971.

Gallahue, D. L., and Meadors, W. J.: *Let's Move! A Physical Education Program for Elementary Classroom Teachers.* Dubuque, Iowa, Kendall/Hunt, 1974.

Haskew, L., and McLendon, J.: *This Is Teaching.* 3rd ed. Dallas, Scott, Foresman and Company, 1968.

Humphreys, A.: *Heaven in My Hand.* Richmond, Virginia, The John Knox Press, 1950.

Some of our best teachers are under twelve. *The Instructor Magazine,* September, 1976.

Jackson, S.: Love. *The Instructor Magazine,* December, 1976.

National Commission on Teacher Education and Professional Standards, N.E.A.: *The Real World of the Beginnning Teacher.* Washington, D.C., 1966.

Peterson, D.: *The Elementary School Teacher.* New York, Appleton-Century-Crofts, 1964.

Purchell, C.: *Teach Me! (A photographic essay on the joys of teaching and learning).* Washington, D.C., National Education Association, 1966.

Sanborn, M., and Hartman, B.: *Issues in Physical Education.* 2nd ed. Philadelphia, Lea & Febiger, 1971.

Vannier, M., and Fait, H.: *Teaching Physical Education in Secondary Schools.* Philadelphia, W. B. Saunders Company, 1975.

Vannier, M., and Poindexter, H. B.: *Individual and Team Sports for Girls and Women.* 3rd ed. Philadelphia, W. B. Saunders Company, 1976.

Wees, W. R.: *Nobody Can Teach Anyone Anything.* New York, Doubleday and Company, Inc., 1971.

PART THREE

Mankind has always felt the need of good leadership,
for the history of the world shows that we have never
had enough leaders in the right place at the right time.
The elementary school is the rich soil in which children
can develop those traits necessary for positive
democratic leadership. The hope for the future is the
education of our present children.

                                        The Authors

THE WHERE AND WHEN

CHAPTER ELEVEN

THE GYMNASIUM, PLAYGROUND, POOL, AND CLASSROOM

Good leadership is far more important than having good facilities. A creative teacher will always provide a developmental and sound physical education program.

The Authors

Usually physical education classes are held in a gymnasium or multipurpose room or outside on a play field. Most public schools are fortunate enough to have one or the other. Schools that use a playground for outdoor recreational activities and a gymnasium for physical education instruction usually have the best programs. The use of the classroom, auditorium, stage, or school corridor has been found to be inadequate and often results in a make-shift program fitted into make-shift space. A well-equipped gymnasium, adequate playground space, and sufficient time for a minimum of 30 minutes daily class instruction plus another 30 minutes of scheduled supervised play or recess period provide an ideal teaching-learning environment.

THE GYMNASIUM

A well-lighted, ventilated, clean gymnasium is a prime necessity in all modern schools. The gymnasium should not be known as a "playroom," but rather as a learning laboratory—the place where children receive instruction not in play but in physical education.

In determining the size of the gymnasium, the immediate concern must be for

1. Adequate teaching space, with a minimum area of approximately 41 by 66 feet for 66 children. For larger classes there should be an increase of 40 square feet for each pupil.
2. Official-size courts for pupil and adult use with a ceiling height of 22 feet under all beams, tresses, or hanging obstacles.
3. Good sunlight and ventilation. The ratio of window space to floor space should be 4:5 with windows preferably placed along the two long sides of the room rather than at the end; room temperature maintained at 60 to 65 degrees.
4. Clean walls on which there are two or more bulletin boards.
5. A clean, smooth-surfaced floor marked with permanent lines or colored chalk or removable tempera paint to indicate playing areas.
6. Removal of all hazards; unremovable hazards, such as posts, radiators, pipes, and so forth, should be covered with mats.
7. Accessibility to drinking fountains, either outside in the corridor or recessed in the wall.

8. An acoustically treated ceiling.
9. Spectator seating.
10. Single doors that swing out away from the play area.

Locker, shower, toilet, and lavatory facilities should adjoin the gymnasium and be accessible from the playground. Pupil enrollment determines the number of lockers needed. Lockers may be the individual steel type measuring 12 × 12 × 36 inches; the narrow type measuring 7 × 18 × 36 inches; the basket type; or the type built flush into the wall. Each student should have a standard combination lock; the teacher should file away two copies of master sheets of all combinations. Each locker room should have stationary long benches, mirrors at the end of each row of lockers, scales, and built-in hair dryers.

The shower room should adjoin the locker room; preferably, it should be a separate unit. There should be one shower head for every four children, all spaced at least 4 feet apart. Liquid soap, properly controlled water and room temperature, and good ventilation should be provided in both the shower and dressing room areas. A well-drained drying room is recommended and should be located between the locker and shower rooms to prevent a flow of moisture and tracking of water into the dressing area. A special towel service booth should be located near the drying room, or towels may be issued at the main equipment counter or exchanged in baskets. *Preferably,* towels, swimming trunks, and pool suits, as well as regulation gymnasium uniforms, should be furnished by the school and provided, newly laundered and sanitary, for each pupil at the beginning of each class.

Adequate well-lighted, sanitary, ventilated rest rooms with sufficient toilets, urinals, and wash basins should be provided. Liquid soap, hot and cold water, and towels should be furnished.

Pupils should be encouraged rather than required to take showers after class periods at the fourth grade level when they begin wearing special uniforms for class instruction. Required showers are not only hard to enforce but can lead to serious teacher criticism from some parents. Pupils should be sold on the idea that taking a shower is a privilege as well as a social obligation to fellow students in the next class to which they will go following physical education, rather than a requirement. The positive approach provides for positive action. Sufficient time should be allotted to include showers in the daily program. For some few, taking showers will be a big part of their physical education program.

THE POOL

Increasingly, schools are building swimming pools that have been planned for maximum use by both the school and the community throughout the entire year. Others, who recognize the great value of having each child learn to swim, are using local pools in the community. The swimming pool should have a southern exposure, be 75 feet long and at least 35 feet wide. Depths should vary from 2 feet 6 inches at the shallow end to 4 feet 6 inches at the outer limits of the shallow area, and the deeper area should taper from 9 feet to 12 feet. The shallow, instructional area should comprise two thirds of the pool area. Troughs at the water level should be used for hand-gripping by beginners. The deck space around the pool should be composed of nonslippery tile and be large enough for land instruction. The walls and ceiling should be acoustically treated. Recessed ceiling lights and the use of natural light coming through side windows will reduce glare as well as provide a more comfortable area for

FIGURE 11–1. All equipment should be chosen carefully from the viewpoint of safety and valued educational use. (© J. A. Preston Corporation 1971.)

teaching. An office adjacent to the pool should be used for keeping records and first-aid equipment. Water temperature should be kept about 80 degrees for elementary children. Shower, dressing, and toilet areas should be provided adjacent to the pool; these might also be used for physical education purposes, thus avoiding expensive duplication. All of the pool facilities should be designed for maximum use and supervisory control. Spectator space is also recommended.

Because the swimming pool is a costly operation, it is essential that it be planned by expert architects and swimming specialists. Such a facility should also be used to its maximum, for swimming is one of our finest physical activities and has high carry-over value throughout life. At all times when the pool is not being used by the school, it should be made available to people of all ages in the community for after-school instructional and recreational use throughout each week yearly.

Many schools are now using neighborhood pools and are training parents to teach swimming and then using them as assistant instructors[1] with their own children.

THE CLASSROOM

The specific objectives the teacher should have in mind when conducting physical education activities in the classroom are to

1. Use all available space to the best advantage.
2. Set up rules of conduct with the pupils while playing so that people in other classes will not be disturbed.
3. Discover with the pupils hazards that should be avoided in the room.

The general objectives the teacher should have when teaching active games and contests in the classroom are to

1. Develop within the child the knowledge, skills, and appreciation favorable to his fullest and wisest use of free moments in the present and future.
2. Guide the student toward mastering social response in a variety of situations.
3. Familiarize the pupil with a wide variety of activities.

FIGURE 11–2. If need be the teacher and the children can make or collect their own equipment for class use. (© J. A. Preston Corporation 1971.)

4. Develop understandings and abilities involved in the planning, selecting, and conducting of games.

Although the classroom is not suitable as a place in which to do physical activities, it can be used during bad weather, provided the children have their physical education classes outdoors whenever weather permits. All children need, among other things, plenty of vigorous big-muscle activity, fresh air, and sunshine.

INCREASED USE OF FACILITIES

School programs and facilities should serve the needs of the total community—both children and adults. Because of the increased national concern for the well-being and education of people of all ages, communities throughout the nation are becoming aware that less than 4 per cent of public school buildings are being used as community centers. Because school buildings belong to the people, they should be opened to serve all the people day and night and especially during Saturday and the summer months. If the school widens its service to the community, it enriches the lives of everyone. In turn, the prestige of the school will rise, its influence will grow, and its support will be strengthened.

The school gymnasium, pool, and multipurpose outdoor play areas should be designed for program flexibility and year-round use by people of all ages in the community.

LEGAL LIABILITY

Few school boards can be sued for negligent acts of omission or commission because of their common-law immunity. This theory states that because the "king can do no wrong" and the state represents him, the state cannot be sued. Consequently, because each school district is a division of government, the school board is immune to lawsuits. Because school districts conduct nonprofit governmental functions, they are also nonliable. In contrast, all organizations that carry on profit-making or pro-prietary functions can be held liable. Teachers, on the other hand, as well as activity directors in profit-making organizations can be sued for proven acts of negligence. Legally, negligence is (1) conducting an act that any reasonable person would have known to be too unreasonable and risky for others to do and (2) failing to do an act necessary for the protection of others.

Physical educators can be held liable for proved negligence for the following reasons:

1. Pupil injuries where playground or gymnastic equipment is defective. (Physical educators should make and periodically report in *written form* to their administrators known defective, dangerous equipment and hazardous areas. They should keep a carbon copy of this report.)
2. Injuries that occur to pupils who attempt to do exercises or activities beyond their skill, such as handstands, running-jump somersaults, and so forth. (Teachers should not permit students to attempt exercises or activities for which they have not developed the necessary skills or for which they have not been danger-warned.)
3. Injuries caused by the negligence of another pupil. The other pupil's misconduct must be foreseeable. (All teachers should know what to expect from each student in behavior as well as performance.)
4. Leaving assigned groups, even temporarily to get a drink of water, go to the bathroom, or answer a phone call. (Physical educators who teach class by throwing in the ball and leaving or other such types of instruction by remote control are *asking for trouble.*)

Accidents sometimes happen in spite of precaution, safety education programs, adequate emergency measures, or routinized habits drilled into students of what to do in case of fire or an air raid. Periodic surveys should be made and carefully studied to determine the real effectiveness of the school safety program. Only when comparative figures show (1) a reduction in the number of school accidents and (2) a lessened degree of the severity of individual injuries can progress be claimed or the program said to be of value.

THE PLAYGROUND

Playground space should be planned so that there is opportunity for the greatest number to play safely at one time. At least five acres should be provided for elementary schools. A minimum of 100 square feet per pupil should be an absolute requirement. Separate areas should be set off for the primary grades for safety purposes, and this group should be assigned the space that is the furthest away from the oldest, most active group. Space should be planned for use by as many age groups as possible. For example, baseball diamonds may be used for kickball with the lower grades and for softball with the upper grades at different periods of the day. The area should also be enclosed by a metal fence.

Playground surfacing is usually of dust-treated dirt, hard cement, black-top, grass turf, or sawdust combined with asphalt. Regardless of which type is used, the area should be a safe and healthful one for children's play. It should be well planned so that it can be adequately and easily supervised, fenced, well shrubbed, and shaded. Primary-grade children should be assigned permanent play areas near the shaded side of the building where they will be well protected and safe at all times. Backstop fences for softball, and enclosed swing and apparatus areas are highly recommended. Space should be provided for sandbox and creative play for the younger children. The entire playground area should be attractive, clean, and safe. It should look like and be a place for great adventures!

FIGURE 11–3. The railroad tie maze serves as a focal point for the playground. Children find it to be one of the most unique facilities on the playground. Sand is spread throughout the entire area. Directionality, balance, and cooperation are some of the skills taught using the maze. (Courtesy of the Scotia-Glenville Central Schools, Scotia, New York.)

The Adventure Playground

The old-fashioned playground is outmoded. The trend is to provide facilities that have creative possibilities and to provide equipment that can have many uses, such as giant Lincoln logs, rocket ships, climbable towers, old discarded boats, climbing nets, and "pretend" ships. Children need things to move, mold, and manipulate, as well as lots of tiny things they can use to build bigger ones that can easily be moved from place

FIGURE 11–4.   The alternating serpentine stepping logs, made of utility poles and beams, develop timing, an awareness of space limitations, and confidence. Varying in height from 8 inches to 3 feet, the poles are securely set 3 feet into the ground. (Courtesy of the Scotia-Glenville Central Schools, Scotia, New York.)

FIGURE 11–5. These children "created" a vertical tunnel with tires. Taking turns, students crawl down through the tires and out at the bottom of the cable spool jungle. The rule is that the tires must be put back in position after use. (Courtesy of the Scotia-Glenville Central Schools, Scotia, New York.)

to place. One of the most popular newer pieces of equipment is the "stack sack," which is many cotton bags filled with dry cement.[2] The children stack them any way they like and then douse them with water. When hardened, these new child-created forms bring them much challenge and delight. Old car tires, wheels, metal poles, and other discarded objects thrill children far more than standardized equipment ever could and can be used to help develop their own creative efforts for their after-school play.

Sixteen fourth and fifth grade children in the Quaker Ridge School of Scarsdale, New York, recently formed a Playground Design Club. From their models, a Space Platform resulted, which is an 8 × 12 foot redwood platform 8 feet from the ground, with bright red, yellow, and blue railings.[3] It is the most popular object on the school's playground.

As one authority on school playgrounds has said, "We really haven't taken full advantage of the only thing children offer us freely—their desire to play."[4] It is true that as children we adults had many more chances to create our own fun, to run at will, to make treehouses, or to wander and explore. Consequently, playground designers of today try to put back into the child's environment such things as cages, nets, ropes, trees, and walls to climb; dirt hills and sandboxes; tunnels and crawl barrels; rockers; bar rollers and barrels; tire walks and jump pits; tire, boat, and rocket swings; all kinds of slides of varying heights; old cars; hills, flowers, and trees to look at; water to wade and even play in; and a lighted school play area for night use for children, supervised by parents if need be. In such play areas, vandalism has been a very minor

[2]Sanders, J.: *Swings and sandboxes are out of style.* Dallas Morning News, March 16, 1972.
[3]Holter, P.: *Playground Design Club.* The Instructor Magazine, March 1972, p. 76.
[4]Pennington, G.: *Slide down the cellar door—the new approach to playgrounds.* The Instructor Magazine, March 1972, pp. 74–76.

FIGURE 11–6. The 24 foot balance beam provides an excellent opportunity for children to develop confidence, coordination, and balance, as well as cooperation and appreciation for the rights of others. (Courtesy of the Scotia-Glenville Central Schools, Scotia, New York.)

problem in contrast to that found in traditional areas. These adventure playgrounds are loved by children, and they flock to them. Like any good playground, the users can constantly rearrange it. Play to these children is not just physical activity; it is a rich learning experience! It influences the mind, emotions, and body of the child as he partakes in a learning adventure called play.

Outdoor play equipment should be chosen carefully from the viewpoint of safety and valued use. Jungle gyms and horizontal hanging bars should be provided that hang 36 inches from the ground for primary-grade children and up to 54 inches for those in the upper elementary grades. Swings with canvas seats from 10 to 12 inches high, monkey rings, and parallel bars are highly recommended. Some physical educators believe that, because seesaws, slides, and merry-go-rounds do very little to develop physical fitness or coordination, they are an unwise investment of public funds.

Other than the above-mentioned items, the following permanent playground facilities should be included:

Apparatus:

Wood or pipe climbing apparatus.
Horizontal ladders.
Low-graded to high circular traveling rings.

FIGURE 11–7. The tire mountain is among the more popular activity centers for both primary and intermediate age children. Each tire weighs about 2500 pounds and is anchored by bolts to another. The tires are brightly painted and serve as an ideal piece of climbing apparatus. (Courtesy of the Scotia-Glenville Central Schools, Scotia, New York.)

Hemp or manila climbing ropes suspended from poles or securely fastened to the building or trees.
Heavy rope giant stride.
Sets of six swings in a frame 12 feet high.
Slides 8 feet high and approximately 16 feet long.
Balance beams of various heights from the ground.
Tether ball poles.
Horseshoe stakes.
Bicycle racks.
Automobile tires suspended on ropes.
Several outdoor bulletin boards.
Vertical climbing poles.

Play Equipment for Younger Children:

Sandboxes and tools.
Wide and narrow horizontal planks and boards several inches off the ground for running and balancing.
Barrels, kegs, and hoops for rolling.
Inclined boards for running up and sliding down on.
Stairs built with varied step heights to climb up and over and jump from.
Wheelbarrows.
Small tables and work benches.
Large wooden boxes and cartons.
Telephone poles laid flat on the ground for climbing on and jumping from, and others holed securely in the ground for vertical climbing.
Numerous tires and wheels of varying sizes for rolling with hands or a crossed T-shaped board.
Pipe tunnels of reinforced concrete sewer pipe arranged in units of three and set at different angles 3 feet apart.

FIGURE 11–8.   The cable spool jungle consists of electric cable spools of varying sizes arranged in such a fashion that children can climb around them and crawl through them. (Courtesy of the Scotia-Glenville Central Schools, Scotia, New York.)

FIGURE 11–9.   The walk-on-top horizontal ladder provides primary grade children with exercises in balance, timing, and coordination. The facility is expansive enough to accommodate large numbers of children without conflicts. (Courtesy of the Scotia-Glenville Central Schools, Scotia, New York.)

A "Whatnot," or small platform of 9 × 6 feet surrounded on three sides by a low wall and
  reached on the fourth open side by steps.
Tables and benches.
As many box hockey sets as feasible.

The school administrator, assisted by a committee of classroom teachers and the
physical education teacher or supervisor or both, should give serious consideration to
the following factors regarding playground facilities and their use: location; arrange-
ment for the protection of all pupils, especially the youngest ones; regular safety
inspection forms and procedures, fencing and marking hazardous zones; care of the
ground underneath the apparatus, instruction in the correct use of the apparatus; and
necessary safety rules.

Courts and playing fields laid north and south should be designated as permanent
play areas and marked with paint or whitewash. Dry slaked lime or tennis tape markers
can be used on turf or dirt areas. Fixed posts are superior to movable standards for
paddle-type games. Iron nets are better and cheaper in the long run than oil-treated
ones, substituted wire fencing, or ropes. Track and field facilities should be laid out
according to the recommendations made at the National Facilities Conference sponsored by the Athletic Institute.[5]

Multiple purpose courts of cement or macadam should be laid and marked
on all permanent play areas. A tennis court can also be used for paddle tennis, volleyball, badminton, shuffleboard, basket shooting, hopscotch, and ice and roller skating.
Electric outlets, if provided, will make it usable for dancing or showing films at night.
Lighted courts and play areas increase participation to such an extent that they are
wonderfully inexpensive investments.[6]

Standard game areas that should be established are

Outdoor badminton courts	Softball and baseball diamonds
Basketball courts	Speedball court
Croquet courts	Speed-a-way fields
Handball courts	Tennis courts
Shuffleboard courts	Touch football field
Soccer fields for both boys and	Volleyball court
girls, if possible	Paddle tennis courts
Lawn bowling courts	

Outdoor equipment, other than balls of varying size, include

Aerial darts	Individual and long jump rope sets
Badminton sets	Jumping standards and crossbar
Basketball or Goal Hi standards	Lawn bowling sets
Bat-O-Net sets	Marbles
Box hockey sets	Putting game sets
Croquet sets	Shuffleboard sets
Deck tennis rings	Tennis equipment
Horseshoe sets	Tether ball sets
Hurdles	

[5]Athletic Institute: *A Guide for Planning Facilities for Athletics, Recreation, and Physical and Health
Education.* Revised ed. Chicago, Illinois, 1970.
    [6]Vannier, M., and Fait, H.: *Teaching Physical Education in Secondary Schools.* 4th ed. Philadelphia,
W. B. Saunders Company, 1975, p. 123.

Activities for the playground should add to the pleasure of the moment and enrich the recreational life of the child so that he uses new activities in his leisure time away from school. By teaching obedience to rules and regulations, games help teach children to get along with others. Activities should be selected that are suitable to sex, playing space, clothing, weather, and age level.

Some suggestions to assure proper conduct on the playground are to

1. Provide a varied program appealing to all.
2. Have a few concise rules and enforce them.
3. Make frequent tours of the playground with pupils, looking for hazards, and have the children paint these hazards bright yellow.
4. Always maintain a spirit of fairness and justice.
5. Foster a spirit of self-government by giving children a share in the making of conduct rules on the playground, and have them help supervise and officiate at activities.
6. Use pupil-game rotation plans so that all get equal use of the best facilities and equipment.

For recess and supervised free-play periods pupils should be assigned to a specific play space. Those in the primary grades should be given a section near the building and have certain pieces of fixed equipment such as swings, slides, and a jungle gym for their exclusive use.

Children in the upper elementary grades should also have a section of the play field that is their own. Boys should not be allowed to monopolize the baseball diamond or soccer field but should rotate with the girls the privilege of using all marked areas. A weekly schedule of play space assignments should be worked out by a student committee and teacher. Coeducational games can be encouraged when at least one assigned weekly period is set aside for them.

HANDLING EQUIPMENT

All equipment, uniforms, and gear should be marked by stenciling the name or initials of the school on it. All items of one type should be numbered consecutively. There should be a definite set of rules and procedures for handing out and returning all equipment. A good plan is to have each squad leader do this. The teacher should make certain that all equipment is ready before each class enters the gymnasium or goes out to the playground. All bats, balls, squad cards, and other needed items should be easily accessible and as many items as possible placed together. Baseballs should be stored near bats, croquet mallets and wickets near balls.

A complete inventory of all items should be made at the beginning and end of each semester's work. Worn-out equipment may be sent to charitable institutions if the items are in good enough shape to be repaired and used.

SUPPLIES AND EQUIPMENT NEEDED

The materials listed below are minimum essentials needed to conduct an adequate program in elementary schools. The amount and variety to be purchased will be dependent upon class size. Rubber balls are cheaper than leather ones and may prove to be just as serviceable.

Supplies

Balls
  Basketball, official
  Basketball, rubber
  Football, official
  Football, rubber
  Indoor, 12 inch
  Rubber, 5, 6, 8, 10 foot
  Soccer, official
  Soccer, rubber
  Volley, official
  Volley, rubber
Baseball gloves, balls, bats,
  protective equipment
Beanbags, 6 × 6, and targets
Broomsticks of various lengths
Chalk

Deck tennis rings
Five-pin bowling sets
Hoops
Hula hoop rings
Indian clubs
Jump-off boxes
Jump ropes, 3 foot 8 inch sashcord
  Individual, 6, 7, 8 foot
  Long, 12, 15, 20, 25 foot
Phonograph needles
Phonograph records
Shuffleboard sets
Squad cards
Tape measure, 50 foot
Tempera paint

Equipment

Balance beams of varying height
  from the floor
Ball inflator
Bases
Bats
Bicycle racks
Blackboard, portable and permanent
Bulletin board
Cabinet, steel
Canvas bags in which to carry balls
Chinning bars
Equipment box
Flying and stationary rings
Game nets
Hurdles, 12, 15, 18, 20 inch
Jump and vault standards
Jungle gym
Junior jump standards
Landing nets
Lime and markers
Low parallel bars
Mats, 33 × 60 inch, 3 × 5 foot, 4 × 6 foot

Microphone and speaker system
Net standards
Percussion instruments
Portable phonograph
Recreational games (checkers, horseshoes, and
  so forth)
Slides
Stall bars, vertical and horizontal bars
Stop watch
Storage cabinets or lockers
Surplus parachutes
Swim fins, unsinkable boards, hair dryers
Swings
Table hockey
Targets
Teeter boards
Tin can walkers
Traveling rings, vaulting buck and horse, Swedish
  box, springboard, parallel bars, climbing stairs
Wooden stilts of varying heights
Whistles, timers

All equipment should be carefully selected, stored, and repaired. The pupils can aid in oiling balls, repairing nets, and sewing ball rips. Sporting goods companies can usually provide better equipment for the money spent than local department stores.

Each teacher needs to have a yearly budget provided for the purchase of equipment, rather than being given a certain sum upon the sudden whim or urge of the school principal.

Uniforms

Beginning in grade 4 many physical educators find it desirable for both sexes to wear regulation uniforms for their class work in the gymnasium or on the playground. One-piece suits of dark material and white tennis shoes and socks are recommended

FIGURE 11–10. The use of rings can be an integral part of both the playground and the gymnasium program. (Courtesy of Los Angeles City Schools, Los Angeles, California.)

for girls. Dark trunks, a white "T" shirt, tennis shoes, and heavy socks are recommended for boys.

In order to secure the cooperation of the parents, letters may be sent to them explaining the costume requirement and places from which the clothing may be bought. They should also be informed that the clothing may be used for several years, and that provisions will be made to re-sell used garments. Upon request, parents from low-income groups and mothers who sew should be sent patterns for making the uniforms.

Companies that sell regulation gymnasium uniforms usually provide superior garments at lower cost than can local stores. Recognized serviceable companies are advertised monthly in the *Journal of Physical Education and Recreation*.

Regulation class uniforms aid in building desirable attitudes regarding the program; they also allow for freedom of movement and build group unity and morale.

Then, too, this is one way to encourage boys and girls to keep clean, because parts of their bodies are seen by their classmates.

ACCIDENT SAFEGUARDS

Physical education includes activities in which children can have adventurous, joyful experiences. Many of the games and sports can be dangerous if improperly supervised. With proper guidance and good teaching, however, a physical education class need not be any more potentially dangerous than one in any other subject. One way of safeguarding against accidents is to be sure that pupils engage only in those activities for which they are prepared in coordination, strength, and skill.

Children are not as interested in safety or being careful as they are in taking chances, in being daring. Consequently, adults must help them see that they can have the most fun over a longer period of time if they can avoid handicaps that may result from injuries. Safety education is learning to take chances wisely.

Accidents, when they do happen, can often be the best teachable moments to instruct youngsters to be careful. A boy who sprained his ankle while running in the shower room may help impress upon his classmates the importance of obeying the no-running rule. However, it must be remembered that parents whose children are hurt at school often develop negative attitudes toward the school or the teacher in charge of the activity in which the child was injured.

All teachers of physical education can safeguard against accidents by

1. Checking all apparatus and equipment periodically and keeping both in good repair at all times.
2. Finding and marking all hazards with the pupils.
3. Directing all pupils and, especially, squad leaders in safety measures.
4. Using plans, materials, and programs that will reduce the possibility of accidents.
5. Insisting that all pupils wear suitable apparel for all activities.
6. Organizing and classifying pupils for class participation according to the results of physical examinations and motor ability tests.
7. Insisting that all rules for playing games be obeyed at all times.
8. Never leaving an assigned class or group.
9. Reporting all safety hazards immediately both orally and in writing to the school administrator.

Pupils have a right to enjoy all their physical education periods in clean, safe, and attractive surroundings. Although elementary-school children are not safety-conscious, it would be educationally foolish and costly to remove all hazardous equipment, facilities, and activities from their physical education experiences, for they must learn early in life how to survive in an ever-increasingly danger-filled world. Teachers should stress *how* to play safely and wisely in order that students may play longer and more skillfully. The following suggestions will prove helpful for increased protection for pupils during physical education and after-school activities.

The Gymnasium, Pool, and Locker Rooms:

1. Check to see that all equipment is in good condition. Discard and replace that which is not.
2. Avoid slippery floors.
3. Cover all exposed dangerous areas with protective pads, or paint them bright yellow.
4. Have all doors swing out.
5. Fountains should be in safe recessed locations.
6. Post, and strictly enforce, all rules regarding the use of the pool, restrictions against running

and horseplay in the showers, and rules concerning the use of the equipment when the instructor is not present.

7. Require all students to be properly dressed for athletics; require all to wear socks and tennis shoes.
8. Stay with all assigned classes for the entire time of duty. Strive for close supervision of the whole class. Stand where you can see and be seen by the majority or the entire group.

Playgrounds, Sports Fields, and Intramural Areas:

1. Allocate space so that all teams and individuals can participate without danger to themselves or others.
2. Check all equipment. Discard and replace that which is dangerous.
3. Discover hazards with each class group; encourage them to point these out to you. Paint all immovable hazards bright yellow.
4. Mark fields and play areas; play according to the official rules, for they have been made for the safety of the players.
5. Supervise all groups; place yourself on the field where you can best do so. Do not leave the area until your assigned duties are over.
6. Help all assume responsibility for their own safety and that of others.

Competitive Athletics:

1. Lay out all playing areas from the standpoint of the best player and spectator safety protection.
2. Remove all hazardous obstructions.
3. Use only equipment approved or recommended by the governing association for secondary school competition in your locality.
4. Provide all players with properly fitting and safe protective clothing. Require them to keep it on while playing.
5. Receive medical approval for every participant.
6. Allow only those who have been properly trained and "warmed up" to play or enter games as substitutes.
7. Supervise all practices and competitive events; keep player safety uppermost in mind.
8. Supply proper first-aid treatment and needed medical care for all injured.
9. Insist upon adherence to training rules; avoid too frequent competition and long distance travel.
10. Make all players safety conscious.

In spite of all precautionary measures, accidents do occur in physical education classes, intramural programs, and competitive interschool contests. Both their frequency and their degree of severity can be reduced by taking the following measures:

1. Play all games according to the official rules.
2. Develop skills; it is the clumsy player who is most frequently injured.
3. Allow students to participate only in those activities that are suitable to their skill maturation levels.
4. Be on the lookout for fatigue, realizing that it is the tired student who is most apt to be injured. Know that fatigue levels differ with each individual.
5. Encourage students to report all injuries to you regardless of how minor they are at the time, and see that they receive proper treatment for them.

All children injured at school should receive first aid from a qualified school nurse or teacher. In small schools the physical educator often gives first aid and suggests the purchase of supplies to the school principal. First-aid equipment for all schools should include

1. One-inch compress on adhesive in individual packages.
2. Sterile gauze squares—3 × 3 inches—in individual packages.
3. Assorted sterile bandage compresses in individual packages.
4. Triangular bandages.
5. Sterile gauze in individual packages of about 1 square yard.
6. Picric acid gauze.
7. Burn ointment—such as 5 per cent tannic acid jelly.
8. Iodine, mild.
9. Aromatic spirits of ammonia.
10. Inelastic tourniquet.
11. Scissors.
12. Three-inch splinter forceps.
13. Paper cups.
14. One-inch and 2-inch roller bandages.
15. Wire or thin board splints.
16. Castor oil or mineral oil for use in eyes. This should be sterile; it may be obtained in small tubes.

Teachers should remember that they are not medical doctors and can neither diagnose nor treat injuries. A complete record must be kept of all accidents. Accident reports should be filled out in duplicate or triplicate, depending upon the size of the school. The school teacher should keep one copy on file and send remaining copies to the administrators. Each accident report form might well include

1. The name of the person injured and date of the accident.
2. The place of the accident and condition of the environment.
3. What the teacher did for first aid.
4. Names and addresses of two or more witnesses.

Suggested Accident Report Form

Name of injured student _____ Sex _____
Age _____ Class _____ Address _____
Phone _____
Description of the accident _____
_____
_____
Condition of the environment _____
_____
What was done for first aid treatment _____
_____
_____
Name and address of witnesses _____
_____
_____
Additional comments _____
_____
Final disposition of the case _____
_____
_____

Signature _____
Date _____

SUGGESTED READINGS

American Red Cross: *First Aid Textbook*. Philadelphia, The Blakiston Company, Current ed.
Bengtsson, A.: *Adventure Playgrounds*. New York, Praeger Publishers, 1972.
Bryant, J. E.: *Don't knock your facilities*. The Physical Educator 28:74, May 1971.

Carter, J.: *How to Make Athletic Equipment.* New York, The Ronald Press, 1960.

Eriksen, F. B.: *Planning the new P. E. center.* Scholastic Coach 44:68, January 1975.

Gallahue, D.: *Developmental Play Equipment for Home and School.* New York, John Wiley & Sons, Inc., 1975.

Hewes, J.: *Build Your Own Playground.* Boston, San Francisco Book Company/Houghton Mifflin Company, 1974.

Kelsey, L. F.: *Sports facilities: the new breed.* Phi Delta Kappa 61:32, January 1975.

Kidder, W.: *A rebuilt playground.* Journal of Physical Education and Recreation. September 1976, pp. 17–18.

Lederman, A., and Trachsel, A.: *Creative Playgrounds and Recreation Centers.* New York, Praeger Publishers, 1968.

MacLean, J.: *Leisure and the Year 2000–Recreation in Modern Society.* Boston, Holbrook Press, 1972.

National Education Association: *Who Is Liable for Pupil Injuries?* Washington, D.C., 1966.

Odde, L.: *Super kids.* Journal of Physical Education and Recreation, September 1976, pp. 43–45.

SOURCES OF EQUIPMENT AND SUPPLIES

A. G. Spaulding & Brothers, 161 Sixth Ave., New York, New York

American Athlete and Educational Supply Co., 13609 Normandie, Gardena, California

Atlantic-Pacific Manufacturing Corp., 124 Atlantic Ave., Brooklyn, New York

Creative Playgrounds Corporation, 1234 East 99 Drive, R.R. 23, Terre Haute, Indiana 47802

Creative Playthings, Inc., Edenburg Road, Hightstown, New Jersey

Jayfro Plant, 30 Hynes Ave., Groton, Connecticut

The MacGregor Co., Cincinnati, Ohio

Miracle Equipment Company, Grinnell, Iowa

Nissen Medart Company, Cedar Rapids, Iowa

Paneltrol, Inc., 9 N. Colonial Ave., Wilmington, Delaware

Peterson Mat Co., Division of Wayne Iron Works, Wayne, Pennsylvania

Premier Athletic Corp., Riverdale, New Jersey

Rawlings Company, St. Louis, Missouri

Safe Fencing Company, 21 Harrison Avenue, Glens Falls, New York

W. J. Voit Rubber Corp., 45 W. 18th St., New York, New York

CHAPTER TWELVE

THE MODERN PHYSICAL EDUCATION PROGRAM

The results of a good physical education are not limited to the body alone, but may extend even to the soul itself.

Plato

INTRODUCTION

The elementary school physical education program is an integral part of the total school curriculum. As such, it incorporates a broad series of movement experiences that aid the child in developing and refining movement abilities, along with enhancing social, emotional, and mental development. The modern elementary physical education curriculum that is well planned, well taught, and based on the needs, interests, and capabilities of children is not a "frill" or "appendage" to the total school curriculum. It is a positive force in the education of the *total* child and contributes to his development in each of the following ways:

1. *Neuromuscular skills* are developed and refined in a wide variety of stability, locomotor, and manipulative movements.
2. *Physical fitness* levels, knowledge, and attitudes are enhanced.
3. *Perceptual-motor abilities* are enhanced through directed movement experiences.
4. *Social and emotional behaviors* that are valued by society are fostered.
5. *Academic concept development* is enhanced through integrating classroom concept development with the gymnasium program.
6. *Development of leisure-time abilities* is increased by movement activities that are challenging and fun.

In order to enhance these abilities the physical education program uses a variety of movement activities that serve as the vehicle by which the objectives of the program are achieved. These activities are viewed as "tools" and not as an end in themselves in the elementary school, for it is the role of the teacher to teach *children through* activities. The focal point must always be the *child* and *not* the activity.

The movement activities of the elementary physical education program are classified into five major content areas: Games and Sports, Rhythmics, Self-Testing, Camping and Outing, and Aquatics. Each of these content areas is subdivided further into secondary headings under these five major activity areas. Each of these secondary headings is further subdivided into the specific experiences that the child is engaged in, such as Red Rover, Circle Soccer, or The Shoemaker's Dance. These specific

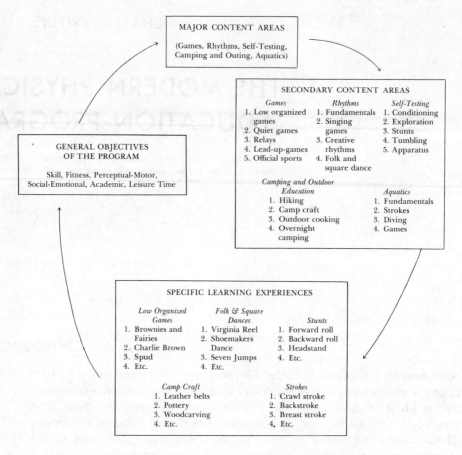

FIGURE 12-1. The elementary physical education program.

activities are selected by the teacher in order to help achieve one or more of the objectives of the program. The specific learning experiences that are used by the teacher at any one grade level are based on the needs, interests, and capabilities of the children. The program should contain a logical progression of activities moving from simple movement experiences to more complex ones. The readiness level of the children is taken into consideration before any activity is utilized. Readiness, or being "ripe" for learning, is an individual matter, and it is difficult to predict exactly when a given child or given class of children will be ready to be involved in particular games, dances, or self-testing activities. *Appropriate levels for the introduction of new skills can only be approximated.* The astute teacher will be able to select activities without relying solely on any one suggested progression. He will realize that grade level placement is relative to each individual child's level of readiness and to that of the class as a whole. A wise plan to follow is one that provides the most challenging, exciting, and educationally sound program of varied activities for the benefit of the most children.

THE CONTENT OF THE PROGRAM

The content of the elementary physical education program should be balanced and should contain a wide range of activities. The content areas of the elementary

FIGURE 12-2. Movement exploration should be a big part of the program for children. (Reprinted by permission of © J. A. Preston Corporation 1971.)

program are subdivided into a broad variety of secondary headings. There is no single best way of making these classifications. The problem has been compounded in recent years by the introduction of new types of programs that use a problem-solving approach in the teaching of movement skills. The following is one way in which the content areas of physical education are commonly subdivided:

1. Games and Sports
   a. Low organized games
   b. Quiet games
   c. Relays
   d. Lead-up games
   e. Official sports

2. Rhythmics
   a. Fundamental rhythm
   b. Singing games
   c. Creative rhythm
   d. Folk and square dance
   e. Social dance

3. Self-Testing
   a. Conditioning activities
   b. Movement exploration
   c. Stunts
   d. Tumbling
   e. Hand apparatus
   f. Large apparatus

4. Camping and Outdoor Education
   a. Hiking
   b. Campcraft
   c. Outdoor cooking
   d. Overnight camping

5. Aquatics
   a. Fundamental aquatics
   b. Swimming strokes
   c. Diving
   d. Water games
   e. Synchronized swimming

Camping, outdoor education, and aquatics should be included in the program whenever possible along with games and sports, rhythms, and self-testing activities. Outdoor living and aquatics are a basic part of our culture, for both of these activities play a major part in the recreational pursuits of the American people. The majority of elementary schools, however, are not equipped with the facilities for aquatics or outdoor education at the present time. This does not mean that these programs should not be included in the curriculum. In recent years there has been a trend to using portable swimming pools that can easily be transported on a flatbed truck and set up in a few hours. Many school systems are also utilizing swimming facilities made available by other public and private organizations. There has also been an expanded use of city parks and recreational facilities for the camping and outing portion of the program. The Future Farmers of America (4H) along with the Boy Scouts and Girl Scouts are making inroads into urban communities through the public schools that heretofore have been practically devoid of such organizations. Because such programs are not available in all or even a majority of our elementary schools does not mean that we should disregard these two content areas of the total program. On the contrary, we should continue to seek new ways and means of implementing these worthy programs in our schools.

If these content areas are included in the program, approximately 10 per cent of the physical education programs should be devoted to aquatics in the preschool and primary grades and 15 per cent to outdoor education and aquatics combined in the intermediate and upper elementary grades. These percentages should be deducted equally from the other activity areas of the program.

THE NEED FOR PROGRESSION IN THE PROGRAM

The primary consideration in planning the physical education program is the developmental level of the children. Although it is difficult to determine the exact grade placement at which specific activities are appropriate, it is possible to categorize the progression of movement-skill acquisition that children are in at various grade levels. Knowledge of each of these phases enables one to more accurately utilize a sound vertical sequence of progression in the program.

Fundamental Movement Abilities (Ages 2 to 7)

The preschool and the primary-grade child is involved in developing basic abilities in numerous fundamental locomotor, manipulative, and stability movements. It is at this phase of motor development that children learn how to run, jump, skip, throw, catch, and so on. Children explore and experiment with the movement potentials of their bodies. The fundamental movement abilities that they develop and refine during these early years form the basis on which all future motor learnings will be based.

At this level of development, the teacher should not be particularly concerned with the child's ability to perform movements with high degrees of form, skill, and accuracy. The teacher should, however, be interested in the student's ability to perform a wide range of fundamental movements in an *acceptable* manner.

General Sport Skills (Ages 8 to 10)

The intermediate-grade child (third and fourth grades) is involved in developing movement abilities in the same areas as the preschool and the primary-grade child; however, stress should now *begin* to be placed on a more skilled performance. The child begins to use larger kinds of equipment and to learn specific sport skills. Although these skills utilize the same movements that were developed during the preschool and primary years, they are now gradually adapted to specific sports. For example, the

FIGURE 12–3. Children need to develop strength in all parts of their bodies. (Courtesy of Jayfro Corporation, Montville, Connecticut.)

fundamental movement of striking is now incorporated into the sport skills of hitting a volleyball, tennis ball, softball, and golf ball and used in a variety of appropriate lead-up games, from Newcomb to volleyball, Tennis Volley to tennis, or the game Twenty-One to basketball.

Specific Sport Skills (Ages 11 to 13)

The upper elementary–grade child (fifth and sixth grades), as well as the junior high school student (this level has come to be known as the Middle School [sixth to eighth grades] in many areas of the country), is involved in the development of more specific movement skills. This phase is similar to the previous one in most ways except that the child is now physically, mentally, and emotionally ready to have greater amounts of emphasis placed on precision, form, skill, and accuracy in his performance in a wide variety of sports, dances, and other movement activities.

Specialized Sport Skills (Age 14 to Adulthood)

Not until the high school years and adulthood does the individual enter the final phase of motor development. In this stage the student selects a *few* activities from among the many movement experiences that he or she has had over the years and concentrates on enhancing abilities in them to his or her fullest potential. Participation in interscholastic or intercollegiate athletics and perfection of one's abilities in a sport for the intrinsic recreational satisfaction are examples of specialized skill development.

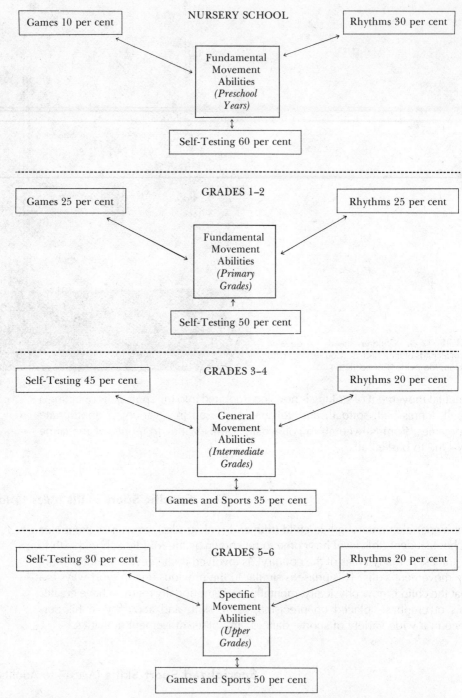

FIGURE 12-4. Suggested division of time for activities based on the developmental level of the child.

THE TOTAL PROGRAM

The total program of activities for the primary, intermediate, and upper elementary grades should be based upon the developmental characteristics of children at each particular grade level. The child's needs, interests, and capabilities are

TABLE 12–1.   SUGGESTED YEARLY TIME PERCENTAGES FOR THE ELEMENTARY PHYSICAL EDUCATION PROGRAM

	K	1	2	3	4	5	6
GAMES AND SPORTS	10%	15%	25%	30%	40%	50%	50%
Low organized games	10	15	20	10	10	0	0
Relays	0	0	5	10	5	5	5
Lead-up games	0	0	0	10	25	45	45
Official sports	0	0	0	0	0	0	0
RHYTHMICS	30%	25%	25%	25%	20%	20%	20%
Fundamentals	15	10	10	5	5	5	5
Creative rhythm	15	10	10	10	5	5	5
Folk and square dance	0	5	5	10	10	10	10
SELF-TESTING	60%	60%	50%	45%	40%	30%	30%
Conditioning	0	5	5	10	10	10	10
Movement exploration	40	30	30	15	10	0	0
Stunts	10	10	5	5	0	0	0
Tumbling	0	5	5	5	10	10	10
Hand apparatus	10	10	5	5	0	0	0
Large apparatus	0	0	5	5	10	10	10

paramount in determining what activities and how much variety and depth to include in the program. Each activity that is in the curriculum must contribute to the objectives of the program and should be appropriate to each child's particular phase of motor development as well as to that of the classes as a whole. Figure 12–4 illustrates suggested percentages of time to be spent in the three primary content areas of the program. These percentages are based on knowledge of the characteristics of children.

Table 12–1 presents a more specific breakdown of suggested time percentages for a balanced program from kindergarten through grade 6. It should be noted that there is no differentiation between boys and girls in this breakdown and that there is no indication that boys and girls should be separated at the fourth grade as has been done traditionally in the past. It is obvious that there are numerous physical differences between boys and girls, but in the elementary school *similarities* between them far outweigh the differences. Classes can be effectively combined in most areas of the program, particularly in self-testing activities, dance, aquatics, camping and outdoor education, gymnastics, and other individual activities. Coeducational instruction and play in contact sports is not recommended, particularly at the upper elementary level.

PLANNING THE PROGRAM

The percentages presented in Table 12–1 are merely *suggested* total time allotments for various types of activities at each grade level in the curriculum. These percentages are based on knowledge of the general developmental level of children at each grade level. There are, however, many outside factors that influence what is included in the curriculum as well as how much of it is included. Each of the following factors must be taken into account prior to planning the program:

1. Ability of the teacher in presenting materials, demonstrating, and correcting movement errors.
2. Educational goals of the teachers, administrators, and taxpayers.
3. Facilities available.
4. Equipment available.

5. Geographic area.
6. Number of pupils in the class.
7. Length of class period.
8. Number of times classes meet per week.
9. Pupil's estimated level of ability.

The following are the five steps that should be followed when planning the program:

General Objectives

Once the preoperational decisions and survey of the factors listed above have been made, actual construction of the curriculum may begin. The first step is to determine the general objectives of the program. General objectives are just that. They are broad general outcomes that you as the teacher have established for the learner to achieve. These objectives might well involve the development of the child in each of the following areas: (1) movement skills, (2) levels of fitness, (3) perceptual-motor efficiency, (4) social-emotional development, (5) academic understandings, and (6) constructive use of leisure time.

Specific Objectives

Once the general objectives of the program have been established, the specific objectives should be determined. The specific objectives that the teacher wishes the students to accomplish within the program may be stated in *relatively broad product terms,* which might well include:

1. Good health, happiness, character, and democratic spirit.
2. Leadership and "followership" skills.
3. Basic skills in as many kinds of activities as possible.
4. In each child, abilities to plan, conduct, and evaluate the things he can do as an individual and a class member.
5. Good safety habits.
6. Proper attitudes toward playing, winning, and losing.
7. The ability to reason and to give directions.
8. Independence.
9. Courage and initiative.
10. Vigor and physical fitness.
11. Skills in games and activities suitable for after-school play.

The trend now, however, is to also state specific objectives in terms of the *process* (behavior) that the child must be involved in in order to satisfy the above *product* objectives. These objectives have three important characteristics. (1) They are observable, (2) they are measurable, and (3) they establish the criterion by which their achievement may be evaluated. The following are samples of some process objectives that may be found in the elementary school program. The student will be able to

1. Correctly perform two consecutive forward rolls from a squat to a squat position.
2. Perform three types of soccer kicks.
3. Recognize the difference between a zone defense and a man-to-man defense in basketball.
4. Execute three out of five stunts involving inverted support.
5. Distinguish the difference between an even and an uneven beat in a musical composition and demonstrate it through appropriate movements.

Content

After the specific objectives of the program have been determined, the next step is to determine the general content areas of the program that will be used to help satisfy each of these objectives. For example, the teacher will determine whether to utilize games, rhythms, or self-testing activities to enhance the running abilities of first grade boys and girls. This stage in planning only requires that the *general content headings and their subheadings* be determined. The following stage involves the actual selection of specific activities from within each of the selected content areas.

Specific Learning Experiences

This is the stage of planning in which the actual activities engaged in by the child are selected. These activities are directly related to the content areas that are being used to satisfy the objectives of the lesson. For example, the chasing and tagging games of Brownies and Fairies, and Crows and Cranes might be used in the lesson along with a variety of movement exploration and problem-solving activities in order to help enhance the child's running abilities.

Evaluation

Evaluation is the final step in planning the program. Evaluation is an important part of the total process, for it is only through evaluation that one can determine whether one's pupils have achieved the objectives of the program. Evaluation also serves as a method of determining the strong and weak points of your program and your teaching. It may take many forms and be either subjective or objective in nature (see Chapter 15, Evaluating the Results).

The important thing to remember in planning the curriculum is that each of the five steps is directly related to the others and that the entire process proceeds in an orderly sequential manner (see Fig. 12–5).

SUGGESTED PLACEMENT OF ACTIVITIES

In the preschool and primary grades, emphasis should be placed upon including activities in the program that develop fundamental movement abilities. Young children are not interested in or capable of learning how to perform intricate movements or game skills. They are more interested in being active and just plain moving. Consequently, movement exploration activities are especially appropriate for younger children. At the intermediate and upper elementary grade levels, children are involved in developing general and specific movement abilities. Emphasis should now begin to be placed on skill and accuracy. More direct teaching should be used because the pupils will receive greater pleasure from their physical activities program when they are motivated and encouraged to move more skillfully.

Instead of including a variety of activities in the beginning of the school year, the teacher should start with those familiar to the pupils and gradually introduce new material into the program. He should go from the known to the unknown, reviewing the familiar and gradually including the new in a developmentally sound sequence of progression. The following is a list of activities suitable for inclusion at various ability

	MONDAY	WEDNESDAY	FRIDAY
W E E K 1	Soccer Film REVIEW: Kicking 　　　　　Trapping	NEW: instep kick 　　　　inside of foot kick 　　　　outside of foot kick 　　　　sole of foot trap 　　　　double knee trap ACTIVITIES: 　　　kicking drills 　　　line soccer	REVIEW: Wednesday's lesson NEW:　　dribbling ACTIVITIES: 　　　　dribble relays
W E E K 2	REVIEW: Friday's lesson NEW:　　Passing and 　　　　Tackling ACTIVITIES: 　　　Skill drills 　　　Alley soccer	REVIEW: Monday's lesson NEW:　　Heading ACTIVITIES: 　　　Heading drills 　　　Alley soccer	NEW:　　Positioning ACTIVITIES: 　　　Crab soccer
W E E K 3	REVIEW: Friday's lesson NEW:　　goal kicking 　　　　free kick ACTIVITIES: 　　　skill drills 　　　crab soccer	NEW:　　basic rules ACTIVITY: 　　　six man soccer	REVIEW: rules NEW:　　strategy ACTIVITIES: 　　　six man soccer
W E E K 4	REVIEW: all skills briefly NEW:　　modified soccer	NEW:　　Skill testing 　　　　1. objective 　　　　2. subjective ACTIVITIES: 　　　modified soccer	REVIEW: finish testing ACTIVITIES: 　　　modified soccer

FIGURE 12–5.　Sample soccer unit plan for 6th grade.

levels. *Level I* activities are considered appropriate for boys and girls from kindergarten through the third grade. *Level II* activities are generally appropriate for children in grades 4, 5, and 6. *Two important things must be kept in mind before referring to this list. First, these activities are intended to serve as a means of achieving the objectives of the program and not as ends in themselves. Second, the level placement of these activities represents only an approximation of the child's suitable level of readiness for learning them.*

Level I (Grades 1, 2, and 3)

Rhythmic Activities
Folk Dances
　　I See You
　　Shoemaker's Dance
　　Danish Dance of Greeting
　　Chimes of Dunkirk
　　Bleking
　　Kinder Polka
　　Gustaf's Skoal
　　Seven Jumps
　　The Crested Hen
　　Broom Dance
　　Rovenacka
　　Polka
　　Ace of Diamonds
　　Green Sleeves
　　Indian War Dance
　　Norwegian Mountain Dance
　　Tantoli
　　Finger Polka

Singing Games
　　A Hunting We Will Go
　　Farmer in the Dell
　　How Do You Do, My Partner
　　London Bridge
　　Hokey Pokey
　　Muffin Man
　　Soldier Boy
　　Hippety Hop to the Barber Shop
　　Thread Follows the Needle
　　I'm Very, Very Tall
　　Old King Cole
　　Jenny Crack Corn
　　Captain Jinks
　　Indian Braves
　　Looby Lou
　　Pop Goes the Weasel
　　Rig-A-Jig
　　The Needle's Eye

Level I (Grades 1, 2, and 3) (Continued)

Movement Exploration
Explore locomotor movements
Explore manipulative movements
Explore stability movements
Explore combinations of movements
Interpret action words
Interpret moods
Interpret feelings
Imitate objects
Imitate events
Interpret song titles
Explore force
Explore level
Explore direction

Games of Low Organization
Have You Seen My Sheep?
Crows and Cranes
Dodgeball
Fox and Geese
Flying Dutchman
Cat and Rat
Squirrel and Trees
I Say Stoop
Slap Jack
Circle Pass Ball
Old Mother Witch
Jump the Brook
Statues
Do This—Do That
Back to Back
Midnight
Call Ball
Charley Over the Water
Steal the Bacon
Poison Tag
Garden Scamp
Squat Tag
Red Light
Wood Tag
Line Dodgeball
Caboose
Stride Ball
Bull in the Ring
Three Deep
Boiler Burst
New York
Target Throw
Last Couple Out
Hill Dill
Circle Club Bowls
Hopscotch
Loose Caboose

Stunts, Tumbling, and Self-testing Activities
Log roll
Forward roll

Push-up from knees
Running
Jumping
Activities on the jungle gym
Bear walk
Duck walk
Elephant walk
Seal walk
One-leg hop, changing directions
Rope jumping
Wheelbarrow
Measuring worm
Crab walk
Leap frog
Rocking horse
Chicken fight
Knee dip
Cartwheel
Coffee grinder
Push-up
Cross leg stand
Foot clap
Walrus walk
Backward and forward roll
Chimney
Fish hawk dive
Twister
The swan

Mimetics and Story Plays
Rope jumping
Figure skating
Branding cows
Fishing
Bicycling
Acting out sports
Animals
Follow the Leader
Building a House
The Trip to the Country
Cowboys and Indians
Christmas tree and Santa
Playing in the Wind
Going to the Grocery Store
Modes of travel

Dance Fundamentals
Accent
Tempo
Intensity
Rhythmic pattern
Dances created to songs, poems, and stories

Team Games
Soccer keep away
Capture the flag
Kickball

Team Games (Continued)
- Dodgeball
- Boundary Ball
- Kick It and Run
- Throw It and Run
- Corner Dodgeball
- Long Base
- Line Soccer
- Circle Dodgeball
- Steal the Bacon

Relays
- All four relay
- Throw and sit relay
- Down and up relay
- Soccer dribble relay
- Run and throw back relay
- Automobile tire relays
- Basketball pass
- Over-and-Under
- Three-legged relay
- Dizzy-Izzy
- Basic sport-skill relays

Level II (Grades 4, 5, and 6)

Rhythmic Activities
Folk Dance
- Minuet
- Broom Dance
- Highland Schottische
- Seven Jumps
- Sellinger's Round
- Sailor's Hornpipe
- Maine Mixer
- Starlight Schottische
- Irish Washerwoman
- Varsovienne
- Kerry Dance
- Troika
- Sextur
- Trip to Helsinki
- Sicilian Tarantella
- Sicilian Circle
- Irish Song Dance
- Jesse Polka
- Badger Gavote
- Raatikko
- Cherkessia
- Road to the Isles
- Jarabe Tapatio
- Trilby
- Laces and Graces
- Ranger Polka

Square Dance
- Grand March
- Virginia Reel
- Red River Valley
- Take a Little Peek
- Jump Jim Joe
- Soldier's Joy
- Oh, Johnny
- Sally Goodin
- Around That Couple, Take a Peek
- Chase the Snake
- Swing the Girl Behind You
- Arkansas
- Arkansas Traveler

- Birdie in the Cage
- Heel and Toe Polka
- Cotton-Eyed Joe
- Rye Waltz
- Dive for the Oyster

Dance Fundamentals
- Walk, run, jump, hop to even rhythm
- Skip, slide, gallop, leap to uneven rhythm
- Creative movements of work, play, sports
- Creative dance to records
- Waltz
- Schottische
- Fox trot
- Waltz Hesitation
- Skip, slide, gallop
- Jump and hop
- Space aspects of movement
- Striking and dodging
- Dance creations
- Slide
- Schottische variations
- Waltz variations
- Propulsive and sustained movements

Games of Low Organization
- Hook-on
- Streets and Alleys
- Vis-a-Vis
- Animal Chase
- Red Rover
- May I
- Charades
- Skin the Snake
- Merry-Go-Round
- Running
- Jumping
- Keep It Up
- Pinch-O
- Cross Tag
- Fire on the Mountain
- Wood Tag
- Buddy Spud
- Keep Away

Level II (Grades 4, 5, and 6) (Continued)

Games of Low Organization (Continued)
Stealing Sticks
Ante Over
Horseshoes
Hand Tennis
Box Hockey
Tug-of-War
Giant Volleyball
Overtake Softball
Long Base
Target Toss

Camping and Outing
Hiking
Compass reading
Trail blazing
Fire building—tepee
Wood gathering
Menu planning
Outdoor cooking
Garbage disposal
Blanket rolling
Crafts from native materials
Camp project
Fishing
Fire building—reflector oven, crisscross,
   travels
Wood chopping
Wood sawing
Fishing-hunting
Simple shelter construction
Camp soil conservation project
Overnight camping
Bicycle trip camping
Use of two-handed axe
Making things with knife, with hatchet
Overnight camping utilizing all skills
   learned for sleeping, playing, and cooking
   in the woods
Fire building—altar fire, charcoal stove
Fishing, hunting, trapping
Construction of three types of shelter
Lashing

Team Games
Soccer Dodgeball
Pin Soccer
End Ball
Club Snatch
Bronco Tag
Floor Hockey
Prisoner's Base
Nine-Court Keep Away

Field Ball
Skills of Baseball
Progressive Dodgeball
Volleyball
Schlagball
Base Football
Softball
Touch Football
Double Dodgeball
Basketball—Twenty-One, Horse
Drop In, Drop Out
Circle Goal Shooting
Basketball
Soccer
Tennis
Speedball
Captain Ball
Hit Pin Baseball

Relays
Rescue relay
Rope climb relay
Kangaroo relay
Leapfrog relay
Run, throw, catch relay
Goal shooting relay
Zigzag relay
Skip rope relay
Family relay
Rabbit jump relay
Soccer relay
Basketball couple passing
Goal shooting relays
Football pass couple relay
Siamese twin relay
Jump the stick relay
Human croquet
Rope jumping relay
Running at increased distances
Squat, jump relay
Juggle relay
Pony express relay
Base running relay
Shuttle-pass-soccer relay
Obstacle dribble relay
Dribble and pass relay
Bounce, pass, and shoot relay
Base-running relays

Stunts, Tumbling, and Self-testing Activities
Chinning
Rope jumping
Goal shooting
Soccer kick for distance
Soccer kick for accuracy
One-leg-squat

*Stunts, Tumbling and Self-Testing
Activities* (Continued)
  Push and pull ups
  Russian bear dance
  Jump the Stick
  Hand wrestle
  Human bridge
  High kick
  Dive
  Handstand
  Seal slap
  Jump over stool
  Track and field events
  Indian leg wrestle
  Stick wrestle
  Rope skipping for speed and time
  Bar hanging by arms, knees
  Turn over on low-bar
  Throwing, batting, kicking for accuracy
  Throwing, batting, kicking for distance
  Base running
  Standing broad jump
  Sprinting
  The top
  Knee spring
  Handstand
  Floor dip
  Dives
  Pyramids
  Simple apparatus

Aquatics (Minimum Skills)
  Fear elimination
  Floating
  Crawl
  Backstroke
  Sidestroke
  Elementary diving
  Elementary life saving
  Diving

  Breast stroke
  Advanced skills in all swimming strokes

Track and Field
  50-yard dash
  Standing long jump
  Pull up and/or jump and reach
  Softball throw for distance and accuracy
  Obstacle relays
  Triple jump
  Running long jump
  High jump
  100-yard dash
  440-yard dash
  600-yard dash
  9-minute run
  Broad jump
  Low hurdles
  Track meet
  100-yard shuttle relay
  Special obstacle relays

Elementary Gymnastics
  Conditioning and free exercises
  Balance beam
  Stall bars
  Stairs
  Swinging and traveling rings
  Side horse
  Rope climbing
  Foot and leg climb
  Stirrup climb
  Rolled mat activities
  Still rings
  Elementary horizontal bar
  Fundamentals for using the buck, horse,
    Swedish box, single springboard
  Parallel bars
  Trampoline
  Balance board

DEVELOPING THE PROGRAM

Once the general and specific objectives of the program have been established, the content of the program and its specific learning experiences should be determined. The first step is to develop a total curriculum plan. The total plan is a very general outline that usually takes the form of a chart that indicates what will be covered throughout the school year at each grade level. This total curriculum outline is sometimes referred to as a *scope and sequence chart*. It tells you three important things about the program:

1. The scope or range of activities covered throughout the year at each grade level.
2. The sequence of progression of the program on a grade-to-grade basis, proceeding from fundamental movement abilities to general and specific sport-skill abilities in a developmentally sound progression.

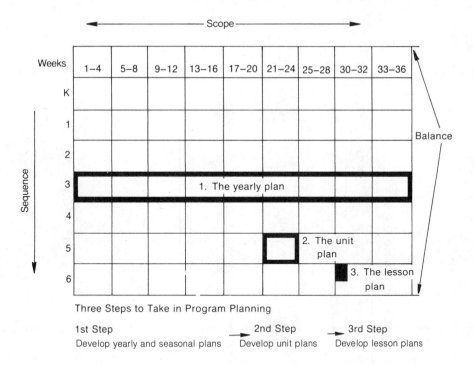

Three Steps to Take in Program Planning

1st Step	2nd Step	3rd Step
Develop yearly and seasonal plans	Develop unit plans	Develop lesson plans

3. The balance of the program in its use of a wide variety of game, rhythm, and self-testing activities, along with camping and aquatics whenever possible.

The Yearly and Seasonal Plan

The yearly plan represents the scope of activities to be included in the curriculum at any one grade level for an entire school year or season. It is more detailed than the total curriculum outline and generally reflects a seasonal influence that is based either on climatic conditions that permit or prevent conducting classes outdoors or the time of year in which particular activities are traditionally engaged in. The yearly plan should provide an outline of the skills to be engaged in by the child in each particular unit of instruction (see Table 12–2).

The Unit and Weekly Plan

The unit plan is developed after the yearly and seasonal plans. It represents one particular area of instruction (such as touch football, gymnastics, or track and field) to be covered in a block of time, usually from three to six weeks long in the elementary school. The unit plan is broken down into the particular skills that will be covered each week and the activities that will be used to develop these skills. Although the unit plan can be organized in numerous ways, basically each should contain the following information:

1. The title of the unit.
2. The general and specific objectives to be achieved by the learner.
3. The skills to be taught and the desired sequence.
4. The specific activities to be used to develop these skills.
5. The equipment needed.

TABLE 12-2.   A SAMPLE YEARLY PLAN FOR SIXTH GRADE BOYS AND GIRLS

Weeks	1–4	5–8	9–12	13–16	17–20	21–24	25–28	30–32	33–36
	Class organization	Touch football	Soccer	Rhythmics	Gymnastics	Basketball	Volleyball	Softball	Track and field
G R A D E 6	Skill and fitness testing	Passing Catching Punting Centering Blocking Pass defense Rules Strategy	Kicking Trapping Dribbling Passing Heading Tackling Rules Strategy	Creative rhythmics Dances without partners Folk dance	Parallel bars Side horse Tumbling Pyramids Free exercise	Dribbling Shooting Pivoting Passing Rules Strategy	Serving Overhead pass Setting Digging Spiking Rotating Rules Strategy	Batting Pitching Throwing Fielding Catching Rules Strategy	Long jump High jump Dashes 600-yard run Hurdles Relays
	Review of skills from previous year								

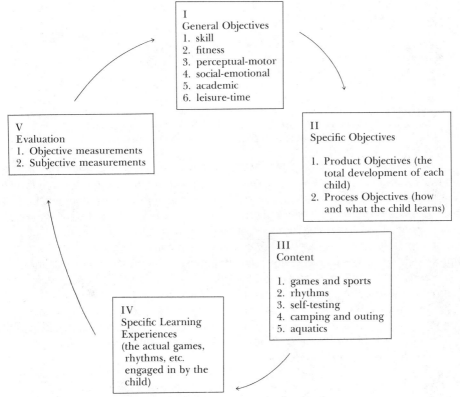

FIGURE 12–6.   The five primary steps in planning the program.

6. The methods of evaluating the students' achievements of the objectives.
7. Sources of information for teachers and students.

Figure 12–6 provides an illustration of a unit plan in soccer for sixth grade boys and girls that has been further subdivided into weekly plans.

The Daily Lesson Plan

Careful planning is basic to good teaching every day. Although all plans should be flexible, they must be made with a definite purpose to shape all learning experiences to the needs and development of each child *and* to the society of which he is a vital part.

Lesson plans are both time and energy savers. They help to assure progression and the building of skill upon skill through a carefully planned and progressively challenging school curriculum. They also

1. Lead to a faster setting of goals and the attainment of education, group, and individual objectives.
2. Help keep all program offerings in a proper balance, so that no one area is overemphasized (such as team relays) to the detriment of another area (such as movement exploration).
3. Make the teacher feel more secure and confident in her role as an educator who does teach something new to every child every time each class meets.
4. Spur on the learner's interest and ability to accept and master greater learning challenges.
5. Clarify thought and, through periodic review and practice, help make learning more accurate and permanent.

6. Set desirable patterns for students to follow when developing their own study and work habits, as well as when planning their own goals.
7. Ensure that during the regular teacher's absence, the substitute instructor can carry out previously planned lessons, thus keeping learning continuous.
8. Provide for periodic measurement at times that are best for the evaluation of certain kinds of learning results.
9. Take into account pupil readiness to move on to new learning experiences.
10. Aid in making the best use of each previous class period for increased pupil learning.
11. Help teachers develop and improve teaching skill.
12. Can be used as evidence to parents, administrators, and others that education plans have been devised and that students are being presented new materials.

Daily lesson plans enable a teacher to make the best use of each class period, are both an energy and time saver, and assure progression in the program. Each lesson should be a meaningful experience through which the pupils learn something new as well as refine previously learned materials and skills. *Build skill upon skill* is a motto recommended for all teachers and, most especially, for physical educators. Writing comprehensive lesson plans out on 5 × 7 inch cards and storing them along with the appropriate unit plans is an excellent way of keeping an up-to-date record of what you have done. It also allows the teacher to quickly, easily, and neatly update lessons by removing outdated or poor lessons and inserting new ones.

Daily lesson plans should include the objectives, needed equipment, techniques for linking yesterday's lesson with that of today, new activities to be taught with a time allotment given for each, and techniques for evaluating progress.

A well-planned and conducted lesson will provide for

1. Maximal participation in meaningful activities for all pupils in the group.
2. The growth and development of each class member in accordance with stated objectives and educational goals.
3. Increased pupil interest in, appreciation of, and enthusiasm for physical education.
4. A variety of well-selected activities that have educational value and lead toward more abundance and healthier living for the future as well as the present.
5. Opportunities to correlate and integrate physical education with health and safety education, as well other subject areas in the curriculum.
6. Opportunity for self-evaluation of daily accomplishments.

Teacher _____

School _____ Class _____ Date _____ Lesson _____
Unit: _____

Specific Objectives	Procedures To Be Followed	Time Allotted	Formations To Be Used	Skill Analysis

Equipment and Materials: _____
Methods of Evaluation: _____
References: _____

FIGURE 12-7. A well-balanced program that is well taught can and will produce physically, morally, mentally, and emotionally fit youths and adults. (Courtesy of Dr. Joan Tillotson, Plattsburgh Public Schools, Plattsburgh, New York.)

Lesson plans enable the teacher to review and relate to overall program objectives, serve as a review and help in the preparation of the coming lesson, provide an organized and progressive procedure that aids in class interest and individual motivation, often help prevent disciplinary problems from arising, help the teacher to emphasize important points and skill elements, and aid in evaluating teacher as well as pupil growth. There are many formats possible. You should develop a plan that is suitable to your needs.

COMPETENCIES TO BE DEVELOPED

What is taught at each grade level depends largely upon where pupils are on the ladder of their social, emotional, mental, and physical development. First graders who have been to kindergarten are often ready for activities usually taught on the second grade level, whereas those who have not been are more apt to respond to activities thought best for four year old children. Likewise, pupils transferring from one school to another even in the same city often find they are ahead or lag far behind their classmates. Certainly much experimentation is needed to determine more satisfactorily (other than by expert opinion) what should be taught where. Although there is a wide gap between the skills that a first grader and sixth grader can do, there is not always such a gap when comparing second with third or fourth with fifth graders. Consequently, devising a list of competencies that should be developed at each grade level is wiser and leads to a sounder educational program in all grades. The following table (Table 12-3) of competencies can be used as an idea springboard for doing so.

TABLE 12-3.   COMPETENCIES TO BE DEVELOPED[1]

Optimal Physical Qualities of Fitness (Developed to Maximal Capacity)	Grades					
	1*	2*	3*	4*	5*	6*
Strength	S†	S	M‡	M	Ex§	Ex
Power	S	S	M	M	Ex	Ex
Endurance	S	S	M	M	Ex	Ex
Flexibility	S	S	M	M	Ex	Ex
Agility	S	S	M	M	Ex	Ex
Functional Skill and Coordination	*	*	*	*	*	*
Locomotion (walking, running, skipping, hopping, jumping, climbing, galloping, sliding)	M	M	Ex	Ex	Ex	Ex
Balancing	M	M	M	Ex	Ex	Ex
Rhythmic Response in Movement						
Moving to a rhythmic sound	M	M	M	Ex	Ex	Ex
Moving in simple patterns	M	M	Ex	Ex	Ex	Ex
Skip, slide, polka, schottische, step-hop, waltz, fox-trot, two-step	S	S	M	M	Ex	Ex
Patterns—honor, swing, circle, allemande, do-si-do, grand right and left balance, promenade, ladies' chain, right and left through			S	M	Ex	Ex
Ball Skills						
Rolling	S	S	M	M	Ex	Ex
Tossing	S	S	M	M	Ex	Ex
Throwing—distance and accuracy	S	S	M	M	Ex	Ex
Dribbling and juggling			S	S	M	M
Volleying			S	S	M	M
Goal shooting			S	S	M	M
Kicking, dribbling, trapping		S	S	M	M	
Striking—hand, bat, club		S	S	S	M	
Rope Jumping	S	M	Ex	Ex	Ex	Ex
Beginning Swimming				S	M	M
Creativity, Exploration, and Self-Expression	*	*	*	*	*	*
Efficient and Attractive Posture	*	*	*	*	*	*
Standing	M	M	M	Ex	Ex	Ex
Sitting	M	M	M	Ex	Ex	Ex
Moving	M	M	M	Ex	Ex	Ex
Increasing Emotional Maturity	*	*	*	*	*	*
Social Adaptability	*	*	*	*	*	*

*It is possible to play and work harder and for longer periods in the upper elementary ages.
†S = Some competency.
‡M = Much competency.
§Ex = Excellent competency.

[1] Reprinted by permission of The President's Council Program. *Youth Fitness.* Revised ed. Washington, D.C., Superintendent of Documents, 1963.

FIGURE 12–8.   You can use simple equipment such as this in a variety of ways if you are a creative teacher. (Courtesy of Snitz Manufacturing Company, East Troy, Wisconsin.)

PROGRAM IMPROVEMENT SUGGESTIONS

The following is a list of suggestions for improving programs in elementary schools:

Grades Kindergarten to 3

1. Stress activities in which movement exploration and experimentation play a vital role.
2. Provide the children with a wide variety of locomotor, manipulative, and stability experiences that are designed to enhance their perceptual-motor functioning.
3. Stress rhythmic activities and combinations of locomotor movement, such as hops with runs or skips with slides.
4. Provide many large group games and a happy, secure, noncompetitive social climate in grades 1 and 2.
5. Use a wide variety of exploratory movement skills with many kinds of equipment—climbing and jumping ropes, objects of various heights from which to jump, the balance beam, and stilts or tin-can walkers. (All of this equipment can be easily improvised.)
6. Use variously sized balls for developing throwing and catching skill.
7. Stress big-muscle activities such as running, jumping, hopping, and skipping in grades 1 and 2; begin skill refinement in grade 3.
8. Introduce a variety of small-group games for six to eight pupils, such as Crows and Cranes or Froggie in the Sea.
9. Stress climbing, hanging, and balancing activities.
10. Develop arm strength in stunts and tumbling activities such as wheelbarrow races, kneeling-position half push-ups, and inch-worm relays.
11. Use dual and combative stunts to develop strength, such as Pull Across the Line, or Indian Leg or Arm Wrestle.
12. Stress creative play; provide for free play at least twice weekly in grades 1 and 2.
13. Avoid highly competitive activities, for children during these formative years will often push themselves too far.

14. In the second and third grades, use many chasing and fleeing games that require agility and change of direction.
15. Help each child "feel" through rhythmic movements the differences between up and down, quick and slow, soft and hard.
16. Provide opportunities for each child to experiment with ball skills, using such activities as O'Leary, and throwing a ball against a wall and catching it; start modified basketball shooting in the third grade using a volleyball and a covered ring.
17. Discuss play situations, "cheating," "taking turns," and so forth with the class; let each express what he feels, sees, and thinks about these.
18. Provide opportunities to keep hands and bodies busy in grades 1 and 2; change activities often.
19. Have children help to make rules regarding safety, equipment use, and other rules they are expected to understand and obey.
20. Begin swimming instruction if at all possible. If not, urge the parents to do so. Provide shorter periods for those not physically able to keep up with the group, or those who chill easily.
21. Stress good posture, health habits, and desirable social and developmental activities.
22. Provide many opportunities for each child to make suggestions by having free-play choices.
23. Proceed slowly with skill development; stress playing for fun.
24. Emphasize the need of safety in play, in work, in the home, in coming to and from school, and while in school.

Grades 4 to 6

1. Use longer activity periods in which skills receive more stress.
2. Provide opportunities for groups and individuals to release emotions and tensions through more rugged physical activities, and cheering one's team.
3. Stress vigorous exercise; help pupils know how exercise assists growth; alternate strenuous activities with less active ones.
4. Teach good body mechanics, posture, and movement in daily life as well as in sports.
5. Gradually emphasize movement accuracy and good form; use a wide variety of throwing, catching, and hitting activities through lead-up games to softball, volleyball, and basketball.
6. Avoid highly competitive activities; stress good sportsmanship, player consideration, and team loyalty.
7. Use many activities that involve rhythm and balancing; teach social, folk, and square dances.
8. Give as much individual attention and help to each pupil as possible in skill development tasks; develop good individual and group support.
9. Teach a variety of activities using apparatus for chinning, vaulting, balancing, and hand traveling.
10. Have a more strenuous class program for every pupil.
11. Provide for the need of belonging through team and squad games and relays.
12. Keep competition at the children's level; provide many kinds of intramural activities for all pupils.
13. Emphasize tumbling, body dynamics, swimming, and rhythmics for girls and boys.
14. Stress track and field events for both sexes.
15. Seize upon "teachable moments" in class for health and safety instruction and shaping life values.

SUGGESTIONS FOR ESTABLISHING A GOOD PROGRAM

In recent years there has been a concentrated effort at establishing quality elementary physical education programs and informing the American people of the contribution that physical education makes to their youth. In 1971 a Physical Education Public Information (PEPI) project was initiated by the American Alliance for Health, Physical

Education, and Recreation.[2] It is the avowed purpose of this project to develop public awareness of the value of physical education. Regional and state PEPI coordinators have promoted this public awareness through news releases, spot announcements on radio and television, local workshops, and printed information sheets. The Texas Education Agency has produced an interesting and informative information sheet entitled *Physical Education in the Elementary School*[3] that tells why physical education is important, the characteristics of a good program, and how to establish a quality program. The following is a list of suggested guidelines for setting up a good program from this manual:

1. Have an up-to-date course of study.
2. Provide vigorous activities for each class.
3. Develop units in progressive sequence.
4. Provide an organized program on a daily basis.
5. Use the achievement standards in the Texas Agency elementary physical education guides.
6. Direct efforts toward all children's attaining a high level of fitness.
7. Provide either indoor or outdoor apparatus for instruction.
8. Provide suitable instructional supplies for primary and upper elementary children.
9. Have marked areas (hopscotch, four-square, and so on) for activities.
10. Set up a central area for equipment and supplies.
11. Maintain the same class size as in language arts or mathematics.
12. Provide an adapted program for the underdeveloped child.
13. Provide a progressive jogging program leading up to the 12-minute run-walk.

PROGRAM GUIDES

Although most states and local school systems have courses of study available as well as teaching guides, such materials should be used mainly as idea-launching pads.

---

[2]Biles, F.: *PEPI*. Journal of Health, Physical Education, and Recreation, September 1971, pp. 53–55.
[3]*Physical Education in the Elementary School*. Texas Education Agency, Austin, Texas, 1972.

FIGURE 12–9. Outdoor play equipment made of sturdy treated lumber is becoming increasingly popular. (Courtesy of Creative Playgrounds Corporation, Terre Haute, Indiana.)

FIGURE   12–10. Wood equipment is attractive and durable and can be used for a great variety of activities. (Courtesy of Creative Playgrounds Corporation, Terre Haute, Indiana.)

An ideal physical education class is one devised and conducted skillfully for each particular class in each particular school, for no course of study or teaching guide will "fit" (or even be fit) for every child. However, such materials do have value, for from them teachers can build upon and create a new and better framework for their own unique teaching situation and class groups.

Every teacher is a builder—a superior, average, or poor one. The superior one will design and construct a magical place in which children have wondrous experiences of joy and accomplishment. The average builder will stick closely to a preplanned blueprint made for and by someone else, and the results will be about the same as everybody else's, or just another house. The poor builder is totally unaware that somewhere a blueprint does exist, or even of where to start to devise one. Her house is never built, and eager pupils who are longing to accomplish something merely mill around instead feeling disinterested, disillusioned, and disappointed.

Educators seldom capitalize upon their gains. They could do so by capitalizing upon what has been accomplished before, instead of going back to a starting point again and again. Already devised and obtainable courses of study, teaching guides, and other materials are, in reality, such starting points. Like medicine, they work the best miracles when taken in just the right amounts, for if a little is good, more may *not* be necessary.

SUGGESTED READINGS

AAHPER: *This Is Physical Education.* Washington, D.C., 1966.
AAHPER: *Desirable Athletic Competition for Children of Elementary School Age.* Washington, D.C., 1968.
AAHPER: *Promising Practices in Elementary School Physical Education.* Washington, D.C., 1968.
AAHPER: *Essentials of a Quality Elementary School Physical Education Program.* Washington, D.C., 1970.
Dowell, L.: *Strategies for Teaching Physical Education.* Englewood Cliffs, New Jersey, Prentice-Hall, Inc., 1975.
Goodlad, J. I., Von Stoephasius, R., and Klein, M. F.: *The Changing School Curriculum.* The Fund for the Advancement of Education, 477 Madison Avenue, New York, New York, 1966.

LaPorte, R.: *The Physical Education Curriculum (A National Program).* 8th ed. Los Angeles, California, The College Book Store, 1976.
MacKenzie, M. M.: *Toward A New Curriculum in Physical Education.* New York, McGraw-Hill, Inc., 1969.
Mager, R. J.: *Preparing Instructional Objectives.* Belmont, California, Fearon Publishers, 1962.
Nixon, J., and Jewett, A.: *Physical Education Curriculum.* New York, The Ronald Press, 1974.
Taba, H.: *Curriculum Development: Theory and Practice.* New York, Harcourt, Brace & World, 1962.
The New Physical Education. Journal of Health, Physical Education, and Recreation, September 1971, pp. 24–39.

PART FOUR

THUS A CHILD LEARNS

. . . Thus a child learns; by wiggling skills through his fingers and toes into himself; by soaking up habits and attitudes of those around him; by pushing and pulling his own world.

. . . Thus a child learns; more through trial than error, more through pleasure than pain, more through experience than suggestion, more through suggestion than direction.

. . . Thus a child learns; through affection, through love, through patience, through understanding, through belonging, through doing, through being.

. . . Day by day the child comes to know a little bit of what you know; to think a little bit of what you think; to understand your understanding. That which you dream and believe and are, in truth, becomes the child.

Frederick J. Moffitt, Chief,
Bureau of Instructional Supervision
New York State Department of Education

THE HOW

CHAPTER THIRTEEN

TECHNIQUES OF SUCCESSFUL TEACHING

If I hear it, I forget
If I see it, I remember
If I do it, I know!

An Old Chinese Proverb

To teach means to guide, lead, inspire, share, and discover with others. Success in this all-important profession is due largely to skill in human engineering and to one's professional preparation. Those best prepared to teach know something not only about *what* to teach but a great deal more about *how* to go about it. The latter comes from experience, experimenting, and tailoring once-learned principles and the methods used by admired former teachers to fit one's own unique situation. To teach means also to inspire others to want to seek learning treasures. To educate means bringing forth latent capabilities and to "lead forth."

Good teaching results when each instructor, through the use of teacher-guided group planning, helps individuals (1) set up desired group goals and individual objectives to be reached, (2) select and see values in materials to be learned in order to obtain these desired ends, (3) share planned, purposeful learning experiences, and (4) evaluate the final results in light of sought goals. Through the use of a variety of well-mastered methods of instruction, the skilled teacher will see pupils improve in skills; make positive attitude changes; deepen and broaden understanding of themselves, others, and life itself; and be able to use what they are learning in their daily lives.

TEACHING METHODS

Just as adequate professional preparation is the prerequisite for successful teaching, so also is the careful planning of each lesson. This can be done best by the whole-part-whole method, in which the teacher begins by (1) planning the course content for a semester or a single unit, (2) devising plans for each class period of this larger whole, and (3) evaluating the results when the unit is completed.

Group plans are the prerequisites for successful group experiences. Consequently, the teacher and pupils (rather than the pupils and teacher) should set up desired individual goals and class objectives, choose the materials to be mastered, share a teaching-learning experience, and measure their success or failure to obtain their goals.

263

Each of the many teaching methods is valuable, but there are times when one is superior to another. The best one to use depends upon ever-changing factors, which the successful instructor learns to sense. Certainly, any method is worthy of use only if desired results can be obtained through it and if it is socially approved. Also, a teaching method that has proved to be successful for one teacher may be a failure when used by another.

TEACHING APPROACHES

The traditional, exploratory, and combination methods are among the most popular teaching approaches utilized in elementary school physical education. Ways of teaching others are patterns that must be tailored to fit one's own situation. The many approaches for successful teaching include

Chalk talks	Class discussions
Drills	Workshops
Lectures	Forums
Questions and answers	Assignments
Reports	Field trips
Demonstrations and participation	Debates
Supervised practice	Workbooks
Role playing	Projects
Visual aids	Combinations of all listed
Experiments	

The Traditional Method

The traditional method, or direct method of teaching as it is often called, is the time-honored way for teaching motor skills in North America. In the traditional method the teacher makes the major decisions for the students, i.e., what is to be performed and how it should be performed. After selecting the skill or activity to be taught, the teacher gives a brief explanation and demonstration of how it is to be done correctly. It is the duty of the students to emulate the model established by the teacher as nearly as possible. The demonstration may be done by the teacher, by the student leader, or by the use of visual aids such as films, diagrams, or wall charts. Immediately following the demonstration phase of the traditional method, the student practices the skill and the teacher observes the student's performance and then diagnoses problems that he or the class may be encountering. Comments or suggestions are then made to the student or class concerning ways of improving performance. Another demonstration and further explanation of the activity may also be presented at this time, after which the students are again given an opportunity to practice. During this practice session the teacher circulates through the group and gives help to individuals with specific problems. The class is then given an opportunity to use the skill in a game, relay, or other appropriate activity. During this activity the teacher continues to work on improving the student's level of performance. Briefly summarized, the steps in the traditional method include

1. Explanation	6. Student practice
2. Demonstration	7. Individual assistance
3. Student practice	8. Implementation of the skill
4. Teacher diagnosis	in appropriate activity
5. General comments	

There are a number of advantages in using the traditional method. It is direct, to the point, and efficient in terms of time, and it provides a high degree of structure to a class. Therefore, it can be used effectively with poorly disciplined students, as well as provide the beginning teacher with a greater degree of security. The traditional method can be effectively used when the general skill level of the group is low and in teaching specific movement skills.

There are, however, a number of disadvantages in using the traditional method in the elementary school that should be considered. First and foremost, it does not allow for individual differences among children. A model is presented, and the child is expected to duplicate that model as nearly as possible. It often fails to provide for individualization of instruction to meet the particular developmental needs, interests, and capabilities of *each* child. The traditional method also restricts the child's participation in deciding what is to be included in the lesson and how it is to be practiced. It also fails to give the child an opportunity to express himself in a creative manner. He is expected to perform the activity in the single "best" manner, which is the one presented by the teacher.

The Exploratory Method

Movement exploration is an indirect method of teaching children that has come into vogue in the United States. It gained popularity in the English primary schools[1] and has been enthusiastically heralded by many in this country as an effective method of teaching young children. The principal uniqueness of movement exploration is that it uses a problem-solving approach and accepts any *reasonable* solution as correct. The teacher structures problems or questions that are appropriate to the developmental level of the children and then encourages them to explore and experiment to find the solution to these problems. No model for correct performance is established by the teacher. The teacher is not particularly concerned that the children perform the activity all in the same manner or with a great deal of precision. The teacher is, however, interested in giving each child an opportunity to (1) explore the movement potential of his body, (2) develop fundamental movement abilities, (3) experience success within the limits of his abilities, and (4) express himself creatively. After the class has had an opportunity to work on the task, the teacher may ask a number of individuals to demonstrate their particular solutions to the problem. The students then continue solving the problem posed to them while the teacher circulates among the group challenging and questioning individuals.

The key to effective use of the exploratory method is thoughtful construction and use of movement problems that allow for a variety of interpretations but still remain within the confines of the stated objectives of the lesson. Although *every* reasonable solution to the problem is considered correct, one should not infer that the lesson will take its own course simply by the teacher's posing one or two questions to the class. The teacher must constantly rephrase and restructure questions in an effort to continually probe and challenge each student. Briefly summarized, the steps in the exploratory method are the following:

1. The teacher establishes the problem or question.
2. The class explores and experiments with solutions to the task.

---

[1] Bilbrough, A., and Jones, P.: *Physical Education in the Primary Schools.* London, University of London Press, 1965.

3. Class members are permitted to demonstrate their solutions to the problems.
4. The class continues to practice and refine the solutions offered by its members.
5. The teacher circulates among the class giving individual assistance in the form of further questions and challenges.

The primary advantages of the exploratory method are that it permits greater involvement on the part of the student in the learning process, and it accounts for individual differences among children by permitting them to solve in any reasonable manner problems presented to them. With no one "best" way to perform, each child works at his own particular level of ability and experiences some degree of success, which is an important aid to the developing self-concept of the young child. The exploratory approach helps the child (1) to develop a movement vocabulary, and (2) at the same time, to express himself creatively. It also encourages him to think and to develop self-direction in his learning attempts.

The disadvantages of the exploratory method are that it is time consuming and that teachers unprepared professionally for its use often find it difficult to structure problems in a meaningful way. It fails to provide the teacher with the more formal class organization found in the traditional method and, as a result, is difficult and frustrating for many teachers to use comfortably. It is also difficult to anticipate the students' responses to questions, and lack of structure may inhibit goal-directed behavior on the part of some children. The exploratory approach works best with younger children when skill, form, and accuracy are not of prime importance to the teacher or the pupils. It is often less effective with older children when used in its pure form.

The Combination Method

This teaching approach is a union of the traditional method and the exploratory method of teaching, and as such, it utilizes the best of each. In this method children are given both specific instructions and problems to solve. For example, after the pupil has been taught to do a movement skill correctly, such as the tennis serve, he is given problems to solve, e.g., "How can you put a spin on the ball?" or "How high should your ball be tossed to enable you to hit it harder?"

The combination method can be used effectively with both younger and older children. Its advantages are that its use allows for creativity and pupil experimentation, that it is not a completely new method for the teacher unprepared professionally to use

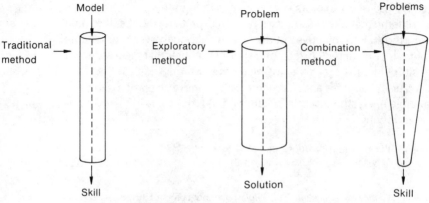

FIGURE 13–1.   Teaching methods.

the exploratory method and will help bridge the gap between the new and the old, and that it leads to a more informal approach toward teaching. It also leads to guided discovery on the part of the learner. But most of all, it is a method of teaching physical education not by teacher command but by pupil discovery.[2]

Among the disadvantages of the combination method are that it is more time-consuming than the traditional method. It is also difficult to structure questions in their proper sequence and to anticipate the student's responses to questions. Practice in the use of this method is necessary before it becomes a natural part of one's teaching behavior.

Each of the previous general methods of teaching children may be effectively used. There are, however, several factors that will influence the use of one or more of these methods by the teacher. Among these are

1. The teacher's philosophy of education and physical education.
2. The teacher's expertise in using the various methods.
3. The type of activity being taught.
4. Growth and developmental factors of the child.
5. Safety considerations.
6. The personality of the teacher and her ability to stimulate children to respond and joyfully react to her.
7. The objectives of the program.
8. The equipment and facilities available.

TEACHING MOTOR SKILLS

The three D's of teaching motor skills are (1) demonstration, (2) diagnosis, and (3) direction. Successful physical educators have mastered all of these techniques.

Demonstration

Most of our learning comes through our eyes and ears. It has been said that one picture is worth many words, but one *experience* is superior to many pictures. This implies that when students copy what they see, they learn from this experience through their mistakes. The teacher should be able to demonstrate when necessary and recognize that children often need and want a visual model of correct performance. Mastery in a wide variety of sport and game skills should be required in the professional training period of all physical educators. If the teacher is unable to execute the skill well, however, student leaders can be trained to do it in front of the class instead, although this may cause some loss of face on the part of the teacher.

Diagnosis

A few students in every class have skill-learning difficulties. There are many reasons for this, including emotional blocks and poor coordination, body structure, and physical condition. The teacher must be an expert in diagnosing difficulties. Some excel in this area and can direct and produce new movement patterns quickly by a few well-chosen words. These master teachers say, ''*Press* your left arm closer to your

---

[2]Mosston, M.: *Teaching from Command to Discovery*. Belmont, California, Wadsworth Publishing Company Inc., 1972.

body," and "*Glide* through the water," or give other simple directions using key words to gain quick results. The novice instructor stumbles, is unsure, and passes this uncertainty on to the student when he remarks, "I *think* your trouble is poor balance," or "Your trouble *may* be that you release the ball at the wrong time." Teachers, like physicians, should *know* what is wrong, not guess what the difficulty is. Ability to diagnose learning difficulty comes largely from (1) ability to perform the skill correctly, (2) knowledge of what each part of the correct movement pattern is, (3) experience, and (4) recognition of the fact that such detection is a vital part of the teaching-learning process that every educator must master.

Direction

The teacher should next direct new movement patterns, for he or she must not only spot the learning snag but also lead the student around it. Success quickens learning. Consequently, when the student follows the teacher's directions and then hits the bull's-eye, makes the basket, or hits the ball, he is eager to repeat those new movements that led to success. However, each physical educator must realize that form is an individual matter and that each student should be assisted to discover his own most productive movement patterns.

It is impossible to isolate skill learning from attitude development or behavior change. How the student *feels* about the teacher and about what he is learning is as important as *what* he learns. The teacher's presence, encouragement, patience, and faith in the student's desire and ability to master what he sets out to do helps longed-for goals become a reality.

TEACHING TECHNIQUES

Suggested Practices

The following techniques for teaching physical education are suggested for trial and each teacher's revision.[3] In each class,

1. Explain briefly what the class will do.
2. Establish a need for learning by having pupils experiment (for example, by having them listen and move to music to get the rhythm of the dance before teaching actual steps).
3. Demonstrate the correct way to do the whole activity. (Show the class how the complete dance looks, or the complete bat swing.)
4. Use squad leaders to demonstrate to their squads.
5. Demonstrate the correct way again to each person who is having difficulty.
6. Explain as simply as possible how to do the skill. (Say "Hook elbows" rather than "Bend your arm and then place it through the bent left arm of your partner.")
7. Encourage pupils by praising what they do correctly so that they will keep trying until they master the skill.
8. Integrate isolated skills in a game, dance, or other activity as soon as possible. (In a soccer class, for example, ten minutes may be spent on learning how to kick, dribble, and trap the ball; the remainder of the period should be spent in playing a game so that these skills will be used. No class period should be devoted entirely to practicing isolated skills.)
9. Work toward 100 per cent pupil participation throughout the class period.

---

[3]Specific techniques for teaching various parts of the total program are given in each of the following chapters.

10. Choose, whenever possible, activities that relate to the season, weather, day, or pupils' interest.
11. Keep plans flexible; overplan rather than underplan.
12. Have a high degree of expectancy for each child, and stimulate him through it to do his best.
13. Analyze classes that did not go well; realize that the reason may be your fault more times than not.
14. Build skill upon skill.
15. Employ techniques that will help each child learn something new every day.
16. Do not begin until everyone is listening.
17. Stand where everyone can see and hear you.
18. Do not "talk down" to students, but use a vocabulary that is understandable to them.
19. Do not attempt to stoop to the pupils' height when talking or working with them.
20. Summarize, using key words or phrases.
21. Analyze students' initial performance of the task. Comment on general problems, and assist students individually with specific problems.
22. When asking for questions from the class be specific in nature.
23. Select pupils to demonstrate who perform the skill reasonably well (no need that they be highly skilled) or have solved the problem in a unique manner.
24. Utilize group or squad demonstrations and audio-visual aids.
25. Place emphasis on the techniques employed during the demonstration rather than on the results.
26. Give everyone chances to demonstrate at various times during the year.
27. Constantly observe and evaluate your pupils' performances. Alter your approach and emphasis to meet the pupils' needs.
28. Encourage self-evaluation of progress by students.
29. Utilize the final few minutes for review, self-evaluation, and planning for the next lesson.
30. Evaluate the lesson yourself in terms of achievement of your specific objectives.
31. Be cheerful, and show a genuine interest in your students, but don't become "buddy-buddy" with them, or "one of the boys."

Pitfalls to Be Avoided

New and experienced teachers alike often make simple errors in planning and in their techniques of teaching. These errors lead to problems and confusion on the part of both the teacher and the student. The experienced teacher will avoid

1. *Verbiage.*   Teaching is *not* telling; it is getting others to teach themselves through participation.
2. *Faulty Planning.*   Provide enough equipment or activity so that all are active. Physical education is a *doing* process, not a watching one. Ten pupils may use the baseball equipment, but 100 others should not stand and watch them have all the fun. If there is insufficient equipment, use what you have to the fullest degree, but add squad play and squad rotation of games that do not require equipment. Give each group a chance to use what you do have.
3. *Shot Scattering.*   Do not attempt to talk *above* the students' level of understanding or while pupils are talking. Make a direct hit every time you do talk and give directions by training the pupils to be quiet when you are speaking. Insist upon observance of this rule, but be wise enough to know *when* to talk, *what* to say, and *how* to say it.
4. *"Letting George Do It."*   Do not pass the buck or send an offending pupil to the principal. Handle discipline cases when they occur in a firm but fair fashion. Group pressure and group discussions can work sometimes when teachers' reprimands fail.
5. *Not Dressing for Class.*   Teachers should not attempt to teach physical education while wearing street clothes except in the primary grades in which the classroom teacher conducts playground activities. If pupils are required to wear special costumes, so should the teacher. Like the pupils, the instructor should be neatly dressed and clean. Soiled sweat shirts and pants are out for men, as well as for women. All-white shorts and shirts or blouses are recommended for both sexes.

6. *Being Too Friendly With Pupils.*   Physical educators are usually the most popular teachers in the school. Some few gain their reputations for being "good Joes" or "good Janes," by being backslap-happy and too friendly with pupils, especially the highly skilled ones. A leader often loses the respect of the group if and when he comes down too near the group level. All youth need to have heroes and teachers worthy of emulation. Big Brothers or Sisters or Buddies who are also their public school teachers often are not followed by children for a long period of time.

7. *Failing to Plan or See Relationships.*   Growth follows patterns. Teachers can help children build shacks or temples, make mud pies, or bake cakes—but only when they utilize building blueprints. Skills must be built upon skills. Daily, weekly, monthly, and yearly plans are the blueprints of this creation.

8. *Window Pecking.*   When children have playground periods and physical education classes the teacher assigned to teach the physical education cannot do this by remote control. Some older teachers, as well as a few unprepared younger ones, believe physical education is staying in one's own warm classroom and peering out of the window to watch children playing on the cold playground, pecking on the icy glass at them when they get into fights. Teachers of this type are gaining experience in the fine art of window pecking while the children are being cheated out of a real educational opportunity.

9. *Becoming Whistle-Happy.*   The whistle may be used as a means of gaining group attention at the beginning of each year's work, semester, or class. Children can be trained to be quiet when the whistle is blown. But whistles can also become a nuisance, as well as a source of annoyance, when used too often. Children can be taught to be automatically quiet when the teacher speaks. A gymnasium of 100 or more children *can* be a controlled teaching-learning environment. The teacher who has something exciting for children to learn has little trouble gaining their attention if she has also trained them to react to her leadership position and ability. Whistles are recommended, however, for playground use when the children are scattered over large areas where it may be difficult for them to see or hear the teacher.

10. *Throwing Out the Ball.*   Too often children in elementary grades are taught physical education classes by the coach. His primary duties too often are to produce winning teams, not to teach unskilled boys how to play. Too often he is not as interested in teaching all boys as he is in training the few who are highly skilled. Coaching takes time and energy spent in after-school hours. It is easier to sit in one's office to conserve energy by drawing up plans for team practice than it is to teach classes. So the ball is thrown out on the gymnasium floor, like a wee bone to a pack of howling wolves, and physical education classes are taught by remote control. Luckily, such practices are diminishing in our better schools. Physical education for all in school is quite a different thing from high-pressured athletics for a few highly skilled or coordinated players.

Individualizing Instruction

Simply making groups or classes smaller does not necessarily individualize instruction, nor does it produce better education unless the teacher really knows how each student can best learn. As one authority has pointed out,

Nongraded schools, team teaching, differentiated staffing, flexible scheduling, optional class attendance, and similar devices have often been set up for administrative expediency and have, in many cases, promoted—not reduced—conformity.[4]

It must be remembered that every child learns in his own unique way and is motivated to master a learning problem according to his own response to problems. For some, learning comes easiest through verbal stimulation; for others, through pictures; for still others, through kinesthetic-tactile approaches; and for a vast number, through the multisensory approach.

---

[4]Stein, J.: *Individualized Instruction in Physical Education.* New London, Connecticut, Croft Educational Services, March 1972.

FIGURE 13–2. All teachers should know that skill mastery is one of the great desires of youth. This boy is working hard on his own to develop muscular and sensory coordination at the school playground during after-school hours because he has been motivated to do so. (Courtesy of Youth Services Section, Los Angeles City Schools.)

The whole key to meeting individual needs is to master an understanding of cause-and-effect relationships. Alice cannot walk the balance beam. Is this because she does not understand the mechanics of walking and balancing? Is she afraid? Is she gaining needed extra attention by failing in her attempts? Does she have a visual or an inner ear problem? Could it be that she sees no reason for learning this skill because there are no balance beams to play on anywhere else except in this gymnasium? Alice, like thousands of children who have difficulty in learning a physical skill or any other type of skill, greatly needs help. To individualize instruction in working with Alice, the teacher needs to know as much about her as possible, *how* she can best be motivated, *why* she is having problems, *what* is the basic problem, and *how* to help her go around and past mastery stumbling blocks. The teacher, in short, must use any or all of those techniques that are the very best means of helping Alice. She must also discover what combinations of techniques are the best to use for all other children in each of her other classes.

Although the teacher has the problem of how to help those most needing it when she has so many children in class, expert instructors find their own unique ways for doing so. Student assistants, squad leaders, paraprofessionals, and team teaching can all be of help. Remember that some people respond more to one person than to any other. Often an older child can help a younger one learn a skill more quickly than the teacher can.[5] What then is her role? Simply, it is to find the right combination that will unlock and free a child who needs help in escaping difficulties. Other suggested ways to individualize instruction are to

1. Use diagnostic tests to learn the strengths and weaknesses of each pupil. Then plan goals to master each weakness based upon these findings.
2. Watch every child closely in order to "see" what his learning problem apparently is.
3. Use a variety of approaches in order to help the child accomplish his own goals and those you want him to gain.
4. Use many problem-solving and exploratory activities in your program. This will help you to spot quickly the uniqueness of each pupil and how each goes about solving learning problems.
5. Provide children with many chances to solve simple movement problems before presenting them with more complex ones, and help them gain self-confidence as well as self-understanding.
6. Find out as soon as possible which ones can learn more effectively in a short time and need long practice periods, and which ones need long trial-and-error periods and short practice sessions. Regroup the class homogeneously according to this discovery.
7. Use circuit or training areas for those of equal ability to work together in small groups.
8. Know as much about each pupil in your group as you can. Know where each *really* is on his own developmental scale. Help him to grow, change, and develop in order to reach his own unique short- as well as long-range goals as a member of his class group.

COMMUNICATING WITH STUDENTS

Teaching is a learned behavior and, as such, it is susceptible to alteration, modification, and change. The good teacher will recognize the fact that if there is no learning on the part of the student, there has been no real teaching. Good teaching requires much more than whistle blowing and the dissemination of information. It requires the establishment and maintenance of clear, open lines of communication between the teacher and the learner. Only when the lines of communication are open and the child is receptive to what is being presented, is there any true learning and, hence, true teaching.

Communicating with students is both a verbal and nonverbal process. It is important to recognize that one's verbal and nonverbal communication skills have a tremendous effect on the individual and on his learning. The following section deals with some of the important requirements of successful communication with students.

Verbal Communication

The spoken word is an important tool for the physical educator whether he is utilizing traditional teaching approaches, which require verbal explanations and descriptions of skills and tasks, or movement exploration techniques, which require the structuring of challenges and movement problems. No matter what teaching method or methods are being used, it is important for the teacher to

1. Keep verbalization to a minimum.
2. Stand in a position where all can see him.
3. Be sure everyone is listening before beginning to speak.
4. Insist on quiet while speaking.

---

[5] See a provocative book by Gartner, et al.: *Children Teach Children* (New York, Harper & Row, Publishers, 1971), in order to discover how effectively children can teach their peers.

5. Use good voice projection. Gymnasiums are large structures, and playgrounds are open, so it is necessary to talk so that all can hear him.
6. Be sure to have sufficient inflection in his voice. Many a teacher has lulled students to sleep with a monotone presentation.
7. Maintain a steady pitch when speaking but be able to alter it as the situation warrants.
8. Talk *to* students, not *at* them.
9. Remember that elementary-school children are not babies; the teacher should refrain from talking down to his pupils or in monosyllables. A "sing-song," condescending manner is unacceptable.
10. Be sure that his presentation is clear and demonstrates the use of good grammar.
11. Avoid the use of slang and colloquialisms. It is not necessary for the teacher to demonstrate that he is "one of the gang."
12. Summarize, using key words or phrases. This helps students conceptualize the content of the lesson.
13. Ask for specific questions concerning the lesson. Avoid general statements such as "Are there any questions?"

The importance of observing the preceding verbal guidelines should not be minimized. Your voice is a teaching tool, and *how* something is said is just as important as *what* is said. The length of verbal discourse, use of your voice, and delivery all play an important role in successful teaching.

Nonverbal Communication

Nonverbal communication, or body language as it is often termed, is another important mode of communication. Our verbal vocabulary ranges from about 28,000 to 40,000 words, but our nonverbal vocabulary is endless. It is important that we learn to see the subtleties in nonverbal communication and recognize the messages we are transmitting.

We project a variety of messages to those around us, including our students, through subtle and often unconscious changes in our facial expressions, postures, and gestures. We convey our feelings and attitudes through our nonverbal mannerisms and are more likely to convey them in their *true* form through body expression than through verbal expression. It is important that our body language convey to students that they matter and are valued and that we are pleased to be with them. We must fully recognize the significance of this mode of communication in our dealings with children and understand the messages we are transmitting either consciously or unconsciously through it. The following is a list of some facial expressions, postures, and gestures and the messages they convey:

1. Pointing of an index finger forcefully at a student singles that student out in a threatening manner.
2. Pointing of the index finger forcefully down reinforces a point.
3. Pointing of the index finger upward indicates a higher authority.
4. Standing with the body weight on one foot indicates a relaxed, carefree, easy-going attitude.
5. Shifting of body weight from foot to foot indicates uneasiness, nervousness, and restlessness.
6. Standing erect with weight evenly distributed shows confidence, assuredness, and readiness to tackle the world.
7. Standing with hands on hips and thumbs back displays confidence and authority.
8. Standing with hands on hips and thumbs forward indicates uneasiness.
9. Staring out of the window signifies a lack of interest, boredom.
10. Staring at lecture notes or a lesson plan indicates disinterest, apprehension, and uncertainty.

11. Staring at students shows condescension.
12. Raising of the eyebrows displays suspicion.
13. Eye rolling says, "How could you be so dumb?"
14. Rubbing of the hands together manifests expectation.
15. Steepling of the hands and fingers says, "I have the advantage."
16. Mutual glances indicate a desire for approval.
17. Arm folding indicates a need for comfort and security.
18. Quick turning of the head at the blackboard says "I can't trust you" and "I am quick to catch you misbehaving."

Teachers also receive a variety of nonverbal messages from students. These messages should be studied carefully so that you can understand how to "read" students and become more sensitive to what they are saying nonverbally. The following is a list of some nonverbal clues transmitted by students and their corresponding messages:

1. Fidgeting—"Let's get moving."
2. Lying on the gym floor—"I am not interested."
3. Staring out of the window—"I am bored."
4. Head nodding—"I want your approval."
5. Avoidance of eye contact—"I am not really here."
6. Double take after making an error or mistake in a game or sport activity—"That wasn't really my fault; some outside force caused me to do it [drop the ball, miss a shot, and so forth]."
7. Holding of a raised hand in a propped-up position—"Please take pity on me and let me answer your question."
8. Hesitant raising of the hand—"I think I know the answer, but I'm not sure."
10. Wild waving of raised arm—"Teacher, teacher, call on me!"
11. Eyes glued to the floor—"I am not here; don't call on me."
12. Eyes looking up with pensive look—"I am thinking; don't disturb me now, or you will break my train of thought."
13. Grimacing—"I don't like you" or "I don't like what we are doing."

Another factor to be considered in the world of nonverbal communication is distance. The distance at which we stand from those we are speaking to has a great effect on what they hear and attend to. The closer the distance between the teacher and the learner, the greater the attention given to the teacher, up to a point. The greater the distance between you and the learner, the less you and the learner are able to attend to each other. See Table 13–1 for a list of approximate distances and the messages they generally communicate.

CLASS CONTROL

The term "classroom discipline" may mean many things to today's physical educator. To some it is indicative of a condition existing in one's class: "Mr. Jones has good discipline." To others it may signify a form of punishment or a method of gaining control over an individual or group. Some may look upon discipline as an important ingredient in the traditional method of teaching physical education, in which structure and regimentation often play an important role. Still others may view discipline as a negative feature that must be omitted from the newer movement exploration method, which stresses experimentation and freedom of response. In the following paragraphs, classroom discipline will be considered to be a means of enabling pupils to use their time in an educationally desirable way and in such a manner that their behavior does

**TABLE 13–1.   PHYSICAL DISTANCES BETWEEN TEACHER AND LEARNER
AND THEIR MESSAGES**

Feet	Distance	Message
1 to 3	Intimate	"You are too close and threatening." (This is known as personal space and is reserved for special people and occasions.)
4 to 6	Near Social	"I feel more comfortable and relaxed." (This is an informal, friendly distance.)
7 to 9	Far Social	"We can still communicate effectively but on less friendly terms." (This is a more formal friendly distance.)
10 to 15	Near Psychological	"I can move into or out of immediate contact with the situation at will." (This is a formal distance.)
16 to 20	Far Psychological	"I am removed and out of contact." (This is a remote distance.)

not inhibit others from working effectively and achieving the specific objectives of the lesson.

Good discipline in the classroom or gymnasium does not require that every student be in rigid lines and formations, every eye focused in rapt attention on the teacher, every pupil silent, or every pupil responding only on command. A setting such as this does not often ensure positive or long-lasting learning. Over-use of rigidity and structure, when not essential to the lesson, may even stifle it. In order for maximal effective learning to take place, the student must be actively involved in the learning process and the teacher must serve as a helpful guide, as well as a motivator of desirable responses. Again, it is wise to remember that the more the child is engrossed in learning things that *he* deems to be important, the greater his learning will be.

The learner, not the teacher, controls what and how much of anything will be learned. Unfortunately, as children strive to learn, their actions are often misinterpreted as a breach of proper or desirable behavior by the inexperienced or the insecure teacher. The lack of guidelines, on the other hand, and the absence of an element of structure in the learning environment may also hinder or stifle this effort. Often those individuals pursuing the exploratory method of teaching fall into this trap, which is brought about by their incomplete understanding of this freer, more informal approach or their own insecurity as a teacher. They lose sight of the fact that the basic concept of movement exploration requires them to *guide* the child in discovering for himself the movement potentialities of his body in solving movement-related problems. Exploration does not free the child from externally imposed guidelines or self-imposed restraints. It merely alters the method of teaching physical education by permitting greater involvement in the learning process on the part of the student. Discipline has not failed if the would-be learner overtly expresses his enthusiasm or excitement in exploring the movement potentialities of his body. It has not failed if the gymnasium is humming with task-related conversation, or when eight eager youngsters simultaneously burst out with an idea, suggestion, or solution, as long as other children are willing to listen to one another. Discipline has failed, however, if the rights of the class are infringed upon by one or more individuals. It has failed if the specific objectives of the lesson cannot be effectively achieved, owing to the climate of the classroom, or if interest, initiative, and individuality of any person or the whole class are curbed by one or a few disruptive individuals.

The following are some remedial actions that have been found to be useful under various circumstances by experienced teachers:

1. Disapproving glances.
2. General comments to the class.
3. Stationing yourself close to student.
4. Placing a *gentle* hand on student's shoulder.
5. Singling out troublemakers for comments.
6. Rearranging the class in order to separate troublemakers.
7. Excluding the child or children for a *portion* of the class period.
8. Isolating the child from the rest of the group for a portion of the class period.
9. Teacher-pupil conferences.
10. Exclusion or isolation for the entire class period (to be used in extreme cases only).
11. Sending the child to the principal (a last resort).
12. Home-school conferences.

It must be remembered that these techniques for handling discipline problems do not get at the *source* of the problem. They are merely methods of handling overt signs of behavior problems. The best method of handling behavior problems is a program designed to prevent them from occurring. This can best be done by understanding the behavior and each child's individual background and personality problems. There are many things that the teacher can do to *prevent* discipline problems from arising.

Negative Results of Punishment

Though it is possible that punishment can be an effective management procedure, it is very difficult to use it effectively in the typical classroom and gymnasium. Because of large class size, the teacher cannot punish a particular behavior every time it occurs. There may be times when a teacher may use an inappropriately severe punishment, or there may be certain people who relish giving punishment; in both cases, normal standards of ethics are violated. Because of these difficulties and the negative consequences of punishment listed below, the appropriateness of punishment should always be very carefully weighed for each situation. The following paragraphs delineate some of the negative results of punishment.

NEGATIVE GENERALIZATION.   Worry, fear, anxiety, hatred, guilt, shame, and avoidance may be instilled by punishment as a reaction not only to the undesirable behavior, but also to study, books, the teacher, the classroom, the child himself, and other things or thoughts present when punishment occurs.

WITHDRAWAL.   A student who is repeatedly punished or reprimanded may try to avoid class or school by being "sick," tardy, or truant, or he may attempt to leave school permanently. Some students may genuinely fear school, just as many people fear a visit to the dentist because of the pain incurred there. Withdrawal may be accomplished by daydreaming, doodling, humming, or otherwise not paying attention even though the student is present in body.

INCREASED EMOTIONALITY.   The more severe the punishment, the more it increases fear, anxiety, anger, and general emotionality in the punished person. Increases in emotion make it *more* difficult for an individual to change his behavior and learn new habits and may even increase the likelihood of future misbehavior.

AGGRESSION.   Punishment usually leads to aggression, but the amount of punishment necessary to cause aggression differs among individuals, as does the strength or kind of aggression. Almost any punished student is likely to make hostile remarks about the teacher or other punishing adult when out of that adult's immediate range of attention. The student is almost certain to like the adult less or dislike him more. Sometimes punished students, even those who may seem to take it well in class, may seek revenge with threatening telephone calls, vandalization of property, and so on. Aggression is largely incompatible with learning; it is difficult to learn from and pay attention to a disliked person.

REACTIONS OF PEERS.   Though other students in the classroom may not immediately imitate either the act of punishment or the punished act, it has been found that both of these acts tend to increase in frequency in the absence of the teacher or other punishing adult. Children who witness shouting, shaking, sarcasm, spanking, and so on are more likely to do these things to other people who frustrate them than are children who witness calmer reactions. Most human behavior is learned from models, and these should be models of fairness and temperance.

LOWERED SELF-ESTEEM.   An individual's behavior and self-concept are influenced strongly by how he *thinks* others perceive him, regardless of how they might *say* they perceive him. Punishing a student increases the chance that he will come to believe that others have a negative view of him and increases the chance that he will develop a negative self-concept. *Self-esteem or a positive self-concept has been found to be predictive of school success.* There should be acceptable alternatives explicitly made available to the student when he is punished that provide opportunities for praise, success, and reward.

Punishment

If it is necessary to punish a child, punishment should be for the *behavior*, not the *person* himself. It should be explicitly combined with a statement of what would have been the appropriate behavior in the situation in which the child misbehaved; praise should be given when good behavior does occur. Punishment should occur immediately after the undesirable behavior to be effective in decreasing its frequency. Physical punishment, unless immediate, will be of little benefit other than for the reduction of frustration in the *punisher*. Punishment should occur every time the undesirable behavior occurs, and it is most effective when introduced at full intensity.

The use of punishment for extended periods of time reduces its effectiveness. When the punishment or threat of immediate punishment is removed, the undesirable behavior almost always returns in the more extroverted individual. The more introverted individual may remain afraid much longer than intended and may actually develop a phobia or neurosis as a result of the punishment.

Although punishment is the most frequently used method of control, it is the *least* effective. Punishment merely represses the undesirable behavior; it fails to get to the "heart" of the matter. It often creates harmful anxiety and escape and avoidance behavior on the part of the child. Physical punishment (spanking) provides children with adult models of aggression; as a result of this example, they will think aggression is acceptable. Punishment should be used in *emergencies* only. It must be used *immediately* to be of any value and with an explanation, so that the child can anticipate the same consequences in the future.

Alternatives to Punishment

It must be remembered that most techniques for handling discipline problems do not get at the *source* of the problem. They are merely methods of handling overt signs of behavior problems. The best method of handling behavior problems is a program designed at preventing them from occurring. This can best be done by understanding the behavior and each child's individual background and personality problems. There are many things that the teacher can do to *prevent* discipline problems from arising. Among these are

1. Being thoroughly prepared for each class.
2. Overplanning, for this is far better than underplanning each class.
3. Having something to interest each child.
4. Challenging the students.
5. Structuring situations so that all may achieve some degree of success.
6. Always maintaining emotional control of himself.
7. Maintaining voice control, and trying to make his voice pleasant to hear.
8. Not regarding children's actions as a personal affront.
9. Maintaining a distinction between teacher and pupil by keeping social distance. Children need adult friends as models and not would-be peers.
10. Avoiding the use of sarcasm in the classroom.

Rewarding desirable behavior when it occurs is much more effective in increasing the desirable behavior than is punishing the *un*desirable behavior and hoping that the punished person will automatically change for the better. Praise, approval, privileges, extra credit, and with younger children, more concrete rewards such as gold stars should be given as soon as possible after the desired behavior occurs.

Teachers and other adults should give clear guidelines and models of correct behavior so that students can know exactly what is acceptable and what is not and so that they know what to expect if they act in certain ways. The danger here is that some adults will expect everyone to act, think, and dress the same and may thus stifle individual differences, which are the very heart of child-centered teaching.

The most effective way of dealing with disruptive behavior in the classroom and gymnasium is with rewards such as privileges, quiet praise, and approval (saying, for example, "That's good," "I like that," or "You're doing well," or patting the child on the back or shoulder, nodding, winking, smiling, and so forth) for desirable behavior, combined with a *gentle* reprimand or correction of the undesirable behavior. The second most effective way of dealing with behavioral problems is to reward good behavior and totally ignore the undesirable behavior. Quiet reprimands of undesirable behavior alone and loud reprimands alone are the least effective forms of class control.

CLASS MANAGEMENT

What the pupils learn, feel, or think about their physical education classes are concepts gained outside as well as during the class instructional period on the gymnasium floor, for their locker-room and showering experiences may be negative enough to counteract positive ones previously obtained in class.

BEFORE CLASS.   The teacher should be dressed in a costume that allows freedom of movement. If possible, she should greet each pupil by name as he enters the gymnasium or locker room. All needed equipment for the class should be ready, and she should have planned well the activities she will teach.

LOCKER-ROOM REGULATIONS.   Each pupil should know where he is to put his clothing when changing for class; each should lock his locker before coming into the gymnasium. A combination lock is recommended, and the teacher should have a master key for all combinations.

COSTUMES. Recommended costumes for girls are one-piece gym suits with a skirt or short pants. For boys, white or dark shorts and a T-shirt are recommended. All pupils should be required to wear these costumes, with their names clearly marked on each item, plus socks and tennis shoes for each class. The teacher should require the class to appear in clean costumes periodically. The importance of neatness, good grooming, and cleanliness should be stressed. Her own example in dressing will work wonders in motivating the pupils.

ROLL CALL. Although roll call is generally not necessary in the primary grades, it is on the upper elementary level. It can be done speedily and accurately by using any of the following methods:

1. By squads. The squad leader is responsible for finding out who is absent in his squad.
   Advantage: Allows for leadership training. Roll is taken quickly.
   Disadvantage: Could allow for cheating. The teacher does not learn students' names and faces as quickly.
2. By seating plan. The teacher marks down names or numbers of vacant seating or standing places.
   Advantage: Fairly quick method of taking roll. The teacher is better able to coordinate names with faces.
   Disadvantage: Does not allow for leadership training. Takes more time than squad method.
3. Roll call. The teacher calls the roll with students answering if present.
   Advantage: Teacher may learn students' names with very little effort. Teacher may be assured about who is present or absent.
   Disadvantage: Too time consuming. Allows for no leadership training.

Increasingly, classes in our better schools are becoming smaller and, since groups are limited in number, the teacher knows each pupil and can soon tell who is absent without checking the roll. Each teacher should develop her own system for recording absences, tardiness, excuses from daily participation, and unsuitable costume. Roll should be taken at the beginning of each class period. Requiring each pupil to wear a name tag will enable the teacher to learn each child's name more quickly, which in turn is a means of class control, because telling John Marsh to "sit up straighter and stop talking during roll taking" is far more effective than referring to a "certain person in squad three" who needs correction.

CLASS EXCUSES. Each teacher with the approval of the principal should devise written policies regarding daily excuses because of temporary illness or for other reasons. No pupil should be excused from physical education because of a physical handicap. However, when temporary excuses are needed, the school nurse or anyone else in the school health department should authorize them. Alternate plans should be devised for each pupil who cannot participate, whether this requires him to dress in the regulation uniform and observe or to take part in as much of the class as possible. Permitting the pupil to go to the library is not recommended, unless he is given an assignment related to the physical education class activity. Some teachers have these pupils keep score, help officiate during games, or work on making an attractive class bulletin board. Regardless of what procedure is established for such cases, it must help the excused pupil spend his class time wisely in accordance with the objectives of the physical education program. Upper-class girls who have menstruation difficulties should be encouraged to take part in as much of the class as they deem possible. Requiring all to wear gym suits when they have their monthly period will encourage them to take part in at least some forms of activity.

Use of Space

Although the American Alliance for Health, Physical Education, and Recreation recommends that there never be more than 35 students in each physical education class in elementary schools, few teachers are fortunate enough to have this ideally sized group. Probably in the near future all classes will be even larger. Consequently, teachers must devise ways to use all available teaching stations in the best manner. This plan, coupled with use of squad leaders, will enable the teacher to rotate around space-assigned groups and to supervise them all adequately. In this way, a wide range of activities can be conducted in one gymnasium.

Methods of Grouping

A wide variety of student groups should be used throughout the year, for opportunities for many working groups to be squad leaders and team captains help pupils develop leadership and "followership" skills, good sportsmanship, and a widened circle of friends. Suggested means of grouping pupils include

1. Homerooms.
2. In homogeneous groups of skilled pupils or heterogeneous groups of skilled and unskilled pupils, skill being determined by tests or observation.
3. Numbering off by 2's, 3's, or 4's, depending upon class size.
4. Electing captains and having each one choose his team (although this may be used infrequently, care must be taken that those last chosen become group leaders or gain recognition in other activities.)
5. Dividing the tallest members among various squads.
6. Teacher-formed teams or squads.
7. Special-skill-practice groups.
8. Dividing a circle in half.
9. Asking pupils to stand behind selected team leaders, such as Jack, George, and Tom.
10. Dividing the class by numbers, the first ten going to this corner of the floor to tumble; the next ten to another area, piece of equipment, and activity; and so forth.
11. The same as above, except the pupils choose the activity and equipment they wish.

Through the entire year, the teacher should stress the qualities of good democratic leadership, and the duties and responsibilities of being a team captain or squad leader.

Checking and Moving Equipment In and Out

If there is no custodian available to render this service, a procedure for doing so should be established. A student should be assigned to this responsibility in each class. All equipment needed for each period must be ready before the class meets so that instruction time is not lost. This should be readily accessible so that all needed items can be gathered at once. Large laundry sacks are ideal for this purpose and are easily carried back and forth to playing fields. Commercial equipment is also available in the form of carts, movable boxes, and so forth.[6]

---

[6]See the appendices for sources.

Keeping Records

Records should be functional and practical and used as a means of evaluating student progress and program content or for recording administrative details. They should not be time consuming or energy draining for the teacher. Such records include essential health information, basket or locker master sheets, cumulative physical education forms, grades, attendance records, inventory, and accident reports. Records and reports should be kept in a locked steel file. All recorded information should be for present or future use and never just busy work, for accurate and meaningful records and reports are as essential to good teaching as efficient and effective class management.

Planning with Pupils

Pupils should work closely with the teacher in developing weekly programs. The approach may well be for the teacher to have suggested activities to present to the group, rather than asking "Well, what shall we do today and the rest of the week?" Children tend to like most the things they can do best, and to get into a rut consisting of old favorite games. Weaning them away from favored activities will lead to growth. The teacher may have to use initiative coupled with force in order to incorporate new activities. However, she need not superimpose all her ideas upon the group; as the adult leader she should eagerly be followed by the pupils. She will be as long as they have enjoyable and meaningful experiences as they learn to master new skills.

Some techniques of evaluating outcomes are observations, comparisons, questions, class discussions, analyses, and skill and written tests. Children can be taught to appraise what they have accomplished. So can the teacher. Evaluation, which is a method of thinking through an accomplishment so that one can revise purposes and procedures for the next effort, is an important part of teaching. When the teacher and pupils share in evaluating outcomes, democratic procedures are being used.

The process of thinking through a project is a valuable achievement in education and life. It can be used effectively with young children, for in spite of their age they have an uncanny way of seeing through things, of sizing up others as well as themselves. Their charming frankness can be utilized for individual as well as group development.

An illustration of how planning and evaluation appears in a physical education lesson follows:

Objectives: To teach children how to play "end ball."
Procedure:
1. ORIENTATION. Give the class a preview of the game by observing an upper class play a demonstration game.
2. PLANNING. Discuss with the class the object of the game and help them to identify skills used, team position, and the rules. Form color teams of squads, and let players take assigned positions on the playfield.
3. EXECUTING. The pupils will walk through or explore their team positions and then play the game.
4. PUPIL'S EVALUATION. Following the playing of the game, the teacher will lead the children to consider what they should have done to play the game more effectively. They may compare the way they saw the demonstration game played with the way they played or analyze only their own play and establish their needs. The children will discover through this procedure what they need to learn or practice in order to play more skillfully. Thus they will discover their need for learning, which through increased interest will cause them to learn more

rapidly than if the teacher had pointed out what she thought they needed to learn. Through such evaluation, teacher and pupils share a new purpose and agree upon objectives for the next lesson. They may include

a. Practicing a straight throw for distance.
b. Practicing catching while standing or while running.
c. Playing "end ball" again.

CLASS ORGANIZATION

Physical education classes are often vastly overcrowded. The ideal number of pupils per class is 20; and there should be not more than 35 at most. Lack of sufficient time, poor facilities, and inadequate equipment, coupled with large numbers of pupils, present gigantic problems to the teacher. Careful planning for the best type of class organization possible will ensure the most fruitful results. Pupils should assist the instructor in planning, conducting, and evaluating the program on each grade level. Primary children can gradually be given more responsibilities in determining what they will do and how they will learn the subject matter, and in evaluating their results. Skillful organization and wise planning will assure that each period of instruction is meaningful to the learner, educationally sound, and fruitful. The class should be informally conducted but well controlled.

The teacher should have a definite beginning and ending to each class period. She should condition the students to listen automatically when she is talking, to get into a circle or squad formation when the class starting signal is given, and to sit in assigned groups at the end of each class for a short evaluative discussion of the period. Because children experiment with each new teacher in order to learn how far they can go or how much they can get away with, it is of primary importance that from the first class to the last one in each semester the teacher be firm, fair, and consistent in her methods of controlling the group. Good class organization helps children feel secure and ready for each new challenging experience.

Formations for Instruction

Far too much precious class time can be lost by reorganizing groups for relays, teams, or skill drills. In order to eliminate such waste, students should be conditioned to form quickly into desired groups when directed to do so. Squads or teams of six to eight usually are best. Placing each group to cover the floor area fully allows the teacher to supervise the entire class effectively. The following formations can be quickly learned and formed. In each, S.L. means Squad Leader.

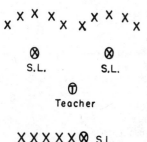

Fan

Players are spread before the leader in a fan formation. This is especially effective in skill drills for throwing, catching, and kicking balls of various sizes. The teacher works as a group supervisor.

Line

This is the easiest of all formations for beginners to learn. It is good for relays, basket shooting, and games in which children take turns. Not more than five should be in line if possible.

Circle

Groups can get into a circle quickly from the line or fan formation by following their leader. This one is especially good for simple games and ball skill drills with the leader in the center throwing the ball to each player and correcting faulty movements when he throws it back.

Shuttle

This grouping is best for ball passing or kicking skill drills.

Zig Zag

Two lines face each other. Player 1 throws to 2 who throws to 3, and so forth. This formation is best for soccer kicking, volleying, throwing, and catching.

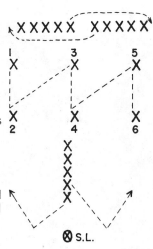

Corner

The leader facing the line gives a signal for 1 and 2 to form a **V** corner. The odd numbers go right, the even to the left. This grouping is ideal for skill drills and teaching response to command movements necessary for marching.

Square

Have four groups form a square. One forms West; two, North; three, East; four, South. The leader stands to the left with his squad. This one is effective for ball-passing drills and team games such as line dodgeball.

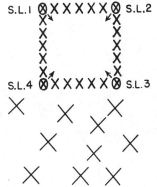

Scatter Formation

This is a random type of formation in which students may sit or stand anywhere they wish.

The Use of Squads

Squads can be started as early as the end of the first half of the first grade. Ideally they should be started when the pupils have reached that stage in their social development that enables them to move easily in groups. The squad leader may be selected for the first time by the teacher, but the children should be given opportunities to select their own leader by the second or third week of each semester. The length of the leadership period can best be pupil-teacher determined. Elements of leadership are superior knowledge and skills. These take time, patience, and determination to develop. Some children are seemingly born leaders, but others can be taught how to lead, too. It is important, however, that every child be given an opportunity to be in a key position in the class several times each semester, either as the squad leader or the leader of some specific activity.

Duties of the squad leader include

1. Checking the attendance of squads.
2. Assisting the teacher in planning the daily, weekly, and semester program.

FIGURE 13-3.   Couple and squad formations.

3. Assisting the teacher with demonstrations and helping each squad member learn each activity.
4. Assisting the teacher and squads in evaluating the program.
5. Setting patterns of good sportsmanship and fellowship as an example for the others to follow.
6. Checking equipment in and out to squad; assisting in the repair of equipment.

A real teacher becomes progressively unnecessary. After the pupils have been taught a number of games they can be given opportunities to play their favorite ones during the supervised free-play period on the playground or in the gymnasium. Suggested techniques for letting the children choose what they want to play are

1. Assign a play space to each squad leader, who will remain at the space. Each squad rotates around each leader, who will lead the same game, assigned to him by the teacher, that the other squads are playing.
2. Assign a play space to each group of 10 to 15 children who want to play a specific game. The entire squad plays the game all period. A variation of this method is to have each squad made up of three who want to play two or three of the same specific games throughout the period.
3. Assign each squad leader to a specific area and give one an opportunity to choose the game or games he would like to play. Other pupils who also want to play those games with that particular leader can join his group.
4. Assign each squad and their leader to a specific piece of equipment and have all squad groups use each piece during the period.

Use of Student Leaders

A good teacher often leads from behind. If teaching is guiding people to learn how to help themselves to become independent and to grow as citizens, then boys and girls must learn early in life how to solve their own and group problems, how to cooperate, how to choose leaders, how to follow, and how to lead others.

The use of a squad leader can produce more efficient, effective teaching. It can also enable the teacher to work more in the role of a supervisor. As soon as possible, the pupils should select the leader they believe to be most qualified. A Leader's Club may be organized at the fourth grade level as a means of teaching pupils how to lead. This group should meet regularly with the teacher to plan and evaluate the work to be done with the rest of the students. The group may also learn new activities to be presented later in class. Squad leaders may serve for a semester's term or be changed more frequently. The former method adds unity to the program as well as increased leadership skill, whereas the latter passes leadership opportunities around, just as a ball is passed from one to another.

Younger children often tend to dominate rather than democratically lead others. All groups in our culture, regardless of age, must have additional training and experience in choosing leaders wisely, in leading and following others. Mankind has always felt the need for good leadership, for the history of the world shows that we have never had enough leaders in the right places at the right time. The elementary school is the rich soil in which children can develop those traits necessary for good leadership.

Team Teaching

Team teaching is now being used successfully in many schools. Under this plan, two or more instructors teach the same subject to separate classes. They plan and organize together the course content for each grade and class group, and then each presents to all classes that part of the subject area (such as dance) for which she is best prepared. This is real team teaching, as opposed to mere "turn" teaching, in which there is no dovetail planning or real unity in the resulting program.

Some schools are organizing teaching teams that include noncertified personnel, such as parents and older students. Through this design, in which the assistants are known as aides, many work as clerks, graders, or supervisors or perform other nonteaching duties. Such a plan, when perfected, can do much to help teachers devote most of their time to planning and conducting more individualized instruction. It can do much also to develop closer adult-parent-school relationships, as well as to help older teenagers develop leadership skills.

SUGGESTED READINGS

Canter, D. (ed.): *Environmental Interaction*. New York, International Universities Press, 1975 (Chapter 5).

Carter, R. D.: *Help! These Kids are Driving Me Crazy*. Champaign, Illinois, Research Press, 1972.

Fast, J.: *Body Language*. New York, Evans, 1970.

Galloway, C.: *Teaching is Communicating: Nonverbal Language*. Washington, D.C., The Association for Student Teaching, Bulletin 29, 1970.

Ginott, H.: *Teacher and Child*. New York, Avon, 1972.

Gray, J.: *The Teacher's Survival Guide: How to Teach Teenagers and Live to Tell About It*. Palo Alto, California, Fearon, 1974.

Kounin, J. S.: *Discipline and Group Management in the Classroom*. New York, Holt, Rinehart, and Winston, 1970.

Krumboltz, J. D., and Krumboltz, H. B.: *Changing Children's Behavior*. Englewood Cliffs, New Jersey, Prentice-Hall, Inc., 1972.

Mosston, M.: *Teaching: From Command to Discovery*. Belmont, California, Wadsworth Publishing Company Inc., 1972.

Whaley, D., and Mallott, R.: *Elementary Principles of Behavior*. Boston, Appleton-Century-Crofts, 1971.

CHAPTER FOURTEEN

MOVEMENT EXPLORATION

A mind stretched by a new idea can never go back to its original dimensions.

Oliver Wendell Holmes

To move is to live! Movement, learning, and living are closely linked experiences through which we, regardless of age, are constantly learning about our ever-changing selves and the world of which we are a vital part. Movement itself is the foundation upon which all educational experiences are built. It is at the very heart of every good physical education program, in which each student has opportunities to learn to master through his own experiences a wide variety of movement problems of ever-increasing complexity in sports and games, rhythms and dance, aquatics, and self-testing activities that require body control and flexibility, strength, quick reaction time, accuracy, and the ability to make quick decisions.

Through movement, the child can improve his health and fitness and gain an understanding of how his own body works, as well as acquire better control of it, develop a better understanding of himself and others, communicate his own feelings and creative ideas, and learn how to respond to challenges that he has set for himself or that have been set for him by others.

THE TEACHER'S ROLE

The teacher should strive to utilize best all available space in this exploratory program and should plan for progressive program activities that will take children from what they can already do well to new movement discoveries and challenges that they must strive hard to master. Often the same movement problems can be presented in many different ways. The children should be encouraged to express their own ideas for new problems and should be increasingly exposed to greater challenges. As one authority in this field suggests,

Basic to the success of the program is the willingness and eagerness of the teacher to experiment with movement. The teacher truly seeking individual expression from children will usually avoid moving herself or giving demonstrations. This attitude will prevent children from imitating her patterns and restricting exploration on their part. Carefully planned sequences for building a vocabulary of movement, for establishing a comfortable emotional climate, and for understanding children's movement potential create an ideal setting for the encouragement of movement expression.[1]

---

[1] Hussey, D.: *Exploration of Basic Movement in Physical Education.* Publication 4–322 TCH, Detroit, Michigan, Detroit Public Schools, 1960, pp. 6–7.

FIGURE 14–1. To move is to live! To live is to learn! (Courtesy of the Detroit Public Schools, Detroit, Michigan.)

The teacher's role in movement exploration, although indirect, is of paramount importance. Through the use of the problem-solving method of teaching and learning, she poses increasingly more challenging movement problems that each child solves in his own unique way through his body movements.

As children explore the various ways to solve these movement problems, they discover the sheer joy moving through space by running, leaping, climbing, hanging, balancing, and using a wide variety of manipulable objects, such as balls of various sizes, hoops, and ropes. They also discover for themselves how to balance their bodies, jump off both high and low places skillfully without falling or injury, how rapidly or slowly they can move, how tightly they can curl themselves into a ball, or how big they can stretch themselves, as well as what their bodies can do at various levels in space. As they move, experiment, and explore, they gain body control and come to see how they can express themselves, their moods, and their ideas by "talking" nonverbally with their bodies. And through these wide exploratory experiences, one authority points out, "In time, movement becomes so automatic that they concentrate on other experiences which affect movement—space, rhythm, and ideas and the ways of organizing these into tangible forms: studies and compositions.[2]

[2]Andrews, G.: *Creative Rhythmic Movement For Children.* Englewood Cliffs, New Jersey, Prentice-Hall, Inc., 1974, p. 46.

FIGURE 14–2.   The unique contribution of physical education to education is in the area of effective, efficient, and purposeful movement. (Reprinted by permission of © J. A. Preston Corporation 1971.)

Posing Movement Problems

The following are a few of the many possible movement problems for children to solve through their own experimentation:

How high can you jump? How can you go higher? Can you find six different ways you can jump? Eight different ways? ten ways?

Lie stretched out on the floor on your back. How many ways can you move your arms and legs? How can you make yourself into a circle? A bridge? Turn on your tummy. Can you move any part of your body in this position that you could not before?

Run as fast as you can. Then stop when I signal. What did you do to stop? What did your knees do? Did you lean forward or backward to set the brake so that you could stop? What did you do to keep from falling? Run slowly. Are the discoveries you made before true when you do not run so fast?

How low can you move to the floor without sitting or lying down? How many different ways can you move your body in this position? Can you gradually come up higher on my first signal? Find out all the things you can do at that level. Come up even higher on my second signal. Can you move at this level in all the ways you did before? Why or why not?

Using this type of approach, the child can discover how his body works, what it can or cannot do as a whole, or what any part of it, such as an arm or leg, can or cannot do. This gaining of body awareness or body image is basic to self-understanding, as well as to self-control. In all these experiences, the teacher is the starter, the stage

FIGURE 14–3.   We learn through movement. (Courtesy of James Wheeler of the Dayton Public Schools, Dayton, Ohio.)

setter, the resource person, the emotional stabilizer, the security provider. She does not tell the children what to do, nor does she demonstrate various movements for the children to copy. Instead, each child is given a movement problem and equipment to use to find the solution and is allowed to move in his own way at his own ability level to discover the answers and solutions to the question or problem.

Program Content

Movement exploration per se is *not* new, and the problem-solving approach to education is the very oldest of all teaching methods. What *is* new is the content of the program. It is an educational breakthrough. Physical activity retains the fun and joy that teachers have taken away from elementary physical education by forcing 30 or more nonskilled children to watch a few skilled ones playing volleyball or other games or stand in long lines to wait their turns to walk on the balance beam or use any other equipment, or by making children, who are anxious to play, sit through long explanations of how you play a game or lengthy demonstration periods, or by having an exercise physical fitness program *be* the program for the school year. Movement exploration should be *added* to the program content of an already well-planned graded program of physical activity for children wherein they progressively are being challenged and *do* learn something new that *they* value every class period. Through its addition, we can get away from the dullness, drabness, and the basic sameness of the program and its unrealistic single standard requirements of perfection that all children are to meet, regardless of their physical limitations, skill level, interest, or innate abilities. As one authority who strongly endorses movement education and is well known in the field of human movement has so aptly stated, "If physical education is to make a *real* contribution to the total education of each student, it must do more than give him a few isolated skills, most of which can only be used in recreational situations. If physical education is to make any contribution at all, it must do much more than give a child an in-school opportunity to learn games he would learn on his own."[3]

Following are program content ideas suggested by Bonnie Gilliom, whose book *Basic Movement Education For Children, Rationale and Teaching Units* can be of tremendous help to all teachers who want to add a graded movement education program to their physical education curriculum and need more specific and detailed help in doing so than can be given here.

SUGGESTED TEACHING UNITS[4]

My body . . . moves . . . in space. . . .

Body parts
Head
Neck
Shoulders
Chest
Waist
Stomach
Hips
Legs
Arms
Back
Spine
Upper arm
Elbow
Lower arm
Wrist
Fingers
Thumb
Hands
Toes
Feet
Heels
Ankles
Shins
Knees
Thighs

Body surfaces
Front
Back
Sides

Body shapes
Curved
Straight and narrow
Straight and wide
Twisted

Body relationships: body part to body part
Near to each other (curled)
Far from each other (stretched)
Rotated with one part fixed (twisted)

Dimensions of space
Directions
Forward
Backward
To one side
To the other side
Up
Down
Levels
High
Medium
Low
Ranges
Large
Medium
Small
Planes
Pathways (floor or air)
Straight
Curved
Zigzag

---

[3]Broer, M.: *Efficiency of Human Movement.* Philadelphia, W. B. Saunders Company, 1973, p. 28.
[4]Gilliom, B.: *Basic Movement Education For Children.* Reading, Massachusetts, Addison-Wesley Publishing Company, 1970, pp. 212–213. Reproduced by permission of the publisher.

FIGURE 14-4.   In how many different ways can you move your hands? (Courtesy of Barbara Mettler, Tucson Creative Dance Center.)

Relationship of body parts to objects:
on, off, over, around, across, under,
near to, far from
      Walls, floor
      Boxes, benches, beams

Manipulating
      Balls (bouncing, catching, tossing, pushing)
      Ropes, hoops

Relationship of one person to another
or others
      Near to
      Far from
      Meeting
      Parting
      Facing
      Side by side
      Shadowing
      Mirroring
      Leading
      Following

By transfer of weight
      Steplike actions
      Rocking
      Rolling
      Sliding
      Flight

Dimensions of space
      Speed
          Slow
          Medium
          Fast
          Accelerating
          Decelerating
      Rhythm
          To pulse beats
          To phrases and rhythmic pat-
          terns

Degrees of force
      Strong
      Medium
      Weak

Qualities of force
      Sudden, explosive
      Sustained, smooth

Creating force
      Quick starts
      Sustained powerful movements
      Held balances

Absorbing force
      Sudden stops on-balance
      Gradual absorption ("give")

By balancing (active stillness)
    Balancing weight on different body parts
    Balancing on different numbers of parts

Division of space
    Self space
    General space

Dimensions of flow
    Free flow
    Bound flow
    Movement sequences
    Smooth series of movements
    Beginning and ending
    Preparation, action, and recovery
        smoothly linked
    Transitions

TEACHING TECHNIQUES

It is only from creative teaching that creative movement experience for children can evolve. The following suggestions, however, can help make these richly shared educational experiences valuable to both the teacher and the learner:

Class Organization

Scattered formations with plenty of space available for children to run, skip, and move freely about are needed for this program. From the beginning the teacher should condition the children to stop, look, and listen when they hear a given signal, such as a drum beat, piano chord, or even a whistle.

Problem Posing

Although each teacher should develop her own technique for presenting problems, suggested ones are: "Can anyone . . . ?" "What . . . ?" "See if you might do this . . . ?" "Who can do it in a better, faster, louder, quieter (and so forth) way . . . ?" or "Let's make up a game using this. . . ."

Safety

Since the element of competition is removed in movement exploration, few children will overtax their limits, and most will set the more difficult tasks for themselves. It is suggested, however, that having the children all run clockwise or counterclockwise in a circle, start to move at the same time, or play in a designated area will help them to become more safety-conscious.

SUGGESTED EQUIPMENT

Use as wide a variety of equipment as possible in this program. Suggested are

Many ropes of varying lengths
Balls of all sizes
Blocks of all sizes
Wands, broomsticks, dowel rods
Parachutes
Horizontal and window ladders
Telephone poles, large tree trunks
   for climbing

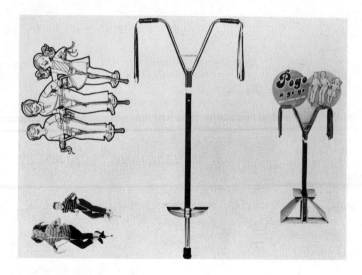

FIGURE 14–5. How many ways can you bounce on the pogo stick? (Courtesy of Things from Bell, Incorporated, Homer, New York.)

Tumbling mats
Phonograph records
Magic ropes
Hoops[5]
Barrels to roll
Car and bicycle tires, inner tubes, hula hoops
Balance beams and boards
Boxes of all sizes and weights
Climbing steps and ladders
Beanbags (one for every one or two children)
Low turning bars
Teeters
Many 2 × 4 boards to be used in balancing
  and jumping activities
All the equipment suggested
  in the chapter on Rhythms and Dances
Drums, tambourines, wooden blocks,
  rhythm sticks, rattles, maracas
Masking tape for marking floor spaces
Benches of varying heights
Cargo nets
Large building blocks
Long stilts and tin can walkers
Traffic cones
Floor scooters
Individual mats

SUGGESTED DEVELOPMENTAL ACTIVITIES WITHOUT EQUIPMENT

Body Awareness Activities

Two helpful rules in guiding children in movement exploration are "Don't bump" and "Freeze on signal."

---

[5]Available from Ed-Nu, Inc., 5115 Route 38, Pennsauken, New Jersey 08109.

1. While in a big circle make yourself as big as you can, then as small as you can. Then expand slowly like a balloon, and then like a tall tree growing from a seed.
2. Run around the room in various floor patterns. Move sideways, backwards, in zigzags, and in circles.
3. Make your body thin, fat, round, like a crooked tree, and so forth.
4. Make various body parts—head, trunk, arms, and legs. Combine these with floor patterns.
5. Experiment with *levels* by taking high, medium, or low positions while moving across the floor. Get in a circle with one child in the middle. The center child takes a high, medium, or low position, and the others move in a circle using that level in locomotion.
6. Explore *balance* by having other points of contact with the floor besides the feet. Try the knees, hands, rear, and back. Try having one point of contact, then three, four, six, or all points.
7. Lie on your back with both feet in the air, and pedal as if riding a bicycle. Pedal slowly, quickly, alternately fast and slow; pedal fast, and then apply brakes suddenly to come to a fast stop.
8. Place your right hand on the ground; then extend your body, resting your weight on your right arm and your feet. Rotate clockwise and counterclockwise with a stepping movement. Repeat with the left hand.
9. Make circles: large circles with your hands, small circles with your fingers. Make circles with your right foot, your left foot, whole body, just your head, both feet, both hands together, and one hand going one way and the other the opposite, and so forth. Move across the floor leading with one body part—elbow, head, back, right hand, and shoulder. Make a floor pattern of a circle, square, or triangle.
10. Walk in slow motion, fast motion, like your shoes are stuck in mud, like you are in a marching band, on your toes, in giant steps, on your heels, without bending your knees, like you are walking on ice, like you are wearing snowshoes, and so forth.
11. Be a growing thing. Begin as a seed, break through the ground, grow leaves and flowers, then wilt and die.

Walking Activities

1. How many tiny or giant steps does it take you to cross this room?
2. Can you change your direction (level, speed) and still keep walking?
3. Can you express joy (sorrow, anger) when walking?
4. Can you walk on only your toes, your heels, the insides of your feet, the outsides of your feet?
5. Discover how many ways you can walk.
6. Can you walk fast around the room without running into anyone?
7. Can you walk turning your feet in different ways? What is the easiest and best way to walk?
8. Can you walk only on your toes, only on your heels, without bending your knees? Of all the ways to walk, which one is the most comfortable way?
9. Can you walk as if you were stuck in gooey mud, on slippery ice, on eggs, stepping over big boxes, on the moon?
10. Can you make up a patterned sequence of all the ways you can walk and change each way after every eight steps?

Running Activities

1. Run and stop fast when you hear the whistle.
2. Who can run in the greatest number of different ways?
3. Can you combine a run with any other kind of movement, such as a jump?
4. If you can run forward, how many other ways can you run?
5. Can you run using your arms in a way other than swinging them forward and backward?
6. Can you run very close to the floor and change on a signal to go to your highest running position?
7. Using a hoop, can you run forward pushing it and then run inside and out of it?
8. Run with a partner. On a signal, you run forward while he runs backward, staying close together. Can both of you move in a zigzag pattern?

9. Make up a running game with the help of three classmates. Teach it to the rest of the class.
10. Make up a sequence pattern using running, walking, leaping, and hopping.

Hopping Activities

1. Hop as fast as you can on one foot.
2. Jump as lightly as you can on both feet.
3. Combine a hop with another movement.
4. If you can hop in a circle, see in how many other patterns you can hop.
5. Jump as high as you can five times; then lower your body every time you hop for five more times. Who can hop lowest to the floor?
6. Hop in a big circle and then make it get smaller and smaller each time you hop to make a complete circle.
7. Hop as any animal does, and we will guess what one you are trying to be.
8. How many different ways can you bend your body as you hop around the room?
9. Hop, and land with your knees bent. Do it again, and land with your knees straight. Which is the easiest and most graceful to do?
10. With a partner try to bump your partner out of balance as he tries to do the same to you. Keep your arms folded at your chest. Play a game giving a point to the one who causes his partner to put one foot down first to keep his balance. Which one can score five points first?

Sliding Activities

1. See how many ways you can slide other than forward.
2. Combine a slide with any other kind of movement.
3. Slide around in a circle with a partner.
4. Slide in a big circle with two others. Can you find a way to go in and out of a circle while sliding?
5. Can you slide face-to-face and then back-to-back with a partner?
6. Take slides of varying sizes.
7. How low to the floor can you slide? How high above the floor can you do it?
8. Make up a movement pattern combining slides with hops and skips.
9. Make up a pattern showing how many different ways you can slide.
10. Slide as if you were on ice, on glue.

Skipping Activities

1. Skip forward, in a big circle, then on a diagonal.
2. Can you skip holding hands with a partner?
3. How many others can skip with you holding hands?
4. How fast can you skip? How slowly?
5. Can you change from a skip to a slide or a gallop?
6. Skip at different levels.
7. Skip as high as you can. Discover what helps you go higher.
8. See how many different ways you can use your arms as you skip.
9. Skip and bend your body in as many different ways as you can.
10. Can you skip a rope with a partner?

Jumping Activities

1. How many times can you jump up and down on one foot? On both feet?
2. Can you jump around in a circle? In a square? Forward? Backward?
3. Who can jump first on one foot and then on the other for the longest time?
4. Can you jump from the top of this box or table to the mat below?
5. Can you jump, run, jump, skip?
6. Jump in and out of a hoop. How many different ways can you jump and do this?

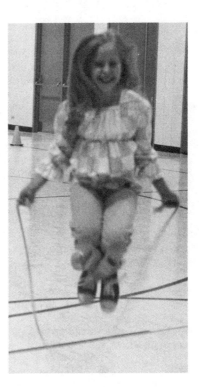

FIGURE 14-6. Oh, How I love to jump rope! (Courtesy of the WHA-TV Photo Department, Madison, Wisconsin, and the AAHPER, Washington, D.C.)

7. How many different ways can you jump off a chair or a long bench?
8. Can you jump and land on all fours? On two feet and one arm?
9. Make a patterned sequence of jumping with your legs crossed and uncrossed.
10. Jump in place and then vary the speed of your jumps in as many different directions as you can.

Locomotor Partner Activities

1. Each person has his hands on the partner's shoulders. Make a pattern across the floor in unison, trying to keep the movement flowing smoothly. Try sitting down, dancing in a circle, hopping, galloping, and so forth.
2. One partner is the leader, and the other follows his actions like a reflection in a mirror. Try various levels and movement sequences. Change leaders. Try it one time without specifying a leader. Is that easier or more difficult?
3. Designate one partner to be the sounder and one to be the mover. The sounder makes various noises that direct the movement of the mover. As the sounder makes noise, the mover attempts to "look" like the noise sounds. Try very high tones, low tones, animal noises, soft noises, loud noises, and so forth. Change roles.
4. Stand around a circle on the floor or a rope in the shape of a circle. One partner is inside the circle, facing his partner who is on the outside. The inside person is the leader, and when he jumps out of the circle, his partner will jump in. Follow the leader's actions, using two feet, then one foot.
5. In partners, scatter across the room. When a whistle blows, everyone must find his partner, join hands, and sit down quickly. The last couple to sit down is eliminated. Have the children run, skip, slide, hop, and so forth before they must quickly find their partners.

Other General Locomotor Activities

1. Choose a corner in this room. Run to it fast when I say "Go!" Now do it very slowly.
2. Bend as far as you can forward, backward, and to the side as you walk forward.

3. Make yourself squat as low to the floor as you can. Stretch high as near to the ceiling as you can.
4. Raise your right arm and left leg, then your left arm and right leg, while marching in place. Now march around the room.
5. As you run forward change from being a tall giant to a tiny mouse, but keep moving.
6. Working in groups of threes, see how many locomotor movements you can make into a rhythmical movement pattern.
7. Walk as if you were in a parade. What else can you imitate doing as you walk?
8. Using a hoop, make up a patterned rhythmical movement using running, skipping, and one other locomotor movement of any kind.
9. Can you leap backward using different levels and directions?
10. Make up a sequence of locomotor movements to your partner's drum beats. Change roles.

Imitative Activities

Show me how you can move like

1. Falling snowflakes
2. Baby kittens
3. Bubbles bursting
4. Firecracker
5. Accordion
6. Electric fan
7. Wind storm
8. Inchworm
9. Waves
10. Airplanes
11. Bears
12. Squirrels
13. Flower growing
14. Cowboy riding a pony
15. Popcorn popping
16. Rocket
17. Ice skaters
18. Humming birds
19. Big eagles flying
20. Elephants
21. Old man
22. Frog jumping
23. Horse prancing
24. Seesaw (partners)
25. Swimming fast
26. Elevator going up and coming down

Show me how you can move like

1. Rocking chairs. Get on your knees. How far back can you rock? How far forward? To the side?
2. A person and his reflection in a mirror (using partners). One copies the other's movements as if he were his reflection in a mirror.
3. Rag doll. Be limp, and act as though you have wooden legs, body, and head.
4. Snowmen. Melt slowly from your head down.
5. You are happy, sad, tired, fast, stuck in glue, on ice, stepping over big boxes.
6. Gliders. Take off, fly around high and low, land, and fly over mountains.
7. You are pulling a cloud down to the ground.
8. You are pushing a car, a lawnmower, a swing, a big box.
9. You are climbing a rope.
10. You are jumping on a feather bed. How high can you jump?

SUGGESTED DEVELOPMENTAL ACTIVITIES USING EQUIPMENT

Turning Bar

1. Can you make a circle over this bar?
2. Who can chin himself on the bar?
3. Can you circle the bar using just one leg?
4. Who can "skin the cat" using this bar?

5. Can you reach behind you and by grasping the bar make a circle over it with your body?
6. What other movements can you do on the bar using only your arms?
7. See how many times you can chin yourself on the bar.
8. Can you "skin the cat" by holding the bar with a double overgrip, then kicking your feet up, pulling your knees to your chest, moving your feet between your hands, and lowering your feet and legs below your shoulder, and then land on your feet as you release your grip?
9. Can you jump up and bring your body over the bar to support your stomach with your arms as you hold your body outstretched in a diagonal line?
10. Can you do a one-leg turn on the bar? See if you can (1) jump to an erect body position, (2) change the grip of your left hand to an undergrip, (3) reach with your right hand beyond your left hand to take an overgrip, and (4) at the same time, shift your weight from your right to your left leg and bring it over the bar to support your extended body by locking your outstretched arms.

Climbing Ladder

1. See how fast you can go up and down the ladder.
2. Can you climb up the ladder without using your feet?
3. Can you weave in and out of the rungs to go up and come down the ladder?
4. Can you skip any rungs while climbing it?
5. What else can you do using this ladder?
6. Race a partner up and down the ladder using only your arms going up and back down. How fast can you do this?
7. See if you can hang from the ladder with your head down.
8. Try bringing your feet down to touch the floor as you hang from the ladder with your head down. How must you hold your hands to do this?
9. What different things can you do with a partner on the ladder?
10. Can you hang by your toes from it?

Stairs

1. Who can go up and down the stairs without holding onto a railing?
2. Can you go up and down them by hopping on two feet? One foot?
3. Can you go up and down backward? Jump up and down them facing sideward?
4. Can you walk up and down them balancing yourself by your hands?
5. Can you go up and down by moving over one, two, or more steps?
6. See how many different things you can do while still in the air as you jump off.
7. What different movements can you and a partner do on each step of the stairs?
8. How fast can you go over the stairs? How slowly? Which is harder to do? Why?
9. Can you use your hands to balance your body as you do a mule kick? What must you remember to do when you do a mule kick?
10. Can you jump on and off of the stairs and make a half-turn? A full turn? How can you use your arms more to do this better?

Wands

1. Can you balance the stick in the palm of your hand? On two fingers, then on one finger?
2. Can you throw it up into the air, spin around, and catch it before it hits the floor?
3. Can you play pitch-and-catch with it with a partner, using the same hand you catch it with to throw it to her?
4. Can you balance the stick while kneeling on one knee? Both knees? While slowly lying down and getting back up?
5. Can you twirl the stick while pretending to be a drum majorette?
6. What kinds of relays can you do using them?
8. Make squares on the floor using four sticks, and hop in and out of the complete square using one foot. What other locomotor movements can you use to go in and out of them?

9. Use a stick and a hoop to make up a good exercise to develop your body.
10. How can you use the stick for a good developmental exercise sitting down? While lying on your back?

Tires

1. See how fast you can roll the tire.
2. See if you can roll it in a circle. In a straight line. Backward.
3. Jump in and out of it moving around in a circle, if the tire is flat on the floor.
4. Can you crawl through it when someone holds it up?
5. Can you throw a volleyball through it? A baseball?
6. What simple games can you make up using four to six tires?
7. What kind of a relay can you do using three tires?
8. Standing on your hands, can you go in and out of the whole circled tire without falling?
9. Can you do a cartwheel over the tire? Two of them in a row? Two on top of each other?
10. Can you and a partner have a tug of war with a bicycle tire? What must you do with your body in order to throw your partner off balance or pull him across the line?

Cargo Nets[6]

1. Can you climb the net using only your hands?
2. Using your hands and feet, who can climb the net the fastest?
3. Can you make up a relay for two teams to play on the net?
4. Can you climb over the net? Through a net hole?
5. Can you hang by your knees on any part of the net?
6. What can you do with a partner on the nets that you could not do by yourself?
7. Can you swing on the net? How many different ways can you do this?
8. Can you climb, swing, and jump off on to the mat, and then do a forward roll?
9. How slowly can you climb in and out of each hole in the net?
10. What developmental exercises can you do on the net for your body? For only your arms? For only your legs?

Grovee Loop[7]

This new type of equipment develops motor skills, hand-eye coordination, and many opportunities for self-expression. It can be used indoors or outdoors, with or without teacher supervision, to provide numerous challenging movement problem experiences that develop manual dexterity as well as other aspects of neuromuscular skill.

1. Can you roll the loop forward, backward, around in a circle, in a square?
2. Can you make a full U-turn with it?
3. Can you push the loop forward with the stick, let it roll ahead of you, and then reinsert the stick in order to roll the hoop around in a circle?
4. Can you balance the loop on the stick? Can you do it and gradually sit down while keeping it balanced, and then come back up to an upright position?
5. Can you use the loop for a jump rope?
6. Can you swing the loop around your left arm and then transfer it to the other and still keep it swinging continuously? Can you transfer it from your right to your left arm, too?
7. Can you swing the loop around your left foot, then jump over it every time it passes your right foot? Can you do this by jumping on your right one and swinging it with your left foot?

---

[6]Available from Sterling Recreation Products, 7 Oak Place, Montclair, New Jersey 07092.
[7]Available from Ed-Nu, Inc., 5115 Route 38, Pennsauken, New Jersey 08109.

8. Can you roll the loop around an obstacle course without touching any of the objects?
9. Can you find other things you can do with the loop by yourself? What can you do with a partner? What can three of you do? Four of you?

Wooden Stilts

Although wooden stilts and tin-can walkers can be purchased commercially, they can also be easily made from scrap lumber and junk materials. The use of both or either will help children gain better total body control and balance, as well as add new program materials. The children will learn, among other things, that their hands and feet must work together, if they are to maintain an upright position.

Find out if you can

1. Keep your balance on your stilts.
2. Walk forward, backward, sideways and around in a circle on them.
3. Race with a partner on them.
4. Step in and out of a hula hoop without touching it.
5. Go around an obstacle course.

Benches

A wide variety of movement skills can be mastered through the use of low balance benches. Not more than four children should use one bench. Mats should be placed at the end of the bench for older groups, but for the youngest, the benches should be placed on large mats and spotters used for greater safety. The children should learn a short, routinized, proper bench approach and how to bend the knees and brake the body when dismounting. This piece of equipment is excellent for developing total body control and directionality, for through its use children will master movements to the left as well as to the right.

Suggested activities include

1. Running, galloping, skipping, moving backward and sliding sideward on it, and jumping on and off of it using both feet, only your right foot, your left foot, and then alternate feet.
2. Doing a forward roll on it, a backward roll, a cartwheel, and a handspring.
3. Balancing on it while sitting with both feet and arms held high into the air (the **v** sit).
4. Doing push-ups on it; discovering what other exercises you can do on it.
5. After you learn how to dismount quickly and well, finding out how many stunts you can do on the mat and still keep moving forward (i.e., the forward roll, jackknife hand and toe touch, and so forth).
6. Crawling over obstacles and through hoops or tires that are on the bench without falling off it or touching them.
7. Doing the wheelbarrow stunt with a partner. What other stunts can you two do on the bench?

Tires

Old bicycle and car tires can be used for a wide variety of movement exploration activities. They can also be placed in a number of different patterns, for example, number figures such as a 7 or various geometric patterns piled on top of one another. They can also be rolled for a locomotor movement exploration experience, as well as placed stationary on the floor.

Find out if you can

1. Walk in and out of all the tires without touching a single one of them.
2. Run and hop in and out of them using both feet, just your right one, just your left, and then alternate feet.
3. Walk around the top of them without touching the ground. Run, skip, and hop around them.
4. Jump around the tops of them like a rabbit or a kangaroo. Be any other kind of animal as you go around the top of them and we will guess which one you are.
5. Roll a tire. How many different ways can you roll it?
6. Stack the tires up on top of each other. How many different movements can you do on them?
7. Can you and a partner do at least three different tricks or stunts on them? Can you do five? How many different things can three of you do on them?
8. Can you crawl through one, three, five or more tires while someone holds them up for you?
9. Can you throw a big ball through a tire? A little one ?

Gym Scooters

Gym scooters can bring much freshness into the physical education program. A wide variety of activities can be played with them, but best of all, children using them are quick to discover new games and exploratory movements they can do with them. For class use, every child should have a scooter. These can be homemade or obtained commercially.

Find

1. The best way to go forward and backward while sitting down. Which swimming strokes are like those you used to do?
2. What and where are the best places to sit and what is the best way to move your feet to gain speed.
3. What you can do with a partner pushing you (pulling you) as you sit on the scooter. Can you do as many as five different things?
4. What different things you can do using two scooters. Can you move in more than two directions?
5. What games you can play using scooters. Can scooters be used to play football and baseball?
6. How many different simple games, such as tag or dodgeball, you can play using scooters.
7. How three, four, five, or seven people can move together as a single unit. What must each of you do?

Parachutes[8]

1. With each person holding a piece of the parachute, see if you can make big waves with it. Can you make little waves turn into big ones?
2. How high can you make the chute go up in the air? How low can you make it come down to the floor?
3. When I throw these volleyballs on the chute can you make them pop up and down like popcorn in a hot pan? Can you pop any off the chute? How many can you pop at one time?
4. Can you make one volleyball roll around the chute without stopping? When I add a second one see if you can make it catch up to the first one.
5. Can all of you run fast to the right (to the left), and turn the chute like a big wheel? Can you skip and do this? Slide? Gallop?
6. Raise the chute quickly. Can you all turn and get under it before it touches the floor?

---

[8]See the clever booklet *Oh, Chute!* by Doug Evans for other suggested activities. It is available from Raven Industries, Applied Technology Division, P. O. Box 1007, Sioux Falls, South Dakota 57101.

The record *Parachute Play*, obtainable from Educational Activities, Freeport, Long Island, has both lively music and directions for the teacher to use.

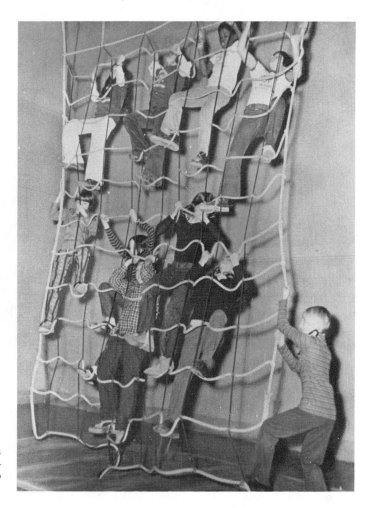

FIGURE 14–7. Cargo nets should be part of the movement exploration equipment. (Courtesy of Jayfro Corporation, Montville, Connecticut.)

7. Can you do any stunt, such as turn a cartwheel, under the chute and run back to place before it comes down to touch you? Who can do another stunt? Can you do two before it touches? Who can do two different ones? Who can do more?
8. Give each child a number. Call out two numbers and have these two exchange places before the chute comes down to touch them. Could they do it if four numbers are called?
9. How many things can you and a partner make up that we could do with this chute?
10. What else could we use this chute for in our class to learn more about how our bodies move?

CREATIVE PLAY

The beginning of the century found children with few toys and the capacity to play for hours on end with "findings." A pile of sand, a few bits of broken glass or china, and twigs furnished materials for full-scale villages complete with houses, barns, schools, and churches. Tea parties with mud pies were held with great formality at a pedestal table made of dirt. From large leaves and twigs young designers fashioned hats, capes, skirts, and dresses, which were modeled with an amusing exactness of adult patterns. Labor-saving devices were few and mothers too busy, except to call children for meals, naps, and baths.

FIGURE 14–8.   The parachute can be used in a number of different ways. (Courtesy of Raven Industries, Inc., Sioux Falls, South Dakota.)

Today, the infant lies in a toy-bedecked crib and collects more toys as birthdays and Christmases pass. Sand is to be had by the load, and woe to the child who dares pluck a leaf from a guarded and nurtured tree. Labor-saving devices have left mothers time to play nursemaid, a job made easier by access to parks, well-equipped libraries, recreation centers, nursery schools, neighborhood movie houses, radio, and television sets. Urban children are gradually being deprived of all stimuli that once enabled them to play without direct instruction and supervision, and mothers complain that the children cannot amuse themselves over a thirty-minute period without being bored.

Today's teacher is completely aware of the short span of attention present in her new pupil, which is characteristic of the age level but is not entirely physiological or psychological. The classroom teacher and the special teachers have tried to remedy this and to give the child a measure of security and self-sufficiency by equipping him with the tools for living. It cannot be said that real effort has not been made to develop the "whole" child mentally, physically, and emotionally, but how near have we come to meeting this objective? Pâté de foie gras is palatable, but is the process good for the goose? We still stuff children and expect magic results in the way of initiative. How many of us ask "Is there a child in the class who could create from his own background of experience an enjoyable period of play acceptable to his classmates?" It is far easier with age, poise, and experience to direct play than to develop in one child the ability to do the same thing "free hand." The art teacher can take potential talent and draw from it the maximum in imagination, reality, or originality. Play is laughter, high spirits, and joy unlimited. In this field where sheer enjoyment is the key it would be shameful if teachers did not meet the challenge of the children's needs and at least give them the *chance* to be ingenious leaders.

Creative play is not new, but its possibilities are comparatively untouched. There are several reasons that explain this fallow corner in a field rich with all the newest trends in progressive education, the most prevalent being the overcrowded conditions that exist in the majority of public schools. The average teacher finds it difficult to deal with a class two to four times the normal load without assuming full or partial leadership. Creative play calls for small, intimate groups, managed in the most informal manner. The ideal group would not exceed 20, and each child would have frequent chances for expression. A certain amount of regimentation is required in all large schools, especially where the platoon system is used, but although it is necessary, the routine subdues latent creativity. The time element is another reason why creative play has not flourished. Creativity cannot be nurtured by bells. Nevertheless, creative play can and has been developed in many schools, in recreation centers, and on playgrounds. It takes a gifted teacher to hold on to a vision gained and to reproject it into the minds of the participants with sustaining and refreshing enthusiasm the next day.

There can be no static method for developing creative play. The group—its individual characteristics and its dominant field of experience—will dictate to the resourceful teacher the plan of procedure. An imaginative six year old child may invent a game that will keep a class engrossed for thirty minutes. There are also people who play a piano by ear, whereas others must learn scales and notes before tackling the simplest of piano selections. Thus, one may find a group of fourth graders who must be reintroduced to the fundamentals of play, for example, chasing, fleeing, tagging, seeking, dodging, guessing, and following, before one child comes forth with an original game. However, we, as teachers, cannot complain too loudly, since we have leaned with monotonous regularity on tried and true game books for years. One must face innumerable presentations of questionable originality. Tact and patience will reward the persistent teacher. In any case, the reward will be adequate when the child can competently lead a game.

This does not mean that every child will immediately burst forth with new and exciting games. Games of dubious creativity will still crop up, but the group will become more discriminating and take the criticizing chore out of the hands of the teacher by observing "Ah, I learned that at Daily Vacation Bible School" or "We learned that at camp." The hard sledding is over. From then on original ideas will start appearing with encouraging regularity. Do not be too critical and, above all, try to gear your evaluation to the grade level.

Children are innately creative, but the current, consuming interest will always be reflected in games. At present "Spaceman" and "Man from Mars" are "It." Children from Spokane to Los Angeles, Dallas to Duluth, and New Haven to Key West are make-believe cowboys, roping, cutting calves,[9] chasing rustlers, packing six-shooters, slapping leather,[10] and addressing playmates as "podner." Sex does not enter into the picture. There is an "Annie Oakley"[11] for each "astronaut." Even now cowboys are becoming "old hat," for youthful "prospectors" are industriously beginning to search out atomic materials with toy Geiger counters or fly to the moon in a rocket. This does not make any difference as long as the child is creating a type of play that includes mental and physical activity, and as long as he is guided into democratic channels.

Creative play involving movement fundamentals will be found in its most productive form from the first through the fourth grades. Thereafter, new games will still appear that concern themselves largely with skills in lead-up games, but the child's interest has shifted to team sports, and creativity is manifested through methods for

---

[9]Round-up—separation of calves from stock ready for market.
[10]Hitting leather chaps with bridle reins to urge on horses and cattle.
[11]Real life character who was a crack shot.

FIGURE 14–9. Creativity can often be best expressed through movement. (Courtesy of Los Angeles City Schools, Los Angeles, California.)

improving offensive and defensive play. However, games related to subject matter may be created through the eighth grade and on into high school as a method for motivating learning.

Numerous European physical educators are experimenting successfully with providing educational and creative play situations for children. The child is challenged to perform a movement but is not told how to do it, for each must create his own solution to the challenging problem posed by the teacher or group. Special emphasis is given to tasks that strengthen the trunk and feet, increase body flexibility and elasticity, develop a "feel" for movements such as bending and stretching that will develop good posture, perfect movement skills in running, jumping, throwing, and supporting activities, and develop rhythmic beauty for movement. The foremost exponent and leader of this new and creative elementary physical education is Liselott Diem of Germany. From her work, as well as from that done experimentally in other European countries, the new approach to elementary physical education, known as "movement education," has developed.[12]

[12]A copy of her book translated into English, entitled *Who Can,* is available at $1.60 per copy from Mrs. Paul Dunsing, George Williams College, Downers Grove, Illinois 60515. It is also available from The Wilhelm Limpert Company, Frankfort, Germany. A wonderful film of her experimental work with primary children is available from Robert Freeman, Metropolitan YMCA, 19 S. La Salle St., Chicago, Illinois 60601.

FIGURE 14–10. Movement exploration in the elementary school curriculum is vital to the child's development of body control, expressiveness, and creativity. (Courtesy of Mr. Ray Sacker, Victor Record Division, Radio Corporation of America.)

Examples of the movement tasks posed as creative problems for children to solve that Mrs. Diem has found to be successful and satisfying for children include

Who Can *(using a box)*
> Run the most lightly, land on the top of the box, then jump off?
> Jump from the box and touch the floor for the briefest time with his finger tips?
> Place his hands on the box, jump upright on it, and take a flying jump down the most gracefully?

Who Can *(using no equipment)*
> Stretch his legs the highest while turning a cartwheel and land on his feet softly like a cat?
> Skip forward, skip sideways, and alternate running with skipping first alone, then with partner, and then in rows?
> Skip backwards with long reaching skips, next with a basketball on his head, and then with his arms crossed behind the back? Then skip facing and away from a partner in unison with him?
> Roll backwards and forwards quickly and quietly; sit touching his knees with his forehead?
> Walk like a little man and then a giant, and change the fastest from these?
> Sit on the floor alternating a toe and heel; change the fastest while sitting the tallest?
> Frog jump from a squat position?
> Bounce up and down in the air, turning and spinning?
> "Merry-go-round" with a partner, changing from high to low, slow to fast?
> Run on his hands and feet forward, backward, sideward?

Who Can *(with broomsticks or wands)*
  Run like a big snake with ten others around the sticks, then run the fastest alone over the sticks?
  Walk forward, backward, and then sideward on the stick?
  Stand the stick upright, turn around quickly, and catch it before it touches the ground?
  Run, walk, and skip forward, backward, and sideward while juggling the stick on the palm of his hand?
  Juggle the wand on his finger, sit down, and stand up while still balancing it?

Who Can *(with a hoop or tire)*
  Roll the hoop forward, backward, and around in a circle while walking, running, and then skipping?
  Pick the hoop up with his toes?
  Roll the hoop and run through it?
  Use the hoop like a skipping rope and jump through it?

Who Can *(with a telephone pole, skinned tree trunk, or beam)*
  Walk upright up the inclined pole and then walk on it on all fours?
  Walk across the pole when it is three, four, then five feet above ground in horizontal position?
  Walk halfway across and sit down and get up without using his hands?
  Travel on the underside while hanging by his hands and feet?
  Walk across throwing and catching a ball, rolling a hoop, or doing something else?

Who Can *(with a ball)*
  Skip forward and backward while bouncing the ball?
  Turn around and catch it while skipping?
  Sit like a tailor and roll the ball around him the fastest?
  Lift his legs high into the air and roll the ball under, around, and over them?
  Start from a sitting position, throw the ball up, and catch it standing?
  Serpentine run around five balls in squads without touching any ball?
  Jump like a bunny over five balls one at a time?
  Bounce the ball completely around himself without turning his whole body or moving his feet?
  Sit on the floor and dribble the ball around himself? Do the same while stretched out on his stomach or on his back? Get up from any of these positions while still dribbling the ball?

What Mrs. Diem and other European physical educators have done, as illustrated above, can be used as a pattern by any creative teacher and can be enlarged upon with the help of his students. The carry-over values of such creativeness are vast. A physically educated individual is one who can use his whole body wisely with the maximum of output and the minimum effort in our ever-changing and problem-ridden world. Children will gain skill in movement and problem solving through this type of creative play, which can have great carry-over value into their own adulthood.

Mimetics

Mimetics can be presented in the first through the sixth grades. A child loses self-consciousness quickly in interpreting the suggested subject. At first the movements will be actual imitations of toys, machines, or animals. Later the movements can become more subtle and suggestive rather than purely imitative. Mimetics serve as a smooth lead-up to creative dance. Musical accompaniment is not always necessary for mimetics but will be suggested when there is a need for music in each of the following activities.

1. Mechanical
   a. Bicycle—Series I, Ruth Evans.
   b. See-Saw—Series I, Ruth Evans.
   c. Airplane—Series I, Ruth Evans; Rhythms for Children—Vic. 20162.
   d. Jumping Jack—Series II, Ruth Evans.
   e. Fire Engine—No music; pantomime sirens, driving through the streets, unwinding the hose, and so forth.
   f. Train—Series I, Ruth Evans.
   g. Dolls—Dance of Chinese Dolls, RCA Victor 22163-A.
   h. Tops—Series I, Ruth Evans.
   i. Clocks—Series II, Ruth Evans.
   j. Elevator—Series II, Ruth Evans.
   k. Swing—Series I, Ruth Evans.
   l. Railroad Rhythms.
   m. Windmills.
2. Animals
   a. Horse—Series I, Ruth Evans.
   b. Bear—No music; pantomine slovenly walk, rolling gait, looking for honey. Bear in the zoo sits, claps paws, and catches a thrown piece of bread.
   c. Elephant—Series I, Ruth Evans—Arms form the trunk, which swings from side to side; elephant sits up, eats, drinks water, and sprays water on the crowd.
   d. Puppy—Does tricks: rolls over, plays dead, sits up, covers face, prays, and walks on hind feet and then on front feet.
   e. Kitten—Plays with a ball of yarn, retreats, stalks, and pounces on prey.
   f. Kangaroo—No music; pantomime hop.
   g. Deer—No music; pantomime being chased by hunters and hounds.
   h. Squirrel—No music; pantomime hiding nuts, using short, jerky movements.
   i. Beasts.
   j. Puppy.
   k. Cat stretches—Stanley Bowman 206.
   l. Rabbit—Stanley Bowman 203.
3. Insects
   a. Butterfly—Butterfly Dance—Indian Rhythms, RCA Victor 22174; Ponies and Butterflies, RCA Victor 22079.
   b. Bee—The Flight of the Bumblebee.
   c. Cricket—No music; pantomime lively jumping movements, rubbing arms together.
   d. Firefly—No music; pantomine quick flitting movements, interspersed with pauses.
4. Miscellaneous
   a. Birds—Rhythms for Children, 20401.
   b. Witch—Series I, Ruth Evans.
   c. Giant—In the Hall of the Mountain King, Victor 11835; The Giants, Victor 20743.
   d. My Shadow.
   e. Bubbles.
   f. Snowflakes and Skating.
   g. Little Fishes.
   h. Elf—Gnomes and Dwarfs, Victor 19882.

Creative Movement Using Stories and Themes

Creativity can often be best expressed in movement. Creative movement is an activity that releases seeds of creative ability that grow with great abandon when sown at an early age. The child on the primary level is full of energy and free of inhibitions. This provides an opportunity for the teacher to help him develop his innate creative ability at a productive age.

Every child intensely feels his surrounding environment and is acutely conscious of change or new additions. Generally, each child naturally reacts in a different way to these stimuli; this is as it should be, but such is not the case when creative dance is introduced. There will always be the more aggressive leader who sets a pattern that will be followed sheep-like by less imaginative children. Participation may be accepted as a goal but is an inadequate one. Aping should be discouraged from the first and differences pointed out to develop pride in the originality of individual expression.

Whether the exercise involves abstract feeling or a story or theme, a picture should be painted by the teacher to fire the imagination. The instructor may select one group and accompany their rhythm with a drumbeat, accenting exciting moments with a heavier beat.

1. *Story or theme*—The use of a story or theme offers excellent transition from mimetics and story acting to creative rhythm.
   a. *Story Example:*
      Little Red Riding Hood
         Divide the class: Girls are Little Red Riding Hoods and the boys are the wolves. Little Red Riding Hood skips through the forest with her basket. She arrives at her grandmother's and is tired and out of breath. In her encounter with her strange-looking grandmother, she shows surprise, bewilderment, and horror. The boy (wolf) shows pleasure, satisfaction, and greed.
      The Three Bears
         Divide the class into groups of four. Go through the story, letting Goldilocks run and skip, eat the food, and lie down to sleep. The bears enter and show chagrin and anger as they find their porridge eaten. They discover Goldilocks who awakens and flees with the bears close behind.
      Snow White and the Seven Dwarfs
         Divide the class into groups of nine. To the slow beat of the drum the dwarfs march with Snow White who is in the center in a trance as a sleepwalker. The prince releases her from her sleep by tapping her on the shoulder. Sadness gives way to joy as the entire group leaps and jumps.
   b. *Theme Example:*

Circus Day	Special Days
Clown	Halloween
Marionettes, RCA Victor 22163	Easter
Transportation	Valentine's Day
Walking	Christmas
Bicycling	Thanksgiving
Riding in cars	School's out!
Trains	Sport Movements
Plane	Rowing
Horse	Swimming
Other People at Work	Football
Eskimos	Skating
Indians	Track
Dutch	Fishing
Sailors	Parade
Farmers	Horses
Big game hunters	Elephants
Songs	Dancing Bears
Peter Cottontail	The Seasons
Rudolph the Red	Visit to the Park
Nosed Reindeer	Visit to the Farm
Santa Claus Is	Seasonal Characters
Coming to Town	Witch
Stories	Santa Claus
Three Little Pigs	Cupid
Billy Goat Gruff	Easter Bunny
Jack and the	
Beanstalk	

2. *Free feeling*—Examples:
   a. Walk in the leaves—The first frosts have painted the leaves with many colors, and they lie in a heavy carpet on the ground. The leaves are dry and crackle underfoot; a kick sends them sailing into the air.
   b. Wind in the trees—The wind sighs in the tall pines as they sway back and forth. The limbs of the large oaks sway more gently while the leaves of the elm, aspen, and cottonwood quaver and chatter at an excited pace.
   c. Fire—The freshly built fire crackles, and the flames leap high, gradually dying down to coals and then embers.
   d. The world is big, big.

And I am small, small

But you should see me
When I stand tall, tall.

Giants don't scare me
I can climb to the stars.

Jack used his beanstalk.
I prefer a moonbeam by far.

Sometimes I'm a puppy
Who rolls, leaps, and barks.
Sometimes I'm a fierce tiger
Who slinks through the parks.

My mom says I'm a tomboy,
With springs here and there,
For making like a pogo stick,
But she's really not fair.
For at the end of the day
It's still in our house,
I put my dolly to bed
And we're quiet like a mouse.

   e. Growing things—The planted seed swells, sprouts, and pushes through the ground to take on leaves, buds, and flowers.
   f. Feeling for color—Using the primary level for observation, the following reactions were recorded (construction paper was used for colors):
   Red—exciting; pugnacious; challenging.
   Blue—calm in light shade; intriguing in intense shade.
   Green—soothing; restful; lazy.
   Yellow—happy; delightful; uplifting.
   Black—depressing; still; quiet.
   If these exercises seem too abstract, the color may be tied in with tangible things such as:
   Red—bullfighter's cape; football jersey; rubber ball; shoes.
   Blue—sky; water; eyes; bluebird; glass.
   Green—grass; trees; moss; fish.
   Yellow—sun; light; canary bird; fire; gems.
   g. Balloon—The balloon is released and soars through the air, rocking with the blasts of wind until it hits a thorn on a tree and slowly deflates.
   h. Emotions—The instructor sets the scene and uses the drum cadence, which the students follow.
   Anger, strength, and power require a strong drumbeat with an occasional resounding drumbeat.

Anger   Power

Joy   Happiness   Contentment

Sorrow   Sadness   Weakness

Joy requires a light and quick drumbeat that invites skipping, leaping, and jumping. Sadness, sorrow, weakness, and disappointment require a low, slow beat that finally dies away as an echo.

i. Adult activities—The following adult activities in the house and yard are suggested for first grade boys and girls. The boys have seen all of these activities and enjoy imitating their mothers' and fathers' familiar chores. In the second or third grades the boy balks at doing women's work and is interested only in the manly chores. Half of the class may do the activities, and the other half guess what they are doing. The teacher should suggest some activities and lead the class into making up their own:

Cleaning house—running the cleaner, sweeping, mopping, and dusting.

Washing and ironing, folding clothes, and putting them away.

Making beds, baking a cake, and putting baby to bed after bathing.

Washing dishes, putting them into the drainer, drying them, placing them on the shelves, setting the table, and clearing it.

Father barbecues a steak, hamburgers, and corn.

Father paints the house and washes and waxes the car.

Father mows the lawn, edges it, prunes it, and waters it.

j. Space adventures—Today we are all concerned with space, and our children have seen space shots, missile launchings, and landings on the moon. Let us see what we can do with these stimuli. We know that the air is very rare and light, so let us get off the earth first and imitate the possible locomotor movements used in outer space where the body is weightless.

Missile shot—Squat with head bowed and arms close to body. Start rotating hands toward body. Gradually increase the size of rotation and slowly rise until the arms are making huge circles and a standing position is achieved. Raise arms straight overhead, jump into the air, and run, run, run.

Space walk—All movements seem to be in slow motion. Slowly jump from spacecraft. Arms wave slowly to maintain balance as the body bends sideways, backward, and forward.

Moon trip—We have landed on the moon. Our boots are weighted. Hop forward as in slow motion, hop backward, and walk slowly forward with legs raised high and stretched forward. Roll forward slowly, roll backward slowly, and jump slowly toward objects or classmates.

FIGURE 14–11. What a way to learn about giving and receiving force! (Courtesy of Things from Bell, Incorporated, Homer, New York.)

IMPORTANCE OF IMAGINATION

Imagination is innate in all children. It flowers richly in some but must be extracted with consummate skill from others. An idea presented may bring an alert look, a sparkle in the eye, or the dead look of flat unconcern. An idea must fit the known field of experience, or ground must be spaded to prepare the soil for growth. Fundamental activities, such as chasing, fleeing, dodging, and reaching, are accepted by all children. Known games succeed; this is also true of rhythms. A child who has been raised on the prairie is unable to feel the wind in the pines, but he has a definite feeling for a whining wind that blows sand into dunes of ever-changing patterns or rolls tumbleweeds crazily across vast, open spaces. The child from the north has visions of the soft fall of snow that is feather light, the drifts, and the eerie cry of the blizzard. Smudge pots often darken the skies of California and Florida, but more familiar is the smell of orange blossoms, the waxy white of the trees, and the fruit-laden abundance of a warm climate. There is the beach with scampering waves; the sun by day and the moon by night painting the ripples. There is also the hard, cold winter of northern days and nights, frozen with a hard pristine sparkle; the stream that runs through great canyons and moves later at a sedate pace by flat, shallow banks. The sun shines on maple, aspen, fir, cottonwood, spruce, and pine; on corn, cotton, tobacco, and wheat our land over. These things children see and can express if teachers guide and help them to release their feelings.

SUGGESTED READINGS

A physical education resource center for every elementary school classroom. Physical Education Newsletter, April 1, 1976.

AAHPER: *Movement Education: A New Direction in Elementary Physical Education.* Washington, D.C., 1967.

Barrett, K. R.: *Exploration: A Method for Teaching Movement.* Madison, Wisconsin, College Printing, 1965.

Beanbag challenges to help promote a variety of physical education skills. Physical Education Newsletter, November 1, 1976.

Broer, M.: *Efficiency of Human Movement*. Philadelphia, W. B. Saunders Company, 1973.

Cratty, B. J.: *Movement Behavior and Motor Learning*. 2nd ed. Philadelphia, Lea & Febiger, 1967.

Diem, L.: *Who Can*. Frankfurt, Germany, Wilhelm Limpert, 1965.

Gilliom, B. C.: *Basic Movement Education for Children: Rationale and Teaching Units*. Reading, Massachusetts, Addison-Wesley Publishing Company, Inc., 1970.

Hackett, L., and Jensen, R.: *A Guide to Movement Exploration*. Palo Alto, California, Peek Publications, 1970.

How to use stilts to promote balance and physical fitness. Physical Education Newsletter, December 1, 1976.

Marzollo, J., and Lloyd, J.: *Learning Through Play*. New York, Harper & Row, Publishers, 1970.

McClenaghan, B. A., and Gallahue, D. L.: *Fundamental Movement: A Developmental and Remedial Approach*. Philadelphia, W. B. Saunders Company, 1978.

Metheny, E.: *Movement and Meaning*. New York, McGraw-Hill, Inc., 1968.

Mettler, B.: *Materials of Dance as a Creative Art Activity; This Is Creative Dance; Creative Dance for Children; Children's Creative Dance Book; Ten Articles on Dance*. Tucson, Creative Dance Center, 1970.

Shurr, E.: *Movement Experiences for Children*. Appleton-Century-Crofts, 1975.

Sweeney, R.: *Selected Readings in Movement Education*. Reading, Massachusetts, Addison-Wesley Publishing Company, 1970.

Teaching the concepts of coordination to second and third graders. Physical Education Newsletter, October 1, 1976.

Using a parachute to teach movement skills and develop overall physical fitness. Physical Education Newsletter, January 1, 1975.

Using individual mats to develop physical fitness and movement skills. Physical Education Newsletter, March 1, 1976.

Werner, P., and Simmons, R.: *Do It Yourself: Creative Movement with Innovative Physical Education Equipment*. Dubuque, Iowa, Kendall/Hunt Publishing Company, 1973.

Wickstrom, R.: *Fundamental Movement Patterns*. Philadelphia, Lea & Febiger, 1977.

Words and props that motivate children to move differently and creatively. Physical Education Newsletter, October 15, 1976.

SUGGESTED RECORDS

The following phonograph records are available from Educational Activities, Inc., Freeport, Long Island, New York 11520. They are excellent, and children find them fun as well as challenging.

Developing Perceptual Motor Needs of Primary Level Children. AR–606–7.
Discovering Through Movement Exploration. AR–534.
Homemade Band. AR–545.
Getting to Know Myself. AR–543.
Learning Basic Skills Through Music. Vol. 1, AR–514; Vol. 2, AR–521.
Music for Movement Exploration. KEA–5090.
The Development of Body Awareness and Position in Space. AR–605.
To Move Is To Be. KEA–8060.

The following phonograph records are available from Kimbo Educational Record Company, P.O. Box 477, Long Branch, New Jersey 07740:

Walk Like The Animals. KIM 7040–C.
Fun Activities for Perceptual Motor Skills. KIM 9071–C.
Heel, Toe, Away We Go. KIM 7050–C.
Perceptual-Motor Activities Using Rhythm Instruments. KIM 9078–C.
Simplified Lummi Stick Activities. KIM 2015–C.
Pop Rock Parachute. KEA 6025–C.
Rhythmic Parachute Play. KEA 6020–C.
Roomnastics I and II. KEA 1131–A, KEA–C.
Jumpnastics. NEA 6000–C.

CARD FILES AND OTHER TEACHING AIDS

Frostig, M.: *Move–Grow–Learn*. (A card file of over 200 activities.) Available from the Follett Publishing Company, Box 5705, Chicago, Illinois.

Getman, G. N.: *Pathway School Program I. Eye-Hand Coordination Exercise*. Available from Teaching Resources, 100 Boylston St., Boston, Massachusetts 02116.

Latchaw, M.: *A Pocket Guide of Movement Activities for the Elementary School.* Englewood Cliffs, New Jersey, Prentice-Hall, Inc.

SUGGESTED FILMS

A Time To Move (16 mm., black and white, 30 min.). Sale, $230.00; rental, $30.00. Available from Early Childhood Productions, P.O. Box 352, Chatsworth, California 91311.
Shows the significance of movement for the three to four year old child.

Basic Movement; Movement Awareness; Manipulative Skills; Functional Fitness (super 8 mm. technicolor, silent, loop film cartridges). Sale, $24.95 each. Available from Ealing Productions, 2225 Massachusetts Avenue, Cambridge, Massachusetts 02140.
A series of 24 loop films, each three to four minutes long, depicting children from kindergarten to second grade in action, developed in cooperation with AAHPER. Designed to show children and teachers a wide variety of activities and equipment with an entire class participating at one time. Problem-solving approach is used in all films. Descriptive note accompanies each cartridge.

Dance For Joy (16 mm., color, 20 min.). Sale, $155.00; rental, $17.50. Available from Documentary Films, 3217 Trout Gulch Road, Aptos, Calif. 95003.
An early childhood movement education film featuring two, three, and four year olds.

Free Expression In Sound and Movement.
Two group improvisations using voices, drums, and a variety of instruments—created by dance students—recorded at Mettler Studios, 78 r.p.m., $3 postpaid. Available from the Tucson Creative Dance Center, 3131 North Cherry Avenue, Tucson, Arizona.

Innovations in Elementary School Physical Education (16 mm., sound, color, 30 min.). Sale, $229.00. Available from Crown Films, West 503 Indiana Avenue, Box 890, Spokane, Washington 99210.
Produced as a part of an ESEA Title III project granted Washington State University for an experimental program in the elementary schools of Pullman, Washington. Depicts a wide variety of activities and equipment for kindergarten to sixth grade programs from ideas gleaned by author's world travels.

Learning Through Movement (16 mm., black and white, sound, 32 min.). Sale, $165.00; rental, $20.00. Available from S-L Film Productions, 5126 Nartwick Street, Los Angeles, California 90041.
Shows experiences with grades 1 to 6, in creative dance and the physical, emotional, and intellectual involvement of the children, and explores the multiplicity of learning concepts.

Movement Education (16 mm., sound, color; six films, 25–40 min. each). Sale, $200.00 each; rental, $25.00. Available from Audio-Visual Center, Simon Frazier University, Burnaby 2, B.C.
A series of six films for kindergarten to sixth grade. Titles are: (1) Introduction to Movement Education; (2) Teaching Direction and Level; (3) Teaching Awareness of Body Movements; (4) Teaching Qualities of Body Movements; (5) Ideas for Theme Development; and (6) Use of Small Apparatus. An instructional manual is included.

Movement Education in Physical Education (16 mm., black and white, 10 min.). Sale, $145.00; rental, $25.00. Available from Hayes Kruger, Department of Physical Education, Madison College, Box 3208, Harrisonburg, Virginia 22801.
Two men teachers from the program provide much information on a variety of activities for kindergarten through sixth grade. The film demonstrates the methodology of the problem-solving approach and emphasizes the importance of a well-structured environment.

Movement Experiences For Primary Children (16 mm., color, sound, 17 min.). Sale, $150.00; rental, $5.45. Available from Department of Instructional Media Distribution, Altgeld 114, Northern Illinois University, DeKalb, Illinois 60115.
Stresses need for children to move and to learn to move well. Emphasizes a problem-solving approach to teaching.

Movement Exploration (16 mm., sound, color, 20 min.). Sale, $185.00; rental, $20.00 first day; $10 each additional day. Available from Documentary Films, 3217 Trout Gulch Road, Aptos, California 95003.
A film designed for kindergarten to sixth grade teachers and major students with a wide range of activities for primary and elementary children, such as locomotor skills, ball handling, hoops, jump ropes, apparatus, and improvised equipment. Emphasis is on involvement of each child for maximum participation, with a problem-solving approach.

Physical Education—Lever To Learning (16 mm., color, sound, 20 min.). Sale, $200.00; rental, $15.00. Available from Stuart Finley, Inc., 3428 Mansfield Road, Falls Church, Virginia 22041.
Educable mentally retarded child from a special education program are shown taking part in a varied activity program emphasizing development of motor skills and physical fitness with limited, improvised equipment.

Ready, Set, Go. Two instructional television series for closed circuit use in large school systems. Available for purchase from the National Instructional Television Center, Box A, Bloomington, Indiana 47401.
Two series (Levels I and II) of 30 television lessons, 20 minutes each, on the basic movement approach to elementary school physical education for primary children. Accompanied by a manual with guidelines for supplementary lessons each week for the teacher, which provides continuity for a year's curriculum. Developed in consultation with AAHPER.

Thinking, Moving, Learning (16 mm., sound, color, 20 min.). Sale, $210.00. Inquire Bradley Wright Films, 309 North Duane Avenue, San Gabriel, California 91775.
Shows a comprehensive developmental program with 26 perceptual-motor activities for preschool and primary grade children for use in the classroom and on the playground.

CHAPTER FIFTEEN

EVALUATING THE RESULTS

Evaluation is finding out where you are in relationship to where you want to go.

The Authors

Evaluation is a method of appraising, measuring, and checking progress. When correctly used, it can help the teacher discover (1) the pupil's progress, health status, behavior, and reaction to the program and his fellow classmates, (2) her own ability to teach and reach successfully individuals as well as a class, (3) the strengths and weaknesses of the program, and (4) better ways to explain to parents, professional colleagues, school administrators, and the general public what physical education is all about. To be most effective, evaluation should be continuous, be done by all who participate in or are affected by the program, and be concerned with both end-products and the means with which to reach these ends.

METHODS OF EVALUATION

Methods of evaluating pupil progress and the physical education program include

Skill tests
Written tests
Observation
Check lists
Rating scales
Interviews
Case studies
Diaries
Parental conferences
Self-appraisal
Group discussions
Questionnaires

Posture tests
Attitude tests
Social development tests
Physical examinations
Health records
Personality inventories
Progress reports by school health personnel
School surveys of the use of school facilities for after-school recreation

The results gleaned from such measuring techniques may be used for motivation, self-evaluation, grading, grouping, guidance, and other purposes.

The elementary-school teacher most frequently uses observation, a type of subjective evaluation. To be of value, such appraisal must be precise and skilled. Both appearance and behavior can be observed and accurate deductions made by those with educated eyes and ears who are adept in noting "telling things" children say and do. Every effort should be made to discover what each child thinks, feels, knows, and does. A teacher must be more than a sounding board, yet each should realize that to an educated, child-sensitized adult, everything a youngster does is revealing; the more freely the child can and does communicate to the adult, the more he will divulge about himself. Children will and do "speak" in *every* way to the *real* teacher. The more the teacher talks, the less she will learn from and about each child in the class.

Success in objective evaluation, which is often more accurate than subjective measuring, requires careful, detailed, planned step-by-step procedures. The effective administration of such tests includes

1. *Preplanning, which involves*

    a. Selecting the test.
    b. Gaining complete knowledge and understanding of the test to be used and how it is to be administered.
    c. Obtaining needed equipment and facilities.
    d. Preparing score cards for individuals by class roll or squads.

2. *Administering the test*

    a. By paired groups with one-half scoring, the other taking the test, in reverse order.
    b. By squads, by the squad leader or other trained class assistants.
    c. Using the station-to-station method, rotating groups to certain testing areas.
    d. Using any combination mentioned above.

3. *Devising scoring methods, recording results by the teachers, assistants, squad leaders, or paired partners.*

4. *Performing necessary duties during the test, which include*

    a. Providing a warm-up period.
    b. Demonstrating each item.
    c. Motivating each pupil to do his best.
    d. Taking many safety precautions.

5. *Performing necessary duties following the test, which include*

    a. Collecting score pads.
    b. Converting raw scores to percentage on a scoring table.
    c. Comparing results with norms, and constructing profiles.
    d. Informing pupils of the results.
    e. Using the results for classification, guidance, research, grading, and motivation.

THE PURPOSE OF EVALUATION

Good testing can produce more orderliness in teaching and effectiveness in gaining desired results. The following specific purposes can be achieved through physical education testing:

1. Determination of the status of boys and girls with regard to fundamental human values amenable to improvement through physical education activities and methods.
2. Determination of the status of boys and girls with regard to basic body traits that affect physical performances.
3. Classification of pupils according to their abilities in physical activities.
4. Measurement of the results of instruction in physical and motor skill activities.

FIGURE 15–1. To a child-sensitized adult everything children do is revealing, for they speak in every way to a real teacher. (Courtesy of AAHPER, Washington, D.C. Photograph by Marjorie Blaufarb.)

EVALUATION OF HEALTH STATUS AND PHYSICAL GROWTH

Although some school authorities believe in annual physical examinations, others recommend four periodic examinations from grades 1 to 12, to be given when the child enters first grade, during the middle elementary period, at the beginning of adolescence (during the junior high school years), and before leaving the senior high school. However, throughout a child's school experience he may be referred to the school physician or a specialist because of a teacher's observation or the result of a screen test. The physical examination should include

Nutritional status
Eyes and eyelids
Ears and eardrums
Skin and hair
Heart
Lungs
Nervous system
Pulse rate when resting and after exercise

Muscle tone
Posture
Bones and joints
Abdomen
Nose, throat, and tonsils
Thyroid glands
Lymph nodes
Teeth and gums

A record should be kept of all findings, and there should be a follow-up corrective or remedial program if necessary, for this appraisal is not an end in itself, but rather a means of helping each pupil gain better health. Because of the number of children to be examined by the available physicians, it is sometimes difficult to allot more than a little time to each child. In such cases, a minimum of ten minutes should be given per pupil to be examined at school by one or more doctors.

Children should be weighed and measured regularly in the elementary school, and an accurate record should be kept for each pupil. Although weight norms are available from insurance companies, each teacher should use these only to compare the records of *each* pupil in relationship to those of many children of the same age and grade in school, for each child may have inherited a small, large or medium skeletal frame, may have had a recent or lingering illness, or a deep-seated emotional problem—all of which affect growth.

The Wetzel Grid is often used in elementary schools for recording a child's growth pattern over several years. Such a record is valuable in noting growth patterns and deviations.

It is important that those conducting screen tests for vision, hearing, and posture capitalize upon teachable moments as they arise, as well as know how to answer the questions children ask, for it is then that they *want* to learn and then that they can best have their fears eliminated. Educators call this "having a need for learning" and have discovered that "wanting to know" is basic to "getting to know."

EVALUATION OF SOCIAL GROWTH AND PUPIL BEHAVIOR

The following suggested chart can be used for recording and studying pupil behavior:

Pupil Behavior Sheet

Name _____ School Year _____ Age _____

Physical Education Class _____

Does the child

	Frequently	Seldom	Never
Take an active part in planning group activities?			
Take an active part in playing?			
Express himself (herself) confidently?			
Accept criticisms and suggestions from peers?			
Accept criticisms and suggestions from adults?			
Take turns with others?			
Show above average leadership ability?			
Have many consistent friends?			
Change friends often?			
Play fairly?			
Seem interested in improving skills or learning new ones?			
Assume responsibility with being reminded or threatened?			
Seem happy and well adjusted?			

Comments

1. _____
2. _____
3. _____
4. _____
5. _____

Areas in which the child needs help:

1. _____
2. _____
3. _____
4. _____
5. _____

What I will do to help:

1. _____
2. _____
3. _____
4. _____
5. _____

Signed_____

Date _____

These records can be of invaluable help to the teacher in gaining insight into all of her pupils. Changes in behavior that indicate growth and improvement should be noticed and commented upon to the pupil by the teacher.

The use of a sociogram is also recommended. In this case, the children are asked to help the teacher group them into an activity, and write the names of class members they would like on a team. By this device, the teacher can identify group isolates, rejects, and leaders.

Children are not miniature adults. We, who are older, must help them to develop their own unique personality. Above all, we need to help them develop necessary work and recreational skills, good health and character, and all else needed for them to find true happiness in life.

EVALUATION OF MOTOR SKILLS AND PHYSICAL FITNESS

Numerous tests have been developed to measure motor abilities, motor intelligence, and physical fitness. Almost all attempt to measure strength and endurance, coordination, speed, reaction time, balance, kinesthesis, flexibility, agility, and body explosive power. Suggested tests for doing so on the elementary level are[1]

---

[1] See Clarke's book listed in the bibliography for complete directions for giving each test.

FIGURE 15–2. Some parts of the program can be more easily measured than others. (Courtesy of WHA-TV Photo Department, Madison, Wisconsin, and AAHPER, Washington, D.C.)

Brace Motor Ability Test
Vertical Jump Test
Burpee Test
Carpenter Motor Ability Test
Iowa Brace Test
Kraus-Weber Floor-Touch Test for Flexibility
AAHPER Youth Fitness Test
New York State Physical Fitness Test
Oregon Motor Fitness Test
Amateur Athletic Union Junior Physical Fitness Test[2]
President's Council on Physical Fitness Test[3]
Washington Motor Fitness Test[4]
California Physical Performance Test[5]

EVALUATION OF PUPIL KNOWLEDGE AND ATTITUDES

Written tests include objective questions that require short answers, longer essay answers to general questions, rating scales, and problem-situation questions that require short but well-thought-through answers.

Written tests are of the greatest value when the teacher fully understands what it is she wants to test, knows what to do with the results, and has found the best measuring instruments for these purposes.

[2]Available from The Amateur Athletic Union, 233 Broadway, New York, New York.
[3]Available from U.S. Government Printing Office, Washington, D.C.
[4]Available from Dr. Glenn Kirchner, Eastern Washington State College, Cheney, Washington.
[5]Available from The Bureau of Health Education, Physical Education and Recreation, California State Department of Education, Sacramento, California.

True-or-False Tests

Educators contend that these are the poorest and weakest kind of objective test questions to use. Pupils tend to read meaning into each statement; few can tell the difference between a correct or incorrect statement or can resist mentally tinkering with it; few things are really completely true or entirely false.

All true-or-false statements should be short and simple. Avoid using the words "never" or "always." Have the pupils use the symbols (+) or (0) instead of (T) or (F), because those unsure of the answer often deliberately make the marks hard to tell apart. Other ways to score the test include encircling T if the statement is entirely true, or F if it is only partly true, or blocking out X in the first column if the sentence is correct and encircling it if the second one is wrong. In the first grade, have the children draw a face ☹ with the mouth turned down if the statement is false and a face with the

mouth turned up if it is true. ☺

Example: Write + if the statement is true, 0 if it is false.

Hit pin baseball for sixth grade pupils.

__0__ 1. Five Indian clubs are used in this game.

__0__ 2. Each scores two points.

__+__ 3. The ball, when kicked fairly, must be sent to first, second, third, and home bases, in this order.

__0__ 4. The pitcher may throw the ball to the kicker.

__+__ 5. The kicker is out on the third strike.

Multiple Choice Tests

These questions should be short, clearly written, and not copied word for word from a textbook. Care must be taken not to make all possible answers so wrong that it is obvious which one is correct or not to set a pattern through which the correct answer can usually be found.

Example: Place the letter of the most correct answer in the provided blank.

Tennis

__c__ 1. A lob is a stroke used in (a) serving, (b) smashing, (c) sending the ball high into the air, (d) driving it directly to the net player.

__d__ 2. The term deuce is used in (a) serving, (b) volleying, (c) rallying, (d) scoring.

__a__ 3. A fast hard drive that "kills the ball" or "puts it away for keeps" is a (a) smash, (b) lob, (c) volley, (d) line drive.

__d__ 4. A point made by the server after a deuce score is called: (a) add out, (b) 40–15, (c) 30–40, (d) add in.

__b__ 5. A set is won by a player who first wins (a) four, (b) six, (c) eight, (d) three games, providing he has won two games more than his opponent.

Matching Tests

These questions are best for measuring the mastery of "where," "when" and "who" types of information. They do not develop in a person the ability to interpret or express oneself. The responses to the matched items should be placed alphabetically or numerically in the right-hand column. Blank spaces should be provided in the left column before each item to be matched. There should be at least two more answers in the right column than in the left.

Example: Match the items in the left column with those in the right. Some answers in the latter may be used twice:

Folk Dance

_c_ 1. Crested Hen	a. England
_b_ 2. Jig	b. Ireland
_a_ 3. Sellinger's Round	c. Denmark
_c_ 4. Little Man in a Fix	d. France
_a_ 5. Green Sleeves	e. Spain
_b_ 6. Broom Dance	f. America
	g. Scotland
	h. Germany
	i. Italy

Fill-in Blanks

The chief drawback to this type of examination is that pupils have difficulty filling in blanks in the exact words the teacher expects; thus, they are often given the benefit of the doubt or cause the teacher to become irritated and more exacting as she continues to grade the paper. Also, it is time-consuming to grade such questions. One advantage to using this type of test is that the pupil is not guided to the answer.

Example: Write the correct answer in the blank provided for it below.

Square Dance

1. The __head__ couple is usually standing with its back to the caller.
2. The lady usually is on the gentleman's __right__ side.
3. "Honor your partner" means to __bow to your partner__ .
4. The last line of the call "all jump up and never come down" is __swing your honey round and round__ .
5. Three running steps followed by a hop is done in a __schottische__ .

Essay Questions

These questions provide pupils with opportunities to write complete sentences and whole paragraphs using good grammar and to think through problems carefully. Their drawback is that they are time-consuming to read and difficult to grade. However, such questions help teachers to gain additional insights concerning their pupils and their unique personal problems. Suggested questions are

1. What are the values of being physically educated?
2. How have your own recreational patterns been improved as a result of taking this class?
3. What is your definition of good sportsmanship?

Rating Scales

Pupils enjoy rating and evaluating their work or habits in school. The best scales for doing so are those devised by the class. Teachers can help children benefit from this type of experience by a personal follow-up conference with each child.

Example: Pupil's Personal Evaluation of Daily Health Habits.

	Always	Frequently	Seldom	Never
1. I brush my teeth after eating.	_____	_____	_____	_____
2. I eat fruits and vegetables every day	_____	_____	_____	_____
3. I drink a quart of milk daily.	_____	_____	_____	_____
4. I usually go to bed before 9:00 p.m.	_____	_____	_____	_____
5. I worry about my school work.	_____	_____	_____	_____

EVALUATION BY THE PUPILS

Children should be given many opportunities to evaluate the progress they have made in relationship to the goals set individually and by the class. Teachers should appraise their progress with them, as well as be ever observant of their reactions to what they are doing and their attitudes toward the teachers, the class, themselves,

FIGURE 15–3. Children, too, should be given many opportunities to evaluate what progress they have made. (Courtesy of Los Angeles City Schools, Los Angeles, California.)

and life in general. Time should be taken frequently to discuss these reactions, problems that have arisen concerning individual or group behavior, and good sportsmanship, as well as to formulate future goals and plans.

Deeper insight and a clearer understanding of the group as a whole, as well as the feelings of the class toward the teacher, can be gained by having each pupil write on an unsigned paper answers to the following questions at the end of a semester or a major class project:

1. Did you enjoy this experience? Why?
2. List the new things you have learned in order of importance to you.
3. What activities did you do away from school that you learned here?
4. What person do you most admire in our class? Why?
5. How could you be like this person, if you wanted to?
6. What did you hope to do or learn that you did not?
7. What pupil do you think improved the most? In what ways?
8. Are the pupils here learning to be good citizens? In what ways?

Much information can also be gained concerning each pupil by having him complete statements that show his inner feelings, fears, or inner thoughts. Suggested statements include the following:

1. My greatest fear when I am in the class is that I _____
   _____ .

2. I think my ability in sports and games is _____
   _____ .

3. I dislike_____ because_____ .

4. I would like to be just like_____ when I grow up because_____
   _____ .

5. I_____ this class, because here I_____
   _____ .

There is great educational value in having pupils submit sample objective test questions with their correct answers and in having them grade one another's paper in class as the teacher reads the correct answer. Every real educator will find ways to utilize any time spent in evaluating progress to its utmost and will make good use of test findings in order to improve as an effective youth leader.

	Always	Frequently	Seldom	Never
Do you enjoy classes in physical education?	_____	_____	_____	
Do you feel as though you are getting enough individual attention in learning to do new things?	_____	_____	_____	_____
Do you play the activities learned in class after school and during leisure time?	_____	_____	_____	_____
Do you like to take showers after class?	_____	_____	_____	_____

Do you feel as though your class gives you enough opportunities to get to know a number of activities and people? _____ _____ _____ _____

Do you feel as though you have gained in skills? _____ _____ _____ _____

List the things you like most about physical education.

1. _____
2. _____
3. _____

List the things you like least about physical education.

1. _____
2. _____
3. _____

How do you think our class could be made better?

1. _____
2. _____

TEACHER EVALUATION

Every teacher should take a frequent realistic look at herself and her work. A suggested evaluation sheet for doing so follows:

	Always	Frequently	Seldom	Never
1. I like teaching.	_____	_____	_____	_____
2. I enjoy my students and try to understand them.	_____	_____	_____	_____
3. I am democratic.	_____	_____	_____	_____
4. I feel inadequately prepared to do my job well.	_____	_____	_____	_____
5. I make the best use of student leadership.	_____	_____	_____	_____
6. I make the best use of facilities and equipment.	_____	_____	_____	_____
7. I have my own teaching objectives clearly in mind for each class.	_____	_____	_____	_____
8. I have my objectives clearly in mind for the development of each unique individual student.	_____	_____	_____	_____
9. I plan my work ahead.	_____	_____	_____	_____
10. I teach something new every class period.	_____	_____	_____	_____
11. I am cognizant of carry-over values in what I am teaching.	_____	_____	_____	_____

	Always	Frequently	Seldom	Never
12. I give skill and written tests periodically and use them to evaluate my work.	____	____	____	____
13. I feel that the students admire me.	____	____	____	____
14. I have discipline trouble.	____	____	____	____
15. I try to cooperate with my administrators.	____	____	____	____
16. I feel the other teachers respect me.	____	____	____	____
17. I join professional organizations, attend their meetings, and read their periodical literature.	____	____	____	____
18. I feel that I am making a real contribution to my professional field.	____	____	____	____

Things I should do to improve myself as a teacher are

a. _____   e. _____

b. _____   f. _____

c. _____   g. _____

d. _____   h. _____

My progress on this so far has been   Date_____

a. _____   c. _____

b. _____   d. _____

                                            Date _____

EVALUATION BY THE PHYSICAL EDUCATION SUPERVISOR

Although the classroom teacher in most primary grades teaches physical education and other subjects, many of them, as well as those specialized physical educators on the upper elementary level, have supervisors to assist them in their work. The use of a supervisor's evaluation sheet, seen below, should be followed by personal conferences, so that improvement, if needed, can be made:

Name of teacher_____   Name of school _____

Date of rating_____   Rated by _____

Instructions: Using a scale of 1 to 3, rate each teacher in each item below. Rate 3 for above average, 2 for average, 1 for below average.

Usually this teacher

	1	2	3
1. Shows an understanding of people.	____	____	____
2. Uses democratic methods.	____	____	____
3. Has an understanding of the community and the school and is aware of their relationship to each other.	____	____	____

4. Shows ability to organize and plan his work carefully.   ___ ___ ___

5. Shows ability to measure pupil progress.   ___ ___ ___

6. Recognizes individual differences.   ___ ___ ___

7. Understands group behavior.   ___ ___ ___

8. Helps groups plan, conduct, and evaluate their own program under his direction.   ___ ___ ___

9. Develops student leadership.   ___ ___ ___

10. Has ability to build group unit.   ___ ___ ___

11. Can solve discipline problems.   ___ ___ ___

12. Is respected and liked by students and fellow teachers.   ___ ___ ___

13. Can demonstrate well.   ___ ___ ___

14. Can speak well, using correct grammar.   ___ ___ ___

15. Safeguards the health and safety of all.   ___ ___ ___

16. Provides a well-balanced graded program that is up-to-date and covers a variety of activities suitable for each grade.   ___ ___ ___

17. Provides definite progression in a graded program.   ___ ___ ___

18. Uses well a wide variety of teaching methods.   ___ ___ ___

19. Is attractive, neat, slim, trim, and a good example of how a leader should look.   ___ ___ ___

20. Is creative.   ___ ___ ___

21. Shows knowledge of the entire school curriculum and realizes the contribution of his own area.   ___ ___ ___

22. Uses the bulletin board often, realizing that it is a silent teacher.   ___ ___ ___

23. Keeps adequate records and realizes their importance.   ___ ___ ___

24. Shows ability to maintain proper teacher-pupil relationships.   ___ ___ ___

25. Shows professional promise.   ___ ___ ___

EVALUATION WITH THE PRINCIPAL

The school administrator should be aware of the work accomplished by all teachers during the school year. The principal should visit each teacher regularly and offer suggestions for improvement. As the chief administrator of the school system, the principal often must be the go-between for teachers and the general public. By observing classes in physical education and reading reports submitted by the teacher, he may gain insight into the program.

The task of teaching also includes that of educational diagnosis. The teacher's analysis of each class should include consideration of what the children accomplished during their class period, learning problems that were evident in the entire group as well as in individuals, and possible solutions for learning stumbling blocks.

Tests are useful tools for evaluating learning in skills, rules, and attitudes. Each unit of work should include a written and skill test. These should be easily administered and not be too time-consuming to grade or record. Not more than two class periods should be taken for these tests.

EVALUATION OF THE SCHOOL PROGRAM

Three major areas of the elementary school physical education program should be evaluated periodically: the effectiveness of the teacher conducting the program, the facilities, and the program content. Such an evaluation could be made by a visiting team of physical education experts, the teachers involved in the program, and the school administrator. Periodic meetings should be held to review the results of such an evaluation made by any two of these groups, and specific plans should be drawn up to eliminate existing weaknesses. Consultants should be brought in to work with the teaching staff to improve offerings, if need be.

The following evaluative form might well be used by those reviewing the program in its entirety:

Program Evaluative Form

A. *The Instructional Staff*

	Yes	No
1. Is the teacher a college graduate with a major in elementary physical education?	___	___
2. Has the teacher had at least one three-hour course in elementary physical education within the past five years?	___	___
3. Has the teacher attended any clinics or workshops in elementary physical education within the past three years?	___	___
4. Is the classroom teacher assisted by an elementary school physical education specialist in planning and conducting the program?	___	___
5. Can the teacher demonstrate a wide variety of movement skills or sport skills correctly?	___	___
6. Can she diagnose faulty movement patterns and correct movement imperfections?	___	___
7. Does the teacher follow a graded course of study in elementary physical education?	___	___

B. *The Facilities*

Outdoor

1. Is the outdoor play space a safe place for children to play?	___	___
2. Is the area fenced?	___	___
3. Are all playing areas well marked, drained, and free of debris?	___	___
4. Are the youngest children assigned a place to play that is (a) farthest away from the oldest children's area; (b) near the school building?	___	___

5. Is there sand, tanbark, or sawdust under all apparatus to protect pupils from injury? ___ ___

6. Are all pieces of equipment thoroughly checked periodically for safety purposes? ___ ___

7. Are all pupils taught the safest way to use all indoor equipment? ___ ___

8. Are the pupils well supervised during recess, before and after school when playing, and during noon hour? ___ ___

Indoor

1. Is there a well-lighted, well-ventilated gymnasium used for both instructional and free-play purposes? ___ ___

2. Is the gymnasium a safe place for pupils at active play? ___ ___

3. Do the girls have the same opportunity to use the facilities as the boys? ___ ___

4. Are all court and boundary lines well marked? ___ ___

5. Is there adequate storage space for all equipment and supplies? ___ ___

6. Can all needed equipment be easily and quickly moved to all teaching areas? ___ ___

C. *The Program*

1. Do teachers help plan and revise periodically a printed graded course of study curriculum? ___ ___

2. Are the teachers and pupils aware of the objectives of the program in its entirety and of each daily lesson therein? ___ ___

3. Does the program contain a variety of activities under the broad headings of aquatics, rhythmical activities, movement exploration, stunts and tumbling, elementary gymnastics, simple games, lead-up games to team sports, and camping and outdoor education? ___ ___

4. Does the instructional program really produce skill learning in a variety of activities? ___ ___

5. Are there adequate established ways in which the program can be evaluated by the teacher, the pupils, and the school administrator? ___ ___

6. Is the program correlated with the school health and safety programs? ___ ___

7. Does the program meet the amount of time designated for daily class instruction in physical education set by state law? ___ ___

According to the above findings, the weaknesses of our total physical education program seem to be

a. _____

b. _____

c. _____

d. _____

Things we should do to improve our program starting now are

a. _____

b. _____

c. _____

d. _____

GRADING AND REPORTING TO PARENTS

It is usually not customary to record separate physical education grades other than Pass or Fail for primary children. However, most report cards for this age group contain blanks for the teacher to rate each child's ability to play well with others and show good sportsmanship and development in play skills. In grades 4, 5, and 6, many schools report a separate grade in physical education for each pupil. Such a grade may be of the number or letter type and is based largely upon achievement, attitude and attendance. All grades should be given on an educational basis, and those who have done the best work in accordance with the stated objectives of social, physical, and academic development should receive the best grades.

The far-reaching influences of a good physical education program should extend into the home and local community. Individual conferences with parents, home visits if possible, and telephone conversations can help teachers gain needed information regarding the effectiveness of their teaching. When parents and teachers become working partners, their joint efforts can and will produce many fruitful results.

SUGGESTED READINGS

AAHPER: *Knowledge and Understanding in Physical Education; Archery Skills Test Manual; Basketball Skills Test Manual; Football Skills Test Manual; Softball Skills Test Manual* (separate manuals for boys and girls); *Volleyball Skill Test Manual* (separate manuals for boys and girls), Washington, D.C.

American Association of School Administrators, Council of Chief State School Officers, and National Association of Secondary-School Principals: *Testing, Testing, Testing.* Washington, D.C., National Education Association, 1962.

Baumgartener, T., and Jackson, A. S.: *Measurement for Evaluation in Physical Education,* Boston, Houghton-Mifflin Company, 1975.

Dauer, V., and Pangrazi, R.: *Dynamic Physical Education for Elementary School Children.* 5th ed. Minneapolis, Burgess Publishing Company, 1975.

Latchaw, M., and Brown, C.: *The Evaluation Process in Health Education, Physical Education and Recreation.* Englewood Cliffs, New Jersey, Prentice-Hall, Inc., 1962.

Lewis, G.: *The Evaluation of Teaching.* Washington, D.C., National Education Association, 1966.

Mathews, D.: *Measurement in Physical Education.* 4th ed. Philadelphia, W. B. Saunders Company, 1973.

Meyers, C. R., and Blesh, T. E.: *Measurement in Physical Education.* New York, The Ronald Press Company, 1962.

Rothney, J. W. M.: *Evaluating and Reporting Pupil Progress: What Research Says to the Teacher.* No. 7. Washington, D.C., National Education Association, 1960.

PART FIVE

Teach them all! teach them all!
The stout, the thin and the tall;
The shy and the others,
The sisters and brothers,
The handicapped, awkward and small.

Teach them love, teach them speeds;
The balance, endurance—their needs;
Respect and good manners,
Three R's and the grammars,
The ethics, principles and creeds.

Let them search and explore
Their space, the walls and the floor;
The sciences of motion,
The creative notion,
Decisions and problems galore.

What's OUR task? OUR main goal?
To guide and develop the "whole"!
Not merely athletics
Nor alphabetics
Teach *them* all—Teach it all, is our role!

Ambrose E. Brazelton

THE WHAT

CHAPTER SIXTEEN

ACTIVE "LOW-ORGANIZED" GAMES

Play for the child is the gaining of life. Play for the adult is the renewal of life.

Joseph Lee

Active games are part of the cultural heritage of all boys and girls. Although environmental conditions and standards of living change, the urge to play games remains a dominant characteristic found in every race and in every country. Geographic location does not alter the original theme or idea, for games are built upon the age-old urges to run, jump, hop, chase and flee, hide and seek, hunt, guess, and dodge. One may find hundreds of variations of these themes, with as many different names, but the original theme remains the same. Thus, we hear of Indians in Mexico playing a game that resembles the familiar London Bridge is Falling Down and of South Pacific islanders playing an aboriginal version of Hull Gull, Hand Full, How Many? with sea shells.

Games *can* be of value in elementary school physical education if used properly and for the right reasons. Too often, however, physical education programs have become little more than glorified recess periods, in which games are endlessly played for their own sake and because they are fun. As noted earlier, fun is a *by-product* of any good educational program. It is not, however, the *primary* purpose of the physical education program. With this important concept in mind, it is possible to view the playing of "low-organized" games as a means to an end, that is, the development of more efficient locomotor and manipulative abilities, rather than as an end in themselves.

The term "low organized games" is used to denote game activities that are easy to play, have few and simple rules, require little or no equipment, and may be varied in many ways. "Low organized" game activities may be easily modified to suit the objectives of the lesson, the size of the room, and the number of students in the group. They are easy to learn and can be enjoyed by both children and adults but are used as an educational tool primarily during grades 1 through 3.

CHOOSING GAMES

The inclusion of "low organized" games in the physical education lesson generally begins in the first three grades; the group spirit of preschool-age children is generally not conducive to group game activities. After this time children are usually more interested in sport-related lead-up games. Figure 16–1 depicts the "golden age" for "low organized" game activities.

NURSERY SCHOOL THROUGH KINDERGARTEN ↓	FIRST THROUGH THIRD GRADE ↓	FOURTH THROUGH SIXTH GRADE ↓
Fundamental Movement ↓	Game Age ↓	Sport-Skill Age ↓

Self-Testing Activities
  Imaginary and Creative Ac-
  tivities (pp. 303–313)
Perceptual-Motor Activities
  (pp. 85–89)
Individualized Activities
	"Low Organized" Games
	  Locomotor Games (pp.
	  339–347 and 355–360)
	  Manipulative Games (pp.
	  347–354)
		Lead-Up Games
		Individual and Dual Sports
		  (pp. 515–531)
		Team Sports (pp. 533–581)

FIGURE 16–1.   The golden age of games (grades 1 through 3).

"Low organized" games are used by the astute teacher as an educational tool. Every game that is played should be chosen for specific reasons. These specific reasons may vary depending upon the nature of the lesson and may range from practicing specific movement skills and enhancing various components of physical fitness to promoting social learnings and academic concept development. If the teacher has clearly defined objectives for the use of a particular game or games in a lesson and these objectives are articulated in a variety of ways, then we may be sure that "low organized" games will serve an educational purpose. If, however, our objective is primarily fun with only remote consideration given to neuromuscular, social, fitness, or academic objectives then we have "missed the boat" entirely and are making little or no contribution to the physical *education* of children.

When choosing a game for inclusion in the lesson one must not limit selection to the "appropriate" grade level placement so often seen in textbooks and card files of games. Children with a sound movement background can easily play and master games graded one or two levels above the level generally used for children their age. The process recommended for choosing a game for inclusion in the lesson includes the following steps:

1. Determine the specific objectives of your lesson.
2. Select a game activity that will satisfy the objectives of the lesson.
3. Modify the game to fit the objectives of the lesson.
4. Modify the game to fit the ability and interest level of your class.
5. Modify the game in terms of the movement skills utilized.

The list of active games is almost endless. Textbooks and card files are filled with thousands of different games. It is not, however, necessary to be familiar with all or even most of these games if the principles of game selection and modification listed above are adhered to. Remember, a "low organized" game is only a vehicle that you use to achieve an end. It is not, or should not be, an end in itself in the developmentally based physical education program.

OBJECTIVES OF GAME PLAYING

Game activities are fun. They add a dimension of group interaction to the lesson and promote skill development. The selection of a game for inclusion in a lesson may be made for one or more of the following reasons:

1. Neuromuscular Skill Development

   a. To enhance fundamental locomotor abilities (running, jumping, leaping, and so forth).
   b. To enhance fundamental manipulative abilities (throwing, catching, kicking, and so forth).

2. Fitness Development

   a. To promote improved physical fitness (strength, endurance, flexibility, circulatory/respiratory endurance).
   b. To promote improved motor fitness (speed, agility, coordination).

3. Social-Emotional Development

   a. To promote positive interaction with others (group spirit, group cooperation, sportsmanship, competition).
   b. To promote positive self-growth (tension release, self-discipline, self-acceptance).

4. Cognitive Development

   a. To promote readiness skills (learning to listen, following directions).
   b. To reinforce academic concepts taught in the classroom (science, math, language arts, social studies).
   c. To stimulate thinking (creativity, strategy, knowledge of rules).

MODIFYING GAMES

Once the objectives of the lesson have been determined and you have decided to use a certain game or games, it is time to modify the activity to suit the objectives of your lesson, the ability and interest level of your students, and the movement skills involved. This may be done simply by carefully reading the description of the game and then modifying it to fit your own particular needs and those of your students.

The game itself may be modified in a variety of ways. The following is a sampling of some of these ways:

1. Change the movement skills used to play the game.
2. Modify the duration of the game.
3. Modify the number playing in a group.
4. Change the formations used or boundaries.
5. Modify the game by stepping up the intensity or pace of the game.
6. Change the game by adding rules or deleting rules.
7. Change the game to incorporate additional movement skills.
8. Modify the game to stress group initiative and teamwork.
9. Modify the game to encourage problem solving.
10. Modify the activity to stimulate creativity by making up new games.
11. Modify the activity to promote total inclusion in games that may otherwise promote exclusion.
12. Modify the game to promote maximal active participation of all students.
13. Modify the activity to encourage increased teamwork.
14. Modify the activity to heighten the group or team spirit.
15. Modify the game to reinforce or develop specific academic concepts.
16. Modify the game to increase or decrease its difficulty.

Once the principles of game modification have been learned, it is possible to devise from a limited number of resources an endless variety of meaningful, educationally sound games for inclusion in the physical education program. A solid grasp of the lesson objectives, a good imagination, and willingness to experiment will greatly aid the teacher in successfully incorporating games into the lesson.

TYPES OF ACTIVE GAMES

Active games may be classified in a variety of ways. In this chapter we have chosen to classify games by the general skill areas involved and their appropriate use. Therefore, the reader will find the following types of games:

1. Active locomotor games (for enhancing locomotor movement abilities).
2. Active manipulative games (for enhancing basic object-manipulation abilities).
3. Active circle games (for enhancing a variety of locomotor and manipulative abilities).
4. Active games for special occasions (Halloween, Thanksgiving, Christmas, and so forth).
5. Active constructed games (for indoor and outdoor use).

ACTIVE LOCOMOTOR GAMES

The following is a compilation of active games to develop a variety of fundamental locomotor abilities. These games may be modified and varied in a variety of ways in order to satisfy the objectives of the lesson.

Automobiles (or Airplanes)

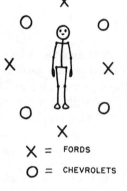

Skills:	Running
Equipment:	None
Players:	30 to 40
Formation:	Circle
Directions:	The players number off, each taking a number from 1 to 4 or 6, depending upon the size of the group. No. 1's are Fords, No. 2's are Chevrolets, and so forth. "It" calls the name of an automobile, and all players who are designated as that type of automobile run counterclockwise around the circle, return to their original places, and dash to the center to touch "It." The first runner to touch "It" wins the race of that kind of automobile. When each type of automobile has raced, "It" calls "All winners," and this race determines the big winner.
Variations:	Use names of racehorses or airplanes; modify skills to include hopping, skipping, and so forth.

X = FORDS

O = CHEVROLETS

Back to Back

Skills:	Running, pivoting, dodging
Equipment:	None
Players:	12 to 16
Formation:	Scattered partners
Directions:	"It" calls "Back to back." Each player must back up to a partner. "It" calls "Face to face," and partners face each other and shake hands. On the next call of "Back to back" and each time thereafter, all players must change partners. "It" tries to get a partner during the change, and the player left out becomes "It."

FACE TO FACE   BACK TO BACK

Beater Goes Round

Skills:	Running, starting, stopping
Equipment:	Knotted sock
Players:	12 to 20
Formation:	Circle
Directions:	One player is outside the circle and carries a knotted sock or folded newspaper. He walks around the circle and gives it to a player. This receiver turns to his right and beats the player lightly on his back. The player runs around the circle to his own place with the beater chasing him. The original starter steps into the place of the first receiver.

Bird, Beast, Fish

Skills:	Running, starting, stopping, dodging
Equipment:	None
Players:	18 to 24
Formation:	Circle
Directions:	The group forms a three-deep circle. The inside player is a "bird," the middle player is a "beast," and the outside player is a "fish." "It" is in the center of the circle. He calls a name—bird, beast, or fish. The players in the group he names must all change places. When the group is changing places, "It" runs to an empty place, and the person left without a place becomes "It."

O – FISH
O – BEAST
O – BIRD

Catch the Bat

Skills:	Running, starting, catching
Equipment:	Wand or bat
Players:	8 to 16
Formation:	Circle
Directions:	Players form a circle and number off. One player stands in the center and balances the bat or wand with his fingertips. The center player calls a number and releases the bat. The player with the number called tries to catch the bat before it falls to the ground. If he succeeds, he becomes "It" and if he fails, he returns to his place in the circle and "It" calls another number.

Club Snatch

```
          1  2  3  4  5  6
          X  X  X  X  X  X
               ⊂○ CLUB

          O  O  O  O  O  O
          1  2  3  4  5  6
```

Skills: Running, starting, dodging
Equipment: Indian club or milk carton
Players: 12 to 18
Formation: Double line
Directions: Divide the players into teams, numbering each player. Place an Indian club or any type of object in the center between the two teams. The instructor calls a number, and the members of each team with the number called run out and try to get the club. The member of the team that gets the club and gets across the restraining line without getting tagged wins the point for his team. The team with the most points wins.

Dog Catcher

```
          KENNEL
                        BOXER
             CATCHER    BEAGLE
               •        SCOTTIE
                        COCKER
                        TERRIER
                        MUTT

             POUND
```

Skills: Running, dodging
Equipment: None
Players: 20 to 80
Formation: See diagram.
Directions: Name three or four kinds of dogs. Each child chooses the kind he wants to be. All go to one "kennel." The "dog catcher" calls one kind of dog. They run to the opposite kennel. If caught, they are put into the "pound." After the dog catcher has had three turns, he tells how many dogs he has caught and chooses another to take his place until all are caught. The last one caught starts the new game.

Double Circle

```
              O
          O   x   O
            x       x
          O             O
            x       x
          O   x   x   O
              O
```

Skills: Skipping, galloping, or hopping
Equipment: None
Players: 8 to 24
Formation: Double circle
Directions: The class is arranged in two concentric circles, one having one more member than the other. On signal they begin to skip around in opposite directions until the whistle is blown or the music stops; then each player endeavors to secure a partner from the other circle. One player is left without a partner. If any player is left out three times he must pay a penalty—do some stunt, sing a song, and so forth.

Weave In

Skills: Running, changing direction
Equipment: None
Players: 12 to 20
Formation: Circle
Directions: One person is "It" and tags a person in the circle. "It" and the tagged player start weaving in and out of the circle running in opposite directions. The first one back to the empty space wins. The other player is "It" for the next game.

Have You Seen My Sheep?

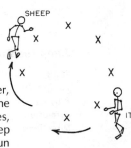

Skills:	Running, tagging, chasing, fleeing
Equipment:	None
Players:	8 to 12
Formation:	Single circle
Directions:	One player is "It" and walks around circle and asks any player, "Have you seen my sheep?" The player queries, "What does he look like?" "It" describes his "sheep" (a player), that is, his eyes, hair, clothes, and so forth. If the player guesses correctly, the sheep runs and he chases and tries to tag the sheep before he can run around the circle and return to his place. "It" steps into the vacated place in the circle. The player, if caught, becomes "It"; if he is not caught, the chaser becomes "It" for another game.

High Windows

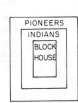

Skills:	Running, tagging, chasing, fleeing
Equipment:	None
Players:	8 to 12
Formation:	Single circle with "It" in center
Directions:	"It" runs around inside the circle and tags a player. "It" runs outside of the circle attempting to run around the circle three times before being tagged by the player chasing him. When he completes three rounds, the players in the circle raise their joined hands and cry "High windows." The runner comes into the circle and is safe. He continues to be "It." If "It" is caught, the chaser becomes "It."

Pioneers and Indians

Skills:	Running, tagging, chasing, fleeing
Equipment:	None
Players:	Two equal teams of any number
Formation:	See diagram.
Directions:	Play in two ten-minute halves.
	Use slips of paper with names of supplies with numbered values. These slips are given to each "pioneer." Station a pioneer in the "blockhouse." The object is for the pioneers to deliver supplies to the blockhouse without letting the "Indians" catch them. If an Indian catches a pioneer, he searches him for the hidden supplies. If the Indian cannot find it before 50 counts, the pioneer goes free. If he is caught again, he must surrender his supply. The team with the most supplies wins.

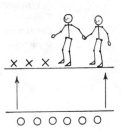

Hook On

Skills:	Pivoting, dodging, running
Equipment:	None
Players:	Entire class
Formation:	Two lines facing each other
Directions:	Pick four children to go to one end of the gymnasium. Others go to the opposite end. Both line up. The leader blows the whistle. All try to hook on to one of the four. The others try to keep back end of line away from children trying to hook on. Move fast. The chain with fewest "hook-ons" wins.

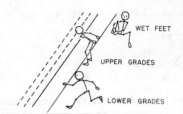

Jump the Creek or Brook

Skills: Jumping
Equipment: Two long ropes
Players: Entire class
Formation: Scatter along the line
Directions: Two lines made of ropes placed apart on the floor represent the creek. The last child over gets to draw the new line, which widens the creek each time. Any child who lands in the creek must take off his shoes and put them back on before he can re-enter the game. For inside activity, it is suggested that third and fourth graders jump with both feet together (standing long jump).

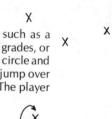

Jump the Shot

Skills: Jumping
Equipment: Long rope
Players: 8 to 12
Formation: Circle
Directions: Knot the end of a long jump rope or attach a weight such as a beanbag or ball in a sack to it. The teacher, in the lower grades, or any player, in the upper grades, stands in the center of the circle and turns, taking the rope under the feet of the players, who jump over it. Any player who touches the rope is out of the game. The player who stays in the circle longest wins.

Loose Caboose

Skills: Pivoting, dodging, changing direction
Equipment: None
Players: Entire class
Formation: Circle
Directions: Players stand in groups of three in a circle. The first player is Engine, the second is Chair car, and the third is Caboose. There are two (or any number) of Loose Cabooses, who try to attach themselves to the end of a line. When this occurs, Engine becomes Loose Caboose, and the game continues.

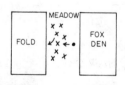

Midnight

Skills: Running, chasing, fleeing, tagging
Equipment: None
Players: 20 to 80
Formation: See diagram.
Directions: The "fox" stands in his den and the "sheep" in their fold. The fox wanders out into the meadow, and so do the sheep. The sheep ask "What time is it?" and the fox answers "Two o'clock," "Ten o'clock," and so forth. The sheep keep milling around, but when he answers "Midnight," they scamper for the fold. All the sheep that are tagged become foxes, and the same procedure is repeated. The last sheep caught becomes the new fox, and a new game starts.

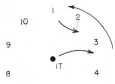

Number Change

Skills:	Starting, running
Equipment:	None
Players:	Entire class
Formation:	Circle
Directions:	All the players are given a number, and one is chosen to be "It." The players stand in a circle with "It" in the center. He calls any two numbers. The players whose numbers he calls exchange places, while the one who is "It" attempts to get one of their places in the circle. The one of these left without a place is "It" for the next time, and he calls the two numbers to change.

Plug (An Old Broken-Down Horse)

Skills:	Pivoting, dodging, tossing
Equipment:	Playground
Players:	Entire class
Formation:	Lines of five players
Directions:	Five players make Plug by locking their arms around the waist of the players in front of them. The other players are "throwers." A thrower tries to hit Plug's "tail." When hit below the waist the person who is the tail becomes a thrower. The player who hit him becomes Plug's "head." Repeat.

Poison

Skills:	Changing direction, agility
Equipment:	Indian club or milk carton
Players:	8 to 12 per group
Formation:	Circles
Directions:	Players join hands and form a circle with an Indian club in the center. One player, chosen as the leader, signals for the start of the game. Players try to pull one another toward the club to knock it down. The player who knocks down the club is eliminated, and the leader replaces the club. If the circle is broken, players on either side of the break are eliminated. The last player to be eliminated is the winner and the leader in a new game.

Come Along

Skills:	Running, changing direction, dodging
Equipment:	None
Players:	20 to 30
Formation:	Circle
Directions:	One player is "It." On signal players face to the right and extend their right arms out in line with their shoulders. "It" runs around outside the circle, touches one of the outstretched arms saying "Come along," and continues to run around the circle. The second player touches an outstretched arm and does the same. This continues until about 10 players are running around the circle. The leader cries "Home," and the players try to get to their spaces. The player left without a space becomes "It."

Red Light

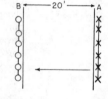

Skills:	Walking, starting, stopping
Equipment:	None
Players:	20 to 40
Formation:	See diagram.
Directions:	One player chosen as the "traffic policeman" stands on the finish line with his back to the group. The policeman calls "Green light," and the players advance cautiously while he counts. The policeman may call "red light" at any time and turn quickly and face the players. Any player in motion must return to the starting line. The first player to cross the finish line becomes the traffic policeman. This game can be used in teaching safety.

Red Rover

Skills:	Running, changing level
Equipment:	None
Players:	16 to 36
Formation:	Running line
Directions:	Players join hands and form two lines facing each other about 20 feet apart. One player in each line is the leader or caller. The leader in Line B calls "Red Rover, Red Rover, let Johnny (any child) come over." Johnny runs from Line A and tries to break through Line B. If he succeeds, he returns to his own line. If he fails, he stays with Line B. The leader of Line A calls to a child in Line B and so forth. The side that finishes with the most players wins. Callers should be changed at intervals.

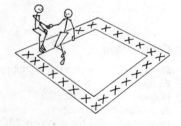

Skip Tag

Skills:	Skipping
Equipment:	Chairs
Players:	20 to 80
Formation:	Square
Directions:	The group is seated around the sides of room with right hands extended. "It" skips around and slaps the palm of one player. The chosen player skips after "It." If he is successful in tagging, he becomes "It" and the tagged player takes his seat; otherwise he returns to his seat. If "It" is not tagged in three tries, he chooses a new "It." In mixed groups, girls should tag boys and boys tag girls. Players must skip and cannot cut corners.

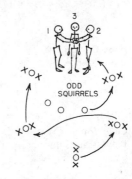

Squirrels in Trees

Skills:	Running, changing direction and level
Equipment:	None
Players:	16 to 80
Formation	Groups of three scattered players
Directions:	Number off by threes. Nos. 1 and 2 form the tree by facing and holding hands. No. 3 is the "squirrel" inside the tree. Odd players are the "homeless squirrels." On a signal, all squirrels must change trees, and in the scramble the homeless squirrels try to find a tree.
Variation:	In small groups play as tag with one odd Squirrel and one chaser (hunter). The odd squirrel ducks into a tree and the other squirrel must vacate and find another tree. If the squirrel is tagged, he becomes the chaser. Change positions of the trees and squirrels often to allow running for all.

Tag in Brief

Skills:	Running, tagging, chasing, fleeing
Equipment:	None
Players:	Entire class
Formation:	Scatter

Nose-and-Toe Tag
Runners cannot be tagged when holding nose with one hand, toes with other hand.

Hindu Tag
Safe when kneeling, with forehead touching ground.

Ostrich Tag
Safe when holding nose with right hand, with right arm under right leg.

Hang Tag
Safe when hanging on to something, such as tree limb or post.

Stoop Tag
Safe when stooping down.

Squat Tag
Squat for safety.

Hook-On-Tag

Players hook onto the arm of another player to keep from being tagged.

Color Tag

Players are safe when touching a certain color.

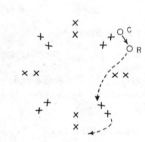

Arm's Length Tag

Equipment: None
Players: Entire class
Directions: Two players stand each with an arm extended at full length at
              shoulder level. Each tries to touch the other above the wrist without
              being touched in return. A touch on the other's extended hand does
              not count.

Three Deep

Skills: Running, starting, stopping
Equipment: None
Players: Entire class
Formation: Double circle
Directions: Players get into a double circle. The chaser (C) chases the runner
              (R). R may save himself by getting in front of a group, making it three
              deep. When a group is three deep, the outside person becomes R. If
              and when R is caught, he becomes C. R must go into the circle from
              the outside when making it three deep. When being chased he may
              cut through. Variations may be made of this game by making it two
              deep, or four deep, depending upon the number in the group.

Weather Cock

Skills: Pivoting, starting, running
Equipment: None
Players: Entire class
Formation: Scatter
Directions: Children should know directions (North, East, South, and West).
              One player represents the "weather bureau" and stands in front of
              the others and tells the way the wind blows. When he says "The
              wind blows north," the players quickly turn to the north, and so
              forth. When he says "Whirlwind," the players spin around three
              times on their right heels. Play rapidly for interest.

WEATHER COCK

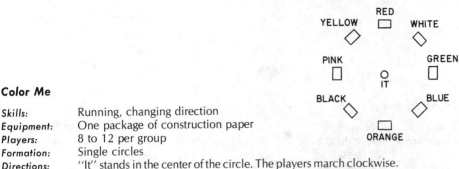

Color Me

Skills: Running, changing direction
Equipment: One package of construction paper
Players: 8 to 12 per group
Formation: Single circles
Directions: "It" stands in the center of the circle. The players march clockwise.
             "It" says "Color me red." "It" tries to get to the red construction
             paper before the other players. If he does, the last player to get
             behind the color is "It."

Blast Off

Skills: Running, starting, stopping
Equipment: None
Players: 20 to 30
Formation: Two lines
Directions: Players squat on line 1. The "captain" does the "count-down"
             from 10 to 0 as the players gradually rise to standing positions. As
             the captain counts "Zero" the players run to opposite line 2. The
             first player across becomes captain.

ACTIVE MANIPULATIVE GAMES

The games included in this section may be varied in a number of ways to enhance
a variety of fundamental manipulative abilities.

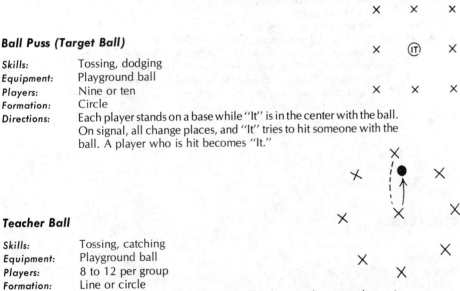

Ball Puss (Target Ball)

Skills: Tossing, dodging
Equipment: Playground ball
Players: Nine or ten
Formation: Circle
Directions: Each player stands on a base while "It" is in the center with the ball.
             On signal, all change places, and "It" tries to hit someone with the
             ball. A player who is hit becomes "It."

Teacher Ball

Skills: Tossing, catching
Equipment: Playground ball
Players: 8 to 12 per group
Formation: Line or circle
Directions: A ball is thrown around the circle. The player in the center throws it
             to each player in the circle, who each return the ball to the thrower.
             Concentrate on throwing and catching, and as skill improves,
             increase speed.

Boundary Ball

Skills:	Throwing
Equipment:	Playground balls
Players:	20 to 40
Formation:	Parallel lines
Directions:	Draw two parallel lines 60 feet long and 60 feet apart. Draw a center line. Divide the players evenly and place teams at opposite ends of the field facing center. The line behind each team is that team's goal. Give each team a ball. At a given signal each tries to throw the ball so as to cross the other team's goal. The ball must bounce or roll across the goal. The players move freely in their own end of the field, trying to keep the opponent's ball from crossing the goal. The team that gets the ball across the goal first wins.

Call Ball

Skills:	Vertical tossing, catching, throwing
Equipment:	8-inch rubber ball or volleyball
Players:	8 to 12 per group
Formation:	Line or circle
Directions:	One player is the thrower. The thrower calls the name of a player and tosses the ball into the air. The player whose name is called attempts to catch the ball. If he succeeds, he changes places with the thrower. If a player misses, the thrower calls names until the ball is caught. In a new and unacquainted group, number off and call a number or call colors of clothing.

Circle Kick Ball

Skills:	Kicking, trapping
Equipment:	Soccerballs
Players:	12 to 18 per group
Formation:	Two teams in a circle
Directions:	Each player attempts to kick a ball between the legs of two opposing players. Score one point for a successful kick. If a player kicks the ball over the heads of the opposing team, the opponents score one.

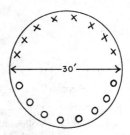

Circle Kick Ball

Skills:	Kicking, trapping
Equipment:	Soccerballs
Players:	16 to 24
Formation:	Two teams in a circle
Directions:	A ball is put in play by a player who kicks it toward an opponent. While the ball is in play all players must stay in their half of the circle, except the captains who may move out of position to kick balls that have stopped out of reach of their teammates. One point is scored for a team each time a player kicks the ball through the opponent's half circle or over their shoulders. Opponents kick the ball out on their own side. Opponents play ball with their hands (except girls using their hands to protect their faces or chests). The player who receives the ball when it goes out puts it into play again.

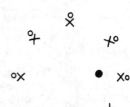

Circle Club Bowl

Skills:	Throwing, dodging, trapping
Equipment:	Indian clubs and softball or volleyball
Players:	12 to 24
Formation:	Circle or line
Directions:	Form a circle. Place a club behind each player, who stands in stride position. Each player tries to throw the ball through the legs of another player. The player whose club is knocked down is out of the game.

Corner Spry

Skills:	Throwing, catching
Equipment:	8-inch rubber ball
Players:	30 to 40
Formation:	Line relay, with 3 feet between each player and those on either side of him
Directions:	Divide the class into four teams, with a captain at the head of each team. The captain throws the ball to each player, who returns it. As soon as the last player catches the ball, the captain calls "Corner spry" and runs to the head of the line, and the last player becomes captain. The first team that gets back to its original position wins the game.

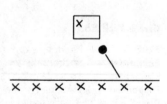

Line Dodgeball

Skills:	Throwing, catching, dodging
Equipment:	Volleyballs
Players:	12 to 24
Formation:	Two lines facing each other
Directions:	Two lines are drawn about 20 feet apart. Halfway between the lines a box about 4 feet square is drawn. One player stands in the box. Half the players stand on one line and half on the other. Players on both lines take turns throwing and trying to hit the center player below the waist. The center player may dodge but must never have both feet out of the box at any time. If hit, the center player changes places with the player who threw the ball.

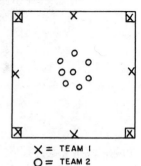

X = TEAM 1
O = TEAM 2

Square Ball

Skills:	Throwing, dodging
Equipment:	Playground ball
Players:	12 to 16 per group
Formation:	Square
Directions:	Team 1 takes its places on the bases, team 2 in the center of the square. The players on bases begin passing the ball around the square. Unexpectedly, a player on base tries to hit an inside player with the ball. If the center player is missed, the ball continues around the square. If the player is hit, team 1 runs around the bases until the player hit picks up the ball and calls "Halt." The player with the ball tries to hit one of the halted players. Score one for each player hit and score one for the opposing team for each miss. Set the game at ten points. Teams change places at the end of the game.

Stride Ball

Skill:	Rolling, striking
Equipment:	Any large ball
Players:	12 to 16
Formation:	Circle
Directions:	Players stand in a circle with their legs in stride position. "It" stands in the circle and tries to roll or bat the ball between the legs of the other players. If the ball is out of reach, a player may retrieve it but must return to the circle before he puts it back into play. If the ball goes through a player's legs three times he must drop out of the game for *one* turn.

CLASS ORGANIZATION

Division of Teams

Some teachers divide classes into teams and keep the same teams through the entirety of a sports unit. This procedure saves time and offers the participants the opportunity to become thoroughly familiar with teammates and the way they play. Others divide teams each week. The latter method has the advantage of exposing the participants to more and different playing situations; hence, it develops the alertness and versatility necessary to meet the unexpected. A teacher must judge which method best meets the situation and needs in that particular school, but it is recommended that teams be divided with an equalization of skill. Selected teams may wear distinguishing colors or pinnies given to them by their squad leaders. Skill segregation makes for dull competition. Then, too, a child with poor motor ability or skill weakness often improves more rapidly while playing with others more highly skilled.

ACTIVE CIRCLE GAMES

Children thoroughly enjoy active circle games. They are easily organized and may be modified in a variety of ways in order to satisfy the particular objectives of the lesson. The following is a compilation of the most popular and educationally sound active circle games available. These game activities may be utilized for developing and reinforcing a variety of locomotor and manipulative abilities, as well as for developing listening and group play skills.

Kick the Pin

Skills:	Kicking, trapping
Equipment:	A volley or rubber play ball and an Indian club or milk bottle for each group
Players:	Ten for each group
Formation:	Circles
Directions:	Each circled group, which have approximately 6 feet between each player, tries to kick the ball so as to knock down the centered pin. All kicking is done from this circle. Each team tries to knock over the pin first. The successful team scores one point. Ten points constitute a game.

Ring the Bottle Neck

Skills:	Eye-hand coordination
Equipment:	A catsup or pop bottle and a brass or wooden ring suspended on 20 inches of string from the end of a 2-foot stick for each group
Players:	Four to six on each team
Formation:	Circles
Direction:	A player holds the stick at the end opposite the end the string is fastened to and tries to get the ring over the neck of the bottle. Each player on each team gets one try while the leader counts slowly from 1 to 10. Score one point for each successful attempt. The team scoring ten points first wins.

Ball Bounce

Skills:	Bounce pass for accuracy
Equipment:	A soccer, rubber playground, or tennis ball, a chair, and one wastebasket for each player.
Players:	Four to six on each team
Directions:	From a distance of 8 feet each player tries to bounce the ball over the chair and into the upturned wastebasket. Each player gets one turn. The team scoring ten points first wins.

Stride Ball

Skills:	Rolling, agility, eye-hand coordination
Equipment:	One volley, soccer, or basketball
Players:	Ten players in each group
Formation:	Circles
Directions:	"It" stands in a circle. Outside, the players stand with their feet in straddle position touching those of the players on their right and left sides. "It" tries to roll the ball outside the circle between the legs of some players. The players try to stop the ball with their hands. If they can, they roll the ball back to the center player. When "It" rolls the ball between the legs of a player, the two exchange places.

Poison Circle

Skills:	Agility, dodging
Equipment:	Chalk
Players:	Eight to ten per group
Formation:	Circles
Directions:	Draw a circle 4 feet in diameter. Place players around the ring. The object of the game is to keep out of the poisoned circle by trying to pull others into it. When a player steps in or on the poisoned circle he is out.

Circle Ball Catch

Skills:	Tossing, catching
Equipment:	Volley, soccer, or basektball for each group
Players:	Eight to ten per group
Formation:	Circles
Directions:	"It" stands inside the circle of players standing 3 feet apart. Players throw the ball around or across the circle to one another while "It" tries to catch the ball. If he succeeds, he trades places with the person who last threw the ball.

Club Guard

Skills:	Throwing, agility, eye-foot coordination
Equipment:	Indian club and volley or playground ball
Players:	Eight to ten in a group
Formation:	Circles
Directions:	Players form a circle around one guarding the club in the middle. The object is to knock the club down with the ball. The guard protects it with his legs or body or bats it with his hands. The new guard is the one who gets the club down. Divide a large group into several smaller circles for greater success and fun. Avoid having more than eight in each group, if possible.

Schoolroom Tag

Skills:	Running, dodging, tagging
Equipment:	Chalk
Players:	Entire class
Directions:	A circle is drawn about 4 feet across in the front of the room. "It" stands near the circle. The leader names any three children, who try to get into the circle without being tagged. The one tagged first becomes "It." If no one is tagged, the first player becomes "It."

Ringmaster

Skills:	Imagery
Equipment:	None
Players:	Entire class
Formation:	Circles
Directions:	All players form a circle without holding hands. A ringmaster stands inside and pretends to flourish a whip. As he turns, he calls out the name of some animal and all move around the circle imitating that animal. When the ringmaster says "Now all join the circus parade" each imitates any animal he wants to. The teacher or class chooses the one who has done the best imitations.

Exchange Tag

Skills:	Running, dodging, tagging
Equipment:	None
Players:	Entire class
Directions:	"It" faces the group and calls out the names of any two players, who must exchange seats. "It" tries to tag one of them before he reaches a seat. The tagged player becomes the new "It."

Indian Running

Skills:	Running, visual memory
Equipment:	None
Players:	Entire class
Directions:	Six are chosen to leave the room. They arrange themselves in any order, return to the room, run around it, and then go out again. When they return, the children try to name their running line-up. The child who is successful may choose five others to leave with him, and the game continues.

Palm Ball

Skills:	Running
Equipment:	A rubber ball for each side
Players:	Entire class divided into small groups
Formation:	Circles
Directions:	Circled players cup hands behind their backs. "It" places the ball in someone's hands, who must turn and run in the opposite direction. Each tries to get back to the vacant spot first. The loser becomes "It."

Numbered Chairs

Skills:	Listening skills
Equipment:	A chair for each player, plus one extra
Players:	Entire class
Formation:	Line
Directions:	Seat players and place the extra chair in a line. Players number off. The space retains the number throughout, though the players change. No. 1 calls "four." Immediately 4 responds with another number. When a player whose number is called does not respond immediately he must go to the end of the line. Thus 9 becomes 8 and so forth. Numbers are called rapidly. The object of the game is to send the top players to the end of the line.
Variations:	Have players clap their hands on their knees and then together. Then have them snap the fingers on their left hands. Then have them do the same with their right hands in rhythm to 1, 2, 3, 4 count. All players must keep this rhythm up while calling out or responding to a number. Failure to keep the rhythm going will send a player to the end of the line. This game may also be played in a circle.

Birds Have Feathers

Skills:	Listening skills
Equipment:	None
Players:	Entire class
Directions:	One player is the leader. He and all others flap their arms like birds. He calls out names of things with feathers. If a player flaps his wings on calling out something that does not have feathers, he is out. The leader flaps his wings on almost all things to confuse the group and calls as rapidly as possible "Birds have feathers, bats have feathers, babies have feathers," and so forth.
Variations:	Have players put their thumbs up and down instead of flap their arms. Fur, leaves, or some other item can be mentioned instead of feathers (for example, "Cats have fur" or "Trees have leaves").

Center Pitch

Skills:	Throwing for accuracy
Equipment:	One beanbag, eraser, or ball for each team
Directions:	Players on each team take single turns throwing the beanbag into a metal wastebasket 8 feet away. Add the players' scores. The winner is the team scoring 21 points.
Variations:	(1) The players begin and stop pitching the bags at the leader's whistle. The winner is the team scoring the most points in five minutes. (2) Draw chalk circles at one end of the room. Players throw the bags into the circles. (3) Draw three circles on a board or cardboard. Each player gets three tosses. The team scoring the largest number of points in a given time wins. The first circle counts 25, the second 15, and the third 5.

ACTIVE GAMES FOR SPECIAL OCCASIONS

Halloween

In order to add variety and spice to the games played during the physical education period the teacher will find the following games for special occasions helpful. Several active games for play during Halloween, Thanksgiving, and Christmas are described in the following pages.

Catch the Witch

Skills: Running, changing direction and level
Directions: The players form a circle around the "witch," who tries to break through their joined hands. If he escapes, all chase him and the one who succeeds in catching him becomes the new witch.

The Cup of Poison

Skills: Running, chasing, fleeing, tagging
Directions: The players form a circle around a drawn ring, inside of which is a cup. They try to pull one another inside the ring in order to get someone to knock over the cup. Whoever does so runs as the others chase him. The game continues until one or more players catch three or more persons.

The Witches Ride Their Brooms

Skills: Carrying a heavy load
Directions: One player mounts the back of another, putting his legs around his waist and arms around his shoulders. All mounted riders race to a goal. The players change roles; the first couple to return to the starting line wins.

Go Pick A Pumpkin

Skills: Hopping, walking, jumping
Directions: The leader calls one's name and says "____, hop to the garden and bring me a pumpkin" (a ball or any object). She counts to 10, trying to finish before the child returns to place with the object. Vary actions by instructing the player to walk, hop, run sideways, crawl, and so forth.

Scat, Cat!

Skills: Running, chasing, fleeing, tagging
Directions: The leader goes through a variety of exercises as the rest follow. When he cries "Scat, Cat!" all run to touch any wall as he chases. Whoever is caught becomes the new leader.

Goblins Run!

Skills: Running, chasing, fleeing, tagging
Directions: Three fourths of the players are goblins, and the rest are police who try to catch them when the leader says "Goblins, run!" Those caught become police.

Who Has The Witch's Hat?

Skills: Tossing, catching
Directions: The players are scattered and throw the witch's hat (a ball) from player to player. When the leader says "Stop, I want my hat," the person holding the ball is out. Play continues until there are only two trying to get each other out.

Witch, Jump Over the Moon

Skills: Jumping
Directions: Two hold a rope, and the others jump over it in single file. It is raised higher after each time all have jumped. The winner is the person who jumps the highest. Next, the players jump sideways over the rope, run over it, or crawl under it.

Roll The Pumpkin

Skills: Rolling, coordination
Directions: A bat or stick is used to push a ball to an end line as each team, in turn, goes to an end line, runs back, and gives the bat and ball to the next. The winning team finishes first.

Follow The Leader Over The Graveyard Trail

Skills: Running, hopping, skipping
Directions: The leader runs, hops, crawls, and so on around the room or the playground as the others imitate his actions. Having several groups and a leader will provide more activity for the entire group.

Bats and Goblins, Fly!

Skills: Running, dodging, chasing, fleeing
Directions: Players form two sides, one group is the bats, one the goblins. Each imitates a flying motion as he runs. When the leader says "All fly!" both sides change places as the leader tries to catch them. Those tagged help the leader catch the rest. Play continues until all are caught.

Thanksgiving

Pilgrims and Indians

Skills: Tagging
Directions: One group, the Indians, tries to find the hidden Pilgrims. All must be caught before the group changes roles.

Gathering Goodies For The Feast

Skills: Running, chasing, fleeing, tagging
Directions: The children imitate picking up nuts from the ground, catching the wild turkey, and preparing the vegetables and so forth for the feast. All flee to safety as one player, a wild boar, tries to catch and eliminate them from the game.

Trap The Animals

Skills: Running, changing levels and directions
Directions: One half forms a circle; the others scatter and each is any animal he wishes to be for a big Thanksgiving dinner. On the leader's signal, they run in and out of the circle as the others try to trap them with their circled hands. All who are caught inside join the circle. When all are trapped, positions change.

Turkey Feather Pull

Skills: Running, dodging
Directions: Each of two teams has a home base. One, the "turkeys," all have a cloth strip or handkerchief tucked inside their belts or shorts. All go to the center ring and move around it. On the leader's signal, "Run, turkeys, run!" the turkeys try to reach their home base without an opposing player snatching his cloth or feather to pull him out of the game. Play continues until the turkeys have lost a team total of five feathers, then roles change.

Animal Chase

Skills: Running, chasing, fleeing, tagging
Directions: Players in teams are named for animals used for the Thanksgiving dinner (deer, turkeys, pigs, hens, and the like), and each group has its own pen. One player is the chaser and stands in the center. He calls the names of two groups of animals or of all four groups if he wishes, and each group must run to a new pen as he tries to catch the players. Those caught also become catchers.

Did You See Anyone Going To Grandma's House For Dinner?

Skills: Imitation
Directions: Players are in lines with each having a leader, who says "I saw someone going to grandma's house and he was trotting like a horse." The rest follow him as he trots around the room. The next in line may say ". . . he was riding on a motorcycle" or ". . . he was flying in an airplane" or whatever. Each child in each line has his turn as leader.

Feed The Hen

Skills: Tossing
Directions: Place a cardboard funnel inside a wastebasket (use as many of these as possible for the size of the group, striving to provide action for as many players as possible). Each player, in turn, tries to toss small balls or other objects into the hen's mouth. Points can be given to individuals or count toward a team's total. Play for ten or more points.

Drive the Pig to Market

Skills: Rolling, coordination
Directions: With a bat or broom each player in turn, in relay formation, drives a ball or other object to an end line and back. The team finishing first wins.

Hawk and Hen

Skills: Changing direction and level, running
Directions: Players stand in a circle of six or more with arms on one another's shoulder to make a pen. One player is the hen and another one is the hawk. On a signal, the hen runs inside the pen as his team tries to keep the hawk out. If the hawk gets in, he chases the hen, trying to catch her. If the hen can get back into the pen, she is safe and chooses a teammate to become the new hen as the hawk chooses one to take his place. If the group is large, have several pens, hawks, and hens.

Christmas

Guard the Toys

Skills: Starting, stopping, dodging, changing direction
Directions: One is the chaser; all others are runners. The chaser stands in a 20-foot circle along with 10 or more Indian clubs (the toys). The players run in and out of the circle trying to carry away the Indian clubs without being tagged by the chaser. The one caught becomes the new chaser, and a new game follows.

The Reindeer's Bell

Skills: Controlled running, listening
Directions: All players are chasers who are blindfolded except one, the runner, who can see. The runner has a bell, which he rings continuously as the others try to catch him. The one who does so trades places with him.

Santa's Parade

Skills: Running, dodging
Directions: All players except one, who is "Santa'" and stands on the outside, are in a circle. Santa walks around the group, and touches various players who follow him when he says "Come be in my parade." Suddenly, after several are following, Santa says "A snow storm is coming, hurry home." All try to return to their original place in the circle. The last one to do so is out, and a new game starts.

Catch the Candy Cane

Skills: Tossing, catching
Directions: Use a sawed-off broom stick (10 to 12 inches long) as the cane. Players stand five in a row with a leader in front of the group. He gently tosses the stick with one hand to the first player who catches it with one hand and tosses it back. Then the leader tosses to the second one, and so on. He starts back to the first player again when the stick has been thrown to all five. Have several groups with a leader and stick for each team. See which group can toss the stick back and forth for the longest time without missing. Next, see which group can toss it for 25 times without missing, counting in succession as it goes from one player to the next. Then see which team can throw it 50, then 100, times without missing. When anyone misses on any team, that group must go back to the count of 1.

How Many Presents Can You Get?

Skills: Running, changing direction
Directions: Place corks, small blocks of wood, erasers, or other objects (the presents) in the center of the room. The players, in two teams, stand behind opposite lines. On the signal, "Go!" all on both teams run to the center, each picking up just one object and running with it to his place back across his home or the base line. He runs to pick up another, takes it home, then another, and so forth. The winner collects the most presents in the shortest time.

Dance Around the Christmas Tree

Skills: Sliding, skipping
Directions: Using sliding or skipping steps, the children join hands and circle clockwise around a real or make-believe Christmas tree, singing Christmas songs as they do so. The type of action to be followed should vary with each new song chosen to be sung.

The Night Before Christmas

Skills: Imitation
Directions: As the teacher reads this poem, some children act out the story. Then have those not chosen act out going into the woods to find a Christmas tree, chopping it down, carrying it home, and decorating it. Change the role of each group.

The Christmas Clowns

Skills: Simple stunts
Directions: Each child becomes a clown doing stunts. Some act out juggling, others balancing, tightrope walking, somersaulting, and so forth.

Santa's Reindeer

Skills: Trotting, galloping, listening
Directions: One child plays Santa. When he claps his hands once, all the rest trot anywhere around the room; when he claps twice, they form a circle and trot to the left; on three claps they trot to the right. When he claps four times, they gallop; on five claps they pace by using short, high steps.

Toyland

Skills: Imitation
Directions: When the leader takes toys singly from a pack, all children act out what each toy does. Use toys such as an airplane, racing car, horse, jack-in-the-box, ball, and so on.

Santa's Pack

Skills: Running
Directions: All children, seated in a circle, are given the name of certain things
that would be in Santa's pack—a doll, ice skates, a drum, candy, a
football, and so forth. Santa starts naming all things he will put into
his pack. As he names each article each child has been given, those
having that name get up and follow him around the circle, putting
their hands on the shoulders of those preceding. When Santa
mentions reindeer in his story, all run to be the first to return and sit
down in his place in the circle. The first to do so becomes a new
Santa.

Piñata

Skills: Striking
Directions: This Mexican Christmas game becomes a favorite of all children
once they learn how to play it. A large paper bag filled with sweets
is hung from the ceiling. Each child, in turn, is given a stick, and his
eyes are blindfolded. Each tries to break the piñata by hitting at it
with the stick. When the bag is broken, the players scramble for the
sweets.

ACTIVE CONSTRUCTED GAMES

In the average school an inventory of board games would include checkers and
boards, Chinese checker boards, marbles, and a few bingo sets. Private schools
would rate higher, for student bodies and staffs are smaller, and often there is more
money left from the equipment budget to buy new games. Many active Parent-
Teacher Associations in the public schools have felt the need for more equipment

FIGURE 16–2. I can do lots of different kinds of movements. (Reprinted by
permission © J. A. Preston Corporation.)

FIGURE 16–3. Come on gang, let's get 'em! (Courtesy of *The Instructor.*)

and have raised money to buy ping-pong tables and shuffleboard sets. They could, likewise, help establish game libraries. The game library functions as any library. For example, a child who is giving a party could check out a number of games and return them at a designated time. Such a library should include puzzles of metal or wood, magic tricks, manufactured table games such as dominoes, checkers, Monopoly, and larger constructed games.

Actually, there is no point for having a poverty game program in any school, for children are interested primarily in play and are creative enough to make their own games if given encouragement. The rag bag, the button box, the attic, the garage, or the grocery store yields adequate materials for constructing a multitude of games. Building contractors are Santa Clauses for enterprising youngsters who really want to help build permanent games for their schools. Cheese boxes, fish buckets, apple and orange

FIGURE 16–4. Bumping and pulling activities such as this help to release tension and pent-up feelings. (Courtesy of AAHPER, Washington, D.C.)

crates, and hundreds of feet of beaver board, sheet rock, molding, plyboard, and lumber go each day into junk heaps that would supply the demands of game-hungry children.

There are numerous manufactured games available to schools with money allotted for such purposes. The games described below can be made by the children in the upper elementary grades; they are as inexpensive as the resourcefulness of teacher and pupils. The actual outlay of money should be for the purchase of nails, tacks, paint, thinner, and paint brushes. Few homes exist in which one could not find small amounts of usable enamel that will eventually harden. Paint is essential—the attractiveness of the finished game will depend largely on the eye appeal of bright, clear colors.

FIGURE 16–5. A healthy child is happy: he radiates and sparkles. (Courtesy of Dr. Joan Tillotson, Plattsburgh Public Schools, Plattsburgh, New York.)

Board Games

Because the bulletin board type of game has many uses, it is as much at home in the classroom as in the playroom. The classroom teacher will find such games most helpful in checking absorption of subject matter covering states, capitals, terrain, industries, foodstuffs, and so on. The inserts can be made in art class. Manila, tag board, wrapping paper, or detail paper is satisfactory. The design may be done in watercolor or tempera paint. Rubber darts are cheap and available at five-and-ten stores.

Frame as for a picture. Back with heavy paste board, beaver board, or wall board. Secure on three sides, leaving an opening at the top to permit removal of game inserts.

Map Games

Integration of subject matter using a map of the United States is shown in the following game. The room may be divided into two teams by numbering off by seat rows, or by sex if the boys and girls are equally divided. The first three rows are the blue team, and the second three rows form the red team. A member of the red team throws a dart at the map and must name the capital of the state the dart hits. If his identification is correct, the red team scores one point. The blue team throws next. The team scoring ten points first win.

Target Games

Most of these games may be played individually on cork, plywood, or different types of ceiling or wall board. Storage space is an item to be considered. Vacuum darts will adhere easily to glass but will not stick to uneven surfaces. Plyboard must be painstakingly sanded and heavily coated with varnish or shellac. Metal darts will stick in any soft wood or heavy cork but are taboo in most school systems because of the safety hazards.

Bombs Away!

Paint a salt box. Cut a round hole in one end the size of a quarter. Teach pupils how to drop five marbles accurately, one at a time, into the box. The best scorer with five tries wins. A cigar box may be used in place of a salt box.

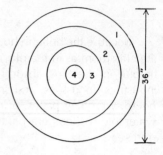

Target Throw

Use overhand throw. Inside use beanbags or a rubber or tennis ball; outside use a tennis or softball

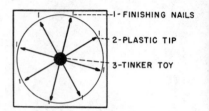

Wheel or Dial with Numbers

Class is divided into two to four teams and each team numbers off from 1 through 10. A selected leader spins the dial and asks a question. Teams may alternate, or the first one who raises his hand after the number is called may answer the question. The questions may be made by the class or teacher on any desired subject. This is also a good party game.

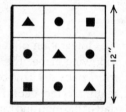

Peg Board

This board has holes for round, square, and triangular pegs. This game is suitable for the first and second grades and is excellent for children with poor manual coordination. Couples may make the play more interesting by counting the length of time it takes to get each peg in its proper place. The boards and pegs can be made in the manual training shop. The board should be painted a light color and the pegs dark red, blue, and green.

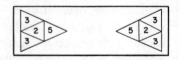

Finger Shuffleboard

Board may be painted on wrapping paper for table use or painted on wall or plyboard. Use checkers or bottle tops for pucks, and thump with the middle finger. Four may play as in horseshoes, and the game point may be set by the players.

There are many pitching games that may be made at little expense. Rings may be tenniquoits of rubber or may be made in class from rope, tubing, or rubber fruit-jar rings. Boards may be made to hang on the wall, stand like an easel, or lie on the floor.

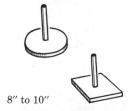

8" to 10"

Horseshoes for Inside

Set stakes a certain distance apart according to age level. Use regular rules for pitching horseshoes. Small rope rings, 6 inches in diameter, are suitable. The rings are secured with string and Scotch or bicycle tape. If tenniquoits are used, lead washers should be imbedded in the bottom of the board for weight.

Wall Boards

Floor boards that lie flat may be made any desired size from 12 × 12 inches to 36 × 36 inches. Nails or dowel stakes are vertical. The size of the ring will be indicated by the size of the board and stakes.

Schnozzle

Large numbers of children can be entertained in true carnival spirit while developing skill in pitching accuracy. Small rubber balls or beanbags may be pitched into wastebaskets, nail kegs, syrup buckets, or shallow cheese boxes. The bags or balls can be pitched through holes cut in boards in different shapes such as circles, squares, triangles, or half circles. Faces or any design may be painted on the board to fit the need. The underhand pitch should be used, and the holes should be large enough to permit easy passage of the bag or ball.

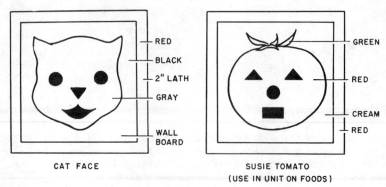

CAT FACE

SUSIE TOMATO
(USE IN UNIT ON FOODS)

Pitching

Use four rubber balls, 2 inches in diameter, or four beanbags, 5 inches square, filled with beans, peas, or gravel. Duck is the most durable of fabrics, but colored Indian Head domestic is attractive and is available in all colors to tie in with the color scheme of the board. The teacher or players can set the game. One point is given for hitting the eyes, two for the nose, and three for the mouth. It is suggested that the children set and draw their own pitching line and set up penalties for stepping over this line.

Put a Spook in a Haunted House

A box is decorated to look like a haunted house. Ghosts are made of white cloth with beanbag heads. Each ghost has a number written on it. If the first grader is able to give the correct number, he may throw the spook in the haunted house.

Santa Claus's sleigh or pack, the Easter Bunny's basket, and other seasonal characters with their unique equipment may be used. A Jack-o'-lantern toss game made from a scooped-out pumpkin and played with numbered beanbags is also a good seasonal game.

SUGGESTED READINGS

Arnold, A.: *The World Book of Children's Games*. New York, World Publishing Company, 1972.

Bentley, W.: *Indoor and Outdoor Games*. Belmont, California, Fearon Publishers, 1966.

Dauer, V., and Pangrazi, R.: *Dynamic Physical Education for Elementary School Children*. Minneapolis, Burgess Publishing Company, 1975.

Fluegelman, G.: *The New Games Book (Play Hard, Play Fair, Nobody Hurt)*. Garden City, New York, Dolphin Books/Doubleday & Company, Inc., 1976.

Kraus, R.: *The Family Book of Games*. New York, McGraw-Hill, Inc., 1960.

Latchaw, M.: *A Pocket Guide of Movement Activities for the Elementary School*. Englewood Cliffs, New Jersey, Prentice-Hall, Inc., 1970.

Lincoln, E.: *Backyard Games*. New York, Stadia Sports Publishing, 1973.

Lowenfeld, M.: *Play in Childhood*. New York, Wiley Press, 1967.

Parker, A. W. H.: *Find Your Own Summer Thing; Getting Together Is The Thing; Kool Summer Fun* (three card files of over 200 activities each). Washington, D.C., National Park and Recreation, 1972.

Sullivan, G.: *Sports for Your Child*. New York, Winchester Press, 1973.

Vannier, M.: *Recreation Leadership*. 3rd ed. Philadelphia, Lea & Febiger, 1977.

CHAPTER SEVENTEEN

SIMPLE GAMES FOR CLASSROOMS AND LIMITED SPACES

To enable youngsters to adjust and live in a democratic world, help them to develop skills necessary for growth and development. Skills are the basic movements which the child will use throughout life.

A Children's Book of Rhymes and Games
Nan Roberts and Jeanette Wieser

GENERAL TECHNIQUES

Adverse weather conditions create few problems to the master teacher who has learned to utilize the classroom for active games and contests during stormy, unpleasant days. This emergency period can be one of bedlam for the novice and one of boredom for the pupils. Scheduled playground play need not be canceled during cold, wet days. Instead, the classroom, corridors, lunchroom, or other space can be used. This makeshift period of classroom play should never be substituted for rugged outdoor activity or daily instruction in physical education. Rather, it can be an addition to the total program. Although children must learn how to run, skip, and jump, and use their bodies in other types of the fundamental big-muscle movements in order to develop properly, they also need to learn how to play the less active, quiet games that will enable them to use skillfully the smaller muscles of the body. Like adults, children need to know how to have fun with things in their everyday environment—how to entertain themselves rather than be entertained.

Specific objectives to be realized through classroom activities might well include

1. Sharing with the child interesting, "fun-to-do" activities for classroom and after-school play.
2. Adding variety and completeness to the total physical education program.
3. Helping the child develop a sense of fair play and the ability to play with others.
4. Helping the child develop good leadership and fellowship techniques.
5. Aiding the child in developing good all-round social, physical, and emotional development.

In order to reach these worthy objectives, the teacher needs to utilize all available indoor space to the greatest advantage in carrying out a carefully planned program. If she is fortunate enough to have movable chairs in the room, circle tag and "It" or other such active games are desirable. If, however, desks and chairs are fastened to the floor, quiet games are more suitable. Knowledge of a wide range of activities and how to modify them to fit into one's own particular situation is imperative.

Rules of conduct should be set up by the children with the help of the teacher. Activities chosen by the group should not infringe upon the rights of others in nearby classrooms.

FIGURE 17-1.   Look, I can jump the rope! (Courtesy of James Wheeler of the Dayton Public Schools, Dayton, Ohio.)

CRITERIA FOR CHOOSING ACTIVITIES

In selecting games for indoor play the teacher should strive for participation of the whole class. Good questions to keep in mind when selecting activities are

1. How many children can be active safely at one time?
2. How quickly can new players replace those who have been active?
3. How much activity will each child actually engage in during the period?
4. Do the chosen games reach our pupil-teacher objectives?

SAFETY PRECAUTIONS

Learning to take chances wisely should be stressed throughout the period. Over-protected children often are denied rich learning experiences. This does not imply that they should be encouraged to cut their fingers in order to learn that a knife is sharp, but it does suggest that many dangers can be avoided best when one learns from a painful experience. Pupil-teacher safety rules are most adhered to; group-discovered hazards are most avoided.

Suggested safety precautions are

1. Avoidance of running around in small circles or changing directions suddenly.
2. Establishment of goal lines away from wall.
3. Use of beanbags or balloons rather than regulation balls and reduction of amount of equipment used.
4. Limitation of the number of players in a given space, but being certain that each child gets a turn and takes part in meaningful activities.
5. Keeping of noise at a minimum.

Additions to this list should be made after the teacher gains from the experience of playing with the children in the classroom. It is wise to make a list of activities most favored by the children and be constantly on the search for new materials.

EQUIPMENT

A "magic box," which is used only on stormy, dark days, can help turn a dull day into one of great adventure. Checkers, cards, table games, beanballs, ring toss, jacks, and miniature bowling pins are among the treasures inside. Small-group or couple play should be encouraged, or a group of six might choose games they want to play. Each group might be allowed to play their favorite games for the entire period or change with any other willing group at half-period time.

A construction box is often found in the rooms of creative, experienced teachers. In it are found games made by the pupils on previous rainy days, along with some half-completed ones. Some children can make checkerboards, and others, tossboards from fruit-jar rubbers. Still others may construct miniature table-shuffleboard sets on which checkers can be finger snapped up, down, and into given areas. Jumping standards may be made by driving nails into two boards and using an old fishing pole

FIGURE 17–2. The classroom can be used by the classroom teacher for some kinds of physical education activities if no gymnasium is available. (Courtesy of *The Instructor.* Photograph by Edith Brockway.)

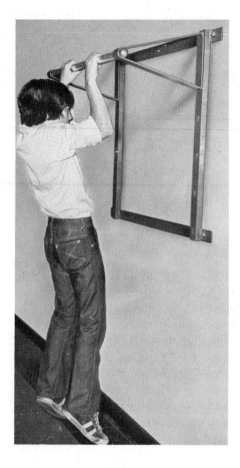

FIGURE 17–3. A chinning bar can be placed in any corner of the classroom. (Courtesy of Jayfro Corporation, Montville, Connecticut.)

to move up and down on the nails to show how high one must jump. A balance beam using blocks to steady a 2 × 4 may be easily made.

These and numerous other pieces of equipment and games can be made for use in the classroom. Home- or class-made equipment often is more meaningful to pupils than expensive items furnished by the school. The creative teacher, when and if she has a will, will find the way to get equipment.

The suggested minimum of equipment for use in the classroom includes

1. Four ring toss games
2. Four rubber balls
3. One treasure box
4. Card and table games

5. Jump ropes
6. One long rope
7. Phonograph or piano
8. Empty milk cartons
   and tin cans of varying sizes

ACTIVITY LEADERSHIP

Successful game and play leadership requires skill. The leader must know games best suited for the group, how to get play started, when to stop one activity and go on to the next, and a wide range of things to play. Mastery of these skills comes from experience, providing one has learned from past mistakes. The novice may gain additional experience with church or neighborhood groups in order to become more expert.

Mastery of a best method to gain attention is important. Suddenly clapping one's hands, playing a piano chord, and saying "Freeze" are recommended techniques. Although the teacher may ordinarily have control over the group, it may be lessened or even lost during this classroom recreation. The teacher may find it necessary to stop activities entirely or momentarily in order to regain control. However, the pupils should not be bargained with when they are "bad" or have been particularly "good." The plea "Please let us play five minutes longer and we will be quieter" or the promise "Now children, if all of you get your arithmetic lesson we will play ten minutes longer this afternoon" are significant signs of this type of leadership technique. In the former, the children have found that they can bargain with the teacher. In the latter, the teacher is promising "dessert" so that the pupils will "eat" the "healthy foods" they do not enjoy. Next to compulsion, bargaining is the lowest form of leadership.

An atmosphere of fun should permeate the classroom. If the first game has been wonderful, obtaining class cooperation will be easier when the second one to be played is introduced. If, however, a game that looked like fun when described in the book falls flat, it is best to change to another rather than insisting "Now children, this game really *is* fun" when obviously it is not.

Rules and the setting of necessary boundaries should be briefly explained. A description of how to play, coupled with actual demonstrations, is ideal. If when saying "Everyone get into a circle," the teacher joins hands with a youngster on either side, the pupils will quickly get into this formation. The use of imitation is a standard teaching method, for children are "copycats." A major portion of their learning comes through what they see and try to do. Educators call this trial-and-error learning through imitation.

Changing activities at their fun peaks adds to their enjoyment. Children often say then "Oh, let's keep on playing please!" Grownups realize that stopping the activity at the climax will cause the children to have greater desire to play the game again because it was such fun. This need for completeness, as psychologists call it, drives us to take up willingly or return joyfully to interrupted tasks or pleasures. Recognition of fun peaks can be developed.

Going from the known to the unknown is an educational principle applicable to game, as well as subject, material, for basically the same principles of teaching underlie all learning materials. Each new game period should begin with the most favored game from the previous period. Because we all like to do those things we can do well, the wise teacher aids children to gain above-average ability in many skills. It is wise to learn at least two new activities during the game period as well as to review others. It is unwise to insist upon skill perfection if an unpleasant experience or unfavorable attitude is anticipated.

QUIET CIRCLE GAMES

There are a wide variety of fun and exciting circle games that can be played in a limited space. These games stress cooperation, group spirit, and listening. They may also be used to enhance fine motor coordination.

Electric Shock

Skills: Visual memory
Equipment: None
Players: 10 to 15
Formation: Circles
Directions: Players sit or stand in a circle. "It" stands inside and tries to guess where the "shock" is. All players hold hands; one player begins the shock by squeezing a player's hand on his right or left. The shock may move in any direction, and at any time a player may send it back the other way. "It" tries to find the position of the shock. The caught player becomes "It."

Air Balloon

Skills: Cooperation, eye-hand coordination
Equipment: One balloon per group
Players: Eight to ten players per group
Formation: Circles
Directions: Divide the group into equally numbered circles. On a count of 3 each group competes with the others to see which one can keep the balloon in the air longest by tapping it. Each player may tap the balloon only once at a time; he may tap it again after another player has tapped it.
Variations: Music may be played. Each player may tap in rhythm to the music or on one separate rhythmic beat.

Poison Ball

Skills: Passing, catching
Equipment: Two rubber balls for each circle
Players: Eight to ten per group
Formation: Circles
Directions: Players form into circles; each circle has two balls. When the music stops or the whistle blows, players in possession of either ball are poisoned and must leave the group. When the group gets down to four players only one is used. The last player to stay in the circle is the winner.
Variations: Musical chairs

Who Has Gone?

Skills: Visual memory
Equipment: None
Players: Entire class
Directions: "It" closes his eyes. One player leaves the room. "It" tries to guess who has gone. If he guesses correctly, he and the player who went out change places. If not, the game begins again.

Electric Tag

Skills: Teamwork
Equipment: None
Players: Entire class
Directions: Players sit in rows with their hands in their laps and eyes closed. At a signal, the last pupil in each row touches the shoulder of the person in front of him. That player touches the next person, and so forth. The row that has its first pupil stand wins.

Still Water

Skills: Listening skills
Equipment: None
Players: Entire class
Directions: "It" faces the rest and picks out the quietest player when he says "Still water." On the words "Running water," the pupils can move around and talk. The winner chooses the quietest, who becomes "It."

Angels Do It

Skills: Listening skills
Equipment: None
Players: Entire class
Directions: The pupils put their hands behind their necks to look like angel wings. The leader gives the direction "Touch your nose; angels do it." All players must quickly touch their noses and get back to angel position. The first team to do so scores one point. Suggested "do its" include "Touch your right foot," "Touch your left foot," "Clap twice behind you," "Stand up," "Touch wood," and "Whistle a tune."

Stagecoach

Skills: Auditory memory, agility
Equipment: None
Players: Entire class
Directions: Players are each given the name of a stagecoach part. One starts telling a story of the stagecoach, mentioning all the parts assigned. As the child's part is named he gets up and runs around his chair. When the leader says "Stagecoach" each player must change chairs with anyone except the player on his left and right. The leader tries to get a seat. The person left seatless becomes the new storyteller.

I Pass These Scissors to You

Skills: Visual scanning
Equipment: A pair of scissors
Players: Entire class
Directions: Players are seated in circle formation. The leader passes a pair of scissors. The next player passes them on, saying "I have received them crossed and I pass these scissors to you uncrossed." The crossed and uncrossed refers to the passer's legs or feet and not to the open or closed scissors being passed as the players think. If the receiver's feet were crossed when the scissors were passed and are crossed as he passes them, he says "I received them crossed and I pass these scissors to you crossed." The game continues until everyone catches on.

The Guessing Blind Man

Skills:	Auditory memory
Equipment:	A blindfold and a stick or ruler
Players:	Entire class
Directions:	Players are seated in circle formation. One is blindfolded and turned around three times while all others change seats. The "blind man" walks forward and touches someone with the stick, saying "Can you guess?" The touched player, trying to disguise his voice, repeats this question three times. If the blind man guesses who is speaking, he and the discovered player exchange places. Otherwise, he continues as the blind man in the next game.

Bug

Skills:	Memory, concentration, cooperation
Equipment:	Two or more hexagonal tops with the letters B, H, T, E, L, and F on the six sides (one letter to a side); paper; and pencils
Players:	Individual, or four to ten per team
Directions:	Each player spins the top. If "B" comes up, he draws the body of the bug and spins again. If he gets an "E" he loses his turn, for there is no head into which to fit the eyes. The best second throw, therefore, is an "H" for the head. "T" means tail, "L" means leg, and "F" means feeler. Each bug must have two eyes, two feelers, and six legs along with its body, tail, and head before it is a complete bug. When a player tosses something he already has, he loses his turn. A player cannot start drawing his bug until he gets a "B" for body. The team or individual player drawing a complete bug first wins.

Muffin Pan Bowling

Skills:	Rolling
Equipment:	One muffin pan and one small rubber ball for each group
Players:	Four to six on each team
Directions:	Set the pan upright against a wall or on a table. Place a board against one edge of the pan to form an incline. Roll the ball up the incline into the compartments. Score one point for each successful attempt. Each player is given three trials. The team scoring ten points first wins.

Ring on a String

Skills:	Fine motor control, visual scanning
Equipment:	A ring on a string
Players:	Ten players per group
Formation:	Circles
Directions:	One player stands in the circle. A string with a ring on it is held loosely in both hands by all players in the seated circle. The object of the game is to slip the ring along the string from one player to the next while "It" tries to locate the ring or the player who has it. If he is successful, he exchanges places with the one under whose hand it was. If unsuccessful, he continues as "It."

Catch the Cane

Skills:	Agility
Equipment:	Cane or yardstick
Players:	Entire class
Formation:	Circle
Directions:	"It" stands inside the circle. All players, including "It," are given a number. "It" holds the cane upright with one end on the floor. As he calls out a number he lets go of the cane. The player whose number has been called attempts to catch it before it touches the floor. If he fails he becomes "It." If he catches the cane the first player remains "It."

The Toy Shop

Skills:	Imagery, creativity
Equipment:	None
Players:	Entire class
Directions:	One child is chosen shopkeeper and one the customer, who leaves the room while the others choose which toy they want to be. When the customer returns he asks to buy some toys. If he asks for a ball, the player representing a ball bounces up and down; if he asks for an airplane, the player designated as that toy "flies" around the room. The shopkeeper guides his buying by suggesting and showing certain toys. The customer selects the three best toys.

How Many Can You Remember?

Skills:	Visual memory
Equipment:	A wide variety of objects
Players:	Entire class
Directions:	Place 20 to 30 objects on a table. Have everyone look at them for two or three minutes. Then place a cover on them. The winner is the person who writes down the names of the greatest number of objects.

GAMES FOR LIMITED SPACES

Not all schools are fortunate enough to have a gymnasium for the children to use during bad weather, although most of them have a large outdoor play area, which should be used to its utmost. The following games can well be played in the classroom, hallways, and on the auditorium stage:

I Say Stoop

This game is like Simon Says. One player is the leader who gives directions for the others to do what he says as he demonstrates each action. If he says one thing and shows another movement, anyone who does what he does and not what he says is out. He may say stand when he stoops, say to bend over to touch your toes as he stretches high, and so on.

Mother Carey's Chickens

In groups of six, players form a line with their arms around the waists of the players in front of them. Mother Carey is the first in each line. One player is the fox, who throws a rubber ball trying to hit any player in any line. Each Mother Carey tries to protect her "chickens" by swinging them away from the ball or warding it off with her hands. Any chicken hit by the ball thrown by the fox is out, as is any player in any line who lets go of the waist of the one in front of him. Those eliminated retrieve the ball for the fox, but only he can throw it. Play continues until all chickens and all Mother Careys are hit with the ball.

Find The Leader

"It" leaves the room. The players in the circle choose a player to be the leader, who does various motions that they follow. They clap their hands vigorously to call "It" into the room. He tries in three guesses to find who is the leader starting each new motion the group follows. This game is much fun to play, especially if the leader (1) changes action often, such as turning around in a circle, doing jumping jacks, and so on, and (2) players look at three others who quickly follow the leader as the rest follow their actions, instead of all players looking at the actual leader.

Back to Back

Each player has a partner in circle formation with all boy partners on the inside. All players move clockwise on "Go!" from the leader. When she says "Back to back," each couple turns back to back or does other actions upon command, such as "Toes to toes," "Thumbs to thumbs," or "Elbows to elbows." When the leader says "Find a new partner," all on the outside must find a new partner before being tagged by the leader who stands inside the circle. No player may seek a new partner to his immediate right or left. Whoever is caught first becomes the new leader.

Red or White

"It" holds a cardboard, one side of which is red and the other white. From behind opposite homebase lines, each team (one the Reds, the other the Whites) comes to the center of the room. The leader tosses the card into the air. If it lands white side up, the Whites must run to safety behind their homebase line as the Reds chase them. If it lands red, the Whites chase the Reds. All who are caught may be out, or one point may be counted for each one caught until one team first has five or more points.

The Magic Carpet

Make several large squares on the floor with chalk or masking tape. The children follow the leader who skips, runs, hops, gallops, or crawls through the magic carpet squares. When he says "Stop!" all who are inside or on a line in any carpet must lead the class in an exercise or be allowed three misses before they are out.

The Mouse Trap

Six or more couples join hands and hold them up to make traps. The rest are mice who run in and out of the various traps. When the leader says "Snap!" all traps fall and those caught also make traps. Play until all mice are caught. Change roles.

Blackboard Relays

All players sit in rows of equal teams. All in each line must leave their desks from the left side and return to them from the right. In turn, each player runs, skips, hops, gallops, or slides to the blackboard, writes his first name on the board or makes a mark, and writes one word of any sentence, which the last player in each line must finish. The winning team finishes first.

Overtake

Players stand in a circle. One larger ball is passed from one player to the next while a smaller ball is passed clockwise as the players try to have it overtake the larger one. Several circles, each with two balls, should be used, if the group is large.

Do This Do That!

When the leader asks the group to "Do this!" the others must imitate his action immediately. Should he say "Do that!" any player imitating his action has a point scored against him. Three mistakes of this kind put a player out of the game. The leader may choose any action familiar to the group—knee bending, hopping, arm stretching, hammering, and so forth.

Ducks Fly

The players stand in the aisles of the schoolroom. The player who is "It" stands in front, faces the group, and calls "Ducks fly! Birds fly! Horses fly!" When he names an animal that does fly, the players go through the motions of flying: raising their arms high above their heads and lowering them to the side. When he names an animal that does not fly, they must not "fly." Anyone who "flies" at the wrong time or does not "fly" at the proper time becomes "It," and the game is repeated.

I Saw

One child who is "It" stands in front of the room. He says "On my way to school this morning I saw _____." He then imitates, in movements or gestures, what he saw and the others try to guess what it was. The child who guesses correctly becomes the leader, and the game starts again. If no one guesses correctly, the leader tells what he saw, and another "It" is selected.

What To Play?

The children in the circle begin singing the following words to the tune of "Mary Had a Little Lamb":
>   Mary, show us what to play,
>   What to play, what to play,
>   Mary, show us what to play,
>   Show us what to play.

When the class stops singing, the leader says "Play this!" and then makes a pantomime action such as hopping, jumping, shaking hands, combing hair, or washing clothes. The entire group imitates this motion until the leader says "Stop." The leader chooses another player to take his place. The song begins again, and the game continues.

Animal Blind Man's Bluff

One player, blindfolded, stands in the center of a circle with a wand, stick, or cane in his hand. The other players walk around him. When he taps three times on the floor with his cane, they must stand still. The blind man thereupon points his cane at some player, who must take the opposite end of the cane in his hand. The blind man then commands him to make a noise like some animal, such as a cat, dog, cow, sheep, lion, donkey, duck, or parrot. From this, the blind man tries to guess the name of the player. If he guesses correctly, they change places. If he is wrong, the game is repeated with the same blind man.

Huckleberry Beanstalk

The object is hidden by the leader while the players have their heads down on their desks and their eyes closed. They are called to hunt for the hidden object. Anyone seeing it takes his seat and calls "Huckleberry beanstalk!" The object of the game is not to be the last one to find the hidden object.

Dog and Bone

One child is selected to be the "dog." He sits on a chair or stool in front of the children who are sitting at their desks. The dog closes his eyes and turns his back to the other players. The dog's "bone," an eraser or any article of similar size, is placed near his chair. A child selected by the teacher attempts to sneak up to the dog and to touch his bone without the dog hearing him. If the dog hears someone coming, he turns around and says, "Bow! Wow!" That player must return to his seat. If the dog "bows-wows" when no one is trying for his bone, he must return to his seat. A child who is successful in touching the bone before the dog hears him becomes the dog, and the game is resumed.

Spin The Platter

Each child is given a number. "It" spins a tin pie plate on the floor in the center of the circle as he calls a number. The child whose number is called tries to catch the plate before it stops spinning. If successful, he may be "It" and the game is repeated.

Squirrel and Nut

In the classroom, all children but one sit in their chairs with heads down and hands outstretched. The standing player is the "squirrel." He tiptoes around the chairs and drops the "nut" into one of the outstretched hands. The child who gets the nut chases the squirrel, trying to catch him before he reaches the chaser's chair. If the squirrel is caught, the chaser becomes the squirrel. If the squirrel reaches the chaser's seat before being tagged, he will name a squirrel from the group.

Who Has Gone From The Room?

"It" stands in front of the seats or in the center of the circle as the case may be. He closes his eyes while the teacher indicates which child shall leave the room. After this child has left, "It" opens his eyes and guesses who has gone. If he names the child correctly, that child is "It" the next time. If he fails to name the child, he closes his eyes again, the child returns to the room, and "It" opens his eyes and guesses who has returned. If he fails, he must be "It" again.

Numbers

Number each seat consecutively and have each player write this number on a sheet of paper which he places on his desk. To begin the game, the leader calls a number. The player whose number was called immediately responds with another number. Failure to respond immediately is a miss. When a player misses he moves to the last seat with each player moving up one place. The seats retain the same numbers when players move. The object of the game is to get to seat No. 1.

Change Seats

In this game children change seats on their teacher's commands "Change right!" "Change left!" "Change front!" or "Change back!" When the shift is forward, children in the front row of seats stand until the command is given to change back. Children in the outside rows to the right or to the left must also stand when the change is made in their direction. The last to stand or sit at attention is given a point. The lowest score is the winner.

Streets and Alleys

All players are in equal lines. Those who face the front of the room are the Streets, and the others are the Alleys. All players in each line join hands. Two other players become "It" and the runner. Both can only run through the aisles formed by the others. When "Streets!" is called by the leader, all who are the Streets face front and join hands. When "Alleys!" is called, all drop hands, turn to the side and rejoin hands. These changing aisles may help or hinder the runner. When he is caught, a new runner and chaser are chosen.

LIMITED-SPACE GAMES OF SKILL

The following games of skill may be performed by a class or group of children in the classroom or other area where space is limited:

Hand Touch

Skills:	Body awareness
Equipment:	None
Players:	Individual
Directions:	Tell the players to put one hand where the other cannot touch it. After the players try unsuccessfully, have them put their right hands to their left elbows, for this is the secret of the trick.

Jump the Shot

Skills:	Jumping
Equipment:	A long rope with a shoe tied on it for each group
Players:	Six to eight in each group
Directions:	Pupils form a circle around the center player, who swings the rope in a circle. He gradually increases the swinging part of the rope until it reaches the knees of the group, and at the same time, he increases the speed of the swing. All try to jump over the weighted rope as it reaches them. A player touched by the rope is eliminated.

Circle Squat

Skills:	Locomotor skills
Equipment:	None
Players:	Entire class
Directions:	Players skip, hop, and march as directed by the leader. All must squat when the leader's whistle blows. Play continues until all but one have been eliminated.

Clothespin Drop

Skills:	Visual-motor coordination
Equipment:	Milk bottles and five clothespins for each group
Players:	Groups of four to six
Directions:	Each player in each line drops five clothespins, one at a time, into the milk bottle from an upright position. The scores for each player are added together. The winner is the team that scores 20 points.

Ping-pong Bounce

Skills:	Visual-motor coordination
Equipment:	Three ping-pong balls and a box for each group
Players:	Groups of four to six
Directions:	Each player in each line bounces all of the ping-pong balls into the box from a 10-foot line. Team scores are added together. The winner is the team that scores 25 points first.

Pick Up

Skills:	Body awareness
Equipment:	A coin
Players:	Individual
Directions:	Stand with your back against a wall and your heels touching it. Try to pick up the coin without moving your heels away from the wall.

Circle Two

Skills:	Body awareness
Equipment:	None
Players:	Individual
Directions:	Move the arms in large circles in opposite directions—the right hand away from the body, the left toward the body.
Variations:	(1) Swing the right foot in a circle moving left; then swing the left foot in a circle moving right. (2) Pat the head with one hand and rub the stomach with the other simultaneously.

Stand Up

Skills:	Body control
Equipment:	None
Players:	Individual
Directions:	Lie flat on your back with your arms to the side and your hands flat against your hips. Rise without using your hands. First come to a sitting position; then stand up.
Variations:	Lie flat on your back; cross your arms on your chest. Stand up without uncrossing your arms or using your elbows.

Balance Writing

Skills:	Visual-motor control
Equipment:	A milk carton, pad of paper, and pencil
Players:	Individual
Directions:	Sit down on an upright milk case. Cross your legs, allowing only the heel of one foot to touch the floor. Write your full name on the pad while trying to maintain your balance.
Variations:	(1) Light a match. (2) Thread a needle.

Jump the Brook

Skills:	Leaping, jumping, hopping
Equipment:	Chalk or two ropes
Players:	Class divided into two groups
Directions:	Players line up in two single lines. Each runs and jumps across the brook (chalk marks or ropes placed about 8 inches apart). If a player misses, he must drop out to get his feet dry. After each round the brook is made wider until one is proclaimed champion.

Beanbag Toss

Skills:	Tossing for accuracy
Equipment:	Plywood with three holes and a beanbag for each group
Players:	Groups of four
Directions:	The board has three holes with 5-, 10-, and 15-point values. Players toss the beanbag through the holes and play for total individual or group points.
Variations:	Paint a clown's face on the plywood. Score five points for hitting the mouth hole, ten for each eye.

Card Toss

Skills:	Visual-motor control
Equipment:	Ten cards for each group
Players:	Four to six on a team
Directions:	Each pupil tosses ten cards singly into a propped-up hat or waste-basket 10 feet away. Score one point for each successful toss.

He Can Do Little

Skills:	Imitations, memory
Equipment:	A cane or stick
Players:	Entire class
Directions:	Players sit in a circle. The leader starts the game by saying "He can do little who can't do this." He passes the cane to the player to the left, who must repeat the action as nearly as possible and then pass the cane on to the player on his left. The leader tells the player whether he has done the stunt correctly. The secret is that tapping is done with the cane in the right hand, and the cane is then taken in the left and passed on to the next person. The leader may beat out a special rhythm and go through extra flourishes to distract attention.

ACTIVE RELAYS FOR LIMITED SPACES

Chinese Hop

Skills: Hopping
Equipment: Ten sticks, candles, or tenpins
Directions: The sticks are placed in a straight line 1 foot apart. Each player hops on one foot over the sticks without touching any of them. He is disqualified if he touches a stick. After jumping over the last stick, the player, still on one foot, picks up that stick and hops back over the other nine. Next he hops over the nine sticks, then the eight, and so forth, each time hopping back down the line of remaining sticks. He continues until all sticks have been picked up. A player is disqualified if he fails to tag the next player to start hopping up his line, if he touches both feet to the ground at any time, or if he touches a stick with his foot. The second player puts down the ten sticks. The third picks them up. The game continues in this way down the line.

Hurdle Race

Skills: Leaping
Equipment: A rope or broomstick
Directions: Players 1 and 2 on each team hold a broomstick or rope between them 6 or more inches from the floor. They run down the line with their teammates between them, jumping the hurdle as it moves to the end of the line. As soon as they reach the end, No. 2 returns to the head of the line and starts down with No. 3 in the same manner. No. 3 then runs with No. 4, and the game continues in this manner until No. 1 is back at the head of the line.

Blackboard Relay

Skills: Mathematics concepts
Equipment: Blackboard and chalk
Directions: This game is played like any relay except that the player writes a number on the board in a line instead of touching a goal. The last player must add all the numbers correctly. The team with the first correct answer wins.

Tag the Wall Relay

Skills: Running
Equipment: None
Directions: Seat players in even-numbered rows. On a signal, the last player in each row runs forward and tags the wall. As soon as this player is past the first seat in the row, everyone moves back one seat, leaving the first seat vacant for the runner. As soon as the runner is seated, he raises his hand and the last person seated begins. The line whose players all finish running first wins.

Newspaper Race

Skills: Leaping, stepping
Equipment: Two newspapers
Directions: Each contestant is given a newspaper, on which each step of the race must be made. He puts down a sheet and steps on it, puts down another sheet and steps on it, reaches back to get the first sheet and move it forward, and so on until he reaches the goal line, from which he returns in the same fashion and tags the second player.

Spider Race

Skills: Running, cooperation
Equipment: None
Directions: Player No. 1 in each line faces the goal. No. 2 stands with his back
              toward No. 1, and they link elbows and race to the goal. No. 2 runs
              back facing the end line while No. 1 runs forward. Players 3 and 4
              and on down the line repeat the actions.

Rapid Fire Artist

Skills: Teamwork
Equipment: Pencil or crayon and paper
Directions: Divide the group into equal teams. Each group sends an "artist" to
              the leader, who tells him an animal, person, tree, or other thing to
              draw. The artist rushes back to his group and begins to draw the
              likeness of the person, place, or thing given him. As soon as the
              group recognizes what is drawn, the members yell it all together.
              The group guessing first scores one point. Ten points constitute a
              game. The artist cannot talk or give any hints other than his draw-
              ing.

Nature Guess

Skills: Imagination
Equipment: None
Directions: Divide the group into four teams. Each group sends a different
              member up each time to the leader, who tells him an animal or
              person to act out. The first group to guess who or what the player is
              acting out scores one point. Ten points constitute a game.

QUIET GUESSING GAMES

The following is a compilation of quiet guessing games that are enjoyed by
children of all ages. The teacher may wish to utilize these activities during rest periods
or between high-activity sessions in the lesson.

Grocery Store

Skills: Recall, listening, and auditory memory
Equipment: None
Players: Entire class or teams of four to ten
Directions: Divide the group(s) into equally numbered lines. One player from
              each line steps forward. The leader calls out any letter. The player
              who first calls out the name of any grocery article beginning with
              that letter scores a point for his team. Ten points constitute a game.
Variation: Players call out the name of any animal, person, state, or other
              thing.

Nursery Rhymes

Skills: Imagery, creativity
Equipment: None
Players: Entire class
Directions: Give each pupil or a group of three pupils a nursery rhyme to act
              out for others to guess.
Variations: Use a poem or a song.

Hand Puppets

Skills:	Finger dexterity, creativity
Equipment:	Paper sacks and crayons
Players:	Entire class
Directions:	Each pupil or group of four makes hand puppets out of paper sacks and puts on a brief show.

Magic Music

Skills:	Listening skills, visual scanning
Equipment:	None
Players:	Entire class
Directions:	One player leaves the room while the others hide a small object. The player returns and tries to find the hidden treasure by getting his clue from the singing of the group. As he draws nearer the object, the singing grows louder; it grows softer when he moves away. Piano music may be substituted.
Variations:	The class may say the words "hot," "warm," "cool," and "cold" to indicate "Its" degree of closeness to the hidden object.

What Am I?

Skills:	Reasoning, thinking, recalling
Equipment:	Any picture from a magazine and one straight pin for each player
Players:	Entire class
Directions:	Pin a picture onto the back of each pupil. Each player mingles with the others, trying to find out what the picture is that he is wearing. He may only ask questions calling for a "no" or "yes" answer. When he discovers what he represents, he reports to the leader who pins the picture on his lapel. Pictures of animals, cars, famous people, flowers, and so forth may be used.

I Saw

Skills:	Imitation
Equipment:	None
Players:	Two groups
Formation:	Circles
Directions:	An "It" stands in each circle and says "On my way to school today I saw—" and imitates what he saw. The others guess what he saw. The one guessing correctly becomes "It." If no one guesses, "It" tells what he was imitating and chooses a new "It."

Alphabetical Geography

Skills:	Social studies concepts, memory
Equipment:	None
Players:	Entire class
Directions:	One pupil calls out the name of a state or city. The next player must call out the name of a state or city that begins with the last letter in the name just called.
Example:	New York, Kansas City, Yucatan, New Hampshire, and so forth.

GAMES FROM OTHER CULTURES

Boys and girls from all over the world enjoy playing games. The following is a compilation of several games from other cultures. They may be effectively integrated with the social studies unit to heighten the children's understanding and appreciation of the activities of children in other lands.

Stone, Paper, Scissors (Japan)

Skills:	Visual memory, fine motor control
Equipment:	None
Players:	Entire class
Directions:	Divide the players into two equal lines. Each player faces his partner with his hands behind him. The leader counts to 3; on 3, each player brings his hands forward in any one of the three possible positions. The stone is represented by clenched fists, the paper by open hands with the palms down, and the scissors by the extension of the first two fingers. Because the stone dulls the scissors it beats them. The scissors beat the paper because it can cut. The paper beats the stone because it wraps the stone. The team scoring the most points wins.
Variations:	(1) All players advance. On the count of 4, one, two, three, or four fingers are held out to represent the stone, scissors, and paper (one finger = stone, two = scissors, three = paper, and four = stone). (2) Man, gun, rabbit, and bear can be substituted for stone, scissors, paper, and stone. (3) Man, gun, and tiger may be substituted for stone, scissors, and paper.

Chicken Market (Italy)

Skills:	Strength, social control
Equipment:	None
Players:	Entire class
Directions:	All players are chickens except the two strongest class members. One becomes the buyer, the other the seller. All other players squat down and clasp their hands around their knees and are told not to smile or laugh. The buyer comes to test each chicken by pinching, chin chucking, or tickling. At last he says "This one is just right." He and the seller take hold of the chicken's arms and swing him, counting to 3. If the chicken laughs while they are swinging him, he is eliminated. If he does not laugh, he is not sold but remains safe.

Hen and Wild Cat (Africa)

Skills:	Running, tagging
Equipment:	None
Players:	Entire class
Directions:	The "hen" leads her flock of other players around a chosen "cat." She warns them of danger, and the "cat" tries to catch any foolish chickens who come too near.

The Tied Monkey (Africa)

Skills:	Eye-hand coordination
Equipment:	A handkerchief with one end tied into a knot for each player
Players:	Entire class
Directions:	One boy is chosen to be the "monkey." He sits in a chair. The others try to hit him with their handkerchiefs while he tries to catch them. If he is successful, he changes places.

Calabash (Africa)

Skills: Strength, quickness
Equipment: None
Players: Three in each group
Directions: Two players lock arms to pen in a third one, who stands between them. The middle player is locked in. He tries to wiggle out while his jailers move their locked arms up and down to keep him in.

Sandbag Ball (Alaska)

Skills: Visual-motor coordination, cooperation
Equipment: One playground volleyball or balloon per group
Players: Ten per group
Formation: Circles
Directions: Players kneel in a circle. The ball is batted into the air, and the players try to keep it aloft by striking it with one hand. A player is out if he uses both hands or if he tries to strike the ball and misses. The winner is the last remaining player.

Guessing Game (Alaska)

Skills: Visual recall
Equipment: 20 or more sticks
Players: Entire class
Directions: "It" arranges the sticks in small bundles while others cover their eyes. Each player guesses quickly how many sticks are in each bunch. The new "It" is the first to call out the correct number.

Frog Dance (Burma)

Skills: Coordination, endurance
Equipment: None
Players: Entire class
Formation: Circle
Directions: Pupils squat in a circle. They hop forward around the ring by throwing out one foot and then the other. As each hops, he claps his hands first in front of his knees and then in back of them and tries to make the others fall over. A player who falls is out. The winner is the one who frog dances longest without falling.

Call the Chickens Home (China)

Skills: Running, dodging, tagging
Equipment: A blindfold
Players: Entire class
Directions: A blindfolded player stands apart from the "chickens" who run by and touch him after he says "Tsoo, Tsoo, come and find your mother." Any chicken caught exchanges places with the blind man.

Catching Fishes in the Dark (China)

Skills:	Chasing, fleeing
Equipment:	A blindfold
Players:	Entire class
Directions:	A blindfolded player tries to catch the "fish" who run past. If one is caught, the blind man tries to guess what kind of a fish the player has chosen to be. If he succeeds, the fish and he exchange places; otherwise, one fish has won freedom.

Catching the Fish's Tail (China)

Skills:	Agility, dodging
Equipment:	None
Players:	Ten in each group
Formation:	Line
Directions:	Each player wraps his arms around the waist of the person ahead of him so that the line becomes compact. The first player is the "head," and the last is the "tail." The head tries to catch hold of the tail. Any player who breaks his hold on the person in front of him is eliminated.

Skin the Snake (China)

Skills:	Cooperation, concentration
Equipment:	None
Players:	Ten in each group
Formation:	Line
Directions:	Players stand in a single line, each putting his right hand between his legs and holding the left hand of the person behind him. All walk backward. The last one lies down. The others pass over him and also lie down. The last one gets up first and walks forward outside the line and helps pull the next player up until all are standing again. All players must keep holding hands.

Menagerie (England)

Skills:	Imitation, creativity
Equipment:	Chalk, blackboard
Players:	Entire class
Directions:	Each chooses an animal sound he wishes to imitate. The leader writes down all names given on the blackboard and tells a story weaving in each animal. When a pupil hears the name of his animal, he imitates the sound. When the leader calls out "Menagerie" all give their sounds at once.

Pebble Game (Greece)

Skills:	Fine eye-hand coordination
Equipment:	Ten or more pebbles or jacks for each player
Players:	Entire class
Directions:	Place the pebbles on the back of your hand. When a signal is given, turn your hand over and try to catch as many pebbles as possible with the same hand.

Phugadi (India)

Skills:	Cooperation, balance
Equipment:	None
Players:	Couples
Directions:	Two players stand facing each other with toes touching. They grasp each other by the waist, lean back as far as possible, and turn together.

Painting Colored Sand Pictures (Italy)

Skills:	Creativity
Equipment:	Bags of colored sand for each group and white notebook paper
Players:	Groups of four
Directions:	Give each group bags of yellow, red, black, blue, and white sand. The white sand is scattered over the paper to form a frame. Next, the outline of a bird, person, animal, or object is formed by letting the black sand slowly ooze between the fingers. The remaining colors are used to complete the design. Groups can compete to "paint" the most attractive picture.

Satsuma Ken (Japan)

Skills:	Guessing
Equipment:	A blindfold
Players:	Entire class
Directions:	The pupils stretch out the fingers of one or both hands simultaneously. "It," who is blindfolded, tries to guess the total number of extended fingers of all players.

Bead Guessing (American Indian)

Skills:	Guessing
Equipment:	A bead
Players:	Entire class
Directions:	One player holds a bead in one hand behind him. He stops before one player, who tries to guess in which hand the bead is held. On each guess the one holding the bead must bring his hands forward and open them. If the guesser guesses correctly three times, the one holding the bead runs to his seat. If the "guesser" catches him, he is permitted to hold the bead. Each player may guess three times, but unless he guesses correctly all three times the one holding the bead moves on.

Chinese Hold Up (China)

Skills:	Body awareness, quickness
Equipment:	None
Players:	Entire class
Directions:	Seat players in a circle. One starts the game by holding his hands to both ears. Immediately, the players to the right and left of him must hold their ears. The last one to do so is out and starts the game again by pointing to any player. This player grasps his own ears and players on his right and left grasp theirs. The eliminated player starts the game again. The game continues until only two are left.

Yemari (Japan)

Skills:	Striking, eye-hand coordination
Equipment:	One tennis or rubber ball for each group
Players:	Six in each group
Formation:	Circles
Directions:	Players stand in a circle. One bounces the ball up and catches it with his open hand. He continues as long as the ball is in reach, but he may not move from the circle. When the ball moves near another player, that person keeps it bouncing. The game continues until someone fails to hit the ball and is eliminated. The last remaining player wins.

SUGGESTED READINGS

AAHPER: *How We Do It Game Book*. Washington, D.C., 1964.

Boy Scouts of America: *Scout Field Book*. New York, 1971.

Culin, S.: *Games of the Orient (Korea, China, Japan)*. Rutland, Vermont, Charles E. Tuttle Company, Inc., 1960.

Doray, M.: *See What I Can Do!* Englewood Cliffs, New Jersey, Prentice-Hall, Inc., 1973.

Fandek, R.: *Classroom Capers*. Bellington, Washington, Department of Physical Education, WWSC, 1969.

Harbin, E. O.: *Games of Many Nations*. Nashville, Tennessee, Abingdon Press, 1964.

Macfarlan, A.: *Book of American Indian Games*. New York, Association Press, 1958.

Macfarlan, A., and Macfarlan, P.: *Fun with Brand-New Games*. New York, Association Press, 1961.

Ripley, G. S.: *The Book of Games*. New York, Association Press, 1960.

Roberts, N., and Wieser, J.: *A Children's Book of Games and Rhymes*. New York, Greenwich Book Publishers, 1960.

Vannier, M.: *Recreation Leadership*. 3rd ed. Philadelphia, Lea & Febiger, 1977.

CHAPTER EIGHTEEN

ACTIVE RELAYS

Play is the process through which the child is educated. From the standpoint of total adjustment, and of optimum health and character, play must be classified as one of the most basic needs of childhood.

Jay B. Nash

Active relays can be a useful teaching aid to the teacher who has large classes. Relays permit a large number to participate with a minimum of organization, but the end results are manifold. Most children enjoy relays while developing a variety of fundamental movement and sport-related skills. Relay-type activities promote group identity, team cooperation, and sportsmanship. They also contribute to the child's level of physical fitness and sense of well-being. Relays can be used as an effective organizational and teaching tool. They should not, however, be overused or serve as a primary focus of the physical education program.

ORGANIZATION

Relay activities are best suited to the developmental levels of children in grades 3 through 6. They may, however, be adapted from time to time to be of use with primary-grade children. The following is a list of several suggestions for the successful organization and inclusion of relays into the physical education program:

1. Permanent teams in which there is an equality of skill and size are organizational time-savers.
2. Change team captains at regular intervals.
3. Train and assign student officials.
4. Divide your class by counting off "One, two, one, two" and so forth, all the ones being in one line and all the twos in another line. It is unwise to let the children choose their team members too often, for one child always tends to be the last one chosen.
5. Keep teams small, placing no more than eight students on a team. It is better to have more groups with fewer numbers in each group in order to maximize participation and interest.
6. Be sure that all teams have an equal number of children. The first person in line in those that have a smaller number should be assigned to run twice.
7. Be sure that teams having a smaller number of participants assign a different person to run twice each time in order to promote additional participation by others than the most skilled.
8. Explain and demonstrate the rules carefully and enforce them. Children need to learn that they will be penalized for breaking the rules.
9. Establish a definite procedure to indicate when each team has finished. Having all sit with arms folded upon finishing is a good procedure to follow.
10. Carefully indicate and mark the boundaries, turning lines, and other limits to be abided by.
11. Show your enthusiasm and interest by encouraging children to do their best within the rules of the activity. Do not overemphasize winning.

12. Utilize student leaders or nonparticipants to aid in seeing that the rules of the relay are abided by.
13. Choose teams carefully and do not hesitate to rearrange teams from time to time. Each team needs an even chance at winning.
14. Do not permit bickering, quarreling, or name calling among teams or between groups.
15. Place poorly skilled participants in the middle of the team in order that their lack of skill not be as obviously exhibited as it would be if they were performing in first or last position.
16. Do not over use relays as a teaching approach. Interest and enthusiasm for them will soon wane if they are over-used.
17. Make relays a fun and enjoyable experience for all children and be sure that each serves a specific purpose.

RELAY FORMATIONS

Relays may be conducted utilizing a variety of formations. The most popular formations include the following:

Shuttle Formations

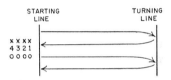

The players are divided into teams of 8 to 16 members. No. 1 runs to the opposite line, touches off No. 2, and goes to the foot of the line. No. 2 runs in the same manner, then No. 3, and so forth. All runners end up on opposite sides.

Single File or Double Line Formations

The players are divided into teams of four to eight. No. 1 runs, turns, runs back, touches off No. 2, and goes to the foot of the line. No. 2 then runs, as do the other team members in turn.

Circle Formations

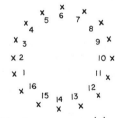

The players are divided into teams of four to eight members. No. 1 runs around the circle clockwise or counterclockwise and returns to his place. Nos. 2, 3, and so forth, run the circle until all have run.

TYPES OF ACTIVE RELAYS

Modified relays can be used with primary-grade children, since the details of the true relay may seem too complicated. Modified relays are run in heats, and each child who comes in first in his heat wins a point for his team. The team scoring the most

FIGURE 18–1.   Can you do the crab walk? (Courtesy of Northlake Elementary School, Dallas, Texas.)

points wins. The directions for the true relays found on the following pages should serve as an adequate guide for selecting and organizing relays.

Most of the relays contained in the following pages use a parallel line or file formation. Distance indicates the number of feet from the starting line to the goal or turning line. The types of relays described include the following:

1. Stunt-type relays
2. Relays without equipment
3. Relays requiring equipment
4. Sport-skill relays
5. Obstacle relays
6. Novelty relays

STUNT-TYPE RELAYS

Stunt-type relays may be utilized in either modified or their true form, but they are especially enjoyed by primary-grade children. They should be performed for a distance of 15 to 20 feet. The children race using the prescribed stunt from the starting line to the turning point and back. Some stunts that may be used are listed here. These and other stunts are described fully in the chapter on stunts and tumbling.

Bear Walk
Crab Walk
Duck Walk
Frog Jump
Kangaroo Hop
Lame Puppy Walk
Monkey Run
Rabbit Hop
Log Roll
Double Line Formation
Wheelbarrow Relay
Forward Roll Relay

RELAYS WITHOUT EQUIPMENT

A wide variety of fundamental locomotor-skill relays may be incorporated into the program as either modified or true relays. They may be performed at a distance of 20 to 40 feet depending on the age and ability level of the children involved. They include (1) point-to-point relays, (2) line relays, and (3) rescue relays.

Point-To-Point Relay

Skills: Starting, pivoting, turning, various locomotor skills
Directions: On the command "On your mark, get set, go!" the first players on each team run to the turning line and return. They touch the hand or shoulder of the next teammate. Players in the first and second grades use a standing start. Those in the third through sixth grades use a crouch start.

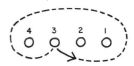

Line Relays

Skills: Agility, various locomotor skills
Directions: The teams number off consecutively from front to back. The teacher or leader calls a number. The child with this number in each team steps out of the line to his right and runs counterclockwise around his team, returning to his original place in line. The winner scores a point. The team with the highest score wins.

GOAL LINE

Rescue Relays

Skills: Running and other locomotor movements, cooperation
Directions: A leader stands behind a goal line facing his team, which is lined up behind the starting line. On a signal, the leader runs to the first player of his team, grasps him by the wrist, and runs back to the goal line. The rescued player then runs back and gets another player, and the game continues in this way until all have been rescued. The relay may be altered to incorporate jumping, skipping, and other locomotor movements.

RELAYS REQUIRING EQUIPMENT

There are many popular relays that may be used with a minimum of equipment. Several of these relays may be adapted for use with young children. The movement skills stressed, along with the equipment needed and the procedures to follow, are described for several relays requiring equipment. Each relay may be performed at a distance ranging from 20 to 40 feet depending on the participants.

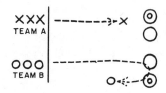

All Up Relay

Skills: Running, agility, coordination
Equipment: One to three Indian clubs or milk cartons for each team
Directions: Chalk two circles the desired number of feet from the starting line. Place one, two, or three Indian clubs in one circle. The first player in line runs and takes the club out of one circle, places it in the second circle, runs back, and touches the second player, who returns the club to circle No. 1. If a club falls over, the player must return and stand it upright.

Balance Relay

Skills: Dynamic balance, posture
Equipment: Beanbags, erasers, or books
Directions: Walk erectly, arms at side, balancing one of the listed objects on top of the head. If the object falls off, the player must stop in his tracks, replace it, and then continue.

PIN REPLACER

Bowling Relay

Skills: Rolling, running
Equipment: Six Indian clubs and one baseball for each team
Directions: Assign one child on each team to replace pins and call out score. Place pins 6 inches apart in a triangle. Roll the baseball, and knock over as many pins as possible. A player gets one point for each club knocked over. Each bowler retrieves the ball and rolls it to the next in line.

Cap Transfer

Skills: Running, manipulation, coordination
Equipment: Three sticks and one cap for each team
Directions: The first three children on a team are given sticks. No. 1 is stationed at the turning point. No. 2 places a cap on the end of his stick, runs to No. 1, transfers the cap to his stick. No. 1 returns to the starting line, transfers the cap to No. 3, gives his stick to No. 4, and goes to the foot of the line. The game continues in this manner until all have run. The team regaining its original position first wins. If a cap falls off, it must be picked up with the stick without the aid of hands.

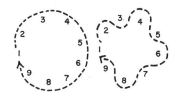

Circle Relay

Skills:	Running, agility, speed
Equipment:	Handkerchief or beanbag for each team
Directions:	Give starting player a handkerchief. On signal, the player runs around the circle and passes the handkerchief to person in front of him. First team to finish wins.
Variation:	Zigzag in and out between members of the team.

Driving the Pig to Market

Skills:	Coordination
Equipment:	Wand or paddle ball for each team, and a chair or stool
Directions:	Ball must be rolled up to and around stool. Ball is controlled by sliding wand or paddle back and forth along its surface.

Fetch and Carry

Skills:	Running, agility, coordination
Equipment:	Three beanbags
Directions:	Draw a 15-inch circle about 5 feet ahead of each team's starting line. Twenty to 30 feet from the starting line draw three crosses about two feet apart. No. 1 picks up beanbags one at a time, making three trips to place them on the crosses, and runs back and touches off No. 2 who returns the beanbags to the circle in three trips. No. 3 does as 1, and 4 as 2, and so forth.

Goat Butting

Skills:	Coordination, body awareness
Equipment:	Any large ball, such as a basketball
Directions:	Start in crouch position with ball on starting line, butt ball to turning line and back over starting line.

Hoop Rolling Relay

Skills:	Manipulation, coordination
Equipment:	Hoop and flat board for each team
Directions:	Roll the hoop to the turning line, pick it up, and roll it back.

Merry-go-round or Dizzy-Izzy

Skills: Balance
Equipment: Baseball bat for each team
Directions: First player stands the bat up straight, places his palms down on the top and his head on the back of his hands. He walks around the bat eight times, drops it, and runs to the turning line and back to the foot of the line. No. 2 picks up the bat as soon as it is dropped and repeats the action of No. 1.

Over and Under

Skills: Ball handling, teamwork
Equipment: Volleyball, soccerball, or basketball
Directions: Stand in stride position, about 14 inches apart. No. 1 passes ball overhead to No. 2, who passes it through his legs to No. 3, and so forth. No. 4 runs to head of line and starts ball overhead to No. 1. When No. 1 returns to head of line, relay is finished.

UNDER   OVER

Push Ball

Skills: Coordination, teamwork
Equipment: Any large or heavy ball, such as a medicine ball
Directions: All team members push the ball with sticks over the goal line. One picks it up and carries it back to the finishing line.

Skip Rope Relay

Skills: Rope skipping
Equipment: Short rope
Directions: Skip to turning line and back. Children learning to jump a short rope find it much easier to run than to stand still.

Stride Ball

Skills: Rolling, passing, teamwork
Equipment: Volleyball or soccerball for each team
Directions: Teams stand in deep-stride position and pass or roll the ball between their legs to the back of the line. Last player in line carries the ball to the head of the line, passing the team to the left. He then starts the ball again through their legs.

SPORT-SKILL RELAYS

Relays may be used to develop and reinforce specific sport skills. Practice of these skills in a relay-type activity adds a new dimension of fun and competition to the program. The following pages contain samples of sport-related relays for developing soccer, football, volleyball, basketball, and softball skills. They may be modified and performed in a variety of ways and are geared for boys and girls in grades 3 to 6.

Soccer-skill Relays

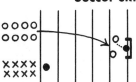

Soccer Pass Relay

Skills:	Dribbling, passing, kicking, cooperation
Equipment:	Soccerballs
Directions:	On signal, couples in a double line formation pass the ball back and forth to each other down the field, make a goal, and pass the ball back to the starting line. Only the feet may be used, and neither player shall play the ball twice consecutively.

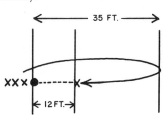

Run and Kick Relay

Skills:	Kicking, trapping
Equipment:	A soccerball for each team
Directions:	The first player runs to and across the turning line, returns to the 12-foot line, and kicks the ball to No. 2. If the waiting player cannot reach the ball, No. 1 must retrieve the ball, return to the 12-foot line, and kick again.

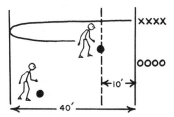

Soccer Relay Variations

Skills:	Kicking, passing, trapping
Equipment:	Soccerballs
Directions:	Dribble to the turning line and back to within 10 to 12 feet of the line and pass with the inside of the foot. In the fourth grade the waiting player may be allowed to stop the ball with his hands. In the fifth and sixth grades the waiting player traps the ball.

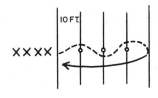

Zigzag Relay

Skills:	Dribbling, ball control, running
Equipment:	Soccerball for each team, three Indian clubs or milk cartons
Directions:	Space Indian clubs 10 feet apart between the starting and turning lines. Dribble in and out between the clubs to the turning line, pick up the ball, and run straight back to the team.

Football-skill Relays

Refer also to Cross Over Relay and Baseball Relay in softball section of relays and to Circle Volley and Zigzag Volley in volleyball section of relays.

Run and Punt Relay

Skills: Punting, running
Equipment: Football for each player
Directions: First player is given a ball. On signal, he runs to turning line and punts to the waiting player and moves back to make room for him. The team that gets all team members to the opposite side first wins.

Center Pass Relay

Skills: Centering
Equipment: Football for each team
Directions: Teams line up on parallel lines spaced about 8 to 10 feet apart. The first player places the ball on the ground and on signal passes the ball between his legs to the player behind him. No. 2 places the ball on the ground and repeats the action. The last player to receive the ball runs to the front of the line and sits. The line that finishes first wins.

Volleyball-skill Relays

Throw and Catch

Skills: Tossing, catching
Equipment: Volleyball for each team, long rope, and jump standards
Directions: In front of the teams, stretch a rope across the standards at a height of 6 to 8 feet. On signal, the first player runs forward, tosses the ball over the rope, catches it on the other side, returns to his team, hands the ball to player No. 2, and passing to the right, goes to the foot of the line. *Fouls:* Failure to throw the ball over the rope; failure to catch the ball after it has cleared the rope.

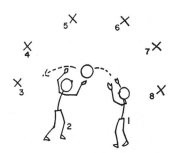

Circle Volley Relay

Skills: Volleying, passing
Equipment: One volleyball for each team
Directions: Divide the group into teams of eight; each team forms a circle with a 7- to 9-foot space between players. No. 1 starts the ball by throwing it in a high arch, slightly above the head of No. 2, who receives the ball and hits it to No. 3. Each player may play the ball as many times as is necessary to get it into a favorable position for passing. If a player drops the ball, he retrieves it, takes his position, and throws it to the next player. Groups that are more advanced in skills may put the ball in play by hitting the ball up in the air, then hitting it to the next player. The team that gets the ball back to No. 1 first wins. *Fouls:* Holding and throwing except in cases mentioned.

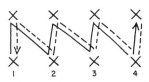

Zigzag Volley

Skills: Volleying, passing
Equipment: One volleyball or balloon for each team
Directions: Team is divided equally into parallel lines facing each other. The ball is volleyed back and forth down the line and back. The team that gets the ball back to the starter first wins.

Basketball-skill Relays

Basket Shooting Relay

Skills: Shooting, dribbling
Equipment: Basketball for each team
Directions: On signal, the first player runs to shooting position and tries to make a basket. He shoots until a basket is made and runs back to the line and gives the next player the ball. The team finishing first wins.
Variation: Dribble the ball into position, try for a basket, and pass the ball back to next in line. Run to the foot of line. Determine the pass to be used before the relay starts. It may be overhead, side, two arm, shoulders, or another. See Basketball Skills.

FIGURE 18–2. Basketball dribbling relays can add spice to the program. (Courtesy of Refugio Public Schools, Refugio, Texas.)

Post Ball

Skills:	Passing
Equipment:	Two basketballs, one post or base
Directions:	Only two teams should use one post. On signal the first player runs around the post to the foot of the opposing team's line and throws the ball to No. 2 on his team, who repeats the action of No. 1 and throws the ball to No. 3. The last player who reaches the end of the opposing line raises the ball high above his head to indicate that his team has finished.

Basketball Pass Relay

Skills:	Passing
Equipment:	Basketball for each team
Directions:	Player may take one step before passing; he then runs to the end of the opposite line, moving to the right. Stipulate the type of pass (chest pass, bounce pass).

Arch Goal Ball Relay

Skills:	Passing, shooting
Equipment:	One basketball for each team
Directions:	On signal, the first player passes the ball over his head to the player behind him; this action is repeated by all down the line. When the last player receives the ball, he runs forward past the line and attempts to shoot for a goal. He is allowed three tries. Whether he is successful or not, he takes his position at the head of the line and passes the ball overhead. To determine the winning team, score one point for finishing first and two points for each goal. Deduct one point for each foul.

Softball Relays

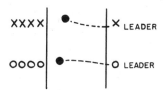

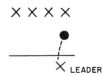

Post or Baseball Relay

Skills: Throwing, catching

Equipment: Softball or beanbag

Directions: Choose a leader for each team. Leaders stand about 10 to 12 feet in front of teams in parallel lines. On signal, the leader throws the ball to the first player using the underhand throw. The first player catches the ball, throws it back to the leader, and immediately squats in line. The leader throws to the second in line, and so forth. Game continues until all players are squatting. The winning team finishes first with the fewest errors. *Errors:* Failure to catch the ball or dropping the ball.

Variation: *Pass and Squat* (Grades 4 to 6). This relay is played in the same manner except for the formation. Players line up side by side.

Cross Over Relay

Skills: Running, throwing, catching

Equipment: Softball for each team

Directions: Give a ball to the first player on each team. On signal, No. 1 runs to the goal line, turns, throws the ball to next player in line, and steps back. No. 2 catches the ball, repeats the action of No. 1, and steps in front of No. 1. The team that finishes first with the fewest fouls wins.

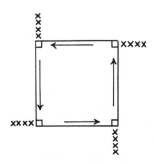

Round the Bases

Skills: Base running

Equipment: Bases

Directions: One team lines up at second base, and the other team lines up at home plate. If there are enough teams, then line up behind all bases. On signal, No. 1 starts around the four bases, touching off No. 2 at the base he started from. The team finishing first wins. *Fouls:* Running over 3 feet outside base line; failure to touch each base.

OBSTACLE RELAYS

Obstacle relays add a dimension of challenge and excitement to the program. They are fun and can be used to develop and reinforce a variety of movement skills. The following is a sampling of obstacle relays.

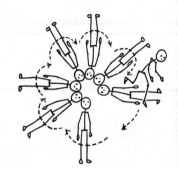

Human Hurdle or Spoke Relay

Skills: Leaping
Equipment: None
Directions: Each team forms a circle, and all lie on the floor with heads touching in the center. One player is designated as the starter. On signal, he jumps up and leaps over each player (clockwise), and when he returns to his place, he touches off the next player and takes his original place on the floor.

Human Obstacle

Skills: Running, crawling, leaping
Equipment: None
Directions: Place four children between the starting and turning lines, spaced several feet apart. No. 1 stands upright, No. 2 stands in stride position, No. 3 stoops in leapfrog position, and No. 4 stands upright. The first player runs around No. 1, crawls through the legs of No. 2, leaps over No. 3, runs around No. 4 and returns in a straight line to his team. The game continues in this way until all players on a team run the obstacle course.

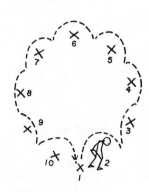

Leapfrog Relay

Skills: Leaping
Equipment: None
Directions: Each team forms a circle and bends over in leapfrog position, facing the same direction. The player designated as the starter leaps over each player, returns to original position, and touches off the player in front of him.

Serpentine

Skills: Running, agility

Equipment: Indian clubs for each team

Directions: Place the clubs about 2 feet apart, starting 2 feet from the turning line. Players zigzag between the clubs and run straight back to the line.

Stool Hurdle

Skills: Hopping, jumping, leaping, running

Equipment: Stools or cones

Directions: Place the stools 5 feet apart. Each player straddle-hops the first, does a flat-footed jump over the second, leaps over the third, runs to the turning line, and returns in a straight line to his team.

NOVELTY RELAYS

Novelty relays are typically reserved for special days and parties. They are great fun and often involve silly activities. Some of the popular novelty relays are listed below.

Balloon or Feather Relay

Skills: Cooperation, control

Equipment: A balloon or feather for each team

Directions: Each player blows a balloon or feather to the turning line and back. If it falls to the floor, it must be picked up at that point and put in the air again before proceeding.

Box Relay

Skills: Coordination

Equipment: Two shoe boxes for each team

Directions: The players are divided into two teams. Each leader runs to the turning line and back wearing two shoe boxes. If any player steps out of a box, he must begin again from the starting line.

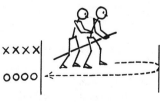

Bronco Relay

Skills: Running, galloping

Equipment: A broom for each team

Directions: Lines number off by 2s to form couples. The first couple in each line straddles a broomstick and races to the turning line and back. The second couple takes the stick and repeats the actions of No. 1, and so forth.

Paper Bag Relay

Skills: Running
Equipment: Paper bags for all participants
Directions: Blow up the bag at starting line, run across turning line, pop the bag and return.

Pilot Relay

Skills: Running in different directions
Directions: No. 1 faces turning line and grasps hands of 2 and 3 who face in opposite direction. No. 1 runs forward to turning line and 2 and 3 run backwards. On the return, No. 1 runs backwards and 2 and 3 run forward.

Sack Relay

Skills: Jumping
Equipment: Sack of burlap or duck
Directions: Players jump with the sack pulled up well above the hips.

Spoon and Ping-pong Ball Relay

Skills: Eye-hand coordination
Equipment: Tablespoon and ping-pong ball for each team
Directions: Balance the ball in the spoon and walk rapidly to the turning line and back. If the ball rolls off, it may be replaced with the free hand of the player; the player then returns to the place where it rolled off. The relay is more interesting and difficult if the ball is picked up without aid from the free hand.

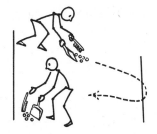

Sweep Up Relay

Skills: Eye-hand coordination, running
Equipment: Five ping-pong balls, broom, and dust pan for each team
Directions: Five ping-pong balls are placed directly in front of the starting line. On signal, the first player sweeps the balls into the dust pan with a whisk broom and races to the turning point and back, dumping the balls gently to the floor so they will not scatter. The second player repeats the action of the first, and the game continues in the preceding manner until all players have raced.

Three-legged Relay

Skills: Hopping, cooperation
Equipment: Short lengths of rope
Directions: Each team forms a double line. With their inside legs tied together, the first couple run to the turning line and back; then the second couple do the same, then the third, and so forth.

Toothpick and Ring Relay

Skills: Coordination, cooperation
Equipment: Toothpick for each team member and a ring for each team (small celluloid curtain ring is light and suitable)
Directions: The first player puts a toothpick in his mouth and places a ring on it, walks to the turning line and back, and transfers ring to toothpick in mouth of player No. 2.

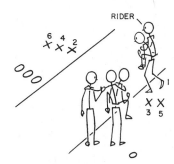

Paul Revere Relay

Skills: Carrying, strength, endurance
Equipment: None
Directions: This is a shuttle relay. After each team selects a rider the players number off, the even numbers standing on one side and the odd numbers on the opposite side. On signal the rider mounts the back of No. 1, who carries him to No. 2; the rider, without touching the ground, exchanges mounts and No. 2 carries him to No. 3. This action continues until the last man carries the rider across the finish line. If a rider falls off he must mount again at the point of the fall. If he falls off in changing mounts, he must get on his original mount again before making the change.

SUGGESTED READINGS

Arnold, A.: *The World Book of Children's Games.* New York, World Publishing Company, 1972.

Latchaw, M.: *A Pocket Guide of Movement Activities for the Elementary School.* Englewood Cliffs, New Jersey, Prentice-Hall, Inc., 1970.

Lincoln, E.: *Backyard Games.* New York, Stadia Sports Publishing, 1973.

Parker, A. W. H.: *Find Your Own Summer Thing; Getting it Together Is the Thing; Kool Summer Fun* (Three card files of over 200 activities each). National Recreation and Park Association, 1700 Pennsylvania Avenue, N.W., Washington, D.C., 1972.

Sullivan, G.: *Sports for Your Child.* New York, Winchester Press, 1973.

CHAPTER NINETEEN

RHYTHMS AND DANCE

Physical education is primarily concerned with the physical manipulation of the most perfectly developed, complex, and interesting of known organisms—the human body.

Paul Smith

A child's body is a thing of wonder! It is his own unique "native instrument" through which he expresses himself. Children intuitively feel rhythm and spontaneously respond to it with their bodies. They have a natural love for running, jumping, skipping, for they are most joyfully in love with life. A child moves to rhythm because of happiness but does so mainly *because it is fun!* Watch a child fill a bucket of sand or run while holding on to a string attached to a kite that he is trying to fly. See how rhythmically he moves!

It is easy to teach rhythms to children, but it can be difficult for them to learn how to gain body control, to change directions gracefully, or to suddenly stop when moving rapidly through space. Thus, one begins from the known (rhythm) to the unknown (dance activities) when teaching rhythms and dance to children.

RHYTHMS
How to Introduce Rhythms

TIME

Have children recite and clap in rhythm familiar nursery rhymes such as Pat-a-cake and Little Bo Peep (Nursery Rhymes—Frank Luther, Decca Records, CU 100, CU 101, and 75522–3). Clap to known songs such as Yankee Doodle. From the third grade on, the rhythm pattern and underlying beat can be explained; the groups can clap the two parts and then do it in rounds. Most children above the first grade know a number of radio commercials and enjoy clapping out the rhythm.

Example 1.

Row, row, / row your / boat

Gently / down the / stream

Mer ri ly, / mer ri ly, / mer ri ly, / mer ri ly /

Life is / but a / dream.

Rhythm pattern $\frac{3}{4}$

Underlying beat $\frac{3}{4}$

FIGURE 19–1. Rhythm is a vital part of all life. (Courtesy of Barbara Mettler, Tucson Creative Dance Center, Tucson, Arizona.)

Also use the wonderful record "The Beat Goes On" as well as "And The Beatles Go On And On For Physical Education" by Ambrose Brazelton[1] to teach simple activities to do while the child is learning to snap his fingers, stamp his feet, bend and twist, and so forth to various rhythmic beats and changing tempos. "Movement Fun," a record by Paul Smith available from the same company, is also highly recommended to use when introducing rhythms. Children will greatly enjoy mimicking to lively music the movements of circus animals and a Jack-in-the-box and doing simple ball activities and swimming movements. All activities can be used in poorly equipped self-contained classrooms as well as in large areas.

BOUNCING BALLS

1. Bounce balls to music.
2. Bounce balls to each other in couple or circle formation.
3. Children act as balls and bounce around the floor as the music indicates.
4. Form couples: one child is the ball; the other the bouncer. Bounce to music, alternating as ball and bouncer.
5. Perform combinations of bounces to music.
6. Do the rhythm combinations by Ruth Evans—Record 203–204.

---

[1] Available from Educational Activities, Inc., Box 392, Freeport, New York 11520.

ROPE JUMPING

This may be introduced as a self-testing activity or offered along with rhythms because it requires skill and timing. In any case it is a must in any elementary program. Long ropes of 12 to 16 feet are more practical, but additional individual ropes can be used to good advantage.[3]

GAMES

Rhythmic Limbo (Caribbean)

Record:	Hoctor Dance Records, Inc.—1608B
Formation:	Double line
Directions:	Two students may walk under the pole at the same time. Each time the entire group has gone under, the pole is lowered 2 inches.
Position:	Keep knees flexed, pelvic girdle tilted back, hips and shoulders dropped, and head back. Knees turn out and ankles roll in as knees come closer to the floor. Go forward with rhyme, with the bar set at shoulder height of the smallest in the class.

Wiggle the ankle,
Wiggle the knee
Under the bar
Like a willow tree.

Lemme or Lummi Sticks (Indian Game)

Equipment:	One set of sticks for each player. These are made of ¾-inch dowel rods cut 18 inches long. Paint half of the sticks one color and half another. Educational Activities, Inc., sells a kit with 24 sticks, instructional record, and illustrated instruction sheets.
Rhythm:	1 – 2 – 3 – 4. Rhythm background may be played by a drum.
Position:	Players sit in cross-legged position on the floor, facing each other. Sticks are held in the center, with the thumb next to the body, four fingers on the opposite side, and fingers spread slightly. To match sticks simply strike together. In throwing the sticks, hold them perpendicular and throw them straight across and catch them on the diagonal.
Position 1:	Heads of sticks rest on floor.
1 – 2 – 3	Strike heads of sticks on floor in rhythm.
– 4	Match sticks with partner. (Repeat four meas.)
Position 2:	Stand sticks upright.
1 – 2 – 3	Strike sticks on floor in rhythm.
– 4	Match sticks with partner. (Repeat four meas.)
Position 3:	Put sticks in position 1.
1 – 2	Strike sticks on floor.
– 3	Hold sticks off floor and cross the right over the left.
– 4	Match sticks with partner. (Repeat four meas.)
Position 4:	Return sticks to position 2.
1 – 2	Strike sticks on floor.
– 3	Partners exchange right sticks by throwing to each other.
– 4	Strike floor with sticks.
1 – 2	Strike sticks on floor.
– 3	Partners exchange left sticks by throwing them to each other.
– 4	Strike floor with sticks. (Repeat eight meas.)

[3]See Chapter 26 for specific directions on teaching this activity and for jump-rope ditties.

Position 5:

1 – 2   Strike sticks on floor.
 – 3   Partners exchange *both* sticks by throwing.
 – 4   Strike sticks on floor. (Repeat eight meas.)
        Note: One partner throws both sticks to the inside and the other
              throws toward the outside.
        Repeat movements 3, 2, and 1; as a finale, cross the sticks. For the
        primary grades it would be wise to use only positions 1, 2, and 3.

Tinikling or Bamboo Hop

Area: Gymnasium, playroom, playground
Equipment: Educational Activities, Inc., sells a kit that includes the record, 12
              instruction sheets, music, and six 5-foot bamboo poles.

MARCHING

This is an excellent way to introduce and review time and floor spacing without the self-consciousness that often exists among children. First and second graders like to march but are indifferent to left and right feet and complicated directions, so this phase of rhythms should be confined to the upper elementary grades, if any measure of excellence in performance is expected. There is no need to motivate this activity because older brothers and sisters in bands and drill teams have already created an enthusiastic acceptance.

Previous training in the fundamental locomotor movements, that is, walking in rhythm to cadence, should make the following easy:

Marching to Music

Any good march with a sound beat is suitable. Record BOL 54, available from Record Center, 2581 Piedmont Road N.E., Atlanta, Georgia 30324, contains five marches and 15 theme charts, giving a wide range of feeling and themes.

Fundamentals in Marching

1. Clap hands to the rhythm of the march music or drum.
2. Take steps in place, stepping first on the left foot, in time to the march music or drumbeat.
3. Maintain good posture: eyes straight ahead and rib cage pulled up.
4. March forward in time to music; let arms swing easily at the sides in opposition to the feet.
5. Try to keep an even spacing in relation to the person in front.
6. Keep in step and learn to do a rapid step-close-step if you get out of step.

Marching Patterns

First and Second Grades

1. In a circle formation march single file, by 2s, and then by 3s.

2. In a square formation march single file, by 2s, and then by 3s. Make square turns at corners in single file, by 2s, and then by 3s; those on the outside pivot around the inside marcher.

Third Grade

1. March up center by 2s, boys going left and girls right.
2. March up center by 2s; all march left in single file.
3. March up center single file and all left by 2s. The boy marks time as the girl marches to his right side. Both turn and march to the corner.

Fourth Grade

1. March up center by 2s; the first couple then marches left and the second couple marches right; the third couple goes left, the fourth couple right.
2. March up center by 4s; form a single file going left and one going right.
3. Cross diagonally. Repeat.
4. March up center by 2s.

Fifth and Sixth Grades: Sequence

1. March up center by 4s; the first four march left, the second march right; the third march left, fourth march right; at the foot march single file.
2. March up center by 8s; march left and right as in Figure 1.
3. March up center by 8s; lines 1 and 3 complete the circle to the left. Lines 2 and 4 complete the circle to the right. Leave enough space between the lines of eight and take small steps on the turn to keep the lines straight.
4. Break into single file formation and spiral inward.
5. The boys wind in and out (serpentine), passing to the left and right of the girls, who remain stationary. As the last boy reaches the last girl all form a circle and march off single file.

In the fifth and sixth grades, according to the proficiency of the group, many figures may be worked out using the diagonal cross by 2s, double circles moving in opposite directions, and a combination of the various figures done in sequence. The figures do not have to be complicated because if the marchers maintain correct time and proper spacing, the movements are effective. This type of controlled rhythm is enjoyable when introduced at intervals with free-flowing movement.

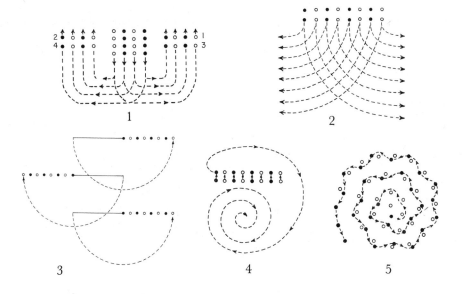

Fundamental Movements

Each fundamental movement should be defined and demonstrated without and with the drumbeat. If the space is large, the whole class may execute the movements in unison. Where the space is limited, such as in a playroom, take the class by couples, lines, or waves. The use of records adds interest. Book sources for all the following dances can be found at the end of this chapter. Record references, listed alphabetically, are also to be found at the end of this chapter.

LOCOMOTOR MOVEMENTS[4]

Even movements are walking, running, jumping, hopping, and leaping. Uneven movements include skipping, sliding, and galloping. Define and demonstrate each of the following:

1. *Walking* to the beat of the drum around the room
   a. Move forward eight counts, then reverse for eight counts.
   b. While walking, bring up knees and slap each knee with hands on each step.
   c. Take four fast steps, then four slow steps.
   d. Introduce waltz step. Clap only on the first beat, then on beats 2 and 3 only while sitting. Then walk accenting the first count: 1,2,3,4, 1,2,3,4.
   e. Walk on tiptoes, then on heels.
   f. Walk with toes turned in, then turned out.
   g. Walk like penguin, then duck.
2. *Running* (to recorded music)
   a. Run and stoop when music stops.
   b. Stop with one foot up when music stops.
   c. Walk during one phrase, then run in another phrase.
   d. Drive car through traffic, stopping at red lights when music stops.
3. *Skipping*
   a. Skip with partner, using inside joined hands for swinging.
   b. Skip in place with high knees.
   c. Skip in circle, around square, around triangle, on diagonal lines.
      (These patterns should be drawn or pointed out on floor for beginners.)
4. *Sliding.*   Have them form four lines at end of gym and have them sit when they get to other end.
   a. Slide sideward with arms at shoulder level.
   b. Slide sideward, four facing one way and four the other.
   c. Slide face to face, then back to back, then alternating front and back.
   d. Slide sideways in a big circle, eight going one way, then eight the other, then four (two, one) going first one way and then the other.
5. *Hopping.*   Formation—in lines going around gymnasium.
   a. Hop in circle, triangle, and square.
   b. Alternate big and little hops.
   c. Hop on one foot five times, then on other, finally decreasing to one. This is done without record.
   d. Act like mechanical toys hopping as you move about.
6. *Jumping*
   a. Land with your feet forward, back, apart, and crossed as you say words in rhythm. Increase tempo gradually, then return to slow pace.
7. *Leaping.*   Formation—four lines at one end of gymnasium, with everyone sitting except those in line performing.

---

[4]Highly recommended records for these basic movement skills are *Movement Fun—Grades 1–6,* Educational Activities, Inc., and *Fitness Fun for Everyone* (grades kindergarten to 3), two long-playing records or cassette tapes with a teaching manual. These are also available from Educational Activities, Inc., Box 392, Freeport, Long Island, New York 11520.

a. Walk, walk, walk, leap to other end of room.
b. Run, run, run, leap to the other side. Use drum for above or have class say words to poem with you. Stress that they must stay with you so everyone will be together.
8. *Galloping*
a. Gallop without changing speed.
b. Change leading foot after series of eight gallops with same foot leading; then work down to two gallops (this will be helpful in learning polka step later).

AXIAL MOVEMENTS

Have the class stand in a big circle with plenty of room between each person. Use two circles if the class is large. One child is in the center performing one of the following movements while all others copy.

1. Bending
2. Turning
3. Twisting
4. Circling
5. Flexion
6. Extension

Formations and floor patterns can be introduced at this time that will lend interest and variety to the simplest locomotor movements. On the primary level, children are inclined to lump themselves into a knot like a bunch of sheep, and it will be necessary at times to chalk formations on the floor such as the following:

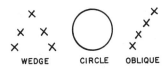

WEDGE   CIRCLE   OBLIQUE

ARC   SQUARE

Accompaniment

1. Hand clapping (refer to section 1 on how to introduce rhythms)
2. Drums
a. Manufactured—A small snare-type drum open on one side and played with a large lamb's-wool hammer is fairly inexpensive and will last a long time if properly cared for. The closed leather drum made in India or China is played with a small, hard hammer. This type of drum requires careful handling and is expensive, but it does have a good, decisive tone.
b. Homemade drums:
(1) American Indian—Buckskin stretched tightly and tacked to a hollowed-out piece of wood such as a tree limb, stump, or mixing bowl.
(2) Cheese box—Remove the lid, and stretch tightly and attach with tacks or staples a piece of unbleached muslin. Wet the muslin and allow it to dry thoroughly. Decorate the box and muslin and apply one or two coats of white shellac.
(3) Oatmeal box or similar round container of paper. A 2-pound coffee can may be used, but the sound is not as pleasing. Cut two circles of leather or an inner tube. With a leather punch place holes 1 inch apart. Lace the top and bottom together with leather or plastic thongs or strips cut from an old inner tube. This type of drum is not durable but is easily made and gives out a resonant tone when played with the hand.

3. Hard sticks or paddles
    a. Round doweling or 1 × 1 sticks, 12 inches long, of hard wood such as maple, oak or teak wood.
    b. Paddles, ½-inch thick, cut out of any wood give a sharp sound.
4. Vocal accompaniment
    a. Half the class recite a poem and the other half follow cadence or suggested thought.
        (1) *Example: With Your Hands*[5]
            With your hands go clap, clap, clap;
            Now with your feet go tap, tap, tap;
            Join your fingers in a ring with me
            And jump in the circle one, two, three.
        (2) *Formation:* Single circle. Children face toward the inside of the circle and execute the action indicated in the song. On the last line all join hands and move clockwise with the movement in the words of the song, which may be a hop, skip, run, gallop, or other movement.

5. Piano
    a. The piano is excellent for accompaniment because the teacher can accent each beat, stop at any time, and take up again at the same place. The use of the piano requires special talent, aside from the ability to play, because instruction and demonstration must be interwoven with the accompaniment, requiring a great deal of change from piano to floor. It is ideal in schools where an accompaniment is available.
6. Record player
    a. The record player has become standard equipment in most schools and the supply of available records is becoming more complete each year. The most satisfactory machine has a speed regulator and will play 33, 45, and 78 r.p.m. records.
    b. Best use of records
        (1) Buy records that carry six to eight rhymes, singing games, or dances. Albums seem expensive but are actually economical because of the number of recordings on each record. The playing time on a standard 78 record is too long for elementary-grade children.
        (2) Play the record and clap the rhythms lightly, accenting change of phrasing with a heavy clap.
        (3) Dance with prescribed steps. Listen to the music. Do the first step without music, then with music. Master and proceed to the second step. Do the first and second, and so forth.
7. Tape recorder
    a. The tape recorder is a reasonably expensive piece of equipment but has many advantages and pays for itself many times over a period of years. A small school system can build a record library, tape the records, and allow teachers to check out the tape and machine as they do films. The teacher can tape drumbeat sequences for the teaching of fundamental movements and creative experiences and be left free to observe, demonstrate, suggest, or correct.

SINGING GAMES

Primary children greatly enjoy four kinds of rhythmic activities: basic rhythmic skills, creative rhythms, singing games, and simple dances. In basic rhythmic skills they learn to do locomotor movements moving through space to 4/4, 2/4, 3/4, and 6/8 times as well as axial movements, such as bending and stretching, to these various tempos. In creative rhythms or movement exploration, for both younger and upper elementary groups, their own bodies become the instrument of expression in response

---

[5]Record No. 1184, Folkraft Record Company, 7 Olive Street, Newark, New Jersey.

to dramatic, exploratory, and imitative rhythmical activities.[6] Singing games are made up of actions the children do as they sing the various songs. Dances for the various grades should be simple, easily learned ones that become more complex for the older children to master.

There is a variance of opinion regarding the best method of presenting singing games and dances. Some teach children to listen for phrasing; some describe a step in rhythm, with the music as step, close step; still others count as for the waltz—one, two, three. A combination of all three is suggested.

Come Let Us Be Joyful

Record: Educational Dance Recordings, FD-1 (German)
Formation: Three pupils in a line around a circle, like the spokes of a wheel
Action: VERSE 1. Each group of three, with inside hands joined, walks three steps forward and bows to opposite group on the fourth count. They walk back to place in four steps, and repeat.
VERSE 2. Center child turns his partner on his right with a right elbow turn in four skips. He turns his partner on his left with a left elbow turn with four skips. He repeats all of this.
VERSE 3. Each group of three takes three steps forward, bows, and takes four steps backward. All walk forward, drop hands, and pass through to face a new group of three without turning.

Captain Jinks

Record: Victor 20639 (American)

VERSE 1. I'm Captain Jinks of the Horse Marines
I feed my horse good corn and beans,
VERSE 2. I swing the ladies in their teens,
For that's the style in the army!
VERSE 3. I teach the ladies how to dance, how to dance,
How to dance, I teach the ladies how to dance,
For that's the style in the army!
VERSE 4. Salute your partner, turn to the right,
And swing your neighbor with all your might,
Then promenade with the lady right,
For that's the style in the army!

Formation: Start with partners in a single circle facing clockwise.
Action: VERSE 1. All march forward to music.
VERSE 2. Partners face each other and do a two-handed swing skipping clockwise.
VERSE 3. They form a double circle, girls on the inside, boys on the outside; they join inside hands and skip forward.
VERSE 4. Each faces his partner; the boy bows (boys may salute) while the girl curtsies; the boy moves to his right to swing his neighbor two times around and promenades his new partner (the boy stays on the outside of the circle).

---

[6]See Chapter 14, Movement Exploration, for detailed suggestions for teaching these creative activities.

Way Down in the Paw Paw Patch

Record: Victor 45–5066B (American); Folkraft 1181

VERSE 1.   Where, oh where is dear little _____ ?
Where, oh where is dear little . . . . ?
Where, oh where is dear little . . . . ?
'Way down yonder in the paw paw patch.

VERSE 2.   Come on boys and let's go find her,
Come on boys and let's go find her,
Come on boys and let's go find her,
'Way down yonder in the paw paw patch.

VERSE 3.   Pickin' up paw paws, puttin' them in a basket,
Pickin' up paw paws, puttin' them in a basket,
Pickin' up paw paws, puttin' them in a basket,
'Way down yonder in the paw paw patch.

Formation: Five or six couples form a double line as follows:

Boys: X X X X X X
Girls: O O O O O O

The first name of the girl is sung as each new lead couple takes its place.

Action: VERSE 1.   First girl turns to her right and skips clockwise around the entire group.

VERSE 2.   She encircles group again and the line of boys follows her and comes back to original place.

VERSE 3.   Partners join hands and skip clockwise. When the head couple reaches the foot of the line, they hold joined hands high to make an arch and the other couples skip under it. The second couple is now the head couple. The game is repeated; singing out of the name of the new girl continues until all couples have been at the head of the line. On the last verse, the children act out the motion of putting paw paws in a basket.

Here We Go Over the Mountain Two by Two[7]

1. Here we go over the mountain, two by two
Here we go over the mountain, two by two
Here we go over the mountain, two by two
Rise up, Sugar, rise.

2. Show us a lively motion, two by two
Show us a lively motion, two by two
Show us a lively motion, two by two
Rise up, Sugar, rise.

3. That's a very lively motion, two by two
That's a very lively motion, two by two
That's a very lively motion, two by two
Rise up, Sugar, rise.

Formation: Single circle of partners, facing in. One couple stands in the center.

VERSE 1.   Children sing and walk counterclockwise while the center couple thinks of some movements to perform.

VERSE 2.   The center couple performs the chosen movements.

VERSE 3.   Entire group imitates the action demonstrated by the couple in the center. The center couple chooses a couple to take their place, and the game is repeated.

---

[7]Available from Barnett, C. J.: *Games, Rhythms, Dances.* 22 W. Monroe St., Chicago, Illinois, Arrow Business Service, 1950.

Hokey Pokey

Record: Capitol 1496 (American)

1. You put your right hand in,
   You take your right hand out,
   You put your right hand in,
   And you shake it all about,
   You do the Hokey Pokey and turn yourself about,
   That's what it's all about—Yeah!
2. You put your left hand in . . . .
3. You put your right elbow in . . . .
4. You put your left elbow in . . . .
5. You put your right shoulder in . . . .
6. You put your left shoulder in . . . .
7. You put your right hip in . . . .
8. You put your left hip in . . . .
9. You put your head in . . . .
10. You put your whole body in . . . .
11. You do the Hokey Pokey,
    You do the Hokey Pokey,
    You do the Hokey Pokey,
    That's what it's all about.

This singing game is a modernized version of Looby Loo and finds favor in primary-grade through adult groups.

Formation: Single circle facing in

Action: Players follow calls by performing the action indicated.

VERSES   When the song calls for the "Hokey Pokey" the elbows are bent, and hands are up (palms out) and wig-wagged backward and forward in front of the face. The player takes a quick turn clockwise and claps out the rhythm of the song, thrusting the right hand toward the center of the circle at the conclusion.

LAST VERSE   Hands are held high and waved in a trembling motion. Players kneel, slap the floor with both hands, and rise and shout as the music finishes.

Rig-A-Jig

Record: Disc 5038; Childhood Rhythms, Series VI, Record 602; Folkraft 1199

As I was walking down the street,
Heigh-o, heigh-o, heigh-o, heigh-o
A little friend I chanced to meet,
Heigh-o, heigh-o, heigh-o

CHORUS

Rig-a-jig-jig, and away we go
Away we go, away we go,
Rig-a-jig-jig, and away we go
Heigh-o, heigh-o, heigh-o

Formation: Single circle facing center. One player stands inside the circle.

Action: The child in the center walks around the inside of the circle until the words "a little friend" are sung. He chooses a partner and skips around the circle. As the chorus is repeated, each child inside the circle chooses a partner until all have been chosen.

Bluebird

Record: Folkraft 1180

Bluebird, bluebird, in and out my windows,
Bluebird, bluebird, in and out my windows,
Oh! Johnny, I am tired.

CHORUS

Take a little boy and tap him on the shoulders,
Take a little boy and tap him on the shoulders,
Oh! Johnny, I am tired.

Formation: Single circle facing center with players' hands joined and held high to make arches. One child, the "bluebird," stands in the center of the circle.

Action: LINES 1 AND 2. Bluebird walks around the circle, weaving in and out under the arches.
LINE 3.   Bluebird stops behind the boy.
CHORUS.   Bluebird places his hands on the shoulders of the child and taps lightly through chorus.

The dance is repeated with the boy becoming the leader and the girl following behind with her hands on his shoulders. Continue the game until all are chosen. Substitute "Jenny" for "Johnny" when girls are chosen.

Jingle Bells

Record: Any recording of this tune with a lively rhythm, such as Folkraft 1080 (American)

Formation: Double circle facing counterclockwise

Action:

PART I.

Dashing thru the snow | With hands in skating position, partners slide forward four slides with right foot leading.

In a one horse open sleigh | Leading with left foot, they repeat the above action.

O'er the field we go
Laughing all the way.
Bells on bob-tail ring
Making spirits bright,
What fun it is to ride and sing
A sleighing song tonight! | They continue this "skating step," alternately leading with right foot and left foot.

PART II.

Jingle bells! Jingle bells!
Jingle all the way! | Partners face each other and clap in rhythm to words.

Oh! What fun it is to ride
In a one horse open sleigh. | Partners link right arms and skip about each other eight skips, making two complete circles.

PART II. (REPEATED)

Jingle bells! Jingle bells!
Jingle all the way! | Partners face each other and clap.

Oh! What fun it is to ride | They link left arms and skip four skips.

In a one horse open sleigh! | The boy moves forward to the next girl.

Repeat all.

Shoo Fly

Record: Folkraft 1102 and 1185
Formation: Circle with partners' facing in with hands joined. Boys stand with
                girls on their right.
Action:

MEASURE SONG	PATTERN
	The dance is in two parts and finishes with a change of partners.
1–2 Shoo, fly, don't bother me; Shoo, fly, don't bother me.	Partners walk forward four steps toward the center of the circle, swinging arms back and forth.
3–4 Shoo, fly, don't bother me, For I belong to somebody.	They walk four steps backward to place with arms swinging.
5–8 (Repeat all of above.)	They repeat all of the above actions.
9–16 I feel, I feel, I feel like a morning star; I feel, I feel, I feel like a morning star.	Each boy turns to the girl on his right, takes hold of both of her hands, and skips around in a small circle, finishing so that this girl will be on his left when the dance is re-formed. His new partner is on his right. The dance is repeated with new partners.

How D'Ye Do My Partner

Record: Folkraft 1190 or RCA Victor 21 685
Formation: Double circle in partners with girls on the outside
Action:

MEASURE SONG	PATTERN
1–2 How d'ye do my partner	Boys bow to their partners.
3–4 How d'ye do today?	Girls curtsy to their partners.
5–6 Will you skip in a circle?	Boys offer hands to their partners.
7–8 I will show you the way.	They join inside hands and turn counterclockwise.
CHORUS	With joined hands, they skip around the circle.
1–8 Tra, la, la, la, la, la Tra, la, la, la, la, la Tra, la, la, la, la, la Tra, la, la, la, la, la	
1–6 Repeat song	Repeat the directions for measures 1–6.
7–8 And I thank you, Good day.	They stop, release hands, face each other; boys bow and girls curtsy. They change partners by moving one step to their right. They repeat the singing game.

Did You Ever See A Lassie

Record: Folkraft 1183, RCA Victor 45–5066, Bowmar Album 1
Formation: Single circle facing center with the players' hands joined. One
                child is in the center of the circle.
Action:

MEASURE SONG	PATTERN
1–8 Did you ever see a lassie, ("laddie" when a boy is in the center) A lassie, a lassie, Did you ever see a lassie, Go this way and that?	All join hands and skip to the left swinging their joined hands.

Chorus

9–16   Go this way and that way.   All stop, release hands, face the child in the center, and imi-
      Go this way and that way.   tate his movements. They repeat the singing game with a new
      Did you ever see a lassie   leader in the center.
      Go this way and that?

Teaching   After the children learn this one, have them choose a new leader
Suggestions: each time who will do creative movements such as run in place,
      clap and stomp in place, sway with the wind forward, backward,
      to each side, and so forth.

Baa, Baa, Black Sheep

Record: Childhood Rhythms, Series 7, No. 701
Formation: One child is in the center, and the rest are in a circle with their
      hands joined.
Action:

MEASURE SONG	PATTERN
1–8 Baa, baa, black sheep, Have you any wool? Yes sir, yes sir, Three bags full.	Take eight walking steps right. Place hands on hips and nod on the word "yes"; hold three fingers up on the word "three" and arms out to show a large bag.
1–8 One for my master, One for my dame, And one for the little boy Who lives in the lane.	Turn right and bow or curtsy, Turn left and bow or curtsy, Face center and bow or curtsy.

Hickory, Dickory, Dock

Record: Childhood Rhythms, Series 7, No. 702
Formation: Double circle of partners with inside hands on their partners'
      shoulders and both partners facing counterclockwise. One child is
      the "mouse," the other the "clock."
Action:

MEASURE SONG	PATTERN
1–4 Hickory, dickory, dock!	Sway toward the center of the circle.
5–8 The mouse ran up the clock	Sway toward the outside. Stamp one foot, then the other.
1–4 The clock struck one, The mouse ran down,	Mouse runs clockwise around his partner, then stamps feet as above. Clock claps hands on the word "one." Mouse runs
5–8 Hickory, Dickory, Dock.	counterclockwise. They repeat swaying and stamping move- ments.

Sally Go Round The Moon

Record: Folkraft 1198, RCA Victor 45–5064
Formation: Single circle facing center with hands joined
Action:

MEASURE SONG	PATTERN
1–8 Sally, go round the stars, Sally, go round the moon, Sally, go round the chimney pots, On a Sunday afternoon Whoops! (or Woo-ee)	Walk, run, skip, or slide around the circle. On the word "whoops," all jump into the air and clap their hands or per- form any movement they wish.
1–8 Repeat above.	Repeat the action in the opposite direction.

The Muffin Man

Record: Folkraft 1188, RCA Victor 45–5065
Formation: Single circle facing center with one child (the "muffin man") in the center of the circle.

Action:

MEASURE SONG	PATTERN

1–2 Oh, have you seen the muffin man,	Children join hands and circle to the left using a walk or a slow skip step.
3–4 The muffin, the muffin man,	
5–6 Oh, have you seen the muffin man,	
7–8 Who lives in Drury Lane?	
1–2 Oh yes, we've seen the muffin man,	Children in circle stand facing center and clap hands while singing "The Muffin Man". The child in the center chooses a partner from the circle and brings him or her back to the center (skater's position). This child becomes the new muffin man, and the "old" partner returns to the circle.
3–4 The muffin man, the muffin man	
5–6 Oh yes, we've seen the muffin man, Who lives in Drury Lane.	

A-Hunting We Will Go

Record: Victor 45–5064

Oh, a-hunting we will go,
A-hunting we will go.
We'll catch a fox and put him in a box.
And never let him go.

Formation: Couples in two parallel rows
Action:

LINE 1. The head couple slides four times down between the rows.

LINE 2. The couple heads back to place.

LINES 3–4. Each partner skips behind his own row to the end. The second couple repeats these steps. Every succeeding couple repeats the steps.

LINES 1–4. Then all join hands and circle left.

LINES 3–4. All circle back to the right. Then all jump one step into the center yelling "Ya!" at the end.

The Snail

Record: Victor 45–5064

1. Hand in hand you see us well,
   Creep like a snail into its shell;
   Ever nearer, ever nearer,
   Ever closer, ever closer,
   Who'd have thought this little shell
   Would have held us all so well?
2. Hand in hand you see us well,
   Creep like a snail out of its shell;
   Ever farther, ever farther,
   Ever wider, ever wider;
   Who'd have thought this little shell
   Would have held us all so well?

Formation: Dancers join hands in a semicircle.
Action:

VERSE 1. All walk to the left in time to the music following the leader around a series of circles, each getting smaller, all resembling a snail crawling into its shell.

VERSE 2. The line reverses, and the one at the end of the line leads the rest back to their original places.

Hippity Hop to the Barber Shop

Record: Victor 45–5064

Hip-pit-y hop to the barber shop
  To buy a stick of candy;
One for you, and one for me,
  And one for sister Annie.

Formation: Partners forming a double circle.
Action: LINES 1–2.   Partners skip around the circle clockwise.
      LINE 3.   They face each other and point to each other and
        then to themselves.
      LINE 4.   Each child in one of the circles moves up one to a
        new partner.

The Needle's Eye

Record: Victor 45–5067

The needle's eye, it doth supply
  The thread that runs so true;
There's many a beau I've let go
  Because I wanted you,
You, oh you,
  Because I wanted you.

Formation: The same as that used in London Bridge
Action: The two players who form the arch by raising and joining their
      hands catch the last one going through the arch at the end of the
      song. After all have been caught and lined up behind one of the
      two players forming the arch, a tug of war tests the "thread's"
      strength.

Skip to My Lou

Record: Victor 45–5066

1. Flies in the buttermilk, two by two,
   Flies in the buttermilk, two by two,
   Flies in the buttermilk, two by two,
   Skip to my Lou my darlin'.
2. Little red wagon painted blue . . . .
3. Purty as a red bird, purtier too . . . .
4. She is gone and I'll go too . . . .
5. Get me another'n as purty as you . . . .

Formation: A circle of partners
Action: One couple chooses another player, and all three skip around in
      the center of the circle while those forming the circle go the op-
      posite way. On the word "Skip," the chosen player in the center
      skips under the arch formed by the arms of the couple in the center.
      The original couple joins the circle while the odd dancer chooses
      another couple. He(she) takes the new girl(boy) for his(her) partner.
      They form the next arch, and the dance continues for as long as
      desired.

SUGGESTIONS FOR TEACHING DANCE SUCCESSFULLY

Dance, movement exploration, and rhythmical activities should constitute a major portion of the elementary physical education program. On the fourth grade level, where the sexes are still sometimes separated for instruction, coeducational classes in dance should be scheduled at least once weekly or during an entire unit. The program for this age level should include the solving of rhythmical movement exploratory problems, square dance, folk dance, and social dance.

Facilities, Equipment, and Supplies

1. Gymnasium, recreational room, or creative dance studio
2. Floor space free from obstructions, with a smooth, clean, nonslip waxed surface
3. Piano
4. Record player and record carrying case
5. Hand or stationary microphone
6. A full-length mirror
7. Reference books
8. Bulletin board and materials to post

Teaching Techniques

Several approaches can be used to introduce a new dance. One is through the music itself. Telling the story of the dance is another. The dance may be related to any dance the group already knows or to a dance that the group has previously done, possibly one that includes some of the same steps as this particular dance. Whatever method is used, keep the introduction brief and begin dancing as soon as possible.

Start with a circle dance so that everyone will be doing the same steps and each person can see all the others in the group. Progress from the circle to couple dancing. Have an intermission before the group becomes tired. It is better to stop for rest than to let one couple after another drift away from the floor. Other suggestions include the following:

1. Stand where everyone can see you. Stand as part of the circle rather than in the center of a circle.
2. If you have an accompanist, stand where he can see you.
3. Give the name of the dance. The nationality may be mentioned at this time, or you may prefer to wait until after the music is played in order to give the group opportunity to guess the origin.
4. After listening to the music, discuss the kind of dance movements it suggests (skip, slide, walk, or other).
5. Give some information concerning the background of the dance and any other facts of interest. Be brief and select interesting details.
6. Demonstrate the entire dance with music.

7. If the dance is short, use the whole method. If it is longer, use the whole-part teaching method. Teach with the music unless practice without it will speed learning.
8. Have the group walk through the first pattern. Use cue words to help them recall the steps and give these in rhythm with the music.
9. Select a signal with which to start both the dancers and the music. If you use a record, play the introduction at least twice so that the dancers will recognize the first measure of the dance.
10. Demonstrate with your back to the group. Arrange all in a line behind you. Demonstrate and give directions at the same time. (Step, hop, step, and so forth. Have all repeat and do step, hop, step with you.)
11. Dance the first pattern; then proceed to the next series of steps. Each time you dance with the music start from the beginning.
12. Be on the lookout for anyone who is having trouble. Analyze the way he is doing the steps and help him discover his mistake.
13. Have the dancers change partners often so that no one has to dance with a poor partner for very long at a time and each has opportunity to dance with many others.
14. Select dances that are difficult enough to challenge the group.
15. Have everyone take part, but do not insist that they do so.
16. Provide for review of familiar dances as well as for learning new ones in every session.
17. Progress as fast as is wise for your particular group.

A folk dance festival given as a climax to a class or club session does much to stimulate and sustain interest. Committees add to the working efficiency of the group.

SQUARE DANCE

Folk dancing has been enjoyed by limited groups in the larger cities of the United States for a long period of time. The repertoire of these groups has been composed chiefly of international dances. The eagerness of these groups has given a tremendous

FIGURE 19–2. Around you go! (Reprinted by permission of © J. A. Preston Corporation.)

boost to all folk dancing, for they have gradually added couple and group dances from all countries to their "know-how."

Square dancing patter and calls vary in different parts of the country and even in different towns in the same state. However, the fundamental formations and steps are the same.

A teacher may start square dancing in the third or fourth grades using circle or round dances. In the fifth or sixth grades the children should be able to execute a number of simple round, square, and longways dances.

Teaching Suggestions

1. Discuss with your group the beginning of square dancing so that they will not get lost in a maze of terms. The first figures will soon be forgotten unless they are tied in directly with dancing. Explain briefly.
2. Demonstrate the step that is used during the dance. This is a smooth, shuffling step done with the knees flexed and relaxed. The dancers may add a two-step now and then for variety. Almost without exception, the beginner will either skip or jump with each step. Review the shuffle step over and over, and remind dancers individually to keep their dance smooth.
3. Begin with a grand march. Line the boys up on one side of the room, the girls on the other, with both facing one end of the dance area. When the music starts, the first "gent" in each line comes to the center of the room, meets his partner there with an elbow swing, and moves down the center of the room. Others in the lines follow. At the opposite end of the dance floor the first couple turns right, the second left, and the dance continues in this way until all couples return to the other end of the floor. Next the couples come down in groups of four; then they come down in groups of eight. As soon as the last group of eight is complete, stop the music and explain how to "square your sets."
4. The Square: Explain the positions of the couples—partner, corner, home position.
5. Mention that calls are directed to the boys.
6. Walk through the following: circle left, allemande left, grand right and left, sashay, and promenade.
7. Practice the two-step swing and the pivot swing.
8. Call these basic figures with the music.
9. Walk through a simple dance. Then dance it with the music. If you use a record with the call recorded with the music, go over the directions carefully and, in addition, tell the dancers the extra patter the caller includes. For the first experiences in dancing with the music, turn the speed of the record to slow tempo. If you have an accompanist, variation of tempo can easily be made.
10. Teach the do-si-do; practice it several times with various patter calls. Use it in a dance. Then review the allemande left, pointing out the difference between it and the do-si-do.
11. Explain that each dance will begin with an *opener,* and then the figure will be called until one couple has danced the figure with every other couple. After each figure, a *filler* or *mixer* may be included, and the last call is the *close* or *ending.*

12. Introduce a new dance. Walk through it at least once. Have one set dance through the figure. Teach any part of the dance that is new to the group. Start the music, and dance. Review and begin again if the dancers become confused. Introduce another new dance. Review the dances already learned. People enjoy being exposed to the new, but they like best the old dances they can do well.

Suggested Teaching Progressions

THE CIRCLE[8]

Have the children form a single circle, boys alternating with girls. The boy's partner is on his right; his corner is on his left. The following terms and figures may be taught in the circle.

HONOR YOUR PARTNER.   The boy bows from the waist with his right arm in front and left arm in back (avoiding stomach-clutching and head-ducking). The girl does a simple curtsy by placing one foot behind the other and flexing her knees slightly. She may hold her skirt at the side.

HONOR YOUR CORNER.   The boy does the same as above to the corner (the boy turns and bows to the girl on his left).

CIRCLE LEFT.   All join hands and move forward around the circle.

CIRCLE RIGHT.   Move to the right as above.

PROMENADE.   Couples move counterclockwise around the circle; the girl is on the boy's right. The boy has the girl's right hand in his right hand and her left hand in his left hand. His right arm is crossed over the girl's left arm.

GRAND RIGHT AND LEFT.   Partners face each other, touch right hands, pass on to the next person, touch left hands. They continue in this way around the circle, weaving in and out until partners meet again. The boys move counterclockwise, the girls clockwise. It may be necessary to have the children hold on to their partners' hands until they can touch the next persons' left hands, release their partners' hands, hold the new persons' left hands, and so forth.

SWINGS

TWO-HANDED SWING.   Partners face each other, clasp both hands, and swing around. This swing is recommended for children up to the sixth grade.

ELBOW SWING.   Hook right or left elbows and swing around once. Use alternately with the two-handed swing.

WAIST SWING.   In the social dance position, the boy takes the girl and swings her around to the right, stepping left, right, left, and so forth. Usually a waist swing calls for two turns.

ALLEMANDE LEFT.   The boy and corner face each other, join left hands, walk around each other, and return to home position. Practice this figure a few times, then add the allemande left to the grand right and left and end up with the promenade home.

---

[8]*Ye Old Time Night: Cowboy Dances*, Decca Album A-524.

THE SQUARE

Break the large circle into small circles of eight, each constituting a set. Teach the sets to "square-up." Each couple in the set forms one side of the square which should be large enough to allow free movement and tight enough to prevent running back to home position. First couples have their back to the Caller or music. Proceeding counterclockwise are couples two, three and four. The first and third couples are called "head couples," and the second and fourth are called "side couples." A couple's starting position is "home." Have the couples identify themselves by raising their hands. After reviewing all fundamentals learned in the circle you are ready to teach a dance.

SQUARE DANCE ACTIVITIES

The square dance has four parts: (1) an introduction or opener, (2) the main figure, the trimmings, (3) fill-ins or mixers, and (4) the ending. Numerous examples of patter for all dances may be found in the references listed at the end of the chapter. There is no doubt that the Allemande left and grand right and left take on color when called in this way "On your corner with the old left hand, why in the world don't you right and left grand." Calls at this level, however, should be kept simple, with just enough variation to avoid monotomy.

Red River Valley

Record: There are any number of good recordings of this tune. This simple version is a favorite among the youngsters of the Southwest. Many groups sing as they dance, which helps them know what steps to do next. Different versions may be found in the listed references.

Formation: Squares of eight dancers

Action:

SONG	PATTERN
The first couple lead down the Valley, And you circle to the left and to the right. Then you swing with the girl in the Valley, And now you swing with your Red River Girl.	The first couple moves to couple No. 2, and all form a circle. They move to the left and then to the right. Each boy swings the girl opposite him one-and-one-half times around. Each boy swings his partner one-and-one-half times around. Couple No. 2 should be in home position, and couple No. 1 should be in the center of the square.
Then lead right on down the Valley, And you circle to the left and to the right, Then you swing with the girl in the Valley, And now you swing with your Red River Girl.	Couple No. 1 moves on to Couple No. 3, and the action of the first four lines is repeated.
Then you lead on down the Valley, And you circle to the left and to the right, Then you swing with the girl in the Valley, And now you swing with your Red River Girl.	Couple No. 1 moves on to couple No. 4, and the action of the first four lines is repeated.
	The whole dance is then repeated, with couples No. 2, No. 3, and No. 4 each leading out in turn.

Examples of introductions are

>Honor your partner, the lady by your side *(corner)*
>All join hands and circle wide *(move to left)*
>Break and swing and promenade home.

>All eight balance, all eight swing,
>Now promenade around the ring.

Examples of endings are

>Bow to your partner, bow to your corner,
>Bow to your opposite, and there you stand.

>Promenade (add girls' names) two by two,
>Take her home like you always do.

LONGWAYS FORMATION

There are two types of longways formations used in dances. The type shown in Figure A is formed by a double line with partners facing forward. This formation is used in the party game Way Down in the Paw Paw Patch. The type shown in Figure B is used in the Virginia Reel, which remains one of the most popular of American folk dances among all age groups. It serves as an excellent introduction to square dancing as a number of the basic movements are learned. Third and fourth graders prefer the skip as the basic step, but fifth and sixth graders show a preference for the shuffle step, which is less strenuous and more dignified.

```
Fig. A      Fig. B
O   X       O→X
O   X       O   X
O   X       O   X
O   X       O   X
O   X       O   X
O   X       O→X
Head of Set
O—girls
X—boys
```

Virginia Reel

Record: Folkraft 1249, with calls; Folkraft 1312, no calls
Formation: Six to eight couples longways, with partners facing each other
Action: In the first six steps the head boy and girl move forward to the center to execute the movement and move backward to their places. The head girl and foot boy repeat the same action by moving to the center of the set and returning to their places.

PATTERN	MEASURE
STEP 1. Boys bow to their corners, and girls curtsy to their corners. The head girl and head boy move to the center, bow, and return to their places.	1–4
The head girl and the foot boy repeat the action.	5–8
STEP 2. Dancers hook right arms and swing around clockwise once.	1–4
Repeat.	5–8
STEP 3. Dancers hook left arms and swing around clockwise once.	9–12
Repeat.	13–16

STEP 4.   Dancers join both hands and turn clockwise.
Repeat.
STEP 5.   Dancers dos-a-dos, passing right shoulders.
Repeat.
STEP 6.   Dancers dos-a-dos, passing left shoulders.
Repeat.
STEP 7.   The head couple face each other, join hands, move sideward to the foot of the set in four slides, and return to the head of the set in four slides.
STEP 8.   The head couple hook right elbows and turn around one-and-one-half times, until the boy is facing the girls' line and the girl is facing the boys' line. The boy hooks left elbows with the second girl as the girl hooks left elbows with the second boy. They swing halfway around counter-clockwise, meet back in the center, hook right elbows, and turn halfway around clockwise. This is repeated down the line, with the head couple turning each dancer with their left arms and each other with their right arms. When they have turned the last dancer at the foot of the line, they turn around one-and-one-half times, join both hands, and slide back to the head of the set. (If there are more than six couples, 12 measures of music may not be enough to complete the action. Repeat the music if necessary.)   5–16
STEP 9.   All face the head of the set. The head boy turns outward and leads the line of boys toward the foot of the set with a slow shuffle. At the same time, the head girl turns   Cast
outward and leads the girls to the foot of the set with the   off
same step.   music

Couple Dances

Jesse Polka (American-Bohemian)

Record: Beer Barrel Polka—RCA Victor 25–1009, Folkraft 1071, or Folkraft 1263—or any good polka

Formation: Couples in varsouvienne position, with the boy and girl on the same foot

Action:

PATTERN	MEASURE

STEP 1.   Touch your left heel forward and take your weight on your left foot. Count 1, and
STEP 2.   Touch your right toe backward. Count 2. Step beside your left foot without removing your weight from it, touch your right heel forward, and step back. Count 3, taking
your weight on your right foot, and   2–3
STEP 3.   Touch your left heel forward. Lift your left foot, cross your left toes in front of your right foot (cut), and   4
STEP 4.   Take four two-steps, beginning with your left foot.   5–8
Repeat the entire dance.

Cotton-eyed Joe (Texan)

Record: Columbia 37658—Foot N' Fiddle, September 1947; Folkraft 1255 (calls)

Formation: Partners in social dance position, with the boys beginning on the left foot, the girls on the right foot.

Action:	STEP 1. Touch your right heel in front; then touch the toes of your foot behind you (two-step). Repeat in the reverse direction. STEP 2. Turn away from your partner (boys to the left, girls to the right) with three two-steps. Complete a circle and face your partner with three stamps. STEP 3. Boys take four slides to the left and, then, four slides to the right. STEP 4. Take four steps in social dance position. Repeat all.
Variations:	This vigorous Texas frontier dance usually follows the description in steps 1, 2, and 4. In step 3, one finds many variations. In one of these, boys and girls go in opposite directions, clapping and sliding in four counts and returning to their original position in four counts. In another, boys push or paddle-step to the left for four counts and to the right for four counts.

Veleta

Record:	Michael Herman; Folkraft 1065
Action:	

PATTERN	MEASURE
Open position:	
STEP 1. Partners join inside hands. Starting with their outside foot (boys' left, girls' right), they take two waltz steps forward.	2
STEP 2. Face your partner, change hands, and take two draw steps to the left.	2
STEP 3. Repeat in the opposite direction.	4
Closed position:	
STEP 4. Start backward (the boy on the left foot, the girl following on the right foot).	
STEP 5. Do two waltz steps.	2
STEP 6. Do two draw steps (the boy with the left foot, the girl with the right foot).	2
STEP 7. Do four waltz steps.	4
Repeat the entire dance.	

MIXERS

Teachers who are working with children who have had rhythmic training from the first grade up will encounter little trouble in directing or teaching mixed groups. However, when groups are new to each other or shy, it is well to warm up with a grand march, a group dance, or a mixer to get everyone acquainted and relaxed. A child should not be allowed to "sit out" too often. If there is an odd dancer, make a game of the mixer and let the boy or girl try to get a partner as a change is made. The children should be allowed to choose their own dance partners at intervals, but if they get in a rut, partners should be juggled with a mixer. Mixers are fun and an excellent method of juggling partners in shy groups.

Maine Mixer

Record:	Glowworm—Imperial 1044
Formation:	Double circle of partners facing right (counterclockwise). All join hands with the boy or girl on the right of them. The group sings or chants instructions until the mixer is learned.

Action:

SONG	PATTERN
Everybody goes to town	
You pick 'em up, you lay 'em down	Dancers take eight steps right.
Back away and say adieu	They take one step away, face their partners, and wave.
And balance to the right of you.	Boys and girls balance to the persons opposite and to the right of them. These are their new partners.
Dos-a-dos and watch her smile	The new partners circle back to back, returning to their original places.
Step right up and swing her awhile	The boy swings the girl with a waist swing.
Give that girl an extra swing	The boy twirls the girl and takes promenade position.
And promenade around the ring.	

Mexican Mixer

Record: Labios de Coral—Imperial 119

Formation: Couples in social dance position form a circle, with the boys facing counterclockwise and the girls facing clockwise.

Action: STEP 1.   Do the grapevine to the inside of the circle. The boy steps with his right foot to the back of his left, to the outside with his left, and forward right; then he swings his left leg out. The girl does the same, starting on her left foot.

Repeat the same to the outside of the circle.

Reverse feet: Step with the left foot to the back, the right to the side, the left forward, and then swing out the right leg.

STEP 2.   With a wrist hold, the couple turns right with four step-hops—right, left, right, left.

STEP 3.   The boy claps while the girl moves away (step 1) with a step right, left, and right, a swing, and four step-hops and turns with her hands on her hips.

They repeat, moving left to their partners.

FIGURE 19–3. By the sixth grade children should be able to do well a number of simple round, square, and longway dances. (Courtesy of AAHPER, Washington, D.C.)

The girl claps and the boy does same; the girl moves to inside of circle and back. As the boy does the step-hops, he turns to his left (counterclockwise) and moves on to the next girl.

Circassian Circle

Record:	Folkraft 1167 and 1115; Windsor Album A–753
Formation:	Single circle of partners with joined hands, the girls to the right of their partners.
Action:	

PATTERN	MEASURE
Dancers walk four steps forward toward the center of the circle.	1–2
Dancers walk four steps backward from the center of the circle.	3–4
They repeat the action of measures 1 to 4.	5–8
They drop hands; the girl steps forward to the center of the circle and bows.	1–2
The girl walks three steps backward to her place.	3–4
The boy walks three steps forward toward the center, turns halfway around on the fourth count, and walks four steps slightly to the right away from the center to his new partner.	5–8
He swings his partner using buzz steps.	1–8
They promenade counterclockwise with 16 walking steps.	1–8

Circle Waltz

Record:	Folkraft 1064
Formation:	Single circle of partners facing center with their hands joined and the girl on the right
Action:	

PATTERN	MEASURE
PART I. Balance forward (the boys on the left, the girls on the right).	1
Balance backward (the boys on the right, the girls on the left).	2
The girl dances two waltz steps as she turns in front of the boy on her right; she finishes on his right. The boy does two balance steps.	3–4
Dancers repeat the action of measures 1 to 4 three times. They finish facing their partners and holding their hands (the boys on the right, the girls on the left).	5–16
PART II. Dancers take two balance steps, starting on the outside foot.	1–2
Dancers drop hands, take two waltz steps, starting on their outside feet and turning from their partners. They finish facing their partners and holding their hands (the boys on the left, the girls on the right).	3–4
Dancers repeat the action of measures 1 to 4. They finish in a closed dance position.	5–8
They take two step-draw steps toward the center of the circle.	9–10
They take two step-draw steps back to their places.	11–12
They take four waltz steps turning clockwise with their partners and progressing counterclockwise in the circle. They finish in a single circle with the girls on the right of their partners. All hands are joined. `	13–16

Georgia Twirl

Record:	Sweet Georgia Brown—Windsor 7630
Formation:	Double circle of dancers in varsouvienne position facing counter-clockwise

PATTERN	MEASURE
Partners take two-steps forward, starting on the left foot; partners drop left hands as the boy takes four walking steps forward, and the girl twirls under their joined right arms. They finish in varsouvienne position.	1–4
With their backs to the center of the circle, dancers take four grapevine steps right.	5–12
Dancers face counterclockwise, balance left, hold, balance right, and hold. The boy walks four short steps forward to the next girl as the girl turns in place.	13–16

Josephine (A Jazz Mixer)

Record:	Josephine—Russell 141
Formation:	Double circle facing counterclockwise, with girls on outside and partners' inside hands joined
Action:	

PATTERN	MEASURE
Starting on the inside foot, walk four steps forward and finish with a step-bend.	1–4
Drop hands. Dance one two-step away from your partner, ending with a slight knee bend. Clap your hands once.	5–8
Take one two-step back to your partner, ending with a slight knee bend; clap your hands once.	9–12
Turn one complete circle away from your partner, ending in your original position.	13–16
Join inside hands with your partner, and dance one two-step forward, ending with a slight knee bend.	17–20
Drop your partners' hands; the girl dances two step-touch-steps in place as the boy walks four steps forward to the new partner.	21–24
In closed dance position, the boy steps forward to the left as the girl steps backward to the right, ending with a slight knee bend. Repeat.	25–28
The girl turns under the boy's arm with four steps; they finish side by side with their inside hands joined.	29–32

Lili Marlene Two-Step

Record:	MacGregor 1010A; Folkraft 1096
Formation:	Double circle facing counterclockwise, with the girls on the outside and partners' inside hands joined.
Action:	These directions are for boys; those for girls are the reverse.

PATTERN	MEASURE
Starting on your left foot, walk four steps forward, face your partner, join hands with her, take four slides counterclockwise.	1–2
Repeat the action of measures 1 and 2.	3–4

Step sideward with your left, and swing your right foot in front of your left; repeat these directions using the right foot where the left was indicated and vice versa.	5
Repeat the action of measure 5, ending with only inside hands joined.	6
Walk forward three steps, starting on the left foot. Drop hands, and turn right to face the opposite direction. Join inside hands with your partner. Walk backward three steps, starting on the right foot.	7–8
Repeat the action of measures 7 and 8.	9–10
Take four two-steps forward starting with the left foot; the boy meets the girl ahead, who becomes his new partner.	11–12

The Mountain Romp

Record: Teton Mountain Stomp—Windsor 7615 and A 7S3
Formation: Double circle of partners with both hands joined and with girls on the outside
Action: The directions are for boys; those for girls are the reverse.

PATTERN	MEASURE
Step left on your left foot. Slide your right foot to your left foot; step to the left again. Tap your right toe.	1–2
Repeat the action of measures 1 and 2, starting on your right foot.	3–4
Step sideward to the left; tap your right toe. Step sideward to the right; tap your left toe.	5–6
Drop outside hands (boy's left, girl's right). Take four short walking steps forward.	7–8
The girl walks four steps forward as the boy turns to face clockwise and walks four steps backward.	9–12
Drop inside hands. The girl walks four steps forward as the boy walks four steps forward to meet his new partner. He swings the new partner around once. The dance ends with partners facing each other with their hands joined.	13–16

Oh Johnny Sashay

Record: Oh Johnny Oh—Bowmar B 205; Folkraft 1037
Formation: Single circle with girls on the right of boys, all facing center, and all hands joined
Action:

PATTERN	MEASURE
Take eight sashay steps to the right.	1–4
Release hands. Swing your partner with a right-elbow swing.	5–8
The boy swings the girl on his left with a left-elbow swing.	9–12
He swings the partner with a right-elbow swing.	13–16
He does an allemande left with the girl on his left.	17–20
He does a do-si-do with his partner.	21–24
He promenades with the girl on his left, singing "Oh Johnny, Oh Johnny Oh."	25–32

St. Bernard's Waltz

Record: Folkraft 1162
Formation: Double circle in closed dance position

Action:

PATTERN	MEASURE
Take two draw-steps left.	1–2
Take one draw-step left. Stamp right and stamp left.	3–4
Take two draw-steps right.	5–6
Take two walking steps forward.	7–8
Take two walking steps backward.	9–10
Dancers take two waltz steps forward as the girl turns under the boy's arm. They finish in closed dance position.	11–12

The Southern Waltz

Record: Tennessee Waltz—MacGregor 649; Tempo 126 M
Formation: Double of circle of partners in varsouvienne position, with the girls on the outside and all facing counterclockwise

Action:

PATTERN	MEASURE
PART 1. Balance forward to the left; balance forward to the right. The boy takes six small steps forward as the girl takes six small steps forward but slightly toward her right, holding her partner's hand on the last three steps.	1–4
Repeat the action of measures 1 to 4.	5–8
PART 2. Step forward to the left, put your right foot behind your left, and step sideward to the left. Repeat, starting on your right foot.	1–2
Balance forward to the left. Balance backward to the right.	3–4
Repeat the actions of measures 1 to 4. Finish in closed dance position with the boy facing counterclockwise.	5–8
PART 3. (Directions are for boys; girls do the opposite.) Balance forward left. Walk forward three short steps. Balance forward left. Balance backward right.	1–4
PART 4. (Directions are for boys; girls do the opposite.) Step-swing forward left. Step-swing forward right.	1–2
Do-si-do using six walking steps.	3–4
Starting from open dance position, step-swing forward on your outside foot; then step-swing forward on your inside foot.	5–6
Do-si-do using six walking steps.	7–8

Ten Pretty Girls

Record: Folkraft 1036; World of Fun M 113
Formation: Double circle of partners facing counterclockwise in open dance position, with girls on the outside.

Action:

PATTERN	MEASURE
Point your left foot forward and then sideward.	1
Take one grapevine step.	2
Repeat the action of measures 1 and 2, beginning with your right foot.	3–4
Take four slow steps forward, beginning with your left foot.	5–6
Swing your left leg forward and lean backward. Swing your left leg backward and lean forward.	7

Stamp three times in place, beginning with your left foot.   8
Repeat the entire dance, this time beginning with your right   9–16
foot.

    Variation: When this dance is done as a mixer, the boy may move forward
                             on the last measure while the girl remains in place and stamps
                             three times.

MIXER GAMES

Dance games, or change-partner dances and elimination dances, should be an integral part of both dance classes and scheduled dance sessions. They serve to motivate the group to practice a particular step, emphasize important points to remember, and add interest.

The success of any mixer depends entirely upon the leader, who must constantly note the atmosphere as the game progresses. He should keep each moving in tempo with the reaction of the dancers toward it. Elimination dances should not be used too long or too much.

The Double Circle (Paul Jones Mixer)

Girls form in a circle facing away from the center, the boys form a circle facing them. Both circles move with the music to the right until the leader gives a signal to dance. Then each boy takes as his partner the girl directly in front of him. The signal may be simply the call "Let's dance!" A sure way to attract everyone's attention is to stop the music until each person has a partner and then begin it again for the dance.

Multiplication

Three or more couples, depending upon the size of the group, are asked to begin dancing. When the music stops each chooses a new partner from those not dancing. The dancing with each new partner should be short until everyone has been included. Play one complete number dancing with the last partner chosen.

Characteristics in Common

Everyone with a certain characteristic or trait finds another with the same feature. For example, "All blond girls find a blond partner" or "Dance with someone whose birthday is in the same month as yours."

Matched Shoes

Each girl tosses one of her shoes into the center of a circle. At a given signal, all the boys rush to pick up a shoe, then find its owner to be his partner for the next dance. This procedure may be reversed (the males take off their shoes). The similarity among boys' shoes causes quite a scramble to find the right owners.

Puzzles

Anything that can be divided into two parts when matched together again is a suitable prop. Two decks of cards can serve, a picture may be cut in half with a zigzag edge, and so forth. Give each person half a song title or half a word and have him find his better half for the next dance.

Blind Date

The boys form a line outside the room. Inside on the dance floor the girls also form a line. As each boy walks through the door, he begins dancing with the first girl in line.

Broom Dance

A broom is given to the person without a partner. He dances with it for a while, then drops it as the signal for everyone to find a new partner. He then grabs a partner, leaving someone else to dance with the broom. Each partner of the broom should give time for new partners to dance a reasonable length of time before he drops the broom, or there will only be a contest instead of a dance.

Grand March

The grand march is ideal for getting new partners. The boys and girls each form a line facing the same direction on opposite sides of the room. When the music begins, the first boy and girl in each line march toward each other until they meet. They continue to march or walk down the middle of the floor until all others in the line have met dance partners.

Paul Jones Mixer

Record: Any square dance record without calls
Formation: Single circle of partners facing center with hands joined and the girl on the boy's right side
Action: PART 1.   All join hands and circle left, then right. All move to the center and back.
PART 2.   Dance with the girl on your left (polka). (Whistle.)
PART 3.   All promenade. (Whistle.) Girls stand still; boys move forward to the fourth girl. They promenade. (Whistle.) Boys stand still; girls move forward to the fourth boy.
PART 4.   All dance with the girls behind them (polka). (Whistle.)
PART 5.   All promenade. (Whistle.) They make a big circle. Face partners and take their right hands. Take a grand right and left. (Say hello, howdy, and so on, to each dancer as you meet him.)
PART 6.   Dance with the girls you now have (polka). (Whistle.)
PART 7.   Make a big circle; circle left, circle right. All move to center and back. Girls move to the center (form a circle); boys circle left. (Whistle.) Boys find their partner from the center.
PART 8.   Dance with your partner for the last dance. (Whistle.)

Rye Waltz

Record: Folkraft 1470, MacGregor 398
Formation: Couples take social dance position: The boy holds the girl's right hand in his extended left while his right arm is placed around her waist. The girl's left hand rests on the boy's right shoulder.
Action: The boy starts with the left foot and the girl with the right foot. Measures are in 2/4 time.

PATTERN	MEASURE
Extend foot to the side and touch floor lightly with toe. Draw same foot just behind heel of other foot with toe touching the floor. Repeat, then slide sideward three slides. (Out, in, out, in, slide, slide, slide.)	4
Repeat starting on other foot.	4

Waltz for one bar.   8
End with three slides.   1

Old Town Stomp

Record: Educational Activities, Inc. Album 32
Formation: A single circle facing center (hands may be joined if desired) or a
                series of lines facing forward with no hands joined.
Action: STEP 1.   Walking Steps and Foot Placing: Beginning left, walk
                backward left, right, left, and right ending with feet together. Move
                forward left, right, left, and right, ending with feet together. Place
                the left heel forward and then step on the left beside the right.
                Place the right heel forward and then step on the right beside the
                left. Bend the knees in place and then straighten the knees. Clap
                your hands twice, waist high. Repeat Step 1.
                STEP 2.   Two-step, Step and Stamp, Four Steps: Moving sideward
                left with a two-step; step sideward left, close right to left, step
                sideward left, and stamp on right beside left. End with your weight
                on left foot. Step sideward right on right, close left to right, step
                sideward right and stamp on left beside right. Weight ends on the
                right foot. Step sideward on left, and stamp right beside left; step
                sideward on right and stamp left beside right. In place take four
                steps left, right, left, and right. Repeat Step 2.

Butterfly Schottische

Record: Educational Activities, Inc. Album 33
Formation: A single circle facing counterclockwise. Hands may be joined
                or free.
Action: STEP 1.   Schottische Forward and Backward; Schottische In and
                Out: Step forward on the right, step forward on the left, and step-
                hop on the right, lifting the bent left knee by the right foot. Step
                back on the left, step back on the right, step-hop back on the left,
                lifting the bent right knee. Step forward on the right, step forward
                on the left, and step-hop on the right, lifting the bent left knee by
                the right foot. Step back left, step back right, step back left, and
                hop on the left, making a quarter-turn left to face center. Beginning
                on the right, schottische in, backward on left, in on right, and
                backward on left.
                STEP 2.   Step-Close and Slide: Moving sideward right, step side-
                ward on the right and close left to right, step sideward right and
                close left to right, step sideward right and close left to right, and
                step sideward right and close left to right with weight on the right
                foot. Move sideward left; take eight fast slides. Repeat the four
                step-close patterns right and the eight slides left.

Bingo

Record: Victor 45–6172, 45 rpm 41–6172
                1. There was a farmer had a dog
                   And Bingo was his name, Sir.
                   The farmer's dog's at our back door,
                   And begging for a bone, Sir.
                2. B and an I and an I with an N
                   N with a G and G with an O
                   B—I—N—G—O—go
                   Bingo was his name, Sir.
Formation: Double circle of partners facing counterclockwise, with girls on
                the outside

Action:

PATTERN	MEASURE
VERSE 1. All walk forward in a circle. They continue walking; on the word "Sir" the boys turn and face clockwise.	1–2
VERSE 2. Boys skip clockwise; girls skip counterclockwise; on the word "Sir" each boy takes the girl nearest him for his partner, ready to repeat the dance.	3–6

The Cindy Dance

Record:	Hot Pretzels—Victor 25–1009; Columbia 12422–F; Imperial 1146
Formation:	Double circle of partners in varsouvienne position, with the girls on the outside
Action:	

PATTERN	MEASURE
Place your left heel to the left and hold; take one grapevine step, starting with the left foot.	1–2
Place your right heel to the right and hold; take one grapevine step, starting with the right foot.	3–4
Repeat the action of measures 1 and 2.	5–6
Walk four steps forward, starting with the right foot.	7–8
Brush the right foot forward and back; take one grapevine step, starting with the right foot.	9–10
Brush the left foot forward and back; take one grapevine step, starting with the left foot.	11–12
Repeat the action of measures 9 to 12.	13–16
Repeat from the beginning.	

Note: After repeating the dance two times there is a four-measure break; walk five steps forward and repeat the grapevine step, starting with the right foot.

Cotton-eyed Joe

Record:	Folkraft F 1035; MacGregor 849 and 604; RCA LPM 1621; World of Fun M 118
Formation:	Double circle in close dance position, with girls on the outside
Action:	(Directions are for boys; girls do the opposite.)

PATTERN	MEASURE
Touch your left heel to the left side; touch your left toe to your right foot; take two quick two-steps counterclockwise in a circle.	1–2
Repeat the action of measures 1 and 2, starting with your right heel.	3–4
Drop your hands; turn once around to the left, away from your partner, with three two-steps; finish facing your partner; stamp in place three times.	5–8
Starting from closed dance position, take four short push-steps left.	9–10
Take four short push-steps to the right.	11–12
Starting on your left foot, take four two-steps, turning clockwise in a circle.	

Jessie Polka

Record: 632; Folkraft 1093 and 1071
Formation: Double circle in open dance position facing counterclockwise
Action:

PATTERN	MEASURE
Touch your left heel forward; step left in place.	1
Touch your right toe back; step right in place.	2
Swing your right foot forward; step right in place.	3
Point your left foot to the left; place your left foot in front of the right.	4
Dance four two-steps counterclockwise in a circle.	5–8
Repeat as many times as the music permits.	

INTERNATIONAL DANCES

Increasingly, educators are teaching children that other countries are not foreign if one knows enough about them. In any metropolitan city, a teacher has a wealth of material in one class with which world fellowship could be taught with live authenticity. The mores, habits, and folklore of a people cease to be strange when explanations throw light on their origin.

Folk dancing is one phase of education for international understanding that should not be tampered with if one desires a true picture of a people. A way of life and the very character of a people is expressed in its folk music and dance. Hence, if we use these dances, they should be taught as near the original as possible, the student receiving a rich background in the country, costume, and reason for the dance. The Czechs take on new stature when one has seen the *Beseda*. A Slav is a person to be admired once the intricate and subtle steps of a *Kolo* have been mastered. The child who has been taught the *Ländler* will think of the Germans as a happy, hardy, fun-loving people who like to "stomp" out a good tune. Likewise, the beautiful strains of *Alexandrovski* remind one that Russians love beauty in movement. The barrier of race falls limply as one joins in a circle to dance the friendly *Cherkessia,* which is both joyous and sad with its undercurrent of the tragic Jewish past. Folk dancing can be an invaluable adjunct to the teacher who is trying to present world geography in an honest way. While the child is learning through the dance how his "world-neighbors" feel, the time is ripe to develop a project through which he can learn how they look in festive costumes. Children may bring dolls to school dressed in native costumes or may dress them as an art or social studies subject.

There are other facets to folk dancing. Coordination and skill can be developed that carry over into all dancing, particularly social dancing. Children need to learn how to do social dancing as much as they need to know almost any other subject taught in schools. Folk dance develops in one the ability to move to rhythm and to coordinate hands and arms with feet and legs. Often our most polished social dancers of the high school level have been the best dancers in a fourth grade folk dance class.

The European and American folk dances that appear in published form have been acknowledged in this book. The sources of a number of American dances are unknown, for a dance will pop up in one community and a visiting folk dance devotee who is present will take it back to his own group with slight changes. Credit has been given to known individuals who have introduced dances to folk dance groups. In many folk dances the music practically calls the steps. In describing these simpler dances in which the music phrasing speaks for itself, counts and measure have been excluded.

Kalvelis (Lithuanian)

Record: Sonart Folk Dance Album I; Folkraft 1051A
Formation: About eight couples form a single circle facing counterclockwise.
Action:

PATTERN	MEASURE
STEP 1. All polka (without hopping) eight steps right.	1–8
All polka (with hopping) eight steps left.	1–8
CHORUS. Clap your hands; clap your hand to your partner's right hand. Clap your hands. Clap your hand to your partner's left. Grasp both your partner's hands and skip four times; skip to the right four times.	9–16
Repeat.	9–16
STEP 2. Girls do four polka steps into a circle, turn, and	1–8
do four polka steps back to their place. Boys do the same.	1–8
CHORUS (twice)	9–16
STEP 3. Girls weave around the circle, going behind the	1–16
first dancer and in front of the next, and so forth, they do	1–16
16 polka steps. Boys do the same.	
CHORUS	
STEP 4. All do grand right and left.	1–16
CHORUS (twice)	1–16
STEP 5. All join hands and polka eight times right as in	
Step 1.	1–8
Polka eight times left.	1–8

Tantoli (Scandinavian)

Record: Crampton, *The Folk Dance Book* and record (Simple Version)
Formation: Couples in double circle facing counterclockwise with inside hands joined and free hands on hips
Action:

PATTERN	MEASURE
STEP 1. With the outside foot, put your heel forward to the floor and your toe backward on the floor.	1
Polka, hopping on the inside foot.	2
Repeat three times, beginning on the inside foot, then using the outside, and then the inside.	3
STEP 2. Partners face each other, join hands at shoulder level, and turn clockwise with 16 step-hops, the boys starting on the left foot, the girls on the right. (This step has been called the windmill because the arms are lowered toward the foot that the hop is taken on and raised on the opposite side.)	8

Hambo (Swedish)

Record: Folkraft F 1048 A and 1164 B
Formation: Double circle facing counterclockwise in open dance position, with girls on the outside.
Action:

PATTERN	MEASURE
Take two dal steps, starting with the outside foot.	1–2
Take three light running steps forward, starting with the outside foot.	3
Take four hambo steps, turning clockwise with your partner in shoulder-waist position and progressing counterclockwise.	4–7
Take three steps or a balance step, boys starting with the right foot and girls with the left, opening into original starting position.	8

Horra (Israeli)

Record: Folkraft F 1118 B; Folk Dancer 1052; Folkraft F 1110 B
Formation: Single circle of dancers facing center with their hands on their neighbors' adjacent shoulders
Action:

PATTERN	MEASURE
Step sideward to the left on your left foot; cross and put right foot behind your left foot; step sideward left on your left foot; hop on your left foot and swing your right foot across in front of the left.	1–2
Step sideward to the right on your right foot; hop on your right foot and swing your left foot across in front of your right foot.	3
Repeat as often as the music allows.	

Road to the Isles (Scottish)

Record: Folkraft 1095 and 1416; MacGregor 728; World of Fun M 110
Formation: Double circle facing counterclockwise in varsouvienne position, with girls on the outside
Action:

PATTERN	MEASURE
Point your left toe diagonally forward left and hold; put your left foot behind your right; step sideward right.	1
Put your left foot in front of your right and hold; point your right toe forward and hold.	2
Put your right foot behind your left; step sideward to the left. Put your right foot in front of your left and hold.	3
Point your left toe diagonally forward to the left and hold; touch your left toe behind you and hold.	4
Take one schottische step diagonally forward to the left.	5
Take one schottische step diagonally forward to the right. Make one half-turn right on a hop, facing clockwise in the circle and holding the adjacent hands of those on either side of you.	6
Repeat the action of measure 6, moving instead to the left. Finish facing counterclockwise with hands still joined.	7
Beginning on your right foot, walk three short steps forward.	8

Csebogar (Hungarian)

Record: Victor 20992; Folkraft 1196
Formation: Partners join hands and form a single circle facing the center; the girl is to the right of the boy.

Action:

PATTERN	MEASURE
STEP 1. All move clockwise with eight slides.	1–4
STEP 2. All move counterclockwise with eight slides.	5–8
STEP 3. With hands still joined and held high, take four skips toward the center of the circle.	9–10
Lower your hands; skip backward to your original place.	11–12
STEP 4. Partners face each other and place their right arms around waist and raise left arm high, with elbow straight.	
Skip eight times turning clockwise.	13–16

(Variation. Upper grades may use eight paddle steps, or the Hungarian. Turn twice, around with a hop right, step left, and step right.)

STEP 5. All face partners; join both hands and step sideways toward center of circle, closing with opposite foot in four slow slides, or draws.	17–20
Repeat to outside of circle.	21–24
STEP 6. Repeat action of Step 5 with two draw steps.	25–28
STEP 7. Repeat Step 4.	29–32

Gustaf's Skoal (Swedish)

Record: Victor 20988; Folkraft 1175
Formation: Square of four couples
Action: "Skoal" is a formal greeting.

PATTERN	MEASURE
STEP 1. The head couples take three steps forward and bow on the fourth count.	1–2
STEP 2. The head couples take three steps backward and put their face together on the fourth count.	3–4
STEP 3. The side couples do the same.	5–8
STEP 4. Repeat all.	1–8
STEP 5. The side couples join inside hands and form an arch. The head couples skip toward each other and take new partners. They skip through the arch, the girls going right, the boys left. They leave their new partners and return to their original positions, meeting their own partners.	9–12
STEP 6. All clap hands, join both hands with partners, and make one complete turn.	13–16
STEP 7. The side couples repeat Step 5, with the head couples forming the arch.	9–16

All repeat Step 6.

Danish Dance of Greeting

Record: Victor 17158; Folkraft 1187
Formation: Single circle of dancers facing the center with their hands on their hips

Action:

PATTERN	MEASURE
STEP 1. Clap hands twice; turn to your partner and bow. Clap hands twice; turn and bow to your neighbor.	1–2
STEP 2. Stamp right; stamp left; turn in place four running steps.	3–4

Repeat measures 1 and 2.	1–4
STEP 3. All join hands and take sixteen running steps to the right.	5–8
Repeat to the left. Repeat the entire dance.	9–16

Chimes of Dunkirk (Flemish)

Record:	World of Fun Series, M-105
Formation:	Double circle of partners facing each other, the boys having their backs to the center
Action:	

PATTERN	MEASURE
STEP 1. Clap three times; pause.	1–4
STEP 2. Partners join both hands and walk around the circle in eight counts.	5–8
STEP 3. Partners join right hands and balance. Repeat.	9–12
STEP 4. Partners walk around each other once and the boy moves on to his left to the next girl.	13–16

Ace of Diamonds (English)

Record:	Victor 20989; World of Fun Series, M-102
Formation:	Double circle of partners facing each other, the boys having their backs to the center of the circle
Action:	

PATTERN	MEASURE
STEP 1. Partners clap hands once, stamp a foot once, and hook right arms and swing around once.	1–4
Repeat, using left arm.	5–8
STEP 2. The girl puts her hand on her hips and moves backward toward the center of the circle with a step and a hop. She steps left and hops left. She steps right and hops right. She repeats this movement. The boy follows with his arms crossed on his chest. He steps right and hops right twice. He repeats this action.	
They return in reverse.	9–16
STEP 3. They polka in skating position, going counterclockwise.	1–16

Troika (Russian)

Record:	Kismet S112; Folkraft 1170
Formation:	Groups of three facing counterclockwise. The center dancer is a boy; the outside dancers are girls. Their hands are joined; their free hands are on their hips.
Action:	

PATTERN	MEASURE
Figure I.	
STEP 1. Take four running steps forward diagonally to the right.	1
STEP 2. Repeat diagonally to the left.	2

STEP 3. Take eight running steps forward around in a circle.	3–4
STEP 4. Still holding her partner's hand, the girl on the boy's right runs under the arch made by the boy and girl on the left. The other two run in place.	5–6
STEP 5. The girl on the left runs under the arch and back to her place in eight steps.	7–8

FIGURE II.

STEP 1. Each group of three joins hands in a circle and runs to the left (clockwise) for 12 steps, beginning on the left foot.	9–11
STEP 2. Stamp in place—left, right, left. Repeat Steps 1 and 2 running to the right (counterclockwise).	12 13–16
Release hands and repeat the entire dance with the same partners. Partners may change in measure 16. Girls raise outside hands to make an arch and release the boy, and he runs with four steps to the next group while the girls stamp in place.	16

Green Sleeves (English)

Record:	Folk Fun Funfest (Dick Kraus) Educational Dance Recordings, P.O. Box 6062, Bridgeport 6, Connecticut
Formation:	Double circle in sets of two couples, numbered 1 and 2, facing counterclockwise, with the girls on the right
Action:	STEP 1. Holding hands, the couples walk forward 16 steps. STEP 2. The couples form a star in sets. Boy No. 1 gives his hand to girl No. 2, and boy No. 2 gives his hand to girl No. 1. They walk clockwise eight steps; they change to left hands and walk back to their place counterclockwise. STEP 3. Couple No. 1 join hands and walk backward under the arch made by couple No. 2, who walk forward four steps, then walk backward while couple No. 1 makes the arch. Repeat the entire dance.

Tropanka (Bulgarian)

Record:	Folk Dancer Record—Disc Album 635
Formation:	Single circle of dancers with little fingers joined
Action:	Stamping step: Cross your foot over in front in ballet position with the heel turned out.

PATTERN	MEASURE
STEP 1. Beginning on the right foot, take five running steps to the right and stamp twice with the left foot. Turn and run to the left five steps and stamp twice with the right foot.	1–2 3–4
Repeat the first four measures.	1–4
STEP 2. Facing center, all step on the right foot, hop on the right foot, and swing the left foot in front. Step, hop, and swing, starting on the left foot.	5
Step on the right foot; cross the left foot over and stamp twice.	6
Repeat measures 5 and 6, starting on the left foot.	7–8
Repeat measures.	5–8

STEP 3.   Moving toward the center of the circle, all starting
on the right foot, they step-hop right, step and hop left. They   5
step right and stamp twice with the left foot. With their arms
raised high, they shout "Hey!"   6
They repeat the action of measures 5 and 6, dancing backward and starting with their left feet. Gradually they lower
their arms. They dance to measures 9 through 16 as in
measures 1 through 9.

Cherkessia (Israeli)

Record:	Sonart Folk Dance Album M8
Formation:	Single circle of dancers with hands joined
Teaching Suggestions:	There should be quite a bit of bending backward and forward and swinging of joined hands as the dance progresses. On the verse the circle moves to the right; on the chorus the circle moves to the left.
Action:	

PATTERN	MEASURE
CHORUS. The dance begins with the chorus and is repeated after each figure. The circle moves to the left. All leap on the right foot across and in front of the left (count 1), step to the side with the left foot (count 2), step across and behind the left foot with the right foot (count 1), and step to the side with the left foot (count 2).	1–2
Repeat the first two measures three times.	3–8
Bend forward on steps to the front and lean backward on steps to the back.	
FIGURE I. The circle moves to the right with 16 steps. All step to the side on the right foot, extending the left leg to the side (count 1); they place the left foot behind the right and bend both knees slightly (count 2).	9
Repeat seven times.	10–16
CHORUS	1–8
FIGURE II. Step-hop—all turn to the right and step on the right foot with the left leg (bent at the knee) extended backward; they hop on the right foot (count 1). They do the same on the left foot (count 2).	9–10
Repeat the actions of measures 9 and 10 for the remainder of music.	11–16
CHORUS	1–8
FIGURE III. The feet are held close together. All move toes to the right (count 1); all move both heels to the right (count 2). Repeat.	9–16
CHORUS	1–8
FIGURE IV. All kick alternate feet forward 16 times, beginning with the right.	9–16
CHORUS	1–8
FIGURE V. All kick alternate feet backward 16 times. Lean forward.	9–16
CHORUS	1–8
FIGURE VI. All turn to the right and move forward in the circle with 16 shuffle steps done in a semicrouch position. The shuffle is a step right, close left, step right. End the dance by raising joined hands high in the air.	9–16

Tinikling⁹ or the Bamboo Hop¹⁰ (Philippine)

Action:

PATTERN	MEASURE

Leap from the left foot (outside poles) onto the right foot
and hop right (inside poles).

INTRODUCTION. Stand. The boys have their hands on their hips; the girls hold their skirts.	3/4
	4
Stand (count 1) and tap your right foot twice between the poles (counts 2 and 3).	4
Repeat the above directions three times.	3

FIGURE I.   The front tiniklings start with the left foot and
do seven tinikling steps. When starting from the left foot
the right hand is at about head level.

1	2	3

When starting with the right foot, the left hand is up.	7
The front tiniklings do one turning bamboo hop. They repeat	1
Figure I, starting with the right foot. The girl must back up to finish at the opposite end of the pole, facing the boy.	8
FIGURE II. The walking tiniklings walk three steps forward (left, right, left) and then do one turning tinikling step, starting with the right foot. The girl holds her skirt; the boy has his hands on his hips.	2
Repeat twice moving.	

⁹The "Tinikling" is a bird with long legs and neck. This dance imitates the movements of the birds
as they are trying not to be trapped by the movement of the sticks.

¹⁰Reproduced by permission from Texas Education Agency, Austin, Physical Education in the Elementary School. 1971, Grade 6. pp. 649–651.

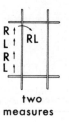

two
measures

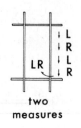

two
measures

Repeat twice, moving to the other end of the poles. Walk forward three steps (right, left, right), and then do one turning bamboo hop.

4

Repeat Figure II, this time moving in the opposite direction. The last hop is done outside, ending with both feet outside, facing the pole. The boy and girl are on the same side, inside hands joined.

2

8

first
measure

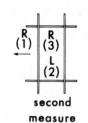

second
measure

FIGURE III.   The side tiniklings take one tinikling step forward, followed by a leap forward (outside), a step backward (inside), and a step in place.

Repeat, alternating forward and backward across the poles. End outside of the poles by stepping forward (outside) and then taking one turning step in place (outside).

1

Repeat Figure III, starting across the other pole. End facing your partner.

8

1   2

Do a double bamboo hop 16 times. Jump, placing your feet apart (outside). At the same time, bring your arms up; then jump twice with your feet together (inside), bringing your arms to your sides. The girl turns at the end so that both are facing in the same direction, the girl being in front of the boy.

16

Cross Bamboo Hop (Philippine)

Action:

PATTERN

MEASURE

FIGURE I.   Facing forward, take one bamboo hop, crossing your left foot in front of your right (outside). The girl holds her skirt; the boy has his hands on his hips.

1

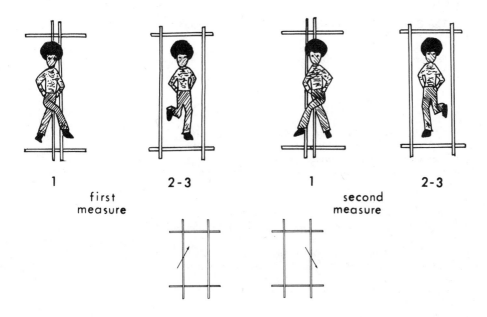

1   **2 - 3**   1   **2 - 3**

first   second

measure   measure

Bamboo hop (without crossing to the left side of the poles).	1
Repeat A, 1 and 2 twice.	4
Repeat A, one bamboo hop turning right.	2
Repeat the figure. The girl backs up to end in the same position as for the end of the first figure.	2
FIGURE II. Diagonal tiniklings step in place (count 1), bring their arms up, step diagonally forward (inside), and step (inside).	1
Bringing their arms down, they leap diagonally backward (outside the other pole), step, and step (inside).	
Repeat 1 and 2 twice, moving diagonally forward and backward, crossing one pole and then the other.	4
Repeat 1, and then do one turning tinikling.	2
Repeat the figure.	8
At the end, bow or curtsy.	

Broom Dance (German)

Record: Victor 20448
Formation: Couples form a double circle facing counterclockwise. One child is left in the center of the circle with a broom.
Action:

PATTERN	MEASURE
PART 1. Couples march around the room to the music, and the child in the center gives the broom to someone in the circle and takes his place. This one gives the broom to another quickly and takes his place, and so on for eight measures.	1–8
PART 2. The child who has the broom at the end of the eighth measure must dance with the broom in the center of the circle while the couples skip around singing "Tra, la, la" through eight measures; the dance begins again with the center dancer passing the broom on.	9–11
The verse and music may be found in the listed references.	

The Crested Hen (Danish)

Record: Folkraft 1194[11]
Formation: Sets of three (one boy with a girl on either side).
Action:

PATTERN	MEASURE
STEP. The hop-step is done through the entire dance. Step on the left foot on count 1, hop on the left foot; swing the right foot in front of it on count 2, keeping the knee bent. Reverse and step-hop on the right foot; swing the left foot to the front.	
FIGURE I. The three dancers in each set join hands to form circles. Moving to the left (clockwise) they stamp their left feet and do eight step-hops. Dancers lean back as they circle.	1–8
FIGURE II. Girls release hands and place their free hands on hips. Boy never releases the hands. The girl at the left of the boy dances (step-hops) in front of him and under the arch made by the raised hands of the boy and the girl on the right.	9–12
Repeat the same action with the girl on the right, passing through the arch.	13–16

Mayim[12] (Israeli)

Record: Folkraft 1108a
Formation: Students stand in a circle facing center with hands joined and down.
Action: STEP 1.   Take four circasia combinations to the left. For each circasia combination, place the right foot in front and across the left (accent right foot); bring the left foot alongside the right foot; place your right foot back, across the left foot, to the left; and hop on left foot alongside the right foot.
STEP 2.   All take eight steps toward the center of the circle, lifting their hands gradually, accentuating the first step by raising the right knee.
STEP 3.   All face left and take four walking steps toward the left, starting with the right foot.
STEP 4.   While hopping on the right foot, tap with the left foot over the right foot. Then tap with the left foot to the left side. This combination is done four times.
STEP 5.   While hopping on the left foot, tap the right foot over the left foot. Then tap with the right foot to the right side. Slap hands on the odd beat. This combination is done four times.
This dance is supposed to convey the movement of water, of waves, and of going toward the well, and the joy of discovering water in an arid country.

Raatikko (Scandinavian)

Record: Folk Dancer Record 1123 (Finnish Polka—Old Maid's Dance).
Formation: Couple in social dance position
Action: STEP 1.   Take right polka steps, turning clockwise.

---

[11]Neilson, N. P., and Van Hagen, W.: *Physical Education for Elementary Schools.* New York, A. S. Barnes & Company, 1960.
[12]Maine Folk Dance Camp. Contributed by Michael Herman.

STEP 2. Do four draw-steps. The boy has the girl by one arm, pulling her, and the girl moves reluctantly toward the rock.
STEP 3. Take eight slide steps away from the rock.
STEP 4. Repeat Steps 2 and 3.
Repeat all.

Background: On the coast of Finland, there is a large rock close to the beach. According to the story, if a boy succeeds in pulling a girl behind the rock, she will be an old maid.

Gie Gordon's (Scottish)

Record: Beltona Record BL–2455; Folkraft 1162 (The Gray Gordons)
Formation: Couples in varsouvienne position
Action: STEP 1. Both start on the left foot. They take four walking steps forward. They reverse and take four walking steps backward but continue in the same line of direction.
Repeat.
STEP 2. The boy holds the girl's right hand high with his right hand and polkas forward as the girl does four polka steps (clockwise) turning under the boy's arm.
STEP 3. In social dance position, they do four polka steps turning clockwise. Repeat the entire dance.

Finger Polka (Lithuanian)

Record: Standard Record 2001A
Formation: Couples form a double circle facing counterclockwise, with boys on the inside of the circle
Action: STEP 1. Couples take eight polka steps in open position (holding inside hands, starting the hop on the outside foot and so forth, back to back and face to face).
STEP 2. They take eight polka steps in closed position, turning clockwise.
STEP 3. They drop hands and face their partners. They stamp three times; they clap their own hands three times, and repeat. They shake right fingers at their partners; they make turns on their own left, slapping their right hands against their partners' right hands as the turn is taken. They stamp three times.
Repeat the entire dance.

Road to the Isles (Scottish)

Record: Imperial 1005A
Formation: Couples in varsouvienne position
Action:

PATTERN	MEASURE
STEP 1. Point your left toe forward and hold. Do a grapevine step, moving to the right. Step your left foot behind your right foot; step your right to your side; step your left foot in front of your right foot and hold.	1 2–3
Point your right toe forward and hold, and do the grapevine step to the left, stepping right, left, and right and holding.	4 5–6
Point your left toe forward and hold.	7
Point your left toe backward in a deep dip and hold.	8
STEP 2. Schottische forward diagonally to the left, beginning on your left foot (left; right; left; hop).	9–10

	MEASURE
Schottische forward diagonally to the right, beginning on the right foot (right; left; right; hop). On the hop, on measure 12, half-turn to the right, facing in the opposite direction and keeping hands joined.	11–12
Schottische, beginning on the left foot. On the hop, take a half-turn to the left, facing original direction.	13–14
In place, step right, left, and right, and hold.	15–16

Bleking (Swedish)

Record: Victor 20989; Folkraft 1188
Formation: Partners face each other with both hands joined.
Action:

PATTERN	MEASURE
STEP 1. Bleking step: Jump lightly to your left foot, placing your right heel to the floor (count 1). Seesaw your arms by extending your right arm forward with the elbows straight and your left arm backward with the elbow bent. Reverse arms and jump lightly on the right foot, placing your left heel to the floor (count 2).	1
Repeat Bleking step three times in quick succession (count 1 and 2).	2
Repeat measures 1 and 2 three times.	3–8
STEP 2. Extend your arms sideward and turn in a clockwise direction with 16 step-hops, alternately raising and lowering your arms and kicking your free leg to the side. Repeat the entire dance.	9–16

Polka (Polish)

Record: 2/4 or 6/8 Time Record—Basic Polka Steps, Educational Activities, Inc.
Formation: Couple in social dance position, with the boy and girl starting from opposite feet. Skaters or varsouvienne positions may also be used.
Action:

PATTERN	MEASURE
Basic Polka Step	Measure 1
Hop on the right foot.	Count "and"
Step forward on the left foot.	Count 1
Bring the right foot to the left foot (transfer your weight to the right foot).	Count "and"
Step forward on the left foot.	Count 2
	Measure 2
Hop on the left foot.	Count "and"
Step forward on the right foot.	Count 1
Bring the left foot to the right foot (transfer your weight to the left foot).	Count "and"
Step forward on the right foot.	Count 2
Heel and Toe Polka	Measure 1
Touch the heel of one foot forward and lean backward.	Count 1 "and"
Touch the toe of the same foot to the rear and lean forward.	Count 2 "and"
	Measure 2
Step to the side (partners facing each other) or step forward on the left foot (side by side).	Count 1

Bring the right foot to the left foot (transfer the weight to the right foot).	Count "and"
Step forward on the left foot.	Count 2 "and"
Face to Face—Back to Back (partners facing each other and the boy and girl on opposite feet)	Measure 1
Hop on the right foot.	Count "and"
Step to the side on the left foot.	Count 1
Close the right foot to the left foot (transfer your weight to the right foot).	Count "and"
Step to the side again on the left foot.	Count 2
	Measure 2
Hop on the left foot, and while hopping, pivot and be back to back with your partner.	Count "and"
Step to the side on the right foot.	Count 1
Close the left foot to the right foot (transfer your weight to the left foot).	Count "and"
Step to the side again on the right foot.	Count 2

Schottische

Record:	2/4 or 4/4 Time Record—Basic Schottische Steps, Educational Activities, Inc.
Formation:	Social dance position, with the boy and girl on opposite feet. Skaters or varsouvienne positions may also be used.
Action:	

PATTERN	MEASURE
Basic Schottische	1
Step forward on the left foot.	Count 1
Bring the right foot to the left foot (transfer your weight to the right foot).	Count 2
Step forward with the left foot.	Count 3
Hop on the left foot (the right foot may be raised and the knee may be bent during the hop).	Count 4
	2
Step forward on the right foot.	Count 1
Bring the left foot to the right foot (transfer your weight to the left foot).	Count 2
Step forward with the right foot.	Count 3
Hop on the right foot (the left foot may be raised and the knee may be bent during the hop).	Count 4
Running Schottische	1
Step forward on the left foot.	Count 1
Step forward on the right foot.	Count 2
Step forward on the left foot.	Count 3
Hop on the left foot.	Count 4
	2
Step forward on the right foot.	Count 1
Step forward on the left foot.	Count 2
Step forward on the right foot.	Count 3
Hop on the right foot.	Count 4

La Raspa (Mexican)

Record:	Methodist World of Fun Series M-106
Formation:	Couples facing each other holding both of each other's hands
Action:	

PATTERN

MEASURE

PART I. Take one Bleking step, beginning right.
(Bleking step: Kick your left foot forward, touch your heel
to the floor, and hop on your right foot. Kick your right foot
forward and touch your heel to the floor, and hop on your
left foot. Repeat this action. Hop on your right foot; kick
your left foot forward, touching your heel to the floor. Repeat
this action three more times.

1–4

Turn so that your right shoulders are together.
Partners are facing opposite directions. Repeat measures
1 to 4.

5–8

Turn your left shoulders together. Repeat 1 to 4 again.

9–12

Repeat 1 to 4, facing your partner.

13–16

PART 2. Hook right elbows; take eight running steps; clap
your own hands on the eighth step.

1–4

Turn to hook your left elbow. Run eight steps. Clap on the
eighth step.

5–8

Repeat measures 1 to 8.

9–15

Variation: Variation of the measures of Part 2 is as follows: Skip eight counts
clockwise, then reverse direction and skip eight counts counterclockwise. Partners hold both hands; for the first eight counts, right
shoulders are together and arms are extended to right. This position
is reversed for the next counts. Polka in skaters' position.

St. Bernard's Waltz (Scottish)

Record: Victor 200FOB
Action: The main steps are the waltz step and the draw step.
PART 1. The boy starts from the left foot, the girl from the right.
Both take three slides and one stamp counterclockwise. They
repeat this action, going clockwise.
PART 2. Beginning on the boy's left and going forward on the
girl's right, they take two draw steps toward the center of the
room; they take two draw steps away from the center. The boy
takes two draw steps to the left while the girl turns under his arm
with two waltz steps.
PART 3. In social dance position, the partners waltz counterclockwise in four waltz steps.

Ten Pretty Girls (American)

Record: Folkraft F1036B
Formation: Circle of partners with hands held in skater's position
Action: The main steps are the grapevine step and the stamp.
PART 1. Both point their left toe across and in front of their right
toe. They then point their left toe sideward to the left. They step
their left foot behind their right foot, step sideward to the right,
and bring their left foot alongside their right. They repeat this
action, starting with the right foot this time.
PART 2. They join inside hands, with elbows held high, and walk
four steps forward. They kick the left foot forward and backward,
and beginning on the left foot, they stamp three times. The boy
moves forward to a new girl partner on the second and third
stamps.

Finnish Spinning Waltz (Finnish)

Record: MacGregor 607; Imperial 1036–A, Methodist World of Fun M-110
Formation: Couples in a double circle. The boys have their backs to the center; the girls face their partners. Their hands are joined.
Action: The main steps are the step swing and the waltz step.

PATTERN	MEASURE
Dancers step on the outside foot (the boy's left, the girl's right).	1
They swing the inside foot across and point the toe.	
They repeat this action, stepping on the inside foot.	2
They slide two steps to the left, side-step, close, and step.	3–4
They repeat.	
The girl turns clockwise under the boy's right arm.	
They turn toward the opposite direction. They repeat the figure with the girl turning the boy.	5–8
They join both hands and slide twice to the boy's left and twice to his right.	9–12
They waltz, turning in a clockwise circle.	13–16

Variation: For a mixer, the boy twirls the girl under his arm during the last two measures and then takes the girl behind him.

Danish Schottische (Danish)

Record: Methodist World of Fun M-102B
Formation: Skater's position
Action:

PATTERN	MEASURE
Take a schottische step to the right, beginning with the right foot.	1
Take a schottische step to the left, beginning left.	2
Step-hop forward—right, left, right, left.	3–4
Repeat the action of measures 1 to 4. On the last step-hop partners turn to face each other. They hold left hands.	5–8
Take a schottische step to the right (away from your partner).	9
Take a schottische step to the left (back to your partner).	10
Sweep your right hand in a big circular motion over your partner's head; place your right hand on your partner's back.	11
Partners look at each other and turn clockwise with four-step-hops.	12
Repeat from the beginning.	

Rumnjsko Kolo (Yugoslavian)

Record: Folk Dancer, Balkan 525
Formation: Single circle of dancers with joined hands held down
Action: The main steps are the walking step, rocking step, and stamp.

PATTERN	MEASURE
Moving backward counterclockwise, take three steps beginning with the right foot. Then hop.	1

	MEASURE
Turn to face the counterclockwise direction and repeat the three steps and hop.	2
Repeat measures 1 and 2.	3–4
Face the center of the circle and step your right foot across your left foot. Rock back to the left. Step right again and then hop on the right foot.	5
Step your left foot across your right foot. Rock back to the right.	6
Step forward on the left foot. Hop on the left foot.	
Repeat measure 5.	7
Stamp three times with your left foot.	8
Repeat measures 5 to 8, beginning on your left foot, and finish with a stamp on your right foot.	9–12
Repeat dance from the beginning.	

Note: Hissing to express pleasure is characteristic of Yugoslavian dances. Also, the feet are barely lifted from the floor.

Eide Ratas (Estonian) (Spinning Wheel)

Record: Folk Dancer MH-1018
Formation: Couples in closed social dance position in a counterclockwise circle.
Action: The main steps are rocking steps and running steps.

PATTERN   MEASURE

	MEASURE
Walk forward two steps, beginning on your outside foot (boy's left, girl's right), and then hop in place on the inside foot (step, step, close). On the first step, leap onto the outside foot and bend forward. Then straighten with the hop on the inside foot.	1
Repeat measure 1.	2
Take six running steps turning clockwise.	3–4
Repeat measures 1 to 4.	5–8
Repeat the entire figure.	9–16
Partners face each other, boys with their backs to the center of the circle. Hands are on hips. Partners take three steps away from each other, beginning on their left feet and turning their right shoulders toward their partners.	17
They take three more steps away, beginning on their right feet and turning their left shoulders toward their partners.	18
Repeat measures 17 and 18.	19–20
Partners move toward each other with running steps. When they meet they lock elbows and continue running for 12 more steps in clockwise direction. The girl now has her back to the center of the circle.	21–24
Repeat measures 17 to 24, hooking left elbows and finishing in your original position.	25–32

Patch Tanz (Clap Dance) (Israeli)

Record: Folk Dance Service 137
Formation: Single circle, with the girls on the boys' right sides. Arms are bent at the elbow, causing the hands to be held at shoulder level.
Action: The main step is the walking step (step, and then bend the knee of the stepping foot to the count "one and").

PATTERN	MEASURE
Take eight walking steps counterclockwise, beginning on the right foot.	1–4
Take eight steps clockwise (to the left), beginning on the right foot.	5–8
Walk two steps forward into the center of the circle, beginning with the right foot.	9
Clap three times (three counts). Pause (one count).	10
Join hands with your partner again. Walk two steps backward; this time the boys begin on the left foot and the girls begin on the right.	11
Stamp three times with your heel.	12
Repeat measures 9 to 12.	13–16
Partners face each other, join hands, and then move to position with their right shoulders almost touching and their arms outstretched to the right. They turn counterclockwise with eight walking steps.	17–20
Turn to the right, counterclockwise, with four walking steps.	21–22
Release outside hands (girl's right, boy's left). The girl walks in front of the boy's left, where she remains. They take four walking steps.	23–24

Lili Marlene (American)

Record:	MacGregor 310A
Formation:	Partners facing counterclockwise with inside hands joined
Action:	The main steps are walking and polka steps.

PART 1. Walk four steps counterclockwise. Face your partner and join both hands. Move in the same direction with four slides. Turn to face clockwise, with the boy still on the inside. Join inside hands and move clockwise with four walking steps and four slide steps.

PART 2. Partners face each other and drop hands. They step right, swing the left foot across and in front of the right, step left, and swing right.

PART 3. Join left hands and go back to your place. Face counterclockwise with inside hands joined, and polka four steps forward, alternating open and closed positions. The girl turns under the partners' joined inside hands and moves forward to the next boy in four walking steps.

Repeat from the beginning.

SOCIAL DANCING

Children who have advanced progressively through fundamental rhythms, singing games, and creative, folk, and square dancing sometimes find themselves ready in the sixth grade for social dancing. Because this is the type of dancing the majority will be doing as they grow older, it is well to expose them to at least the simple fundamentals before they enter junior high school. Basic steps learned in group and couple dances pave the way to this more restrained type of movement; the desire to emulate adult patterns serves as a useful motivating force. The children will get some practice at parties in their own homes, but it is suggested that at school affairs the social dancing be interspersed with folk dances such as mixers, couple and group dances. In this way the future Fred Astaires, Gene Kellys, and Arthur Murrays get an opportunity to "let off steam" and are less likely to become tense in this new field of experience.

Basic fundamentals such as body position, leading, following, turning, the fox trot and the waltz adequately introduce sixth graders to social dancing. Teachers who desire additional information will find it worthwhile to read the listed references.

If you have seen the latest in the Hustle and other "disco" dances and wonder where one should start with social dancing, you are not exactly alone. True, this text is Victorian by comparison, but we cannot help feeling that with a little aging the young ones will come around to a more sedate form of dancing. In the meantime, let them shake, rattle, roll, and jerk. We do not feel that instructions are necessary.

DANCE TERMINOLOGY

ALLEMANDE LEFT.   The boy and the corner face each other, join left hands, and walk around each other and back to their places.

ALLEMANDE RIGHT.   Partners join right hands and walk around each other and back to their places.

BALANCE.   Step forward on your left foot; step your right foot forward beside your left and rise slightly on your toes. Step backward on your right, step back your left beside your right and rise slightly on your toes. In square dance, take two steps backward and bow to your partner.

BREAK.   Release hands (used in square dances).

CORNER.   The girl is on the boy's left; the boy is on the girl's right.

DOS-A-DOS.   The boy and girl circle each other, passing right shoulder to right shoulder and back to back, returning to original position.

DO-SI-DO.   The boy faces his partner; both join left hands and walk around (counterclockwise) until each is facing his corner; they join right hands with their corners and walk around (clockwise) to their original positions.

DRAW STEP.   Step to the side on the left foot and draw the right foot to the left, shifting your weight to the right foot.

ELBOW SWING.   Hook right or left elbows and swing around once.

FOOT COUPLES.   Last couples in a longways set.

GRAND RIGHT AND LEFT.   Partners face, touch right hands and pass on by to the next person, touch left hands, and continue in this manner around the circle until the partners meet again. The boys move counterclockwise, the girls clockwise. In square dancing, an allemande left usually precedes the grand right and left and partners promenade home when they meet.

GRAPEVINE.   Step your left foot to the side; step your right foot behind the left; step your left foot to the side; step your right foot in front of the left.

HEAD COUPLES.   First and third couples in a set.

HOME POSITION.   Original position of each dancer in the set.

MARCHING.   Walking in a military or dignified manner with even steps.

PADDLE STEP.   Weight is on the left foot. Pivot on the left, turning clockwise and stepping around with the right.

POLKA.   Weight is on the left foot. Hop on the left; step on the right; bring the left to the right and transfer the weight to the right foot. Hop on the right, and so forth (very often in folk dancing the hop is left off). Hop; step; close; step.

POSITIONS

CLOSED POSITION.   (Ballroom or social dance position.) Partners face each other; the boy has his right arm around the girl's waist; the girl has her left hand on the boy's right shoulder. The boy holds the girl's left hand in his right hand at about shoulder level with the elbow slightly bent.

OPEN POSITION.   Partners are side by side facing the same direction. The boy has his right arm around the girl's waist, and the girl has her left hand on the boy's right shoulder. The free hands may, as the dance demands, hang loosely or be placed on the hips.

SKATER'S POSITION.   See Promenade.

VARSOUVIENNE POSITION.   Partners face in the same direction, the girl slightly to the front of the boy. The boy holds the girl's left hand in his left hand at shoulder level and extends his right arm across the girl's shoulders and holds her right hand in his right hand.

PROMENADE.   Each boy takes his partner in skater's position, and all couples move counterclockwise around the circle. Partners stand side by side; the girl is on the boy's right. The boy takes his girl's left hand in his left hand and her right hand in his right. His right arm is over her left arm.

SCHOTTISCHE.   Step left; step right; step left; hop left—run, run, run, hop, or one, two, three, hop.

SHUFFLE.   A flowing one-step with feet in contact with the floor. This is the principal step in square dancing and when done properly gives the impression that the dancer is moving without any apparent effort.

SIDE COUPLES.   Couples 2 and 4 in a set.

STEP-HOP.   Step on the left; hop on the left; step on the right; hop on the right.

STEP-SWING.   Step on the left, swinging the right leg forward in front of the left. Step right and swing your left leg over.

TWO-STEP.   Step forward left; bringing your right foot to your left; step forward left. Step forward right; bring your left foot to your right; step forward right. Teach: Step, close, step.

WALTZ.   Step forward left on count 1; step forward right on count 2; close your left foot to your right on count 3. Step right; step left; close your right to your left.

SUGGESTED READINGS

Andrews, G.: *Creative Rhythmic Movement For Children.* Englewood Cliffs, New Jersey, Prentice-Hall, Inc., 1975.

Bucher, C., and Reade, E. M.: *Physical Education in the Modern Elementary School.* New York, The Macmillan Company, 1972.

Burton, E.: *The New Physical Education for Elementary School Children.* New York, Houghton Mifflin Company, 1976.

Clarke, H. H., and Harr, F. B.: *Health and Physical Education for the Elementary School Classroom Teacher.* Englewood Cliffs, New Jersey, Prentice-Hall, Inc., 1964.

Gilbert, C.: *International Folk Dance at a Glance.* 2nd ed. Minneapolis, Burgess Publishing Company, 1974.

Hall, J. T.: *Dance: A Complete Guide to Social, Folk and Square Dancing.* Belmont, California. Wadsworth Publishing Company, 1963.

Jensen, C., and Jensen, M. B.: *Beginning Square Dancing.* Belmont, California, Wadsworth Press, 1966.

Kraus, R.: *A Pocket Guide of Folk and Square Dances and Singing Games for the Elementary School.* Englewood Cliffs, New Jersey, Prentice-Hall, Inc., 1966.

Latchaw, M.: *A Pocket Guide of Games and Rhythms for the Elementary School.* Englewood Cliffs, New Jersey, Prentice-Hall, Inc., 1970.

Lidstir, M. D., and Tamburini, D. H.: *Folk Dance Progressions*. Belmont, California, Wadsworth Publishing Company, 1965.

Murray, R.: *Dance in Elementary Education*. New York, Harper & Row, Publisher, 1975.

Mynatt, C., and Kaiman, B.: *Folk Dancing For Students and Teachers*. Dubuque, Iowa, William C. Brown Company, Publishers, 1968.

Spiesman, M.: *Folk Dancing*. Philadelphia, W. B. Saunders Company, 1970.

Taylor, C.: *Rhythm: A Guide for Creative Movement*. Mountain View, California, Peek Publications, 1973.

Vick, M., and Cox, R.: *A Collection of Dances for Children*. Minneapolis, Burgess Publishing Company, 1970.

Wakefield, E.: *Folk Dancing In America*. New York, J. Lowell Pratt Company, 1966.

Winters, S.: *Creative Rhythmic Movement for Children of Elementary School Age*. Dubuque, Iowa, William C. Brown Company, Publishers, 1975.

PERIODICALS

Country Dancer. The Country Dance Society of America, 31 Union Square West, New York, New York 10003. Published irregularly.

Let's Dance. Folk Dance Federation of California, Inc., 1604 Felton Street, San Francisco, California 94134. Published 10 times per year.

Northern Junket. Ralph Page, editor, 117 Washington Street, Keene, New Hampshire 03431. Published monthly.

Resin the Bow. 115 Cliff Street, Paterson, New Jersey 07522. Published quarterly.

Sets in Order, the Official Magazine of Square Dancing. 462 N. Robertson Blvd., Los Angeles, California 90048. Published monthly.

Square Dance (formerly *American Square*). Arvid Olson, editor, 1622 N. Rand Road, Arlington Heights, Illinois 60004. Published monthly.

RECORD SOURCES

Bowman Records, 4921 Santa Monica Boulevard, Los Angeles 29, California.

Stanley Bowmar Company, 12 Cleveland Street, Valhalla, New York.

Burns Record Company, 755 Chickadee Lane, Stratford, Connecticut.

Capitol Records, Sunset and Vine, Hollywood, California.

Childhood Rhythms (Vols. I, II, VI), 326 Forest Park Avenue, Springfield, Massachusetts.

Educational Activities, Inc., P.O. Box 392, Freeport, Long Island, New York 11520.

Folkraft Record Company, 7 Oliver Street, Newark, New Jersey.

Folkways, 117 W. 46th Street, New York, New York.

Henlee Record Company, 2404 Harris, Austin, Texas.

Michael Herman, Folk Dance Records, Box 201, Flushing, Long Island, New York.

Hoctor Dance Records, Waldwick, New Jersey 07463.

Israeli Music Foundation, 731 Broadway, New York, New York.

Kimbo Records, Box 55, Deal, New Jersey 07723.

Le Crone Rhythm Record Company, 9203 Nichols Road, Oklahoma City, Oklahoma 73120.

MacGregor Records, 2005 Labranch, Houston, Texas.

David McKay Company, Inc., 119 W. 40th Street, New York, New York. Rhythms for primary and intermediate grades, folk dances, and social dances.

Methodist World of Fun Series, Methodist Publishing House, Nashville, Tennessee. Singing games, folk dances, couple dances, and so forth.

Phoebe James Products, Box 134, Pacific Palisades, California.

Playtime Records. These records are nonbreakable, cost very little, and are found in most drug stores and record shops. Each contains a simple rhyme or singing game.

Radio Corporation of America, RCA Victor Division, Camden, New Jersey.

Record Center, 2581 Piedmont Road N.E., Atlanta, Georgia 30324.

Rhythms Productions, Capricorn Records, Affiliates of Woodcliff Productions.

VISUAL AIDS, WORDS, AND MUSIC

Bertail, I.: *Complete Nursery Song Book*. New York, Lathrop, Lee and Shephard Company, 1947.

Building Children's Personality Through Creative Dancing. Extension Department, Bureau of Visual Instruction, University of California, Berkeley, California (film).

Durlacher, E.: *Honor Your Partner.* New York, The Devin-Adair Co., 1949.
Gomez, W. L.: *Merry Songs for Boys and Girls.* New York, Follett Publishing Company, 1949.
Lomax, J., and Lomax, A.: *The 111 Best American Ballads, Folk Songs, U.S.A.* 2nd ed. New York, Duell, Sloan and Pearce, 1947.
Materials for Teaching Dance, Vol. III, Selected Visual Aids for Dance. Washington 6, D.C., National Section on Dance by the AAHPER, 1201 16th Street, N.W.
Wilson, J.: *Children's Pieces.* 56 Jane Street, New York, N.Y. Book I, six pieces, Book II, 7 pieces. Include such as "Night Magic," "The Sick Lamb," "Early Morning Song," and "The Lost Balloon."

SUGGESTED RECORDS FOR CREATIVE MOVEMENT EXPERIENCES

Activity Songs—Facts, Fancies and Experiences of Children. Record A 102. Rhythms Productions, Capricorn Records, Affiliates of Woodcliff Productions.
All-American Dance Winners. Educational Activities, Inc., P.O. Box 392, Freeport, Long Island, New York 11520.
American Folk Dances. Imperial Records.
And the Beat Goes On For Physical Education. KEA 5020–C. Folk rock. Kimbo Educational Record Company, P.O. Box 477, Long Branch, New Jersey 07740.
Ball Gymnastics. KIM 4031–C, 4030–C. Kimbo Educational Record Company, P.O. Box 477, Long Branch, New Jersey 07740.
Balloons. Educational Department, RCA Victor Records, 155 E. 24th Street, New York, New York.
Ballroom Dance Record Series. RRLPS–1007. Kimbo Educational Record Company, P.O. Box 477, Long Branch, New Jersey 07740.
Baltic Dances. Imperial Records.
Basic Latin Dances. HI11 1–C. Kimbo Educational Record Company, P.O. Box 477, Long Branch, New Jersey 07740.
The Brave Hunter. Educational Department, RCA Victor Records, 155 E. 24th Street, New York, New York.
Burns, J., and Wheeler, E.: *Creative Rhythm Album.* A visit to a farm, park, and circus. Stanley Bowmar Company, 12 Cleveland Street, Valhalla, New York.
Clap, Snap and Tap. EA 48–C. Kimbo Educational Record Company, P.O. Box 477, Long Branch, New Jersey 07740.
Come Dance with Me. RRLPS–1010. Kimbo Educational Record Company, P.O. Box 477, Long Branch, New Jersey 07740.
Contemporary Tinikling Activities. KEA 8095–C. Kimbo Educational Activities. Record Company, P.O. Box 477, Long Branch, New Jersey 07740.
Cooperative Activities. Educational Activities, Inc., P.O. Box 392, Freeport, Long Island, New York 11520.
Creative Rhythms for Children. Phoebe James Products, Box 134, Pacific Palisades, California.
Dance Me A Story. Educational Department, RCA Victor Records, 155 E. 24th Street, New York, New York.
Dances Without Partners. Educational Activities, Inc., P.O. Box 392, Freeport, Long Island, New York 11520.
Durlacher, E.: *Honor Your Partner.* Square Dance Associates, 102 N. Columbus Avenue, Freeport, Long Island, New York.
Exercise is Kid Stuff. KIM 2070–C. Kimbo Educational Record Company, P.O. Box 477, Long Branch, New Jersey 07740.
Flappy and Floppy. Educational Department, RCA Victor Records, 155 E. 24th Street, New York, New York.
Folk Dance Funfest. Educational Dance, FD–1, FD–2, FD–3, FD–4 (Dick Kraus). David McKay Company, 119 W. 40th Street, New York, New York.
Folk Dances from 'Round the World, Series I through V. Records LP–106, A 110. Instructions included. Rhythms Publications, Capricorn Records, Affiliates of Woodcliff Productions.
Holiday Time Album. No. 302. Bowman Records, 4921 Santa Monica Boulevard, Los Angeles 29, California.
Israeli Folk Dances. Direction book included. 731 Broadway, New York, New York.
Jewish Folk Dances. Vols. I and II. Ultra Records, New York, New York. Also available from Michael Herman, Box 201, Flushing, Long Island, New York.
Keep on Steppin'. Educational Activities, Inc., P.O. Box 392, Freeport, Long Island, New York 11520.
Library of International Dances. Folkraft Record Company, 7 Oliver Street, Newark, New Jersey.
Little Duck. Educational Department, RCA Victor Records, 155 E. 24th Street, New York, New York.
Living With Rhythms Series—Basic Rhythms for Primary Grades; Animal Rhythms; Rhythms and Meter Appreciation; Rhythms for Physical Fitness (Dick Kraus). David McKay Company, 119 W. 40th Street, New York, New York.
The Magic Mountain. Educational Department, RCA Victor Records, 155 E. 24th Street, New York, New York.

Make Believe in Movement. KIM 0500–C. Kimbo Educational Record Company, P.O. Box 477, Long Branch, New Jersey 07740.

Modern Jazz Movements. KIM 3030–C. Kimbo Educational Record Company, P.O. Box 477, Long Branch, New Jersey 07740.

Move Along Alphabet. KIM 0510–C. Kimbo Educational Record Company, P.O. Box 477, Long Branch, New Jersey 07740.

Music for Modern Dance. KIM 6090–C. Kimbo Educational Record Company, P.O. Box 477, Long Branch, New Jersey 07740.

Noah's Ark. Educational Department, RCA Victor Records, 155 E. 24th Street, New York, New York.

Primary Musical Games. Educational Activities, Inc., P.O. Box 392, Freeport, Long Island, New York 11520.

Railroad Rhythms. Record AF 101. Musical score by Ruth White. Instructions included. Rhythms Productions, Capricorn Records, Affiliates of Woodcliff Productions.

Rainbow Rhythms. Piano recordings arranged and recorded by Nora Belle Emerson, edited by Thomas E. McDonough. Four series, 78 rpm with instructions included in each set. P.O. Box 608, Emory University, Atlanta, Georgia.

RCA Victor Record Library for Elementary Schools. Includes *Music of American Indians,* with instructions and suggestions for 16 dances; *Rhythmic Activities*—five volumes for primary and upper grades; and *Singing Games.* Radio Corporation of America, RCA Victor Division, Camden, New Jersey.

Records for Folk Dances and Games. Educational Activities, Inc., P.O. Box 392, Freeport, Long Island, New York 11520.

Rhythmic Rope Jumping. Educational Activities, Inc., P.O. Box 392, Freeport, Long Island, New York 11520.

Rhythms for Basic Motor Skills. KIM 9074–C. Kimbo Educational Record Company, P.O. Box 477, Long Branch, New Jersey 07740.

Rhythms of the World. Birds, Beasts, Bugs, and Little Fishes. Folkways, 117 W. 46th Street, New York, New York.

Russian Folk Dances. Imperial Records.

Scandinavian Folk Dance Album. Michael Herman, Box 201, Flushing, Long Island, New York.

Sonart Folk Dance Album. M-8. Sonart Record Corporation, 251 W. 42nd Street, New York, New York. Can be ordered from Michael Herman.

Square Dance Albums. Capitol, Disc, Keystone, and others.

Square Dances: (Without calls). Jimmy Clossin. Imperial Records.

Square Dances: (With calls). Lee Bedford, Jr. Imperial Records.

Swiss Folk Dance Album. M-8. Columbia Recording Company, Bridgeport, Connecticut.

Texas Square Dance Music. Without calls. Henlee Record Company, 2404 Harris, Austin, Texas.

Tinikling. KEA 9015–C. Kimbo Educational Record Company, P.O. Box 477, Long Branch, New Jersey 07740.

To Move Is To Be. Educational Activities, Inc., P.O. Box 392, Freeport, Long Island, New York 11520.

World of Fun. Educational Activities, Inc., P.O. Box 392, Freeport, Long Island, New York 11520.

Ye Old Time Night: Cowboy Dances. Decca Album A–524. Called by Lloyd Shaw. Book of instructions included. Decca Records.

CHAPTER TWENTY

STUNTS, TUMBLING, PYRAMIDS, AND TRAMPOLINING

Your body is a marvelous machine. As its manager-engineer you regulate it almost as you wish.

Bruce Frederick

A program that excludes self-testing activities, stunts, and tumbling has missed a golden opportunity in aiding the development of the whole child. The abundant use of large muscles in these activities, plus the development of fine coordination, flexibility, balance, and timing, round out the muscle-building process in a most satisfactory manner. The resultant body control gives a sureness of movement and confidence to the child that cannot be gained through any other aspect of the total physical education program.

Physical and social end-results more than justify the inclusion of these activities. The pleasure derived from viewing one's progress gives stature to all, but particularly to the boy or girl who does not take naturally to sports, i.e., the frail or obese child. Individual disciplined control necessary for good performance in class carries over into play and social life.

FIGURE 20–1. The crab walk is great fun for children. (Courtesy of *The Instructor.* Photograph by Edith Brockway.)

Elementary school children do not have to be sold on this part of the program if it is scaled to their age and skill level. The majority will look forward with enthusiasm to periods spent learning stunts and tumbling. The cause for the small percentage of holdbacks can be traced generally to family objections, where the word tumbling is used in a general way to include all self-testing activities. Parents have visions of their children hurtling through space with resulting neck and back injuries. This fear is inevitably transferred to the child. Public demonstrations of grade-level accomplishments coupled with thorough explanations of each activity will give parents and children alike new appreciation of the program. People support things in which they believe!

EQUIPMENT

The size of the budget is always a deciding factor in the purchase of equipment. However, many activities require only limited space, little equipment, and can be done inside or outside the school. Wands are inexpensive, but a sanded mop or broom handle serves the same purpose. Mats are comparatively expensive equipment but, with proper care, will last for years. Ingenious instructors have used cotton mattresses with good results. These may be purchased at Army-Navy surplus stores or from local mattress factories. The cotton filling will lump in time but washable covers hold the mat firm. Athletic firms make mats of all sizes. A 5′ × 7′ mat is small enough to be handled by four children and heavy enough to hug the floor.

If storage is available, it is best to store mats flat. Where mats must be hung from the walls, safety brackets are best, as they push flush against the wall, preventing sagging, which is a safety hazard. *Never* allow a mat to be pulled or dragged across the floor, and *never* allow hard-soled shoes on a mat. Canvas-covered mats should be beaten often and cleaned with a vacuum cleaner. Cotton covers should be laundered frequently, and plastic-covered mats should be washed regularly with a mild soap and rinsed with a cloth wrung out in clear water.

SAFETY PRECAUTIONS

Safety instruction should be given by the instructor, but children become more aware and cooperative when they write and post their own version of precautionary safety measures. A fourth grade group worked out the following list of suggested directions:

Four on a mat. Do not move mats that are too heavy.
Place mats clear of walls, bars, and benches.
Leaders check mats before and during the class to see that they do not separate.
Do not walk, jump, or play on mats except in class periods when a teacher is present.
Lines should stand a good 12 inches from the mat and *always* move in the same direction.
Get off the mat as soon as the stunt is completed.
Do your clothes keep you from moving or get in your way?
Are your pockets *empty?*
Do you have on socks or tennis shoes?
Girls, have you taken off all bobby pins, hair ornaments, and jewelry?

Alert teacher spotting is necessary for children in the elementary grades to anticipate and forestall accidents. Men are often physiologically better equipped as

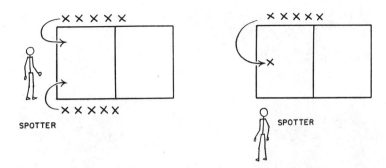

spotters, but women can work safely with most children on this level if they will observe a few simple suggestions. A spotter should assume a position that permits easy, quick assistance and rapid shifts to avoid hampering the activity and to escape flying arms and legs. The stronger arm (generally the right) should receive the weight of the child and slightly flexed knees allow quick movements in any direction. Kneel on the knee away from the performer. It is not wise to give too much assistance as it is frustrating and robs the child of the feeling of accomplishment. In less difficult stunts the presence of the spotter is all that is necessary to instill confidence. Two pupils standing on either side of each mat can be trained as assistant spotters.

CLASS ORGANIZATION AND PRESENTATION

Each activity should be analyzed and all possible risks eliminated by

1. Explanation and demonstration from start to finish.
2. Teacher spotting.
3. Teaching progressive skills to permit easy transition from known to unknown.
4. Being sure in couple stunts that the two pupils are approximately the same size and of the same skill.
5. Having classes prepare posters with rules and regulations for procedure with safety and the best learning conditions in mind.
6. Taking into consideration physical limitations. *Watch* for fatigue and do not allow tired children to continue the activity. Do not allow children recuperating from recent illnesses to participate. Allow only minimum participation by and watch carefully children with chronic sinusitis, bronchitis, asthma, epilepsy, and heart conditions.

Activities that follow have been labeled as *Level I* or *Level II* activities. Level I activities are generally suitable for boys and girls in grades 1, 2, and 3. They may also be of interest to children both younger and older than this depending on their background. Level II activities are best suited to children in grades 4, 5, and 6. They are more advanced than Level I activities and require a greater degree of strength and coordination. *Some* children who are younger, however, may benefit from these activities if they have advanced beyond Level I. It is important that class interest be held by introducing enough material each period to challenge the more proficient students and by organizing the class in squads to allow frequent individual turns at trying. In large groups of the lower elementary level, simple stunts may be done in double lines on either side of the mats. To avoid long lines have children perform across the mat when possible.

Try to develop a group feeling of pride in good execution, and discourage laughter or critical remarks directed toward poor performers. Give praise and attention to the ones who *try* as well as to those who show excellent form.

FIGURE 20-2. Pyramid building offers excellent training in body control and group cooperation. (Courtesy of C. G. White, Director, Kanakuk Kamp, College Station, Texas.)

It is wise to keep the activity on the ability level of the group, as adventurous youngsters will try to do stunts they have observed that are too difficult for their background of experience.

STUNTS FOR LEVEL I (GRADES 1, 2, and 3)

SINGLE STUNTS

Dog Run p. 469
Monkey Run p. 473
Rabbit Hop p. 473
Frog Hop p. 470
Duck Walk p. 469
Turk Stand p. 475
Egg Roll p. 469
Crab Walk p. 468
Jumping Jack p. 471
Inch Worm p. 470
Free Standing p. 469
Full Squat p. 470
Wicket Walk p. 476
Balance Stand p. 467

Tight Rope Walking p. 475
Push Ups p. 473
Seal Crawl p. 473
Lame Puppy Walk p. 472
Human Ball p. 470
Spanker p. 474
Backward Kick p. 467
Bent Knee Hop p. 468
Knee Lift p. 472
Kangaroo Hop p. 471
Mule Kick p. 473
Bear Dance p. 467
Stiff Leg Bend p. 474
Frog Dance p. 470

Weather Vane p. 476
Log Roll p. 472
Sit-Ups p. 473
Forward Roll p. 474
Bear Walk p. 468
Step Over the Wand p. 474
Jump and Slap Heels p. 471
Backward Roll p. 479
Cartwheel p. 480
Egg Sit p. 469
Thread the Needle p. 475
Forward Roll p. 481
Tripod p. 481

PARTNER STUNTS

Bouncing Ball p. 476
Wring the Dishrag p. 477
Row Boat p. 477
Leapfrog p. 478

Chinese Get-Up p. 478
Rocker p. 477
Churn the Butter p. 476
Wheelbarrow p. 477

Rooster Fight p. 477
Hand Wrestle p. 476
Double Walk p. 476

STUNTS FOR LEVEL II (GRADES 4, 5, and 6)

SINGLE STUNTS

Stiff Knee Pick Up p. 474
Folded Leg Walk p. 469
Bells or Clicks p. 468
Knuckle Down p. 472
Knee Mark p. 472
Stoop and Throw p. 474
Grasp the Toe p. 470
Fish Hawk Dive p. 469
Headstand p. 481
Headspring p. 481
Handspring p. 481

Under the Bridge p. 475
Long Stretch p. 472
Jump and Reach p. 471
Knee Dip p. 471
Cut the Wand p. 468
Backward Jump p. 467
Dip p. 469
Forearm Headstand p. 480
Jump Over the Stick p. 471
Corkscrew p. 468
Crane Dive p. 468

Single Squat p. 473
Up-swing p. 475
Up-spring p. 475
Human Rocker p. 470
Jump Foot p. 470
Coffee Grinder p. 468
Handstand p. 481
Knee Walk p. 472
Through the Stick p. 475
Dive Over One p. 480
Shoulder Stand p. 485

PARTNER STUNTS

Cock Fight p. 478
Leapfrog p. 478
Skin the Snake p. 479
Toe Wrestle p. 479
Indian Wrestle p. 478

Merry-Go-Round-It p. 479
Bull Dog Pull p. 477
Hog Tying p. 478
Walking Chair p. 479
Pull Across p. 477

Pyramids pp. 482–487
Toe Wrestle p. 479
Elephant Walk p. 478
Eskimo Roll p. 480
Back-to-Back Roll p. 479

DESCRIPTIONS OF SINGLE STUNTS[1]

Backward Jump—II

Stand on mat with toes at the edge, heels toward center. Jump backwards as far as possible, swinging arms forcibly. Land lightly.

Backward Kick—I

Jump in place on both feet four times. On fourth jump, kick both heels backward. Land lightly on toes.

Balance Stand—I

Stand on either foot, bend body foward to right angle, with body supporting free leg slightly bent from knee, head up, arms horizontal to sides.

Bear Dance—I

Squat on one heel, and extend other foot forward. Draw extended foot under body and shoot other foot out to front. Arms are folded across chest.

[1]The number following the name of the stunt indicates the approximate level for which the stunt is best suited. Level I stunts are geared for children in grades 1 to 3. Level II stunts are appropriate for most children in grades 4 to 6.

Bear Walk—I

Place hands on floor with arms and knees straight. Body sways from side to side as a lumbering bear would walk.

Bells—II

Hop on left foot, extend right leg to side, and bring left heel to click with right heel.

Bent Knee Hop—I

Child squats and takes a tuck position (arms and hands wrapped around knees). Walk on balls of feet.

Coffee Grinder—II

Child places one hand on floor and the other in an upright position. He straightens legs and arms and walks around using hand on the floor as a pivot.

Corkscrew—II

Stand with feet 15 inches apart. Place piece of paper at toe of right foot. Swing left arm across body and between legs to pick up paper.

Crab Walk—I

Put hands and feet on floor, with face up and back straight. Walk backward, using right arm and right leg, then left arm and left leg.

Crane Dive or Nose Dive—II

Toe a line. Place a piece of folded paper, at least 6 inches high, 6 inches in front of feet. Bend forward, raising one leg to rear, and pick up paper.

Cut the Wand—II

Hold a wand about 3 feet long vertically in front of the body, grasping one end and resting the other end on the floor in front of the feet. Release the wand and lift right leg over and catch it before it falls.

Dip—II

Place crumpled paper 12 inches in front of body. Kneel with hands behind back, and bend and pick up paper with teeth.

Dog Run—I

Place hands on floor in front of body, with knees and arms slightly bent. Imitate a dog walking, then running.

Duck Walk—I

Squat with knees wide, and hands under armpits. Swing feet wide to the side with each step and flap wings. First-graders love to bring the arms to the back and make a tail by placing the hands together.

Egg Roll—I

Cross legs and kneel. Wrap arms across chest. Roll using arms and knees to start.

Egg Sit—I

Sit on floor with knees bent close to chest. Grasp ankles, rock back, and extend legs.

Fish Hawk Dive—II

Kneel on one knee with the other leg entirely off the ground. Bend forward and pick up an object which is directly in front of the resting knee.

Folded Leg Walk—II

Sit on mat. Take left foot and place it as high as possible against the right thigh. Cross right leg over the left and place high on the left thigh. Fold arms or extend to side for balance. Rise to kneeling position, and walk across mat on knees.

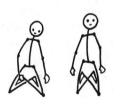

Free Standing—I

Lie on back on mat with arms folded across chest. Come to standing position without unfolding arms or using elbows.

Frog Dance—I

Squat, keep back straight, and fold arms across chest. Hop on left foot, and extend right leg to side. Hop again on left foot, draw the right leg under body, and extend left leg to side.

Frog Hop—I

Squat with arms between legs and hands on floor. Take short hops by placing hands ahead of feet and bringing feet up to hands.

Full Squat—I

Clasp wrist with right hand behind the body. Keep back straight, bend knees deeply, and touch floor with fingers. Knees are spread wide.

Grasp the Toe—II

Stand on one foot, and grasp the other foot at the arch with two hands. Bend forward and, at the same time, lift the foot, attempting to touch the toe to the forehead.

Human Ball—I

Sit on mat with knees up and feet together. Reach arms under inside of legs and lock fingers over ankles. Roll over.

Human Rocker—II

Lie face down, bend knees, arch back, and grasp right foot with right hand and left foot with left hand. Rock forward on chest and backward on thighs. Rock in open position, holding arms and legs together tightly.

Inch Worm—I

Lean in prone position. Keep hands stationary and walk feet to hands. Walk back with hands to starting position keeping legs straight.

Jump Foot—II

Stand with one foot against wall, about 12 inches from floor and in front of inside leg. Spring from inside foot and jump over leg.

Jumping Jack—I

Take a squat position, with arms across chest. Spring to erect position with weight on heels, back straight, and arms horizontal to sides.

Jump Over the Stick—II

Hold wand in horizontal position in front of body, with palms down. Swing wand forward and backward, and jump over wand.

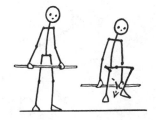

Jump and Reach—II

Stand facing wall. Without lifting heels reach high with both hands and mark with chalk highest point reached. Stand with side to wall. Start from crouch position, jump, and mark point reached with chalk held in nearest hand.

Jump and Slap Heels—I

Jump into air, and bring heels up to side. Slap heels.

Kangaroo Hop—I

Squat with arms folded over chest. Spring into air and come back to squat position with knees flexed to prevent jarring.

Knee Dip—II

Stand on one foot and grasp the other foot behind the back with opposite hand. Bend down with arm outstretched for balance, touch knee lightly to floor, and return to standing position.

Knee Lift—I

Stand with feet apart and hands extended forward at hip level. Jump up and try to touch the knees to the palms. Repeat, raising hands higher.

Knee Mark—II

Kneel on both knees behind a line on the floor. Place one hand behind the back and reach forward with a piece of chalk and mark point reached.

Knee Walk or Stump Walk—II

Kneel and grasp ankles or toes with hands. Walk on knees, leaning forward slightly to maintain balance.

Knuckle Down—II

Place toes on line. Without moving toes from line or using hands, kneel and rise.

Lame Puppy Walk—I

On all fours, raise one foot in air and walk like a dog on three legs.

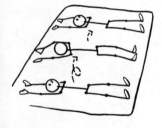

Log Roll—I

Lie on back with arms extended over head and legs straight, and roll slowly over to end of mat. The body must move as "one piece" to keep direction straight.

Long Stretch—II

Stand with feet together, toeing line. Hold piece of chalk in one hand. Bend knees deeply, and place free hand on floor. Walk forward on hands as far as possible without moving toes from line, and mark on floor. Walk back to squat position and stand.

Monkey Run—I

On all fours scamper agilely, imitating a monkey. Put down hands, then feet.

Mule Kick—I

Bend forward, place hands on floor, bend knees, and kick into air as a mule.

Push-ups—I

Get on hands and knees with arms below shoulders and shoulder-distance apart. Extend legs backward until hips and knees are straight. Lower body by bending elbows until nose touches floor. Raise body and repeat.

Rabbit Jump—I

Squat with hands in front of feet. Push with feet and lift hands from floor. Catch weight on hands and bring feet to hands.

Seal Crawl—I

Lean in prone position with fingers turned to side like flappers. Keep legs together, weight on toes. Drag body along by walking on hands and let hips swing.

Single Squat—II

Stand on mat, and raise arms to side for balance. Raise one leg in front, keeping knee straight. Squat, keeping weight well over supporting leg. Return to standing position without losing balance.

Sit-ups—I

Lie flat on floor with arms extended above head and legs bent and together. Come to sitting position and keep legs tight to floor. Lie down slowly.

Somersault—Forward Roll—I

Stand on floor at end of mat with feet astride. Place hands on mat between feet without bending knees. Touch back of head to mat. Body will roll forward and somersault will be completed.

Spanker—I

Take position as for Crab Walk. Raise both feet in the air and slap seat with right hand, then left hand. Advanced: Hop and extend right leg and spank with left hand; hop and extend left leg and spank with right hand.

Step Over the Wand—I

Grasp a wand at both ends with the backs of the hands toward the ceiling. Keep wand close to floor, bend forward, and step over the wand first with one foot, then with the other. Stand straight. Step back over wand in same manner. Stand.

Stiff Knee Pick-up—II

Stand with feet together, bend forward, and pick up article placed 3 inches in front of toes without bending knees.

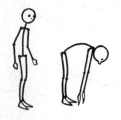

Stiff Leg Bend—I

Stand with heels together and arms at side. Bend forward and touch floor with fingertips.

Stoop and Throw—II

Stand in stride position, toeing a line. Hold beanbag behind back with both hands. Bend knees deeply and throw beanbag between legs, using both hands. Keep a record of distance for competition.

Thread the Needle—I

Clasp the hands in front of body, bend the trunk forward, and step through clasped hands with right foot, then left foot. Return by stepping backward with right, then left foot.

Through the Stick—II

Grasp a wand behind the back, keeping palms forward. Bring wand over head to position in front of body without losing grasp. Swing right leg around right arm, between the hands from front, and over stick. Crawl through head first and back over with left foot.

Tight Rope Walking—I

Walk a line drawn on the floor (10 feet long). Use arms to balance.

Turk Stand—I

Arms folded across chest. Sit cross-legged on floor. Stand without using hands or changing position of feet.

Under the Bridge—II

Stand toeing a line with the feet about 12 inches apart. Have chalk in one hand. Squat, and with the hand holding the chalk reach forward between the legs to mark the floor as far forward as possible.

Up-spring—II

Kneel with ankles extended and toes flat. Swing arms backward, then forward vigorously, pushing with the feet at the same time. Bring body to erect position.

Up-swing—II

Knee with the weight on the balls of the feet. Swing arms backward, then forward, coming to standing position.

Weather Vane—I

Stand with feet apart, hands on shoulders, and elbows up. Turn from side to side.

Wicket Walk—I

Simple: With knees straight, bend forward touching floor with hands. Walk forward and backward with small steps, keeping legs and arms close together. *Advanced:* Grasp ankles and walk without bending knees.

DESCRIPTIONS OF PARTNER STUNTS

Bouncing Ball—I

One child is the ball and another the bouncer. Try to achieve the feel and rhythm of a bouncing ball.

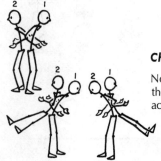

Churn the Butter—I

No. 1 and No. 2 stand back to back, with elbows locked. No. 1 bends forward from the hips. No. 2 springs from floor, leans back, and lifts his feet from floor. Repeat action with No. 2 bending forward.

Double Walk—I

A couple face each other and grasp upper arms. No. 2 steps diagonally across insteps of No. 1, who walks forward. No. 2 shifts weight as No. 1 walks.

Hand Wrestle—I

Two children face each other and joing right hands, and each raises one foot behind him. On signal, each attempts to cause the other to touch either free hand or foot to floor.

Pull Across—II

Divide class into two equal groups. Draw line on floor, and have teams stand on opposite sides of the line. On signal, each child grasps his opponent by the right hand and attempts to pull him across the line. Limit bout to two minutes.

Rocker—I

Partners sit facing each other and extend legs so that each child is sitting on feet of other child. They grasp upper arms and rock. One leans backward and lifts other child up. Alternate.

Rooster Fight—I

Couple face each other with arms folded across chest and weight on one foot. On signal, each tries to throw the other off balance by pushing with his arms. First one to lose balance, by putting down a foot, loses.

Wheelbarrow—I

No. 1 grasps legs of No. 2 at knees and walks as guiding a wheelbarrow. No. 2 walks on hands and keeps back straight.

Row Boat—I

Facing parnter, child sits cross-legged on mat. He grasps partner's hands. When he leans back, he will pull the partner forward.

Wring the Dishrag—I

Partners face each other and join hands. They lower arms on one side and turn away from each other and under the raised arms. They stand back to back. They raise other pair of arms and turn under.

Bulldog Pull—II

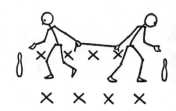

Number of participants: 10 to 20. Equipment: Rope 3 to 5 feet long and two Indian clubs. Place rope on floor between two clubs. Divide group into two teams. Line them up facing and parallel to rope. Two opponents step forward and grasp ends of rope. On signal each pulls rope and tries to pick up Indian club in one- to two-minute bouts. Keep score.

Cock Fight—II

Sit on floor facing partner. Draw up knees close to body and have toes touching partner's toes. Clasp hands in front of knees. Place wand under knees and over arms at elbows. Try with toes to lift partner's feet so he will roll over backward.

Chinese Get-up—I

Partners stand back to back with elbows locked. They sink to floor and rise by taking small walking steps and pressing against each other's backs.

Elephant Walk—II

Couple face each other. No. 1 stands in wide stride. No. 2 springs forward and upward around waist of No. 1. No. 2 bends backward and crawls between legs and grasps ankles. No. 1 bends forward and walks with swaying motion.

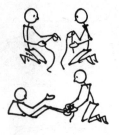

Hog Tying—II

Two face kneeling on hands and knees, each with a 4-foot rope in hands. On signal, each tries to tie the opponent's ankles together. Any fair wrestling hold is permissible.

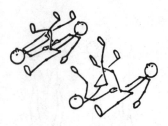

Indian Leg Wrestle—II

Two children lie side-by-side, facing opposite directions. They place hips at opponent's waistline. They hook inside legs and hook inside arms. They raise inside legs to count three times. On the third count they bend knees, hook them and try to force opponent into backward roll.

Leapfrog—I and II

Base takes wide stance, bends forward from the hips, and braces hands on knees. Top runs forward and jumps both feet over base's back. He places hands on base's shoulders and pushes, extending legs to side. He lands on both feet, knees and ankles relaxed.

Merry-Go-Round—II

Group of eight to ten forms circle. Children take double wrist lock, 1, 3, 5, 7, sit on floor with knees straight and feet together in the center. On signal, 2, 4, 6, 8 take a step outwards and 1, 3, 5, 7, raise hips until body is in inclined position with back straight. 2, 4, 6, 8 walk around circle, and the center group are the spokes of a wheel.

Skin the Snake—II

Forward: All line up directly behind one another in stride position. All bend forward and reach right hand between knees to person behind and reach forward with the left hand and grasp right hand of person in front. Last person in line crawls through and assumes stride position. Next in line follows until all have crawled through. *Backward:* All line up as before. Last one in line lies down flat, and the rest of the line moves backward. As each person reaches the end he lies down. The last performer to lie down rises and walks forward straddling the line and pulls the next performer to feet. Players continue until all return to original position.

Toe Wrestle—II

This is same as Cock Fight, p. 478, but instead of using a wand, the arms are wrapped around knees.

Walking Chair—II

Line up behind each other. Hold hips of person in front. All sit back so legs touch thighs of one behind. Each supports own weight. On signal, all move forward in step.

DESCRIPTION OF TUMBLING ACTIVITIES

All of the following stunts require "spotters."

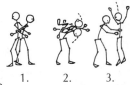

Back-to-Back Roll—II

Review Churn the Butter as a lead-up stunt. One child is base, and another is top. Base and top stand back to back, lock elbows, with base's on outside of top's. Base stands with one foot forward and one foot backward for better balance; he bends knees, gets hips in small of top's back. On signal, top springs from mat, brings knees to chest, and throws head well back to lean over base. Base at same time bends forward slightly and pulls up on top's arms to roll him over base's back and head.

1.   2.   3.

Backward Roll Progressions

Basic: Start in sitting position. Place hands at shoulders, with palms up and thumbs toward neck. Roll back, pushing with the feet, tuck head forward, and bring knees close to chest. As hips are vertical to shoulders, push with hands. Land on toes in squat position. *Stand to stand:* Start in standing position. Sit, keeping feet as close to body as possible. Roll back, pushing forcibly with hands, and extend legs in a vigorous snap to finish in a standing position.

Cartwheel Progressions

1. No hip extension: Stand with right side to mat. Bend sideways and place both hands in line on the mat. Push off with feet, first right, then left. Swing legs over arms and push with right hand, then with left hand. Finish in crouched position.
2. Alternate, starting from right, then left.
3. Hip extension: Hold elbows and legs straight, head up, and back slightly arched.
4. Click heels in air: as you reach vertical position, quickly click heels before lowering one leg.
5. Cartwheel on one hand: With free hand on hip, make push from mat more vigorous. This stunt should be done only by those with excellent arm and shoulder development.

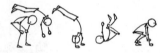

Dive Over One

1. Place obstacle close to edge of mat. This may be rolled mat or child in tuck position or kneeling on all fours. Take short run and when 1 foot from obstacle, extend arms, duck head, and roll forward to standing position.
2. Dive over person kneeling on hands and knees.
3. Dive through spread legs of child doing headstand.

Eskimo Roll—II

Forward: Base lies on mat with legs raised and knees flexed. Top stands behind base's shoulders, reaches forward, and grasps base's ankles with fingers to outside, thumbs to inside. Base grasps top's ankles in same grip. Top does forward roll between base's legs and pulls top to feet. They continue to roll, changing positions.
Backward: Players start in same position as above. As top rolls backward base pushes forcibly against top's ankles and against mat with head and shoulders. They stay close together.

Forearm Headstand—I

Kneel and place forearms, palms down, on mat. Place forehead between hands. Walk up and kick up one leg, secure balance, and raise other leg slowly to vertical position.

Forward Roll Progressions—I

1. Squat-to-sit (somersault): Squat with weight on toes and hands on mat just ahead of toes. Round back by tucking head between knees. Push with hands and feet and roll over to sitting position. Keep body in tight ball to prevent slapping back.
2. Stand-to-stand: Execute as in No. 1. Bend forward and place hands on mat. Finish in standing position.
3. Running and taking off from one foot.
4. Springing from both feet.
5. Continuous forward rolls.
6. Forward roll with arms folded across chest.

Handstand—II

Stand on hands, feet raised straight in air with head and hands making a triangle. Arch back slightly for balance. Walk on hands. Shift weight gently and keep it over hands.

Handspring Progressions—II

1. Over back: Do handstand about 1 foot from base, arch back, and drop legs to floor, pushing forcibly with hands.
2. Handspring with assistance of base.
3. Handspring over base's arms.
4. Handspring over two rolled mats.

Headstand—II

Start with tripod position. Gradually raise legs high in rear, keeping legs and ankles together.

Headspring—II

Place two rolled mats in center of mats. Place head and hands on top. Spring from feet, push hard with head and hands, arch back, and snap legs down toward mat. Land in squat position and rise to erect position.

Tripod—I

Form a triangle by placing hands on mat, fingers forward, and bend elbows to form a shelf. Place right knee above right elbow and left knee above left elbow. Lower one leg at a time or go into a forward roll.

FIGURE 20–3.   Children learning the human rocker. (Courtesy of Dr. Joan Tillotson, Plattsburgh Public Schools, Plattsburgh, New York.)

PYRAMID BUILDING

Pyramid building not only offers excellent training in body control and group adjustment but also has a dual value in its salesmanship. The simplest of pyramids, if executed in a clean-cut and decisive manner, is showy. Pyramid building is the cherry that tops a sundae. The part below may be more filling and nutritious, and it definitely required more work, but the bright red has eye appeal. Physical educators should not overlook showmanship in selling their program to the public even though they are completely aware that there is no substitute for hard-earned skills learned with slow, patient, and sometimes monotonous repetition.

The basic requirements for simple pyramid building are

1. Strength
2. Balance
3. Timing
4. Knowledge of fundamentals
5. Ability to work as a team

The last requirement explains why this activity is postponed, generally, until the sixth grade. Many fourth graders who have progressed through a well-planned program show excellence in performance in individual stunts but are not interested in working as a team. However, the teacher working with small and skilled groups would be justified in introducing this activity at a lower level.

Finished pyramids should meet the requirements of good design, namely, balance, proportion, and interest (varying levels). The structure may start from a line, circle, square, rectangle or triangle, but all units, whether they are composed of two,

FIGURE 20–4. Can you touch your toe to your chin? Children respond to such challenges. (Courtesy of Camp Yonahlossee, Blowing Rock, North Carolina.)

three, or five performers, should give the whole a feeling of continuity. This should not be dependent upon physical contact. In the most commonly used pyramids one finds the high point in the center, but the sides can be higher if symmetry is maintained. In simple elementary pyramids the base looks and is more secure if the ends taper to the floor.

The teacher or a pupil may give the counts or signals vocally, with a whistle, with a snapper, or by a sharp clap of the hands. All move to the edge of the mat in a formation arranged to enable first positions to be taken with a minimum of walking.

Count 1: Bases move to positions on the mats.
Count 2: Tops move to positions.
Count 3: All tops mount.
Count 4: Tops dismount.
Count 5: All return to place.

The pyramid is good if

1. Performers have moved quickly with good posture and precision to their positions.
2. Movements have been executed in unison to count.
3. The completed pyramid is maintained until steadiness is attained. (The rhythm of the building is impaired if it is held too long.)
4. It is dismounted in positive and orderly manner.

On the following pages are suggested stunts, listed according to grade level, that may be used in typical pyramids. Once the feel has been attained, classes should be encouraged to create their own pyramids.

Angel Balance—II

Base lies on the floor with legs raised and knees slightly bent and places feet diagonally alongside of top's pelvic bones. They grasp hands. Top springs forward, and base straightens legs. Base lowers arms, and top arches back and raises arms as in a swan dive.

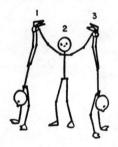

Handstand Archway—II

No. 2 is base. On signal, Nos. 1 and 3 do handstands and base catches them at ankles.

Handstand Supported at Hips—II

Base lies down, places feet across lower abdomen of top, who puts hands to floor. Base places hands on top's shoulders. Top springs, and base extends legs and supports top's hips with feet.

Horizontal Stand—II

Base grasps top's ankles, with thumbs on inside of top's legs. As top springs and shifts weight to hands base straightens arms.

Knee-Shoulder Stand—II

Top does handstand on knees of base, who supports top's shoulders.

Mercury—II

Base clasps hands at back, with palms up. Top places right foot on base's hands and springs from left foot. Top secures balance and extends arms and free leg, bracing supporting leg from knee down on base's back.

Shoulder Rest—II

Extend legs straight above head and support hips with hands. Weight is on shoulders and elbows.

Shoulder Stand—II

(See knee-shoulder stand.) Top and base grasp hands. Top does handstand with support of feet at shoulders.

Sitting Balance—II

Base lies on mat, legs in air and slightly bent. Top sits on base's feet, extends arms backward, and grasps top's hands. Base straightens legs and releases hands. Top extends arms to side.

Sitting Mount—II

Base stands in stride position, and top stands directly behind. Base kneels on one knee and places head between top's legs. Top places legs under base's arms and behind back. Top rises, straightening knees slowly. He stands erect.

Stand on Partner—II

Top stands on lower back of base, with feet placed diagonally or one foot on lower back and one foot on shoulders.

Stand on Partner's Knee—II

Base aids balance by supporting top at knee.

Standing Mount—II

Top stands directly behind base. Base stands in deep-stride position with arms raised up and back. Top grasps base's hands and places right foot on base's thigh, then left foot on base's left shoulder and right foot on base's right shoulder. Top gradually straightens knees, releases hands, and stands tall, with arms extended. Base supports top with hands at back of knees.

Thigh Mount—II

No. 2 mounts thigh of No. 1 with right foot and mounts thigh of No. 3. He stands erect and extends arms to side. Nos. 1 and 3 support him at waist.

Triangle—II

Base lifts one of top's legs to shoulder. Top springs and places other leg on base's other shoulder.

EIGHT PYRAMID VARIATIONS

7.

8.

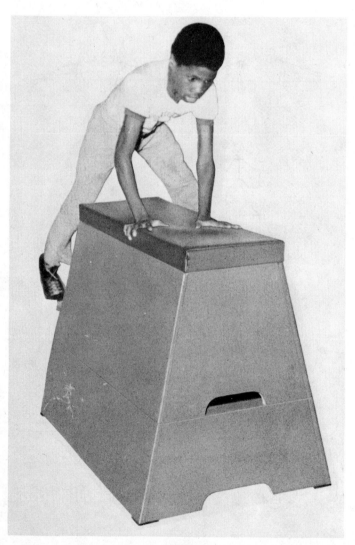

FIGURE 20–5. Self-confidence and courage can be developed in a wide variety of activities such as this one. (Courtesy of Jayfro Corporation, Montville, Connecticut.)

REBOUND TUMBLING (TRAMPOLINING)

Twenty years ago the trampoline was a piece of equipment found in circuses, athletic clubs, and colleges. It was used by a limited number of skilled tumblers, gymnasts, and divers. Today, one encounters the trampoline in the gymnasiums of many schools and recreational centers, in the backyards of private homes.

The trampoline is fun and exciting and gives the child a feeling of being "lighter than air"; consequently, it lends to the simplest routine a sense of power in excelling. With proper spotting and clear instructions, this equipment is quite safe. The following routines are recommended for the elementary school. More difficult routines are eliminated for obvious reasons. Safety factors must be considered at all times. Although training rigs are expensive and time consuming to use in large classes, they are recommended if the school can afford to buy them.

FIGURE 20-6.   You have to have strength and body control to do this. (Courtesy of Jayfro Corporation, Montville, Connecticut.)

FIGURE 20–7.   Learning to do a handstand is a challenging activity which, when mastered, brings delight to children. (Courtesy of Dr. Joan Tillotson, Plattsburgh Public Schools, Plattsburgh, New York.)

Procedures

1. Only one student at a time should be on the trampoline.
2. Jump in stocking feet to protect the bed and to give traction.
3. Follow explicitly the routine set by the instructor.
4. The instructor stands at the side and places a spotter at the other side and ends. If the student loses his balance, a light push with both hands sends him back to the middle of the bed. Spotters should place hands on the frame and keep hands off the suspension system.
5. The class counts off by fours. No. 1 gets on the trampoline. Numbers 2, 3, and 4 take their turns at spotting and jumping on the trampoline. Upon finishing, No. 1 takes the spotting station of No. 4, and No. 4 moves to station of No. 3, and so forth.

Routines

MOUNT

1. Mounting ladders or small tables covered with mats are excellent and speed up the safe and orderly procedure of getting on and off the trampoline.
2. Place hands on the frame and crawl on and off.

3. Skilled students in the upper elementary grades may take a short run, place hands on the frame, and do a forward roll onto the bed.
4. *Never* allow a student to step on the suspension system.

DISMOUNT

1. In dismounting, *never* allow a student to jump from the bed to the floor. The more skilled may place their hands on the frame and vault to the floor or jump with flexed knees from the frame to a mat.

FUNDAMENTAL BOUNCE

1. Stand in the middle of the bed, ribcage pulled high and eyes forward on the frame or end of bed.
2. Arms lift forward and upward in a circular motion as you leave the bed; they return to your side as you come down.
3. Feet are shoulder-width apart on landing and together in the air.
4. Students should be taught that control is more important than height.
5. Mount, bounce ten times, dismount.

KNEE DROP

1. Kneel in the center of the bed with the legs and back straight, and arms at side.
2. Pull your arms hard forward and upward and come to a standing position.
3. Take three bounces to a knee drop. Repeat twice. Dismount.

HANDS AND KNEE DROP

1. Start in erect position.
2. Bounce three times.
3. Land on bed on your hands and knees.
4. Push with hands to come back to erect position.
5. Repeat twice, and dismount.

SEAT DROP

1. Bounce three times.
2. Go to seat drop. Legs are straight, toes pointed, and hands are close to side of hips.
3. Push with hands as you return to erect position.
4. Repeat twice, and dismount.

FRONT DROP

1. Take three bounces and land in prone position.
2. Keep head up and arms extended forward.
3. Push up with arms to return to standing position.
4. Repeat routine twice, and dismount.

BACK DROP

1. Take three low bounces.
2. Land on back with chin pulled in close to chest and arms extended forward.
3. Kick forward and up with legs to return to standing position.
4. Repeat routine twice, and dismount.

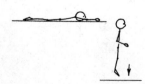

MIXED ROUTINES

1. Take three bounces, one knee drop, three bounces, and one seat drop. Repeat.
2. Take three bounces, one hands-and-knee drop, three bounces, and one front drop. Repeat.
3. Take three bounces, one seat drop, three bounces, and one back drop. Repeat.
4. Take three bounces, one knee drop, three bounces, and one back drop. Repeat.

SUGGESTED READINGS

Athletic Institute: How To Improve Your Trampolining. Chicago, 1970.

Bailey, J.: *Gymnastic Activities in the School.* Boston, Allyn & Bacon, Inc., 1965.

Borkowski, R.: *Rough and tumble: a guide to physical toughness activities in boys' physical education.* Journal of Health, Physical Education, Recreation, April 1967.

Department of Education: *Junior Division Physical Education, Grades 4, 5, 6.* Ontario, Canada, 1967.

Edwards, V.: *Tumbling.* Philadelphia, W. B. Saunders Company, 1969.

Loken, N., and Willoughby, R.: *Complete Book of Gymnastics.* 3rd ed. Englewood Cliffs, New Jersey, Prentice-Hall, Inc., 1975.

Mosston, M.: Developmental Movement. Columbus, Ohio, Charles E. Merrill Publishing Company, 1965.

O'Quinn, G.: *Gymnastics for Elementary School Children.* Dubuque, Iowa, William C. Brown Company, Publishers, 1972.

Pond, C.: *Tumbling in Total Gymnastics.* Champaign, Illinois, Stipes Publishing Company, 1965.

Ryser, O.: *Tumbling and Apparatus Stunts.* Dubuque, Iowa, William C. Brown Company, Publishers, 1976.

Yeager, P.: *A Teacher's Guide For Tumbling and Pyramids.* Statesboro, Georgia, The Wide World Publications, 1963.

INSTRUCTIONAL AIDS

Gym Master. Chart of basic trampoline skills. 3200 S. Zuni St., Englewood, Colorado.

National Sports Company. Basic tumbling chart. 360–370 N. Marquette Street, Fond du Lac, Wisconsin.

Nissen Training Kit. Illustrated wall charts, lesson plans, and progress charts. Nissen Trampoline Company, 215 A Ave. N.W., Cedar Rapids, Iowa.

SUGGESTED FILM

Basic Tumbling. Available for $20.00 per week including postage and insurance from Vannie Edwards, Physical Education Department, Centenary College, Shreveport, Louisiana.

CHAPTER TWENTY-ONE

ELEMENTARY APPARATUS ACTIVITIES

Gymnastic activities can do more toward developing the body physically through the use of big muscles and the development of agility, flexibility, balance and strength than can be accomplished through any other aspect of the physical education program.

Arthur Miller and Virginia Whitcomb

Elementary gymnastics is gaining an increasingly important place in American physical education at all educational levels. Free exercises and stunts are the foundation upon which all gymnastic activities are built. The former are made up of improvised patterns of movement that include vertical and horizontal balances, often done to music. The latter are composed of activities such as the headstand, forearm stand, handstand, handspring, and flip. It is important that a spotter (preferably the teacher) stand by the side of the performer during such activity to help him learn desired skills more quickly and to prevent injury by anticipating which way he is most likely to fall should he lose body control. The best assistance the spotter can give is pushing, lifting, catching, or holding, depending upon the particular activity the pupil is doing and his movement errors.

WARM-UP EXERCISES

Ultimately, the objective of these exercises is to enable the individual to execute any body movement with relaxed ease while expending a minimum of energy. Maja Carlquist[1] believes that "it is essential that we teach ourselves conscious relaxation of muscles; conscious contraction of muscles." This process gradually becomes unconscious and natural as short periods of relaxation and contraction are used alternately and followed by longer periods.

The following exercises are simple, but try to follow the principle mentioned above. They do not have to follow as a unit and may be freely interspersed with exercises on apparatus, but it is suggested that a short period of walking, running, skipping, bending, and stretching releases the tension from sitting in a classroom and,

[1]Carlquist, M.: *Rhythmical Games.* London, Methuen & Co., Ltd., 1955.

FIGURE 21-1. Children like to see who can travel the longest and fastest on the horizontal bar. (Courtesy of Northlake Elementary School, Dallas, Texas.)

consequently, improves performance in activities in which more complex coordination is demanded.

1. Walk using normal steps and holding body in a relaxed posture while arms swing naturally at sides. Gradually increase stride, extending knees and insteps until a run with giant strides is achieved.

2. Pedal in place, alternately shifting weight from one foot to the other. This strengthens feet and gives flexibility to knees.

3. *Skip:* Start with a free, loose skip, arms at side. Gradually increase height until arms are used to pull, knees are high, and feet are used in springlike motion.

4. *Swings:* Swing arms forward and sideward, stopping sideward swing at the point where tension begins. Swing arms forward and sideward, and describe a circle in front crossing arms.

Swing arms forward and backward using entire body. Flex knees and straighten both forward and backward swings. With feet spread wide, swing can be carried backward through legs.

Swing both arms horizontally from side to side. Bend over with body relaxed and start a low swing, alternately transferring weight and gradually increasing perimeter of swing until body is in erect position.

See how many ways children can swing arms, legs, and body, setting own rhythm.

5. *Stretching:*
Standing Position: Extend arms at shoulder level; stretch; relax. Let body fall forward, with head and arms down and knees relaxed. Raise body and stretch arms high, coming up on tiptoes. Vary with bobs up and down and stretch upwards.

With feet comfortably apart, left arm at shoulder level, and right arm curved over head, bend toward left with soft stretches.

Put hands on knees and keep spine straight and head up. Bounce up and down letting hands slide down legs until fingers touch toes. With back rounded, bob and touch toes forward, and bob sideways, alternately touching right and left ankles.

Kneeling Position: Stretch trunk. With arms at side, bend left and right. Lower head, sit with arms curled around head, and return to kneeling position.

Floor Positions: On back, hands at side, lift hips and legs and bicycle pedal in air and lower toward floor, stretching knees and insteps.

On back, make arch of body using back, neck, and leg muscles.
Have body in prone position, arms extended shoulder width, in relaxed position. With feet and arms together, arch body and rock backward and forward.

On back, arms above head, stretch left arm up and right leg down. Now, stretch right arm up and left leg down.

6. *Cross-legged Sit:* Stand erect, cross legs, and sit down. Come back to original position.

7. *Leap Frog:* Straddle vault over child lengthwise and sideways.

TYPES OF APPARATUS

A variety of apparatus and equipment may be used in the elementary school gymnastics program. Although much of this equipment is not used in the formal competitive sport of gymnastics, it is of great value to the physical and movement ability development of children.

Boys and girls in the primary grades should utilize most apparatus at an exploratory and experimental level. Teachers should not be overly concerned about form, skill, and difficulty in the performance of stunts on the apparatus. Rather, the teacher needs to provide an atmosphere of fun and adventure.

At the intermediate and upper elementary grade level, practice may begin on the more traditional apparatus activities contained within this chapter. Skill will develop in conjunction with strength and coordination and will be challenging to all.

The following is a compilation of several types of large and small apparatus that may be successfully used in the elementary physical education program:

Climbing Ropes p. 499
Balance Beam pp. 500–501
Horizontal Bar p. 501
Still Rings p. 501
Stall Bars pp. 502–503
Vaulting Apparatus pp. 503–504
Springboard pp. 504–506
Rolled Mats pp. 507–508
Stairs pp. 508–509
Wands pp. 509–511
Hoops pp. 511–512
Parallel Bars p. 513
Horizontal Ladder pp. 513–514

APPARATUS ACTIVITIES

There are numerous types of large and small apparatus used for gymnastic-type activities. The following is a compilation of several activities on a variety of equipment. These activities are intended to serve only as "starter" experiences. The reader is referred to the excellent texts in the Suggested Readings section for more complete information.

Climbing Ropes

Rope climbing looks difficult but can be fun and safe. At the start, students should only travel a few feet and descend. Never slide down a rope, because severe rope burns can result in permanent injury.

1. Stand close to rope and grasp with both hands, one above other. Place one foot on top of other and grip rope between calves and shins. Hips are now in sitting position, and arms are straight. Practice until climber can hold position securely without slipping.
2. Straighten legs and bend elbows.
3. Reach up with hands and draw legs up to position
   a. Repeat twice.
4. Descend by taking position 3, with body close to rope. Alternately lower hands on rope as the leg grip is released to allow a slow descent. The feet clamp to control the downward movement.

Chinning:
1. Grasp rope high above head.
2. Hang.
3. Pull up until elbows are bent, and lower body to mat.

Inverted Hang:
1. Grasp rope above head.
2. Swing feet forward and upward.
3. Secure position on rope with one foot in front and one in back.
4. Descend by releasing leg grip and lower feet to mat.

Free Double Ropes: Run forward, grasp ropes, and swing feet forward and land on mat with flexed knees.

Stationary Double Ropes:
1. Jump and grasp ropes, hang, and drop.
2. *Inverted Hang:* Hang by hands, draw knees up, drop head back and extend feet upward, one foot in front of rope, the other back of rope.
3. *Skin the Cat:* From inverted hang position, bring feet down to rear, hang, and drop to mat.

Balance Beam

The balance beam can be one of the most rewarding pieces of equipment in the gymnasium. It provides excellent opportunities to develop balance and presents an enjoyable challenge to the child. In earlier days, children in small towns spent hours walking on railroad rails. The beam may range from 18 inches to 3 feet above the floor. The latter size may be used for vaulting.

Suggested activities for the balance beam include the following:

1. Traveling in straddle seat.

2. Traveling sideways across beam.

3. Walking forward and backward.

4. Walking forward and backward on heels.

5. Monkey walking forward on all fours.

6. Duck walking forward.

7. Duck walking sideward.

8. Walking sideward stepping over front foot.

9. Walking sideways stepping over back foot.

10. Squatting on one leg, with free leg forward.

11. Standing, sitting on beam, and then standing.

12. Running lightly length of beam.

13. Slowly skipping length of beam.

14. Kneeling on one knee. Coming to erect position. Repeating, using other leg.

15. Standing facing beam. Jumping to single leg equal with other leg extended down. Doing quarter turn left. Bringing extended leg to beam and holding. Walking two steps forward. Dismounting.

16. Standing on beam. Doing a quarter turn. Dismounting with straddle jump. Landing with your body in full extension.

Horizontal Bar

Adjust the height of the bar for the average height in a class so that no child will have to jump higher than 12 inches.

1. *Front grasp:* Grip bar with fingers forward and thumbs under bar.
2. *Reverse or rear grasp:* Grip bar with fingers turned toward performer and thumbs under bar.
3. *Combined grasp:* Left hand using reverse grasp, right hand using forward grasp.
4. *Chin:* Place hands on bar, shoulder width apart, using either grasp. Pull body up until chin is level with bar. Lower body. Repeat until tired.

5. *Skin the Cat:* With front grasp and fingers away from performer, pull bent knees up to chest and carry through arms. Drop feet to mat and release bar.

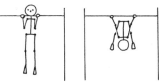

6. *Hip Pullover Mount:* From a standing position, bend knees and grasp bar with undergrip. Using a fast hip-circling movement, curl your body under and over beam. Straighten your body, using full-arm support.

Still Rings

Adjust the rings to shoulder height.

1. *Chin:* Take front grasp as used on horizontal bar. Pull body up until head is even with rings. Keep rings close to chest.
2. *Skin the Cat:* Follow instructions for this stunt on horizontal bar.
3. *Inverted Hang:* Spring from mat and raise hips and knees to chest. Extend legs upward, body arched, head back, and feet together with toes pointed. Keep rings close to sides.

Stall Bars

Floor exercises that generally require spotters, corrective exercises for specific weaknesses such as spinal curvature, and numerous stunts can be performed on the stall bars. The child with a poor sense of balance develops muscles with a sense of security because he has something solid from which to work.

The teacher sets up a unit of exercises, demonstrates, and checks as they are executed by students. It is a good idea to draw stick figures of the unit and tape them to the wall. Then the teacher may supervise other floor activities while the students perform prescribed activities. A few exercises are suggested.

1. Hang, using reverse grasp. Raise right leg; lower. Raise left leg; lower. Raise both legs with bent knees. Keep body flush against bars. Raise both legs until they are in horizontal position.

2. Squat in front of bars with hands on rod at comfortable height. Jump to first rod. Shift hands and jump to second and so forth.

3. *Side Lean:* Stand with left side close to bars, elbow bent. Gradually straighten left arm and extend right arm and leg. Repeat from right side.

4. Lie on back and tuck toes under first bar and put arms above head. Pull to sitting position and return to supine position.

5. *Side Swing:* Face stall bars and put feet on second wall bar with knees bent and hands at comfortable height. Swing to right side stretching knees. Swing to left.

6. *Pendulum Swing:* Hang facing bars. Swing from side to side, lifting alternate hands.

7. *Climb Upward:* Place feet on second wall bar. Grasp bar above and, using alternate hands, climb until body is flush against bars. Dismount by springing backward, landing with flexed knees.

8. *Headstand:* Place mat in front of bars. Do head and handstand following instructions on page 481. Face bars and allow feet to rest against bars for steadiness.

9. *Handstand:* See page 481 for instructions. For children who have difficulty in balancing, bars give steady point of reference.

Vaulting Apparatus

Vaults may be done using the side horse, long horse, buck, low parallel bars covered with a mat, Swedish box, or balance beam. The vaults should be adapted to the size and ability of the elementary-school child. Vaults on the long horse generally require a beat board or springboard and its use should be limited to the well-coordinated student in the fifth or sixth grades.

1. Jump to box; jump to floor.

2. *Squat vault:* The legs are between arms, and knees are pulled up to chest. Push hard with hands and kick feet forward.

3. *Straddle vault:* Use the same technique as in leapfrog. Push with hands as legs are extended to side.

4. *Flank vault right or left:* With both hands on buck, transfer weight to one hand as legs swing to side with body straight and legs and trunk in line. This vault may be executed on low horizontal bar or balance beam.

5. *Front Support:* Stand close to horse, grasp pommels, and spring from both feet to straight-arm position with thighs against horse, back slightly arched, and head up.

6. *Left and Right Leg Half-Circle:* From front-support position, swing left leg over horse and across pommel. Shift weight away from swinging leg to supporting arm. Grasp pommel again. Keep legs straight. Swing right leg over in the same manner. Grasp pommel again. Dismount with light spring or return to front-support position by swinging legs back over horse.

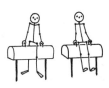

7. Jump to squat, stand in saddle, knees to chest. Release pommels and dismount.

8. *Squat Vault:* Jump, grasp pommels with hips high and knees to chest; push hard with hands and release pommels as body moves upward.

9. *Straddle Vault:* Spring from both feet, with hips high, legs straight, and head up. Release pommels on upward movement.

Springboard

When using this equipment, the pupil should run on the board in quick steps, making the last step about 1½ feet from the end of the board for the spring. Stress gaining height on the forward swing. In most of the activities shown below, pupils should follow one another in rapid succession. A mat should be placed under the take-off part of the board and should extend out in the area where pupils will land. A spotter should stand at the side of the mat ahead of the performer. The following stunts are for upper elementary pupils who have had previous lessons in stunts and tumbling:

Plain Jump and Hand Clap:
1. Run up board.
2. Jump high into air on take-off at end of board.

3. Clap hands overhead.
4. Land in balanced position with knees bent.

5. Repeat: clap hands behind back.

6. Jump, clap hands above head and behind back, and land.

7. Repeat; clap hands under one leg.

Swan Jump:
1. Jump high on board.
2. Swan-jumps, with arms extended sideward, arch body, keep head back.
3. Land with arms forward and knees bent.

Jump and Turn:
1. Run, and jump on board.
2. Run, jump on board, and make quarter turn.
3. Run, jump on board, and make half turn.
4. Run, jump on board, and make full turn.

Jump and Heel Click:
1. Jump high off board.
2. Click heels together in the air, and land with bent knees.
3. Repeat; click heels together twice before landing.
4. Repeat; click heels together three times before landing.

Jump and Kick:
1. Run, jump high, and kick buttocks; keep head back, back arched, and thighs extended.
2. Run, jump, quickly flex thighs, keep knees straight, bend body slightly forward, touch toes in jackknife position, extend body, and land with knees bent.

3. Run, jump high, bring knees to chest with both hands.

Jump and Dive:
1. Reach for mat with hands, keep body straight, make slight spring jump, and land on back of neck and shoulders. Careful spotting is recommended.

2. Dive for height by springing high, reach arms out, and extend body in mid-air; use hands and arms for landing.

Rolled Mats

Large groups can readily use a rolled mat, for two or three performers may use the same one, depending upon the stunt being learned. Simple activities such as running and jumping over the mat are recommended for the younger children, whereas more advanced stunts appeal greatly to older pupils. The rolled mat, 15 to 20 feet in length, which should be placed on top of a large flat mat, can also be used for teaching elementary dives, cartwheels, handstands, armstands, and somersaults for tumbling. Spotters should watch each performer carefully and anticipate faulty movements.

Run and Cross Over:
1. Run, and jump over mat, taking off with one foot forward in stride jump.

2. Run, and jump over mat, taking off with both feet at same time.

3. Run, hop over, and hold left foot momentarily in right hand; repeat, reversing hand and foot.

4. Run, jump over, and clap hands over head.

5. Run, jump over, and kick buttocks.

6. Run, and jump over, facing sideways.

7. Run, jump, turn complete circle in air, and land with bent knees.

Dive Over Roll:
(Beginners should stand at near side and reach over, doing a forward roll.)
1. Dive over roll.
2. Jump, and dive higher over roll.
3. Swan-dive over, arch body, keep arms sideward, tuck, and recover.

Hand Balance on Roll:
1. Stand near roll.
2. Hand-balance by leaning well forward on kick up.
3. Arch, keep body extended, arch forward, bend over, and come to erect position.

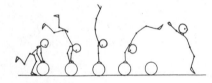

Stairs

This type of equipment can be made easily. Any two sets of stairs can be used when placed back to back and made stationary and secure. When only one set of stairs is available, the stunts can be done by having the pupils go up doing the activity and then jump off onto a mat on which the stairs should be placed. This type of equipment is intriguing to elementary-school children and is especially good for teaching them proper jumping and landing skills. A spotter should stand where he can best assist those who have faulty body movements. Wide stairs will enable two or more children to use this equipment safely at one time. The following stunts are to be done in an upstairs and downstairs fashion.

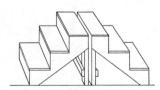

Go Up and Down:
1. Run up and down, using one foot at time.

2. Jump up and down, changing feet at top.
3. Jump up and down, zigzagging by jumping to left side on first step, to right on next one, and so forth.
4. Run up and down at full speed.

5. Run, jump off at top, and land with bent knees.

6. Hop sideward upon left foot; hop down sideward on right foot.
7. Jump up first two steps backward; turn; hop up rest frontward; hop down frontward; turn and hop down last two steps backward.

8. Walk up steps, do handstand on top, and walk down steps in handstand position.

Wands

Cut-down broomsticks or wands made of one-half inch doweling can be used for a wide variety of gymnastic activities to teach hand-eye coordination, body flexibility, and movement exploration, as well as to help children gain a better understanding of their bodies and what they are capable of doing.

1. Balance wand on index finger while standing, sitting, walking forward, and then backward.
2. Balance wand on two fingers, sit, then lie on back while continuing to balance it, and then gradually return to upright position.
3. Jump forward over stick without letting go of it; jump backward; raise it higher after each successful jump.
4. Place stick on two chairs, jump over it, and crawl under it; raise and lower it after each successful jump to discover how high or low you can move.
5. Hold stick in each hand with palms facing out. Bring stick up over head to waist without letting go of it. Bend right leg and step between right hand and stick. Move stick to right and around back. Twist body, then move left foot back over stick, step out of it, and return to your starting upright position. Throughout all movements keep both hands on stick. See how fast you can do it. Which person in your group can do it quickest?
6. Sit and hold stick with both hands. Draw legs over it. Next, extend them over stick without touching.
7. Stand stick up. Before it falls to floor, turn around quickly to right. Then turn left; turn twice either way; stand, stoop, and come back to erect position before it falls to ground.
8. One tosses stick to other who catches it and tosses it back with same hand. They move

FIGURE 21–2. Up you go! (Courtesy of North-lake Elementary School, Dallas, Texas.)

FIGURE 21-3. All children enjoy climbing and hanging from objects. (Courtesy of Refugio Public Schools, Refugio, Texas.)

further apart and continue. Count on each toss but go back to 1 each time a person misses. See which two in your group can get to 25, 50, 100 first without missing.
9. Each hold stick and straddle line. On "Go!" each tries to pull other holding stick across line.
10. Player A holds the wand upright on floor and then gradually lets it fall. B tries to catch it before it falls. They change roles. Play for 25 points.
11. Each holds wand and tries to get other to release it by twisting and turning both it and their bodies.
12. Two put stick through their legs and ride it in relay.

Hoops

Hula hoops, bicycle tires, and wooden or metal hoops can be used for a wide variety of activities. Have the children make up some new ones after they have done the following ones:

1. Each pupil places hoop on floor. Each jumps forward on one foot around it, then on other, and with both feet. Repeat all movements by jumping backward.
2. Arrange several hoops in straight line, then in circle, then in square, then in diagonal line. Jump on one foot forward into each hoop facing north, south, east, and west. Repeat, jumping forward on both feet. Then jump backward using same pattern on one foot; repeat pattern using both feet.
3. Roll hoop forward, around in circle, then backward while walking, running, skipping, jumping on both feet.
4. Hold hoop in front of body with both hands. Raise left leg in back and secure it inside hoop when it is raised over head. Balance on right leg. Hold for five counts. Repeat movement balancing on left leg.

FIGURE 21–4. With proper spotting and clear instructions, tampolining can be safe, fun, and exciting. (Courtesy of the Nissen Corporation, Cedar Rapids, Iowa.)

5. Roll hoop forward and run through it to starting line and back.
6. Using the hoop as jump rope, skip through it while moving forward, backward, in circle, and diagonally.
7. One player runs and rolls hoop as other tries to run faster than it travels. Change roles.

FIGURE 21–5. Elementary gymnastics is gaining an increasingly important place in American physical education programs on all educational levels. (Courtesy of the Nissen Corporation, Cedar Rapids, Iowa.)

Parallel Bar

Stress body control. In spotting from the side, the spotter should take a firm grip on the child's wrist with one hand and, with the other hand, grasp the child on the upper arm.

1. Stand between bars. With hands on top of bars, jump to a straight arm support. Do the following activities: move legs as on bicycle, swing both legs back and forth, move legs sideways so they cross each other, and walk on hands.
2. *On top of bars:* Do animal walks such as crab walk, measuring worm, duck walk, elephant walk, and so on.
3. *Straddle seat–travel forward:* Stand between bars. Jump to straight arm support. Swing legs forward and straddle bars with legs. Place hands in front of legs and place weight on hands. Swing legs down in back and forward between bars to straddle seat position. Continue length of the bars.
4. *Side-saddle position:* Jump to straight arm support. Swing legs over one bar. Let go with hands and sit erect in side saddle position.
5. *Shoulder balance:* Sit in straddle seat position. Lean forward and place upper arms or shoulders on bars, grasping bars with hands to give body control. Slowly raise legs to shoulder balance position.
6. *Simple routine:* (Many can be worked out. Only one is mentioned here.) Stand between bars. Swing legs to side-straddle position on right side. Turn quarter turn to right, placing hands on bar in back, and extend legs to V formation. Hold. Roll half turn to right to front lying position on bar, with arms extended sideways. Hold. Place left hand on opposite bar, right hand on bar next to right leg. Swing left leg forward between bars, turning body as legs come up over bar into straddle-seat position.

Horizontal Ladder

1. Sit facing end of ladder, grasp rung, and travel length of ladder with only feet dragging on floor.
2. Sit under ladder tailor fashion, grasp rung, raise legs off floor, and travel length of ladder.

FIGURE 21-6. Rope climbing is recommended for girls as well as boys. Here we see that a climbing pole can be used with equal results. (Courtesy of the Nissen Corporation, Cedar Rapids, Iowa.)

3. *Monkey Walk:* Same as on single beam but on rungs of ladder.
4. Grasp siderails, and travel with only feet touching the floor.

1. Chin yourself.
2. *Leg hang:* Grasp one rung, bring feet up and over a rung until the feet hook under the next rung, release hands, and hang inverted.
3. *Leg hang:* Do as above, and fold arms over chest and swing back and forth.

SUGGESTED READINGS

AAHPER: *Gymnastic Guide.* Latest ed. Washington, D.C.
Diem, L.: *Who Can?* Wilhelm Limpert, Publisher, 1955. Copyright U.S.A. by George Williams College, Chicago, 1957.
Edwards, V.: *Tumbling.* Philadelphia, W. B. Saunders Company, 1969.
Loken, N.: *How to Improve Your Apparatus Activities.* Chicago, The Athletic Institute, 1960.
Loken, N. C., and Willoughby, R. J.: *Complete Book of Gymnastics.* Englewood Cliffs, New Jersey, Prentice-Hall, Inc., 1976.
Mosston, M.: *Developmental Movement.* Columbus, Ohio, Charles E. Merrill Publishing Company, 1965.
O'Quinn, G.: *Gymnastics for Elementary School Children.* Dubuque, Iowa, William C. Brown Company, Publishers, 1972.
Roys, B.: *Gymnastics for Women.* Philadelphia, W. B. Saunders Company, 1975.
Ryser, O.: *Tumbling and Apparatus Stunts.* Dubuque, Iowa, William C. Brown Company, Publishers, 1976.

SUGGESTED FILMS

Loop films available from The Athletic Institute, 805 Merchandise Mart, Chicago, Illinois 60654:

Boys	*Girls*
Parallel bars (14 loops)	Free calisthenics (6 loops)
Tumbling (8 loops)	Balance beam (6 loops)
Rings (12 loops)	High-low bar (6 loops)
Vaulting (5 loops)	Side horse (6 loops)

CHAPTER TWENTY-TWO

LEAD-UP ACTIVITIES TO INDIVIDUAL AND DUAL SPORTS

If you want to know what children are like, watch their play.
If you are concerned about what they will become, guide
their play.

The Authors

Pupils in the upper elementary grades should have instruction in the basic skills of tennis, badminton, archery, bowling, and as many other of the lifetime sports as possible. Lead-up games to these activities should also be a part of this program and be used to help children learn game strategy as well as to provide them with opportunities to perfect basic beginning skills both in class and in after-school intramural play.

Although schools are increasingly adding instructional facilities for these sports, many of the basic skills, such as bowling, can be taught in the gymnasium or elsewhere in the community during those school hours when the general public would not be using either private or commercial facilities. Improvised or borrowed equipment can be made available. Although classes may be large, the Lifetime Sports Association has available group instructional guides that will enable those teachers who want to bring these new activities with high carry-over value into the program but who hesitate to do so because of class size.[1]

TENNIS

Basic Skills

Only the forehand, backhand, and serve strokes, playing rules, and simple game strategy should be taught on this level to the majority of students. Those more skilled may be taught more skills.

THE FOREHAND DRIVE

Used most often in game play, this stroke is usually the most easily mastered. Stand sideways to the net, feet in a forward-back position, hold the racket in the handshake grip, and hit the ball with a fully extended arm and racket, holding the

---

[1]Write to the American Alliance For Health, Physical Education and Recreation, 1201 16th N.W., Washington, D.C. for information concerning these guides, or consult current issues of The Journal of Health, Physical Education and Recreation, available in most college libraries.

elbow well out and away from the body. Shift the entire body weight forward as the ball is hit.

The wrist should be kept firm and one should move into the stroke, hitting the ball in the center or "sweet part" of the racket so that it travels swiftly in a straight line and barely clears the net. The follow-through should also be in a straight line pattern, and will be if the ball is hit at an imaginary nine o'clock position and the racket swept on through to three o'clock without the racket head's dropping lower than the wrist.

THE BACKHAND DRIVE

Although similar to the forehand stroke, the backhand drive is often more difficult for right-handed players to master, whereas many left-handed ones will develop a backhand superior to their forehand. Hold the racket in the Eastern grip, that has been modified by being moved one-quarter turn forward, and hold the thumb behind the handle for additional support. Stand facing sideways, feet in a forward and back stride, knees relaxed, and body bent forward at the waist so that the racket arm can swing freely back and then across the body at waist height. Hold the racket head perpendicular to the ground, contact the ball, shift body weight forward, and follow through in a straight line pattern.

THE SERVE

A correct serve results from a combination of the correct stance, ball toss, swing, and footwork. In movement it is similar to the overhand baseball throw. The student stands sideways to the base line with feet spread comfortably apart, weight equally distributed, and the forward shoulder pointed in the direction the ball is to go. The racket is held in the Continental grip (similar to the Eastern backhand, with the racket shifted from one-sixteenth to one-eighth of a turn toward the forehand grip). The higher the point of contact with the ball, the better the serve is likely to be. The ball should therefore be thrown straight up in the air as high as the fully extended arm and racket can reach above the head and over the forward foot and be hit at its maximal height when practically motionless, just before it comes back down toward the ground. As the ball is tossed into the air, the weight shifts to the rear foot. When the ball starts down, the racket is swung back behind the head and the whole body weight shifts to the forward foot as contact is made with the ball above the serving shoulder. On the natural follow-through, the racket is brought down and across the body.

Basic Rules and Scoring

The point progress of a game is 15, 30, 40, and game. (Throughout this discussion a point should be understood to mean one of these scoring units.) When the score is tied 40–40, the score is called deuce and the tie must be broken; the game is won by winning two consecutive points. If the server wins the first point after deuce it is called *advantage in,* short for advantage in favor of the server. If the receiver wins the first point it is called *advantage out.* Players speak of it as "ad out" and "ad there." When a player has no score, it is referred to as "love." The server's score is called first during a game, whether officiated by tournament officials or by the players themselves. For example, the server's score would be love–30 if he has lost the first two game points, 40–30 if he gains the next three. Singles and doubles are scored in the same way.

FIGURE 22–1.   Paddle tennis is similar to regular tennis except that the ball is served underhand and is hit with a wooden paddle. (Courtesy of the Los Angeles City Schools, Los Angeles, California.)

SET AND MATCH

A set is won by the player or team who first wins six games, providing they have at least a two-game lead over the opponents. A set can be won at 6–0, 6–1, 6–2, 6–3, and 6–4. It cannot be won at 6–5 but may terminate at 7–5 or, in the case of a hard-won battle, may go to as many as 15 games or even more. A match is made up of the winner of two of three sets for women and for mixed doubles, the winner being the person who wins. (Men's competition requires the best three of five sets.)

General Rules

SERVICE

Each server serves a complete game. The first serve of the game must be from the right half of the court behind the base line. He has two chances to send the ball over the net diagonally into his opponent's service court. If the first ball is good, a second is not used. The next serve is made from the left, the remaining serves thus alternating between right and left. A double service fault (such as hitting the first ball into the net and the second out of bounds) causes a loss of point. The ball must land in the opponent's service court before it can be hit by the receiver, who must wait until it bounces before returning it. After the service, the ball may be hit before it bounces, throughout the game.

The serve is a fault if the server

1. Does not take the proper position before serving.
2. Commits a foot fault.
3. Misses the ball but hits it slightly with the racket. The server may toss and catch the ball on an attempted serve without penalty if his racket does not touch it.
4. Fails to hit the ball into the correct service court.
5. Hits any permanent structure with the served ball other than the net, strap, or hand.
6. Hits his partner or anything he wears or carries with the served ball.

(The penalty for any one of the above is a single fault; it becomes a double fault and loss of point if such an error happens on both serves.)

FOOT FAULT.   It is a foot fault on the serve

1. For the server to change his position by walking or running.
2. To step on or over the back line as the ball is hit.

THE LET

The ball is considered to be a "let" when

1. A served ball touches the net, strap, or band and is otherwise good.
2. Because of interference beyond a player's control, he is unable to play the ball.
3. It is delivered before the receiver is ready. (Call "ready?" before each serve.)

LOSS OF POINT

The player loses a point if

1. He does not return the ball to his opponent's court on the volley or first bounce after service.
2. He or his clothing touches the net on any play.
3. He reaches over the net to play a ball unless it has bounced back over the net because of a spin or a strong wind.
4. He throws his racket at the ball.
5. He hits the ball more than once.
6. He misses the ball or hits it out of bounds or into the net.
7. He plays a served ball before it bounces.

GOOD RETURNS

A ball is considered good if

1. It lands on any line.
2. It touches the top of a net post or the net and falls into the proper court.
3. A player reaches outside the net posts to play a ball and returns it successfully.
4. The player's racket on the follow-through goes over the net but does not touch it.

CHANGING SIDES

Players should change after the first, third, and every following alternate game of each set, and at the end of each set, so that each side will compete under the same sun, wind court, and spectator conditions. If the total number of games won in the set is even, however, courts should not be changed until the end of the first game of the next set.

Doubles Rules

SERVICE

1. The players on one side take turns serving. The order of serving should be determined before the beginning of each set. One of the alternating serving pair should serve games 1, 3, 5, 7, and so on, while those of the opposite side should alternate serving the even-numbered games.
2. The order of serving must be consistent throughout the set but may change at the beginning of a new set.
3. During the serve, the server's partner may stand anywhere on his half of the court.
4. When one serves out of turn, the proper server must serve as soon as the error is discovered, but all points already earned should be counted. If a complete game is played before the error is known, the game counts, and the service order should remain as altered.

Game Strategy

The attacking style is usually played at the net with the defensive players moving back to base-line positions. Although most players "beat themselves" through their own errors, this may be avoided by carefully analyzing all mistakes made and not repeating them. Consistent, steady play is more fruitful than taking unwise chances or trying to "kill" as many shots as possible. Beginners especially should learn (1) to hit the ball away from their opponents, (2) to anticipate where the returned ball will land on the court and be ready to receive it, and (3) to outsmart their opponents by placing returned shots to their weakness (this may be one of the double partners, the backhand of one, or the inability of both to move quickly around the court).

BADMINTON

Basic Skills

Only the grip, forehand, and backhand strokes, basic rules, and scoring of this sport should be taught to the majority of students. Those more skilled may be taught more skills.

THE GRIP

A flexible wrist snap is a must for stroking the bird on both the forehand and backhand. For the forehand, grasp the handle with the handshake grip while the racket face is at right angles to the ground. The fingers are spread slightly apart, with the forefinger extended diagonally and slightly bent behind the handle. The thumb is cocked and wrapped around the inside of the handle, exerting pressure against the forefinger. The handle rests at the base of the fingers but not in the palm, with the V formed by the thumb and forefinger on the inside top of the handle and in line with the racket head. Swing the racket back and forth, snapping the wrist to get the feel of the necessary quick, definite movement.

The backhand grip is similar to the Eastern backhand grip in tennis. To gain the backhand from a forehand grip position, hold the racket by the throat with the left hand and turn the right hand to the left so that the first knuckle is on top of the racket handle. Extend the thumb diagonally up and back of the handle. The V line formed by the thumb and forefinger is somewhat behind the racket when held in front of the player. The advanced player will notice that the backhand grip results in a slight wrist cock as the arm is brought across the body in preparation for a backhand stroke.

THE FOREHAND DRIVE

This stroke, which is similar to throwing a softball, is a flowing, free movement in which the follow-through plays an important part. It is a natural movement used when returning the bird from the right side of the body. The head of the racket should be kept higher than the wrist, and the left foot is brought forward, the body leaning slightly sideward toward the net. The backswing should start at the same time the left foot is brought forward. Simultaneously with a pivotal shift of the body weight from the rear to the forward foot, the bent elbow leads the flexed wrist into the stroking area. The wrist should be slightly ahead of the racket head and snapped at the moment of contact. If the player wants to hit the bird upward, he should swing low, then up to it; to hit it downward, the forward swing is in a downward arc. The arm should be extended and relaxed and the bird hit squarely in the racket center by a quick wrist flick.

THE BACKHAND DRIVE

The backhand drive is made with the right shoulder facing the net and the racket held with a backhand grip. As the bird is hit with the reverse side of the racket, the weight is shifted with the feet in a stride position from the rear to the forward foot. When the bird is played in front of the body, the thumb may be held so that it rests flat against the nonhitting side of the racket for more power and better control.

THE SERVE

The racket is held with a forehand grip. The shuttle should be struck in front of the body with the full arm stretched for a relaxed but forceful movement. With feet in stride position, the body weight shifts from the forward foot to back, then is returned to forward as the bird is hit. The wrist flick, forward arc swing, and follow-through should be easy, natural movements. There is very little follow-through on a short serve. Beginners should drop the bird from the thumb and index finger, held at the extreme feather tip, and play it in front of the forward foot. Advanced players may master the toss serve by throwing the bird slightly into the air and contacting it with a well-timed forward stroke. The majority of serves in singles should be high and deep; in doubles they should be low and land just inside the service court or on a boundary line. To be a legal serve, the bird must be contacted below the waist with no part of the racket higher than the server's hand.

General Rules

A game of women's singles is 11 points; for men's singles and mixed doubles it is 15 to 21 points, according to what has been arranged. The doubles service court extends from the short service line to the long service line and from the center line to the side boundary line. The singles service court extends from the short service line to the back boundary line and from the center line to the side boundary line. The court service boundaries are long and narrow for singles, short and fat for doubles. After service the singles playing court remains the same, whereas the doubles playing area becomes long and wide. Points are scored only by the serving side, with loss of service known as "side out," as in volleyball.

The server serves only one bird into alternate courts (as in tennis) and begins in his right-hand court. To be good the bird must go diagonally across the net and land in the receiver's box. A serve that strikes the net but continues on into the proper court is good. In doubles only one player serves at the beginning of the game (this is called "one hand down in the first inning"), but for the rest of the game both the opposing partners alternate serves. Service in doubles always starts in the right court. In singles the service begins in the right court, but thereafter it is made in this court only when the score is even for that side, and in the left court when the score is odd for that side. The first singles player to reach nine points when the score is 9–all may choose to play for three more points, or for two more when the score is 10–all. In doubles, when the score is tied 13–all, those first reaching 13 determine whether to finish the game at 15 or to "set" it for five more points.

It is a fault (a service or hand loss for the server, or point loss for the receiver) when

1. The bird is served above the waist or the racket head is higher than the hand on a serve.
2. The server or receiver fails to keep his feet within the boundaries of his service area during the serve.
3. The bird is hit into the wrong service area, out of bounds, or into the net or hits a player or any obstruction outside the court.
4. Anyone other than the intended receiver returns the bird.
5. The server feints a serve or balks his opponent.
6. A player reaches over the net to hit the bird or touches the net with any part of his body or racket.
7. A player hits the bird twice or "tosses" or "holds" it instead of stroking it correctly.
8. A player fails to return the bird or hits it twice in a row, or it is hit by one player and then his partner successively before it goes over the net.

A match consists of the best of three games. Players change ends at the start of the second game, and if needed, also at the third game. In the third game players change sides when the first player reaches eight points in a game of 15 points or six points in a game of 11 points.

ARCHERY

Basic Skills

Activities to be included in an archery unit on this level include bracing and unbracing the bow, nocking, drawing, anchoring, aiming, and scoring.

BRACING AND UNBRACING THE BOW

A commercial bow stringer is a common and desirable accessory. Not only does it lessen the labor of bow stringing for the individual, it also lessens or equalizes the stress on the bow while it is being strung.

The push-pull method is frequently used on light target bows. The lower end of the bow is placed against the inside arch of the left foot with the back of the bow toward the body. The bow tip does not touch the ground but is pressed against the foot. The heel of

FIGURE 22-2. A target showing scoring values.

the right hand is placed near the bow tip while the left hand, on the handle, pulls the bow toward the body. The heel of the right hand presses the upper limb of the bow down while the thumb and index finger slide up the bow and slip the noose into the nock.

To unstring the bow, the same bow, hand, and body positions are used. The string is lifted from its nock by the index and middle fingers and slipped down the bow as the left hand pulls the bow toward the body.

For a heavier or recurve bow the step-in stringing method is often used. With the right leg between the string and the belly of the bow, belly facing forward, the lower end of the bow rests on the instep of the left foot. As the right hand pushes the bow forward at the top of the upper limb, the bow at the handle bends against the back of the right thigh. The left hand guides the string into the nock. Use of a commercial bow string for bows usually strung by the push-pull method prevents twisting and possible damage to bow limbs.

THE STANCE

The target archer stands astride the shooting line, the field archer behind the shooting stake, with body weight equally distributed. For the right-handed archer the left shoulder and head are turned toward the target and the feet are spread to shoulder width. The left foot is moved backward approximately 6 inches, and the toes turns slightly to the target to complete the open stance. The body is held in a comfortable, relaxed yet erect position. The stance must be consistent.

THE GRIP AND BOW ARM

The fingers and thumb of the bow hand lightly encircle the bow so that the V of the thumb and forefinger is at the pivot point of the handle. The bow is held parallel to the ground and pointing toward the target with the string toward the body until the arrow is nocked.

The bow is raised upright, and in preparation for the draw, the bow arm is raised to shoulder height. During the draw and release, the bow handle is pushed by the V formed by the fleshy part of the thumb and hand. The forefinger is around the back of the bow, and the thumb may be resting lightly on the forefinger. The other three fingers no longer "hold" the bow but are relaxed in an extended position and point toward the target. The wrist is straight and firm. The arm is comfortably extended with the elbow turned out, away from the bowstring. The bow arm shoulder is kept down and back to avoid leaning toward the target.

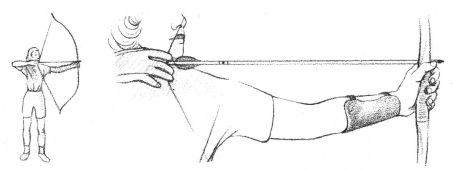

FIGURE 22–3.   The teacher should demonstrate the basic skills of archery.

NOCKING

The bow is held horizontal to the ground with the back of the bow hand facing up. With the cock feather up, the drawing hand, holding the nock of the arrow between the thumb and index finger, slides the arrow across the arrow rest and places the nock on the serving. A 90° angle is formed by the arrow and the string. The thumb remains in contact with the arrow until the index finger and the other drawing fingers reach behind the string to stabilize the arrow. Often the index finger of the bow hand may be needed to support the arrow until it is partially drawn.

DRAWING AND ANCHORING

The first three fingers of the right hand grasp under the string with the fingertips (no farther back than the first joint). The back of the hand remains straight, with flexion only in the first and second finger joints. The large knuckle joints are never flexed during the draw. The arrow is positioned between the first and second fingers. At the same time the bow arm is raised, the drawing arm is pulled backward by the muscles of the back, shoulder, and arm. When fully extended, the right elbow is bent and parallel to the ground. During the draw take a deep breath and hold it.

ANCHOR POINT

Anchor point refers to the point on the archer's face at which she places her hand when the bowstring is fully drawn. The point is often described as low, a point on or under the jaw bone, or high, a point on or directly under the cheekbone. The anchor point, once established, must be used consistently and constantly for all distances.

Scoring

1. Score values are gold—9 points; red—7 points; blue—5 points; black—3 points; white—1 point.
2. An arrow that cuts two colors is given the higher value.
3. An arrow that passes through the scoring face so it is not visible from the front counts 7 points, if shot from 60 yards or less.
4. An arrow rebounding from the scoring face counts seven points if shot from 60 yards or less.
5. Arrows in the petticoat have no scoring value.

BOWLING

Basic Skills

Activities to include in this unit are the proper ball delivery, aiming, and scoring. Plastic pins and balls are also available.[2] Indian clubs or milk cartons filled with sand or pebbles and playground balls (8½-inch) can be used to teach the fundamentals of this game almost anywhere including the gymnasium or in hallways. They should be set in the proper order. However, the children should be taught this challenging sport at a regular bowling alley, if at all possible.

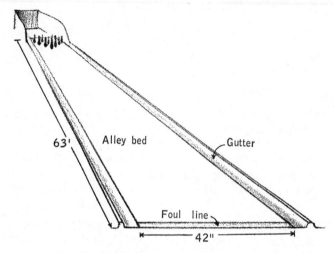

FIGURE 22–4. The bowling alley.

If the class is working without regulation bowling balls, the grip cannot be taught. However, the proper stance and approach can be simulated and practiced. The grip, stance, and approach should be taught by a demonstration accompanied by clear explanations of the movements. The class should then attempt the skills under the close supervision of the teacher.

The four-step approach is recommended for beginners. The approach should be demonstrated, followed by student practice without a ball. Marking the steps on the floor may help those to achieve success who are having difficulty making a smooth approach.

It is well to allow the student to practice the approach with a ball as soon as he understands the rhythm of the steps in the approach, for the release is an integral part of the entire movement. Some teachers even prefer to introduce the release first and have

[2]See the Appendix for a list of suppliers of elementary physical education equipment.

FIGURE 22–5. The proper setting of the pins.

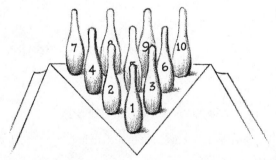

FIGURE 22-6. The correct way to hold the ball with one hand.

the students practice it without the ball six or seven times. Then the approach is learned and practiced, followed by the synchronization of the two movements. When the students are able to move smoothly through the approach and release, they try it with the ball.

The methods of scoring in bowling may be presented following the instruction in the above skills and before the students begin to practice on their own. Because the scoring is difficult for students to comprehend from an oral explanation, it is suggested that a score sheet be reproduced in large size on a blackboard or on a piece of oak tag for the class to view as the teacher keeps score of a real or imagined game. A lesson in picking up spares may well follow scoring. Diagrams, slides, and films may be used to supplement or substitute for actual demonstrations.

If instruction is being given in the gymnasium because no alley is available or if for some reason the class is not going to the alley during a certain class period, there are a number of bowling games which may be introduced to vary the class routine and to provide additional activity. Among the games recommended are soccer bowling, skittles, tire bowling, lawn bowls, miniature bowling, arch bowls, bowl spot ball, cocked hat bowling, and square five bowling (see Suggested Readings).

BALL DELIVERY

If a playground ball is used, it should be grasped in one hand with the fingers used to control its direction when rolled toward the pins. If rolled with the right hand, the left foot should be forward and body weight transferred from front-back-front on the ball release.

If a bowling ball is used at an alley, the right-handed bowler stands on the right-hand corner of the approach with the left foot five to ten boards from the right gutter. Throughout the coordinated approach the ball hand and arm are in line with the floor boards. As the ball is carried toward the foul line, the thumb is in a 12 o'clock position, pointing toward the pins, and the fingers are under and behind the ball. As the release begins the thumb slides from the hole and the ball rolls off the fingertips beyond the foul line and six to eight boards in from the right gutter. There is no rotation of the forearm. As the ball is released, the fingers impart an upward spin; then the open hand, with palm up and fingers and thumb pointing toward the pins, continues in an upward arc.

AIMING

For children, the point of aim should be for the 1–3 pocket (1–2 pocket for left-handers), if only one ball is used. If two are used, the second should be aimed directly at the pin or area.

PLAYER	1	2	3	4	5	6	7	8	9	10		
1	X	6/	8/	X	6/3	X	X	9ı⸍	6/ X⸍ 7 2		182	
WINNER	20	38	58	77	86	115	134	143	163 182			
2												
WINNER												

FIGURE 22–7. A perfect game is a score of 300.

Scoring

A regular bowling game is divided into ten frames. A perfect game is a score of 300—12 strikes in a row. The highest number of pins scored in a game is 30. There are three games to a match.

A strike (all pins knocked down) is marked with a large X in a small box, as shown. The strike is scored as ten points plus the total of the next two balls. If a strike is not scored, the number of pins knocked down is recorded.

In the second and all other frames, all previous scores are added consecutively. The winner has the highest score.

When a playground ball is used, each pin knocked down should count 1 point. A game consists of 25 points.

TRACK AND FIELD

Basic Skills

Dashes

1. *Standing start:* This start is recommended for elementary-school children, as the majority will be running in tennis shoes. The runner places the feet in a comfortable position, one foot slightly behind the other, and arms in opposition. The runner leans forward slightly and, at the gun signal, takes off with the back foot.
2. *Crouch start:* Starting must be adapted to each runner because body measurements vary with regard to trunk, legs, and arms. The following instructions are basic:

On Your Mark:
1. Squat about a foot from the starting line.
2. Place the hands, shoulder width, behind the line, with your weight on your thumbs and fingers.
3. Kneel on your right knee, and the left foot should be even with the right knee. Adjust widith.

Get Set:
1. Rock forward and upward, hips down, head up, and weight on the hands and front foot.

Go:
1. Whip arms.
2. Push with the front leg.
3. Step forward on the back leg.
4. Straighten up gradually

Standing Long Jump

1. Toe the line with both feet.
2. Crouch low with your knees bent and arms behind your hips.
3. Jump forward, carrying your arms and feet forward and upward.
4. Land on both feet.

Running Long Jump

This event includes the approach, jump, and landing.

1. *Approach:* Run 16 to 20 strides. Take off on one foot from the board.
2. *Jump:* The hitch kick is used by many other jumpers. The feet cycle in the air. The tuck jump is simpler. Jump high in the air, tuck the body as if sitting in a chair, and bring your feet together.
3. *Landing:* Legs are forward and arms back. As your heels hit the pit, your arms are thrust forward so the body will fall forward.

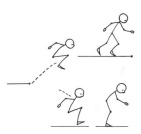

High Jump

All children enjoy jumping, but the child with long thighs and limber hips will excel in this event. The scissors jump will be enjoyed most by children at this age level, though it has been replaced in high school and college competition by the western roll, straddle roll, and Fosbury flop.

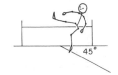

Scissors Jump

1. *Approach:* The child should be allowed and instructed to follow his natural urge to approach the bar from either the left or the right. The jumper stands at a 45-degree angle to the bar and runs to gain momentum. The number of steps, from seven to eleven, required will depend upon the size of the jumper.
2. *Jump:* The jumper approaches with his right side to the bar and takes off from the left foot, swinging the right leg up and over the bar. The left leg follows over the bar in a scissors movement. Legs are kept straight.
3. *Landing:* Land on both feet in the pit, facing in the same direction as at the beginning of the jump.

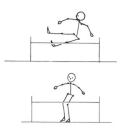

Western Roll

1. *Approach:* Come in from the left and approach as in the scissors jump. The left shoulder is toward the bar at the take-off.
2. *Jump:* Take off on the left foot and swing the right leg forward and over. The left leg tucks at the side of the right and the jumper rolls over the bar.
3. *Landing:* The jumper lands on his left foot and hands.

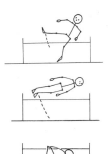

Relay: 240-Yard

The shuttle relay is suited to gymnasiums and can be used with the shorter distances as a training event. A baton may be passed, or the runner may touch off the next runner. The 240-yard relay is run by a team of four, each running a distance of 60 yards and passing a baton to the next runner. The baton, in official relays, must be passed within a 20-yard space. The visual exchange is recommended for the elementary level. When the approaching runner is 5 to 7 yards away, the receiver should start running, looking back with the right arm extended backward, hand open, and palm up to receive the baton. The initial runner may use the standing or crouch start and carries the baton in the left hand.

Softball Throw

1. *Distance:* Throw at a 45-degree angle because this trajectory provides the maximal distance.
2. *Accuracy:* Throw at a target made up of colored circles of various sizes or at an archery target face. Give number values for each colored circle.

Standing High Jump

In a standing high jump, the jumper stands sideways to the cross bar and uses the foot away from the bar for the take-off. With maximal effort, the leg next to the bar is thrown forward, up, and over. The take-off foot trails the inside leg. The arms should assist during the jump. As the jumper improves in body control, he may, after the take-off, throw his head back to raise the buttocks in clearing the bar. He can also either roll away from the bar or cut back to face the bar, depending on which form is easier. This basic jump, the scissors jump, is the one most used by elementary-school children.

Hop, Step, and Jump

Each player, in turn, runs to a designated starting line. Upon reaching the starting line, he hops on his left foot, steps on the right foot, then broad jumps to complete the third phase of the event. Measurement is taken wherever the back of the heel strikes the floor. If the contestant should fall back on his hands or sit down at the completion of his jump, the jump is measured from whatever part of the anatomy is closest to the starting line.

×××××× |←—20'–30'—→| •••••••◆

Starting line

Distance Running

Each student tries to run or fast walk (jog) a distance of 600 yards in as short a time as possible. Keep time of each one as he strives to cover the distance in the shortest amount of time. Increase the distance to be run as the students gain in endurance.

Straddle High Jump

The approach and take-off are about the same as in the western roll. The approach angle should be 30 to 45 degrees. A vertical take-off of the foot is essential. On the jump, the outside arm should swing up sharply and the waist should be as high as the bar before the body is laid out parallel to it. The trailing toe turns out as the hips roll over the crossbar and the trailing arm is on the chest or hip. When over the bar, the head and lead arm drop as the landing is made with the lead arm and leg.

Step, Hop, and Jump

A take-off board and jumping pit are essential. Start with a run and use either foot for the take-off. Land and hop on this same foot. Take one step forward and then jump over the crossbar and on both feet and come to an upright position.

The Baton Hand-Off

The baton can be passed in a number of ways. The underarm extension or the V-pass is best for fifth graders. Just before the passer and receiver are running evenly, the passer A gives the baton to passer B, who takes it with his right hand and quickly transfers it to his left. The receiver's hand is turned to the rear with fingers together to form the V's so that the passer has as large a target in which to leave the baton as possible.

Pursuit Baton Exchange Drill

A baton is needed for each group of five. One child in each group gets into the "on your mark" position, holding the baton in his left hand at the starting line. On "Go" the starter in each group runs forward and gives the baton to the next child in each line of five stationed in a straight line 15 feet apart. No. 2 gives it to 3, and so on. The baton should be passed with the left hand and received with the right. Each receiver must change the baton from his receiving right hand to his passing left one as he is running. After No. 4 gives the baton to No. 5, the line turns and repeats the sequence of passing with each going the other way. If the baton is dropped, it must be picked up before the runner can continue moving.

The Low Hurdles

This activity is best for sixth graders. The hurdles should be 20 inches high. Place four hurdles at a distance of 50 yards. Corrugated boxes can be used first before the pupils actually try jumping over wooden ones. The same start is used in the low hurdles as in dashes. The leading leg is the one going over the hurdle first. It should be in the rear in the starting position. When clearing the hurdle, the lead leg is kept nearly straight and the trailing leg is drawn up with the knee turned to the side. The trailing leg is then whipped quickly over hurdle. The lead leg and opposite arm should clear the hurdle at the same time, and the body should lean slightly forward. When the lead leg clears the hurdle, it should be quickly brought down so that the foot will be in running position. Pupils should practice taking a long stride over the hurdle and know the importance of speed made on the ground before jumping.

FIGURE 22–8.   Boys especially like learning how to jump. (Courtesy of Jayfro Corporation, Montville, Connecticut.)

Jogging

Jogging is a run-walk combination done for one mile against one's own time. It is not a competitive race. Each individual should be timed after several sessions of untimed distance jogging and each strive to increase the amount of running he does, instead of running-walking. He should also try to jog a mile in less time than the 12 minutes allowed for his first attempt.

General Rules

1. Each contestant should not enter more than three events.
2. All contestants must take part in conditioning exercises, including running and jumping, for at least three weeks before the meet.
3. The health record of each contestant should be checked before the meet.
4. Contestants should wear armbands of distinguishing colors and name tags.
5. All spectators must stay away from starting and finishing lines, and student patrols should keep the areas cleared for each event.
6. A first-aid station, easily identifiable, must be provided and be under the direction of a certified first-aider.
7. Inexpensive ribbons or other awards should be given to the winners.

Facilities and Equipment

1. Gymnasium.
2. Playground with 100-yard straightaway or track.
3. 8- × 20-foot pit for broad and high jump, filled with sand or sawdust.

FIGURE 22–9. Flag football is a recommended lead-up team game for left-handed sixth grade boys. (Courtesy of Snitz Manufacturing Company, East Troy, Wisconsin.)

4. Standard for high jump with bamboo pole.
5. Softball.
6. Targets.
7. Whistle or starting pistol.
8. Lime for marking outside starts, finishes, and curved lanes.
9. Tempera for marking starts, finishes, and curves in the gymnasium.
10. Steel tape for measuring.
11. Take-off board, 2 to 3 feet square, for running broad jump. (Optimal–lime marker may be used.)
12. Batons–9 inches. Can use bamboo pole, doweling, broomstick or mailing tubes.
13. Officials.
    Starter.
    Judges–one for each place to be given.
    Scorers.
    Referee.

The equipment and facilities listed above meet minimum requirements. At a scheduled track meet on an official track, starting blocks, stop watch, timers, and so forth, would be present.

SUGGESTED READINGS

AAHPER: *Desirable Competition for Children of Elementary School Age and Track and Field Guide*, Washington, D.C.
Armbruster, D., Irwin, L., and Musker, F.: *Basic Skills in Sports for Men and Women*. 5th ed. St. Louis, The C.V. Mosby Company, 1971.

Breshahan, G., et al.: *Track and Field Athletics*. 7th ed. St. Louis, The C.V. Mosby Company, 1969.

Cheatum, B. A.: *Golf*. Philadelphia, W.B. Saunders Company, 1969.

Cooper, D.: *The New Aerobics*. New York, Bantam Books, 1974.

Gemsemer, R.: *Tennis*. Philadelphia, W.B. Saunders Company, 1969.

Kansas City Public Schools: *Physical Education in the Elementary School*. Curriculum Bulletin No. 167, Kansas City, 1972.

Milwaukee Public Schools: *Physical Education, Intermediate Schools, 1971*. Milwaukee, Wisconsin.

Parker, V., and Kennedy, R.: *Track and Field For Girls and Women*. Philadelphia, W.B. Saunders Company, 1969.

Pszczola, L.: *Archery*. Philadelphia, W.B. Saunders Company, 1971.

Schunk, C.: *Bowling*. Philadelphia, W.B. Saunders Company, 1970.

Texas Education Agency: *Physical Education in the Elementary School, Curriculum Guide For Grade 4; Grade 5; and Grade 6*. Austin, Texas, 1972.

Vannier, M., and Poindexter, H. B.: *Individual and Team Sports For Girls and Women*. 3rd ed. Philadelphia, W. B. Saunders Company, 1977.

CHAPTER TWENTY-THREE

LEAD-UP ACTIVITIES TO TEAM SPORTS

The spirit of playful competition is, as a social impulse, older than culture itself and pervades all life like a veritable ferment.

Johan Huizinga
Homo Ludens: A Study of the Play Element in Culture

Skills required in team games taught from the first grade through the sixth grade will gradually increase proficiency in relays, lead-up games, and modified team games, as well as in formal drill or practice. The desire to play team sports, often manifested in the third and fourth grades, can be fulfilled in the fifth grade, when interest has become sustained instead of sporadic and the participants have reached a level of understanding and skill necessary for thorough enjoyment of games involving group cooperation and complicated rules. When primary-level children start asking for team games, let it be remembered that there is no substitute for skill when the child is ready, as judged by the teacher, for progressive instruction.

In the primary grades one can teach games that introduce simple skills with the ball, such as catching, throwing, kicking, and dodging. These give a general background of mechanics that carries over into all types of games in which a ball is used. The reader is referred to Chapter 16, Active "Low-Organized" Games, for a compilation of appropriate locomotor and manipulative games for primary-grade children. This chapter consists of lead-up activities for a variety of team sports including

1. Soccer
2. Softball
3. Volleyball
4. Basketball
5. Football
6. Floor Hockey

Each section on each activity area has been subdivided into (1) skills, (2) lead-up games, and (3) basic rules.

CLASS ORGANIZATION

Division of Teams

Some teachers divide classes into teams and keep the same teams through the entirety of a sports unit. This procedure saves time and offers the participants the opportunity to become thoroughly familiar with teammates and the way they play. Others divide teams each week. The latter method has the advantage of exposing the participants to more and differing playing situations; hence, it develops alertness and versatility to meet the unexpected. A teacher must judge which method best meets the situation and needs in that particular school, but it is recommended that teams be divided with an equalization of skill. Selected teams may wear distinguishing colors or pinnies given to them by their squad leaders. Skill segregation makes for dull competition. Then, too, a child with poor motor ability or skill weakness often improves more rapidly while playing with others more highly skilled.

Choice of Leaders

Leaders or team captains should be chosen because of their sportsmanship and knowledge of the game. Weekly rotation of captains is advisable in order to develop leadership and acceptance of responsibility within the whole group.

FIGURE 23–1.   How to play on a team is an important thing to learn, especially when you are a sixth-grader. (Courtesy of Snitz Manufacturing Company, East Troy, Wisconsin.)

FIGURE 23–2. Tennis instruction can begin at the elementary level. (Courtesy of Camp Yonahlossee, Blowing Rock, North Carolina.)

Student officials must not only be grounded in the rules of the game but also must remain fair and impartial in their decisions. Daily rotation of officials permits each equal playing time. Student officials will require frequent advice from the teacher; this help should be exact and consistent. Surprisingly enough, fifth and sixth graders can become quite technical in their insistence that games be played according to the rules. Some become more touchy about inconsistencies than do high school students.

Teaching Skills

There are three commonly used methods for teaching skills: (1) the part method, (2) the whole method, and (3) the part-whole method. The first consists of teaching each skill through formal drill until a fair degree of proficiency has been reached. In the second, the teacher briefs the children on the rudiments of the game, demonstrates the fundamental skills, places the players on the field or court, and starts the game, stopping it when necessary to correct errors in form or strategy. In the third, one combines the elements of the first and second method.

Children in elementary grades, as a rule, take a dim view of formal practice. Because they are primarily interested in the game itself, drill should be held to the minimum. Each skill should be explained briefly, demonstrated, then tried individually in a skill drill or lead-up game. Relays are particularly effective in motivating the learning process, for competition serves as a means of stimulating and holding interest while skills are being mastered.

SOCCER

Basic Skills

DRIBBLE

Tap the ball with the inside of the right and left foot alternately, keeping the ball close to the feet and always under control. Beginners are prone to kick the ball too far, then run to catch up.

SIDE

FRONT

PASSING

Take your weight on your right foot and swing your left leg back and forward, hitting the ball with the inside of the left foot. To pass forward left, reverse the action, hitting ball with inside of right foot.

KICKING

Swing the leg back and contact the ball at the instep. Keep the toe pointed down. The inside of the foot may also be used for long, low kicks.

TRAPPING

Slow balls may be stopped with a raised foot, toes up. As contact is made, the toes are lowered to secure the ball. Fast balls are trapped with the leg. If the ball is on the right, take a small step sideways to the left and at the same time roll the right instep in toward the ground and trap the ball with the knee and the inside of the calf.

HEADING

Get under the ball, lower your head slightly, stiffen your neck, and meet the ball with an upward and forward movement to control direction. This skill is too advanced for the majority of elementary-grade children.

Lead-up Games

Circle Soccer

Skills:	Kicking, trapping
Equipment:	Soccerball
Players:	16 to 20
Formation:	Single circle of players with hands joined
Directions:	The ball is rolled into the center of the circle, and the players pass the ball around the inside of the circle. Players trap, block, and pass with their feet and legs but keep their hands joined. If the ball goes outside the circle, the players between whom it passed are eliminated from the game. When all but five are eliminated, the game is over.

Kick Ball

Skills: Kicking, catching
Equipment: Baseball diamond, bases 30 feet apart, and a soccerball or basket-ball
Players: 10 to 24
Formation: Two teams
Directions: Seven innings make a game. The pitcher rolls the ball to the batter, who kicks it into the field. The general rules of baseball apply, with the following exceptions: (1) The base runner may be tagged out or "thrown out"; (2) a runner must be tagged with the ball held in the hand; and (3) "thrown out" means the base is tagged with the ball or touched by some part of the body of the baseman or fielder while the ball is in his hands before the runner reaches base. There may be from 5 to 12 on the team. The pitcher's box is 15 to 20 feet from home plate.

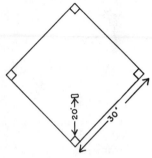

Soccer Keep-Away

Skills: Kicking, dribbling, passing, throw-in (overhead) passing, trapping
Equipment: One soccerball, colored shirts or flags to designate one team from the other, and a stop watch
Players: 12 to 15 players per team
Formation: Team soccer formation
Directions: The rules are similar to those of regular keep-away games with these exceptions: (1) The ball may be kicked or caught in the air but not picked up off the ground. (2) The team may pass the ball around either by kicking or by passing with a two-hand overhead pass (both feet on the ground). (3) Fouls are any roughness, tripping, hitting, picking up of the ball from the ground, or pushing. If a foul occurs, the opposing team is awarded a free kick. (4) The objective is to see which team can keep the ball for the longer time period. (5) No player may hold the ball for longer than 3 seconds. (6) An out-of-bounds ball is thrown in by a member of the opposing team.

Soccer Dodge Ball

Skills: Kicking for accuracy and trapping
Equipment: One soccer ball (should be slightly deflated)
Players: 15 to 20 per group
Formation: Double circle
Directions: Players are divided equally into two teams, with one team on the outside of the circle and one team on the inside. The outside team attempts to kick and hit members of the inside team at waist height or below. Set a time period for each game. One point is given for each player hit. Deduct penalty points for illegal kicks and using hands on the ball.

Soccer Tagger

Skills: Instep kicking, trapping, dribbling
Equipment: Soccerballs
Players: 20 to 30 students

Formation: Scatter, in a designated area
Directions: All players are scattered throughout the designated playing area. One player is chosen as the "tagger." The tagger may dribble anywhere in the playing area in an attempt to kick the ball and hit another player at chest height or lower. Any tagged player goes out of the game to the sidelines. The tagger remains "it" until five players are eliminated. The last eliminated player becomes the new tagger, and the game begins again. No hands are allowed on the ball.

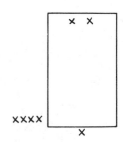

Kick for Distance

Skills: Kicking
Equipment: Soccerballs
Players: Any number
Formation: Single line
Directions: Line up behind the kicking line; two players stand at the end of the field to recover kicks. Each player is given a definite number of tries. The longest kick is recorded. The player with the longest kick is the winner.

Kickover Ball

Skills: Kicking
Equipment: Soccerball
Players: 12 to 14
Formation: Two parallel lines
Directions: Players are divided into two teams and placed in parallel lines facing each other. Teams alternate putting the ball in play. A space is left between the feet of the teams. By superior kicking, one team tries to kick the ball over the heads of those in the other team. After the ball is kicked over the heads of the players in one team, the two end players jump up and try to retrieve the ball and run over a restraining line. The team with the most points wins. The game may continue until all get a chance to retrieve the ball.

Line Soccer

Skills:	Kicking, trapping
Equipment:	Soccerball
Players:	Two teams of 8 to 12 players each
Formation:	Two parallel lines
Directions:	Teams number off and take positions. On signal, the soccerball is rolled in from the sideline, and the No. 1s on each team run out and try to dribble and kick the ball over the opponent's goal line. Guards and linesmen try to stop the ball with their feet or hands. If hands are used, the ball must not be held or moved. Score two points for kicking of the ball across the opponent's goal line. Score one point for a successful free kick. When one player kicks the ball out of bounds, it is given to the other player in the center of the field. A free kick is awarded if the runner uses his hands, pushes, blocks, or holds. For a free kick, the ball is placed in the center of the field and the player tries to kick it over the opponent's goal line. Neither the linesman nor the opposing player must interfere with the kick. The free kick must not pass over the heads of linesmen.

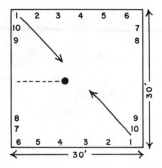

Soccer Kickball

Skills:	Kicking, trapping, dribbling
Equipment:	Soccerballs
Players:	10 to 12 per team
Formation:	Two teams
Directions:	Two equally divided teams alternate as kickers and fielders. The object of the game is for each team member to kick the ball in turn from behind the goal line and then run to the base and back before the fielding team can score a goal. Members of the kicking team stand behind the base line; the fielders are scattered outside the half circle. Each kicker kicks the ball and runs around the forward base and tries to cross the base line before the ball is kicked over the goal line by the fielders. Fielders advance the ball by dribbling it with their feet while outside the semicircle. If the ball goes inside the semicircle, one fielder must enter it, kick the ball out, and leave. A run scores two points. A ball kicked over the base line by the fielders scores one point. The runners gain one point if the ball kicked by the fielders goes over the base line but is outside of the fielders' goal area. They also gain one point if a fielder fouls. Fouls made by a fielder that give the runners one point are (1) touching the ball with the arms or hands, (2) being inside the half circle when the ball is kicked into the field from the goal line, and (3) being inside the half circle when a teammate tries to kick the ball. Kickers are out (1) when they fail to cross the base line before the ball crosses it or (2) if they fail to go around the base on their run. (This game is best played outside. If played indoors, use a slightly deflated ball. Add a goalkeeper to prevent scoring and decrease the length of the goal line when the players develop skill in this game.)

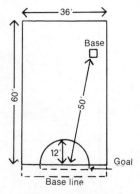

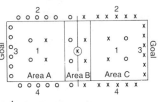

Group Soccer

Skills:	All basic soccer skills
Equipment:	Soccerballs
Players:	Five to eight per team
Formation:	Soccer formation
Directions:	A class of 40 to 64 students is divided into two opposing groups. Each group is then divided into four teams of from five to eight players each. The four teams of each group are then placed in position as follows: Team 1 plays the game on court; teams 2 and 4 defend the sidelines and are placed from the goal line to the center line K; team 3 is placed along the goal line and defends the goal against kicks by the opposing group. (See the diagram for positions of groups and teams; X and O represent the two groups and the team positions are numbered.) Two players from each team in position 1 are placed in Area A and two from each team in position 1 are placed in Area C. These players may not leave the area in which they are placed. Two players from each team in position 1 are located in Area B and may roam all over the court.

Play: The ball is kicked off at the center line (K) in a face-off between a player from each team in position 1. The ball is then kicked and played as in soccer until a goal is scored or until the period ends. If a goal is scored, K starts the ball again.

Time and Scoring: The game is played in four five-minute periods. Any goal kick growing out of regular play or resulting from a foul is scored as one point. The group with the most points wins, the scores of the four teams in each group being added together for the group total.

Fouls: If any player except the goalies (players in position 3) touches the ball with his hands or forearms, the opposing team gets a free kick for one point from the K line. This kick may be blocked only by the goalies. If any player is guilty of unneccessary roughness, then an opponent gets a free kick for one point from K. Only goalies may block this kick. If a player in position 2 or 4 permits the ball to go through the side line, then the opposing team gets a free kick for one point from K. This kick may be blocked by either a goalie or player in position 1.

Suggestions: At the end of each five-minute period, the teams move from position 1 to position 2 to position 3 to position 4 to position 1. This permits each player to have a chance to serve as goalie, line player, and forward or guard.

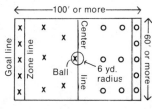

End Zone Soccer

Skills:	Goal kicking
Equipment:	Soccerballs
Players:	10 to 12 per group
Formation:	Two parallel lines
Directions:	Each player is in his own half of the field, and only the kicker is in the circle. After the kickoff, players of either team may advance to the zone line of the opponent in an effort to kick the ball over the goal line. Players may not use their hands while playing the ball. If the ball is kicked for a goal and it goes over the heads of the defenders, a free kick is awarded the defenders at the spot the ball crossed over the goal line. The regulations for out-of-bounds plays and fouls are the same as in soccer. A goal scored by kicking the ball over the opponent's goal line counts one point.

Basic Rules of Soccer

Soccer is a running and kicking game in which the ball is controlled by the foot. The game is played by two teams of 11 players each. These 11 include one goalie, two fullbacks, three halfbacks, and five forwards. The soccerball may not be touched with the hands or arms. The ball is advanced toward the opponent's goal with the foot, body, or head.

At the start of the game, the selection of goals or choice of kicking-off is decided. See the diagram for each team's playing position. The center forward of the offensive or kicking team kicks the ball from the center circle toward a teammate. The ball must travel its circumference. The opposition must remain outside the circle until the ball is touched; then players on both teams may cross the center line and play the ball wherever it goes. The object of the game is to move the ball down the field and into the opponent's goal for a score. The ball is moved by dribbling or by passing to another teammate. A defending player may intercept the ball and thus reverse the field of play.

RULES.   When unnecessary roughness takes place, the offending team is penalized by a penalty kick or a free kick. A penalty kick is awarded when a foul is committed in the penalty area by the defensive team. The offensive team will take the penalty kick from the penalty mark with all the players except the goalie staying outside of the penalty area.

A free kick is awarded for any fouls committed outside of the penalty area. It will be kicked from the spot of the foul. The opponents must be at least 10 yards away until the ball is kicked.

If the ball is kicked over the sideline, it is put into play by the opposite team. A halfback usually puts the ball into play from the sideline by a throw-in, delivering the ball with two hands over the head.

When the ball is kicked over the goal line but not through the goal by the offensive team, the goalie of the defensive team will kick the ball back into the game. The other team must remain 10 yards away until the ball is kicked. When the defensive team causes the ball to go over its own goal line, the offensive team gets a corner kick. This kick is taken by the outside forward from the corner of the field closest to the ball when it went out of bounds.

SCORING.   One point is awarded each goal. After a goal is scored, the team scored against shall kickoff.

FOULS.   Fouls include the following:

1. Carrying—The goalie taking more than two steps with the ball in his hands.
2. Handling—Touching the ball with the hand or any part of the arm between the wrist and shoulder.
3. Pushing—Moving an opponent away with the hands, arm, or body.

PRIVILEGES.   The goalie is permitted to

1. Pick up the ball with his hands.
2. Punt the ball away from the goal line.
3. Throw the ball away from his goal.
4. Take only two steps with the ball.

The other players may

1. Stop the ball with their feet.
2. Dribble, pass, shoulder, or head the ball.
3. Kick the ball to a teammate when trapped by an opponent.
4. Stop the ball by blocking with any part of the body except the hands or arms.

SOFTBALL

Basic Skills

CATCHING

Cup relaxed hands, close them firmly when contact is made and give with the ball. Balls above the waist are caught with fingers up, thumbs together; balls below the waist are caught with hands down, little fingers together.

THROWING

UNDERHAND.   Hold the ball in the hand, palm up, keep weight on the right foot. Swing arm backward, then forward, keeping arm close to body. Simultaneously step forward with the left foot and release the ball at hip level and follow through with weight on right foot. This is a legal pitch.

OVERHAND.   Hold the ball in the hand with palm down and with fingers spread easily around the ball. Draw arm backward with elbow bent; swing arm forward using hand, wrist, elbow and shoulder to deliver ball as weight is shifted to the left foot and follow through with entire arm and body.

BATTING

Stand facing the plate with body parallel to the flight of the ball. Hold the bat close to the end in both hands, with right hand on top. Weight is evenly divided on comfortably spread feet; the bat is held over the plate, back, and at shoulder level. The distance from the box to the plate in softball is short, so it is important to get set to hit every ball. As the pitcher releases the ball, put weight on right foot, shifting to left as the bat is swung parallel to the ground. Drop bat and step off on the right foot for the run to first base.

FIELDING

Stand with feet spread to allow movement in any direction. Ground balls often bounce, so the fielder steps forward with the fingers down and fields the ball off of his toes.

BASE RUNNING

Weight is on the left foot as the pitcher starts the throw. Step off on right foot as the pitcher releases the ball or batter gets a hit. Run close to the base line and touch each base.

Lead-up Games

Bat Ball

Skills:	Batting, fielding, throwing
Equipment:	Volleyball or 8-inch rubber ball
Players:	10 to 14 per group
Formation:	Two teams on ball diamond
Directions:	Divide the players into two teams, one in the field, one at bat. The batter strikes ball with his hand or fist. If his hit is successful, he runs to the base, tags it, and returns to home plate. A fielder tries to hit the runner. He may take only two steps and can pass the ball to teammates. A player is out when (1) a fly is caught, (2) he is hit by a ball, (3) he does not tag the base, or (4) he does not hit the ball beyond the scratch line. The game may be timed or played by innings. Score two points for each complete run and one point for a foul made by a fielder.

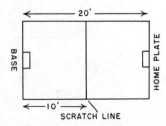

Beat the Ball

Skills:	Running, fielding, throwing
Equipment:	Volleyball
Players:	Two teams of equal size
Formation:	Two teams on a ball diamond
Directions:	Play on the playground ball diamond. The batter throws the ball into the field and runs the bases; he keeps going until he reaches home or is put out. Fielders field the ball and throw it to first base; the first baseman throws it to second and on around the bases. If the runner reaches home before the ball does, he scores one point. Otherwise, he is out.
Variations:	Hand beatball: This is the same except the pitcher pitches the ball and the batter bats it with open hand. Bowl beatball: This is the same except the pitcher rolls the ball and the batter kicks it.

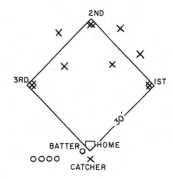

Diamond or Box Ball

Skills:	Striking, base running, fielding
Equipment:	Volleyball or soft rubber ball
Players:	Two teams of equal size
Formation:	Two teams on a ball diamond
Directions:	A "box" or square is made by three bases and home base for the lower grades. A baseball diamond may be used for the upper grades. The pitcher throws the ball so that it bounces once before crossing home plate. The batter strikes the ball with his open hand or clenched fist out into the field. The ball must first strike within the box or diamond for the batter to be safe. If the ball strikes outside the diamond, the batter is out. All other baseball rules apply. One point is scored for each successful run. Seven innings make a game.

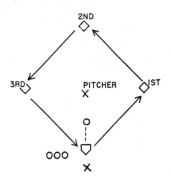

Hand Baseball

Skills:	Throwing, striking
Equipment:	Volleyball or soft rubber ball
Players:	9 to 12 per team
Formation:	Two teams
Directions:	The pitcher delivers the ball to the batter with an underhand throw from 15 feet from home plate. The batter hits the ball with his open hand or fist. A runner is out if he is with a ball any time he is not on base. A game is seven innings. Score one for each completed run.

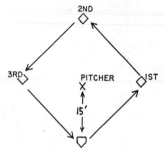

Baseball Overtake

Skills:	Base running, throwing, catching
Equipment:	Softball
Players:	8 to 12 per group
Formation:	Two teams
Directions:	All positions of the infield are occupied except shortstop. The pitcher holds the softball. The runner stands on home base and, on signal, runs the bases. At the same time, the pitcher throws the ball to the catcher on home base, and from there it is thrown around the bases. One point is scored for each base the runner reaches ahead of the ball. After all the players on the running team have run, the teams change positions. The runner throws the ball to any player on the opposite team. The fielder throws the ball to the catcher, and so forth.

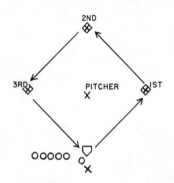

Progressive Bat Ball

Skills:	Striking, throwing, catching
Equipment:	Volleyball
Players:	Ten players per team
Formation:	Rows
Directions:	Teams line up in rows directly behind one another (3 to 4 yards apart), with two arms lengths between each player, whose backs are to the "back line." The team farthest from the "back line" turns and faces the rest. A player tosses a ball and bats it with his hand, then runs to the "back line." The ball must go within the square, and the other players attempt to hit the runner before he reaches the line. The runner is out if the ball is caught in the air or if it hits him. If the runner reaches the "back line" safely, he must return to his team on the next play. Players must maintain their positions and advance the ball by passing only. A batted ball striking outside the square is a foul and the batter is out. One point is scored for each player who reaches the "back line" and returns to his team. Three outs retires a team, which then moves to the "back line"; the next team in line moves into play.

Long Base

Skills:	Batting
Equipment:	Bat and softball
Players:	9 to 12 per group
Formation:	Two teams
Directions:	Divide players into two teams. The pitcher throws the ball to the batter who bats. The runner runs to the long base and remains if he arrives before the ball. The next runner does the same and runner No. 1 comes in. The fielders catch the ball and try to put either one out. The runner may make a home run if he has time. He is out if he doesn't hit in three times. When the team has three outs they change places with the other team.

Target

Skills:	Throwing for accuracy
Equipment:	Targets and softballs
Players:	Six to eight per team
Formation:	File
Directions:	The target is suspended on a wall, fence, or tree 10 feet away from the thrower. The thrower attempts to hit the bull's-eye with the softball. Each has three successive turns, and the best of three scores is counted.

Race Around the Bases

Skills:	Base running
Players:	12 to 14 per group
Formation:	Ball diamond
Directions:	Two players start from home plate. One player runs to first, second, third, and back to home. The second player runs to third, second, first, and home. The player who reaches home plate first wins. If a player fails to touch a base, he must go back and do so.

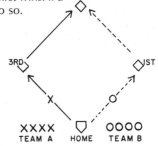

Throw It and Run

Skills:	Base running
Equipment:	Softball or volleyball
Players:	8 to 12 per group
Formation:	Ball diamond
Directions:	A thrower scores a run by throwing a softball (or rubber volleyball) out into the playing field and running to first base and back to home plate. If a fielder catches a fly ball or returns the ball to the catcher before the thrower returns home, the thrower is out. The team scoring most runs wins.

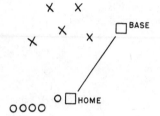

Twenty-Five Throws

Skills:	Ball throwing, catching
Equipment:	Softballs
Players:	8 to 12 per group
Formations:	Circle
Directions:	The player holding the ball throws it to a teammate who is not immediately on either side of him. The object of the game is to complete 25 consecutive throws and catches before an opposing team does. If the ball is dropped or misthrown, the count must begin over again at 1.

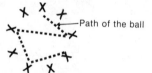

Players in a circle

Leader Ground and Fly Ball

Skills:	Fielding
Equipment:	Softballs
Players:	8 to 12 per group
Formation:	Semicircle
Directions:	Six on each team standing in a semicircle face a leader. He throws a ground ball to each player in turn, who retrieves it and throws it back to him. Next, he bats a fly ball to each in his group, who must catch it in the air and return it.

Each team group moves increasingly farther away from the leader as they gain catching skills. Competition between groups in which each team member scores one point if successful will add interest in this game.

X Players
O Leader

Tee Ball

Skills:	Batting, base running, fielding
Equipment:	Softball, batting tee
Players:	8 to 12 per group
Formation:	Two teams, ball diamond
Directions:	The players on each of two teams count off their batting order and field position rotation—No. 1, catcher; No. 2, pitcher; No. 3, first baseman; No. 4, second baseman; No. 5, third baseman; No. 6, shortstop; No. 7, left fielder; No. 8, center fielder; and No. 9 right fielder. Remaining players are given additional numbers and play in the outfield. Softball rules are played and the game is the same except the pitcher plays fielder and does not pitch the ball. Instead, each batter hits the ball off a batting tee. Nine innings are played and players change positions at the start of each new one.

Basic Rules of Softball

This game is played for nine innings, or more if there is a tie, by two teams, one at bat, the other in the field. The pitcher of the team in the field pitches underhand to members of the batting team in order. If the batter hits a fair ball, he runs to first base, second base, third base, and home while the fielding team tries to put him out by catching the ball and touching him while he is off base. The base runner may stop at any base and continue his run the next time the ball is fairly hit by his team. A complete run around the bases and home scores a point for the batting team. When three men on the batting team have been put out and the teams exchange positions, half an inning has been played.

PITCHING RULES

1. In delivering the ball, the pitcher may take one step forward.
2. The ball must be thrown underhand with the wrist and fingers following through past the line of the body before the ball is released.
3. The pitched ball should cross the home plate between the shoulders and knees of the batter.

BATTING. The batter may swing at a pitched ball or let it go by. If the batter swings at a ball and misses it, it is called a *strike*. A foul ball is counted as a strike unless the batter already has two strikes. After three strikes the batter is declared out.

STRIKES. The following are strikes:

1. A ball swung at by a batter and missed, even if the ball touches the person of the batter.
2. A foul ball, not being caught on the fly, providing the batter does not already have two strikes.

FOUL BALLS. A foul ball is a batted ball that lands outside the foul line between home and first base or home and third base, or a fly ball that lands in foul territory beyond first or third base.

FOUL TIP BALL. A batted ball that goes directly to the catcher is called a *foul tip*. If caught, a strike is called and the ball is in play as for any strike.

FAIR BALLS. A fair ball is one legally batted that settles inside the foul lines. A batted ball that hits foul territory and rolls into fair territory between home and first base or home and third base is also considered a fair ball. If this happens beyond first or third base, however, the ball is considered a foul.

BASE RUNNING

1. A batter becomes a base runner under the following conditions:
   a. When a pitched ball is hit into fair territory.
   b. If the catcher interferes with the batter.

c. If a pitched ball, not struck at, hits the person of the batter, unless the batter did not try to get out of the way of the ball.

2. A base runner is permitted to advance one base when a ball is overthrown into foul territory.

3. A base runner shall return to this base without being put out after a foul ball that is not caught.

4. Base runners may try to advance a base with the possibility of being put out after a fly ball—fair or foul—or a foul tip has been caught.

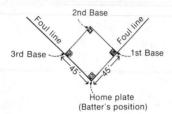

2nd Base

Foul line   Foul line

3rd Base ---   ---1st Base

45   45

Home plate
(Batter's position)

OUTS

1. A batter is out
   a. If he bats out of turn.
   b. If he hits a foul ball, other than a foul tip, and it is caught by a fielder before it touches the ground.
   c. After three strikes.
   d. If, before two are out and while first and second, or first, second, and third bases are occupied, a fair fly is hit that will land within or near the lines.

2. A base runner is out
   a. If a ball hit fair is securely held by a fielder while touching first base before the base runner arrives at first base; or at second, if first is occupied (called a "force out"); or at third, if both first and second are occupied; or at home if all three bases are occupied.
   b. If before reaching base he is tagged by a fielder who holds a legally caught ball.
   c. If he runs outside the baseline in an attempt to avoid being tagged.
   d. If he is caught off base and is tagged by a fielder holding the ball.
   e. If he leaves a base before a fly ball is caught and fails to return before the baseman touches the base with the ball in his possession.
   f. If he fails to tag any base while advancing to another base, and the fielder, holding the ball, touches that base.

SCORING.   One point is scored each time a runner legally completes a run around the diamond, touching first, second, third, and home bases before three outs are made. The runs need not be continuous. If, after two outs, an advance is made from third to home base on or during a play in which a base runner is forced out or put out before reaching first base, the run does not count.

VOLLEYBALL
Basic Skills

SERVICE

The underhand serve is the simplest to teach, easiest to learn, and most practical for use in placement of the ball. Stand facing the opposite court with the ball in the left hand. Weight is on the right foot as the right arm swings backward to shoulder height. Shift your weight to the left foot as the right arm swings forward, knocking the ball out of the left hand. Follow through with the whole body as the ball leaves the right hand. The ball may be struck with the open palm, palm side of the closed fist, or thumb and forefinger side of the closed fist. The assist is generally used in elementary grades.

RECEIVING THE BALL

Take a stance with knees slightly flexed. If the ball is high, flex elbows with hands up, take a small step forward, and meet the ball with fingers relaxed. If the ball is low, flex knees more deeply, step forward, and meet the ball with fingers down and palms forward. Children should be taught from the start to keep their eyes on the ball and to be ready to receive a volley or a pass from a teammate.

PASSING THE BALL

Try to give upward impetus to the ball and direct it by turning the hands and body toward the desired objective. A high ball can be handled more easily and gives a good background for teaching the "set-up" and juggle (girls) which is taught in junior high school.

ROTATION

Snake or "S" type rotation is used because of its simplicity and the fact that generally 30 to 40 play on each side.

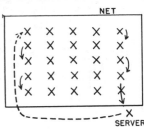

Lead-up Games

Keep It Up

Skills: Volleying
Equipment: Volleyballs or balloons
Players: Entire class
Formation: Scatter
Directions: Divide the players into as many groups as there are volleyballs or balloons. Pitch the ball up in each group and see which group can keep the ball up the longest without its touching the floor. If you have to use basketballs, be sure to alternate the basketball among the groups.

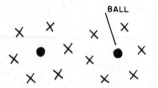

Fist Fungo

Skills: Striking, catching, fielding
Equipment: Volleyball
Players: 10 to 12 per group
Formation: Scattered
Directions: The batter faces scattered players and bats the ball toward them with an open hand or fist. A fielder who catches the ball exchanges with the batter. A player who fields the ball but does not catch it on the fly tries to hit the batter. The batter may not move his feet. If the batter is hit, he exchanges places with the fielder. If he is not hit, he has another turn.

Shower Ball

Skills: Volleying
Equipment: Net and one ball for every ten players
Players: 8 to 12 per group
Formation: Volleyball court
Directions: The ball may be batted or tossed over the net. Only one player on each side may handle the ball, and it cannot be held over three seconds. A player may only take one step with the ball. Points are given for violations and each time the ball touches the ground.

Newcomb

Skills: Tossing, catching, rotating
Equipment: Volleyball, nets
Players: Six to eight
Formation: Volleyball court
Directions: The ball is thrown back and forth over the net, and each team catches it to keep it from touching the ground on their side. Any number of players may handle a ball on one side, but it must not be held over three seconds. A point is scored when the ball touches the ground or is thrown out of bounds.

One Bounce

Skills:	Tossing, catching, rotating
Equipment:	Volleyballs, nets
Players:	Six to eight per team
Formation:	Volleyball court
Directions:	The object of the game is to score 15 points. A point is scored for the throwing team when the ball bounces twice on the opposite side, or when a player on the opposite team tries to catch the ball on the fly and drops it. A point is scored for the receiving team when a player on the throwing team throws the ball out of bounds or into the net, causing it to strike the floor on his side. A player on one team starts the game by throwing the ball over the net. The receiving team must catch the ball on the fly or before it has hit the floor the second time. After catching the ball on the fly or after one bounce, the player may not move but must then throw the ball back over the net. After a point is scored, the team scoring the point starts the game again.

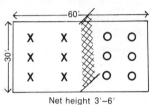

Net height 3'–6'

Ring Toss

Skills:	Tossing, catching, rotating
Equipment:	Rubber deck-tennis rings
Players:	Six to eight per team
Formation:	Volleyball court
Directions:	One team begins the game by throwing the deck-tennis ring over the net. If the opposing team fails to catch the ring, a point is scored for the throwing team. If the thrower fails to get the ring over the net, a point is scored for the other team. A throw that goes outside the boundary lines is a point for the opposite team. A player may not move once he catches the ring. After the ring strikes the floor, the closest player picks it up and starts a new volley for a point by throwing it over the net.

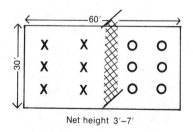

Net height 3'–7'

High Ball

Skills:	Volleying, teamwork
Equipment:	Volleyballs
Players:	Six to eight per team
Formation:	Circle
Directions:	The object of the game is to keep the ball in the air by batting or volleying it. Number the players in each group. On receiving the

signal to play, No. 1 of each group sends the ball into the air by volleying it with the fingers of both hands. He tries to direct the ball to a member of his group. Passing is continued from player to player until one of the following errors is made:

1. A player strikes the ball using only one hand.
2. The ball is hit with the fist.
3. The ball falls to the ground or hits some object other than the hands of players.
4. The ball is handled twice in succession by the same player.

When an error is made, the next player of the group puts the ball into play as rapidly as possible.

Scoring: Each time the ball is successfully batted from player to player, a score of one point is made. The instant an error is made, that score is terminated. A new score begins with each renewal of play. A continuous match may be played by keeping the highest daily score of each group and totaling these scores each week or season.

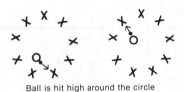

Ball is hit high around the circle

X Players

O Leader

Cageball Volley

Skills:	Volleying, teamwork
Equipment:	Cageball, tennis net
Players:	10 to 14 per team
Formation:	Tennis court
Directions:	The object of the game is to score 20 points. A point is scored when one team can push or hit the cageball over the net and make it strike the floor in-bounds on the opponent's side. One team puts the ball into play by hitting or pushing it over the net. After striking the floor, the ball is put into play by the receiving team. The cageball may be hit by one or more players as many times as is necessary to get it over the net.

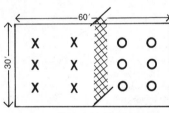

Net height 3'–7'

Modified Volleyball

Skills:	Serving, volleying
Equipment:	Volleyballs
Players:	Six to eight per team
Formation:	Volleyball court
Directions:	Each team is arranged in lines of three or four players. A regulation volleyball game is played with the following modifications:

1. The server may serve from a position in the center of the court.
2. Two or more service trials may be allowed. An assisted serve is permissible; that is, a teammate may relay a ball that has been served in an effort to send it over the net.
3. During the volley, an unlimited number of players may bat the ball before it goes over the net.
4. Although position play should be encouraged, it is not a requirement.
5. The ball may not be hit more than three times in succession by the same player.
6. The ball may be played from a bounce or from the air.

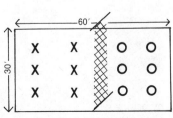

Net height 3'–7'

Basic Volleyball Rules

The official game is played with six on a side on a 30- by 60-foot court. Adjustment may be made according to local conditions. The ball is always served from the back right corner of the court. The server must stay behind the end line while serving. After the serve he should move to his position on the court. The serving team scores when the receiving team fails to return the ball to the opponent's court. Only the serving team may score. The receiving team gains the serve when their opponents fail to return the ball over the net. A team gaining the serve must rotate before beginning the serve. The players may not reach over or touch the net. A player may not play the ball twice in succession. A ball may be played a maximum of three times by any one team before going over the net. A ball touching a boundary line is considered in-bounds. A team wins when it scores 15 points and has a two-point advantage. Play continues until the two-point advantage is obtained. Teams exchange courts at the end of each game. The losing team begins a new game.

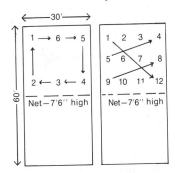

Rotation Systems

BASKETBALL

Basic Skills

STANCE

Stand with feet apart, knees slightly bent to permit shifts in all directions.

PASSING

Concentrate on accuracy, passing with just enough momentum so that the ball may be caught easily. Step in the direction of the pass in order to back up teammates.

Overhead

Two Arm: With arms above head and elbows slightly bent, propel ball straight forward.

Overhead

One Arm: This is the same as above, except ball is balanced on one hand.

Chest

Ball is held to chest with elbows bent. Push ball forward and upward as arms are extended, and release when arms are straight.

Side-arm

Balance ball on one hand, with arm back and weight on foot on the same side. Transfer weight to other foot as ball is thrown.

Bounce

Arms are in position as for chest pass. Keep ball low, as high bounces are easily intercepted. Ball is held to side, with one arm across chest and both elbows bent. Push the ball as arms are extended.

FRONT   SIDE

Roll Pass

Allow children who have not advanced far in skills to roll the ball on the floor as in bowling.

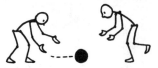

CATCHING

Receive high balls with fingers up, low balls with fingers down. Relax hands and give with the ball. Always keep your eye on the ball.

SHOOTING BASKETS

Arch: Hold ball slightly to the front at about chin level, with fingers up and elbows bent. Look at the basket, straighten arms, and push the ball in a high arch.

Lay-Up Shot: Player receives ball under or close to basket, jumps into air, and tries to lay the ball so that it will enter just over the rim of the basket.

DRIBBLE

Body is in crouch position, head up so that the player can look over the court. Bounce the ball low by flexing the wrist back and hitting the ball with the fingers. Elementary-grade children often do not develop a high degree of skill in dribbling, as they commonly lower their heads to watch the ball.

FOUL SHOTS

Arch: This is the same as the high arch shot, but the knees are flexed more and the toes must not cross the foul line.

Scoop: Small children find it easier to shoot a foul shot by catching the ball with fingers down and throwing underhand in a high arch.

Lead-up Games

Catch, Throw, and Sit

Skills:	Passing (various types)
Equipment:	Basketballs
Players:	Six to eight per group
Formation:	Line
Directions:	Divide the group into teams of 8 to 12. Line them up against the walls of the gym or in a hollow square. The captain faces his team and must keep one foot in a 3-foot circle. The captain stands 15 feet from his team. On signal, he throws the ball to the first player on the right, who catches it, throws it back, and then sits down. This is repeated down the line. If any player or captain fails to catch the ball, he must recover it and return to position before throwing it. The team wins that has all players seated first.

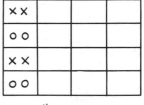

Keep Away

Skills:	Passing (various types)
Equipment:	Basketballs
Players:	Three per group
Formation:	See diagram.
Directions:	Draw a court of four rectangles about 6 × 10 feet. Place two pupils in each rectangle. The alternate rectangles are partners, and they try to keep the ball away from the other two. When a player steps on or out of the line, the ball goes to the opposite team. This can be played either with a baseball or with a basketball.

Twenty-one

Skills:	Shooting
Equipment:	Basketballs, goals
Players:	Two to ten per group
Formation:	Variable
Directions:	Players take a long shot (15 to 20 feet) at the basket and a short shot. Long shot scores two points and short shot one point. Players take turns and the first to score 21 points wins.
Variation:	Players may shoot from the foul line, retrieve the ball and take a short shot. A small, light ball may be used for primary-grade children.

Side-Line Basketball

Skills:	Passing, shooting, dribbling
Equipment:	Basketballs, one-half regulation basketball court
Players:	Six to eight per team
Formation:	See diagram.
Directions:	Two members of each team play on the floor and players line up on the side. Regulation basketball rules are followed except the ball may be passed to teammates on the side lines. Both teams play the same basket. The defensive team becomes offensive by throwing the ball to a player on the side lines. The center line is out of bounds, and stepping over any line gives the ball to the opposing team on their side line. The ball may be put into play by center toss-up, or by giving the ball on the side lines to the team scored against. Players on side lines rotate with players on the floor. Score two points for each basket made and one point for each free throw after a foul.

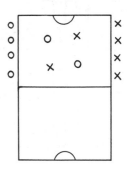

Keyhole Basketball

Skills:	Shooting
Equipment:	Basketball
Players:	Two to ten
Formation:	See diagram.
Directions:	Chalk eight marks around the basket. The No. 1 player shoots from the first mark. If he makes the basket, he moves on and shoots from the No. 2 mark and on around until he misses. The other players shoot in turn and advance counterclockwise. The first player who reaches his original position wins.

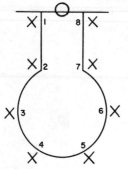

Freeze Out

Skills:	Shooting
Equipment:	Basketballs
Players:	Six to eight to a basket
Formation:	Scatter
Directions:	Players scatter out and take turns at shooting for the basket. The first player shoots a long shot, then a short shot. If he misses the first but sinks the short shot, the next player must make a long shot as well as a short shot. If he does not succeed, he is frozen out of the game. Each player in turn must try to make the same shots as the preceding player. The last player to remain in the game wins.

Nine-Court Basketball

Skills:	All basketball skills
Equipment:	Basketball
Players:	Two teams of nine
Formation:	Basketball court divided into nine equal areas
Directions:	This is played like basketball except each player is assigned an area and must stay within that boundary. Players advance the ball toward their goal by passing and may dribble one time. Only forwards may shoot at the goal. The ball is put in play by a center toss-up. An unguarded free shot, worth one point, is awarded for fouls, such as blocking and holding. The ball is taken out of bounds for infractions such as crossing the line or traveling.

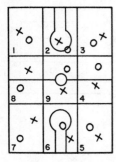

One Basket

Skills:	Shooting
Equipment:	Basketball
Players:	Three or four per line
Formation:	File
Directions:	Arrange groups in file formation. The first player from each team dribbles to the basket and shoots from underneath until he makes one basket. As soon as he does, he dribbles back to his team and gives the ball to the next player. The first team to make 25 baskets wins.

Goal Shooting

Skills:	Shooting
Equipment:	Basketballs
Players:	Three or four per line
Formation:	File
Directions:	Each player gets the number of turns designated by the teacher. Each basketball goal made counts one point. The team with the largest total after the specified number of turns is the winner. The following variation of shots may be used: lay-up shots; foul shots—underhand and overhand; one-handed shots from 5-, 10-, and 15-foot distances, and two-handed shots from 5-, 10-, and 15-foot distances.

Around the World

Skills:	Shooting
Equipment:	Basketballs, basketball goal
Players:	Four to eight per basket
Formation:	Fan
Directions:	Players, in turn, shoot one ball at the basket from each of the several positions. After shooting, each player retrieves his own ball and moves to the next number. A point is awarded the player for each goal. The winner may be the one with the most points. If the game is played that one must make the basket at each number before he moves on to the next, the winner finishes the circuit first.

Dribble, Pivot, and Pass

Skills:	Dribbling, passing, pivoting
Equipment:	Basketballs
Players:	6 to 12 per group
Formation:	See diagram.
Directions:	The first player on each team dribbles the ball to a parallel line 15 feet from the starting line. He pivots on his right foot and passes the ball back to the next player in line for one point. The first team to get 25 points is the winner.

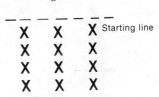

FIGURE 23–3. To throw, push the ball away from your body. (Courtesy of *The Instructor.*)

Half-Court Basketball

Skills:	All basic basketball skills
Equipment:	Basketball, one-half basketball court
Formation:	Basketball
Players:	Two to six per team
Directions:	There are two teams with two to six players on each team. With few exceptions, the rules of basketball govern fouls, penalties, and general playing situations. A throw-in is used to start the game and to re-start play after each score. The player making the throw-in must be standing in the center circle with one foot in the neutral area (see diagram). The player taking the throw-in is unguarded. *Out-of-bounds play:* On an out-of-bounds play, two completed passes must occur before a goal may be attempted. *Violations:* The violations and their penalties are as follows: (1) A player may not attempt a goal when the progress of the ball to the basket was not started by a teammate standing with one or both feet in the neutral area. Penalty: The goal, if made, does not score, and the ball is awarded to an opponent out-of-bounds at a sideline. (2) A player may not try for a goal following a free throw missed by a member of the opposing team until the ball has first been passed to the neutral area and returned. Penalty: The goal, if made, does not score, and the ball is awarded to a member of the opposing team out-of-bounds at a sideline. (3) A player may not carry or cause the ball to go over the center line. Penalty: The ball is awarded to an opponent out-of-bounds at a sideline of the neutral zone. *Scoring:* A field goal scores two points, and a free throw scores one point.

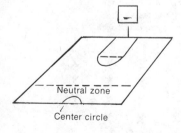

Neutral zone

Center circle

Twenty-Five Throws

Path of the ball

Skills:	Passing
Equipment:	Basketballs
Players:	Six to eight per group
Formation:	Circle
Directions:	Players are in single circles, facing in. Using the two-hand chest pass, players move the ball around the circle until 25 consecutive passes are caught. No one may pass to the person on either side of him. The team to complete 25 passes first is the winner.
Variations:	Vary the types of passes used: chest, underhand, bounce, and hook.

Six-Hole Basketball

Skills:	Shooting
Equipment:	Basketballs, basketball goals
Players:	Six per group
Formation:	See diagram.
Directions:	Each player, in turn, attempts to make a basket, starting at hole 1. Every basket made advances the player one hole. He continues to progress until he fails to make a basket. Holes 2 and 4 are marked "safety." If one player overtakes another in a hole not marked "safety," the first player must return to hole 1 and start over again. The person who first makes the circuit of holes and returns to the starting point is the winner. A player overtaken on the return six holes goes back to hole 6 rather than hole 1.

Basic Rules of Basketball

Basketball is played on a rectangular court with an optimal length of 94 feet and an optimal width of 50 feet. It is played by two opposing teams of five players on both boys' and girls' teams. The object of the game is to gain possession of the ball, to advance it into a scoring position by passing or dribbling, and to throw it through the opponent's goal (one of two baskets suspended horizontally 10 feet above each end of the playing surface). The team that does not have possession of the ball attempts to stop its opponents from scoring and to secure possession of the ball itself in order to score at the other end of the playing court. A field goal counts two points. A free throw, given for an infringement of a playing rule, counts one point.

In basketball, a team is composed of two forwards, two guards, and a center. In general, the forwards play in the half of the court containing the goal the opponents are defending and the guards play in the other half-court.

A jump ball at the center circle starts the game at the beginning of each half. After a field goal, the ball is put back into play by the team scored upon through a throw-in from out-of-bounds behind their basket.

Free throws from the free throw line are awarded to players who have specifically defined fouls committed against them by opposing team members or their representatives. For various less serious violations of playing rules, a team loses possession of the ball. In certain situations, when aspects of a playing situation are not clear-cut, the officials may call for a jump ball between two opposing players.

Substitutions may be made under certain conditions, and a limited number of time outs may be taken by each team. The game is won by the team that scores the most points within the allotted playing time.

TOUCH FOOTBALL

Basic Skills

Arrange squads in a circle or other formations found below. Demonstrate the proper way to pass, receive, punt, and kick the ball. Have squad leaders to whom you have previously taught the skills assist you in correcting movement errors of others. Use small groups and as many balls as possible.

Squad leader in circle

Squad leader's position
in fan formation

```
O⇄×  × × ×
O⇄×  × × ×
O⇄×  × × ×
O⇄×  × × ×
```

Squad leader's position
in file formation

(Arrow shows ball path in all three diagrams.)

BALL HANDLING

Arrange squads in the following ways in order to teach this skill more quickly. Have the pupils

1. Pass the ball left from one to another; then right in a circle formation.
2. Place a squad leader in a circle. He passes the ball to anyone who returns it. Faulty movement patterns should be corrected as they occur.
3. Arrange the groups in two lines about 5 yards apart. Increase the distance as the pupils gain skill.
4. Have two lines in a file formation with one half of the group facing the other. Increase the distance between the line from 5 to 20 yards.

In all ball handling skills stress accuracy of movement. The ball may be thrown with either hand or held in the palm for forward or lateral passing. The ball should be thrown like a softball, with body weight shifting from the right to left forward foot if thrown with the right hand and vice versa if thrown with the left one. Stress watching the ball.

Pass receivers should catch the ball like a softball, away from the body. When catching the ball over the left shoulder, the left arm should be lower than the line of vision and the right slightly above the head. Use an opposite position when the ball is caught over the right shoulder.

PUNTING

Step with right foot, then the left, and kick the ball with the right. Hold the ball waist high. As the right leg swings upward, take the left hand from the ball and guide the ball to the foot. Kick the flat side of the ball with the instep of the foot, keeping the toes pointed downward. The leg should be bent at the knee on the start of the swing, and the leg locked at the joint when the ball is contacted with the foot instep. Although the ball is contacted about knee height, the leg should follow through above the head.

Stress to beginners that the ball should be controlled and not dropped or thrown from the hands to the kicking foot.

PUNTING AND RECEIVING

Divide the class into squads of six with a football for each group. One player punts the ball downfield to the rest who are receivers. Each receiver runs the ball back to the punter as the rest try to tag him. After each player receives two punts, have him in turn become the punter.

Lead-up Games

Three-Step Football

Skills:	Punting
Equipment:	Junior-size footballs
Players:	Eight to ten per group
Formation:	Two parallel lines
Directions:	Have two teams with equally divided players of seven or fewer. Play in an area 80 by 40 yards. The object of the game is to punt the ball over the opponents' goal line. Each team is on its own half of the field. One of the players on team A punts the ball into team B's area. A player of the opposing team, if he catches it, may take three long steps before punting it toward the opponents' goal line. If the ball is not caught in the air, it must be punted from where it first touched ground and the kicker cannot take any steps. Score one point for each punt landing behind the opponents' goal line. Play for five points. Should the ball be missed behind the goal line, it should be brought out to the goal line to be punted.

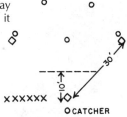

Kick Football

Skills:	Punting, kicking
Equipment:	Junior-size football
Players:	Eight to ten per group
Formation:	Two parallel lines
Directions:	Players on two teams try to advance the ball across the opponents' goal line by passing or running. The ball is put in motion by a place kick from the kickoff line 10 yards behind the midfield. The receiving team must have seven men not closer than 10 yards nor farther than 20 yards from the ball. The other players may be any place behind the 10-yard line. After the kickoff, the receiving team runs or passes the ball up the field as far as it can before the player with the ball is touched or the attempted pass is not completed. The last player on a complete play—either the passer of an incompleted pass or a runner who is touched—returns to the place he was touched or the point from which the incompleted pass was thrown and punts the ball to his opponents. The ball-carrier has been

stopped when a defensive player touches him between the knee and shoulder with one hand. When the ball is passed or carried over the opponents' goal line, it is a touchdown. When a runner is tagged behind his own goal line, it is a safety, unless the ball was thrown by an opponent, in which case it is a touchback. When a ball propelled by the opponent rolls dead in the end zone or rolls out of the end zone, it is also a touchback. *Scoring:* A touchdown scores six points; and a safety, two points. No points are awarded for a touchback. The team with the lowest score has its choice of kicking or receiving. The team with the highest score at the end of the playing time wins. *Onside:* The kicker must wait until his teammates are onside before kicking the ball, or an offside penalty will result. Players are onside when all are in line with or behind the kicker when he contacts the ball. *Offside:* Any opposing or defensive player who is closer than 10 yards to the kicker's line is declared offside, as is an offensive player who is in front of the kicker. *Punted Ball:* The kicker is allowed no more than two steps to get his kick away. If the receiving team catches a punted ball in the end zone or on the playing field, its members may advance the ball by running or passing. If a punted ball touches the ground, it is put into play from that spot with a punt, and cannot be run. *Out-of-bounds:* Any ball that goes out over the sidelines is put into play by the nearest player of the team that did not cause the ball to go out of bounds. The ball is put into play by a punt from the spot it went out. *Touchback:* After a touchback, the ball is put into play by a kick from the nearest goal line by the person who caught or recovered the ball. *Interference:* When there is deliberate interference on a pass play, the pass is considered completed at the spot of the foul. If the foul occurs over the goal line, it is counted as a touchdown. *Fouls:* The penalty for all fouls is a 10-yard advance from the spot the foul occurred or an advance to the place the ball became dead, whichever is the most severe. The following are fouls: tripping, pushing, holding, pass interference, being offside, and unsportsmanlike conduct.

Base Football

Skills:	Kicking, running
Equipment:	Football, bases
Players:	10 to 20
Directions:	The kicker punts (kicks from his hands) and tries to make all bases without getting put out. He may run until the ball is held by the catcher at home plate or is played to the base he is running to. Score one point if the runner completes the circuit. The kicker is out if (1) the ball doesn't go over the 10-foot line, (2) the ball is caught on the fly, or (3) he is touched by the ball when it is in the hands of the opposing team. The player may stay on base and advance on the next kick. The kicking team exchanges places with the opposing team after three outs.

Forward Pass Football

Skills:	Passing, catching, position play
Equipment:	Football, team shirts
Players:	10 to 15 players per team
Directions:	The game objective is to move the ball by completing a series of forward passes. The final pass must be completed across the goal line. Score one or six points. Begin by centering the ball at midfield. Each time a pass is completed another down is made and another

pass attempt is permitted. Pushing, shoving, and pass interference are considered fouls, and the pass is considered good. The opposing team is given the ball on an incomplete pass or on an interception. On an incomplete pass, the team may punt the ball away. On an interception, the ball is assumed where the interception occurred.

Pass Over

Skills: Punting, catching
Equipment: Footballs
Players: Six to eight per team
Directions: Teams are scattered on opposite ends of the field. The object is to pass the ball over the other team's goal line. If the ball is caught in the end zone, no score is made. If the ball is passed beyond the end zone on the fly, a score is made regardless of whether it is caught. A ball passed into the end zone on the fly and not caught is a score also. Begin by one team passing from a point 20 to 30 feet in front of the goal line it is defending. On a pass, if the ball is not caught, the team must pass in a set rotation.

Centering

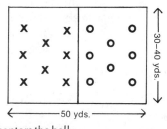

Skills: Centering
Equipment: Junior-size footballs
Players: Six to eight per team
Formation: File
Directions: Teams are in open file. The first player on each team centers the ball through his legs to the next player. If the ball touches the ground because of a fumble or poor pass, it is returned to the center, who must pass it again. If caught, the player catching the ball centers it to the next, and so on. The first team to successfully center and catch the ball in consecutive order up the line and back again is the winner.

Punt Return

Skills: Punting, catching
Equipment: Junior-size football
Players: Six to eight per team
Formation: See diagram.
Directions: Have two teams, one at either end of the playing area. A ball is punted back and forth. A player catching the ball on the fly is allowed three steps forward. If not caught on the fly, the ball is punted from the place it was first touched by a player or where the ball rests when recovered. To score, the ball must be kicked so it hits the ground across the opponents' goal line. Each successful kick counts one point. Balls caught behind the goal line score no points, and the catcher kicks the balls from the goal line. The game can be played for a certain number of points or by time.

Punt, Pass, or Kick

Skills: Punting, passing, kicking
Equipment: Junior-size footballs
Players: Six to eight per team
Formation: See diagram
Directions: Two teams are scattered, one on each side of the playing area. The objective of the game is to punt, pass, or kick the ball over the opponents' goal line before it strikes the ground. Both teams number their players. One team begins the game, with player No. 1 attempting a punt, pass, or kick from his 10-yard line. Players continue propelling the ball back and forth, in turn, until a score is made. A ball caught after striking the ground is returned from the spot at which it was caught. If the ball is caught in the air, an advance of three steps is allowed. A punt over the goal line is awarded one point, a pass two points, and a place kick three points.

Basic Rules of Touch Football

Each of two teams, composed of seven players, tries to retain possession of the ball and advance it across the opponents' goal line. A team's own goal line is always the one it is defending. The game involves most of the basic skills, strategies, and elements of team play found in American football. The offensive team may advance the ball forward by running, passing, or kicking. The center must make a backward pass to a teammate in his backfield before any other player may advance the ball beyond the line of scrimmage.

The defensive team has the right to intercept passes and return kicks. Blocking punts and recovering fumbles are not permitted.

FORMATION.   *On kickoff plays* the players of each team stand in their own half of the field with their backs toward their own goal until the ball is kicked. The players of the receiving team may line up in any formation they wish provided they form no group interference and are behind a line 10 yards away from where the ball is put into play (see diagram).

On scrimmage plays, the offensive team must have three players on the line of scrimmage and four players at least one yard behind the line of scrimmage when the ball is put into play. The defensive team is not restricted to any particular formation.

The positions on each team are as follows: left end, center, right end, left halfback, fullback, right halfback, and quarterback.

The game is started with a kickoff from any point on the 40-yard line. The ball may be place-kicked or punted. It must travel at least 10 yards before it is in play. If the ball goes out of bounds between the goal lines without being in possession and control of a player of the receiving team, it must be kicked over again. If the ball goes out of bounds a second time, the receiving team puts the ball into play on the yardline from which it was last kicked.

The receiving team is allowed four downs, or tries, to advance the ball from the point of possession to or beyond the nearest yard line in the direction of the opponents' goal. If in four downs this is not accomplished, the ball goes to the opponents.

The offensive team may elect to kick the ball from scrimmage rather than run or pass it. This option is used by a team either when it is in danger of losing the ball on downs, that is, not having advanced the ball the necessary yardage to retain it, or as a surprise tactic.

If a kicked ball from scrimmage or a free kick that has traveled the necessary 10 yards is muffed, fumbled, or touched, it is dead where it first touches the ground and is awarded to the receiving team at that spot.

SCORING.   The scoring is the same as in football. Running plays and forward pass plays that result in carrying the ball over the goal line into the end zone for a touchdown score six points each. The team scoring a touchdown may receive an additional point by successfully carrying the ball across the goal line from a scrimmage on the 3-yard line. After each touchdown, the team with the lowest score has the choice of kicking off or receiving. A safety scores two points. After a safety the ball is put into play by a kick or punt from the 20-yard line by the team scored upon.

FOULS AND PENALTIES.   The following fouls are penalized by awarding the team fouled 5 yards from the spot of the foul and a first down: tripping, clipping, tackling, feet leaving the ground when blocking or touching, forming mass interference on the return of a kickoff, rough play, and unsportsmanlike conduct. Whenever a foul occurs, the captain of the team fouled has the option of accepting or declining the penalty. His decision is governed by whether the yardage gained on the play is greater than that received by the penalty.

OFFSIDE.   Offsides occur when any part of a player is ahead of the end of the ball nearest him when the ball is put into play. It is a foul for a player to be offside. The play is not called back until the ball is dead. The penalty is the loss of 5 yards from the spot of the snap.

FIGURE 23–4.   Flag football can give children plenty of exercise. (Courtesy of Jayfro Corporation, Montville, Connecticut.)

FOULS COMMITTED BY THE DEFENSIVE TEAM.   All fouls committed by the defensive team are ruled as first downs for the opponents except for offside, in which case the down remains the same and a 5-yard penalty is assessed. In all cases not otherwise stated, regular football rules should be followed.

BLOCKING.   This is obstructing an opponent by the use of the body. Any player on the offensive team may interpose his body between an opponent and the ball-carrier to prevent a "touch." Both feet must be on the ground while blocking. The forearms should be held against the chest when contact is made with a defensive player. No part of the blocker's body except his feet should touch the ground before, during, or after contact is made with the defensive player.

DEFENSIVE TEAM.   This is the team that does not have the ball.

FORWARD PASS.   A pass made by the offensive team forward from any point behind the line of scrimmage. Any player of either team is eligible to receive a forward pass. The offensive team is permitted to make one forward pass during a play from any point behind the line of scrimmage. If it passes forward more than once, the penalty is 5 yards and loss of a down from the spot of the illegal pass. Forward passes are not allowed on a kickoff, a punt, a pass interception, or by the defensive team on any play. Any forward pass caught by a player of either team before the ball touches the ground is considered to be a completed pass, regardless of the number of players on either side touching the ball. If a forward pass is incomplete, the ball is put into play at the spot of the previous down.

FUMBLED BALL.   This is loss of possession of the ball after it has been received. The ball is dead at the spot it touches the ground and belongs to the team in possession of the ball when the fumble occurred.

HUDDLE.   This is players in possession of the ball grouped together to call a play.

LINE OF SCRIMMAGE.   This is an imaginary line extending across the field. It is as wide as the length of the football and intersects the point where the ball is to be put into play by scrimmage.

MUFFED BALL.   This is an unsuccessful attempt to catch a ball.

OFFSIDE.   This is an infraction in which any part of a player's body is ahead of the ball when it is put into play. Examples are (1) when a player of either team is ahead of the ball before the kickoff occurs and (2) when a player of either team infringes upon or crosses into the neutral area (ground area separating two lines of players or scrimmage line) before ball is snapped.

OUT-OF-BOUNDS.   This is an action in which the ball-carrier steps on or outside a sideline or the ball is fumbled or muffed and hits the ground on or outside a sideline.

RUNNING PLAY.   This is an attempt to carry the ball through or around the defensive team. A wide sweeping play that attempts to advance the ball outside the defensive end is an *end run*.

SAFETY.   This is an action in which a player attempting to advance a ball propelled by his own team across his own goal is touched behind the goal line with the ball in his possession. The team making the safety puts the ball into play by a free kick anywhere along the nearest 20-yard line.

SNAP.   This is a ball passed between the legs to a player in the backfield. It is used by the player occupying the center position when scrimmage play starts.

TOUCHBACK.   This is an action in which (1) a player who receives a ball behind his own goal propelled there by the opponents does not advance it and (2) a ball so propelled comes to a stop behind the defender's goal. The ball is taken to the nearest 20-yard line where the receiving team puts it into play by scrimmage.

TOUCHING.   This is an action in which the ball-carrier is tagged below the neck with both hands simultaneously. The ball is declared dead at the point the touch occurs. No part of the toucher's body, except his feet, may be in contact with the ground throughout the touch. The defensive player may not, while lying or kneeling on the ground, touch the ball-carrier. Pushing or striking the ball-carrier is penalized as unnecessary roughness. After a ball-carrier is touched, the toucher should bring his arms directly above his head to indicate that a touch has occurred.

USE OF HANDS.   Defensive players may use their hands to protect themselves from offensive blockers and to get to the player with the ball. The use of their hands is restricted to touching the shoulders and body of attacking blockers. Offensive players may not use their hands in blocking or screening defensive players.

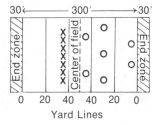

FLOOR HOCKEY

Basic Skills

GRIP

The hockey stick is held with both hands. One hand is at the top of the stock and the other approximately 12 inches below. The stick is held low and carried to the right side of the body (for the right-handed player).

FIGURE 23–5.   All active children love floor hockey. (Courtesy of Jayfro Corporation, Montville, Connecticut.)

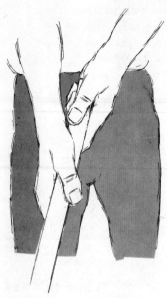

PASSING

The puck is passed with a flicking motion of the wrists. Care must be taken to keep the stick below the level of the waist for all passing and shooting.

DRIBBLING

Dribbling is the manner in which the puck is moved forward under the control; the puck is pushed 10 to 12 inches in front of the leading foot. The player advances on the puck and pushes it forward again with the flat side of the stick. The process is repeated down the field.

FIGURE 23–6.   Floor hockey is an exciting sport for boys and girls. (Courtesy of Shield Manufacturing Company, Buffalo, New York.)

TRAPPING OR FIELDING

When a moving puck is trapped or fielded it is brought under control by a player. The eyes must be kept on the puck, and the flat side must make contact. The player must also "give" with the puck as it contacts the stick. The puck should be trapped in front of the player, who should be ready to continue putting it in play.

SHOOTING

Good shooting differs from passing in that greater speed is imparted to the puck. The player bends over at the waist as the stick is lifted to waist height and brought forcefully down. The flat side of the stick makes contact and then follows through.

TACKLING

Tackling is a means of taking the puck from one's opponent. To do so the player, keeping his stick low, jabs at the puck as it comes off the opponent's stick. Successful tackling takes practice and should represent controlled effort rather than random stick swinging.

DODGING

Dodging is a means of evading an opponent trying to tackle. The player with the puck attempts to fool the opponent by making quick, short, deceptive dribbling actions. Passing to a teammate is suggested rather than a constant one-on-one battle down the field.

FIGURE 23–7. Gym floor hockey is a good game for girls and mixed classes. (Courtesy of Jayfro Corporation, Montville, Connecticut.)

Lead-up Games

Forehand Sweep and Pass

Skills:	Forehand passing, trapping
Equipment:	Plastic hockey sticks and pucks
Players:	Eight to ten per group
Formation:	See diagram.
Directions:	Divide the players into groups of eight to ten. Place one half of the group on one line and the other half facing them 20 feet away on another line. The object of the relay is to pass the puck in a zigzag manner from one line to the other. Start at one end and work toward the opposite end and back again. The first team to finish wins. Remember to stress pushing the puck rather than slapping it.
Variations:	Use backhand sweep pass.

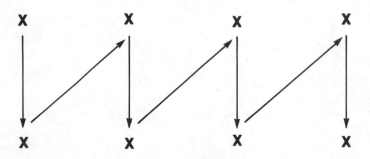

Pivot and Pass

Skills:	Pivoting, passing
Equipment:	Plastic hockey sticks and puck
Players:	12 to 15 per group
Formation:	Three lines
Directions:	Divide the group into three lines. Lines 1 and 2 face each other. Line 2 has its back to line 3. The puck is passed from the first player in line 1 to the corresponding individual in line 2, who stops the puck, pivots, and passes to line 3. The procedure is repeated in a zigzag pattern from one end to the other and back again. The first team finished wins.

Dribble Practice

Skills:	Dribbling, shooting
Equipment:	Plastic hockey sticks, pucks, and chairs or cones
Players:	Four to six per group
Formation:	File
Directions:	Players line up in groups of four to six, one player behind the other. The first player dribbles the puck to the opposite end of the floor, weaving in and out of the markers and back again. The first team finished wins.

Dribble and Shoot

Skills:	Dribbling, goal shooting
Equipment:	Plastic hockey sticks, pucks, and large cardboard boxes
Players:	Four to six per group
Formation:	File
Directions:	Follow the same procedures as in the Dribble Practice above, but have students shoot the puck into the box as they return.

Dribble and Kick Relay

Skills:	Dribbling, kicking with the feet
Equipment:	Pucks
Players:	Six to eight per group
Formation:	File
Directions:	Follow the same procedures as in the Dribble Practice above, but use the feet to handle a puck that is close rather than bringing the stick in close.

Wall-Pass Give-and-Go

Skills:	Rebounding, passing, dribbling, puck control
Equipment:	Plastic hockey sticks, pucks, and markers
Players:	Four groups of six to eight
Formation:	Lines parallel to the wall
Directions:	Players stand parallel to the wall with their left shoulders toward the wall. Player No. 1 dribbles to the marker. The first marker passes the puck so that it rebounds from the wall back to his line of motion. He continues to markers 2, 3, and 4 and returns in the same manner. The first team finished wins.

Dribble-Pass and Shoot

Skills: Dribbling, passing, shooting
Equipment: Hockey sticks, pucks, markers, goal
Players: Six to eight per group
Formation: See diagram.

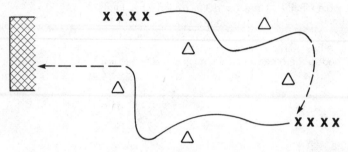

Directions: Groups 1 and 2 stand as shown in the diagram. The first player from group 1 dribbles the puck through the markers. Upon moving around the last marker he passes the puck to the first member of group 2 and goes to the end of that line. The person now with the puck dribbles it around the two markers, takes a shot at the goal from the last marker, and goes to the end of group 1. The process is then repeated. The first team finished or with the most goals is the winner.

Variations: The same drill may be used with the wrist shot, flip shot, and slap shot. It should also be performed from both sides and with shooting down the middle and from the sides.

Pass Behind the Goal

Skills: Rebounding, passing, shooting
Equipment: Plastic hockey sticks, pucks, goal
Players: Six to eight per group
Formation: See diagram.
Directions: Divide the group in half. Station one group on one side of the goal and the other on the opposite side. Player 1 shoots the puck against the wall so that it rebounds behind the goal to player 2. Player 2 passes the puck to player 1, who then shoots at the goal. The team with the most points in a given time period wins.

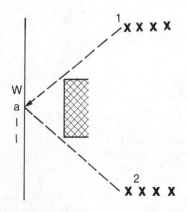

Goal Shooting

Skills:	Goaltending, shooting
Equipment:	Plastic hockey sticks, pucks, goals
Players:	Four to six per group
Formation:	Fan
Directions:	One player serves as goaltender. Other players take five turns shooting at the goal using various shots. The player with the greatest number of goals wins. Switch goaltenders. The goalie with the greatest number of saves (fewest goals scored) is also declared winner.

Three-Person Hockey

Skills:	Stresses teamwork using all the basic floor hockey skills
Equipment:	Plastic hockey sticks and pucks, goalie equipment, goal
Players:	Three per team
Formation:	See diagram.
Directions:	One player is assigned to play center forward (C); the others play the wing positions (RW and LW). Opposing teams play the two defensive positions and goal. After that, the positions are reversed and the opposite team is given three chances to score.

```
                    W        G = goalie
              D
                             D = defense
         G          C
                             W = wing
              D
                    W        C = center
```

Hockey Keep Away

Skills:	Passing, controlling puck
Equipment:	Plastic hockey sticks and pucks
Players:	Three to ten per group
Formation:	Square
Directions:	The players arrange themselves 20 to 30 feet apart in a square, with one player in the middle. The outside players hit the puck to one another while the inside player attempts to break up their passes. If he is successful, he exchanges places with the person passing the puck.
Variation:	Play three on one.

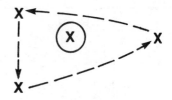

Line Hockey

Skills:	Passing, dribbling, shooting, controlling puck
Equipment:	Plastic hockey sticks and pucks
Players:	Six to eight per team.
Formation:	The two teams line up 30 feet apart. Each team member is given a number. The game begins by the teacher calling a number. The two players assigned the number called run to the center and attempt to shoot the puck through the opposing team's line. A team scores two points if the puck is successfully shot through the opposing team's line. A team loses one point if the ball is shot above the waist.
Variation:	Call more than one number at a time and require at least one pass to a team member before a shot may be taken.

X   X   X   X   X

Ⓧ Puck   ◯

X   X   X   X   X

Modified Hockey

Skills:	All the basic floor hockey skills
Equipment:	Plastic hockey sticks and puck, two goals, goalie equipment
Players:	Six to ten players per team
Formation:	See diagram.
Directions:	Divide the class into teams. Designate teams by different colored hockey sticks, pinnies, or armbands. Assign positions (center, wings, defensive players, and goalie). The number of players in each position will be determined by the size of your class. Two or three goalies are possible, for example, if you simply extend the boundary areas for a goal (use two markers or tape to designate the

G = goalie

D = defense

W = wing

C = center

goal area). Stress playing your assigned position and teamwork. The puck is put into play at the center of the gym with a face-off between the two centers. The entire gym floor is used, and there is no out-of-bounds area unless otherwise designated. No checking, hooking, tripping, or high sticking is permitted. The game is played best with six to ten players per team.

Basic Rules of Floor Hockey

PLAYING AREA.   An illustration of the playing area appears below. It is a basketball court surrounded by rebounding surfaces, such as walls or overturned benches.

The goals are 5 feet 5 inches wide and 3 feet 2 inches high. Each is anchored in the rear by heavy objects, so they are not easily moved. An oversized crease area is marked to substantially protect the goalie from undesirable crowding and body contact. It extends 3 feet beyond both sides of the goal and 6 and one-half feet toward the midcourt line. The center circle of the basketball court serves as the center face-off circle. Auxiliary face-off circles are marked by X's that appear about half way between the goal line and the midcourt line.

Sticks and pucks of hard plastic are used. Goalies may wear baseball gloves. Each team has two time-outs per game. The halftime period is five minutes. Games consist of two 16-minute halves. A sudden-death overtime period is contested, when necessary. The clock runs continuously, except for unusual delays and times out. A constantly running clock standardizes game length and virtually assures that subsequent games start on time.

TEAM ALIGNMENT.   Teams consist of six players: one goalie, two defensemen, two forwards, and one swing person. The two defensemen and the goalie may not cross the center line into the offensive zone. Likewise, the two forwards may not back into the defensive zone. *Only* the swing person may play all over the court.

Zones are separated by the midcourt line of the basketball court. Except as described above, there is no other type of offsides. A penalty shot is awarded to the team against which any offside is made.

By aligning players in the manner designated, heavy traffic around the puck is reduced. Since there is a tendency for all players to follow the puck, instead of having

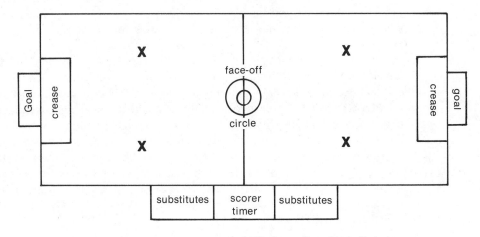

x's indicate auxiliary face-off circles

six to eight players slashing away in the puck area, only two to four are usually there. Freedom of movement and safety are thereby enhanced, and passes to teammates are more easily achieved.

SUBSTITUTIONS.   Substitutes may enter by reporting to the scorekeeper during any period that play is dead. Any form of illegal substitution is penalized by awarding a penalty shot to the opponents.

FACE-OFFS.   To start the game, a face-off takes place at the center circle. Players other than the centers must align themselves in such a way that their feet are outside the circle. For any face-off, the official places the puck on the appropriate spot, steps away from the players, then signifies the start of play by blowing his whistle. Before the whistle, centers must have their sticks on the floor and not touching the puck.

GENERAL PLAY.   The puck is in play until it is hit out of play, a goal is scored, the puck is "frozen," or a penalty is called. The puck is playable off walls, overturned benches, and the like.

Body checking is forbidden. Contact is viewed in the same manner as it is in basketball. Play the puck, not the person. Not only does this rule promote safe play and reduce the incidence of antagonism, but it also allows people unfamiliar with regular hockey rules to officiate, assuming they know basketball.

A player may not raise the blade of his stick to chest level at any time. Furthermore, a player may not hit another player with his stick except when contact is inadvertent in the playing of the puck and is not reckless or unduly dangerous. For doing so, a penalty shot is awarded to the offended team.

Any infraction against another player that involves the use of body or stick results in a penalty shot for the offended player and a foul recorded against the offender. Upon commission of his fifth foul, a player is removed from the game. That procedure is used for simplicity of administration. Normal hockey rules provide for the serving of penalty minutes in a penalty box by offending players. That, however, would require an extra official and at least four extra stopwatches for proper administration of the penalties. It is far easier, much quicker, and less confusing to employ the foul-recording system such as is used in basketball.

The referee may remove from play any person who persistently engages in rough play, commits any single violent act, endangers the well-being of another player, or violates the proper atmosphere of play.

Only the goalies may catch and freeze the puck, as an individual act. Other players may stop the puck with their hands, but they may not catch, pass, or freeze the puck. Two or more opposing players, however, may combine to freeze the puck. The penalty for illegally passing, catching, or freezing the puck is a penalty shot for the other team.

A player may advance the puck with his feet, but any goal scored by a direct kick or push with the foot is disallowed. However, any puck, whether advanced by stick or feet, that deflects off a defender and goes into the net counts as a goal.

PENALTY SHOT.   This involves only the goalie and one offensive player (anyone in the game at the time). All other players must stand to the side. The puck is placed at the center face-off circle, and the goalie must stand, initially, in the crease. On a signal from the referee, the offensive player has ten seconds in which to score. He may take as many shots as possible within that ten seconds. However, the penalty shot period ends immediately when the goalie freezes the puck or the puck is hit out of play by either player. The score-timer is responsible for timing the ten-second period, and he blows his whistle to signify its end.

SUGGESTED READINGS

AAHPER: *Football Skills Test Manual* (Boys); *Basketball Skills Test Manual* (Boys) (Girls); *Softball Skills Test Manual* (Boys) (Girls). *How We Do It Game Book.* Washington, D.C.

AAHPER, Division of Girls' and Women's Sports: *Aquatics,* 1971–73; *Archery, Golf, Bowling, Fencing, Golf; Field Hockey, Lacrosse; Gymnastics,* 1971–73; *Outing Activities and Winter Sports; Soccer, Speedball; Softball; Tennis, Badminton; Track and Field; Volleyball.* (These guides contain official rules for players and officials, and selected articles. Guides are published biannually except the basketball guide. $1.00 per copy.)

AAHPER, Division of Girls' and Women's Sports: Reprint Series: *Selected Aquatics Articles,* 1971; *Selected Basketball Articles,* 1971; *Selected Field Hockey-Lacrosse Articles,* 1963; *Selected Soccer-Speedball Articles,* 1963; *Selected Softball Articles,* 1971; *Selected Tennis-Badminton Articles,* 1970; *Selected Volleyball Articles,* 1970. (All $1.00 per copy.)

AAHPER, Division of Girls' and Women's Sports: Technique Charts: *Aquatics—Swimming and Diving* (18 charts), $2.00; *Badminton* (12 charts), $1.50; *Basketball* (12 charts), $1.50; *Bowling*—Ten Pin (9 charts, boys and girls), $1.00; *Softball* (11 charts), $1.00; *Speedball* (8 charts), $1.00; *Tennis* (12 charts), $1.50; *Volleyball* (11 charts), $1.50.

Blake, William: *Lead-up Games to Team Sports.* Englewood Cliffs, New Jersey, Prentice-Hall, Inc., 1964.

Educational Research Council of American Physical Education: *Physical Education Programed Activities for Grades K–6* (Over 1000 Cards). Columbus, Ohio, Charles E. Merrill Publishing Company, 1971.

Vannier, M., and Poindexter, H. B.: *Individual and Team Sports for Girls and Women.* 3rd ed. Philadelphia. W. B. Saunders Company, 1976.

CHAPTER TWENTY-FOUR

AQUATICS

For their own safety and that of others, all children should learn to swim.

The Authors

There is a great need for aquatics on the elementary level. One finds the most apt pupils in the preschool-age to six year old child. At this age level the child can listen, reason, and take instruction in the basic elements of swimming. Fear of water is absent in the majority of cases, and the learning process is far quicker than at a later period when a "tightening up" occurs, which slows up this process.

Death comes to many small children by drowning because of their ignorance of the simplest forms of water safety and swimming techniques. Various organizations are doing a splendid job of eliminating these unnecessary deaths, but they have their limitations. A summer program of three months cannot be as satisfactory as a nine-month program in which continuous progress is made in an environment conducive to learning.

Aquatics in the elementary school will be limited for a number of years because of facilities, but increasing numbers of schools are including pools in their new plans. The newer unit building that uses one plot of land for senior, junior, and elementary schools permits sharing one pool for teaching and competition. In warmer climates, pools adjacent to school buildings can be used during the spring and fall months, and in some cases, if the water and decks are heated, such pools can be used during the entire year. In some cities the city recreation or park departments have cooperated with the board of education in building pools on the school campuses.

Many six year olds do not have a high degree of muscular coordination, so that skill expectancy should be correspondingly low. This condition exists up to the third grade and sometimes into the fourth. The fifth grader usually has acquired coordination, poise, balance, and timing, which enable him to acquire proficiency in strokes. Individual differences in classes will always determine the speed in teaching new techniques. The suggested methods of teaching follow the steps in progressive learning that with repetition, on different grade levels, lead to the expected skill.

CLASS ORGANIZATION

The organization of a swimming class is of utmost importance on any level but doubly so with young children, whose attention spans are short. Deck space, the size and shape of the pool, and the depth of the water will indicate the best formation,

FIGURE 24–1. Aquatic activities are a must for today's boys and girls. (Courtesy of Camp Yonahlossee, Blowing Rock, North Carolina.)

but in arranging a class for demonstrations or practice, the teacher should keep the following in mind:

1. Safety factors should be attended to.
2. The teacher should be able to see each student.
3. Each student should be able to see and hear the instructor.
4. Formations should give adequate space for practice without interference and should allow maximal participation.
5. If possible, the students should not have to face the sun.

Formations for Demonstrations

In deck demonstrations, a circle or arc may be used in A or B with small groups and in C with large groups. Formation D is ideal for pool demonstrations with small groups; E and C may be used for large groups.

FIGURE 24–2. Learning to swim is easiest for the preschooler and six year old because at this age fear of water, in the majority of cases, is absent. (Courtesy of Los Angeles City Schools, Los Angeles, California.)

Formations for Practice

For static drill in bobbing, breathing, and so forth, use *A, B, F,* and *G.* The double circle, such as in *H,* is a good formation for static drill as the class progresses, especially in large groups. The stronger students from the outside circle help the weaker students in the inside circle.

For drill in skills such as the prone float, leg strokes, and so forth, use formation *I* for small groups. The No. 1's go as a group and are followed by the No. 2's. Formation *J* is best for large groups, and each numbered group progresses in waves. The same formation may be used for distance swimming in the upper elementary grades, and lanes should be observed.

Static   Fluid

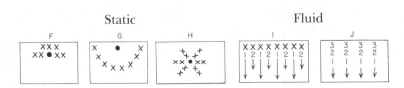

FIGURE 24–3. All elementary children should learn how to swim and have many opportunities to swim at school or in their community. Swimming is one of our best lifetime sports. (Courtesy of Flint Community Schools, Flint, Michigan.)

Methods and Control

From the beginning, students must be taught to *listen* and follow instructions. Short, simple commands should be repeated until a pattern is set up in the mind of the student. Teachers are able to reach the students through repetition of key commands such as "Heads down," for diving; "Squeeze," when the legs are to be brought together; "Push," when the soles of the feet are to push against the water; and "Press," when the palms are down and propelling the body forward.

Repetition is the essence of all learning, but pure drill can become very boring; therefore, diversified activities better accomplish set goals. The whistle should be used sparingly and secure absolute and instant attention. The instructor must have control at all times. There will always be one or two students who wander out of line and do not respond to instruction, but when the lack of attention becomes general it is best to end the class with a game or relay and clear the pool.

PRELIMINARY SKILLS

Entry

It is imperative that the water in which beginners are taught be warm. A child or adult who is cold and shivering will become tense and learn little. Splashing of the wrists, arms, and back of the neck breaks the shock of entry. Jumping up and down helps increase circulation and tempers the body to the temperature of the water. Remember that your one big job is to build confidence in the pupil, which means building confidence in you as an instructor and confidence in his own ability to learn. At this point there can be no hurry, and play must be mixed freely with instruction. Keep in mind the short attention span of your charges and keep in mind that *confidence* and *relaxation* are prime essentials.

FIGURE 24-4. Down at the old swimmin' hole. (Courtesy of Kanakuk-Kanakomo-Kamps, College Station, Texas.)

Ducking

Hold the gutter with one hand and your nose with the other. Squat, and submerge your head.

Breath-holding

Compare the chest to a balloon. Demonstrate by gasping in your breath and showing that the air is held in the chest cavity and not in puffed-out cheeks. Hold your breath above water, and later submerge your head.

Opening Eyes

Hold your breath, submerge your head, and open your eyes under water. Count your fingers or pick up toys, washers, or pebbles from the bottom. This not only gives confidence but eliminates the habit of wiping water from the eyes which slows teaching.

Exhaling

Breath control is of utmost importance. Exhalation should be easy and relaxed. Forcing the breath out through the mouth and nose under pressure as if you were blowing out a candle hurries the process at first, but later the exhalation more nearly resembles a sigh. Hold to the gutter for the first trials. Later, stand in shallow water, bend at the waist, and repeat inhaling and exhaling five times in succession.

Bobbing

Inhale above the water, submerge with knees flexed, and exhale. Shoot the body above water and repeat. This is fun and gives excellent practice in rhythmic breathing. This technique is used later as a safety device in progressing from deep to shallow water.

Relaxing

Take a deep breath, bend at the waist, and drop head into the water. Let arms hang loosely and allow knees to buckle.

Prone Float

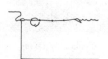

Place fingers tips lightly on the gutter, take a breath, submerge face, and stay underwater long enough to allow feet to float to the top. Tap the gutter four or five times with fingers.

Tuck Float

Once the child has learned to relax, the most needed information is the fact that the water will support the body. There are a few who cannot float easily because of weight displacement; you will find this in the wiry, lean children rather than in the well-padded ones, but propulsion of the body through the water will take care of this handicap later.

Bend forward at the waist, take a quick breath, go into a tuck, drawing knees to chest and chin to knees, and clasp arms around the legs. To recover footing simply straighten the legs and stand up.

Prone Glide and Recovery

Glide back to the side of the pool; put one foot flat against the side wall 10 to 12 inches from the bottom; put your arms and hands on top of the water. Inhale, submerge your face, and give a gentle shove away from the bank with the raised foot. The body is in a straight line from the outstretched arms to the toes. When the forward glide is spent, tuck legs, as you would when sitting down in a chair, press hands down through water toward the knees, and stand.

Back Glide and Recovery

Face side of the pool and place both hands in the gutter. Put one foot against the side of the pool, inhale, and shove into glide. As the forward motion is spent bend knees, drop arms (palms up), vigorously pull arms in an arc toward the surface, lower feet, and stand.

METHODS OF STAYING AFLOAT

Horizontal Float

Divide the class into couples. No. 1s will face the side of the pool in waist-deep water with No. 2s standing directly behind them. No. 1 assumes a semi-sitting position with knees bent and hands in the gutter. He inhales and lies back on the water by gradually straightening his legs and extending his arms obliquely. No. 2 assists, if needed, by placing his finger tips or the palm of his hand on the small of No. 1's back or on the back of his head.

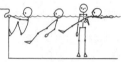

Finning

Check and see how many children have seen fish swim and then imitate the motions of the pectoral fins with the right hand, the left hand, and both hands. Do this first above the water and then on the surface to get the feel of the water resistance. Lower the arms to sides, flex wrists, and push the water toward the feet. Now, get in the horizontal float position and repeat this motion. Better propulsion is obtained if the arms are kept fairly close to the sides.

Sculling

Imagine that the water is sand. With the arms extended and resting on top of the water, pull the hands toward each other until the thumbs touch. There is a mound of sand between the hands. Turn the thumbs down and spread the sand out, pushing to the side. Repeat these motions until it becomes easy and rhythmical. The process of pull-in and push-out resembles that of frosting a cake, only it is done with both hands. Make a figure 8 in the water with both hands. Lie back in a float position and repeat motions.

Treading

Hold to the gutter with one hand and keep your body erect and at right angles to the side of the pool; use your free hand in a finning or sculling motion and at the same time employ galloping, bicycling, or scissor action of the feet and legs. As skill progresses, release your hand from gutter and employ both hands instead of one.

SWIMMING STROKES

The basic swimming strokes taught at the elementary school level are the (1) elementary backstroke, (2) back crawl, (3) front crawl, (4) side stroke, and (5) breast stroke. There are a variety of methods for teaching each of these strokes, and the reader is referred to the Suggested Readings for assistance in selecting the latest techniques for teaching the various swimming strokes to children. The scope of this text does not make a detailed presentation of these materials possible.

Suggested Sequence for Swimming Instruction

Beginner	Intermediate	Advanced

1. Breath holding	1. Leg stroke
	  a. Flutter
	  b. Frog
	  c. Scissor
		1. Crawl stroke

2. Rhythmic breathing	2. Arm strokes
	  a. Crawl
	  b. Back
	  c. Breast
	  d. Side stroke
	  e. Sculling
	  f. Finning
		2. Back stroke

3. Prone float	3. Combined stroking
	  a. Crawl
	  b. Back
	  c. Breast
	  d. Elementary back
	  e. Side
		3. Breast stroke

4. Prone glide	4. Floating	4. Side stroke
5. Back float	5. Treading water	5. Over-arm side stroke
6. Back glide		6. Elementary back stroke
7. Kick glide on the front		7. Butterfly stroke
8. Kick glide on the back		
9. Arm stroke on front		
10. Arm stroke on back		
11. Combined stroke and kick on front		
12. Combined stroke and kick on back		
13. Feet-first jump into waist-deep water		
14. Jump into deep water and swim		

There are many suggested sequences for teaching swimming to children. The reader is referred to the Suggested Readings for other approaches. The following is a sequence of presentation found helpful by many.

AQUATIC FUN TIME

A "fun time" of five to ten minutes is the perfect ending for a learning period in the water. The student leaves the pool relaxed and with a sustained enthusiasm that carries over to the next teaching period. The games and races utilize the simplest to the more advanced skills and give impetus to the desire to master these skills in the formal teaching period.

It is recommended that for the first, second, and third grades this period be used purely for play. In the fourth, fifth, and sixth grades, when the competitive spirit begins to run high, teams may be selected for a semester and a running score kept on the contests. Relays may be used instead of races when the groups are large.

FIGURE 24–5. All children should learn to swim either at school or in the community. (Courtesy of Documentary Films, Aptos, California.)

Shallow Water

1. *See* how many can hold their breath and sit on the bottom of the pool.
2. *See* how many can submerge, holding their breath, and count their fingers.
3. *Blow* small sailboats, balloons, or ping-pong balls across the pool.
4. *Poison Tag:* "It" tries to tag a player who is safe while floating, finning, or sculling.
5. *Corks:* Throw in ten corks. See who can collect the most.
6. *Retrieving:* Throw smooth rocks, lead washers, pucks, and tin plates into the pool. See who can collect the most objects in a prescribed time.
7. *Water Dodgeball:* This promotes ducking, because the player is safe under water.
8. *Tunnel Ball:* Divide students into teams and have them pass ball between the legs.
9. *Can You Do It:* Divide students into two groups, selecting a leader for group. The leader of one group performs a stunt. If the opposing team cannot do it, he receives a point for his team. Teams alternate in performing stunts.
10. *Drop the Puck:* The players form a circle, and "It" drops the puck behind a player, who must retrieve it and try to catch "It" before he returns to the vacant place. If he does not catch him, he becomes "It."
11. *Life Line:* Divide players into teams. One member takes his position on the opposite side of the pool. At the whistle, one at a time drops into the pool and advances, joining hands with Nos. 2, 3, 4, and so forth. Upon reaching the lone player, they see how fast they can get him back to their starting post. This is not only a game but a device for rescuing weak swimmers who have stepped over their depth.
12. *Leap Frog:* Line up teams as for the game on land. The No. 1 player who returns to the head of the line first wins the game for his team.
13. *Races* using finning, sculling, and elementary strokes; limit distance to the proficiency of the swimmers, that is, 10 ft., 20 ft., 30 ft.
14. *Underwater Race:* 10 to 20 feet.
15. *Bobbing Race:* Use bobbing technique and lunge the body forward as the body shoots to surface.
16. *Flutter Board Relay:* Use a flutter board with the flutter or whip kick. This may also be used for advanced swimmers.

Deep Water

The game program for swimmers who can handle themselves in deep water can be as varied and as interesting as the ingenuity of the instructor. Many land games and team games can be adapted to use in the water. Life buoys or floats with lead anchors become floats, hula hoops or old basketball hoops serve as goals, wooden beads float on ropes and describe the playing area, and old volleyball nets may be stretched across the pool on short standards and improvised vises attached to the scum gutters.

1. *Water Baseball:* Use a bat and plastic ball. The diamond may be limited to shallow water, deep water, or both. Use regulation baseball rules.
2. *Water Volleyball:* Use water polo ball. Anchor net 3 feet above the water. Mark limits with floating beads. Follow regulation volleyball rules.
3. *Water Basketball:* Place goals on sides of pool, if width permits. Play like land basketball.
4. *Modified Water Polo:* Because water polo requires a great deal of stamina, its use must be limited to the fifth and sixth grades, and the play area should be limited. The goals, two 3-foot uprights and a crossbar 10 feet wide, may be made of ½-inch galvanized pipe and anchored to the sides and scum gutters. The goal should clear the water by 3 feet. Two teams of seven to ten line up in front of their respective goals.
   a. The ball is put in play in the center of the play area.
   b. The ball may be thrown or carried.
   c. A point is scored when the ball passes between the uprights and below the crossbar.
   d. The game is divided into two halves of five to eight minutes and teams change goals at the half.
   e. A ball that goes out of bounds is brought back by the team that was not in contact with the ball. If the ball goes out over the goals it is brought back to a corner.
   f. If a team holds or interferes illegally with the progress of the ball, a foul is called and a free throw is allowed from a designated line 10 feet from the goal.

FIGURE 24–6.   Overcoming the fear of water is a must for many children. (Courtesy of Documentary Films, Aptos, California.)

Games, Races, and Relays

1. *Front and Back Flutter Kick:* Front with your face in water and back with your head raised, chin on chest, and hands by sides.
2. *Underwater Race:* Start with racing dive and swim under water for distance or in shorter distance for time.
3. *Medley Relay:* Use back crawl, breast stroke, and front crawl. Push balloon or water polo ball with breast stroke.
4. *Carrying Relays:* Race, carrying a lighted candle, an umbrella, a spoon holding an egg or ping-pong ball, or a flag.
5. *Tandem or Centipede Relay:* Four to six swimmers work as one body and stroke as a crew.
6. *Front Crawl:* Swimmers hook feet around the waist of the swimmer behind them and stroke in unison.
7. *Racing Back:* Hook toes in the armpits of the swimmer in front and stroke as crew.
8. *Will-o'-the-wisp:* Divide into groups of six or eight. Blindfold all players except "It," who has a bell or whistle. He swims under water and each time he surfaces he rings the bell or blows the whistle and the players try to catch him. If he is caught, he joins the group and the captor becomes the Will-o'-the-wisp.

TESTING PROCEDURES

Testing (1) gives the instructor a record that aids in pointing out weaknesses to be corrected and (2) provides potent motivational aid. Someone once observed that the man does not live who does not like to see his name in print. Children are not different from adults in this respect, and whereas a good mark is a reward for effort, a poor mark may for some be a spur that challenges them to try harder.

The American Red Cross has graded sheets that are available to Water Safety Instructors. They give a card to a child upon the successful completion of each test, that is, Beginner, Intermediate, Swimmer, and Advanced Swimmer.

The tests that follow have been made simpler and graded down to young children, and, while they require the same skill, the reduced distances demand less stamina. The suggested names for the tests could be changed to fit the need, and the last test could be divided into two if it is too difficult for the group. Small fish made of felt in school colors, with the size increasing for graded tests, would be proudly stitched on bathing suits or trunks. Certain days should be set aside for testing and a routine followed; a child should be given credit for any completed skill whether it is in sequence or not.

FINGERLING TEST

1. Breath-holding: Take a deep breath, submerge, and pick up four objects in a 12-inch radius.
2. Bobbing: This is executed ten times in a deliberate manner. The student should not finish gasping for breath.
3. Prone float, in horizontal position if possible. If the student's feet sink to the bottom, grading should be done on the relaxation of the swimmer.
4. Prone glide and recovery: The body should plane through the water and after the glide is spent, the recovery should be unhurried.
5. Back glide and recovery: Same as front except the head is raised slightly.
6. Back float (horizontal; semihorizontal): Knees should be bent or in vertical position.
7. Finning: Hands should be close to sides.
8. Sculling: Describe a figure 8. There should be definite propulsion through water.
9. Crawl (dog paddle): Arms may be under the water or out. Rhythmic breathing is not required. Distance is the only requirement.
10. Elementary back: A fair amount of form is expected as coordination is simple.
11. Dive and jump into shoulder-depth water: Level off and swim 10 feet.

FINGERLING TEST — GRADES 1 & 2

	BREATH HOLDING 4 OBJECTS	BOBBING 10 TIMES RHYTHMIC BREATHING	PRONE FLOAT & RECOVERY	PRONE GLIDE & RECOVERY	BACK GLIDE & RECOVERY	BACK FLOAT	FINNING	SCULLING	CRAWL 15 FT.	ELEMENTARY BACK 15 FT	SITTING DIVE	KNEELING DIVE	JUMP (SHOULDER DEPTH) LEVEL OFF & SWIM								TOTAL POINTS
	1	2	3	4	5	6	7	8	9	10	11	12	13								
NAME	5	5	5	5	5	5	10	10	10	10	10	10	10								100

KEEPER TEST — GRADES 2–5

	BOBBING 20 TIMES	ELEM. BACK 25 FT.	FLOAT ½ MINUTE	TREAD WATER ½ MINUTE	SIDE STROKE 25 FT.	UNDERWATER SWIM	JUMP INTO DEEP WATER	STANDING FRONT DIVE	SCULLING 20 FT.	CRAWL 25 FT.	SURFACE DIVE	TURN OVER	KICK GLIDE ON FRONT	KICK GLIDE ON BACK	3 MINUTE SWIM						TOTAL POINTS
	1	2	3	4	5	6	7	8	9	10	11	12	13	14	15						
NAME	5	10	5	5	10	5	5	5	5	10	5	5	5	5	15						100

FISH TEST — GRADES 5–8

	ELEM. BACK 25 YDS.	RACING DIVE	25 YDS. SIDE STROKE	FLOAT 1 MIN.	25 YDS. BREAST STROKE	TREAD WATER 1 MIN.	RACING BACK 25 YDS.	TURNS	CRAWL 25 YDS.	FRONT DIVE	SWIM 5 MIN									TOTAL POINTS
	1	2	3	4	5	6	7	8	9	10	11									
NAME	5	5	10	5	10	10	10	5	10	10	20									100

GRADING SHEET FOR SWIMMING STROKES

	ELEMENTARY BACK					SIDE				BREAST				CRAWL				BACK CRAWL		
	ARMS	LEGS	BODY POSITION	COORDINATION	TOTAL															
	1	1	1	2	5															

KEEPER TEST

1. Elementary back: Good form required.
2. Tread water: Hands allowed.
3. Side stroke: Fair form required. Grade 3 (on swimming stroke sheet) should be a passing grade.
4. Underwater swim: Two body lengths.
5. Jump into deep water: Level off and swim to a bank of shallow water.
6. Standing front dive: Do not grade for form. Head-first entry is the only requirement.
7. Sculling: In good form and relaxed.
8. Crawl: Arms should clear the water and a fair degree of coordination is expected in arms and legs; rhythmic breathing is also expected. Grade 3 is passing.
9. Surface dive: Toes should go underwater without swimming assist.
10. Turn over: Change from back to side or front and continue to swim for several feet.
11. Kick glide: Flutter kick for 20 feet on back or front without use of hands or arms.
12. Three-minute swim: Use any stroke and sculling or finning.

FISH TEST

All strokes should be done in good form. If a board is available, the front dive should be done from it; otherwise, it should be done from the bank.

SAFETY PRECAUTIONS FOR TEACHERS

The following is a list of important safety considerations for the swimming pool:

1. Keep entrances to the pool locked when it is not in use.
2. Instructors should be the first to enter the pool area and the last to leave.
3. Provide adequate life-saving equipment.
4. Check equipment frequently to see that it is in proper working condition and in its proper place.
5. Rope off the nonswimmers' area.
6. Schedule small classes.
7. Allow sufficient time to elapse after eating a heavy meal before entering the water.
8. Have some mark of identification for nonswimmers in large classes of mixed abilities.
9. Never swim alone.
10. Never swim if a lifeguard is not present.
11. Girls wear bathing caps in the pools.
12. Adjust to the water slowly by showering or rubbing the extremities first.
13. Enter unknown bodies of water feet first.
14. Call for help when you realize that someone is in danger of drowning.
15. Refrain from yelling for help unless real trouble is present.
16. Keep the diving area clear of swimmers except those who are diving.
17. No running should be permitted on the deck nor horseplay in the water.
18. Allow only one diver at a time on the board.
19. Never swim when you have any type of contagious infection.
20. Do not bring articles to the area that might cause injury to others.
21. Do not overestimate your ability to swim or make a swimming rescue.

SUGGESTED READINGS

AAHPER: *Practical Guide For Teaching The Mentally Retarded To Swim.* Washington, D.C.

AAHPER: *Professional Standards In Aquatic Instruction, Aquatics' Guide For 1971–1973.* Washington, D.C.

American Red Cross: *Swimming and Diving,* Revised ed. Washington, D.C.,

American Red Cross: *Water Safety Instructor's Manual.* Washington, D.C.,

Counsilman, J.: *The Science of Swimming.* Englewood Cliffs, New Jersey, Prentice-Hall, Inc., 1968.

Kauffman, C.: *How To Teach Children To Swim.* New York, G. P. Putnam's Sons, 1960.

Mackenzie, M. M., and Spears, B.: *Beginning Swimming.* Belmont, Calif., Wadsworth Publishing Company, 1963.

Midtlying, J.: *Swimming.* Philadelphia, W. B. Saunders Company, 1976.

O'Brien, R.: *Springboard Diving.* Columbus, Ohio, Charles E. Merrill Publishing Company, 1968.

Official Aquatic Guide. Latest ed. National Section for Girls' and Women's Athletics, American Alliance for Health, Physical Education, and Recreation, Washington, D.C.

Smith, H.: *Water Games.* New York, The Ronald Press Company, 1962.

Vannier, M., and Poindexter, H. B.: *Individual and Team Sports for Girls and Women.* 3rd ed. Philadelphia, W. B. Saunders Company, 1976.

Vickers, B., and Vincent, W.: *Swimming.* Dubuque, Iowa, William C. Brown Company, Publishers, 1966.

CHAPTER TWENTY-FIVE

CAMPING AND OUTDOOR EDUCATION

Now I see the secret of the making of the best persons,
It is to grow in the open air and eat and sleep with the earth.

Walt Whitman

Increasingly, camping and outing activities become an integral part of the total school program. Ideally, these activities can best be stressed from grades 4 through 12, although some may be begun at any time in the first three grades. Crowded classrooms and gymnasiums often create a problem, yet every school in America, whether it be located in a village or teeming city, has access to wide-open spaces, city parks, or even school grounds where a camping program might be initiated. Many cities now operate public school camps on a year-round basis. Still more provide some kind of overnight, day, or weekend camping experiences for their students.

Such camps have been launched primarily as a means of integrating indoor learning centered on verbalized theory with outdoor experiences focused on learning to live in the out-of-doors. At these school camps where there are no truant officers, no school buildings, no bells, no traditional school subjects taught by ordinary school teachers, no detention rooms, and no failures, youths are gaining experiences that cap all others in their educational lives.

Here children are discovering the real meaning of the words "nature," "trees," "hills," "ferns," "cooperate," "share," and "contribute." Boys and girls are living the thrill of seeing, touching, and smelling the earth and all its magic and experiencing the joy of hearing the indescribable music of wind in the pine trees and of rushing water. For many of these children, camping and outing activities are opening up a world about which they have been told, that they have seen in movies or on television, and about which they have dreamed and are eager to learn. And here, too, children from rural areas are having the thrilling discovery of learning to play in the out-of-doors with others. City children are learning new skills in a new world of adventure.

What these far-sighted American school systems have done in establishing school camps and outdoor education programs can and should be duplicated. The local community, the state, and the federal government all have vital roles to play in this educational movement.

TYPES OF EXPERIENCES

Camping and outing activities possible for elementary schools include learning to

1. Live independently of one's family.
2. Adjust and contribute to group life.
3. Care for and select one's own clothing in accordance with changing weather conditions.
4. Make one's bed and care for it.
5. Set and clear tables; act as host and hostess.
6. Plan group meals confined to a definite budget according to nutritional standards.
7. Make a number of different kinds of fires and cook over them.
8. Use a compass; tell directions from trees, sun, and grass.
9. Lay trails.
10. Pace and measure distance.
11. Read maps; construct maps of local areas.
12. Hike long or short distances with the maximum of pleasure and the minimum of fatigue.
13. Know the sky above and the meaning of stars and their use to man.
14. Understand and know as much as possible for one's age about birds, animals, trees, rocks, insects, and flowers.
15. Recognize harmful plants, trees, insects, and animals.
16. Care for and use camp tools, including axes, saws, and ropes.
17. Enjoy outdoor sports and games; the school does not provide such sports as ice skating, free climbing, snow shoeing, wood-chopping contests, fishing, canoeing, and trapping.
18. Make useful articles from native materials—pans from clay, spoons from wood, pan racks from tree branches, hats from reeds and so forth.
19. Take an active part in some community project, such as protection from camp soil erosion, building an outdoor theater, making a new road.
20. Build a number of different kinds of shelters.
21. Use the camp environment to its fullest extent.
22. Practice good health and safety habits.
23. Lash.
24. Roll blankets.

Classes in camping should be held outdoors for a double period or be the last scheduled in the day. The physical education class is the logical place for the inclusion of camping in the school program. Weekend or afternoon camping trips can easily be incorporated in the program, especially if teachers, as well as the students, are camping minded. Interested parents and local Girl and Boy Scout leaders are usually available as chaperones or assistant leaders.

The key person in the program is the teacher. If she is interested in learning as well as teaching others camping and outing skills, and if she is enthusiastic, she will find ways to include and develop this as an integral part of the total school program. Camping experts in the community can and will offer valuable help, for camping-minded leaders are usually eager to sell outdoor education. Increasingly, colleges and universities are requiring camp leadership training courses for majors and minors in physical education.

THE OUTDOOR LEARNING LABORATORY

One of the most vital outdoor education programs in the country is thrilling many youngsters at the Ladera Elementary School in Thousand Oaks, California, where a large, outdoor wooded area has been set aside for new kinds of educational experiences. Part of this large area has been left in its natural state so that conservation, plant, and wild animal projects abound. An adjacent plot of level land is used for mapmaking, digging, landscaping and sheer fun in the out-of-doors.

FIGURE 25–1.   Through camping children can learn much about the wonderful world of nature. (Courtesy of Kanakuk-Kanakomo-Kamps, College Station, Texas.)

The children have built a model weather station. There is a pen enclosing domestic pets and a small lake for fishing, aquatics, and other recreational purposes. The youngsters have also built a model of an early California mission from their own handmade adobe bricks.

In another nearby school, the pupils have used their outdoor education area to dramatize the small size of the "wee" plane Charles Lindbergh first flew across the Atlantic Ocean. Elsewhere children have devised a framework model of the

FIGURE 25-2. Camping activities for children should revolve around food, shelter, nature lore, and recreation in the out-of-doors. (Courtesy of AAHPER, Washington, D.C.)

Goodspeed, one of the first ships to arrive at Jamestown in 1607. Such experiences give children rich educational tools with which to explore their world and that of their ancestors. These and many other outdoor learning experiences, such as that in a New England pine forest where the children sweep the ground clean early every morning in order to learn how to read the tracks made by nocturnal animals, as well as about the animals themselves, all help to make learning the great adventure it can be and to make the world, in which each living thing is a vital part, an exciting place in which to live.

Camping and outdoor education have also been used successfully to help prevent juvenile delinquency as well as to rehabilitate youthful law breakers and emotionally disturbed youth.

THE PROGRAM

The program of outdoor education and school camping should be aimed at helping the child (1) learn to live with others in the out-of-doors, (2) enjoy healthful personal and community living, (3) basic campcraft skills, (4) gain work experiences, and (5) participate in conservation projects. Subjects that have been found to be best taught, in part, outdoors through firsthand experiences are physical education, health education, science and nature, dramatics, music, arts and crafts, mathematics, local history, geography, English, and government or civics.

Program activities at the Tyler Texas Public School Camp include

Intra-group evening programs	Outdoor cooking
Felling, chopping, and splitting wood	Planting trees, grass, gardens
Conservation hikes	Farm chores
Learning how to use an axe, saw, and wedge	Camp maintenance projects

FIGURE 25–3. Dear Mother: Today I caught my first fish! (Courtesy of Kanakuk-Kanakomo-Kamps, College Station, Texas.)

Map and compass hikes	Trail blazing
Trapping animals	Logging
Cabin clean-up duties	Visiting the school farm
Construction, carpentry	Swimming
Weather study	Visits to community places of interest
Making check dams	Scavenger hunts
Making posted signs	Lard making
Pottery	Milking
Fishing	Soap making
	Sketching

This school camp also has a farm and permits children to feed animals, gather eggs, harvest crops, and share in other farming experiences.

Teachers take advantage of the camping experience in many different ways. Children largely operate the dining room, and some teachers stress manners, table setting, proper nutrition, and table conversation. A banking system at the camp provides training in arithmetic.

Fifth-grade teachers usually find the camp useful in teaching about the solar system, seasonal changes, plants, the earth, water and soil conservation, and farming.

Popular sixth-grade topics include the weather, conservation, farming, and animals.

At the camp, children take nature hikes; visit the Nature Den, which has exhibits of local animals and plants; see a weather station; study area soils at a soils laboratory; and participate in other activities.

All the children have assigned duties. There are farm chores as well as the responsibility of making up their beds, cleaning their own rooms, setting tables, and drying dishes.

Classes elect storekeepers, postal clerks, bankers, and health inspectors. Each child usually has at least one community job for which he is responsible.

Not all schools are lucky enough to have a school camp. However, programs in outdoor education, although best taught in a camp setting in a wooded area, can be conducted on a smaller scale through such programs as clubs and class projects, field trips, and garden projects.

CLUBS AND CLASS PROJECTS. Several students can form a club group in almost any area of nature, including insect and rock collecting, raising vegetables and flowers in gardens or window boxes, animal and bird woodcarving, and pet care and training. Class projects might well include the study of and prevention of the destruction of our natural resources (ecology), building of nature trails, beautification of the school and community, leaf printing, and so forth. Special events that could involve the whole school, such as Pioneer Day, featuring wood-chopping and other campcraft contests, corn-husking bees, and outdoor cooking, can provide a learning adventure that most children thrive on, if given an opportunity to have such experiences at school.

FIELD TRIPS. These experiences can be the highlight for some children of an entire elementary school experience. All trips should be carefully planned with a definite purpose in mind, cleared with the proper authorities, arranged with those in charge of the place to be visited, talked about beforehand and after coming back, related to materials being studied at school, safely conducted, and exciting, enriching, and educational for children. Some exciting places to visit include the following:

Nature museum	Veterinarian hospital
Farm	Zoo
Canning and packing plant	Quarry
Farmers' vegetable market	Orchards
Vacant lot	Greenhouses

A field trip can be a meaningful experience or a frivolous lark. To have educational value it must be an important adjunct to problems currently being studied in the classroom. The most fruitful excursions will be those that help pupils to learn from many kinds of firsthand experiences those things that cannot be learned elsewhere. Such experiences can build a bridge between school experiences and community life.

Some schools, however, forbid teachers to take children on trips. Nevertheless, "Where there is a will there is a way," as all teachers who are determined to give their pupils the richest kind of educational experiences possible well know. Such educators often contact the Girl Scouts and Boy Scouts or other youth organizations in the community and enlist their cooperation in helping children learn more about their community through Saturday excursions. Others assign older pupils to visit places such as a recreation center or health museum on their own time and write a paper that describes what has been learned from this experience. Regardless of what method is used to make education positive, purposeful, and functional to youth, the community with all its rich resources for learning should be fully utilized.

GARDEN PROJECTS. Too many of our present-day children are not around things growing from the soil and have little idea of where the many foods they eat come from, other than from the grocery store, and they know still less about how they are produced. Garden projects not only can provide them with these kinds of educational experiences but also can help them learn to care for living and growing things other than themselves. All kinds of fruits and vegetables can be raised by children, and such projects can be related to many phases of the school program, including the earth and biological sciences, health and physical education, and even mathematics if costs are estimated and the ground measured for planting. Many schools are now renting farms for such garden projects for their children. Still others are purchasing school forests to provide outdoor education laboratories for youth.

If our country is ever to solve its many growing problems of ecology and the destruction of our natural resources, it is today's schoolchildren who will do so. Outdoor education, then, has much to contribute as a means of making educational experiences come alive for our youth. The effects of such a program can be far reaching in the remaking of and the keeping of the beauty of America.

School Subjects Related to Outdoor Education

Every school subject has a contribution to make to outdoor education. Such experiences should be conducted outdoors, for it is a vicarious experience for children to hear or read about Indian arrowheads, but it is the real thing to find such treasures.

Found below are program possibilities for outdoor education incorporating various subjects that are included in most school curricula:

ARITHMETIC

1. Pacing hiking distances.
2. Finding geometric shapes in rocks and elsewhere in nature.
3. Counting tree rings to discover age.
4. Building one's own shelter according to dimension.
5. Making scale drawings and maps of local areas.
6. Estimating stream widths, tree heights, and map distances.
7. Learning to use your own watch as a compass.
8. Averaging temperatures and barometric readings.
9. Learning how to predict weather by counting cricket chirps.
10. Compass hiking and stalking games.
11. Construction of check dams, bridges, feeding stations, and an outdoor school bank.

LANGUAGE ARTS

1. Storytelling about any aspect of nature.
2. Planning a daily and weekly camp program and menus.
3. Dramatizations of the life of our early ancestors.
4. Keeping field notes, a diary, or other records.
5. Writing poems or plays about nature or historical events.
6. Camp newspapers.

SOCIAL STUDIES

1. Collecting Indian relics and learning about Indian life.
2. Making miniature pioneer buildings; having a Pilgrim-Indian Thanksgiving party.
3. Making household articles from native materials.
4. Map and model making.
5. Learning to trap by making snares, slings, bows and arrows, and boomerangs.
6. Restoring or visiting historical sites.
7. Learning about the history of one's county, city, and state through visitation and interviewing people in the area.

BIOLOGICAL SCIENCES

1. Learning to use a microscope and hand lens to observe things from nature more closely.
2. Building aquariums, terrariums, feeding stations, and animal shelters.
3. Visiting game and fishing preserves.
4. Studying animal tracks, leaves, flowers, and trees and making plaster molds, spatter prints, or blueprints of them.

5. Learning to forecast the weather through wind and cloud study.
6. Tapping maple trees; planting and caring for trees, shrubs, and grass.
7. Nature treasure hunts.

ECOLOGY AND EARTH SCIENCE

1. Studying soil erosion and conducting soil experiments.
2. Making water and air experiments to test pollution degrees.
3. Visiting a city dump and studying waste disposal; visiting a conservation farm and contrasting it with a visit to a deserted farm.
4. Making weather instruments from junk materials and predicting weather.
5. Studying glacial formations and deposits.

HEALTH AND PHYSICAL EDUCATION

1. Menu planning.
2. Camp skills (outdoor cooking, fire building).
3. Camp safety.
4. Discussing and solving group living problems.
5. Folk, square, and Indian dancing.
6. Fly and bait casting.
7. Ice fishing and skating, skiing, snow skiing, and tobogganing.

ARTS, CRAFTS, AND MUSIC

1. Lashing and making camp furniture, picture frames, and cooking utensils from native materials.
2. Sand and rock painting and sculpture.
3. Making bird houses and feeders.
4. Cutting and polishing stones for making jewelry.
5. Photography, sketching, and painting birds, trees, and other things in nature using watercolors and oil paints.
6. Making collages from native materials.
7. Recording nature sounds and imitating bird calls.
8. Making up songs and composing music about any aspect of nature.

Camping and Outdoor Living Skills

Camping and outdoor living skills that should be included in the school program of outdoor education can best be taught in wooded areas. The following activities may be taught on the play field or on a vacant lot if no other place is available:

CAMPCRAFT

1. Knife selection, use, care, and safety measures; whittling.
2. Selection, use, and care of axe, hatchet, and cross-saw; splitting, chopping, and cutting down of trees; safety measures.
3. Use of saws, shovels, picks, and hammers; safety measures.

FIRE BUILDING

1. Fixing a fireplace.
2. Selection of wood, and common kinds of fires for outdoor cooking.
3. Fire safety hints.

OUTDOOR COOKING

1. Menu planning according to daily nutritional standards.
2. Packing for hikes and overnight trips.
3. Care of food—refrigeration, protection, waste disposal.
4. Types of outdoor cooking devices.
5. Preparation and serving of food.

HIKES AND OUTINGS

1. Kinds of hikes.
2. Where to go, what to do, what to take, and what to do when you arrive.
3. Hiking games, pacing.
4. Camp site selection.
5. Camp making and breaking; tent pitching, ditching and striking.
6. Bed rolls and sleeping bags.
7. Packing a knapsack, personal needs.[1]
8. Light camping equipment.

KNOTCRAFT AND LASHING

1. Rope whipping.
2. Square knots, sheet bend, bowline, clove hitch.
3. Ways to use knots.
4. Square, diagonal, sheer, continuous lashing.
5. Things to lash.

NATURE AND WOOD-LORE CONSERVATION

1. Common plants, edible and poisonous.
2. Common animals—harmful and friendly.
3. Common insects and snakes—harmless and harmful.
4. Common birds.
5. Knowledge of astronomy.
6. Knowledge of common myths and legends concerning the heavens.
7. Common fossils, minerals.
8. Fishing, hunting, and trapping skills.
9. Forestry conservation.
10. Trail blazing, map reading, use of compass.
11. Weather casting.
12. Improvised shelter, equipment, and rustic construction.
13. Soil conservation.

INFORMAL GROUP ACTIVITIES

1. Group singing.
2. Simple dramatics, including stunts, skits, hand puppets.
3. Story telling.
4. Games—active, quiet, folk, nature.
5. Crafts—nature, junk, rise of native materials, sketching and painting, and others suitable for camp.

---

[1]Boy Scouts of America: *The Boy Scout Handbook*. New York, 1971.

CONSTRUCTION PROJECTS[2]

Suggested projects include

1. Making the following:
    a. Rustic entrance for cabin, unit, or camp
    b. Totem poles
    c. Outdoor kitchen
    d. Outdoor theater
    e. Rustic furniture
    f. Rustic bulletin boards
    g. Nature aquarium
    h. Campfire trail
    i. Log cabin
    j. Nature exhibit, nature trail
    k. Rock garden
    l. Campcraft exhibit
    m. Outpost camp
    n. Weathervane
    o. Tree house
    p. Council ring
    q. Pottery kiln
    r. Nature trails
    s. Fernery
    t. Outdoor chapel
    u. Camping equipment and eating utensils
    v. Lean-to-shelters
    w. Bows and arrows
    x. Sundial
    y. Bridge across a creek
    z. Shelves, tables, and benches
2. Damming up a creek.
3. Repairing boats and other equipment and facilities.
4. Clearing paths.
5. Controlling soil erosion.
6. Clearing up the campsite.

Campcraft Skill Contests

Groups will enjoy the following:

1. Water boiling.
2. Wood chopping.
3. Lashing camp tables, bridges.
4. Making functional crafts from materials.
5. Fishing for the most fish, the biggest fish, or a specific kind of fish.
6. Knotcraft relays.
7. Trail blazing.
8. Fire building—with and without matches.
9. Wood saving.
10. Whittling.
11. Pie-, cookie-, and cake-making contests.
12. Casting at white tire targets place at different distances.
13. Knot tying for speed.
14. Tent ditching and pitching for speed.

The teaching of skills in campcraft should be concluded with a day, weekend, or summer camping trip. Activities included in the program must be geared to the interests, needs, and capabilities of the children. Fourth graders may not be as keen

---

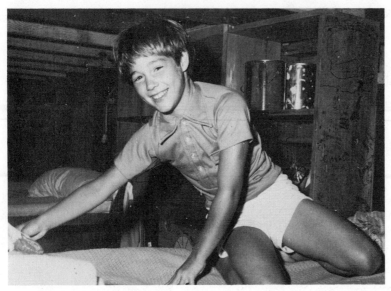

FIGURE 25–4.   You learn lots of new things at camp. (Courtesy of Kanakuk-Kanakomo-Kamps, College Station, Texas.)

about knotcraft as sixth graders; they may, however, be thrilled with going on a vagabond hike or learning how to fry eggs on a heated rock.

Hiking

A hike is a walk with a purpose. It is one of the best of all outdoor activities, for it builds physical fitness through vigorous use of the big muscles of the body. There are many kinds of hikes, ranging from early morning bird walks to mountain climbing.

The teacher and pupils should plan together where they want to hike, what each will take and how it will be packed or carried, what kind of clothes, especially shoes and socks, would be the best to wear, what to do on the way, how to walk on the highway or through the forest, and what to do when the group reaches its destination.

Places to hike to might include some local park, a nearby lake or forest, someone's farm, some place of local interest, the local zoo, or some camp nearby. Group singing or round-robin story telling will add to the fun along the way.

Hiking distances should be increased gradually as the pupils become more expert in covering more ground with a minimum of fatigue and more adept at seeing interesting treasures along the way. Cookouts can add to the joy of the hike's end. Simple meals such as fried bacon and egg sandwiches, carrot sticks, cocoa, and fruit are easily prepared and great fun to make.

Types of suitable hikes, some for class time, others for longer periods include the following:

1. *Nature Hike:* to collect, study, or see as many kinds of wild flowers, birds, insects, or animals as possible.
2. *Treasure Hunt Hike:* Each squad is given a sealed envelope containing a list of clues leading to the hidden treasure. The first squad to find the treasure wins.
3. *Scavenger Hunt Hike:* Each squad is given a sealed envelope containing a list of articles to be brought back to a certain spot in a given time. The group which has found the most articles wins.

4. *The Lost Baby or Object Hike:* Each squad searches for a doll hidden by the teacher or a squad.
5. *Exploration Hike:* A walk along back roads, through forests, or in other places unknown to the children.
6. *Coin Flip Hike:* A coin is tossed in the air at every road crossing to see which direction the group will go.
7. *Star, Sun or Cloud Hike:* A trip to a hill to hear legends about the stars, sun, or clouds.
8. *Moonlight Hike:* A night's stroll to see and hear the beauties of night.
9. *Stream Hike:* The class follows a creek, river, or stream as far as possible in a given time to see how it winds, turns, and changes.
10. *Trail-Blazing Hike:* The class finds and clears a new trail or path.
11. *Compass Hike:* Each squad selects a direction and hikes that way. The groups exchange news of their adventures upon returning.
12. *Walk Out–Ride Back Hike:* One group walks while the second one rides and vice-versa for the return trip.
13. *Overnight Hike:* The group hikes to and from the established camp where they will stay overnight.

What one wears upon a hike depends upon where he is going, when, and the kind of weather expected. However, a good general rule to remember is that old comfortable clothes are best. Blue jeans or slacks may be preferred by the group to shorts. Shoes worn must be appropriate, with room enough in them for the hiker to wear one or two pairs of heavy socks. Both shoes and socks must be free from rips or holes. Sweaters, jackets, or flannel shirts can be tied around the waist. Sandwiches wrapped in bandanas and tied to a stick carried over the shoulder will leave hands and arms free for easy rhythmic swinging attuned to easy rhythmic walking.

Hiking is one of the few cost-free physical activities left in our land. Children who learn early the joy of strolling, seeing, and absorbing the beauty and wonder of life that ever surrounds them can well be started on a life-long, pleasurable hobby.

Fire Building

Fire has many uses: to cook, heat, burn rubbish, and give off warmth. The appeal of fire is omnipresent among all peoples of the earth, for everyone, regardless of age, is drawn to it. Children can be taught how to use fire—the desire for this knowledge can be constructively channeled.

Types of wood best for cooking are the following:

1. For fast flames needed for boiling purposes use pine, spruce, balsam fir, red maple, basswood, or elder.
2. For even flames and coals needed for frying or broiling use the hickories, oaks, birches, sugar maple, white ash, eucalyptus, locust, beech.

Points to remember about fire building are to

1. Clear the ground around the area.
2. Use small, match-sized twigs, shavings, or bark for the foundation.
3. Add finger-size dry sticks laid crisscross or tepee-shaped over the foundation.
4. Have all wood ready before starting the fire.
5. Light the fire with the wind at your back, remembering that fire needs air.
6. Build the fire by adding wood of graduating size.
7. Be sure the fire is out before you leave it; water is best to use.

TYPES OF FIRES

TEPEE FIRE

Tepee or Wigwam

This is used for boiling purposes. Place the wood in a tepee formation.

CRISSCROSS

Crisscross

This is a slow burning fire best for frying, baking, or heat. Start with a foundation of tinder. Make a crisscross of sticks, placing larger ones at the bottom.

Reflector

This is a slow-burning fire used for baking. Bank the wood against larger pieces of green wood so that the heat is thrown forward. Have the baker in place before the fire is lighted.

REFLECTOR FIRE

Indian Star or Lazy Man's Fire

This is a slow burning fire that can be used for heat, comfort, and slow roasting. Start with a tepee fire. Use long poles, which are pushed into the fire as their ends burn.

INDIAN FIRE

Hunter-Trapper Fire

Use for slow boiling, stewing. Two heavy logs of slow-burning wood are laid parallel, with the narrowest end placed facing the wind. Sticks of green wood are laid across the two to be used for supporting pans. Start from a tepee fire, which will catch other tinder laid between the two big logs.

HUNTER-TRAPPER FIRE

Bean Hole Fire

Use for cooking a one-pot meal. Fire is laid in a hole 1 foot wide and 8 to 10 inches deep. Green sticks are laid across the top of the hole for supporting pans.

BEAN HOLE FIRE

Backlog Fire

Use for frying and boiling. The fire is built in front of a backlog for boiling purposes. Coals are raked forward between the two logs for frying purposes.

BACKLOG FIRE

Suggested Easy-to-Prepare Outdoor Meals

Menu planning will aid children in learning the essentials of good nutrition. Outdoor cooking is great fun! Roasting wieners and toasting marshmallows is easy, but real outdoor cooking takes skill. Simple one-pot meals are best for young children to cook.

Each meal should include

1. Meat, fish, cheese, beans, or eggs.
2. Milk for cooking or drinking.
3. Some kind of fruit.
4. One vegetable—preferably two (one cooked, one raw).
5. Enriched bread.

If the child are to be at camp all day the three meals eaten there should include

1. At least 1 pint of milk per person.
2. Fruit of some kind for two meals.
3. Cereals or enriched bread.
4. Two vegetables—one raw, of the green leafy variety, and one cooked.
5. One potato, in addition to the other vegetables.
6. Meat, fish, cheese, beans, or eggs.
7. Butter or fortified margarine.

Various types of outdoor cooking will be fun to try.

Tennis Racket Broiler

Toasting bread on sticks is an easy beginning. Broiling meat on green sticks shaped like snowshoes is more advanced and more fun to do.

TENNIS RACKET BROILER

Tin-Can Stove

Pan broiling, frying, and stewing can be done individually over tin-can stoves made from large-sized, number 10 coffee cans with a wedge cut out of the end from which the lid has been removed. A burner can be made using a smaller can (smaller than a tuna fish can), melted paraffin, and string for a wick.

TIN CAN STOVE

Flat Rock Cooking

On-a-rock cooking is sheer delight to all who can do it. A flat rock is laid across several smaller ones and is used as a frying pan.

FLAT ROCK COOKING

Baking Bread Sticks

Green-stick cooking is an art but also one not difficult to master. Prepared biscuit dough to which water or milk has been added is twisted around the end of a green stick and slowly toasted.

BAKING BREAD DOUGH

Green-Stick Cooking

Barbecues are more advanced, but sixth graders can cook small pieces of meat this way. Two V-shaped sticks driven into the ground support a green stick, on which the meat is speared. A special sauce is used for basting the slowly turned meat. Pans and skillets are used, too, but are not as novel for the novice as the ingenious methods suggested.

GREEN STICK COOKING

Planking

Planking, a method of cooking meat on a board by reflected heat, is great sport, especially for all cowboy fans.

PLANKING

Paraffin Buddy Burners

Buddy burners made of cans smaller than tuna fish cans, paraffin, and cardboard are fun to make and use. One end is taken from the can, and paraffin is made from old candle stubs dripped around a piece of cardboard wound in a loose spiral with one end pulled out as a wick. The burner can be used inside a tin-can stove. It is ideal for frying eggs or cooking pancakes.

PARAFFIN BUDDY BURNER

Suggested things to cook by any of the mentioned methods are

Green Stick or Green-Stick Broiler
Steak, bacon, ham, liver
Bread twists
Kebobs

One-Pot Meals
Chili
Corn chowder
Hunter's stew
Baked beans
Chop suey
Ring tum diddy

Fry Pans
Any meat that can be fried
Eggs—scrambled, fried
Toasted sandwiches
Pancakes
Fried potatoes

Reflector Ovens or Backlog Reflector
Biscuits
Cookies
Cakes
Corn bread
Muffins

REFLECTOR OVEN

Bean Hole Cooking
Stews
Beans
Cooked cereals

Coal Baking
Potatoes
Roast corn
Apples

Barbecue
Pork
Beef
Chicken

Plank Cooking
Fish
Steak
Chops
Liver
Ham

Foil Cooking

Aluminum foil cooking is ideal for beginners. Almost any kind of food that can be baked or steamed can be cooked in it. The secret of success is in folding the food in a double wrapper into a neatly pressed package and placing it on or covering it with coals. Children tend, like the novice adult, to put the food directly into flames and should, consequently, be instructed that this will only ruin it.

Types of food that can be prepared best by beginners include

1. Chicken parts, frozen fish, or other kinds of meat or fowl, thoroughly cleaned; place these and thinly sliced potatoes, carrots, and onions in the package.
2. Hamburger meat or Spam, using the vegetables mentioned above.
3. Canned prepared biscuits, wrapped singly and spread with either brown sugar and cinnamon or butter and jelly, or both.
4. Bacon and eggs. Lay flat two or three slices of bacon and break an egg over them; season, and fold into a package.
5. Corn. Spread butter, salt, and pepper over the corn, sprinkle water or insert ice cubes for steaming purposes, leave the shucks on, and wrap in foil.
6. Apples, squash, potatoes, or other fruits and vegetables.
7. Franks in a blanket.
8. Cakes and cookies.
9. Shish-kebobs made of beef, veal, or franks alternating on skewers or green sticks with slices of onions, tomatoes, potatoes, and mushrooms. Baste each skewerful with barbecue sauce and lay it above the coals for 15 to 20 minutes.
10. Frozen vegetables cooked in a pan with a lid made from the foil.

Foil skillets and pans can also be shaped and used in frying or baking almost every type of meat, fish, or vegetable. Corn popped in foil is especially recommended for beginners.

Camping Recipes

Chili Con Carne

Serves eight   One pot

4 tablespoons of grease
4 chopped onions
1½–2 lbs. of hamburger
2 cans tomatoes
2 cans kidney, red, or ranch-style beans
Salt
Pepper
Chili powder

Fry onions and meat until brown. Season. Add tomatoes and beans. Add chili powder or 2 tablespoons of Worcestershire sauce.

Campfire Stew

Serves eight   One pot

1½–2 lbs. of hamburger
3 teaspoons of grease or cooking oil
4 onions
2 cans of concentrated vegetable soup
Salt
Pepper

Make and fry little balls of hamburger. Fry onions in the bottom of the pan until they and the meatballs are brown. Pour off excess grease. Add the soup. Cover and slowly cook until the meat is thoroughly cooked.

Savory Beans

Serves eight   One pot

6 wieners or 2 slices of ham
1 can of whole corn
2 cans of baked beans
1 can tomatoes
2 onions
Salt
Pepper

Fry onions and meat together. Add tomatoes, corn and beans. Cook slowly.

Fish in a Bag

Individual   No utensils

¼ to ⅓ lb. of fillet fish per person
Salt
Pepper
Small piece of butter
Heavy wax paper
Newspaper

Wrap the seasoned, buttered fish in wax paper so that it is all covered. Wrap it again in wet newspaper. Leave in the coals 20 to 30 minutes, turning it once. Keep paper wet enough to cook the fish by steaming. Season with lemon, if desired. Tin foil may be used instead of wax and wet paper.

Corn Roast

Individual   No utensils

2 to 3 ears per person
Salt
Pepper
Butter

Soak ears of corn in their husks in water 2 or 3 hours. Cook in a good bed of coals. (Or each water-soaked ear may be wrapped in aluminum foil, after removing the husks, and cooked in the coals.) Cook 20 to 35 minutes. Eat with lots of butter.

Pioneer Drumsticks

Eight persons   On-a-stick

2 lbs. of chopped beef
1 cup corn flakes crumbled fine
2 eggs
Pepper
Salt
2 or 3 onions
16 rolls or pieces of bread
8 green sticks, thumb size

Mix chopped beef with onions, two eggs, one cup of crumbled corn flakes, and seasoning. Wrap this around the end of a green stick, squeezing it evenly in place. Cook over coals, turning frequently. Slightly twist to remove it from the stick. Serve on bread.

Kebobs

Individual   On-a-stick

¼ lb. round steak cut in 1-inch squares about
          ¼ inch thick
Small onion, peeled and sliced
Partially boiled potato, sliced ¼ inch thick
2 strips of bacon cut in squares
1 fresh tomato cut in thick slices
2 rolls or sandwiches

Alternate cubes of beef (raw or partially cooked), onion, bacon, potato, and tomato on green stick or pointed wire, leaving little space between pieces. Repeat in same order. Sear quickly all over. Then cook slowly over coals, turning frequently. For variation try alternate pieces of lamb and onion, or bacon and liver, or oysters and bacon.

Lots-Mores

Individual   On-a-stick

3 marshmallows
3 squares of chocolate
green stick, thumb size

Split the marshmallows and insert the chocolate. Toast slowly.

Marguerites

Individual   On-a-stick

2 marshmallows
2 soda crackers
2 walnuts, pecans, or peanuts

Split the marshmallows and place the nuts on top. Insert between the crackers and toast.

Potatoes Baked in Tin Can

Serves eight   Baking

8 potatoes
No. 2 tin cans, with wire handles
Heavy wax paper

Scrub potatoes well and rub with butter or wrap in wax paper. Put in a large coffee can that has five holes punched in the top. Place in the coals, and pile them around the sides. Cook about one hour.

Other recipes for types of dishes that are unique to camping include

BREAD TWISTS.   Add water, according to directions, to prepared biscuit dough or Bisquick. Mix in a paper bag until a stiff dough is formed. Wind this around a green stick or a broom handle covered with foil, browning it slowly. Stuff holes with butter, bacon, or jam.

MIX DOUGH IN A PAPER BAG

USE ROCKS AND STICKS

PANCAKES.   Add water to prepared mix. Have pan hot and well greased. Pour a spoonful on the pan. Cook until bubbles appear, and turn. For variety, add to the batter cinnamon, cooked rice, blueberries, or a cup of whole-kernel canned corn.

SOMEMORES.   Make a sandwich of two white or graham crackers, a piece of chocolate, and one marshmallow. Toast slowly, and sample. Judge for yourself whether you would like "Somemore."

BAKED FISH.   Wrap a piece of frozen fillet in aluminum foil with a piece of raw carrot, potato, onion, and celery. Cook over coals.

BAKED CHICKEN.   As above, wrap your favorite piece of chicken in the foil and cook with the vegetables.

EGGS IN MUD.   Cover eggs or potatoes with wet clay or mud. Cook eggs twenty minutes in hot coals, potatoes one hour.

CAMPER'S STEW.   Have each person wrap the lower part of a large coffee can with foil. Put in alternate layers of chopped onions, carrots, celery, corn, and beef. Sprinkle tomato juice, canned tomatoes, or catsup over the top. Put on lid. Wrap the entire can with foil. Cook in hot coals for fifteen to twenty minutes.

CHILI CON CARNE. Brown diced onions and hamburger. Add meat and cook until done. Season with chili powder. Add 1 can of Mexican chili beans, 1 can of tomatoes, and 2 tablespoons of catsup, and cook slowly.

CAMP COCOA. Use 1 teaspoon of cocoa for every 2 of sugar. Add 1 cup of milk for every person, or 4 tablespoons of powdered milk to every cup of water, or ½ cup of evaporated milk to every ½ cup of water. Mix cocoa and sugar with water in a kettle and cook to a smooth paste. Add milk, a pinch of salt, and stir all together. Heat almost to a boil. Serve with a marshmallow in each cup.

Nature

Too many children are oblivious of their world around them. The role of the adult in helping youth discover the magic and beauty of nature is to help them really see and appreciate living things in their everyday life. A nature lover will never be a nature destroyer. Thus, the earlier nature education begins, the better. Children love it—if it is fun and exciting.[3] In this program, emphasis should be placed on nature *exploration* rather than on nature study, for the former spells adventure, the latter, school and patterned drudgery. Teachers untrained in botany and biology often are more successful in helping children find things to smell, touch, watch, and love than teachers who answer eager questions of "What is this?" or "Why do the birds do that?" in a flat, all-knowing tone that quickly quenches a flickering flame of curiosity. Too often adults have succeeded in robbing children of the thrill of finding things for themselves.

Numerous free and inexpensive sources of help in this area are available from local and federal government sources.[4] Other sources of aid include farmers, rangers,

---

[3]The children and the teacher should subscribe to Ranger Rick, a nature magazine for children, available from the National Wildlife Federation, Washington, D.C. It is written for children and is full of beautiful pictures and exciting textual matter (price is $7.00 per year).

[4]M. Vannier: *Recreation Leadership.* Philadelphia, Lea & Febiger, 1977, pp. 204–205.

FIGURE 25–5. Children should learn things at camp that they cannot learn at school. (Courtesy of Kanakuk-Kanakomo-Kamps, College Station, Texas.)

scout officials, hobbyists, and science teachers. Reference books, beautifully illustrated in color, should be readily available so that those eager to learn more about nature can do so.

Program possibilities in nature education include

1. Trail making in scenic wooded areas.
2. Forestry projects (tree planting, making seed beds, transplanting, or trail blazing by marking trees).
3. Nature guessing games.
4. Rock, fern, flower, or vegetable garden making and care.
5. Building tree houses for the discovery of bird and animal habits.
6. Crafts from native clay, shells, and woods.
7. Vegetable dyeing.
8. Sketching and painting.
9. Cloud, tree, flower, or animal photography.
10. Making a lily pond.
11. Building fish shelters in streams.
12. Constructing bird refuges.
13. Fishing, fly and bait casting, and fly tying.
14. Berry and other fruit picking.
15. Hobby collections of Indian relics, spore prints, rocks, minerals, butterflies.
16. Making a sundial or Indian clock.
17. Driftwood collecting.
18. Making mats, bed frames, and other useful articles from reeds and willows.
19. Tanning skins for purses or belts.
20. Collecting feathers for ornaments.
21. Constructing canoe paddles, arrows, and bows from native woods.
22. Rope making.
23. Bone and sandstone carving.
24. Making a weather forecasting station.
25. Constructing weather flags.
26. Collecting weather signs and sayings.
27. Taking trips to local fire patrol stations, tree nurseries, wild game preserves, and fish hatcheries.
28. Telling star and other nature legends of Indians.
29. Making a camp nature museum of local wildlife.
30. Boat and canoe rides to see the wonders of night on the water.
31. Rainy-day hikes to discover how nature adapts itself to inclement weather.
32. Making and observing rules for conservation of the local natural resources.
33. Composing creative writing, music, dance, and dramatic activities around nature themes.
34. Making musical instruments from gourds, hollow reeds, or corn stalks.

NATURE GAMES

Wise is the leader who has a large supply of carefully selected nature games to add zest and sparkle to his or her program or variety and surprise during adverse weather conditions. Even adults enjoy testing their wits or newly acquired nature knowledge in a game similar to Twenty Questions. Each selected game should add to the effectiveness of the total program and not be a tacked-on, unnecessary fringe to an already attractive garment. The leader might well make a large collection of such games, writing each on a separate card employing the pattern used to describe each of the following active and passive games:

One Foot Square
Outdoor—Quiet

Divide the group into teams. Place a book or other object over a piece of ground approximately 1 foot square. Give each group five minutes or less to collect as many living things as possible in that square. Reward the winning group with the privilege of choosing the next activity.

Retrieving
Outdoor—Active

Divide the group into teams. The leader holds up one specimen (rock, maple leaf, or other) and says "Go!" Award one point to the group that returns first with a similar object. Play for ten or fewer points.

I Saw
Outdoor or Indoor—
Active

Arrange players in a circle. One acts out the animal, fish, or bird he saw recently. He remains inside the circle if anyone or all fail to guess what he saw. The winner remains in the circle longest.

Trailing
Outdoor—Active

The leader goes cross country into the woods, marking his trail by bending twigs, footprints, or similar signs. The group tries to find him 10 to 15 minutes later. The first to find him is the winner.

True or False
Outdoor or Indoor—
Active

Divide the group into two teams, naming one side True, the other False. The leader reads either a true or false statement, such as "Dogs fly." Each side runs behind its own safety line, depending upon the statement. If true, the True group runs while the False chases. The winning team ends up with the most players.

Touch
Indoor—Quiet

Place bird nests, leaves, fruit, and so forth, into a paper sack. All players close their eyes, and each handles all articles inside the bag. When all have removed blindfolds, the winner is the one who records the largest correct number of articles.

Kim's Game
Indoor—Quiet

Place a nut, vegetable, leaf, and so forth, into an uncovered box. Have all players look into the box for two minutes. The winner has recorded the largest correct number of articles.

Sounds
Outdoor—Quiet

Give each player pencil and paper. All remain silent for five minutes, noting down all natural sounds heard during that period. The winner is the one who has recorded the greatest number.

Sharp Eyes
Indoor—Quiet

Show all a bird or animal picture for two minutes. Have all record the answers to specific questions, such as "What color was the bird's left wing?" The winner has recorded the greatest number correctly.

Draw
Indoor—Quiet

Divide players into teams. Call one from each team to see the name of a bird or beast you have written down. Each goes back to his own group and without talking must draw a picture of the bird or animal. The winning team is the one that guesses correctly first and is given one point. Play to five points.

Blind as a Bat
Outdoor—Active

The leader blindfolds and ties a rope to the wrist of one representative from each team. The leader holds the rope ends and allows each 5 feet of rope. All walk around and call out the identity of as many objects as possible in five minutes. The winner is the player who names the most objects correctly.

Flash Nature Game
Outdoor or Indoor—
Quiet

Give each player a number and divide into two teams. The leader has 10 or more specimens from a wide variety of nature objects in a bag. He holds each one above his head, turning it around slowly, allowing all to see. He calls a number and the player with that number guesses what the object is. Award one point to the team member who correctly identifies the object. Play for ten points.

Changing Cover
Outdoor—Active

While the leader counts to 10, all players hide themselves 30 feet away. Leader eliminates anyone he can see. He closes his eyes and counts to 9 while players move closer. He continues counting one less each time and eliminates all those seen as they all move closer each time. Winner gets closest to the leader at the most reduced count.

Number One Man
Outdoor—Active

The leader arranges hikers in single file behind him. He sees an object of nature and asks the person behind him (the No. 1 Man) to identify it. Failure to do so means that player goes to the end of the line and the second person has chance to move up if he can answer. If he fails, he goes to the end of the line, too. The winner remains in first place longest.

Hare and Hounds

Outdoor—Active

Divide the group into Hare and Hound teams. Hares hide in groups of three and must remain in this group. Hounds search until all groups are found. Hares become Hounds and the game continues. The team finding others in shortest time wins.

Curio Collection

Outdoor—Active

The leader names an oddity of nature such as a tree with red leaves, a tree bent by a strong wind, and so forth. Players search until the curio is found. The winner finds the greatest number.

Fetch It

Outdoor—Active

Divide the group into two lines, each player numbered so that the opposite players have the same number. The leader asks any two with the same number to "fetch" a certain object, such as a milkweed. The line scoring ten points first wins.

Who Am I?

Outdoor or Indoor—

Active

One player pretends to be some character in nature. He tells brief facts about himself but conceals his identity; he says, for example "I live along the seashore and am an animal." The one guessing correctly becomes the new leader.

Find Me

Outdoor—Active

Divide the group into teams. Give each team a list of various nature objects to find with points given according to difficulty of finding each article. First group to make 15 points wins.

I Spy

Outdoor—Active

Hike with a group. The leader says "I spy a robin" (or any other nature object). All who also see the object sit down. Others remain standing until they see it. Award points to each of the first three in the group who see the object named. Play until one wins ten points.

Match It or Know It

Outdoor—Active

Divide group into two teams. Allow each team 15 minutes to collect objects of nature (leaves, twigs, seeds, nuts, and so forth) and to take them back to their side. One representative from each goes to the opposite side with an article. If the opposing team can name it, award one point; if they can match it from their collection, award two points. Play for 15 points.

Nature Scavenger Hike
Outdoor—Active

Divide group into teams of six to ten. Give each a list of nature objects to find within a given time. The winning team finds the greatest number within the allotted time.

Nature Scouting
Outdoor—Active

Divide the group into teams and send each on a 15- to 30-minute hike going East, West, North, or South. A representative from each team tells of the most interesting things seen by the group. All vote to determine which team saw the most interesting things.

Tree Tag
Outdoor—Active

"It" tries to tag players. Designate one kind of tree that players are safe when touching. Tagged players assist "It" until all are caught.

Scramble
Indoor—Active

Arrange 20 or more nature objects in a pile. Divide players into teams, giving each corresponding numbers. Call out all No. 2s to find the bird nest or other object and to bring the object to their teams first. Winning team is the one that secures the most objects.

Nature Baseball
Indoor—Quiet

Arrange nature questions on cards. Divide the players into two teams. Draw baseball diamond on the floor with chalk. The leader asks batter a question. If he answers correctly, he goes to first base; if he fails, he is out. Play according to regular baseball rules. Play four innings or for 10 to 15 minutes.

Prove It
Outdoor—Quiet

Arrange players in a circle. One says "From where I sit I see a tree with moss on it" (or any other natural object in sight). If anyone challenges his seeing the tree, he must prove it by touching the tree. If challenged and unable to prove what he saw, he must drop out; if he can prove it, his challenger must leave the game.

String-Burning Contest
Outdoor—Active

Stretch two strings between stakes, one 12 inches above the ground, the other 18 inches above it. Contestants must collect tinder kindling and build a fire to burn the upper string. No wood may be piled higher than the 12-inch string. Each one tries to burn the upper string apart first.

Knotcraft

Although there are hundreds of knots, with a specific use for each, the elementary-school child should learn to tie a few basic ones well and know the unique value of each, rather than trying to master the art of knowing how to tie many. The pupil should learn that a good knot is one that is easily tied and untied and one that will serve its purpose. Knots are used for (1) joining rope, cord, or string; (2) stopping the end of the rope, string, or cord from slipping; (3) looping; (4) securing; (5) shortening other ropes; and (6) holding articles.

The teacher should have each pupil bring a piece of clothesline or small rope. She demonstrates how the knot is tied or shows a picture if she herself cannot tie the knot and has the pupils copy the instructions, step by step. The pupils should tie the knot on a chair, box, or tree and practice until the skill is mastered.

Learning how to tie the following knots and their use might well be included in the program.

Square Knot

Use to join two ends of rope or to tie a bundle, bandage, or shoestring, as well as to make a longer rope from several short ones. Take an end of the rope in each hand. Cross the end in the right hand over the end in the left, twisting it back down and up in front so that a single knot is made. The end you started with should now be in the left hand. Take the end in the right hand and bend it over the left, making a loop that lies along the knot already made. Take the end in your left hand into the loop you have made. Take hold of the knot on both sides, and tighten by pulling the ends in opposite directions. To loosen it, take hold in the same way and push toward the center.

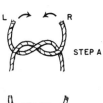

STEP A

STEP B

Sheet Bend

Use to join two ropes of different sizes. Two ropes of different sizes are needed. Make a square knot with two ends. Take the end of the smaller rope *(A)* and cross it under the other piece of the rope at *(B)* and then up and over the loop of the bigger rope at C. This puts one end of the smaller rope on top and one underneath the loop of the larger rope. As you pull the knot tight, the extra turn will secure the small end in place. The knot is completed after making the extra twist with the smaller rope.

SHEET BEND

Bowline

Use to make a loop in the end of a rope to slip over a hook or secure something to a post. Take only one end of the rope but tie the other one to a tree or round object. Make a loop and judge the place where the knot will be. Let the rope lie in the palm of your left hand. With the right hand, make a loop up and in back of the fingers of the left hand, coming down in front and catching the rope with the thumb as it crosses. Slip your fingers out of the loop and take the end of the rope in your right hand with your left thumb and finger. Pass the rope up from underneath to make a small loop. Pull this end to make the main loop the size you want it and then pass the end in back of the standing part of the rope and back to the front and down into the small loop again so that it is beside itself. Take these two pieces of rope in one hand and the main part of the rope in the other and pull the knot by pulling in opposite directions. To make the loop around a tree or round object, pull around it before you pull through the small loop; pull it tightly and proceed as before. Try to tie the knot with one hand as sailors do, but remember that even with both hands you always should use just one end of the rope.

BOWLINE KNOT

Clove Hitch

Use to tie something securely. Take an end of the rope around a tree or rung and cross it over its own part. Take the end around the tree or rung again and under the bend just made.

Slip Knot

Use to tether a horse, to attach a rope to a bucket handle, or to tie neckties. Draw end A (as shown in step A) around a tree or rung and make a small loop in it. Bring A up behind and across the standing part of the opposite rope end (D), then down through bight B, and then up, around, and down through bight B again (as shown in step B).

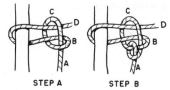

STEP A   STEP B

Knifemanship and Toolcraft

Use of the knife can be taught to girls as well as boys. A Boy or Girl Scout knife is recommended. The pupils should be taught the parts of the knife, safety measures to use when opening and closing it, how to sharpen it, and how to care for it.

The group can be taught how to whittle useful articles such as buttons, name tags, candle holders, letter openers, paper weights, lapel pins, napkin rings, knives, forks, and spoons from native materials. How to make and use fuzz sticks and kindling wood might well be included.

THE USE OF THE HATCHET AND AXE

The Axe

A hand axe is a good tool for general use. To use the axe properly, grasp the end firmly with the thumb around the first finger. Bring the axe down, carried by its head, and strike sharp direct blows on the wood. To cut a heavy log, strike diagonal blows; never cut square across. To fell a small tree, first clear the brush around it. Cut diagonally down the trunk and alternate this with blows up the trunk. To split a log, drive the axe into the wood and raise both together, striking on the edge of a block. Or lean the log against another log or block and strike in the center where it touches the block. Practice splitting larger logs into small pieces of kindling.

Axemanship

STEP I

Teach your pupils to use first a light single-headed axe. Have them first try to chop a log that is on the ground. To hold the axe, grasp it easily in the right hand with the palm under the handle of the axe and with the left palm over the end. These positions are reversed for left-handed pupils. Balance the weight easily and practice letting the axe fall from above your head on to the log. Then (1) raise the axe head with your right hand over your head while your left hand moves up slightly to the front; keep your elbows bent; (2) let your right hand slip down the handle to the other hand as the axe falls, but guide the handle and keep your eyes on the spot to hit; and (3) let the axe head do the swinging and the work. Keep practicing until a rhythmic, easy swing develops. Practice by cutting heavy logs before you begin chopping down small tress.

STEP 2

STEP 3

Sleeping Equipment and Tents

Bed Roll

Sleeping bags are ideal camping equipment. However, blanket rolls are simple to make and prove to be almost as good. First, lay a poncho or raincoat on the ground. Place the first blanket on the poncho near the middle so that half of it extends out on the side. Place a second blanket on its end at the center of the first blanket so that it lies directly above the poncho. Lap each additional blanket over the underneath one. Fold a sheet and place it on last. Fold all blankets over in reverse order—1, 2, 3, and so forth. Pin through all the sides and the bottom with horse-blanket pins. Snap the poncho over and tightly roll all the blankets into a bed roll. Carry the roll over your shoulder or on your back.

BLANKET NO.3   BLANKET NO.1

PONCHO   BLANKET NO.2 OR SHEET

Tents

The simplest type of shelter is a poncho tent made by throwing a poncho over a rope stretched between two trees and pegging it down. A wall tent is also recommended. These can be bought at nominal cost at army and navy stores. The campers can be taught how to pitch and ditch these tents with skill as well as how to make wooden tables and chairs, brooms, waste baskets, and other housekeeping articles from native materials. Caches used for storing food and keeping it cool are also fun to make.

PONCHO SHELTER

Lashing

This skill aids campers in using native materials for needed articles, for lashing is a way to bind sticks or poles together without nails. Its use serves to protect trees, which would be damaged by nails, and adds to the over-all rustic setting of camp. Because it requires only cord and sticks or poles, it is easy to set up or take down.

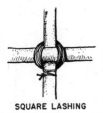

SQUARE LASHING

Square Lashing

This type joins two sticks together at right angles. Tie a clove hitch to the vertical stick at one end of the stick. Bring the standing part across the horizontal stick, and then around behind the vertical stick. Repeat until both sticks are secure. The ends should be made secure, and the sticks made secure by frapping. This is done by winding the cord tightly as you use it.

DIAGONAL LASHING

Diagonal Lashing

This type joins two sticks at a diagonally formed X. Tie a clove hitch around both. Make as many as six turns joining in one direction, then as many the other way. Finish off with a square knot.

ROUND LASHING

Round Lashing

This type is used to join two short sticks to make one long one. Tie a clove hitch around one, then wrap the cord around both. Finish off with a square knot or half hitches.

Continuous Lashing (Paling Hitch)

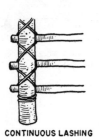

CONTINUOUS LASHING

This type is used to make ladders or bridges. Use small short sticks and long narrow ones. Notch the long sticks where the smaller ones will be lashed. Use a cord four times longer than the long sticks and start at the end of the long stick with a clove hitch made at the middle of the cord, thus leaving equal lengths on either side of the long stick. If the hitch has been properly placed, the ends of cord will pull the knot tight as they come up from the underside of the long stick. Next, bring the cords around this knot over the first small stick, following the lines of the long stick. Pull down and under, crossing the cord on the underside of the long stick. Pull the cords over the second small stick, following the lines of the long stick by going under and crossing underneath the long stick and coming up for the next one. The rope should always run parallel to the long stick on the top and should cross on the underside. End with 2 half-inches and tuck the ends of the rope under the last stick. Lashing is fun to do. It is a useful camp skill, for the campers can learn to lash pieces of wood together to make coat hangers, mirrors, picture frames, tables, shoe racks, suitcase racks, a tripod for pots and pans, bridges, chairs, as well as the other articles previously mentioned.

Other Camp Skills

FINDING YOUR WAY

Knowing how to find one's way in the woods even when lost is a valuable skill. Teach pupils how to find their way by the sun, a watch, stars, tree moss, and a compass. At the same time introduce trail blazing by using trees, rocks, or grass. Map making and reading of places in the local community will be interesting to the students. Signaling by means of the Morse Code or flags and smoke should also be included. Care should be taken, however, not to duplicate skill areas already covered by the pupils in their Girl and Boy Scout work. Use of a skill inventory sheet before classes begin will prevent any duplication.

SOIL CONSERVATION

The pupils can learn much in this area about our land and how to conserve our national resources. Learning about how to build dams and their use, soil erosion and correction, forest conservation, and how to plant trees, shrubs, fruits, and vegetables will give each student a deeper appreciation of the soil and land on which he lives. That we all live on the land is often forgotten in our modern world. Learning how to live simply in the out-of-doors, utilizing what is in one's environment, can add much to a child's wise use of present and future leisure time.

FISHING

Every child should learn how to fish, for this is one sport that can bring lifetime enjoyment. Cane poles can be used, or the children can cut and fashion their own from tree branches. Fly and bait casting is more fun but requires special equipment, which is relatively inexpensive.

Bait casting is done with live, artificial, or fresh bait. Worms, spoons, or pork rind are often used. The rod is made from wood, steel, glass, or bamboo.

1. Hold the rod easily in one hand, with the thumb on the spool where it feels best as you apply pressure to control the speed of the lure. Do the overhead cast on three counts:
   a. Count One—Hold the rod almost horizontal.
   b. Count Two—Bring it back to an imaginary twelve o'clock position, then eleven o'clock.
   c. Count Three—Snap your wrist, bringing the rod back down, slightly above your original horizontal position, and release the line by pressing the button.

Practice to develop a smooth, relaxed, accurate cast. Use the rod tip for aiming, and whip the line straight ahead each time. Avoid back casting too far or tensing up. Stand squarely, or with the opposite leg forward in a stride position (right leg forward for a left-handed person and vice versa for a right handed one).

Fly casting is done with artificial or live bait. Artificial flies are multicolored and have colorful names such as the royal coachman, grizzly bear, and so forth. Live bait includes salmon eggs, worms, grasshoppers, and minnows. The rod is made from tubular steel, split bamboo, or glass.

1. Hold the rod easily in one hand with the thumb on top or at one side (whichever is more comfortable). Learn to cast on these four counts:
   a. Count One—Hold the rod horizontal. Take up the line slack with an outward pull of the opposite hand.
   b. Count Two—Snap the line back over your head to one o'clock position.
   c. Count Three—Make a momentary pause until the lure completes its backward movement.
   d. Count Four—Snap the rod back down, almost to its original horizontal position.

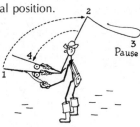

BACKPACKING

Backpacks should be fit directly on the back and be of light yet good waterproof material. When packing the bag place the bulk of the weight close to the shoulders and never near the small of the back, as this can cause early and extreme fatigue. The lightest articles should go on the bottom with the heaviest on top. The best packs are available from sporting goods stores and include a knapsack (small bag), haversack (somewhat larger), rucksack (considered the best), or the Adirondack Pack Basket (best for experienced and older hikers). Ponchos and a ground cloth can also be used but are not as good as purchased packs.

Our American Heritage

The early history of America is a brilliantly colored tapestry recording as its dominant pattern man's struggle to carve a unique life and culture out of a wilderness. Pictured there are Indians, explorers, trappers, prospectors, Pilgrims, lumberjacks, and ranchers—campers all, to whom life itself was camping—rugged human beings dependent upon the land, respectful of it, and seeing in it a good life. These dynamic pioneers, pushing beyond boundaries, blazing new trails into regions marked "unknown," left behind them rich sagas of daring courage. Today's youth needs to learn and appreciate this treasure. They also need to learn about the wisdom of the woods as expressed by Joan Anglund in *A Slice of Show:*

> What need we teach a child . .
> with our books and rules?
>
> Let him walk among the hills and flowers,
> let him gaze upon the waters,
> let him look up to the stars . . .
> and he will have his wisdom.

Campfire programs should be built around folk themes. Songs and stories from all regions of the country will increase appreciation of other groups. Folk and square dancing, and party games will add much sheer fun. Games of low organization, including nature guessing games and contests in campcraft skills, will add much to build group unity and a spirit of good fellowship. Camping has no equal in bringing out and developing the best in youth and helping them find real adventure.

SUGGESTED READINGS

Angier, B.: *Wilderness Cookery.* New York, Stackpole Books, 1970.

Angier, B.: *Home in Your Pack.* New York, Macmillan, Inc., 1972.

Angier, B.: *Wilderness Gear You Can Make for Yourself.* New York, Macmillan, Inc., 1973.

Benson, K. R., and Frankson, C. E.: *Nature Crafts.* Englewood Cliffs, New Jersey, Prentice-Hall, 1968.

Brehm, S. A.: *A Teacher's Handbook for Study Outside the Classroom.* Columbus, Ohio, Charles E. Merrill Publishing Company, 1969.

Brown, R. E., and Mouser, G. W.: *Techniques for Teaching Conservation Education.* Minneapolis, Burgess Publishing Company, 1964.

Donaldson, G., and Goering, O.: *Perspective In Outdoor Education.* Dubuque, Iowa, William C. Brown Company, Publishers, 1972.

Garrison, C.: *Outdoor Education: Principles and Practice.* Springfield, Illinois, Charles C Thomas, Publisher, 1966.

Goodrich, W., and Hutchins, C.: *Science Through Recreation.* New York, Holt, Rinehart and Winston, 1964.

Hammerman, D. R., and Hammerman, W. M.: *Teaching in the Outdoors*. Minneapolis, Burgess Publishing Company, 1964.

Harty, W.: *Science for Camp and Counselor*. New York, Association Press, 1964.

Hug, J. W., and Wilson, P. J.: *Curriculum Enrichment Outdoors*. New York, Harper & Row, Publishers, 1965.

Ickis, M.: *Nature in Recreation*. New York, A. S. Barnes & Company, 1965.

Mand, C. L.: *Outdoor Education*. New York, J. Lowell Pratt & Company, 1967.

Milliken, M., Hamer, A. F., and McDonald, E. C.: *Field Study Manual for Outdoor Learning*. Minneapolis, Minnesota, Burgess Publishing Company, 1968.

Mitchell, V., Robberson, B. A., and Obley, J.: *Camp Counseling*. 5th ed. Philadelphia, W. B. Saunders Company, 1977.

Riviere, B.: *The Camper's Bible*. Garden City, New York, Doubleday and Company, 1974.

Van der Smissen, B., and Goering, O. H.: *A Leader's Guide to Nature-Oriented Activities,* 2nd ed. Ames, Iowa, Iowa State University Press, 1968.

SUGGESTED FILMS

Beyond the Chalkboard. Northern Illinois University, DeKalb, Illinois 60115.

Nature's Classroom. Division of Conservation, Depatment of Natural Resources, Madison, Wisconsin 53701.

Outdoor Education. AAHPER, 1201 Sixteenth Street, N.W., Washington, D.C. 20036.

CHAPTER TWENTY-SIX

RECESS AND NOON-HOUR ACTIVITIES

If we really accept the fact that each child is unique, that his informational background is different from his neighbors, and perhaps his drive for answers is action-oriented, while his companion responds primarily to the spoken word; then our curriculum must be almost as varied as the children themselves.

Sarah Van Camp: How free is free play? Journal of the National Association For the Education of Young Children, April 1972, p. 206.

Playground activities include recess, before- and after-school play, and noon-hour recreation. Such times are for spontaneous free play in which each child engages in games or does things of his own choosing. These are rich educational times, far more so than most teachers realize. The child of today has now, and will have as tomorrow's adult, more free time than his grandparents or own parents ever dreamed possible. As future adult citizens who are prepared for life, our children must learn how to use their ever-increasing free time wisely, how to create their own fun without being constantly or passively entertained, and how to gain refreshment and release from tension.

A small boy once defined recreation as "doing what you do when you don't have to." The college professor explains that it is those activities voluntarily done during leisure that bring satisfaction and joy and are socially approved. Both are right, for recreation does means re-creation, renewal, refreshment, relaxation, fun, spontaneity, joyfulness, and fullness of life. Aristotle, born in 384 B.C., claimed that the whole end and object of education is the right use of leisure. Present-day educators are increasingly seeing the great wisdom of his statement.

Recess and noon-hour play helps the child maintain and develop good health through increased exercise, provides opportunity for him to practice and improve in physical and social skills, and gives him a chance to "let off steam" in legitimate ways. Above all, these are valued free-choice and experimental learning times in which the youth prepares for his own unsupervised adulthood, during which time he must be ably skilled at making his own choices regarding living his daily 24 hours on and off the job. Education for positive use of leisure time is a *must* in our contemporary society. Consequently, children who are "bad" should not be punished by having their recess play denied them. For too many this is the only bright spot in what too often is a dark, dull, and ego-shattering school day. What a child learns on the school playground may prove to be the most significant life lesson learned of them all.

ADMINISTRATIVE DETAILS

It is imperative that the school provide adequate and safe facilities as well as teacher leadership and supervision during these periods of play. Schedules for recess time should be staggered so that not too many children are on the grounds at one time. The allotted period should be long enough to allow each child to use some of the apparatus and run and play with others, as well as have enough time to go to the bathroom, wash his hands, and get a drink of water. For safety reasons primary classes should be assigned a permanent play space next to the main building that has enough shade and sunlight to produce and safeguard health. Older children should be given their own play area far enough away from the younger ones so that both groups can play safely.

All free-play periods should be well supervised. No teacher should be assigned more than 50 to 75 children. Male teachers might well be asked to supervise both sexes on the upper elementary level. A first-aid box should be located on the grounds or just inside the door of the main building. Records and careful study should be made of all accidents that occur. Both students and teachers will profit from making a careful study of these reports and together devising ways to make the play area safer for all classes and individuals.

Noon-hour recreation should follow a supervised and unhurried lunch period. If one hour is allowed for this activity, only half of it should be given over to free-choice play. No child should be permitted to gulp down lunch in order to join friends in rugged play. Such an action is unhealthy and educationally backward. Together, youths and adults should set up rules regarding how long students should be expected to stay in the lunchroom and how much time may be given over to play. Quiet games, social

FIGURE 26–1. Activities for the playground should add to the pleasure of the moment and enrich the recreational life of the child. (Courtesy of Los Angeles City Schools, Los Angeles, California.)

FIGURE 26–2. The noon-hour and recess programs can be fun and challenging. (Courtesy of AAHPER.)

dancing, and such dual games as box hockey or deck tennis are recommended. It is unwise to schedule highly competitive intramural games during this period because the development of good eating habits in a relaxed atmosphere is as important in the life of growing boys and girls as outdoor exercise.

SAFETY PRECAUTIONS

Although there should be few rules regarding the playground, these might well be devised by the children themselves with teacher guidance. All hazardous equipment should be discovered and marked by each class group when taken on a tour of the area by its teacher. Bright yellow paint or white markings striped with red for protruding rocks, swing apparatus, posts, and so forth is recommended. Children should be taught how to use correctly each piece of apparatus and equipment, as well as how to care for perishable articles such as rackets and balls. All apparatus should be inspected by a reliable adult at least once a month.[1]

ACTIVITIES

Most of the games mentioned in this book can be played outdoors. However, the following ones are especially suitable for recess and noon-hour play.

------

[1]See Chapter 11, The Gymnasium, Playground, Pool, and Classroom, for suggested outdoor play areas, apparatus, and equipment.

Marbles

This game is best for two or not more than six players. Ten or more marbles are encircled in a drawn ring. All players stand behind a line 4 to 6 feet away. Each "lags," or rolls, his shooting marble, the largest one being called his "taw," toward the ring, trying to knock out as many of the enclosed marbles as possible. Players then take turns, each shooting his taw by flipping it with his thumb out of his curved hand and from his bent index finger.

Fox and Geese

Two players sit 4 to 6 feet away from and facing each other with their legs spread apart. Each arranges his 20 to 30 marbles in lines or in a flying-geese V-formation before a line drawn in front of his feet. Players take turns rolling four to six big taws (foxes) toward the other's marbles (geese), trying to hit and knock them behind the line. Play continues until one has destroyed all the other's geese.

Hopscotch

Area:	Playground, tennis courts, and sidewalks
Grades:	Girls—1 to 4; boys—1 and 2
Players:	Four to six to a court
Directions:	This game is enjoyed by all children but is particularly suitable for remediable purposes in cases in which limited activity is recommended. In second through fourth grades, a player throws a pebble into square 1, hops in on one foot, picks up the pebble, and hops out. The pebble is then thrown into square 2, and the player hops on one foot into 1, straddles 2 and 3, picks up the pebble, puts his weight on his left foot, and hops into 1 and out. The player may

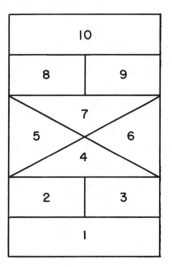

continue until the pebble fails to land in the proper square or until he steps on a line or puts a foot down when he should not. He hops on one foot into squares 1, 4, 7, and 10 and straddles the lines to retrieve the pebble in squares 3, 5, 6, 8, and 9. First graders like more activity so they follow the above instructions but hop to the end and back each time.

Variations: Play the game as above, but hop from one number to the next without missing.

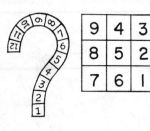  

Jump Rope

Class instruction should be given as follows:

1. The rope is swung back and forth in pendulum fashion. A child jumps from one side to the other.
2. The child stands by the rope and jumps as it describes a large, full circle.
3. *Front door*—The child learns to run in as the rope comes toward him.
4. *Back door*—The child learns to run in as the rope goes away.
5. *Hot pepper*—This is a fast jump.
6. *Jump-rope ditties*—The most popular ditties chanted by today's children as they skip rope are included below. These ditties are made up by the children and are apparently understood by the young fry, although their meaning may sometimes seem vague to adults. In some the words dictate certain movements, whereas others simply give each jumper a fair turn at the rope.

Jump-Rope Ditties

1. Had a little radio
   Put it in free
   Only station I could get
   Was W-B-Z. *(Hot pepper is turned until the jumper misses.)*

2. Bubble gum, bubble gum,
   Chew and blow,
   Bubble gum, bubble gum,
   Scrape your toe.
   Bubble gum, bubble gum,
   Tastes so sweet.
   Get that bubble gum off your feet. *(The jumper runs out.)*

3. Momma, Momma, I am sick
   Call the doctor quick, quick, quick
   How many pills must I take? *(Count 1, 2, 3, until the jumper misses.)*

4. Ice cream soda
   Delaware punch
   Tell me the name
   Of your honey bunch.
   A, b, c. . . . *(When the jumper misses she names a boy to take her place whose name begins with the letter on which she missed.)*

5. Blue bells, cockle shells
   Evie, Ivy, Over. *(Count 1, 2, 3, and so forth until the jumper misses.)*

6. Cinderella dressed in yellow
   Went upstairs to kiss her fellow
   How many kisses did she get? *(Count 1, 2, 3, until the jumper misses.)*
   Cinderella dress in green
   Went upstairs to eat ice cream.
   How many spoonfuls did she eat? *(Count 1, 2, 3, until the jumper misses.)*
   Cinderella dressed in black.
   Went upstairs and sat on a tack.
   How many stitches did it take? *(Count 1, 2, 3, until the jumper misses.)*

7. One, two, buckle my shoe
   Three, four, shut the door
   Five, six, pick up sticks
   Seven, eight, lay them straight
   Nine, ten, big fat hen
   Eleven, twelve, bake her well. *(Count 1, 2, 3, until the jumper misses.)*

8. Down in the meadow
   When the green grass grows
   There sat Mary *(the name of the jumper)*
   As sweet as a rose.
   She sang and she sang
   And she sang so sweet
   Along came Joe *(a boy friend)*
   And kissed her on the cheek.
   How many kisses did she get? *(Count.)*

9. Teddie Bear, Teddie Bear
   Turn around
   Teddie bear, Teddie Bear
   Touch the ground
   Teddie Bear, Teddie bear
   Go upstairs *(This jumper jumps toward the head of the rope)*
   Teddie bear, Teddie Bear
   Say your prayers
   Teddie Bear, Teddie Bear
   Turn out the light
   Teddie Bear, Teddie Bear
   Say good night.

10. Mabel, Mabel
    Set the table
    And don't forget
    The Red Hot Pepper.

11. *Twenty-four robbers.*
    Not last night but the night before.
    Twenty-four robbers came knocking at my door.
    I ran out and they ran in
    And this is the song they sang to me.
    Spanish dancer, do a split
    Spanish dancer, do a high kick
    Spanish dancer, turn around
    Spanish dancer, touch the ground
    Spanish dancer, do the kangaroo *(squat and jump)*
    Spanish dancer, skit, skat, skidoo!

12. The Jackson Five went to France.
    To teach the children how to dance
    A heel and a toe and around you go,
    A heel and a toe and around I go,
    Salute to the Captain,
    Bow to the King,
    Turn your back on the Ugly Ole Queen. *(Jumper runs out the back door.)*

13. *Nonsense.*
 Buster Brown went to town
 With his britches upside down.
 Out rolled a nickel
 He bought a pickle
 The pickle was sour
 He bought some flour
 The flour was yellow
 He bought him a fellow
 The fellow was mean
 He bought a bean
 The bean was hard
 He bought a card
 And on the card
 It said, "Red Hot Pepper."

Rope Games and Rope-Skipping Variations

Swaying Rope Rebound Jump[2]

Use one rope for every three children. Two players hold the rope while the third jumps. Positions are exchanged until all have had the opportunity to be the jumper. The rope is held so that the midpoint touches the floor. Stand alongside the rope so that one side is close to the rope. The players holding the rope cause it to sway away from the jumper and return toward him. As it returns, the jumper springs off both feet, allowing the rope to pass beneath him, and lands on both feet. On landing, he performs a small jump (rebound) readying him to jump over the rope again. Continue this action in time to the music.

Short Rope Swinging

Use a double rope and hold it in the right hand. Swing the rope forward in a counterclockwise circle so that the end strikes the ground. Continue this action in time to the music. Repeat turning the rope backward. Repeat both actions using the left hand.

Long Rope Swinging

Two players hold the rope so that the midpoint touches the floor midway between them. After deciding direction, they swing the rope in a full circle so that it strikes the floor on each turn. Continue this action in time with the music. Repeat swinging the rope in the opposite direction.

Run Through

Two players swing the rope so that it strikes the ground midway between them. The initial move of the rope should be away from the third player, who stands alongside the rope facing it. Timing the swing of the rope, the third player runs under the arch of the rope, beginning his move as the rope strikes the ground again. He then returns to the starting position by walking around the rope.

---

[2]These activities will be more fun for children if they are done to music. Recommended is the album *Rope Skipping* from Educational Activities Company, Freeport, Long Island, and the book, *Rope Skipping, Rhythms, and Routines* by Paul Smith, available from the same address.

Swinging Rope Jump

Two players hold the rope so that it touches the ground midway between them. The third player (jumper) stands in the middle so that the rope is alongside his feet. The players holding the rope swing the rope so that it passes over the jumper's head and down toward his feet. The jumper springs into the air and allows the rope to pass beneath his feet.

Step-Over Skip

Hold the rope with the loop behind your ankles. Swing it overhead and step over the rope with one foot. Transfer weight to lead foot and lift rear foot as the rope swings under. Return your weight to your rear foot and continue the action.

  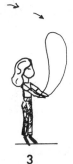 

1   2   3   4

Jump Skip

Hold the rope with the loop behind your ankles. Swing the rope over your head and jump over it as it passes underfoot. Continue this action in time to the music.

1   2   3   4

Rebound Skip

Hold the rope with the loop behind your ankles. Swing the rope overhead and then down toward your feet. As it passes overhead rebound both feet lightly off the floor. Turn the rope again and continue the action.

1   2   3   4   5   6

Hop Skip

Stand on one foot and hold the rope with the loop behind your ankle. Swing the rope over your head and down toward your foot. Hop over the rope. Rebound, and repeat the action.

1   2   3   4

Leap Skip

Stand on one foot (left) and hold the rope with the loop behind your ankle. Swing the rope over your head and down toward your foot. Spring over the rope, and land on your other foot (right). Rebound (on your right foot). Spring over the rope again, landing on the opposite foot (left). Rebound (on the left foot); continue this action.

1   2   3   4   5   6

Stride Skip

Stand with one foot in front of the other and hold the rope with the loop behind your ankle. Swing the rope over your head and down toward your feet. Jump rope, maintaining your feet in the same alignment, your weight equally distributed. Rebound, and repeat the action.

1   2   3   4

Bleking Skip

Stand with one foot (right) in front of the other and hold the rope with the loop behind the ankle. Swing the rope over your head and down toward your feet. Jump rope, changing the front foot and landing on the other (left). Continue turning and jumping with alternating feet forward.

1   2   3   4   5

Straddle Skip

Stand with your feet together and hold the rope with the loop behind your ankles. Swing the rope over your head and down toward your feet. Jump as the rope passes underneath your feet. Land with your feet together. As the rope passes overhead, rebound with your feet together. Jump the rope again with your feet apart (straddled). Rebound with your feet apart as the rope moves overhead.

1   2   3   4   5

Cross Skip

Stand holding the rope with the loop behind the ankles. Swing it overhead and down toward the feet. Jump rope. Rebound as rope swings up overhead; then cross hands and arms at elbows in front of the body. Jump rope. Rebound again as the rope swings up overhead, and uncross arms, bringing them back to normal position. Repeat sequence.

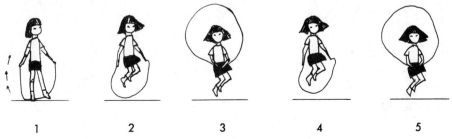

1   2   3   4   5

Paddle Tennis

This game is played like regular tennis except that the ball is served underhand and hit with a wooden paddle. The server stands behind the serving line in the right court and serves the ball diagonally across the net in one or two tries into his opponent's receiving court. After the ball bounces once, it is hit back across the net, and the game continues until one hits the ball into the net or out of bounds or misses it. The game is scored like tennis: 15, 30, 40, game, except when a tie score of 40–40 or "deuce," after which two consecutive points must be made. The game may be played by two or four players. *Variations:* Hand Tennis is played by batting a ball back and forth with either hand. Kick Tennis is played by kicking a soccer or playground ball back and forth across the net using the same rules.

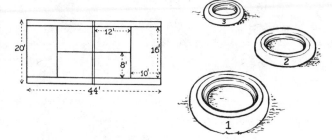

Playground Golf

Tennis balls or beanbags can be thrown into numbered tin cans or rubber tires scattered over the area. Players take turns trying to throw the ball into these in as few tosses as possible. *Variation:* Sink numbered poles in partially buried tin cans in a widely scattered area. Hit a golf, ping-pong, or jack ball into the can with a broomstick.

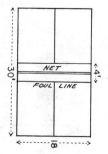

Deck Tennis

This game is played with a round rubber deck-tennis ring or rope ring by two or four players. The rules are similar to volleyball in that one continues serving as long as he wins a point; when he loses it, "side out" is called and his opponent then serves. The server begins the game by throwing the ring underhand, across, or to one side of his body into the diagonally opposite half court. Loss of serve occurs when one catches the ring with both hands, changes it from one hand to the other, steps on or over the serving line, or throws the ring into the net or out of bounds. The game consists of 15 points. If the score becomes tied at 14 all, two consecutive points must be made. As many as 20 players can play, but the game is best for smaller groups.

Tether Ball

The game object is to hit the ball so that it will wind around the pole, one person choosing to hit it always in one direction and his opponent hitting in the other. Score one point for winding the ball around the pole. Play for five or ten points. Players must take turns hitting the ball.

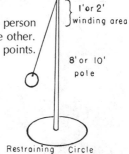

Shuffleboard (Children's Game)

Equipment: Four cues shaped to curve around the disc and eight discs, each set of four having its own color.

Directions: The object is to score the most points. Players take turns. To count, the disc must be inside but not touching any line. A player may move his own disc by hitting it into a better position. Scoring is done after each has shot all of his discs. In doubles, two opponents play side by side at one end, alternating turns until all have been hit. Then their partners play in the same manner, starting from the opposite court end. Their scores are tallied with those previously made by their partners.

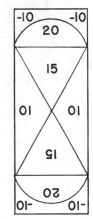

Horseshoes

Equipment: Two stakes placed 20 to 30 feet apart and four hard rubber horse-shoes.

Directions: In singles, two players start from the same stake by taking turns before throwing from the opposite stake. In doubles, each team member takes turns at each court end. The closest shoe scores one point, a ringer three. The game consists of 21 points.

Roller Skating

Upper elementary–grade children greatly enjoy roller skating. Many schools include instruction in this activity in their physical education programs. Although pupils can best be taught to roller skate individually, after the basic movements have been mastered the children can be grouped according to achievement levels for recess and noon-hour activity, as well as for needed practice. The children should learn how to skate forward, stop, make turns, skate with a partner, do the cross-over or corner turn, and skate with a partner and three or more pupils in a single line. More advanced pupils will enjoy skating to music during the noon hour, as well as learning how to waltz, fox-trot, and perform many other kinds of dance steps on skates. Square dancing

FIGURE 26–3.   Recess and noon-hour play help the child maintain and develop good health through increased exercise, provide opportunity for him to practice and improve in physical and social skills, and give him a chance to let off steam in legitimate ways. (Courtesy of Los Angeles City Schools, Los Angeles, California.)

on skates is especially exciting to those older pupils who have already learned how to do successfully the many movement skills this type of dancing offers.

Basic roller skating skills include the following:

Forward Skating

Pretend you are gliding and sliding on ice. Push forward on one skate, glide on the other. Repeat. Make bigger movements, trying to cover more distance on each foot.

Stopping

Put your weight on the inside skate. Point the toe of the outside skate outward; bring your heels closely together. Press your weight down on the outside skate and drag it behind the forward skate.

The Cross-Over Turn

For the two-foot leaning turn, place the inside skate in front of the outside skate and lean to the inside. For the one-foot leaning turn, glide on the inside skate and bring the outside skate forward in front of the body as the turn is made.

Skating Backward

Point your toes in and push one skate backward and glide on the other. At corners, cross the inside skate behind the outside skate.

The Waltz

The boy skates forward, the girl backward. They skate in rhythm, accenting the first beat.

Trio Skating

Three children, two boys with a girl in the middle, hook elbows and all move forward on the right foot or back on the left in unison.

Other Popular Activities

Pit Bowling

Play with up to four individual players or in teams of three. Each player rolls croquet balls or softballs toward three pits dug in the ground 20 feet away. Score three points for each ball that lands in the hole. Play for individual or team points.

Tin Can Golf

Sink tin cans in the ground for holes. Players use improvised sticks and old tennis balls, croquet mallets and balls, or hockey sticks and balls. Arrange the cans like a clock face with each hole across the circle from the preceding one, that is, 1, 3, 5; 7, 9, 11; 6, 8, 10. Use posts that extend about a foot above the ground instead of sunken cans, if desired. Each hole is made when the ball hits the proper post. A ball may be kicked instead of hit with the hands. The winner completes the course in the least number of strokes.

Croquet

Played with a wooden ball and mallet, the object of this game is to be the first to hit the ball through all the arches up and down the court. Simplified rules include the following:

1. Each player alternates turns hitting the ball, starting a mallet's distance in front of the starting stake and attempting to drive the ball through the first two wickets.
2. Each player is given another hit for going through an arch or hitting another's ball or the turning stake at the opposite end of the court. Two more hits are earned if the ball goes through both first arches, but if it goes through any other two arches, the player has the right of a mallet's length ahead in any direction, plus one stroke.
3. One loses a hit for playing out of turn.
4. Each ball must go through each numbered arch in proper progression.
5. A ball driven out of bounds may be put back on the boundary line where it went off.
6. One missing the ball entirely with the mallet may have a second turn.

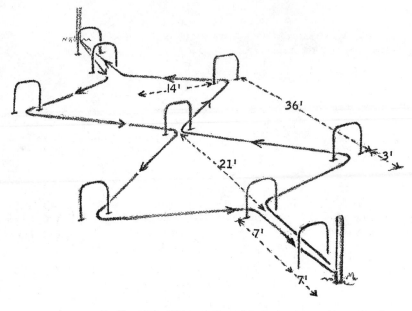

7. If one's ball hits another, the owner may put it next to the one struck and step on it while he hits his own ball hard enough to send the other's far down the court or out of position, or he may measure a mallet's distance in any direction and hit his ball from there.

Shuffleboard

Played by two or four, the game object is to propel discs, using a cue, onto scoring diagrams at the opposite end of the court in order to score, or to prevent one's opponent from scoring. Simplified rules are

1. The red disc is shot first, and then the two players alternate shooting black and red discs until all are shot from one end of the court and then the other.
2. In doubles, after all discs are played at the head of the court, play starts at the foot with red leading. A red player and a black one stand at each end of the court, alternating turns, each shooting two discs.
3. A game consists of 50, 75, or 100 points.
4. After players have shot all four discs, score all within the court area but do not count those on any line.

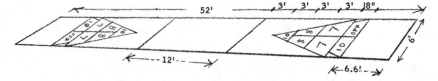

Rope Quoits

This game is played by two or four or any number, with either purchased or improvised equipment. Each player shoots four quoits per frame when it is his time to shoot. Opponents then shoot four quoits in the same manner. "Ringers" count five points each. All other quoits remaining on the base count one point each. Quoits that go off the board are lost and do not score any points. A game consists of ten frames for each player in the game. The player having the highest score wins. Players' feet must be behind the foul line or designated shooting point when the quoit is thrown; otherwise the shot is a foul and does not score. The distance from

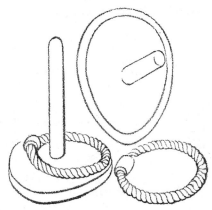

foul line or shooting line to the rope-quoit base should be as near 15 feet as possible. As in shuffleboard or bowling, any number of partners may play in a game. Partners having the highest score win.

Jacks

Equipment:	Six jacks, small rubber ball
Players:	Four to six in a circle
Area:	Sidewalk, hallway, classroom, cafeteria
Directions:	All jacks are tossed on the ground. A player tosses the ball into the air, picks up a jack, and catches the ball before it hits the ground. Each continues until he misses or all single jacks are picked up; players take turns and go as far as possible. After picking all jacks up one at a time, proceed in the same manner picking up two at a time, then three, four, five, and six. All jacks are tossed on the ground, the ball is tossed into the air, and the jacks are brushed singly into the player's cupped other hand (Pigs in a Pen). With all jacks tossed on the ground and the player's ball in air, the player picks up a jack with his other hand and catches it on the back of the hand before catching the ball; he does one at a time, two, three, and so forth. Add as many variations as possible.
Variations:	*Eggs in the Basket:* Jacks are picked up and transferred to the other hand before catching the ball. *Pigs in the Pen:* Jacks are swept into the opposite hand between spread fingers. *Lambs Over the Wall:* Jacks are lifted over the opposite hand held in wall position. *Lazy Susan:* The ball is bounced twice before the jacks are picked up. *Rapid Fire:* The ball is never allowed to bounce or hit the playing surface.

SUGGESTED READINGS

Armbruster, D., and Irwin, L.: *Basic Skills in Sports.* 2nd ed. St. Louis, The C. V. Mosby Company, 1967.

Baker, K.: *Let's Play Outdoors.* Washington, D.C., National Association for the Education of Young Children, 1966.

Blake, O. W., and Volp, A.: *Lead-up Games to Team Sports.* Englewood Cliffs, New Jersey, Prentice-Hall, 1964.

Kraus, R.: *Recreation Today, Program Planning and Leadership.* New York, Appleton-Century-Crofts, 1966.

Latchaw, M.: *A Pocket Guide of Movement Activities for the Elementary School.* 2nd ed. Englewood Cliffs, New Jersey, Prentice-Hall, Inc., 1970.

Mulac, M.: *Games and Sports for Schools, Camps and Playgrounds.* New York, Harper & Row, Publishers, 1964.

Stone, J.: *Play and Playgrounds.* Washington, D.C., National Association for the Education of Young Children, 1970.

Van der Smissen, B., and Knierim, H.: *Recreational Sports and Games.* Minneapolis, Burgess Publishing Company, 1964.

Van Camp, S.: *How free is free play?* The Journal of the National Association for the Education of Young Children, April 1972.

Wallis, E., and Logan, G.: *Exercises for Children.* Englewood Cliffs, New Jersey, Prentice-Hall, Inc., 1966.

CHAPTER TWENTY-SEVEN

INTRAMURAL AND AFTER-SCHOOL ACTIVITIES

Under the auspices of the public schools and community agencies, youth sport programs including baseball, football, soccer, and swimming have grown to such an extent that they are changing the course of childhood.

Magill et al.: *Children in Sport.* 1978, p. 1.

CLASS COMPETITION AND TOURNAMENTS

Competitive class tournaments are suggested for grades, squads, teams, and individuals. Basically, competition for children is good if conducted under the proper conditions of good leadership and if too much stress is not placed upon winning. Children like to compete, to match and test their skill with others. However, games and athletic activities best suited for their own age groups must be selected for competitive purposes. Types of competition possible are (1) single elimination tournaments, (2) winner-loser tournaments, (3) ladder tournaments, and (4) round robin tournaments.

Single Elimination Tournaments

If the original number of contestants is a perfect power of two, no modification of this diagram is necessary. When the number of contestants is not a perfect power of two, byes are added until this is reached. The number of byes should equal the difference between the number of competitors and the next higher power of two. When fifteen are entered there will be one bye (16 − 15 = 1) and so forth.

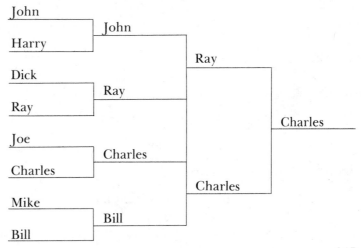

The number of byes should be divided so that one half of them appear at the top of the drawing and the remaining half at the bottom.

Winner-loser Tournament

The principle for adding byes in this type of tournament is the same as in the elimination tournament. Winners move out to the right of the chart; losers move out to the left in the second round, and winners continue to move out to the left or right in all continuing rounds.

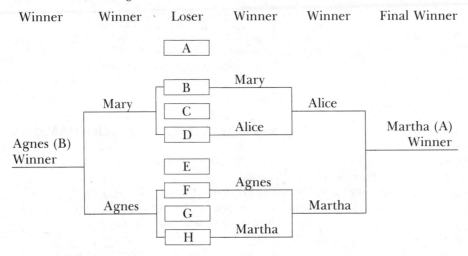

Ladder Tournament

Individuals or teams are arranged in ladder formation. Any player may challenge another player directly above. If the challenger is successful in defeating the opponent, his name takes the place of the defeated team, and vice versa. The final winner remains in the first position at the completion of the tournament.

| Team 1 |
| Team 2 |
| Team 3 |
| Team 4 |
| Team 5 |
| Team 6 |
| etc. |

Round Robin Tournaments

In this type of competition the revolving column is the simplest for pairing opponents. Numbers are given to teams or individuals. A bye is used in the place of teams or individuals if there is an uneven number of competitors. Pairing of competitors is done by placing them in two columns. Once teams or individuals are given a number and once the numbers appear on the tournament chart, that order must be maintained. Competitors are arranged in the following manner:

1	Jack	bye	Ray
2	Agnes	7	Peggy
3	Martha	8	Bill
4	Alice	9	Catherine
5	Harry	10	Greg
6	Charles	11	Betty

Players are moved either clockwise or counterclockwise to meet their opponents. If there is a bye it remains stationary, each number jumping over it to the next place:

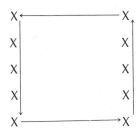

One fewer round is played than the number of teams or individuals entered. The pairings and series for a round robin tournament for eight teams are given below:

First Round	Second Round	Third Round
1 ———— 8	1 ———— 7	1 ———— 6
2 ———— 7	8 ———— 6	7 ———— 5
3 ———— 6	2 ———— 5	8 ———— 4
4 ———— 5	3 ———— 4	2 ———— 3

Fourth Round	Fifth Round	Sixth Round	Seventh Round
1 ———— 5	1 ———— 4	1 ———— 3	1 ———— 2
6 ———— 4	5 ———— 3	4 ———— 2	3 ———— 8
7 ———— 3	6 ———— 2	5 ———— 8	4 ———— 7
8 ———— 2	7 ———— 8	6 ———— 7	5 ———— 6

The pairings will be different in each round. The team winning the most games is declared the winner. The above procedure may be followed for any number of teams if a bye is used for an uneven number. When all players have played each other in each round, the tournament is completed.

TYPES OF COMPETITION SUITABLE FOR CHILDREN

Suggested games and sports for tournament competition for young children include

Athletic games (kick ball, balloon volleyball, and other simple lead-up game activities).

Hopscotch
Jump rope
Kicking soccer balls for distance
Kite making and flying
Marbles
Relays of all kinds
Running races
Stunts and self-testing activities (individual)
Target throws

Suggested competitive activities for upper elementary-grade children include

Team Games

TOUCH FOOTBALL

1. Modified touch football games
2. Football keep-away
3. Centering relays
4. Passing relays
5. Pass or punt back game
6. Place kick, punt, or pass for accuracy or distance

SOCCER

1. Six-a-side, soccer, speedball, or speed-away
2. Circle or line soccer
3. Soccer goal kick
4. Passing and dribbling relays
5. Goal kicking for accuracy

VOLLEYBALL

1. Modified volleyball
2. Ball keep-up
3. Newcomb
4. Serving, passing, or volleyball for accuracy

SOFTBALL

1. Throws for accuracy and distance
2. Timed base running
3. Lead-up games (Beat the Ball, Throw It and Run, and so forth)
4. Modified softball

BASKETBALL

1. Basket shooting contests
2. Dribbling, passing for accuracy and speed
3. Lead-up games (Twenty One, Drop In, Drop Out, and so forth)
4. Sideline basketball
5. Six- or nine-court basketball

OTHER TEAM GAMES

1. Circle team dodgeball
2. Modified floor hockey
3. Modified lacrosse

FIGURE 27-1. In some parts of the country, lacrosse is becoming a popular intramural sport. (Courtesy of Snitz Manufacturing Company, East Troy, Wisconsin.)

Individual Games

SWIMMING

1. Speed and distance team and individual contests using a variety of strokes
2. Swimming for form

TRACK AND FIELD

1. 20–40–60 yard dashes
2. 220–440 yard distance events
3. Hurdles
4. High jumps
5. Running and standing long jumps
6. Light shot put
7. Standing hop-step-jump
8. Throws for distances using balls of various weight and size
9. Shuttle relays

OTHER GAME ACTIVITIES

1. Deck, table, and paddle tennis
2. Badminton
3. Tennis
4. Shuffleboard
5. Horseshoes
6. Rope jumping
7. Yo-yo tops
8. Hula hoop contests
9. Quoits
10. Lawn and alley bowling
11. Handball
12. Archery
13. Roller and ice skating
14. Marbles

ORGANIZATION OF PROGRAMS

Ideally an intramural director should be in overall charge of the program, assisted by the individual leader and student leaders from each competing unit. The last are best peer-elected rather than teacher-selected, and they should assist as team captains, equipment helpers, officials, scorers, timers, record keepers, and news reporters. An intramural council made up of the director and student leaders, which would provide opportunities for student leadership development and act as an overall governing body, is suggested.

The program should be for *all* children, including the handicapped and those of various skill abilities; grouping may be by classroom, grades, age, sex, skills, height and weight, or interest. All school and community facilities should be used for the program.

FIGURE 27–2. Public demonstrations will help gain parental support for your program. (Courtesy of Raven Industries, Inc.)

FIGURE 27–2. *Continued*

Activities can be scheduled before and after school, during extended lunch periods, as a scheduled part of the school day, on Saturdays and holidays, and during school vacations.

Written policies should be drawn up regarding awards, transportation, finances and budget, records, eligibility and parental approval, medical care, safety and first aid, and accident liability insurance. The program should be evaluated frequently to determine its effectiveness in relation to the stated aims, goals, and objectives. No program can be measured realistically by the number of participants it has, for it is the increased growth of each child who takes part in it that matters most.

CLASSIFICATION OF PLAYERS

Intramural activities are those physical activities conducted between groups of students within one school. A successful program depends upon equality among competing teams or individuals. It is advisable to classify students according to a plan that includes the factors of age, height, weight, and sex. For safety reasons, boys and girls should be separated for some competitive sports after ten years of age, for boys at this age tend to surpass girls in strength, flexibility, endurance, and speed. However, because of social values inherent in team play, opportunities should be provided for boys and girls to be members of the same team as many times as possible during each semester. Increasingly classes are now coeducational in physical education.

Children of primary-grade age should be classified in different groups according to their capacity to enter into different levels of graded activities. Physical examinations and skill tests are the best way to determine this capacity.

Individual players may be classified for all competitive events according to age, height, or weight or a combination of these factors.

The teacher, aided by squad leaders, might well select team members, who in turn will elect their captains. This provides for a more reliable equalization of team skill, for children tend to choose their best friends rather than skillful players. Often the class ugly duckling or least skilled child either is left out or is usually the last one chosen. Children, like adults, want to be first; it is ego-damaging to be last always.

Another suggested way for selecting teams is for the group to select the needed number of captains. These chosen leaders stand facing the class, who will count off according to the number of captains. As each one calls out his number, he goes and stands behind the captain having the corresponding number. This method is often superior to having circled groups number off in teams, for some pupils will be wise enough to count ahead and change places with one or two others in order to be on the desired team. Another method is selecting captains by pupil vote, having each player draw a number out of a hat and stand behind the numbered captain drawn.

If the major emphasis is placed upon fun rather than winning, the children will gradually select the method that to them seems fairest for classifying and forming teams. They should be encouraged to experiment with as many methods as possible. We often learn what we want by finding out from experience what we do not want. Experience is not only the best teacher; it can also be an ideal way for learning how to make good judgments.

CLUB ORGANIZATION

Pupils may be organized into clubs for competitive purposes. Class, grade, and homeroom teams are suggested. Group or physical education class groups may compete with members from other classes in after-school play. Interested groups may be organized into teams or as individual players to compete against one another.

FIGURE 27–3. Education for positive use of leisure time is a *must* for all children in our society, for they and all other Americans must learn how to use their ever-increasing free time wisely. Youth must learn how to create their own fun without being passively entertained or constantly supervised by adults. (Courtesy of Youth Services Section, Los Angeles City Schools.)

FIGURE 27–4.   Co-educational activities are highly recommended for intramural fun. (Courtesy of Snitz Manufacturing Company, East Troy, Wisconsin.)

Whatever subdivision or organizational play is followed, the teacher should stress 100 per cent group participation and work toward that end.

An after-school leaders' club might well be developed. Members may be either teacher-selected or pupil-elected. These pupils can be trained to organize competitive groups, assist in officiating, scoring, and record-keeping, and plan and evaluate the complete program for a season, term, or year. The club might also be responsible for issuing, caring for, and checking in equipment. Bulletin board publicity, loud speaker announcements, and newspaper reports offer splendid means for integrating the total program with English as well as other subjects.

Clubs are rapidly growing in popularity throughout our nation's schools. The mood of the times is toward noncompetitive club activities that tax one's mental and physical abilities. Outdoor activities involving cycling, canoeing, rock climbing, and cave exploration are especially popular.

THE SEASONAL PROGRAM

The total after-school program should be organized around seasonal sports and games. Kite-flying contests and marble, jack, or jump-rope tournaments are best in the spring. Lead-up games to football are best in the fall season, whereas basketball-type games are ideal for the winter.

The following seasonal program might serve as a guide to which the leader could make additions:

Fall Season

Line soccer	Pin soccer
Shuttle-pass soccer relay	Relays
Simplified soccer	

Winter Season

Dodgeball	Keep away
Basketball shuttle relay	Captain ball
Newcomb	Relays

Spring Season

Base kickball	Jump rope
Kickball	Kite flying
Jacks	Relays
Hopscotch	Camping-skill contests
Track and field events	Skateboard contests

A seasonal program provides a logical progression from lesson to lesson and season to season. Simple games that use the basic skills of running, throwing, catching, jumping, hopping, creeping, and hanging should be stressed through grade 3. More advanced games into which these fundamental movements are integrated as sport skills should be stressed beginning at the fourth grade levels.

SPECIAL EVENTS

Play Days

Play days or community get-together days are excellent ways to get parents to come see what their children have learned. The primary purpose of the play day is to provide mass participation in all the games, stunts, rhythmic activities, hunting games, campcraft skills, and individual events. Every student should take an active part, not just the best students from each school or class.

Play days may be organized for all the children (1) within one school, (2) in two or three neighboring schools combined, (3) from all schools in the district, or (4) for the whole county. Small play days organized at the close of the fall, winter, and spring programs offer incentive for teachers and children to plan and carry out a systematized progressive program.

Suggestions for conducting a successful play day include the following:

1. Have a definite theme such as a rodeo day, a national airplane, car or horse race, the Olympic Games, or a popular holiday.
2. Separate pupils from each school or class so that each team will be made up of members from different schools or classes.
3. Divide the players into teams built upon the chosen theme:
   a. Rodeo—bronchos, mustangs, cowboys, and so forth.
   b. Airplane race—TWA, Braniff, American, United, and so forth.
   c. Olympic Games—U.S., Germany, England, Italy, and so forth.
   d. Popular holiday (for example, Christmas—trees, toys, reindeer, and so forth).
4. Have each team wear a favor or symbol representative of the theme.
5. Play games known to all, but change their names to fit the theme.
   a. Rodeo—For example, a running race becomes a wild horse race across the plains.
   b. Airplane—A running race becomes a nonstop flight from Los Angeles to New York or another destination.
   c. Olympic Games—A running race becomes a foot race of contestants bringing a lighted torch from Mt. Olympus to the site of the Olympic Games.
   d. Popular holiday—For example, a running race becomes a race for reindeers for an honored place on Santa's Christmas team.
6. Have each group make up a team yell, motto, or song.
7. Have each group compete in other areas, too, such as singing, charades, dancing, and guessing games.
8. If refreshments are served, change the name of the food to fit the theme.
9. Award single prizes to winning team members, such as magazine pictures, ribbons, or tin cups.
10. Have a definite beginning and ending to the entire program and to each event.

Demonstrations

An annual public demonstration should be the outgrowth of the regular physical education program.[1] It should be the best of the year's program but never its goal. All

---

[1] See the helpful article "Demonstrations Show Parents About Physical Education." *Crofts Physical Education Newsletter,* Columbus, Ohio, May 1972.

FIGURE 27–5.   Hoops provide a colorful routine for public demonstration. (Courtesy of Central College, Pella, Iowa.)

children should participate rather than the few selected best. Demonstrations may show (1) a typical class period, (2) a survey of all activities covered during the year, (3) pupil-parent activities in which the pupil demonstrates first, then the parent, or (4) a program centered on a general theme.

Rehearsals of the demonstration should be held largely during class period and little after-school time should be taken up with practice. Mass rehearsals held one or two days before the performance aid in smoothing out rough spots. These practices should include the procession and recession order, the finale and large numbers, each

Rhythms, 5th Grade

FIGURE 27–6.   Children should be provided with opportunities to demonstrate to adults the many skills they have learned in their physical education classes. (Hastings Public School, Hastings, Nebraska.)

separate number on the program taken up in order, and a check of the general effect of costumes and music.

Scenery and costumes should be of secondary importance but should be made, to the extent possible, by the pupils. A scarf tied around the regulation uniform can do much to change its appearance.

The sample program that follows may serve as a suggested guide for a demonstration program showing the work done in six elementary classes.

1. Entrance March   all pupils

2. Singing Games   grades K, 1

   Hickory, Dickory, Dock
   Little Jack Horner
   The Muffin Man
   Did You Ever See A Lassie?

3. Stunts and Tumbling   grades 2, 3

   Inchworm Walk
   Elephant Walk
   Forward and Backward Somersaults
   The Merry-Go-Round
   Pyramids

4. Relays   grade 4

   Wheelbarrow Relay
   Ropejump Relay
   Tenpin Relay
   Forty Ways to Get There Relay

5. Lead-up Games   grade 5

   Line Dodgeball
   Line Soccer
   Hit Pin Baseball
   Newcomb
   Shuffleboard
   Kickball

6. Square Dancing   grades 5, 6

   Old Dan Tucker
   Virginia Reel
   Starlight Schottische
   Butterfly Polka

7. Gymnastic Drills   grades 1–6

   Five minutes of exercises done to command

8. Departure March   all pupils

School Assembly Programs

Special programs given in assembly can be rich educational experiences. They can be excellent means of educating the principal and other teachers and can lead to better understanding and appreciation on the part of the pupils.

The presentation may be (1) a general orientation, (2) a recognition assembly, or (3) a special subject assembly.

The general orientation assembly is best held at the beginning of the new year. It is a grand means of acquainting newcomers with the objectives and activities included in the physical education program. Pupils can demonstrate games, dances, and other activities. Films can be shown that stress good sportsmanship or playground safety. The program can also be used to stimulate interest in coming events. Outside speakers can give illustrated talks or demonstrations.

The recognition assembly is the time leaders are given public acclaim for skill, leadership ability, or some contribution made to the school. Pupils can give short speeches stressing values of good health, fair play, and team loyalty. Songs or short poems may be interspersed with the talks. Awards given to outstanding pupils may be in the form of verbal recognition or actual presentation of an inexpensive object.

The special subject assembly is often used to introduce new activities to the pupils or reacquaint them with familiar ones. Posture, safety, Indian dancing, and games from other lands might be used.

Exhibits

Although exhibits are often associated with a large occasion, such as National Education Week or National Safety Week, the school exhibit can be a separate type of demonstration. A corridor, bulletin board, or room may be used for the display. Pupils should make, gather, and assemble all materials to be shown, working under the guidance of the teacher. Emphasis may be placed on such themes as the total physical

FIGURE 27–7. The martial arts are gaining in popularity all across the country. (Courtesy of Camp Yonahlossee, Blowing Rock, North Carolina.)

education program, safety, good heath habits, leisure time, play, posture, or the work done in the department or class. Snapshots taken of pupils on the playground might be arranged attractively on a bulletin board. Mimeographed material may also be laid out for free distribution. Samples of toothpaste, cereal, soap, and so forth may be obtained from companies interested primarily in using this type of advertising. Hobby samples often make an interesting exhibit and sometimes start new enthusiasts on a pleasurable pursuit of developing a new skill or interest.

Programs for Community Groups

The physical education department or classroom teacher is frequently asked to prepare programs for civic groups. As much as possible, these programs should be drawn from the actual program in the school and be a fair representation of it. Spectacular performances given by a few should be kept at a minimum. Preferably, as many pupils as possible should take part. Such programs often make a valuable contribution toward developing better understanding and appreciation between the school and community, the teacher and parent.

In conducting all special events, the teacher should assume the responsibility for organizing, conducting, and evaluating them. Student chairmen and their various committees should assist with all aspects of the event. Questions to be answered honestly by both the teacher and pupils when evaluating the outcome of each program are

FIGURE 27–8.   Many schools have formed hiking and backpacking clubs. (Courtesy of Camp Yonahlossee, Blowing Rock, North Carolina.)

1. What changes were made in the pupils' development of desirable attitudes, new skills, and new knowledge?
2. To what degree did the program acquaint others with the real purpose and content of our physical education classwork and program?
3. What increased opportunities should be given to students next time in planning, conducting, and evaluating the program?
4. How many school people commented favorably on it? How many parents? What did other pupils say about it?

HIGH-LEVEL COMPETITION

One major problem facing the elementary teacher is when to allow boys and girls to compete on a school-sponsored team against other schools. When the question is raised concerning whether elementary school children should compete against others, teachers take sides on this issue, all almost immediately thinking of competition in basketball and football. Increasingly, competition in these two sports and its place in American schools is being questioned on all levels, but especially in high schools and colleges. Some believe too much emphasis is placed on these major sports and on few players instead of on the majority of students. Actually, competition in itself is not undesirable; it is only what one does when competing that may be negative, or how one feels when winning or losing. In reality, children compete for family status the day they are born. A group of boys playing marbles is competing against one another, as is a group of girls playing jacks for fun. Certainly we, as educated adults, must avoid stereotype thinking, realizing that we all must guard against thinking all policemen are dumb, all detectives smart, all teachers "old maids," all professors absent-

FIGURE 27–9.   Competition for children is good if conducted under good leadership and if too much stress is not placed upon winning. (Courtesy of AAHPER, Washington, D.C.)

minded, or all competition bad. But at the same time, as educated adults, we must be cognizant that outside groups are putting increasingly greater pressure on teachers and parents to allow sixth, fifth, fourth, and in some schools, even second and third grade children to play competitive athletic sports. There are many pro and con arguments to this question.

Arguments For

Some sporting-goods salesmen, sports writers, parents, physical educators, coaches, and teachers present the following arguments in favor of competitive sports:

1. Because children will play these games anyway in sandlots and streets, why not teach them how to play, so fewer will get hurt?
2. Because these are our national games, children should learn how to play them well early in life.
3. We will develop better high school and college players if we can teach players earlier in life, and thus, the game will be more thrilling to play and to watch.
4. The individual player who is beyond his age in growth and skill should not be held back by being forced to play baby or sissy games.
5. It is better to be skilled in one or two sports than just an average player in several.
6. We live in a highly competitive society and the sooner a child learns how to compete, the more successful he is apt to be as an adult.
7. The program gives children a chance to represent their school and to develop school spirit, as well as good sportsmanship.
8. Such a program will help eradicate juvenile delinquency.
9. Our children are maturing earlier, are taller and heavier than their predecessors, and thus need more challenging activities.
10. Competition is good at any grade level, and highly organized athletic contests can stimulate some children, as an advanced academic class challenges the mentally superior child.

Arguments Against

On the other hand, some physicians, leading physical educators, coaches, teachers, and parents argue that

1. Children may receive permanent bone and ligament deformities from playing these adult games while they are in a period of rapid growth and body change.
2. There is little carry-over value in these games, for the modern world offers little opportunity to play these games throughout life. Few will play them when they are 28, 48, 68, or 88.
3. The games are superimposed upon children by adults, often for their own selfish gains.
4. The games tend to "star" some children too early (the softball pitcher, the football quarterback, etc.).
5. Children should learn to do things set aside for children, and have competitive major sports to look forward to when they become adults.
6. Such a program for a few already "good" players diverts attention from all children, thus causing the "poor" to become poorer.
7. Children should be exposed to many generalized activities, whereas specialized activities should be reserved for older children who are more emotionally mature.
8. Although children naturally protect themselves from fatigue or stress, in such sports they are too often pressured by their coach, team, or others to push themselves beyond their physical limits.
9. Too often emphasis is placed upon winning, advertising, gate receipts, and concessions rather than upon children.
10. Experts claim juvenile delinquency is caused by at least five major factors of which not having opportunities to compete successfully is not one.
11. We should devote our energies to broadening and strengthening all existing programs rather than entering into such controversial ones.

A Point of View

Because a challenging, varied program encompassing a wide range of physical activities should be provided for every child of grade-school age, the above pro and con arguments should be viewed in this light. The American Alliance for Health, Physical Education, and Recreation; the American Medical Association; and the American Society for State Directors of Health, Physical Education, and Recreation have all taken definite stands *against* regularly scheduled interscholastic competition below the senior high school level.[2] Any school, therefore, and any grade or junior high school teacher who bases physical education on after-school programs in football, basketball, or any other competitive athletics limits participation to those of certain physical size, strength, or ability, or all three, and does so without the approval of experts in the physical education profession and in medicine.

These leading experts endorse the following recommendations, drawn up at the National Conference on Program Planning in Games and Sports, for desirable athletic competitions for children of elementary-school age:

1. Programs of games and sports should be based on the developmental level of children. Boxing, tackle football, ice hockey, and other body contact sports should not be included in any competitive program for children 12 and under.
2. These programs should provide a variety of activities for all children throughout the year.
3. Competition is inherent in the growth and development of the child and, depending upon a variety of factors, will be harmful or beneficial to the individual.
4. Adequate competitive programs organized on neighborhood and community levels will meet the needs of these children. State, regional, and national tournaments; bowling; and charity and exhibition games are not recommended for these age groups.
5. Education and recreation authorities and other community youth-serving agencies have a definite responsibility to develop adequate neighborhood and community programs of games and sports and to provide competent leadership for them.
6. The competent, professionally prepared physical educators and recreation leaders are the people to whom communities should look for basic leadership.

Although today's children will enter tomorrow our highly complex adult society, their elementary-school teachers are morally and professionally obligated to reserve, as well as provide, for them those simple, unspoiled, carefree and abundant joys of childhood for which they are physically, mentally, and emotionally best suited.

Despite the fact that leading educators and medical authorities have taken a firm stand against interscholastic competition during the elementary years, programs continue to flourish and to grow in all areas of the country. High levels of competition are found in Little League Baseball, Biddy Basketball, Pee Wee Football, and Ice Hockey and are available to elementary-school children in nearly every sport engaged in the United States. National tournaments exist for children under eight years old and even six and seven year olds are involved in local and area tournaments. Educators and medical authorities do not make the decision concerning the availability of competitive athletes in our society—the public does. It is time to recognize this fact and to stop hiding our heads in the sand or blindly taking sides for or against athletic competition for youngsters. Competitive athletics for elementary school–age youth is here to stay, and as educators, we must see to it that parents and coaches are educated in its positive potential values and many detrimental pitfalls and that each child taking part in the program receives proper guidance and supervision.

We must not lose sight of the fact that competitive athletic programs are supposed to be designed for children as *one* of many possible avenues for providing them an

---

[2]AAHPER: *Desirable Athletic Competition for Children of Elementary School Age.* Washington, 1968.

opportunity to develop into more complete individuals. Not all children want or need to be involved in competitive athletics, and they should not be led in this direction unless a sincere desire is indicated. Athletic programs should never be established for the entertainment or glorification of parents and coaches. The abusive and disruptive behavior too often demonstrated by these individuals has been a major stumbling block in establishing good programs of competition. Such behavior as pushing and threatening by referees, tongue lashing of an eight year old for a poor play, and disregarding of general rules of good conduct or the well-being of the child cannot be condoned. If competition is to be a worthwhile experience for children, parents and coaches must be educated in their developmental needs, interests, and capabilities (mental and emotional, as well as physical). They must be made to view competition through the "eyes" of the child in order to provide a developmentally sound program and one that is a genuine credit to the spirit of competitive athletics. *Qualified leadership is a must,* for coaches who intelligently look out for the best interests of their players are of paramount importance. The "win at all costs" attitude or the "winning isn't everything—it's the only thing" philosophy of the late Vince Lombardi must not be a part of competition in schools *at any level,* and most especially not for children, who are too often "used" by adults seeking status or those who are bored and looking for a new entertainment outlet. Providing youths with the opportunity to compete under the best kinds of circumstances is the lifeblood of sport. Winning is important; it definitely beats coming in second, but it must not be regarded as the "only thing." If it is, the entire point of competition is lost and so are all its meaning, purpose, and potential for helping youths develop above-average physical skills and become contributing group members and worthy citizens.

SUGGESTED READINGS

AAHPER: *Desirable Athletic Competition for Children of Elementary School Age.* Washington, D.C., 1968; and *People Makes Ideas Happen,* 1971.

Athletic Institute: *Intramurals for Elementary School Children.* Chicago, Illinois, 1964; and *Desirable Athletic Competition for Children,* 1967.

Bula, M.: *Competition for children: the real issue.* Journal of Health, Physical Education and Recreation, September 1971.

Corbin, C. B.: *The Athletic Snowball.* Champaign, Illinois, Human Kinetics Publishers, 1978.

Daughtrey, G., and Woods, J. B.: *Physical Education Programs: Organization and Administration.* Philadelphia, W. B. Saunders Company, 1971.

Forsythe, C.: *Administration of High School Athletics,* 5th ed. Englewood Cliffs, New Jersey, Prentice-Hall, Inc., 1972.

Freeman, W.: *Physical Education in a Changing Society.* Boston, Houghton Mifflin Company, 1977.

Magill, R. A., Ash, M. J., and Smoll, F. L. (eds.): *Children in Sport: A Contemporary Anthology.* Champaign, Illinois, Human Kinetics Publishers, 1978.

Martens, R.: *Joy and Sadness in Childrens Sports.* Champaign, Illinois, Human Kinetics Publishers, 1978.

Means, L.: *Intramurals: Their Organization and Administration.* Englewood Cliffs, New Jersey, Prentice-Hall, Inc., 1963.

Neilson, N. P., Van Hagen, W., and Comer, J.: *Physical Education for Elementary School.* 3rd ed. Englewood Cliffs, New Jersey, Prentice-Hall, Inc., 1966.

Ogilvie, B. C., and Tutko, T. A.: *Sport: if you want to build character try something else.* Psychology Today, October 1971.

APPENDICES

APPARATUS AND EQUIPMENT

OUTDOOR APPARATUS*

This outdoor apparatus complex, which is similar to that in general use, was designed and installed on each elementary school campus of the Hurst-Euless-Bedford Independent School District, Hurst, Texas. The instructional program for the apparatus is located in the gymnastics section of the guide.

Students travel through the course in a zigzag fashion while using it as either an Obstacle Training Course or a Station Training Course, as follows:

As an Obstacle Training Course: Divide the class into nine equal groups, assign each group to a beginning station, and begin exercises by signal. The children will then travel automatically through all stations by walking down the balance beam; hand-and-leg crawling across the parallel bars; crawling through the rectangle bars and over the vault bar; climbing up to the overhead ladder; swinging by their hands across it, then sliding down the fireman ladder; chinning on the chin bars; climbing to the top of the stall bars; traveling by hands across the overhead travel bar and sliding fireman-style down its anchor pipe; and climbing and descending one vertical climb bar.

As a Station Training Course: Divide the class into nine equal groups, assign each group to a station, and begin exercises by signal. At the next signal all groups advance to the next station. Repeat until all groups have progressed through all stations. Simple exercises selected from the suggested list in the gymnastic section of the guide can be assigned for beginners, while more difficult exercises can be assigned for advanced students.

APPARATUS STATIONS

1. Balance Beams
   The balance beam station consists of six horizontal wooden beams 4 inches × 4 inches × 12 feet long. Each is mounted 6 inches above ground on four flanged 2-inch pipes ground anchored 2 feet deep in concrete.

2. Parallel Bars
   The parallel bars station consists of two horizontal 1¼-inch pipes. They are 16 feet long, 16 inches apart, and anchored 3 feet above the ground. This station is mounted on 2-inch pipe ground anchored 2 feet deep in concrete.

---

*Reproduced by permission of Texas Education Agency: Physical Education in the Elementary Schools Curriculum Guide. Austin, pp. 6–10.

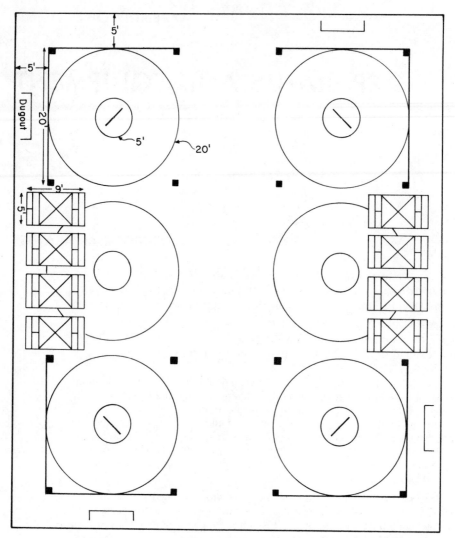

Scale 1"–10'

Suggested Playground Markings for an Asphalt Area, Kindergarten–Primary Grades.

(Reproduced by permission of Athletic Institute: College and University Facilities Guide. Chicago, 1970, p. 81.)

3. Rectangle and Vaulting Bars

The rectangle bars part of station 3 consists of two horizontal 1-inch pipes placed vertical to each other and divided in half by a 12-inch length of 1-inch pipe. They are 4 feet long, 12 inches apart, and anchored 30 inches and 18 inches above the ground. This part of station 3 is at the beginning and anchored to station 2 on one side and station 4 on the other side.

The vault bar station consists of a horizontal 1-inch pipe. It is 4 feet long and anchored 30 inches above the ground. This part of station 3 is at the end and anchored like the rectangle bars.

4. Overhead Ladder and Fireman Pole

The overhead ladder consists of 17 horizontal 1-inch pipes 4 feet long that are

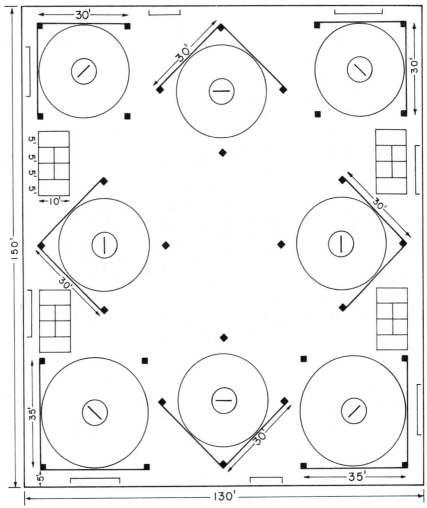

Scale ½"–10'

Suggested Playground Markings for an Asphalt Area, Lower and Upper Intermediate Grades.

(Reproduced by permission of Athletic Institute: College and University Facilities Guide. Chicago, 1970, p. 82.)

anchored at equal intervals along the 16-foot path of travel. This station is mounted on 2-inch pipe ground anchored 2 feet deep in concrete. The height of the ladder should be 7 feet 6 inches for intermediates and 6 feet 6 inches for primary students.

5. Chinning and Stall Bars

The chinning bar part of station 5 consists of a horizontal 1-inch bar. It is 4 feet long and anchored 6 feet 6 inches above the ground for intermediates. This part of station 5 is at the beginning and anchored to station 4 on one side and station 6 on the other side. There are two primary chinning bars, which are anchored at 4 feet and 5 feet above the ground.

The stall bars part of station 5 consists of 11 horizontal 1-inch pipes placed vertical to each other. They are 4 feet long and spaced as follows: 12 inches from the ground to the first bar and 12 inches between the top two bars. This part of station 5 is at the end and anchored like the chin bar.

6. Overhead Travel Bar

   The overhead travel bar station consists of a horizontal 2-inch pipe 16 feet long. It is anchored 7 feet 6 inches above the ground for intermediates and 6 feet 6 inches above the ground for primary students. This station is mounted on 2-inch pipe and ground anchored 2 feet deep in concrete.

7. Vertical Climb Poles

   The vertical climb bars station consists of three vertical 1-inch climbing pipes. They are 16 feet high, 3 feet apart, and attached at the top to a horizontal 2-inch pipe. This station is further supported by two vertical 2-inch pipes attached to the horizontal support and ground anchored 3 feet deep in concrete.

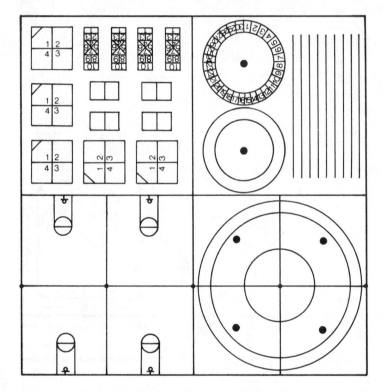

Small circles and a large circle for all types of circle games and activities.

Lines and lanes for locomotor activities such as relays, walking and skipping on a balance-beam line, and so forth.

An activity area of 100 × 100 feet with a variety of markings that include the following:

- One large circle is approximately 48 feet in diameter, and the inner circle is 45 feet in diameter.

- Two small circles are approximately 23 feet in diameter, and inner circles are 20 feet in diameter.

- ●—Locations for tetherball installations (removable poles).

- ●—Locations for volleyball installations (removable poles).

- Lines are 30 inches apart and 40 feet in length for the eight lanes (these lines can also be used for beginning balance-beam work).

- Two basketball goals should be 8 feet in height for third and fourth grade students, and two regulation goals should be used for fifth and sixth grade students.

- Hopscotch areas are 4 × 12 feet.

- Four-square areas are 12 × 12 feet.

- Hand tennis areas are 5 × 10 feet.

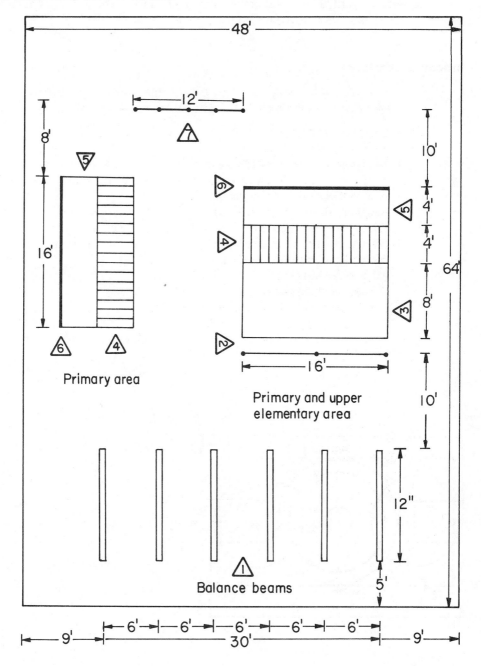

ELEMENTARY PHYSICAL EDUCATION INSTRUCTIONAL LABORATORIES*

In the professional preparation of physical education teachers and elementary school teachers and administrators, increased emphasis is being placed on the program of physical education at the elementary level.

Not only should physical educators know and understand the facilities needed for elementary programs, but classroom teachers and elementary school principals should have an opportunity to study elementary physical education in its proper environment. This environment includes indoor and outdoor instructional laboratories designed and equipped for children.

Indoor Laboratory

A gymnasium designed to house the elementary physical education professional preparation program is desirable. The following guidelines are recommended:

- Dimensions of 54 × 76 feet.
- Minimum ceiling height of 18 feet.
- Maximum ceiling height of 24 feet.
- Tongue-and-groove select maple flooring. (Consideration should be given to the new resilient synthetic materials.)
- Markings should be painted on the floor before completing the final finish coat. (This procedure preserves floor markings for many years.)
- Steel girder beams extending widthwise in this facility should permit installation of overhead apparatus such as
    Four climbing ropes
    Four climbing poles
    Four pairs of wall adjustable flying rings

---

*Reproduced by permission of Athletic Institute: College and University Facilities Guide. Chicago, 1970, p. 80.

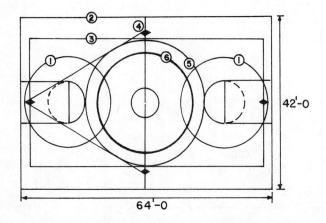

- Wall construction should allow installation of the following:
    One adjustable horizontal ladder
    Stall bars
    Eye hooks for net mountings
    Basketball goals
    A wall-mounted chalkboard, tackboards, and hook strips
- Walls should be painted a light, aesthetically-pleasing color.
- Lighting units should be protected by guards or transparent, nonbreakable plastic coverings.
- Duplex electrical outlets should be located approximately 12 inches from the floor on at least one side wall and one end wall.
- There should be an even distribution of light throughout the room.

Outdoor Laboratory

The following recommendations should be helpful in planning the instructional laboratory for elementary school physical education course work for elementary physical educators, classroom teachers, and elementary-school principals:

- Minimum dimensions of 130 × 180 feet of asphalt or resilient synthetic material.
- Minimum dimensions of 150 × 200 feet of turf.
- Asphalt or new synthetic area should have a smooth surface with line markings, including circles, diamonds, running lines, 4-square, and hopscotch.
- Turf area should have close-cut grass.
- If located next to the school, asphalt areas should be distributed around the building according to locations of the kindergarten, primary, and intermediate levels. (Strategic placing of the asphalt areas reduces traffic through the building and through other group areas.)
- Class organization and care of the area may be more logically planned if the turf area is in one location.
- A chain-link galvanized fence should separate all playground areas from street and sidewalk traffic.
- Openings to the outside area from the playground should be of the baffled type, constructed of chain-link fences.
- Permanent apparatus should be strategically placed on the hard-surface areas according to the kindergarten, primary, and intermediate levels.
- Permanent installations of apparatus should include
    Climbing tower 6 feet long × 6 feet wide × 7½ feet high
    Junior horizontal ladder, crossbars 3½, 4½, and 5½ feet above ground
    Junior horizontal ladder 12 feet long, with gradual slope from 6 to 5 feet
    Senior horizontal bars 16 feet long, with gradual slope from 7½ to 6½ feet
    Apparatus obstacle course
    Sculptured play apparatus
- Placing a resilient synthetic surfacing material under all apparatus has merit.
- Both asphalt and turf areas should allow space for children to play creatively with boxes, benches, balance beams, and cylindrical equipment for climbing over, through, and under.

FIELD AND COURT CHART

Badminton

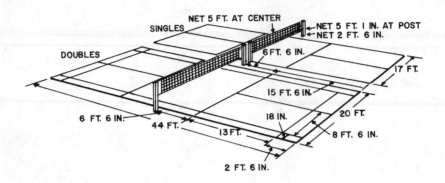

Biddy Basketball

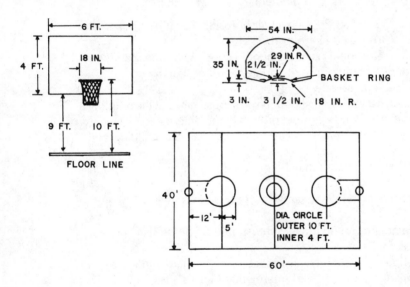

Horseshoes

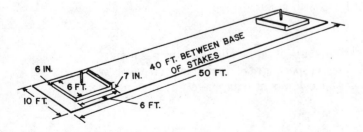

Indoor Ball

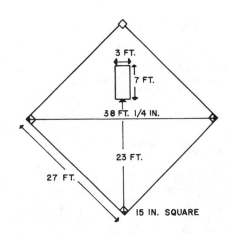

Paddle Tennis

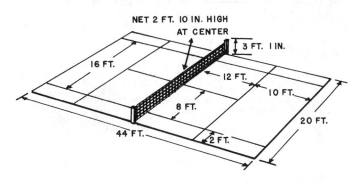

Quarter Mile Track with 220-Yard Straightaway

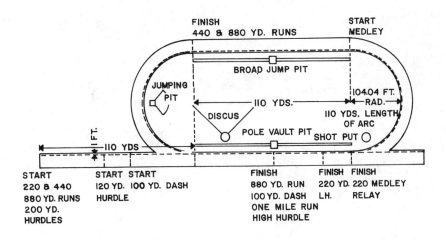

Shuffleboard

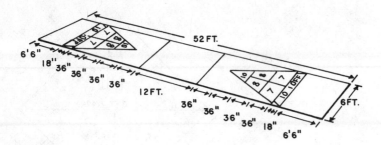

Six Man Football

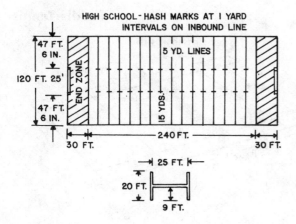

Soccer

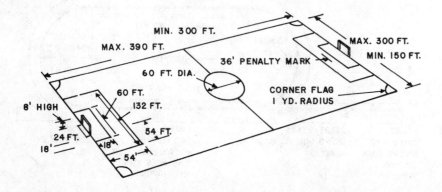

Softball

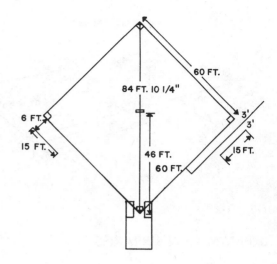

Table Tennis

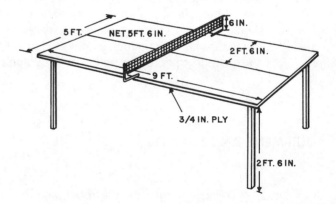

Tennis

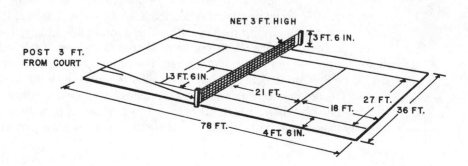

Volleyball

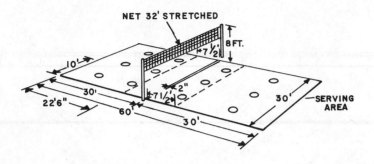

DEPARTMENTAL LIBRARIES

Basic philosophy concerning departmental or central branch libraries must be established before extensive planning can be done. Departmental or branch libraries should provide for adequate shelf space. Reading rooms, carrels, and functional zones should be carefully planned. Librarians who know and understand the problems should assist in checking plans for space requirements, traffic flow, control, and storage space. The common guides used to indicate space requirements specify 30 to 35 square feet per reader station and 8 volumes to 1 linear foot of stack area.

EQUIPMENT AND SUPPLIES

The gymnasium, the playroom, and the outdoor area are the teaching stations used to administer the program. In some situations it may be necessary to augment these facilities by using the classroom. No matter what teaching station is used, the importance of equipment and supplies to physical education should be recognized.

Selection of these tools of learning should be based on the physical education curriculum and provide the children with opportunities to learn many different skills.

Expendable equipment such as beanbags, balls, and ropes should be provided in quantities that will give each child full participation in the activity. The storage area should be centrally located. A few items should be placed in the individual class-rooms for the use of that particular room. Inventory lists of equipment and supplies should be kept up to date and posted for easy reference near the storage space.

The recommended equipment and supplies based on a maximum of *thirty-five students per class period* is listed below. The number in parentheses refers to the quantity that should be available for instruction during a class period.

Suggested Seasonal Program Scheduling Format*

Team Sports	Suggested Season	Boys	Girls	Co-educational
Basketball	Fall-Winter	*	**	**
Soccer	Fall	*	**	**
Softball	Spring	*	*	**
Flag Football	Fall	*	**	**
Volleyball	Optional	*	*	*

Lead-up Games	Suggested Season	Boys	Girls	Co-educational
Four Square	Optional	*	*	*
Newcomb Volleyball	Optional	*	*	*
One-bounce Volleyball	Optional	*	*	*
Deck Tennis	Optional	*	*	*
Captain Basketball	Fall-Winter	*	*	**
20-yard Flag Football	Fall	*	**	**
Punt Back	Fall	*	*	**
Zone Soccer	Fall	*	*	**

Individual Activities	Suggested Season	Boys	Girls	Co-educational
Basket Shooting	Winter	*	*	*
Hand Ball	Optional	*	*	*
Chess-Checkers	Optional	*	*	*
Rope Climbing	Optional	*	*	*
Shuffleboard	Optional	*	*	*
Folk & Square Dancing	Optional	*	*	*
Swimming	Optional	*	*	*
Tetherball	Optional	*	*	*
Track and Field	Spring	*	*	*
Gymnastics	Optional	*	*	*
Wrestling	Winter	*		
Paddle Tennis	Optional	*	*	*

Miscellaneous Activities—Air riflery, fly and bait casting, bicycling, canoeing, rowing, hiking, water skiing, roller skating, marbles, yo-yos, tops, and kite flying.

Program Spice—Parent, student, and teacher special events can be scheduled at opportune times during the year.

*Indicates suitable activity
**Indicates suitable activity if modified

Equipment for Gymnasium and Activity Area

1. Apparatus layout (one)
   a. Six low balance beams
   b. One set of low parallel bars
   c. One set of rectangle and vault bars
   d. One overhead ladder and fireman pole
   e. One set of chin and stall bars
   f. One overhead travel bar
   g. One set vertical climb poles

*Reproduced by permission of Texas Education Agency: Physical Education in the Elementary Schools Curriculum Guide. Austin, Texas, p. 606.

2. Ball inflator (one)
3. Barrels (a single barrel open at both ends or two barrels welded together and open at both ends) (three)
4. Basketball backboards and goals (two 8-foot and two 10-foot goals) (four)
5. Batting tees (seven)
6. Bulletin board (one)
7. Climbing ropes (two)
8. Drum and beater (one)
9. Goal posts for soccer and football (two)
10. Gymnastic apparatus (junior size and adjustable)
    a. One set of parallel bars   d. One horse
    b. One set of uneven bars   e. One set of rings
    c. One balance beam   f. One horizontal bar
11. High jump standards (one set)
12. Marked asphalt areas (which include small and large circles, small and large rectangles, and lines) (one)
13. Phonograph with 10-watt amplifier with variable speed control (one)
14. Sandpit (one)
15. Sawhorses and cleated boards of varying lengths (three sawhorses, six boards)
16. Softball backstops (two)
17. Targets (hoop standards, beanbag boards, wall targets, boxes, tires) (three or four of each)
18. Tether ball standard and ball (three)
19. Trampoline (standard size) (one)
20. Tumbling mats of foam plastic that are 5 × 12 feet or 5 × 10 feet (six)
21. Vaulting box (adjustable height) (one)
22. Vaulting equipment (benches, 12 to 24 inches high) (three)
23. Volleyball net and standards with adjustable heights (one)

Instructional Supplies

1. Balls (a minimum of one ball appropriate to the activity available for each child in the class for primary grades)
    a. Rubber utility balls 6 inches, 8½ inches, 10 inches, 24 inches diameter
    b. Tennis balls or sponge rubber balls
2. Bamboo poles for tinikling (14)
3. Bats of varying lengths and weights
4. Beanbags (35)
5. Blocks for building (two sets for first grade)
6. Catcher's mask (two)
7. Deck tennis rings (four)
8. First Aid Kit (one)
9. Hurdles (pasteboard boxes of 12 inches, 18 inches, and 24 inches high) (15)
10. Jump ropes (one short rope, 8 feet long, for each child; one long rope, 12 feet long, for each group of four to six children)
11. Junior and regular size soccerball, footballs, basketballs, volleyballs for appropriate grades (one of each for every six students)
12. Lummi sticks (two sticks per student)
13. Manipulative toys (an assortment for first grade)
14. Ordinary wooden boxes of various sizes (six)
15. Paddle tennis paddles (20)
16. Percussion or rhythm band instruments (one set)
17. Phonograph records for locomotion, dramatic play, interpretive rhythms, singing games, folk dances (10 to 12)
18. Pinnies or colored bands for identifying teams (35)
19. Softballs (regular) (seven); (soft) (seven)
20. Stop watch (one)
21. Tape for measuring distances (100 feet) (one)
22. Tennis balls (old or new for paddle tennis) (20)
23. Tug-of-war rope (one)
24. Wands (wooden dowels 1 inch in diameter and 36 inches long) (35)
25. Wooden blocks for relays (12)

SELF-EVALUATION SCORE CARD*

PHYSICAL EDUCATION IN THE ELEMENTARY SCHOOL

EVALUATION CRITERIA FOR PHYSICAL EDUCATION
(explanation of column headings)

0. Non-compliance; provisions missing or not functioning
1. Limited compliance
2. Partial compliance; adequacy of provisions questionable
3. Adequate compliance
4. Full compliance

The rating of 0 or 1 is *unsatisfactory;* a 2 represents the *borderline between unsatisfactory and satisfactory;* a 3 or 4 represents a *satisfactory* score. The scale should be applied to the standard under question and the estimate of degree of compliance indicated by placing a check (✔) in the appropriate column.

The needed improvements should be recorded under the proper heading. This list may then serve as a blueprint for improving the quality of services to students through physical education.

---

*Reproduced by permission of Kentucky Department of Education: Planning and Developing the Elementary Physical Education Program. The Department. Frankfort, pp. 355–356.

PART I—PHILOSOPHY

	0	1	2	3	4	Changes Needed and Action Necessary
1. Is there a written statement of the physical education philosophy of the school?						
2. Are administrative policies relating to the physical education program planned, written, and made available to all school personnel?						
3. Do physical education teachers adapt methods of instruction to different teaching situations?						
4. Is each student evaluation made in terms of his progress and achievement?						
5. Does the school attempt to provide a varied program of physical education regardless of whatever substandard conditions might exist?						
6. Is the program designed to meet the needs of youth by providing opportunity for vigorous muscular activities?						
7. Is there an intramural program planned to provide opportunities for all to participate?						
8. Is the welfare of the participant at all times an essential concern of the program?						
9. Is there a planned public relations program for interpreting the physical education program to the community?						
10. Is a concentrated effort made to use all available school and community resources?						
11. Is there continuous evaluation of the program aimed at improvement in terms of accomplishing school objectives?						
Totals						

Possible Score = __44__ points

Actual Score   = ____ points

PART II—PROGRAM ORGANIZATION AND PROCEDURES

	0	1	2	3	4	Changes Needed and Action Necessary
1. Is a 30-minute (minimum) physical education period provided daily for all children?						
2. Are minimal and maximal teaching loads for the physical education teacher the same as those for the classroom teacher?						
3. Is there a physical education specialist available? If there is a. Does he coordinate the physical education program?						
b. Is time allotted for planning with the classroom teacher?						
4. Are pupils given the opportunity to help choose, evaluate, and plan their activities?						
5. Is there opportunity for each child to achieve some measure of success during each physical education period?						
6. Do teachers limit disciplinary measures to action other than restriction from physical education activities?						
7. Is a medical excuse required for children who cannot participate regularly in the daily physical education program?						
8. Are provisions made for children who are temporarily or permanently restricted from participating in the regular program of physical education?						
9. Has the child's adapted program been approved by his physician?						
10. Are activities constantly supervised to avoid possible accidents from unnecessary roughness and other hazards?						

PART II—PROGRAM ORGANIZATION AND PROCEDURES (Continued)

	0	1	2	3	4	Changes Needed and Action Necessary
11. Are there separate areas on the playground where various groups of children may play in safety without interference from other groups of children?						
12. In case of injury, is first aid readily available and promptly given by a qualified person?						
13. Are accurate records kept and data from accident reports used in planning the physical education program?						
14. Does the physical education teacher use daily lesson plans (in written form)?						
15. Does the physical education teacher have written course outline for the current school year?						
Totals						

Possible Score = 68 points
Actual Score   = ____ points

PART III—PERSONNEL

	0	1	2	3	4	Changes Needed and Action Necessary
1. Is the person responsible for teaching physical education specifically trained in this area?						
2. Do the classroom teacher and the specialist work cooperatively in planning the physical education program?						
3. Are there any provisions for in-service education?						
4. Have all teachers had instruction in safety and first aid?						

PART III—PERSONNEL *(Continued)*

	0	1	2	3	4	Changes Needed and Action Necessary
5. Are teachers informed with respect to legal liability concerning accidents?						
6. Does the principal make provisions for the teacher to observe other elementary-school physical education programs?						
7. Are professional elementary physical education resource materials available for use in all activities for program planning?						
8. Does the teacher participate and cooperate in system-wide planning and development?						
Totals						

Possible Score = __32__ points
Actual Score   = _____ points

PART IV—PROGRAM

	0	1	2	3	4	Changes Needed and Action Necessary
1. Does the course of study include written aims and objectives designed to contribute to the education of all children?						
2. Is the outline of the total physical education program on file in the administrative and supervisory offices of the county or independent district?						
3. Is the course of study evaluated periodically and revised accordingly?						
4. Does the program include activities from the following areas: a. Directed play?						
b. Small group games?						
c. Large group games?						
d. Team games?						
e. Body mechanics?						

PART IV—PROGRAM (Continued)

0	1	2	3	4	Changes Needed and Action Necessary

f. Rhythmic activities?

g. Stunts and tumbling?

h. Apparatus activities?

i. Self-testing activities?

j. Individual and dual activities?

k. Classroom games?

l. Movement exploration?

5. Do the activities in the program provide satisfying experiences for the children?

6. Do these activities provide for an increased knowledge of the skills involved?

Totals

Possible Score = __68__ points
Actual Score   = _____ points

PART V—FACILITIES, EQUIPMENT, AND SUPPLIES

0	1	2	3	4	Changes Needed and Action Necessary

1. Is the auditorium, cafeteria, or any large vacant room available, when needed, for activities suitable to its use?

2. Can the classroom be used on rainy days or at other times when the need arises?

3. Is the play area for the primary-grade children separated from that of the intermediate children?

4. Is play apparatus definitely separated from other established play areas?

5. Do the teachers plan for effective use of available facilities?

PART V—FACILITIES, EQUIPMENT, AND SUPPLIES *(Continued)*

	0	1	2	3	4	Changes Needed and Action Necessary
6. Are the play areas so designed that a teacher can supervise more than one group at a time?						
7. Are all facilities maintained properly by a designated person other than the teacher or a child?						
8. Are adequate facilities provided for storage of equipment for daily use and for off-season storage?						
9. Wherever traffic or other hazards exist adjacent to the playground, is the playground protected by a fence at least five feet high?						
10. Is effective use made of available community facilities in addition to school facilities?						
11. Are there sufficient funds set aside in the regular school budget for equipment and supplies?						
12. Are faculty members involved in planning the purchase, use, and repair of physical education equipment and supplies?						
13. If the Parent-Teacher Association or any other organization has available funds for school use, does the physical education department share in the allocation of the funds?						
14. Are the equipment and supplies purchased in accordance with inventory and anticipated needs?						
15. Are bulletin boards, charts, pictures, and other visual aids used as part of the program?						
Totals						

Possible Score = __60__ points
Actual Score   = ____ points

PART VI—PUBLIC RELATIONS

	0	1	2	3	4	Changes Needed and Action Necessary
1. Is the atmosphere in the class such that the teacher and students respect one another?						
2. Does the public relations program involve parents, teachers, and children?						
3. Is a consistent effort made to interpret the program to the public?						
4. Does the teacher participate in community affairs?						
5. Is there willing cooperation with other faculty and school personnel?						
6. Does the school share physical education facilities with the community?						
7. Does the community share its facilities with the school?						
8. Are there opportunities for parents, teachers, and children to participate together?						
Totals						

Possible Score = _32_ points
Actual Score   = ____ points

PART VII—IN-SERVICE MEETINGS

	0	1	2	3	4	Changes Needed and Action Necessary
1. Did the teacher attend the four In-Service meetings held on conference days?						
2. Did the teacher attend physical education meetings on the state level?						
3. Did the teacher attend physical education meetings on the national level?						
4. If the teacher attended the county In-Service meetings, was he able to incorporate new ideas into his program?						
5. If the teacher attended state or national physical education meetings, did he bring back ideas that were shared with his fellow teachers or incorporated into his program?						
Totals						

Possible Score = __20__ points
Actual Score   = _____ points

Summary

AREAS	POSSIBLE SCORE	ACTUAL SCORE
Part I. Philosophy	44	
Part II. Program Organization and Procedures	68	
Part III. Personnel	32	
Part IV. Program	68	
Part V. Facilities, Equipment and Supplies	60	
Part VI. Public Relations	32	
Part VII. Attendance In-Service Programs	20	
Totals	324	

Needed improvements:

RECOMMENDED FILMS ON ELEMENTARY PHYSICAL EDUCATION

After School Activities for Boys and Girls (filmstrip), American Council on Education, Washington, D.C.
Archery for Girls, ten min., Coronet Films.
Ball Handling in Basketball, ten min., Encyclopaedia Britannica Films, Inc.
Ball Handling in Football, 11 min., Encyclopaedia Britannica Films, Inc.
Basketball for Girls—Fundamental Techniques, ten min., Coronet Films.
Beginning Camping, 30 min., Athletic Institute.
Beginning Swimming, 30 min., Athletic Institute.
Beginning Tumbling, 11 min., Coronet Films.
Beginning Volleyball (filmstrip of 208 frames—four units, ten min. each), Athletic Institute.
Careers in Physical Education, 30 min.; *Careers in Recreation,* 30 min., Athletic Institute.
Children Growing Up With Others, 45 min., National Film Board of Canada.
Evaluating Physical Abilities, 15 min., Athletic Institute.
Exercise and Health, eight min., Coronet Films.
Focus on Fitness, 18 mm., American Alliance for Health, Physical Education, and Recreation.
Fundamentals in Track and Field, 26 min., Encyclopedia Films.
Intermediate Tumbling, 11 min., Coronet Films.
Mat Mann's Swimming Techniques for Boys, 18 min., Coronet Films.
Mat Mann's Swimming Techniques for Girls, 11 min., Coronet Films.
Methods of Teaching Physical Education, 40 min., All American Productions, Box 801, Riverside, California.
New Designs in Elementary Physical Education, 30 min., American Alliance for Health, Physical Education, and Recreation.
Play Ball, Son! 20 min., Young America Films, Inc.
Play in the Snow, ten min., Encyclopaedia Britannica Films, Inc.
Play Softball, 86 frames with script, Association Films.
Playground Safety, ten min., Coronet Films.
Playtown U.S.A., 35 min., Athletic Institute.
Primary Safety: In the School Building, Coronet Films.
Primary Safety: On the School Playground, Coronet Films.
Readiness—The Fourth R, Athletic Institute.
Share the Ball, 32 frames with text, Simmel-Meservey, Inc.
Simple Stunts, 11 min., Coronet Films.
Skip to My Lou, five min., Indiana University.
Soccer for Girls, 11 min., Coronet Films.
Social Dancing, 11 min., Coronet Films.
Softball for Boys, ten min., Coronet Films.
Softball for Girls, 11 min. (black and white and color), Coronet Films.
Sports Teaching Aids (3 × 5 card bibliography of films, filmstrips, and slides), Division of Girls' and Women's Sports, American Alliance for Health, Physical Education, and Recreation.
Squirrel in Trees, five min., Indiana University.
Swimming for Beginners, color, Visual Educational Films.
Teaching Aids for Health, Physical Education, and Recreation (a list of free and inexpensive teaching aids), Thomas Flanigan, Box 2, Mokena, Illinois.
They Grow Up So Fast, 27 min., color, American Alliance for Health, Physical Education, and Recreation.
Three Deep, six min., Indiana University.
Trampolining, 28 min., Athletic Institute.
Volleyball for Boys, 11 min., Coronet Films.
Volleyball Techniques for Girls, nine min., McGraw-Hill Book Co., Inc., Text-Film Department.

RECOMMENDED FILM STRIPS

The following films are available both for rental and purchase from The Athletic Institute, 805 Merchandise Mart, Chicago, Illinois:

Apparatus Activities for Boys and Men
Archery
Badminton
Campcraft Shelters
Campcraft Series
Fishing
Gymnastics for Girls and Women
Lifesaving
Skiing
Soccer
Swimming
Table Tennis
Track and Field for Elementary School Children
Tumbling
Volleyball

FILM SOURCES

The following are the full addresses of the sources (sale, rental, or loan) of the films listed:

AAHPER: AAHPER Film Sales, 1201 16th Street, N.W., Washington, D.C.

A.F.R.: American Film Registry, 24 East Eighth Street, Chicago, Illinois.

A.M.N.H.: American Museum of Natural History, Department of Education, Central Park West at 79th Street, New York, New York.

Association: Association Films, Inc., Broad at Elm, Ridgefield, New Jersey.

Bailey: Bailey Films, Inc., 6509 DeLongpre Avenue, Hollywood, California.

Castle: Castle Films—Distributor, United World Films, Inc., 1445 Park Avenue, New York, New York; 542 S. Dearborn Street, Chicago, Illinois; 6610 Melrose Avenue, Los Angeles, California.

Commerce: New York State Department of Commerce, Film Library, 40 Howard Street, Albany, New York.

E.B.: Encyclopaedia Britannica Films, 1150 Willamette Avenue, Willamette, Illinois; 202 E. 44th Street, New York, New York; 5625 Hollywood Blvd., Hollywood, California.

I.C.S.: Institutional Cinema Service, Inc., 1560 Broadway, New York, New York.

Ideal: Ideal Pictures, 1558 Main Street, Buffalo, New York; 233–239 West 42nd Street, New York, New York; 58 E. South Water Street, Chicago, Illinois.

I.F.F.: International Film Foundation, Inc., 1600 Broadway, New York, New York.

Indiana: Indiana University, Audio-Visual Center, Bloomington, Indiana 47401.

N.E.M.P.: New England Movie Production, 83–85 Winter Street, Exeter, New Hampshire.

N.F.B.: National Film Board of Canada, R.K.O. Building, Suite 2307, 1270 Avenue of the Americas, New York, New York.

Simmel: Simmel Meservey, Inc., 321 S. Beverly Drive, Beverly Hills, California.

Syracuse: Educational Film Library, Syracuse University, Collendale at Lancaster Avenue, Syracuse, New York.

U.W.F.: United World Films, Inc., 1445 Park Avenue, New York, New York.

FILM GUIDES

A Directory of 2600 Films (16 mm.). Film Libraries, 1976. Available from Supt. of Documents, Government Printing Office, Washington, D.C.

Educational Film Guide. The H. W. Wilson Company, 950 University Avenue, New York, New York (Contains information on 13,762 films).

Educators' Guide to Free Films. Educators' Progress Service, Randolph, Wisconsin.

Free and Inexpensive Learning Materials. Division of Surveys and Field Services, George Peabody College for Teachers, Nashville, Tennessee.

Sport Film Guide. The Athletic Institute, 2095 State Street, Chicago, Illinois.

Sports Teaching Aids: Audio-Visual. AAHPER, 1201 16th Street, N.W., Washington, D.C.

SOURCES FOR EQUIPMENT AND SUPPLIES

Large Indoor Equipment

Atlas Athletic Equipment Company
2339 Hampton Avenue
St. Louis, Missouri 63139

Gym Master
3200 So. Zuri Street
Englewood, Colorado 80110

Jayfro Corp.
1 Bridge Street, P.O. Box 50
Montville, Connecticut 06353

Lind Climber Co.
807 Reba Place
Evanston, Illinois 60202

Nissen Corporation
930 27th Avenue S.W.
Cedar Rapids, Iowa 52406

Trampoline, Inc.
247 West Sixth Street
San Pedro, California 90733

Large Outdoor Equipment

The J. E. Burke Company
Fond du Lac, Wisconsin 54935

Game-Time Inc.
Litchfield, Michigan 49252

Jamison Manufacturing Co.
510 East Manchester Avenue
Los Angeles, California 90003

Northwest Design Products, Inc.
1235 South Tacoma Way
Tacoma, Washington 98409

Otto Industries Pty., Ltd.
309–313 South Road
Mile End South
South Australia 5031

Playground Corporation of America
29–16 40th Avenue
Long Island City, New York 11101

W. J. Voit Rubber Corp.
29 Essex Street
Maywood, New Jersey 07607

Hand Manipulative and Games Equipment

Adirondack Industries, Inc.
Dolgeville, New York 13329

American Seating
Grand Rapids, Michigan 49502

Childcraft Education Corp.
P.O. Box 94
Bayonne, New Jersey 07002

Cosom Corporation
6030 Wayzata Blvd.
Minneapolis, Minnesota 55416

General Sportcraft Company, Ltd.
140 Woodbine Street
Bergenfield, New Jersey 07621

Interstate Rubber Products Corp.
908 Avila Street
Los Angeles, California 90012

Lojen Apparatus, Inc.
Box 785
Fremont, Nebraska 68025

Mid-Valley Sport Center
5350 No. Blackstone
Fresno, California 93726

Oregon Worsted Company
8300 S. E. McLoughlin Blvd.
Portland, Oregon 97202

Physical Education Supply Associates, Inc.
P.O. Box 292
Trumbull, Connecticut 06611

Playskool, Inc. Dept. E.
Division of Milton Bradley Company
3720 North Kedzie Avenue
Chicago, Illinois 60618

Program Aids, Inc.
161 MacQuesten Parkway
Mt. Vernon, New York 10550

R. E. Titus Gym Scooter Co.
Winfield, Kansas 67156

Wolters Company
9250 South Buttonwillow
Reedley, California

Ed-Nu, Inc.
5115 Route 38
Pennsauken, New Jersey 08110

School-Tech, Inc.
745 State Circle
Ann Arbor, Michigan 48104

Creative Playgrounds Corporation
Terre Haute, Indiana 47808

INDEX

Circle games, active, 351–354
  quiet, 371–375
Circle Kick Ball (active manipulative game), 348
Circle Relay, 395
Circle relay formation, 391
Circle Squat (game), 380
Circle soccer (soccer skill game), 537
Circle Two (game), 380
Circle Volley Relay, 399
Circle Waltz, 432
Circulatory-respiratory endurance, 49
Clap Dance (Israeli), 456
Class, excuses from, policies for, 279
  management of, 278–282
  organization of, 282–286
Class organization, 351
  for aquatics, 583
  for stunts, 465
  for team sports, 534
Class projects, outdoor, 601
Classroom, games for, 367–389
  physical education activities in, 219
Climbing ladder, in movement exploration, 299
Clothespin Drop (game), 380
Clove hitch knot, 622
Club Guard (active circle game), 352
Club Snatch (active locomotor game), 340
Clubs, after-school, 652
Clumsy child, programs for, 178
Cock Fight (stunt), 478
Coffee Grinder (stunt), 468
Color Me (active locomotor game), 347
Combination method, of teaching, 266
Come Along (active locomotor game), 343
Come Let Us Be Joyful (singing game), 415
Communication, between teacher and students, 272
Community groups, programs for, 659
Community programs, for mentally disabled children, 171
Competence, sense of, 95
Competencies, development of, 253
Competition, high-level, for students, 660
  tournament, types of, 647
Conditioning, 186
Conditioning theory of learning, 186
Conflict, arising from unfilled needs, 137–139
Connectionism, theory of, 187
Conservation, of nature, 604
  soil, 625
Constructed games, 360–366
Continuing education, for teachers, 209–213
Continuous lashing, 624
Cooking, green-stick, 610
  outdoor, 604, 609–615
Coordination, 50
  physical, 8
Corkscrew (stunt), 468
Corn Roast (recipe), 613
Corner formation, for class instruction, 283
Corner Spry (active manipulative game), 349
Costumes. See Uniforms.
Cotton-eyed Joe (Texan dance), 429, 439
Crab Walk (stunt), 468
Crafts, and outdoor education, 603
Crane Dive or Nose Dive (stunt), 468

Creative movement, using stories and themes, 309–312
Creative play, 303–313
Crested Hen (Danish dance), 450
Crisscross fire, 608
Croquet, 641
Cross Bamboo Hop (Philippine dance), 448
Cross Over Relay, 401
Cross Skip (rope game), 637
Crossing the Brook (group game), 125
Cross-Over Turn (roller skating skill), 640
Csebogar (Hungarian dance), 442
Cup of Poison (Halloween game), 355
Curio Collection (nature game), 619
Curriculum study, 211
Cut the Wand (stunt), 468

Dance, and rhythms, 407–462
  teaching of, 423
    techniques for, 423
  terminology of, 458
Dance Around the Christmas Tree (Christmas game), 359
Dance games, 436–440
Dances, international, 440–457
Dancing, social, 457
  square, 424
Danish Dance of Greeting, 443
Danish Schottische (dance), 455
Dash, 50-yard, national norms for, 63
Dashes (field and track activity), 526
Deck Tennis, 638
Deep water, activities in, 592
Delinquency, increasing, 131
Demonstrations, aquatic, formations for, 584
  public, 655
Departmental libraries, use of, 678
Developing self, and movement, 98–101
Development, child, and physical education, 3–17
  of academic concepts, 9–11
  of neuromuscular abilities, 18–44. See also names of specific skills and exercises.
  of self, 92–95
  of self-concept, 9
    and movement, 91–101
  of specific skills. See names of specific skills.
  of visual perception, Frostig's program for, 80
Diagnosis, of motor skill difficulties, 267
Diagonal lashing, 624
Diamond or Box Ball (softball skill game), 545
Did You Ever See a Lassie (singing game), 419
Did You See Anyone Going to Grandma's House for Dinner? (Thanksgiving game), 357
Dip (stunt), 469
Direction, in teaching motor skills, 268
Directional awareness, activities for, 86
Disabilities, children with, 155–171
  learning, 74, 84
Discipline, techniques of, 274–278
Dismount, of trampoline, 490
Distance running, 529
Ditties, for jumping rope, 632
Dive Over One (tumbling activity), 480

F

(